American Politics

Classic and Contemporary Readings

Fifth Edition

Allan J. Cigler

University of Kansas

Burdett A. Loomis

University of Kansas

Houghton Mifflin Company   Boston   New York

Sponsoring Editor: Mary Dougherty
Editorial Assistant: Tonya Lobato
Associate Project Editor: Heather Hubbard
Associate Production/Design Coordinator: Christine Gervais
Senior Manufacturing Coordinator: Priscilla Bailey
Marketing Manager: Jay Hu

Text credits begin on page 507.

Printed in the U.S.A.

Library of Congress Control Number: 2001131485

ISBN: 0-618-12307-5

3456789–FFG–05 04 03 02 01

Contents

Topic Correlation Chart   xiii

Preface   xv

Part I
Constitutional Foundations

Chapter 1
THE CONSTITUTION AND FOUNDING   1

1.1   JACK N. RAKOVE
A Tradition Born of Strife   3
Even before the Revolution, the states provided models for representative government, which the framers used to their advantage.

1.2   CHARLES A. BEARD
An Economic Interpretation of the Constitution of the United States   8
The Constitution was drafted by a propertied elite whose objective was to protect its own economic interests.

1.3   JOHN P. ROCHE
The Founding Fathers: A Reform Caucus in Action   15
The framers of the Constitution should be remembered less for their ideological commitment than for their political skill.

1.4   JAMES MADISON
The Federalist, No. 51   28
The separation of powers will provide for a strong central government and limit the opportunity for each branch of government to abuse its authority.

1.5   BURT SOLOMON
What Were They Thinking?   33
For the framers, the Electoral College was about balance—between regions and branches of government.

Chapter 2
FEDERALISM AND INTERGOVERNMENTAL RELATIONS   38

2.1   JAMES MADISON
The Federalist, No. 39   41
The political structure set up in the Constitution is a compromise between a government in which all power rests with a central authority and one in which all power remains with the states.

2.2   *McCulloch v. Maryland* (1819)   47
       The national government has supremacy over the states, even
       beyond the powers made explicit in the Constitution; a state has no
       right to sanction laws or procedures that interfere with the operation
       of the national government.

2.3   JOHN D. DONAHUE
       The Devil in Devolution   53
       Although the return of power and responsibility to state and local
       government is a popular idea, devolution can lead to the
       fragmentation of authority and difficulty in addressing pressing
       national issues.

2.4   MARTHA DERTHICK
       American Federalism: Half-Full or Half-Empty?   61
       Claims that the federal system of government is tending toward
       decentralization may not hold up to close inspection.

CHAPTER 3
CIVIL LIBERTIES AND CIVIL RIGHTS   68

3.1   *Near v. Minnesota* (1931)   71
       Freedom of expression shall not be denied; anticipated malice or
       falsehood by the press toward a public figure is not grounds for
       prior restraint.

3.2   FRED FRIENDLY
       From the Saturday Press *to the* New York Times   77
       Near v. *Minnesota* served as a precedent for *New York Times Co.* v.
       United States (1971). According to the latter, the government's claim
       that national security is at stake does not justify prior restraint.

3.3   *Griswold v. Connecticut* (1965)   81
       Constitutional protection of the right to privacy is made explicit.

3.4   JEFFREY ROSEN
       Why Privacy Matters   86
       Privacy is a hard-won right that citizens must continue to defend
       with vigor, especially in light of recent technological advancements.

3.5   *Gideon v. Wainwright* (1963)   93
       The Sixth Amendment to the Constitution guarantees the right to
       counsel in all criminal cases, and under the Fourteenth Amendment
       the states must protect this right.

3.6   ALEXANDER NGUYEN
       The Assault   97
       The efficacy of Miranda resides in the wording of the Miranda rules
       and not with how the rules are administered.

PART II
PEOPLE AND POLITICS

CHAPTER 4
PUBLIC OPINION 105

4.1 BENJAMIN GINSBERG
Polling and the Transformation of Public Opinion 108
The modern use of polling has fundamentally altered the character of public opinion and the relationship between citizens and their government.

4.2 MOLLY W. SONNER AND CLYDE WILCOX
Forgiving and Forgetting: Public Support for Bill Clinton During the Lewinsky Scandal 122
Clinton's survival throughout the Lewinsky scandal was due, in large part, to the booming economy, to his charisma and to his refusal to crumble in the face of political antagonists.

4.3 DAVID S. BRODER AND RICHARD MORIN
A Question of Values 130
Value differences between generations on moral and ethical matters were glaring in the light of Clinton's impeachment trial.

4.4 DANA MILBANK
I Hear America Ringing 136
Pollsters during election season work overtime to provide Americans with a quasi-scientific snapshot of public opinion; and the media look for explanations behind weighted numbers.

CHAPTER 5
PARTICIPATION 141

5.1 MICAH L. SIFRY
Finding the Lost Voters 144
Growing alienation from the major parties lies at the heart of why many Americans choose not to participate in elections.

5.2 MICHAEL SCHUDSON
Voting Rites: Why We Need a New Concept of Citizenship 153
The Progressive ideal of citizenship, with its expectations of extensive political information and constant attention to public affairs, may set an unrealistic standard in the contemporary political world.

5.3 ROBERT D. PUTNAM
Bowling Alone: America's Declining Social Capital 162
There is an important link between citizens' engagement in the associational life of their communities and government performance; the decline of citizen associational involvement in recent decades threatens democratic values.

CHAPTER 6
POLITICAL PARTIES   173

6.1   KAY LAWSON
       Why We Still Need Real Political Parties   177
       Political parties have been captured by elites and other insiders; real
       parties that are controlled by a broad base of citizens who are able
       to hold public officials accountable are needed.

6.2   EVERETT CARLL LADD
       Of Political Parties Great and Strong   189
       The argument for stronger political parties is an argument for larger
       government, resting more on normative assumptions about the role
       of government than on democratic necessities.

6.3   JOHN KENNETH WHITE AND DANIEL M. SHEA
       Creative Party Finances in the Information Age   201
       Parties in the 1990s have become particularly adept at devising
       creative strategies to test the limits of campaign finance
       regulations.

CHAPTER 7
CAMPAIGNS AND ELECTIONS   213

7.1   BURT SOLOMON
       Presidency—Disunity for All   216
       Clear political distinctions between U.S. regions are masking an
       emerging pattern of less homogeneous party voting patterns
       within certain individual states.

7.2   ALAN EHRENHALT
       Political Pawns   225
       Millions were spent in the battle for the Wisconsin legislature,
       but some candidates, not aware of where the money came
       from, have begun to lose control of their own campaign agendas
       that are increasingly set by the interest groups who finance
       them.

7.3   ROBERT DREYFUSS
       Rousing the Democratic Base   233
       While most campaign strategists focus high-tech tools on
       narrow slivers of the electorate, labor and the NAACP are going
       back to basics: organizing voters to talk to voters about the
       issues.

CHAPTER 8
THE MASS MEDIA   241

8.1   JOSHUA MEYROWITZ
       Lowering the Political Hero to Our Level   **244**
       The electronic media have greatly affected the nation's perceptions
       of political leaders, making it difficult for Americans to trust and
       respect politicians.

8.2   THOMAS E. PATTERSON
       Bad News, Bad Governance   **252**
       The traditional descriptive style of reporting has given way to
       an interpretive style that empowers journalists by giving them
       more control over content, leading to an "antipolitics" bias in the
       media.

8.3   SCOTT STOSSEL
       Echo Chamber of Horrors   **263**
       The unprecedented error in television news media predictions on
       election night 2000 was primarily related to structural changes in
       the news business.

CHAPTER 9
INTEREST GROUPS   272

9.1   JAMES MADISON
       The Federalist, No. 10   **275**
       The factions that naturally arise in a democracy can be dangerous.
       Since trying to do away with special interests would destroy liberty,
       we must control them through checks and balances.

9.2   JEFFREY H. BIRNBAUM
       Lobbyists—Why the Bad Rap?   **281**
       In order to adjust to a changed political and ethical climate,
       lobbyists have altered their strategies away from blatantly unethical
       or illegal activities to more sophisticated methods of influencing
       government.

9.3   THEDA SKOCPOL
       Associations Without Members   **292**
       Since the 1950s, the nature of American civic and political
       associations has slowly become less locally rooted and less
       membership-focused, resulting in little democratic input and
       a decreased ability to mobilize to spawn meaningful political
       reform.

9.4   ALLAN J. CIGLER AND BURDETT A. LOOMIS
       From Big Bird to Bill Gates: Organized Interests and the
       Emergence of Hyperpolitics   303
       Interest groups are involved in an ongoing campaign to influence
       political communication, but they often lack distinguishable voices;
       a barrage of "interested" voices with monetary resources
       undermines their effectiveness.

PART III
INSTITUTIONS

CHAPTER 10
CONGRESS   315

10.1   KENNETH A. SHEPSLE
       The Changing Textbook Congress   318
       Significant developments over the past three decades have
       profoundly changed conventional representations of Congress,
       which is now characterized by large numbers of power centers and
       stronger individual leaders.

10.2   LEE H. HAMILTON
       Ten Things I Wish Political Scientists Would Teach About Congress   331
       Ten simple lessons on Congress will help increase public
       understanding of the institution and, in turn, decrease cynicism that
       threatens to weaken the relationship between voters and their
       representatives.

10.3   SARAH A. BINDER
       Going Nowhere: A Gridlocked Congress?   343
       Gridlock, to some extent, is intrinsic to the American system of
       checks and balances and a natural consequence of separated
       institutions sharing and competing for power; but nudging Congress
       toward the center will likely make gridlock a less inhibiting force in
       the future.

10.4   MARK MURRAY
       King of the Roads   350
       Transportation Committee Chairman, Bud Shuster, succeeded in
       passing two of the most expensive and important pieces of
       legislation regarding highway and airport construction in the late
       1990s by rewarding friends and punishing neighbors.

10.5   RICHARD E. COHEN
       Crackup of the Committees   358
       A major reason for the chaos prevading capitol hill is that committee
       power has eroded to the point of collapse.

CHAPTER 11
THE PRESIDENCY   367

11.1   RICHARD E. NEUSTADT
       The Power to Persuade   370
       Given the limits put on his power by Congress and his own
       administration, a president must be able to persuade both of these
       groups to carry out his agenda.

11.2   ROBERT A. DAHL
       Myth of the Presidential Mandate   377
       The notion that election confers a popular mandate on the president
       is a fallacy that exalts the office within the constitutional system at
       the expense of both Congress and our diverse citizenry.

11.3   EVAN THOMAS
       Why Clinton Won   389
       The president's team was especially clever in demonizing the
       prosecutor and playing to public opinion in the Lewinsky ordeal,
       which they insisted was about sex, not constitutional substance.

11.4   CARL M. CANNON
       Promises, Promises   396
       Presidential candidates make lots of promises on the campaign trail,
       and once in office, they usually try to keep them.

CHAPTER 12
BUREAUCRACY   405

12.1   CHARLES PETERS
       *From Ouagadougou to Cape Canaveral: Why the Bad News
       Doesn't Travel Up*   408
       The present bureaucratic structure discourages communication
       between levels of the hierarchy and is unlikely to prevent such
       policy failures as the space shuttle disaster.

12.2   JAMES Q. WILSON
       Constraints on Public Managers   416
       External political constraints result in public managers' lack of
       control over agency revenues, productive factors, and agency goals.

12.3   NICHOLAS THOMPSON
       Finding the Civil Service's Hidden Sex Appeal   431
       As aging government workers retire in large numbers in the coming
       years, opportunities are opening up that will offer younger workers
       interesting challenges and the potential for advancement.

12.4   NORMAN ORNSTEIN AND THOMAS DONILON
The Confirmation Clog   **440**
The nomination and confirmation process of presidential cabinet officers is breaking down, impeding efficient governance; and the problems will not be easy to solve.

CHAPTER 13
THE SUPREME COURT   449

13.1   ALEXANDER HAMILTON
The Federalist, No. 78   **452**
For the Supreme Court to practice judicial review most effectively, it must be completely removed from legislative and executive influence.

13.2   *Marbury v. Madison* (1803)   **457**
The Supreme Court's declaration of an existing statute as unconstitutional set a precedent for the judicial review of federal legislation.

13.3   RICHARD A. POSNER
What Am I? A Potted Plant?   **463**
A strict constructionist interpretation of the Constitution is not practical; judges are expected to make policy, and their doing so has worked for the public good.

13.4   STUART TAYLOR, JR.
The Tipping Point   **469**
One new appointment could change the balance of power in the Supreme Court

PART IV
PUBLIC POLICY

CHAPTER 14
POLICYMAKING   479

14.1   CHRISTOPHER GEORGES
Sign It, Then Mind It   **481**
An often forgotten part of the policymaking process is planning for effective implementation; overlooking implementation may result in the failure to reach legislative goals.

14.2   DEBORAH STONE
Stories   **489**
Understanding policymaking means, in part, understanding how stories help shape the communication of ideas by lobbyists, intellectuals, legislators, and bureaucrats; because we think in terms of narratives, stories can have great power in shaping acceptable policies.

14.3   PIETRO S. NIVOLA
       Regulation: The New Pork Barrel   **493**
       In an era of reduced levels of governmental spending—especially for
       discretionary items (space travel, highways)—interest groups have
       turned their attention to influencing regulations, which often
       mandate substantial spending to meet governmental standards.

14.4   ALLEN SCHICK
       A Surplus, If We Can Keep It   **500**
       How long the federal budget will remain balanced will depend, in
       large part, on the prudence of Washington politicians over the
       coming years.

Topic Correlation Chart

Although the chapters of this book of readings have been organized to mesh with the coverage of most American government textbooks, many subjects receive attention in more than one chapter. The following chart permits students and instructors to locate relevant readings for twenty-six subjects, ranging (in alphabetical order) from bureaucracy to the Washington establishment.

Topic:	Covered in:
Bureaucracy	Chapter 12; 14.1
Campaigns and Elections	Chapter 7; 4.4; 8.3; 11.2
Clinton Presidency	4.2; 4.3; 11.3; 14.4
Congress	Chapter 10; 12.4
Constitution	Chapters 1, 3, and 13; 2.1, 2.2; 9.1
Domestic Policy	Chapter 14; 2.3; 2.4; 10.4; 12.1
Election 2000	1.5; 7.1; 7.2; 8.3
Federalism	Chapter 2; 1.1; 9.1
The Founding	Chapter 1; 9.1
Impeachment	4.2; 4.3; 11.3
Interest Groups	Chapter 9; 7.3; 7.4; 14.2; 14.3
Leadership	Chapter 11; 8.1; 14.2
Mass Media	Chapter 8; 4.4
Money and Politics	6.3; 7.3; 7.4; 9.2; 9.4
Participation	Chapter 5; 6.1; 7.4; 9.3
Policymaking Process	Chapter 14; 2.4; 7.3; 9.4; 10.4; 11.4
Political Culture	4.3; 5.2; 5.3; 7.2
Political Parties	Chapter 6; 5.1; 7.4; 10.3
Presidency	Chapter 11; 1.5; 8.1; 8.2
Public Opinion	Chapter 4; 5.1; 8.2

Reform   5.2; 6.1; 7.3; 8.3; 9.3

Representation   Chapter 9; 10.1; 10.4; 10.5

Separation of   1.4; 10.3; 11.1; 11.4; 13.1
Powers

Supreme Court   Chapters 3 and 13
and the
Judiciary

Technology and   3.4; 4.4
Politics

Washington   9.2; 11.1; 14.4
Establishment

PREFACE

In the wake of the close election in 2000 and the unsuccessful impeachment of Bill Clinton in 1998–1999, the need to place American politics in a historic perspective has rarely been more important. We find that the framers of the Constitution continue to influence our political life, even as we race toward a global economy and continuous communication. Republicans have captured both the presidency and both houses of Congress for the first time since 1955, yet their margin of victory was extremely narrow—narrow to the point that George W. Bush received fewer popular votes than did Al Gore.

As in previous editions of this book, we have strived to assemble the best possible collection of articles—both established classics and important recent pieces—that will allow students to explore the complexities of American politics. The resulting set of fifty-seven articles (twenty-four of which are new) includes selections, like John Roche's, "The Founding Fathers: A Reform Caucus in Action" and Richard Neustadt's excerpt from *Presidential Power*, that are well-established "classics." Other selections, such as Kenneth Shepsle's "The Changing Textbook Congress" and Richard Posner's "What Am I? A Potted Plant?," have become "new classics" that will stand the test of time. Still other articles, like Allen Schick's "A Surplus, If You Can Keep It," reflects new work by veteran scholars.

We continue to work to make this volume both accessible and sophisticated, as well as to address the major issues of the day (impeachment, the electoral college). In an effort to maintain the essential argument of each selection, some readings may be longer than average. This limits the number of articles that we can incorporate into the book, but it does allow for a bit more depth per topic.

American Politics: Classic and Contemporary Readings, Fifth Edition, is divided into fourteen chapters that correspond with the organization of most American government texts. Each chapter begins with an essay that sets out the themes of that section, and a headnote introduces each selection, thus providing some context for the article. Following each article are "questions for discussion" that address issues raised in the piece.

The book includes two other, useful features. First, each selection is annotated, so that difficult terms and obscure historical references are clarified. Second, we have produced an extensive topic correlation chart, directly following the table of contents, that provides cross-references for twenty-six subjects, such as "impeachment" and "money in politics."

Complementing *American Politics* is an *Instructor's Resource Manual with Test Items*, written most capably by Professor Joel Paddock of Southwest Missouri State University. This manual includes article selection summaries, suggestions for classroom use, and sets of both multiple-choice and essay questions for all readings.

Since beginning this project in the 1980s, Houghton Mifflin has consistently obtained excellent reviewers for examining and reexamining the contents. We are in their debt, once again. They include:

Edmond Costantini, University of California–Davis
James W. Davis, Washington University
Robert Friedman, California State University
Dennis J. Goldford, Drake University
Ange-Marie Hancock, University of San Francisco
Mark S. Jendrysik, University of North Dakota
Mark Landis, Hofstra University
Brad Lockerbie, University of Georgia
Penny Miller, University of Kentucky
Bruce Oppenheimer, Vanderbilt University
Ronald Pynn, University of North Dakota
Robert Y. Shapiro, Columbia University
G. Michael Stathis, Southern Utah University
John W. Winkle III, University of Mississippi

As always, the Houghton Mifflin editors have worked diligently to help produce the very best book possible. Our thanks go to Tonya Lobato, Mary Dougherty, Heather Hubbard, and Jean Woy.

Somewhat to our amazement, as we edit our tenth book together, the authors continue to discover that we complement each other. Our spouses, Beth Cigler and Michel Loomis, long-suffering through all ten books, remain supportive nonetheless. And we continue to hope that, one year, Jayhawk basketball will meet our expectations. Maybe by the twentieth edition.

A. J. C.
B. A. L.

# Chapter 1

THE CONSTITUTION AND FOUNDING

The framing of the Constitution serves as one of the anchors of American politics. The Constitution was written, under pressure, by an extraordinary band of political leaders, whose accomplishments at the Philadelphia convention have proven so workable and lasting that it is difficult not to see them as mythical figures. Still, with the possible exception of George Washington, these were people, not demigods. And Washington's elevated status proved useful to the framers: As they devised the presidency and later pushed for ratification, they, along with the great body of citizens, could easily envision Washington as the first incumbent of the office.

It is difficult to exaggerate the scope of the problems the framers faced. They confronted a system of government under the Articles of Confederation that emphasized the sovereignty of the individual states at the expense of a coherent national identity and hindered the development of the nation. An armed insurrection in Massachusetts (Shays's Rebellion) demonstrated the weakness of the states in coming to terms with problems of commerce, currency, and credit. In addition, this uprising brought home the supposed dangers of the masses within a democratic state. The possible "tyranny of the majority" was a real fear. Domestic challenges were no greater than those from abroad. The United States may have won its war of independence, but European powers certainly did not see American sovereignty as immutable. Throughout the country's first few decades, there were numerous plots to compromise American independence (for example, the XYZ Affair and Aaron Burr's plan for a separatist state in the Southwest).

In writing the Constitution and securing its ratification, the framers proved themselves skillful political engineers and propagandists. As Jack Rakove points out, the framers had to "reconstitute" the government of the new nation by the very act of writing a constitution, and Rakove argues that they learned well from the Massachusetts experience of including "broad statements on the first principles of government" within the document. John P. Roche sees these individuals as a "reform caucus," a label that aptly captures the essentially political nature of their task. Nevertheless, their purposes were more radical than merely carrying out a set of reforms. As Roche notes, "The Constitutionalists went forth to subvert the Confederation," not to enact some modest changes.

Just as the American Revolution has been characterized as conservative, the same can be said of the writing of the Constitution. As historian Charles A. Beard and Richard Hofstadter emphasize, protecting property rights played a central role in the framers' thinking. Given their status as part of the new nation's elite, this is understandable. Still, protecting property rights represented more than a simple appeal to self-interest; for the framers, such safeguards were important guideposts in assessing the reach of governmental power. Property rights could best be protected by the creation of a central government that was strong enough to ensure orderly commerce but not so strong that it impinged on the rights of the minority.

A governmental structure that could protect property rights without becoming oppressive would not only have to make sense theoretically; it would have to win the approval of the states in the ratification process. To address these necessities, the framers created a series of checks and balances, most notably federalism (see Chapter 2) and the separation of powers. In *The Federalist,* No. 51, James Madison argues that liberty can be protected only where the executive, legislative, and judicial functions are divided. The division, however, need not be, and cannot be, complete; there will always be some sharing of powers. Indeed, Madison notes in *The Federalist,* No. 47, "where the *whole* power of one department is exercised by the same hands which possess the *whole* power of another department, the fundamental principles of a free constitution are subverted."

One test of a "fundamental principle" of any constitution is its staying power. The separation of powers has not gone unchallenged over the course of the American republic. The most common conflict has arisen between the executive and the legislature, with critics often arguing that the executive branch needs more power to carry out its electoral mandate and to implement a coherent foreign policy.

In the 2000 election between Vice President Al Gore and Governor George W. Bush of Texas, the staying power of one fundamental element of the American political system—the Electoral College—was challenged by the closest election in more than a century. This jerrybuilt system, the product of political compromises in the 1787 convention, survived and produced a legitimate winner, even though Gore won the popular vote by about 500,000. Burt Solomon provides the constitutional background for one of the framers' decisions that remains relevant (and controversial) in the 21st century.

A Tradition Born of Strife

Jack N. Rakove

When the framers decided to write a new constitution rather than attempt to restructure the Articles of Confederation, they were setting out for unknown territory. Some of them, however, had experience with state constitutions that had been written after 1776. In addition, the framers could reflect on how well these documents had done in establishing a balance of liberty and order. In particular, the Massachusetts delegates to the 1787 Constitutional Convention benefited from their four years of efforts to craft a suitable constitution.

In this article, Jack N. Rakove argues that in writing a new constitution the framers concluded that the Union needed to be completely reconstituted and that the states' constitution-building experiences offered a series of practical lessons for them to draw on. Most important, the state experiences taught the framers to think of a constitution as specifying the broad nature and powers of government, an integral step to making it the supreme law of the land. Their preliminary efforts at writing state documents gave the framers a base of understanding for their more difficult task of constructing a national constitution.

Traditions, by nature conservative, may sometimes have revolutionary origins. So it is with America's constitutional tradition. It was shaped not only by the decade of controversy that carried Americans to independence, but also—and more importantly—by the process of writing a series of innovative governing documents for the states and observing their effectiveness over the decade that followed.

For much of the 18th century, the American colonies and Great Britain had shared a constitutional tradition, though each emphasized different aspects. England, of course, had no single written constitutional document; its "constitution" was the totality of its governing laws and customs. The British held that the Glorious Revolution of 1688–89, which limited the King's authority over Parliament and confirmed that he was bound by constitutional principles, had also made Parliament the supreme source of law within the British Empire. But during

---

Jack N. Rakove is a professor of history at Stanford University.

the Stamp Act crisis of 1765, when Parliament took the position that it had the power to legislate for America "in all cases whatsoever," a grave and prophetic constitutional dispute erupted between the two countries.

In the American view, the Glorious Revolution restrained all arbitrary power, Parliament's as well as the King's. Americans were seeking for their own legislative assemblies the same rights and privileges that Parliament had secured for itself—including the exclusive power to enact laws and taxes for the people whom these bodies represented. That right rested on an ancient and hallowed constitutional principle: that law was binding only when enacted through popular consent.

Each crisis that followed the Stamp Act brought Britain's and the colonies' views of their rights and obligations toward each other into greater conflict. In Massachusetts in 1768, for example, the colony's General Court denied Parliament's authority to impose the Townshend duties. Britain's movement of troops into Boston that year was denounced as an occupation by a standing army. It begat the Boston Massacre in 1770. After the 1773 Tea Party, Parliament closed Boston's port, restructured the General Court, forbade town meetings without the governor's consent and decreed that Americans might be taken to England to stand trial. These actions brought on the convocation of the First Continental Congress and, eventually, the open hostilities at Lexington and Concord.

In the aftermath of these events, Americans were forced to think creatively about constitutionalism. Legal government collapsed in nearly every colony. Governors and officials acting under royal commission could hardly allow the colonial assemblies to enact laws mobilizing arms and men to defy Parliament and the King; colonists, on the other hand, had to reconsider their allegiance to a crown that made war on them. In the traditional view, government meant a contract under which subjects pledged fealty in exchange for the King's protection. Many Americans thus felt they were now absolved of any obligation to George III.

These colonists concluded that war and the collapse of lawful government had placed them in something like the state of nature described by the philosophers Thomas Hobbes and John Locke. It was impossible simply to restore the old colonial government: The judges, councillors and governors who ran it had resigned or fled. Government itself must be reconstituted. Americans had to replace elements of the monarchy under which they'd lived with new institutions appropriate to a republican people.

But how does one reconstitute government? Obviously a new executive must replace the old imperial governors, but the enterprise did not stop there. In the months preceding and after the Declaration of Independence, then, 11 of the 13 colonies decided to write constitutions that would bring their citizens out of the state of nature and give them the benefits of government by consent. These constitutions were revolutionary not only because of the circumstances that gave them birth, but also because the process of writing them enabled Americans to break from the constitutional tradition inherited from England. No longer did the colonists think of a constitution as a set of norms and customs descended from a distant past, or use the word to describe the current practices of a government. Americans gave the concept an entirely new meaning. As they now defined it, *constitution* referred to a single document that specified the nature and powers of the government, written and adopted at a specific moment in time. A later innovation would give the document revolutionary authority: It would be adopted under conditions establishing it as the supreme and fundamental law of the land, limiting government and unalterable by it.

In reconstituting government through written constitutions, the colonists did not consider how to distinguish an act establishing government from statutes or ordinary legislative acts. Although several states had held new elections so that the drafters of these constitutions could come with fresh authority from their citizenry, some observers—notably in Massachusetts—began to think that more might be needed.

In the often contentious Bay State, the legislature's efforts to draft a constitution under its own authority sparked a popular revolt that led to a critical constitutional breakthrough. For a constitution to become supreme law, a number of communities insisted, two conditions had to be met. First, the document had to be drafted by a body appointed for that purpose alone; and second, the proposed constitution then had to be submitted to the people for approval. It took the citizens of Massachusetts four years to reach agreement on these points, but when they adopted the constitution of 1780 on this basis, they had discovered a principle that would be of critical importance to the framers of the federal Constitution.

The precise legal authority of the other state constitutions was in doubt. These constitutions and their accompanying declarations of rights were more than statutes but less than supreme, fundamental law. To a modern reader, these declarations of rights are strange but exciting documents. They are not merely compendiums of legally enforceable rights; they also include broad statements on the first principles of government, the moral obligations and political rights of citizens and the importance of freedom of the press and religious conscience, as well as rules relating to specific issues such as search-and-seizure and compensation for property taken for public use. But rather than compel government to follow their dictates, these statements typically said that such rights "ought to" (not "shall") be respected.

But it is one thing to declare rights and another to set them beyond the reach of politics. To observers like Thomas Jefferson and James Madison, the experience of the states after 1776 offered a continuing lesson in the errors of the "compilers"—as Madison called them—of the first constitutions. Two errors were critical. First, the defective procedures used to adopt those constitutions prevented the documents from becoming fundamental law, unalterable by later legislatures. And second, the real danger to balanced government that a well-constructed constitution should guard against came from the people's own legislative representatives. As Jefferson observed in his *Notes on the State of Virginia* (1785), "An elective despotism was not the government we fought for."

Madison kept these problems in mind as he worked to bring about the Constitutional Convention of 1787. The Articles of Confederation, America's first governing document, had often been denounced as an "imbecility" because of its want of power. Its single-chambered Congress had no authority to legislate or tax in its own right; instead it proposed measures that the state legislatures were expected to carry out. The failure of the states to do so had convinced Madison and others that the national government had to be given the authority to enact, execute and adjudicate law in its own right, without relying on the intermediary authority of the states.

Had the framers simply wished to give the existing Congress a few modest additional powers, the convention could have wrapped up its business in a fortnight or so and headed home. But many of them realized that the Union must be reconstituted as a government in the full sense of the term, and with this insight they embarked on a more ambitious and difficult project. Now they could ask what a well-constructed republican government should look like. And in answering this question, they drew time and again on the past decade of constitutional experience within the states. There were many sources for the framers' ideas of government—from the writers of classical antiquity to the luminaries of the European Enlightenment—but the lessons that mattered most were those they had learned on native ground.

The framers were expected to present the results of the convention's work to the Confederation Congress, which presumably would submit the Constitution to the states for approval. Under the Articles of Confederation, all 13 legislatures had to accept any amendments; but one of those states, Rhode Island, had not even sent a delegation to Philadelphia. Nor were the framers at all confident that the other 12 states, as net losers of power, would comply with so radical a restructuring of the Union and sanction the Constitution.

Obviously, the rule of unanimity had to go. But even if the Constitution won approval, how was its supremacy over state constitutions to be confirmed? Now Madison, James Wilson and other nationalists invoked the Massachusetts discovery, which became a guiding rule of American constitutionalism. They asked Congress to suggest that the state legislatures lay the proposed Constitution before special, popularly elected ratification conventions. Approval by these conventions would establish grounds for making the Constitution the supreme and fundamental law of the land. Ratification by the people would create a Constitution superior in authority to the constitutions and laws of the states, and would give the federal government a persuasive argument for countermanding state measures that ran contrary to national law. Popular ratification would also convey this benefit within the national government. Each of the three federal branches—particularly the weaker executive and the judiciary—would have a rationale for opposing the "encroachments" of the others, especially Congress's.

The possibility, however, that a powerful national government would run roughshod over the states alarmed anti-Federalists, who opposed the Constitution. One of the most vociferous, Maryland Attorney General Luther Martin, left the convention early to organize opposition to the new government. In his view, and those of many states'-rights advocates since, no national constitution can abridge the immutable sovereignty of the Union's original members—the states. This tension between national supremacy and state sovereignty has been a continuing part of America's constitutional tradition. It dominated constitutional discourse for much of the 19th century, and has been revived periodically in the 20th, most recently in the wake of the 1994 congressional elections.

George Mason of Virginia, a delegate to the convention who would refuse to sign the Constitution, opposed it for other reasons. High on his list of objections was his colleagues' refusal to add a declaration of rights such as the one he had drafted for Virginia in 1776. Their failure to do so is often regarded as a political error—and perhaps it was. But the omission also reflected the reexamination of constitutionalism that was going on. Before 1787, a bill of rights recognized those rights existing from time immemorial that had become part of the social contract, a pact formed in some mythic past when people first agreed to live in society. But Americans were writing real compacts of government, and this process raised disturbing questions: Must rights be explicitly stated in these new constitutions to retain their authority? Or would fundamental rights remain intact whether stated or not?

Anti-Federalists had a plain answer to these questions: adopt a bill of rights no matter what. But Federalists were less certain. Suppose you wrote a bill of rights, Madison asked, and failed to enumerate all rights worth protecting? Would those unenumerated rights lose influence? Or suppose you used an ambiguous or watered-down text to secure adoption of an unpopular right. Wouldn't you risk weakening the authority of that right?

Despite these concerns, Madison conceded that a bill of rights should be added to the Constitution—more to allay the fears of moderate anti-Federalists than because he believed it important in itself. In 1789, at the first session of the new Congress, he persuaded his colleagues to propose 12 amendments; of these, the 10 we know as the Bill of Rights were ratified by the states. For more than a century afterward, the seeming irrelevance of these amendments suggested that Madison's doubts about their utility were well founded. Only early in the 20th century did the courts begin to interpret parts of the Bill of Rights to protect individual rights and liberties from abuse by both state and national governments. In the past 50 years, the interpretation and reinterpretation of the Bill of Rights and its great descendant, the 14th Amendment, have generated many of the serious controversies of law and politics that have shaped the American constitutional tradition.

Despite two centuries of debate, urgent political or legal questions repeatedly call the meaning of one or another constitutional provision into doubt. That the Constitution can be continually enlarged and invigorated in this way tells us something important. When Americans began writing constitutions, they did not foresee that these texts—especially the national charter—would acquire such profound authority. Constitutionalism was an experiment; even its greatest adherents—men like Madison, Jefferson and Alexander Hamilton—brooded about its likely success. Both Madison and Hamilton were privately skeptical whether the federal Constitution would last, and Jefferson mused that constitutions should be replaced every generation. Each would be surprised by how deep a hold the Constitution has acquired and retained over our political culture. Revolutionary in its origins, the American constitutional tradition may have grown more conservative in its workings—yet what is most striking about it is its vitality.

Questions for Discussion

1. How did the framers' experiences within the colonies and states (under the Articles of Confederation) shape their approaches to constructing a new constitution?
2. Why did Madison oppose the listing of a particular "Bill of Rights"? You might return to this question in light of the reasoning in *Griswold* v. *Connecticut* (see selection 3.2), which establishes a "right of privacy."

 1.2

An Economic Interpretation of the Constitution of the United States

Charles A. Beard

One central problem in establishing a new constitutional order in 1787 was that of limiting the power of the majority within a centralized political system that drew ultimate legitimacy from the approval of its citizens. Indeed, this was a major task that the framers addressed in writing and seeking ratification for the document.

Charles A. Beard (1874–1948), a professor of history at Columbia University, helped found the New School for Social Research in New York City.

Charles A. Beard argues that the framers, "by the force of circumstances, [were] compelled to convince large economic groups that safety and strength [lay] in the adoption of the new system." This was a neat trick given Beard's assessment of the framers as economic elitists who relentlessly pursued their own interests throughout the process.

Among interpreters of the creation of the Constitution, few scholars have had more impact than Charles Beard. Despite shortcomings in Beard's analysis, his approach has been extremely important in opening up the subject to subsequent demythologizing interpretations. In addition, you should bear in mind historian Richard Hofstadter's assertion that the framers saw prosperity as virtually essential for the protection of liberty.

The Constitution as an Economic Document

I t is difficult for the superficial student of the Constitution, who has read only the commentaries of the legists,* to conceive of that instrument as an economic document. It places no property qualifications on voters or officers; it gives no outward recognition of any economic groups in society; it mentions no special privileges to be conferred upon any class. It betrays no feeling, such as vibrates through the French constitution of 1791; its language is cold, formal, and severe.

The true inwardness of the Constitution is not revealed by an examination of its provisions as simple propositions of law; but by a long and careful study of the voluminous correspondence of the period, contemporary newspapers and pamphlets, the records of the debates in the Convention at Philadelphia and in the several state conventions, and particularly, *The Federalist*, which was widely circulated during the struggle over ratification. The correspondence shows the exact character of the evils which the Constitution was intended to remedy; the records of the proceedings in the Philadelphia Convention reveal the successive steps in the building of the framework of the government under the pressure of economic interests; the pamphlets and newspapers disclose the ideas of the contestants over the ratification; and *The Federalist* presents the political science of the new system as conceived by three of the profoundest thinkers of the period, Hamilton, Madison, and Jay.

Doubtless, the most illuminating of these sources on the economic character of the Constitution are the records of the debates in the Convention, which have come down to us in fragmentary form; and a thorough treatment of material forces reflected in the several clauses of the instrument of government created by the grave assembly at Philadelphia would require a rewriting of the history of the

* A legist is a person learned in law, particularly ancient and Roman law.

proceedings in the light of the great interests represented there. But an entire volume would scarcely suffice to present the results of such a survey, and an undertaking of this character is accordingly impossible here.

The Federalist, on the other hand, presents in a relatively brief and systematic form an economic interpretation of the Constitution by the men best fitted, through an intimate knowledge of the ideals of the framers, to expound the political science of the new government. This wonderful piece of argumentation by Hamilton, Madison, and Jay is in fact the finest study in the economic interpretation of politics which exists in any language; and whoever would understand the Constitution as an economic document need hardly go beyond it. It is true that the tone of the writers is somewhat modified on account of the fact that they are appealing to the voters to ratify the Constitution, but at the same time they are, by the force of circumstances, compelled to convince large economic groups that safety and strength lie in the adoption of the new system.

Indeed, every fundamental appeal in it is to some material and substantial interest. Sometimes it is to the people at large in the name of protection against invading armies and European coalitions. Sometimes it is to the commercial classes whose business is represented as prostrate before the follies of the Confederation. Now it is to creditors seeking relief against paper money and the assaults of the agrarians in general; now it is to the holders of federal securities which are depreciating toward the vanishing point. But above all, it is to the owners of personalty* anxious to find a foil against the attacks of levelling democracy, that the authors of *The Federalist* address their most cogent arguments in favor of ratification. It is true there is much discussion of the details of the new framework of government, to which even some friends of reform took exceptions; but Madison and Hamilton both knew that these were incidental matters when compared with the sound basis upon which the superstructure rested.

In reading the pages of this remarkable work as a study in political economy, it is important to bear in mind that the system, which the authors are describing, consisted of two fundamental parts—one positive, the other negative:

I. A government endowed with certain positive powers, but so constructed as to break the force of majority rule and prevent invasions of the property rights of minorities.

II. Restrictions on the state legislatures which had been so vigorous in their attacks on capital.

Under some circumstances, action is the immediate interest of the dominant party; and whenever it desires to make an economic gain through governmental functioning, it must have, of course, a system endowed with the requisite powers.

Examples of this are to be found in protective tariffs, in ship subsidies, in railway land grants, in river and harbor improvements, and so on through the catalogue of so-called "paternalistic" legislation. Of course it may be shown that the

---

* *Personalty* is a legal term for personal property.

"general good" is the ostensible object of any particular act; but the general good is a passive force, and unless we know who are the several individuals that benefit in its name, it has no meaning. When it is so analyzed, immediate and remote beneficiaries are discovered; and the former are usually found to have been the dynamic element in securing the legislation. Take, for example, the economic interests of the advocates who appear in tariff hearings at Washington.

On the obverse side, dominant interests quite as often benefit from the prevention of governmental action as from positive assistance. They are able to take care of themselves if let alone within the circle of protection created by the law. Indeed, most owners of property have as much to fear from positive governmental action as from their inability to secure advantageous legislation. Particularly is this true where the field of private property is already extended to cover practically every form of tangible and intangible wealth. This was clearly set forth by Hamilton:

> It may perhaps be said that the power of preventing bad laws includes that of preventing good ones. . . . But this objection will have little weight with those who can properly estimate the mischiefs of that inconstancy and mutability in the laws which form the greatest blemish in the character and genius of our governments. They will consider every institution calculated to restrain the excess of law-making, and to keep things in the same state in which they happen to be at any given period, as more likely to do good than harm. . . . The injury which may possibly be done by defeating a few good laws will be amply compensated by the advantage of preventing a number of bad ones.

The Underlying Political Science of the Constitution

Before taking up the economic implications of the structure of the federal government, it is important to ascertain what, in the opinion of *The Federalist*, is the basis of all government. The most philosophical examination of the foundations of political science is made by Madison in the tenth number. [See selection 9.1.] Here he lays down, in no uncertain language, the principle that the first and elemental concern of every government is economic.

1. "The first object of government," he declares, is the protection of "the diversity in the faculties of men, from which the rights of property originate." The chief business of government, from which, perforce, its essential nature must be derived, consists in the control and adjustment of conflicting economic interests. After enumerating the various forms of propertied interests which spring up inevitably in modern society, he adds: "The regulation of these various and interfering interests forms the principal task of modern legislation, and involves the spirit of party and faction in the ordinary operations of the government."

2. What are the chief causes of these conflicting political forces with which the government must concern itself? Madison answers. Of course fanciful and frivolous distinctions have sometimes been the cause of violent conflicts; "but the most common and durable source of factions has been the various and

unequal distribution of property. Those who hold and those who are without property have ever formed distinct interests in society. Those who are creditors, and those who are debtors, fall under a like discrimination. A landed interest, a manufacturing interest, a mercantile interest, a moneyed interest, with many lesser interests grow up of necessity in civilized nations, and divide them into different classes actuated by different sentiments and views."

3. The theories of government which men entertain are emotional reactions to their property interests. "From the protection of different and unequal faculties of acquiring property, the possession of different degrees and kinds of property immediately results; *and from the influence of these on the sentiments and views of the respective proprietors, ensues a division of society into different interests and parties.*" Legislatures reflect these interests. "What," he asks, "are the different classes of legislators but advocates and parties to the causes which they determine." There is no help for it. "The causes of faction cannot be removed," and "we well know that neither moral nor religious motives can be relied on as an adequate control."

4. Unequal distribution of property is inevitable, and from it contending factions will rise in the state. The government will reflect them, for they will have their separate principles and "sentiments"; but the supreme danger will arise from the fusion of certain interests into an overbearing majority, which Madison, in another place, prophesied would be the landless proletariat—an overbearing majority which will make its "rights" paramount, and sacrifice the "rights" of the minority. "To secure the public good," he declares, "and private rights against the danger of such a faction and at the same time preserve the spirit and the form of popular government is then the great object to which our inquiries are directed."

5. How is this to be done? Since the contending classes cannot be eliminated and their interests are bound to be reflected in politics, the only way out lies in making it difficult for enough contending interests to fuse into a majority, and in balancing one over against another. The machinery for doing this is created by the new Constitution and by the Union. (a) Public views are to be refined and enlarged "by passing them through the medium of a chosen body of citizens." (b) The very size of the Union will enable the inclusion of more interests so that the danger of an overbearing majority is not so great. "The smaller the society, the fewer probably will be the distinct parties and interests composing it; the fewer the distinct parties and interests, the more frequently will a majority be found of the same party. . . . Extend the sphere, and you take in a greater variety of parties and interests; you make it less probable that a majority of the whole will have a common motive to invade the rights of other citizens; or if such a common motive exists, it will be more difficult for all who feel it to discover their strength and to act in unison with each other."

Q.E.D. [which was to be demonstrated], "in the extent and proper structure of the Union, therefore, we behold a republican remedy for the diseases most incident to republican government."

The Economic Conflict over Ratification as Viewed by Contemporaries

. . . No one can pore for weeks over the letters, newspapers, and pamphlets of the years 1787–1789 without coming to the conclusion that there was a deep-seated conflict between a popular party based on paper money and agrarian interests, and a conservative party centered in the towns and resting on financial, mercantile, and personal property interests generally. It is true that much of the fulmination in pamphlets was concerned with controversies over various features of the Constitution; but those writers who went to the bottom of matters, such as the authors of *The Federalist,* and the more serious Anti-Federalists,* gave careful attention to the basic elements in the struggle as well as to the incidental controversial details.

The superficiality of many of the ostensible reasons put forth by the opponents of the Constitution was penetrated by Madison. Writing to Jefferson, in October, 1788, he says: "The little pamphlet herewith inclosed will give you a collective view of the alterations which have been proposed by the State Conventions for the new Constitution. Various and numerous as they appear, they certainly omit many of the true grounds of opposition. The articles relating to Treaties, to paper money, and to contracts, created more enemies than all the errors in the system, positive and negative, put together."

Naturally the more circumspect of the pamphleteers who lent their support to the new system were careful about a too precise alignment of forces, for their strength often lay in the conciliation of opponents rather than in exciting a more deep-seated antagonism. But even in such conciliatory publications the material advantages to be expected from the adoption of the Constitution are constantly put forward.

Take, for example, this extract from a mollifying "Address to the Freemen of America" issued while the Convention was in the midst of its deliberations:

> Let the public creditor, who lent his money to his country, and the soldier and citizen who yielded their services, come forward next and contribute their aid to establish an effective federal government. It is from the united power and resources of America only that they can expect permanent and substantial justice. . . . Let the citizens of America who inhabit the western counties of our states fly to a federal power for protection [against the Indians]. . . . Let the farmer who groans beneath the weight of direct taxation seek relief from a government whose extensive jurisdiction will enable it to extract the resources of our country by means of imposts and customs. Let the merchant, who complains of the restrictions and exclusions imposed upon his vessels by foreign nations, unite his influence in establishing a power that shall retaliate those injuries and insure him success in his honest pursuits by a general system of commercial

---

* The term *antifederalists* has attached itself to opponents of the Constitution. Ironically, Madison and Hamilton were nationalists who appropriated the federalist title. True federalists, who desired more power for the states, were left with the less attractive *antifederalist* label.

regulations. Let the manufacturer and mechanic, who are everywhere languishing for
want of employment, direct their eyes to an assembly of the states. It will be in their
power only to encourage such arts and manufactures as are essential to the prosperity of
our country. . . .

Conclusions

. . . The movement for the Constitution of the United States was originated and
carried through principally by four groups of personalty interests which had been
adversely affected under the Articles of Confederation: money, public securities,
manufactures, and trade and shipping.

The first firm steps toward the formation of the Constitution were taken by a
small and active group of men immediately interested through their personal
possessions in the outcome of their labors.

No popular vote was taken directly or indirectly on the proposition to call the
Convention which drafted the Constitution.

A large propertyless mass was, under the prevailing suffrage qualifications,
excluded at the outset from participation (through representatives) in the work
of framing the Constitution.

The members of the Philadelphia Convention which drafted the Constitution
were, with a few exceptions, immediately, directly, and personally interested in,
and derived economic advantages from, the establishment of the new system.

The Constitution was essentially an economic document based upon the
concept that the fundamental private rights of property are anterior to government and morally beyond the reach of popular majorities.

The major portion of the members of the Convention are on record
as recognizing the claim of property to a special and defensive position in
the Constitution.

In the ratification of the Constitution, about three-fourths of the adult males
failed to vote on the question, having abstained from the elections at which
delegates to the state conventions were chosen, either on account of their
indifference or their disfranchisement by property qualifications.

The Constitution was ratified by a vote of probably not more than one-sixth of
the adult males.

It is questionable whether a majority of the voters participating in the elections
for the state conventions in New York, Massachusetts, New Hampshire, Virginia,
and South Carolina, actually approved the ratification of the Constitution.

The leaders who supported the Constitution in the ratifying conventions
represented the same economic groups as the members of the Philadelphia
Convention; and in a large number of instances they were also directly and
personally interested in the outcome of their efforts.

In the ratification, it became manifest that the line of cleavage for and against the Constitution was between substantial personalty interests on the one hand and the small farming and debtor interests on the other.

The Constitution was not created by "the whole people" as the jurists have said; neither was it created by "the states" as Southern nullifiers long contended; but it was the work of a consolidated group whose interests knew no state boundaries and were truly national in their scope.

Questions for Discussion

1. After reading selection 1.3 (Roche), compare his characterization of the framers with that of Beard. Do these scholars reach fundamentally different conclusions, or are they essentially in accord on the nature of the framers' actions and motivations?
2. Why was a strong central government so important for a propertied economic elite? Do you think the framers acted solely on economic grounds?

 1.3

The Founding Fathers: A Reform Caucus in Action

John P. Roche

After two hundred years, the American Constitution remains a vital document, subject to continuing reinterpretation in the courts. At the same time, its status in American mythology has become more firmly enshrined. A balance between tangible and symbolic elements has been central to the success of the Constitution, but we need to put down our rose-colored glasses to view its creation in ways that contribute to both our contemporary and our historic understanding of it.

In this selection, John P. Roche argues that the framers of the Constitution were above all "superb democratic politicians" who constituted an elite—but a demo-

John P. Roche is a professor of political science at Tufts University.

cratic elite. Roche objects to viewing the framers solely through the lens of *The Federalist,* the collection of articles in support of ratification, which he regards as a brilliant set of post hoc rationalizations. Instead, James Madison should be seen as a clever tactical politician and an "inspired propagandist," whose writing in *The Federalist* only incidentally emerges as brilliant political theory. We might well wonder what our political system would have looked like, absent the framers' political acumen.

◆ ◆ ◆ The Convention has been described picturesquely as a counter-revolutionary junta and the Constitution as a *coup d'état,* but this has been accomplished by withdrawing the whole history of the movement for constitutional reform from its true context. No doubt the goals of the constitutional elite were "subversive" to the existing political order, but it is overlooked that their subversion could only have succeeded if the people of the United States endorsed it by regularized procedures. Indubitably they were "plotting" to establish a much stronger central government than existed under the Articles, but only in the sense in which one could argue equally well that John F. Kennedy was, from 1956 to 1960, "plotting" to become President. In short, on the fundamental *procedural* level, the Constitutionalists had to work according to the prevailing rules of the game. . . .

I

The history of the United States from 1786 to 1790 was largely one of a masterful employment of political expertise by the Constitutionalists as against bumbling, erratic behavior by the opponents of reform. Effectively, the Constitutionalists had to induce the states, by democratic techniques of coercion, to emasculate themselves. To be specific, if New York had refused to join the new Union, the project was doomed; yet before New York was safely in, the reluctant state legislature had . . . to take the following steps: (1) agree to send delegates to the Philadelphia Convention; (2) provide maintenance for these delegates . . . ; (3) set up the special *ad hoc* convention to decide on ratification; and (4) concede to the decision of the *ad hoc* convention that New York should participate. New York admittedly was a tricky state, with a strong interest in a *status quo* which permitted her to exploit New Jersey and Connecticut, but the same legal hurdles existed in every state. . . . the *only* weapon in the Constitutionalist arsenal was an effective mobilization of public opinion.

The group which undertook this struggle was an interesting amalgam of a few dedicated nationalists with the self-interested spokesmen of various parochial bailiwicks. The Georgians, for example, wanted a strong central authority to provide military protection for their huge, underpopulated state . . . ; Jerseymen and Connecticuters wanted to escape from economic bondage to New York; the Virginians hoped to establish a system which would give that great state its rightful place in the councils of the republic. . . . There was, of course, a large element of personality in the affair: There is reason to suspect that Patrick Henry's opposition to the Convention and the Constitution was founded on his conviction that Jefferson was behind both, and a close study of local politics elsewhere would surely reveal that others supported the Constitution for the simple (and politically quite sufficient) reason that the "wrong" people were against it.

To say this is not to suggest that the Constitution rested on a foundation of impure or base motives. It is rather to argue that in politics there are no immaculate conceptions, and that in the drive for a stronger general government, motives of all sorts played a part. Few men in the history of mankind have espoused a view of the "common good" or "public interest" that militated against their private status; even Plato with all his reverence for disembodied reason managed to put philosophers on top of the pile. Thus it is not surprising that a number of diversified private interests joined to push the nationalist public interest; what would have been surprising was the absence of such a pragmatic united front. And the fact remains that, however motivated, these men did demonstrate a willingness to compromise their parochial interests in behalf of an ideal which took shape before their eyes and under their ministrations.

As Stanley Elkins and Eric McKitrick have suggested in a perceptive essay, what distinguished the leaders of the Constitutionalist caucus from their enemies was a "Continental" approach to political, economic and military issues. To the extent that they shared an institutional base of operations, it was the Continental Congress (thirty-nine of the delegates to the Federal Convention had served in Congress), and this was hardly a locale which inspired respect for the state governments. . . . "Continental" ideology developed which seems to have demanded a revision of our domestic institutions primarily on the ground that only by invigorating our general government could we assume our rightful place in the international arena. Indeed, an argument with great force—particularly since Washington was its incarnation—urged that our very survival in the Hobbesian* jungle of world politics depended upon a reordering and strengthening of our national sovereignty. . . .

The great achievement of the Constitutionalists was their ultimate success in convincing the elected representatives of a majority of the white male population that change was imperative. A small group of political leaders with a Continental vision and essentially a consciousness of the United States' *international* impotence, provided the matrix of the movement. To their standard other leaders

---

* Thomas Hobbes (1588–1679) was an English philosopher who viewed human nature as brutish and self-seeking to the point of anarchy. The state, with an absolute ruler, thus becomes an agency for maintaining peace and order.

rallied with their own parallel ambitions. Their great assets were (1) the presence in their caucus of the one authentic American "father figure," George Washington, whose prestige was enormous; (2) the energy and talent of their leadership (in which one must include the towering intellectuals of the time, John Adams and Thomas Jefferson, despite their absence abroad), and their communications "network," which was far superior to anything on the opposition side; (3) preemptive skill which made "their" issue The Issue and kept the locally oriented opposition permanently on the defensive; and (4) the subjective consideration that these men were spokesmen of a new and compelling credo: *American* nationalism, that ill-defined but nonetheless potent sense of collective purpose that emerged from the American Revolution. . . .

The Constitutionalists got the jump on the "opposition" (a collective noun: oppositions would be more correct) at the outset with the demand for a Convention. Their opponents were caught in an old political trap: They were not being asked to approve any specific program of reform, but only to endorse a meeting to discuss and recommend needed reforms. If they took a hard line at the first stage, they were put in the position of glorifying the *status quo* and of denying the need for *any* changes. Moreover, the Constitutionalists could go to the people with a persuasive argument for "fair play"—"How can you condemn reform before you know precisely what is involved?" Since the state legislatures obviously would have the final say on any proposals that might emerge from the Convention, the Constitutionalists were merely reasonable men asking for a chance. Besides, since they did not make any concrete proposals at that stage, they were in a position to capitalize on every sort of generalized discontent with the Confederation.

Perhaps because of their poor intelligence system, perhaps because of overconfidence generated by the failure of all previous efforts to alter the Articles, the opposition awoke too late to the dangers that confronted them in 1787. Not only did the Constitutionalists manage to get every state but Rhode Island . . . to appoint delegates to Philadelphia, but when the results were in, it appeared that they dominated the delegations. Given the apathy of the opposition, this was a natural phenomenon: In an ideologically nonpolarized political atmosphere those who get appointed to a special committee are likely to be the men who supported the movement for its creation. Even George Clinton, who seems to have been the first opposition leader to awake to the possibility of trouble, could not prevent the New York legislature from appointing Alexander Hamilton—though he did have the foresight to send two of his henchmen to dominate the delegation. Incidentally, much has been made of the fact that the delegates to Philadelphia were not elected by the people; some have adduced this fact as evidence of the "undemocratic" character of the gathering. But put in the context of the time, this argument is wholly specious: The central government under the Articles was considered a creature of the component states and in all the states but Rhode Island, Connecticut and New Hampshire, members of the national Congress were chosen by the state legislatures. This was not a consequence of elitism or fear of the mob; it was a logical extension of states'-rights doctrine to guarantee that the national institution did not end-run the state legislatures and make direct contact with the people.

II

With delegations safely named, the focus shifted to Philadelphia. While waiting for a quorum to assemble, James Madison got busy and drafted the so-called Randolph or Virginia Plan with the aid of the Virginia delegation. This was a political master-stroke. Its consequence was that once business got underway, the framework of discussion was established on Madison's terms. There was no interminable argument over agenda; instead the delegates took the Virginia Resolutions—"just for purposes of discussion"—as their point of departure. And along with Madison's proposals, many of which were buried in the course of the summer, went his major premise: a new start on a Constitution rather than piecemeal amendment. This was not necessarily revolutionary—a little exegesis could demonstrate that a new Constitution might be formulated as "amendments" to the Articles of Confederation—but Madison's proposal that this "lump sum" amendment go into effect after approval by nine states (the Articles required unanimous state approval for any amendment) was thoroughly subversive. . . .

Basic differences of opinion emerged, of course, but these were not ideological; they were *structural*. If the so-called "states'-rights" group had not accepted the fundamental purposes of the Convention, they could simply have pulled out and by doing so have aborted the whole enterprise. Instead of bolting, they returned day after day to argue and to compromise. An interesting symbol of this basic homogeneity was the initial agreement on secrecy: These professional politicians did not want to become prisoners of publicity; they wanted to retain that freedom of maneuver which is only possible when men are not forced to take public stands in the preliminary stages of negotiation. There was no legal means of binding the tongues of the delegates: At any stage in the game a delegate with basic principled objections to the emerging project could have taken the stump (as Luther Martin did after his exit) and denounced the convention to the skies. Yet Madison did not even inform Thomas Jefferson in Paris of the course of the deliberations and available correspondence indicates that the delegates generally observed the injunction. Secrecy is certainly uncharacteristic of any assembly marked by strong ideological polarization. This was noted at the time: The *New York Daily Advertiser*, August 14, 1787, commented that the ". . . profound secrecy hitherto observed by the Convention [we consider] a happy omen, as it demonstrates that the spirit of party on any great and essential point cannot have arisen to any height."

Commentators on the Constitution who have read *The Federalist* in lieu of reading the actual debates have credited the Fathers with the invention of a sublime concept called "Federalism." Unfortunately *The Federalist* is probative evidence for only one proposition: that Hamilton and Madison were inspired propagandists with a genius for retrospective symmetry. Federalism, as the theory is generally defined, was an improvisation which was later promoted into a political theory. . . .

It is indeed astonishing how those who have glibly designated James Madison the "father" of Federalism have overlooked the solid body of fact which indicates that he shared Hamilton's quest for a unitary central government.* To be specific, they have avoided examining the clear import of the Madison-Virginia Plan, and have disregarded Madison's dogged inch-by-inch retreat from the bastions of centralization. The Virginia Plan envisioned a unitary national government effectively freed from and dominant over the states. The lower house of the national legislature was to be elected directly by the people of the states with membership proportional to population. The upper house was to be selected by the lower, and the two chambers would elect the executive and choose the judges. The national government would be thus cut completely loose from the states.

The structure of the general government was freed from state control in a truly radical fashion, but the scope of the authority of the national sovereign as Madison initially formulated it was breathtaking. . . . The national legislature was to be empowered to disallow the acts of state legislatures, and the central government was vested, in addition to the powers of the nation under the Articles of Confederation, with plenary authority wherever ". . . the separate States are incompetent or in which the harmony of the United States may be interrupted by the exercise of individual legislation." Finally, just to lock the door against state intrusion, the national Congress was to be given the power to use military force on recalcitrant states. This was Madison's "model" of an ideal national government, though it later received little publicity in *The Federalist*.

The interesting thing was the reaction of the Convention to this militant program for a strong autonomous central government. Some delegates were startled, some obviously leery of so comprehensive a project of reform, but nobody set off any fireworks and nobody walked out. Moreover, in the two weeks that followed, the Virginia Plan received substantial endorsement *en principe*; the initial temper of the gathering can be deduced from the approval "without debate or dissent," on May 31, of the Sixth Resolution which granted Congress the authority to disallow state legislation ". . . contravening *in its opinion* the Articles of Union." Indeed, an amendment was included to bar states from contravening national treaties.

---

* Unitary governments such as that of Great Britain minimize the importance of local or regional units. Most major decisions are made at the national level.

The Virginia Plan may therefore be considered, in ideological terms, as the delegates' Utopia, but as the discussions continued and became more specific, many of those present began to have second thoughts. After all, they were not residents of Utopia or guardians in Plato's Republic who could simply impose a philosophical ideal on subordinate strata of the population. They were practical politicians in a democratic society, and no matter what their private dreams might be, they had to take home an acceptable package and defend it—and their own political futures—against predictable attack. On June 14 the breaking point between dream and reality took place. Apparently realizing that under the Virginia Plan, Massachusetts, Virginia and Pennsylvania could virtually dominate the national government—and probably appreciating that to sell this program to "the folks back home" would be impossible—the delegates from the small states dug in their heels and demanded time for a consideration of alternatives. One gets a graphic sense of the inner politics from John Dickinson's reproach to Madison: "You see the consequences of pushing things too far. Some of the members from the small States wish for two branches in the General Legislature, and are friends to a good National Government; but we would sooner submit to a foreign power than . . . be deprived of an equality of suffrage in both branches of the Legislature, and thereby be thrown under the domination of the large States."

. . . Now the process of accommodation was put into action smoothly—and wisely, given the character and strength of the doubters. Madison had the votes, but this was one of those situations where the enforcement of mechanical majoritarianism could easily have destroyed the objectives of the majority: The Constitutionalists were in quest of a qualitative as well as a quantitative consensus. This was hardly from deference to local Quaker custom; it was a political imperative if they were to attain ratification.

III

According to the standard script, at this point the "states'-rights" group intervened in force behind the New Jersey Plan, which has been characteristically portrayed as a reversion to the *status quo* under the Articles of Confederation with but minor modifications. A careful examination of the evidence indicates that only in a marginal sense is this an accurate description. It is true that the New Jersey Plan put the states back into the institutional picture, but one could argue that to do so was a recognition of political reality rather than an affirmation of states' rights. A serious case can be made that the advocates of the New Jersey Plan, far from being ideological addicts of states' rights, intended to substitute for the Virginia Plan a system which would both retain strong national power and have a chance of adoption in the states. The leading spokesman for the project asserted quite clearly that his views were based more on counsels of expediency than on principle; said Paterson on June 16: "I came here not to speak my own sentiments, but the sentiments of those who sent me. Our object is not such a Governmt. as may be best in itself, but such a one as our Constituents have authorized us to prepare, and as they will approve." This is Madison's version; in Yates' transcription, there is a crucial sentence following the remarks above: "I believe that a little practical virtue is to be preferred to the finest theoretical principles, which cannot be carried into effect." . . .

This was a defense of political acumen, not of states' rights. In fact, Paterson's notes of his speech can easily be construed as an argument for attaining the substantive objectives of the Virginia Plan by a sound political route, *i.e.*, pouring the new wine in the old bottles. With a shrewd eye, Paterson queried:

> Will the Operation and Force of the [central] Govt. depend upon the mode of Represent.—No—it will depend upon the Quantum of Power lodged in the leg. ex. and judy. Departments—Give [the existing] Congress the same Powers that you intend to give the two Branches [under the Virginia Plan], and I apprehend they will act with as much Propriety and more Energy . . .

In other words, the advocates of the New Jersey Plan concentrated their fire on what they held to be the *political liabilities* of the Virginia Plan—which were matters of institutional structure—rather than on the proposed scope of national authority. Indeed, the Supremacy Clause of the Constitution first saw the light of day in Paterson's Sixth Resolution; the New Jersey Plan contemplated the use of military force to secure compliance with national law; and finally Paterson made clear his view that under either the Virginia or the New Jersey systems, the general government would ". . . act on individuals and not on states." From the states'-rights viewpoint, this was heresy: the fundament of that doctrine was the proposition that any central government had as its contituents the states, not the people, and could only reach the people through the agency of the state government.

Paterson then reopened the agenda of the Convention, but he did so within a distinctly nationalist framework. Paterson's position was one of favoring a strong central government in principle, but opposing one which in fact *put the big states in the saddle*. (The Virginia Plan, for all its abstract merits, did very well by Virginia.) As evidence for this speculation, there is a curious and intriguing proposal among Paterson's preliminary drafts of the New Jersey Plan:

> Whereas it is necessary in Order to form the People of the U.S. of America in to a Nation, that the States should be consolidated, by which means all the Citizens thereof will become equally intitled to and will equally participate in the same Privileges and Rights . . . it is therefore resolved, that all the Lands contained within the Limits of each state individually, and of the U.S. generally be considered as constituting one Body or Mass, and be divided into thirteen or more integral parts.
>
> Resolved, That such Divisions or integral Parts shall be styled Districts.

This makes it sound as though Paterson was prepared to accept a strong unified central government along the lines of the Virginia Plan if the existing states were eliminated. He may have gotten the idea from his New Jersey colleague Judge David Brearley, who on June 9 had commented that the only remedy to the dilemma over representation was ". . . that a map of the U.S. be spread out, that all the existing boundaries be erased, and that a new partition of the whole be made into 13 equal parts." According to Yates, Brearley added at this point, ". . . then a government on the present [Virginia Plan] system will be just."

   This proposition was never pushed—it was patently unrealistic—but one can appreciate its purpose: It would have separated the men from the boys in the large-state delegations. How attached would the Virginians have been to their reform principles if Virginia were to disappear as a component geographical unit (the largest) for representational purposes? Up to this point, the Virginians had been in the happy position of supporting high ideals with that inner confidence born of knowledge that the "public interest" they endorsed would nourish their private interest. Worse, they had shown little willingness to compromise. Now the delegates from the small states announced that they were unprepared to be offered up as sacrificial victims to a "national interest" which reflected Virginia's parochial ambition. Caustic Charles Pinckney was not far off when he remarked sardonically that ". . . the whole [conflict] comes to this"[:] "Give N. Jersey an equal vote, and she will dismiss her scruples, and concur in the Natil. system." What he rather unfairly did not add was that the Jersey delegates were not free agents who could adhere to their private convictions; they had to take back, sponsor and risk their reputations on the reforms approved by the Convention— and in New Jersey, not in Virginia. . . .

IV

On Tuesday morning, June 19, . . . James Madison led off with a long, carefully reasoned speech analyzing the New Jersey Plan which, while intellectually vigorous in its criticisms, was quite conciliatory in mood. "The great difficulty," he observed, "lies in the affair of Representation; and if this could be adjusted, all others would be surmountable." (As events were to demonstrate, this diagnosis was correct.) When he finished, a vote was taken on whether to continue with the Virginia Plan as the nucleus for a new constitution: seven states voted "Yes"; New York, New Jersey, and Delaware voted "No"; and Maryland, whose position often depended on which delegates happened to be on the floor, divided. Paterson, it seems, lost decisively; yet in a fundamental sense he and his allies had achieved their purpose: From that day onward, it could never be forgotten that the state governments loomed ominously in the background and that no verbal incantations could exorcise their power. Moreover, nobody bolted the convention: Paterson and his colleagues took their defeat in stride and set to work to modify the Virginia Plan, particularly with respect to its provisions on representation in the national legislature. Indeed, they won an immediate rhetorical bonus; when Oliver Ellsworth of Connecticut rose to move that the word "national" be expunged from the Third Virginia Resolution ("Resolved that a *national* Government ought to be established consisting of a *supreme* Legislative, Executive and Judiciary"), Randolph agreed and the motion passed unanimously. The process of compromise had begun.

For the next two weeks, the delegates circled around the problem of legislative representation. The Connecticut delegation appears to have evolved a possible compromise quite early in the debates, but the Virginians and particularly Madison (unaware that he would later be acclaimed as the prophet of "federalism") fought obdurately against providing for equal representation of states in the second chamber. There was a good deal of acrimony and at one point Benjamin Franklin—of all people—proposed the institution of a daily prayer; practical politicians in the gathering, however, were meditating more on the merits of a good committee than on the utility of Divine intervention. On July 2, the ice began to break when through a number of fortuitous events—and one that seems deliberate—the majority against equality of representation was converted into a dead tie. The Convention had reached the stage where it was "ripe" for a solution (presumably all the therapeutic speeches had been made), and the South Carolinians proposed a committee. Madison and James Wilson wanted none of it, but with only Pennsylvania dissenting, the body voted to establish a working party on the problem of representation.

The members of this committee, one from each state, were elected by the delegates—and a very interesting committee it was. Despite the fact that the Virginia Plan had held majority support up to that date, neither Madison nor Randolph was selected (Mason was the Virginian) and Baldwin of Georgia, whose shift in position had resulted in the tie, was chosen. From the composition, it was clear that this was not to be a "fighting" committee: The emphasis in membership was on what might be described as "second-level political entrepreneurs." On the basis of the discussions up to that time, only Luther Martin of Maryland could be described as a "bitter-ender." Admittedly, some divination enters into this sort of analysis, but one does get a sense of the mood of the delegates from these choices—including the interesting selection of Benjamin Franklin, despite his age and intellectual wobbliness, over the brilliant and incisive Wilson or the sharp, polemical Gouverneur Morris, to represent Pennsylvania. His passion for conciliation was more valuable at this juncture than Wilson's logical genius, or Morris' acerbic wit.

. . . It should be reiterated that the Madison model had no room either for the states or for the "separation of powers": Effectively *all* governmental power was vested in the national legislature. The merits of Montesquieu did not turn up until *The Federalist*; and although a perverse argument could be made that Madison's ideal was truly in the tradition of John Locke's *Second Treatise of Government*, the Locke whom the American rebels treated as an honorary president was a pluralistic defender of vested rights, not of parliamentary supremacy.*

It would be tedious to continue a blow-by-blow analysis of the work of the delegates; the critical fight was over representation of the states and once the Connecticut Compromise[†] was adopted on July 17, the Convention was over the hump. . . . Moreover, once the compromise had carried (by five states to four, with one state divided), its advocates threw themselves vigorously into the job of strengthening the general government's substantive powers—as might have been predicted, indeed, from Paterson's early statements. It nourishes an increased respect for Madison's devotion to the art of politics, to realize that this dogged fighter could sit down six months later and prepare essays for *The Federalist* in contradiction to his basic convictions about the true course the Convention should have taken. . . .

VI

Drawing on their vast collective political experience, utilizing every weapon in the politician's arsenal, looking constantly over their shoulders at their constituents, the delegates put together a Constitution. It was a makeshift affair; some sticky issues (for example, the qualification of voters) they ducked entirely; others they mastered with that ancient instrument of political sagacity, studied ambiguity (for example, citizenship), and some they just overlooked. In this last category, I suspect, fell the matter of the power of the federal courts to determine the constitutionality of acts of Congress. When the judicial article was formulated (Article III of the Constitution), deliberations were still in the stage where the legislature was endowed with broad power under the Randolph formulation, authority which by its own terms was scarcely amenable to judicial review. In essence, courts could hardly determine when ". . . the separate States are incompetent or . . . the harmony of the United States may be interrupted"; the National Legislature, as critics pointed out, was free to define its own jurisdiction. Later the definition of legislative authority was changed into the form we know, a series of stipulated powers, *but the delegates never seriously reexamined the jurisdiction of the judiciary under this new limited formulation.* All arguments on the intention of the Framers in this matter are thus deductive and *a posteriori*, though some obviously make more sense than others.

---

* John Locke (1632–1704) was an English philosopher whose writings served as a basis for government rooted in a social contract between citizens and their rulers. Montesquieu (1689–1755) was a French political philosopher whose work emphasized checks and balances in the exercise of authority.

† The Connecticut Compromise advanced the solution of a two-chamber legislature, with each state receiving two senators and House representation in proportion to its population.

The Framers were busy and distinguished men, anxious to get back to their families, their positions, and their constituents, not members of the French Academy devoting a lifetime to a dictionary. They were trying to do an important job, and do it in such a fashion that their handiwork would be acceptable to very diverse constituencies. No one was rhapsodic about the final document, but it was a beginning, a move in the right direction, and one they had reason to believe the people would endorse. In addition, since they had modified the impossible amendment provisions of the Articles (the requirement of unanimity which could always be frustrated by "Rogues [Rhode] Island") to one demanding approval by only three-quarters of the states, they seemed confident that gaps in the fabric which experience would reveal could be rewoven without undue difficulty. . . .

Madison, despite his reservations about the Constitution, was the campaign manager in ratification. His first task was to get the Congress in New York to light its own funeral pyre by approving the "amendments" to the Articles and sending them on to the state legislatures. Above all, momentum had to be maintained. The anti-Constitutionalists, now thoroughly alarmed and no novices in politics, realized that their best tactic was attrition rather than direct opposition. Thus they settled on a position expressing qualified approval but calling for a second Convention to remedy various defects (the one with the most demagogic appeal was the lack of a Bill of Rights). Madison knew that to accede to this demand would be equivalent to losing the battle, nor would he agree to conditional approval (despite wavering even by Hamilton). This was an all-or-nothing proposition: national salvation or national impotence with no intermediate positions possible. Unable to get congressional approval, he settled for second best: a unanimous resolution of Congress transmitting the Constitution to the states for whatever action they saw fit to take. . . .

VII

. . . Victory for the Constitution meant simultaneous victory for the Constitutionalists; the anti-Constitutionalists either capitulated or vanished into limbo— soon Patrick Henry would be offered a seat on the Supreme Court and Luther Martin would be known as the Federalist "bull-dog." And irony of ironies, Alexander Hamilton and James Madison would shortly accumulate a reputation as the formulators of what is often alleged to be our political theory, the concept of "federalism." Also, on the other side of the ledger, the arguments would soon appear over what the Framers "really meant"; while these disputes have assumed the proportions of a big scholarly business in the last century, they began almost before the ink on the Constitution was dry. One of the best early ones featured Hamilton versus Madison on the scope of presidential power, and other Framers characteristically assumed positions in this and other disputes on the basis of their political convictions.

Probably our greatest difficulty is that we know so much more about what the Framers *should have meant* than they themselves did. We are intimately acquainted with the problems that their Constitution should have been designed to master; in short, we have read the mystery story backward. If we are to get the right "feel" for their time and their circumstances, we must, in Maitland's phrase, ". . . think ourselves back into a twilight." Obviously, no one can pretend completely to escape from the solipsistic web of his own environment, but if the effort is made, it is possible to appreciate the past roughly on its own terms. The first step in this process is to abandon the academic premise that because we can ask a question, there must be an answer.

Thus we can ask what the Framers meant when they gave Congress the power to regulate interstate and foreign commerce, and we emerge, reluctantly perhaps, with the reply that . . . they may not have known what they meant, that there may not have been any semantic consensus. The Convention was not a seminar in analytic philosophy or linguistic analysis. Commerce was *commerce*—and if different interpretations of the word arose, later generations could worry about the problem of definition. The delegates were in a hurry to get a new government established; when definitional arguments arose, they characteristically took refuge in ambiguity. If different men voted for the same proposition for varying reasons, that was politics (and still is); if later generations were unsettled by this lack of precision, that would be their problem. . . .

The Constitution, then, was not an apotheosis of "constitutionalism," a triumph of architectonic genius; it was a patch-work sewn together under the pressure of both time and events by a group of extremely talented democratic politicians. They refused to attempt the establishment of a strong, centralized sovereignty on the principle of legislative supremacy for the excellent reason that the people would not accept it. They risked their political fortunes by opposing the established doctrines of state sovereignty because they were convinced that the existing system was leading to national impotence and probably foreign domination. For two years, they worked to get a convention established. For over three months, in what must have seemed to the faithful participants an endless process of give-and-take, they reasoned, cajoled, threatened, and bargained amongst themselves. The result was a Constitution which the people, in fact, by democratic processes, did accept, and a new and far better national government was established. . . .

To conclude, the Constitution was neither a victory for abstract theory nor a great practical success. Well over half a million men had to die on the battlefields of the Civil War before certain constitutional principles could be defined—a baleful consideration which is somehow overlooked in our customary tributes to the farsighted genius of the Framers and to the supposed American talent for "constitutionalism." The Constitution was, however, a vivid demonstration of effective democratic political action, and of the forging of a national elite which literally persuaded its countrymen to hoist themselves by their own boot straps. American pro-consuls would be wise not to translate the Constitution into Japanese, or Swahili, or treat it as a work of semi-Divine origin; but when students of comparative politics examine the process of nation-building in countries newly freed from colonial rule, they may find the American experience instructive as a classic example of the potentialities of a democratic elite.

Questions for Discussion

1. How does Roche's approach to the framers affect our contemporary under-standing of the Constitution? How might the framers have confronted diffi-cult problems such as abortion and affirmative action?
2. What does Roche mean by a "democratic elite"? Is this phrase a contradiction in terms, or does it have real meaning?

 1.4

The Federalist, No. 51

James Madison

As we have seen, among the formidable tasks the framers faced in writing the Constitution was establishing a strong central government while minimizing the possibility that this authority would be abused. The resulting system of checks and balances relies heavily on the separation of powers and a multiple-level, federal relationship between the states and the national government.

James Madison, Alexander Hamilton, and John Jay led the fight for ratification through a series of newspaper articles, *The Federalist.* In the following selection from these papers, Madison articulates a sophisticated understanding of the actual operation of central authority divided into legislative, executive, and judicial branches. Madison observes that regardless of the formal separations embodied

---

James Madison, who was the chief drafter of the Constitution, became the fourth president of the United States.

within a constitution, the different branches in fact will share powers. Such a realistic assessment is reflected today in continuing arguments over the legislature's role in foreign policy (for example, passing legislation to implement the North American Free Trade Agreement) and the Supreme Court's willingness to range beyond narrow constitutional interpretations, as in its 1973 *Roe* v. *Wade* abortion decision.

---

*T*o *the People of the State of New York:* To what expedient, then, shall we finally resort for maintaining in practice the necessary partition of power among the several departments as laid down in the Constitution? The only answer that can be given is, that as all these exterior provisions are found to be inadequate, the defect must be supplied by so contriving the interior structure of the government as that its several constituent parts may, by their mutual relations, be the means of keeping each other in their proper places. Without presuming to undertake a full development of this important idea, I will hazard a few general observations, which may perhaps place it in a clearer light, and enable us to form a more correct judgment of the principles and structure of the government planned by the convention.

In order to lay a due foundation for that separate and distinct exercise of the difficult powers of government, which to a certain extent is admitted on all hands to be essential to the preservation of liberty, it is evident that each department should have a will of its own; and consequently should be so constituted that the members of each should have as little agency as possible in the appointment of the members of the others. Were this principle rigorously adhered to, it would require that all the appointments for the supreme executive, legislative, and judiciary magistracies should be drawn from the same fountain of authority, the people, through channels having no communication whatever with one another. Perhaps such a plan of constructing the several departments would be less difficult in practice than it may in contemplation appear. Some difficulties, however, and some additional expense would attend the execution of it. Some deviations, therefore, from the principle must be admitted. In the constitution of the judiciary department in particular, it might be inexpedient to insist rigorously on the principle: first, because peculiar qualifications being essential in the members, the primary consideration ought to be to select that mode of choice which best secures these qualifications; secondly, because the permanent tenure by which the appointments are held in that department must soon destroy all sense of dependence on the authority conferring them.

It is equally evident, that the members of each department should be as little dependent as possible on those of the others for the emoluments annexed to their offices. Were the executive magistrate or the judges not independent of the legislature in this particular, their independence in every other would be merely nominal.

But the great security against a gradual concentration of the several powers in the same department, consists in giving to those who administer each department the necessary constitutional means and personal motives to resist encroachments of the others. The provision for defence must in this, as in all other cases, be made commensurate to the danger of attack. Ambition must be made to counteract ambition. The interest of the man must be connected with the constitutional rights of the place. It may be a reflection on human nature, that such devices should be necessary to control the abuses of government. But what is government itself, but the greatest of all reflections on human nature? If men were angels, no government would be necessary. If angels were to govern men, neither external nor internal controls on government would be necessary. In framing a government which is to be administered by men over men, the great difficulty lies in this: you must first enable the government to control the governed; and in the next place oblige it to control itself. A dependence on the people is, no doubt, the primary control on the government; but experience has taught mankind the necessity of auxiliary precautions.

The policy of supplying, by opposite and rival interests, the defect of better motives might be traced through the whole system of human affairs, private as well as public. We see it particularly displayed in all the subordinate distributions of power, where the constant aim is to divide and arrange the several offices in such a manner as that each may be a check on the other—that the private interest of every individual may be a sentinel over the public rights. These inventions of prudence cannot be less requisite in the distribution of the supreme powers of the state.

But it is not possible to give to each department an equal power of self-defence. In republican government the legislative authority necessarily predominates. The remedy for this inconveniency is to divide the legislature into different branches; and to render them, by different modes of election and different principles of action, as little connected with each other as the nature of their common functions and their common dependence on the society will admit. It may even be necessary to guard against dangerous encroachments by still further precautions. As the weight of the legislative authority requires that it should be thus divided, the weakness of the executive may require, on the other hand, that it should be fortified. An absolute negative on the legislature [i.e., veto] appears, at first view, to be the natural defence with which the executive magistrate should be armed. But perhaps it would be neither altogether safe nor alone sufficient. On ordinary occasions it might not be exerted with the requisite firmness, and on extraordinary occasions it might be perfidiously abused. May not this defect of an absolute negative be supplied by some qualified connection between this weaker department and the weaker branch of the stronger department, by which the latter may be led to support the constitutional rights of the former, without being too much detached from the rights of its own department?

If the principles on which these observations are founded be just . . . and they be applied as a criterion to the several state constitutions and to the federal

Constitution, it will be found that if the latter does not perfectly correspond with them, the former are infinitely less able to bear such a test.

There are, moreover, two considerations particularly applicable to the federal system of America, which place that system in a very interesting point of view.

First. In a single republic, all the power surrendered by the people is submitted to the administration of a single government; and the usurpations are guarded against by a division of the government into distinct and separate departments. In the compound republic of America,* the power surrendered by the people is first divided between two distinct governments, and then the portion allotted to each subdivided among distinct and separate departments. Hence a double security arises to the rights of the people. The different governments will control each other, at the same time that each will be controlled by itself.

Second. It is of great importance in a republic not only to guard the society against the oppression of its rulers, but to guard one part of the society against the injustice of the other part. Different interests necessarily exist in different classes of citizens. If a majority be united by a common interest, the rights of the minority will be insecure. There are but two methods of providing against this evil: the one by creating a will in the community independent of the majority—that is, of the society itself; the other by comprehending in the society so many separate descriptions of citizens as will render an unjust combination of a majority of the whole very improbable, if not impracticable. The first method prevails in all governments possessing an hereditary or self-appointed authority. This, at best, is but a precarious security; because a power independent of the society may as well espouse the unjust views of the major, as the rightful interests of the minor party, and may possibly be turned against both parties. The second method will be exemplified in the federal republic of the United States. Whilst all authority in it will be derived from and dependent on the society, the society itself will be broken into so many parts, interests and classes of citizens, that the rights of individuals or of the minority will be in little danger from interested combinations of the majority. In a free government the security for civil rights must be the same as that for religious rights.† It consists in the one case in the multiplicity of interests and in the other in the multiplicity of sects. The degree of security in both cases will depend on the number of interests and sects; and this may be presumed to depend on the extent of country and number of people comprehended under the same government. This view of the subject must particularly recommend a proper federal system to all the sincere and considerate friends of republican government, since it shows that in exact proportion as the territory of

---

* For the framers, a republic was essentially a representative democracy. A compound republic placed representative authority at two levels, state and national.

† Madison and his colleagues did not incorporate a separate bill of rights into the Constitution; rather, they relied on the "multiplicity of interests" to protect these rights. In part, a guarantee that a bill of rights would be passed was essential to ratification, especially at New York's convention, where the document won a narrow 30-to-27 victory.

the Union may be formed into more circumscribed confederacies or states, oppressive combinations of a majority will be facilitated; the best security under the republican forms for the rights of every class of citizens will be diminished; and consequently the stability and independence of some member of the government, the only other security, must be proportionally increased. Justice is the end of government. It is the end of civil society. It ever has been and ever will be pursued until it be obtined, or until liberty be lost in the pursuit. In a society under the forms of which the stronger faction can readily unite and oppress the weaker, anarchy may as truly be said to reign as in a state of nature, where the weaker individual is not secured against the violence of the stronger; and, as in the latter state even the stronger individuals are prompted, by the uncertainty of their condition, to submit to government which may protect the weak as well as themselves; so, in the former state will the more powerful factions or parties be gradually induced by a like motive to wish for a government which will protect all parties, the weaker as well as the more powerful. It can be little doubted that if the state of Rhode Island was separated from the Confederacy and left to itself, the insecurity of rights under the popular form of government within such narrow limits would be displayed by such reiterated oppressions of factious majorities that some power altogether independent of the people would soon be called for by the voice of the very factions whose misrule had proved the necessity of it. In the extended republic of the United States and among the great variety of interests, parties, and sects which it embraces, a coalition of a majority of the whole society could seldom take place on any other principles than those of justice and the general good; and there being thus less danger to a minor from the will of a major party, there must be less pretext, also, to provide for the security of the former, by introducing into the government a will not dependent on the latter, or, in other words, a will independent of the society itself. It is no less certain than it is important, notwithstanding the contrary opinions which have been entertained, that the larger the society, provided it lie within a practical sphere, the more duly capable it will be of self-government. And happily for the *republican cause*, the practicable sphere may be carried to a very great extent by a judicious modification and mixture of the *federal principle*.

Questions for Discussion

1. Could governmental powers ever be completely separated into three distinct branches?
2. Madison claims that the legislative branch will be the strongest. Why would this be so? Does such a contention hold true today?

1.5

What Were They Thinking?

Burt Solomon

Although the framers were designing a document that could last beyond their lifetimes, they could accomplish this feat only through skillful politicking within the Constitutional Convention, as John P. Roche demonstrates in selection 1.3. One of their most difficult tasks was to create an executive office that would be relatively strong, yet not so powerful that its occupant might become tyrannical. Investing substantial, detailed power in the legislature was one way to limit the executive officeholder, but the framers still had to work through a method of presidential selection that would balance the interests of the large and small states, while providing the country with a competent head of state.

In this article, which appeared after the 2000 presidential election, Burt Solomon recounts the issues that faced the framers and how the problems were addressed. What resulted was an "artful compromise," but one that did not work out quite the way the framers had envisioned. Indeed, they thought that most presidential elections would be decided in the House of Representatives, where elites could select from among several candidates. But from 1789 on, the people have chosen the president, albeit through the rickety mechanisms of the Electoral College, which may have faced its most profound test in 2000.

One late-summer morning in 1787, in sweltering Philadelphia, John Dickinson of Delaware strode tardily into the Library Room upstairs in the elegant but democratically scaled State House. This was the brick building in which, downstairs, the Declaration of Independence had been passed and signed in 1776 and in which, for nearly four months now, the U.S. Constitution had been arduously and imaginatively drafted. Dickinson was one of 11 members of the Committee on Unfinished Business, which was gathering behind closed doors to chew over an intricate problem: how a redesigned republic should choose its chief political administrator, an office that the delegates referred to as the National Executive.

His fellow delegates, on their feet, told him what they had decided—that Congress would pick the President. The 54-year-old lawyer had been the presi-

Burt Solomon is a staff correspondent for the *National Journal* and author of *Where They Ain't*, a book chronicling the early years of The Baltimore Orioles.

dent of Delaware as well as of Pennsylvania, and he objected. "I observed, that the Powers which we had agreed to vest in the President, were so many and so great, that I did not think, the people would be willing to deposit them with him, unless they themselves would be more immediately concerned in his Election," Dickinson recounted in a letter in 1802. "He should be in a strict sense of the Expression, the Man of the People."

Gouverneur Morris of Pennsylvania, a high-living lawyer with a wooden leg who was known for indulging in sex daily, suggested that the discussion be reopened. It was, and soon James Madison, whose legal brilliance guided the Constitutional Convention, sat down with a pen and paper and sketched out an indirect system of choosing the President, a peculiar institution that came to be known as the Electoral College.

The point of this political mechanism was to permit the election of a strong President free from the clutches of Congress, but in a manner that solved some practical and political problems that remain with us: overcoming a diverse nation's regional and racial complexities, and the fear in relatively unpopulated places about being politically overwhelmed by urban centers and powerful states. The Electoral College was "simply the most practical means by which to secure a free, democratic choice of an independent and effective chief executive," Martin Diamond, an academic expert on the odd electoral device, wrote in 1977.

The story of how and why the Electoral College came to be suggests that its purpose wasn't distrust of a democratic mob. Earlier in the Constitutional Convention, and more than once, the delegates had spurned the idea of allowing the citizenry to elect the President directly. But the reason, most historians say, wasn't the fear of the whims and fury of an unbridled electorate—the voters, in general, were in those days the better classes of men. No, the worry was that, in a vast country with fitful communications, ordinary citizens were likely to know next to nothing about would-be Presidents from afar. Someone in, say, Georgia "would be unable to assess the qualifications" of an aspiring President from Massachusetts, and thus couldn't vote intelligently, explains Walter Berns, a resident scholar at the American Enterprise Institute for Public Policy Research and the editor of a 1992 book on the Electoral College.

The prospect of a direct popular vote also upset the small states, which spent the entire Constitutional Convention trying to stop the populous, powerful states (such as Virginia, New York, and Massachusetts) from taking over. When Gouverneur Morris suggested that the President "ought to be elected by the people at large," Roger Sherman of Connecticut offered a Bronx cheer. "The people at large," he contended, according to Madison's notes of the deliberations, "will generally vote for some man in their own state, and the largest state will have the best chance for the appointment." The Framers assumed that, once the uniquely unifying figure of George Washington accepted and then gave up the presidency, his would-be successors would have regional but not national support.

There was another regional—and also racial—consideration. A direct popular vote would raise the hackles of the South, which had a multitude of slaves who were not permitted to vote but who—in an earlier compromise—had each been counted as three-fifths of a person in calculating a state's seats in the House of Representatives. Madison, a Virginia slave owner, worried that letting the public vote directly, without any representation for slaves, "would hurt the South, which would have been outnumbered by the North." . . .

Madison—the Father of the Constitution and a future President—knew he needed a mechanism to satisfy everyone's concerns, if he hoped to have a Constitution to sire.

An Artful Compromise

The 55 men who argued that summer over the wording of the U.S. Constitution, the first document ever to structure a national government from scratch, had a certain sameness about them. They were mainly wealthy businessmen and lawyers, well-educated and ambitious. But they had their differences—in region, in the size of their home states, in whether they preferred to let the states continue to exercise the bulk of governmental power or to shift the power to a national government.

Some delegates wanted a strong President, while others saw that as a route back to monarchy, which they had so recently struggled—pledging their lives, fortunes, and sacred honor—to escape. The question for Madison and the other Framers was how to satisfy these disparate interests. The Electoral College was the end result of a process of elimination.

At first, the most popular idea among the delegates was for the legislature to choose the President. Having a President at all was a dramatic change from the Articles of Confederation, America's first, and feeble, attempt at a central government. In effect since 1781, the articles had provided for a legislature alone, and a ridiculously weak one at that. "America was thirteen small democratic republics," *The Washington Post*'s Fred Barbash wrote in a 1987 book that told the story of how the Constitution was assembled. He described a one-chamber Congress that was unable to levy taxes, enact a law over a state's objections, or even raise troops to put down Shays's Rebellion of debt-ridden New England farmers in 1786.

Letting a newly powerful Congress choose the President, though, would lead to a legislative body that was too strong. A President who depended on Congress for his political fate, the thinking went, would wind up too ready to deal. Such a situation would upset the clever set of checks and balances that was at the core of Madison's conception of a government designed to police itself. And besides, the affairs of the country had become too complicated to be governed by committee, James Wilson of Pennsylvania argued. An independent President was a must.

Similarly, the delegates took up but spit out the notion of having the state legislatures pick the President. That would make him beholden to the states, when it was a centralized, national government that Madison and many of the other Framers sought.

It was James Wilson, along with Madison and Morris, who is generally given the most credit for the artful compromise of relying on electors in each state to pick the President. Wilson, a strong-minded conservative who had thought as deeply as Madison had about how a national government should be structured, had been a member of Congress and later became a Supreme Court Justice.

The melding of constituencies and influences—its very weirdness, in a way—is what lent the Electoral College its political appeal. It provided the President an independent base of power, one that rested in the states but wasn't controlled by the states themselves. The power behind the closest American equivalent of a throne was to be divvied up in politically sensitive proportions. Each state would be awarded a number of electors equal to its representation in the House plus the Senate. This let the populous states wield more power, benefited the slaveholding South, and still gave the small states an extra measure of influence.

The electors were also intended to bring some expertise to bear on the choice of a President. They were supposed to be people involved with politics, albeit not serving in any federal capacity. But they weren't expected to be attached to particular candidates. Instead, they were to meet in each state as a deliberative body, to assess the qualifications of candidates both near and far. Indeed, the Constitution required electors to vote for two candidates, from two different states—hence the political problem earlier this year because Dick Cheney and George W. Bush were both from Texas. (That's why Cheney changed his legal residency to Wyoming.) The presumption in 1787 was that electors would vote for a favorite son and somebody else, so that their collective second choice might—and, quite possibly, should—ultimately win the presidency.

The Framers anticipated that, once the electors met in every state capital to mull over the possible Presidents, four or five leading candidates would emerge. "Essentially, the electors would serve as nominators of the principal candidates for the presidency," none of which would ordinarily win a majority of the Electoral College, so that the House would decide the victor, explains Mark Tushnet, a law professor at Georgetown University. The Committee on Unfinished Business recommended that this power be bestowed on the Senate. But the other delegates regarded the upper chamber as too powerful already, and so the authority was moved to the House, but to be exercised in a Senate-like fashion: In the lower chamber, apportioned by population, each state was given one vote and therefore an equal say in choosing the President. That helped satisfy the small states.

But the Framers, in directing the electors to meet in their respective state capitals, betrayed some darker fears. This prevented them from meeting in a single, nationwide group that "might form yet another power-hungry, intrigue-ridden branch of government," Barbash wrote.

One Congress, in other words, was enough. Or, as Dickinson recalled the Framers' intentions several years later, "the electors, having performed their ephemeral Duty, melt at once into the common Mass." That hasn't changed, at least yet. Most Americans have no idea who their electors are, even though that is actually who they are voting for every four years when they cast their ballots for President. . . .

Glimpses of Irrelevancy

The Framers never bothered to specify their intentions at the time, but Dickinson recollected that they meant "that the Electors should be chosen by the People and not appointed by the Legislatures of the States." Most of the states did just that, allowing for the popular election of individual electors by congressional district. But as late as 1836, six of the 24 states had their legislatures name the electors. In South Carolina, the practice didn't end until 1860.

This wasn't the only way in which the Electoral College failed to work as its creators expected, beyond the nation's first three presidential elections. The rise of political parties during the 1790s produced national candidacies, and soon the electors had nothing much to discuss. That each party offered its own two-man national ticket inadvertently created a tie in the 1800 election. The winning party's electors each voted twice but didn't specify whom they wanted as President and as Vice President. As a result, Thomas Jefferson and running mate Aaron Burr drew an equal number of votes. The technical, obscure changes embodied in the 12th Amendment, which was ratified in 1804, required each elector to cast separate votes for President and Vice President. This change enabled the fledgling political parties to endorse national tickets; ever since, the President and Vice President have always belonged to the same party.

But in the ensuing years, little about the Electoral College has changed, other than its descent into—except on rare occasions, such as [in 2000]—political irrelevancy. Certainly, many of the conditions that gave rise to it are gone. Lord knows, ordinary voters today don't lack for enough information to make up their minds. The Electoral College was created, says Berns, "largely for a reason that no longer obtains." . . .

Questions for Discussion

1. How does the framers' thinking on the electoral college relate to Roche's notion of the framers as a "reform caucus?"
2. If we had a constitutional convention today, what kind of system would we choose to select the president? Why?

 Chapter 2

Federalism and Intergovernmental Relations

Federalism is a way of organizing a political system so that authority is shared between a central government and state or regional governments. Individuals living in Pennsylvania, for example, are citizens of both that state and the United States, are under the legal authority of both governments, and have obligations (such as paying taxes) to each government.

A country is federal only if the subnational units exist independently of the national government and can make some binding decisions on their own. Some nations, like Britain and France, have unitary forms of government, in which regional and local units exist only to aid the national administration. Such subnational units can be abolished or altered at any time by the national government. In contrast, the central government in the United States (commonly referred to as the federal government) can never abolish a state. Also, the Constitution protects states by providing for two senators and at least one member of the House of Representatives from each state.

The United States embraced the concept of federalism in the Constitution more than two hundred years ago, amid much debate. The Articles of Confederation had proved inadequate because of the weakness of the central government and the almost total autonomy of the states. The nation's domestic economy was chaotic, as individual states' trade restrictions, tariff barriers, and currency weaknesses led to local depressions and encouraged citizens to move from state to state to escape debt obligations. At the same time, neither the central government nor the states could protect citizens from foreign threats or even from domestic insurrection. At the Constitutional Convention in 1787, the founders agreed that the existing government was inadequate; debate arose over the amount of power the central government should be given and how certain aspects of state autonomy could be ensured.

Federalism resulted from a compromise between those seeking a more powerful and efficient central government and those who feared such a government and valued state independence. The founders hoped the national government would act on matters concerning the common good, such as defense, trade, and financial stability, yet not become so strong that it threatened individual liberty and reduced diversity among the states. Federalism as it was understood then, and as it operated until the twentieth century, essentially meant dual federalism: Governmental functions were divided between the state and the national government, each of which was autonomous in its own sphere. For example, the national government had a monopoly on delivering the mail and conducting foreign relations, whereas state governments were in charge of areas such as education and law enforcement.

The framers tried to be as clear as possible in defining the powers possessed by the national government (Article I, Section 8 of the Constitution). But with some exceptions, such as state control of the conduct of elections, they said little about state powers or about what should happen when national and state authorities collide.

In general, the trend has been to expand the central government's powers beyond those enumerated in the Constitution and thus to erode state power and independence. Supreme Court decisions have played a crucial role here, opening the door for the federal government's involvement in many traditionally state functions. In the landmark case of *McCulloch* v. *Maryland* (1819), the Court affirmed the supremacy of the national government over the states and introduced the notion of implied powers. The Court ruled that the purpose of the Constitution is not to prevent Congress from carrying out the enumerated powers; Congress has the authority to use all means "necessary and proper" to fulfill its obligations. For example, broad interpretations of the commerce clause not only have given Congress the authority to regulate commerce with foreign nations and among the states but also have provided it with a basis for intervention within state boundaries on matters such as racial relations.

The variety and scale of the federal government's actions have changed over the years. Since the Civil War (which definitively settled the question of national supremacy), the relationships between the states and the federal government have become increasingly characterized by cooperative federalism, in which governmental powers and policies are shared. Cooperative federalism often involves sharing the costs of needed programs or projects, which requires state and local officials to adhere to federal guidelines. Franklin Roosevelt's New Deal, with its expanded national economic and social agenda, had an especially marked impact on intergovernmental relations. Both states and citizens became dependent on Washington for aid, for many states were incapable of dealing with poverty on their own. In addition, the problems of an industrial society that did not stop at state boundaries, such as water and air pollution, necessitated federal government action.

By the 1960s, American citizens seemed unwilling to let states and localities thwart the national will, and the central government was viewed as an entity to be encouraged rather than feared. Perhaps the greatest cost of federalism has been the systematic oppression of African Americans by localities and states, first as slaves and then as a separate class. The Great Society programs of the Johnson years attempted to eliminate racism and poverty through national initiatives, and federal aid to the states rose greatly during the 1960s and 1970s. By 1980, Daniel Elazar, a leading scholar of federalism, concluded that we have moved to a system in which it is taken as axiomatic that the federal government shall initiate policies and programs, shall determine their character, shall delegate their administration to the states and localities according to terms that it alone determines, and shall provide for whatever intervention on the part of its administrative agencies it deems necessary to secure compliance with those terms.

Still, the boundaries between state and national authority, originally inspired by a fear of a strong central government, have never been fixed, and political conflict between national and state governments has existed since the nation's founding.

There is a great deal of evidence to support the notion that the role of the states was enhanced during the 1980s. But forces such as the mass media and economic interdependence among nations are leading to an increasingly national culture. Further, it is unlikely that the states will have the protection of the courts in defending their rights, as has often been the case in the past. In *Garcia* v. *San Antonio Metropolitan Transit Authority* (1985), the Supreme Court ruled that no constitutional limits contained in the Tenth Amendment or any other section of the Constitution may limit the national government's power over commerce. States' rights, therefore, are to be found only in the structure of the government, such as equal state representation in the Senate. In a sense, states are now considered equivalent to other special-interest groups asking for favors and protection from the national government in Washington.

By the 1990s, however, the political winds were blowing in favor of returning power on many matters back to the states, and "devolution" became the rage among Washington policymakers. The Clinton administration sought to "reinvent" federalism, while congressional Republican majorities aggressively pursued a states'-rights agenda. One consequence was that in a number of program areas, such as welfare, states became more influential.

The four readings in this chapter illustrate various aspects of the controversy over the meaning and changing nature of federalism. *The Federalist,* No. 39, reflects James Madison's views on the relations between states and the national government under the new Constitution and on the importance of the governmental structure as an American innovation. The landmark case *McCulloch* v. *Maryland* resolved two key issues left open by the Constitution: which level of government is supreme when state and national policies clash and whether the federal government is limited by the Tenth Amendment to those powers explicitly enumerated in the Constitution.

The final two selections look at federalism in practice. John Donahue argues that "devolution" has tremendous costs and may be ill suited for a period in history when economic and cultural lines across states are becoming stronger. In the final selection, Martha Derthick suggests that the supposed trend toward devolution is not as clear as it initially seems. A good example is the federal government's growing role in public education—a major issue in the 2000 presidential elections.

2.1

The Federalist, No. 39

James Madison

At the time of the framing of the Constitution, the founders were aware of two basic forms of government: a national government, with total central domination, and a confederation, a loose alliance of states in which the central government has virtually no power. When the Constitution and *The Federalist* were written, a "federal" government and a "confederation" were synonymous. The governmental form that has come to be called *federalism,* in which authority is divided between two independent levels, was the invention of the founders, though the label came later.

Critics of the Constitution believed the document gave so much power to the central government that it was in fact "national" in character. In *The Federalist,* No. 39, James Madison refutes this charge and asserts that the new government is "neither a national nor a federal Constitution, but a composition of both." Being a politician, Madison took great pains to point out that the national government's powers are strictly limited to those enumerated in the Constitution and that the residual sovereignty of the states is greater than that of the national government. The first part of this paper can also be regarded as an elegant statement of what Madison meant by the term *republic.*

To the People of the State of New York: The first question that offers itself is, whether the general form and aspect of the government be strictly republican?* It is evident that no other form would be reconcilable with the genius of the people of America; with the fundamental principles of the revolution; or with that honorable determination, which animates every votary [devotee] of freedom, to rest all our political experiments on the capacity of mankind for self-government. If the plan of the Convention therefore be found to depart from the republican character, its advocates must abandon it as no longer defensible.

---

* A *republican* form of government is one in which power resides in the people but is formally exercised by their elected representatives.

What then are the distinctive characters of the republican form? Were an answer to this question to be sought, not by recurring to principles, but in the application of the term by political writers, to the constitutions of different States, no satisfactory one would ever be found. Holland, in which no particle of the supreme authority is derived from the people, has passed almost universally under the denomination of a republic. The same title has been bestowed on Venice, where absolute power over the great body of the people, is exercised in the most absolute manner, by a small body of hereditary nobles. Poland, which is a mixture of aristocracy and of monarchy in their worst forms, has been dignified with the same appellation. The government of England, which has one republican branch only, combined with a hereditary aristocracy and monarchy, has with equal impropriety been frequently placed on the list of republics. These examples, which are nearly as dissimilar to each other as to a genuine republic, show the extreme inaccuracy with which the term has been used in political disquisitions.

If we resort for a criterion, to the different principles on which different forms of government are established, we may define a republic to be, or at least may bestow that name on, a government which derives all its powers directly or indirectly from the great body of the people; and is administered by persons holding their offices during pleasure, for a limited period, or during good behaviour. It is *essential* to such a government, that it be derived from the great body of the society, not from an inconsiderable proportion, or a favored class of it; otherwise a handful of tyrannical nobles, exercising their oppressions by a delegation of their powers, might aspire to the rank of republicans, and claim for their government the honorable title of republic. It is *sufficient* for such a government, that the persons administering it be appointed, either directly or indirectly, by the people; and that they hold their appointments by either of the tenures just specified; otherwise every government in the United States, as well as every other popular government that has been or can be well organized or well executed, would be degraded from the republican character. According to the Constitution of every State in the Union, some or other of the officers of government are appointed indirectly only by the people. According to most of them the chief magistrate himself is so appointed. And according to one, this mode of appointment is extended to one of the coordinate branches of the legislature. According to all the Constitutions also, the tenure of the highest offices is extended to a definite period, and in many instances, both within the legislative and executive departments, to a period of years. According to the provisions of most of the constitutions, again, as well as according to the most respectable and received opinions on the subject, the members of the judiciary department are to retain their offices by the firm tenure of good behaviour.

On comparing the Constitution planned by the Convention, with the standard here fixed, we perceive at once that it is in the most rigid sense conformable to it. The House of Representatives, like that of one branch at least of all the State

Legislatures, is elected immediately by the great body of the people. The Senate, like the present Congress, and the Senate of Maryland, derives its appointment indirectly from the people.* The President is indirectly derived from the choice of the people, according to the example in most of the States. Even the judges, with all other officers of the Union, will, as in the several States, be the choice, though a remote choice, of the people themselves. The duration of the appointments is equally conformable to the republican standard, and to the model of the State Constitutions. The House of Representatives is periodically elective as in all the States: and for the period of two years as in the State of South-Carolina. The Senate is elective for the period of six years; which is but one year more than the period of the Senate of Maryland; and but two more than that of the Senates of New-York and Virginia. The President is to continue in office for the period of four years; as in New-York and Delaware, the chief magistrate is elected for three years, and in South-Carolina for two years. In the other States the election is annual. In several of the States, however, no constitutional provision is made for the impeachment of the Chief Magistrate. And in Delaware and Virginia, he is not impeachable till out of office. The President of the United States is impeachable at any time during his continuance in office. The tenure by which the Judges are to hold their places, is, as it unquestionably ought to be, that of good behaviour. The tenure of the ministerial offices generally will be a subject of legal regulation, conformably to the reason of the case, and the example of the State Constitutions.

Could any further proof be required of the republican complexion of this system, the most decisive one might be found in its absolute prohibition of titles of nobility, both under the Federal and the State Governments; and in its express guarantee of the republican form to each of the latter.

But it was not sufficient, say the adversaries of the proposed Constitution, for the Convention to adhere to the republican form. They ought, with equal care, to have preserved the *federal* form, which regards the union as a *confederacy* of sovereign States; instead of which, they have framed a *national* government, which regards the union as a *consolidation* of the States. And it is asked by what authority this bold and radical innovation was undertaken. The handle which has been made of this objection requires, that it should be examined with some precision.

Without enquiring into the accuracy of the distinction on which the objection is founded, it will be necessary to a just estimate of its force, first to ascertain the real character of the government in question; secondly, to enquire how far the Convention were authorised to propose such a government; and thirdly, how far the duty they owed to their country, could supply any defect of regular authority.

---

* The Seventeenth Amendment, adopted in 1913, changed the election procedure for U.S. senators from indirect election by state legislatures to direct election by the people of each state.

First. In order to ascertain the real character of the government it may be considered in relation to the foundation on which it is to be established; to the sources from which its ordinary powers are to be drawn; to the operation of those powers; to the extent of them; and to the authority by which future changes in the government are to be introduced.

On examining the first relation, it appears on one hand that the Constitution is to be founded on the assent and ratification of the people of America, given by deputies elected for the special purpose; but on the other, that this assent and ratification is to be given by the people, not as individuals composing one entire nation; but as composing the distinct and independent States to which they respectively belong. It is to be the assent and ratification of the several States, derived from the supreme authority in each State, the authority of the people themselves. The act therefore establishing the Constitution, will not be a *national* but a *federal* act.

That it will be a federal and not a national act, as these terms are understood by the objectors, the act of the people as forming so many independent States, not as forming one aggregate nation, is obvious from this single consideration that it is to result neither from the decision of a *majority* of the people of the Union, nor from that of a *majority* of the States. It must result from the *unanimous* assent of the several States that are parties to it, differing no other wise from their ordinary assent than in its being expressed, not by the legislative authority, but by that of the people themselves. Were the people regarded in this transaction as forming one nation, the will of the majority of the whole people of the United States would bind the minority; in the same manner as the majority in each State must bind the minority; and the will of the majority must be determined either by a comparison of the individual votes; or by considering the will of a majority of the States, as evidence of the will of a majority of the people of the United States. Neither of these rules has been adopted. Each State in ratifying the Constitution, is considered as a sovereign body independent of all others, and only to be bound by its own voluntary act. In this relation then the new Constitution will, if established, be a *federal* and not a *national* Constitution.

The next relation is to the sources from which the ordinary powers of government are to be derived. The house of representatives will derive its powers from the people of America, and the people will be represented in the same proportion, and on the same principle, as they are in the Legislature of a particular State. So far the Government is *national* not *federal*. The Senate on the other hand will derive its powers from the States, as political and co-equal societies; and these will be represented on the principle of equality in the Senate, as they now are in the existing Congress. So far the government is *federal*, not *national*. The executive power will be derived from a very compound source. The immediate election of the President is to be made by the States in their political characters. The votes allotted to them are in a compound ratio, which considers them partly as distinct and co-equal societies; partly as unequal members of the same society. The eventual election again is to be made by that branch of the Legislature which consists of the national representatives; but in this particular act, they are to be thrown into the form of individual delegations from so many distinct and co-equal bodies politic. From this aspect of the Government, it appears to be of a mixed character presenting at least as many *federal* as *national* features.

The difference between a federal and national Government as it relates to the *operation of the Government* is supposed to consist in this, that in the former, the powers operate on the political bodies composing the confederacy, in their political capacities: In the latter, on the individual citizens, composing the nation, in their individual capacities. On trying the Constitution by this criterion, it falls under the *national*, not the *federal* character; though perhaps not so compleatly, as has been understood. In several cases and particularly in the trial of controversies to which States may be parties, they must be viewed and proceeded against in their collective and political capacities only. So far the national countenance of the Government on this side seems to be disfigured by a few federal features. But this blemish is perhaps unavoidable in any plan; and the operation of the Government on the people in their individual capacities, in its ordinary and most essential proceedings, may on the whole designate it in this relation a *national* Government.

But if the Government be national with regard to the *operation* of its powers, it changes its aspect again when we contemplate it in relation to the *extent* of its powers. The idea of a national Government involves in it, not only an authority over the individual citizens; but an indefinite supremacy over all persons and things, so far as they are objects of lawful Government. Among a people consolidated into one nation, this supremacy is compleatly vested in the national Legislature. Among communities united for particular purposes, it is vested partly in the general, and partly in the municipal Legislatures. In the former case, all local authorities are subordinate to the supreme; and may be controuled, directed or abolished by it at pleasure. In the latter the local or municipal authorities form distinct and independent portions of the supremacy, no more subject within their respective spheres to the general authority, than the general authority is subject to them, within its own sphere. In this relation then the proposed Government cannot be deemed a *national* one; since its jurisdiction extends to certain enumerated objects only, and leaves to the several States a residuary and inviolable sovereignty over all other objects. It is true that in controversies relating to the boundary between the two jurisdictions, the tribunal which is ultimately to decide is to be established under the general Government.* But this does not change the principle of the case. The decision is to be impartially made, according to the rules of the Constitution; and all the usual and most effectual

---

* The tribunal to resolve boundary disputes became the Supreme Court (see *McCulloch* v. *Maryland,* which follows this selection).

precautions are taken to secure this impartiality. Some such tribunal is clearly essential to prevent an appeal to the sword, and a dissolution of the compact; and that it ought to be established under the general rather than under the local Governments; or to speak more properly, that it could be safely established under the first alone, is a position not likely to be combated.

If we try the Constitution by its last relation, to the authority by which amendments are to be made, we find it neither wholly *national*, nor wholly *federal*. Were it wholly national, the supreme and ultimate authority would reside in the *majority* of the people of the Union; and this authority would be competent at all times, like that of a majority of every national society, to alter or abolish its established Government. Were it wholly federal on the other hand, the concurrence of each State in the Union would be essential to every alteration that would be binding on all. The mode provided by the plan of the Convention is not founded on either of these principles. In requiring more than a majority, and particularly, in computing the proportion by *States*, not by *citizens*, it departs from the *national*, and advances towards the *federal* character: In rendering the concurrence of less than the whole number of States sufficient, it loses again the *federal*, and partakes of the *national* character.

The proposed Constitution therefore is in strictness neither a national nor a federal constitution; but a composition of both. In its foundation, it is federal, not national; in the sources from which the ordinary powers of the Government are drawn, it is partly federal, and partly national; in the operation of these powers, it is national, not federal; in the extent of them again, it is federal, not national. And finally, in the authoritative mode of introducing amendments, it is neither wholly federal, nor wholly national.

Questions for Discussion

1. According to Madison, why was the new U.S. Constitution neither a "national" nor a "federal" document? Which of its features were designed to curb the national government's domination of the states?

2. Madison believed the Constitution set up a republican rather than a democratic form of government. What features of the document were designed to give the people an indirect rather than a direct influence on public policy?

2.2

McCulloch v. Maryland (1819)

In many areas, the framers of the Constitution were explicit about the powers granted to the national government and to the states. In other areas, however, such as the power to tax, the two were given many of the same responsibilities. The Constitution leaves open the relationship of state and national authority when their policies conflict. In 1819, *McCulloch* v. *Maryland** settled the issue in favor of the national government.

In 1791 Congress created a national bank to print money, make loans, and engage in a variety of banking activities. The bank was deeply resented by a number of state legislatures, which held that Congress did not have the authority to charter a bank, and in 1818 Maryland passed a law that taxed its Baltimore branch $15,000. James McCulloch, a cashier at the bank, refused to pay and was sued in state court. The state's tax was upheld, and the bank appealed to the U.S. Supreme Court.

Chief Justice John Marshall delivered a landmark opinion for the Court with a decision that markedly expanded the powers of the national government over those explicitly stated in the Constitution and affirmed the supremacy of the national government over the states. According to the Court, Congress had the power to charter a national bank because it had been granted the power "to make all laws which shall be necessary and proper for carrying into execution" the expressed powers. In short, Congress has a number of implied powers in addition to its enumerated powers. Further, because the power to tax could be used to destroy an institution that is necessary for the operations of the national government, Maryland's attempt to levy a tax on the national bank was unconstitutional. The Court upheld the supremacy of the national government when policies collide.

M r. Chief Justice Marshall[†] delivered the opinion of the Court.

In the case now to be determined, the defendant, a sovereign State, denies the obligation of a law enacted by the legislature of the Union, and the plaintiff, on his part, contests the validity of an act which has been passed

---

* 4 Wheaton 316 (1819).

[†] John Marshall became chief justice of the United States in 1801. He is probably most famous for his opinion in *Marbury* v. *Madison* (see selection 13.2), which established the principle of judicial review—the power of the Court to declare laws unconstitutional.

by the legislature of that State. The constitution of our country, in its most interesting and vital parts, is to be considered; the conflicting powers of the government of the Union and of its members, as marked in that constitution, are to be discussed; and an opinion given, which may essentially influence the great operations of the government. . . .

The first question made in the case is, has Congress power to incorporate a bank? . . .

The power now contested was exercised by the first Congress elected under the present constitution. The bill for incorporating the bank of the United States did not steal upon an unsuspecting legislature, and pass unobserved. Its principle was completely understood, and was opposed with equal zeal and ability. After being resisted, first in the fair and open field of debate, and afterward in the executive cabinet, with as much persevering talent as any measure has ever experienced, and being supported by arguments which convinced minds as pure and as intelligent as this country can boast, it became a law. The original act was permitted to expire; but a short experience of the embarrassments to which the refusal to revive it exposed the government, convinced those who were most prejudiced against the measure of its necessity, and induced the passage of the present law. It would require no ordinary share of intrepidity to assert that a measure adopted under these circumstances was a bold and plain usurpation, to which the constitution gave no countenance. . . .

In discussing this question, the counsel for the State of Maryland have deemed it of some importance, in the construction of the constitution, to consider that instrument not as emanating from the people, but as the act of sovereign and independent States. The powers of the general government, it has been said, are delegated by the States, who alone are truly sovereign; and must be exercised in subordination to the States, who alone possess supreme dominion.

It would be difficult to sustain this proposition. The Convention which framed the constitution was indeed elected by the State legislatures. But the instrument, when it came from their hands, was a mere proposal, without obligation, or pretensions to it. It was reported to the then existing Congress of the United States, with a request that it might "be submitted to a Convention of Delegates, chosen in each State by the people thereof, under the recommendation of its Legislature, for their assent and ratification." This mode of proceeding was adopted; and by the Convention, by Congress, and by the State Legislatures, the instrument was submitted to the people. They acted upon it in the only manner in which they can act safely, effectively, and wisely, on such a subject, by assembling in Convention. It is true, they assembled in their several States—and where else should they have assembled? No political dreamer was ever wild enough to think of breaking down the lines which separate the States, and of compounding the American people into one common mass. Of consequence, when they act, they act in their States. But the measures they adopt do not, on that account, cease to be the measures of the people themselves, or become the measures of the State governments.

From these Conventions the constitution derives its whole authority. The government proceeds directly from the people; is "ordained and established" in the name of the people; and is declared to be ordained, "in order to form a more perfect union, establish justice, ensure domestic tranquillity, and secure the blessings of liberty to themselves and to their posterity." The assent of the States, in their sovereign capacity, is implied in calling a Convention, and thus submitting that instrument to the people. But the people were at perfect liberty to accept or reject it; and their act was final. It required not the affirmance, and could not be negatived, by the State governments. The constitution, when thus adopted, was of complete obligation, and bound the State sovereignties.

It has been said, that the people had already surrendered all their powers to the State sovereignties, and had nothing more to give. But, surely, the question whether they may resume and modify the powers granted to government does not remain to be settled in this country. Much more might the legitimacy of the general government be doubted, had it been created by the States. The powers delegated to the State sovereignties were to be exercised by themselves, not by a distinct and independent sovereignty, created by themselves. To the formation of a league, such as was the confederation, the State sovereignties were certainly competent. But when, "in order to form a more perfect union," it was deemed necessary to change this alliance into an effective government, possessing great and sovereign powers, and acting directly on the people, the necessity of referring it to the people, and of deriving its powers directly from them, was felt and acknowledged by all.

The government of the Union, then (whatever may be the influence of this fact on the case) is, emphatically, and truly, a government of the people. In form and in substance it emanates from them. Its powers are granted by them, and are to be exercised directly on them, and for their benefit.

This government is acknowledged by all to be one of enumerated powers. The principle, that it can exercise only the powers granted to it, would seem too apparent to have required to be enforced by all those arguments which its enlightened friends, while it was depending before the people, found it necessary to urge. That principle is now universally admitted. But the question respecting the extent of the powers actually granted, is perpetually arising, and will probably continue to arise, as long as our system shall exist. . . .

If any one proposition could command the universal assent of mankind, we might expect it would be this—that the government of the Union, though limited in its powers, is supreme within its sphere of action. This would seem to result necessarily from its nature. It is the government of all; its powers are delegated by all; it represents all, and acts for all. Though any one State may be willing to control its operations, no State is willing to allow others to control them. The nation, on those subjects on which it can act, must necessarily bind its component parts. But this question is not left to mere reason: the people have, in express terms, decided it, by saying, "this constitution, and the laws of the United States, which shall be made in pursuance thereof, . . . shall be the supreme law of the land," and by requiring that the members of the State legislatures, and the officers of the executive and judicial departments of the States, shall take the oath of fidelity to it.

The government of the United States, then, though limited in its powers, is supreme; and its laws, when made in pursuance of the constitution, form the supreme law of the land, "any thing in the constitution or laws of any State to the contrary notwithstanding."

Among the enumerated powers, we do not find that of establishing a bank or creating a corporation. But there is no phrase in the instrument which, like the articles of confederation, excludes incidental or implied powers; and which requires that every thing granted shall be expressly and minutely described. Even the 10th amendment, which was framed for the purpose of quieting the excessive jealousies which had been excited, omits the word "expressly," and declares only that the powers "not delegated to the United States, nor prohibited to the States, are reserved to the States or to the people;" thus leaving the question, whether the particular power which may become the subject of contest has been delegated to the one government, or prohibited to the other, to depend on a fair construction of the whole instrument. The men who drew and adopted this amendment had experienced the embarrassments resulting from the insertion of this word in the articles of confederation, and probably omitted it to avoid those embarrassments. A constitution, to contain an accurate detail of all the subdivisions of which its great powers will admit, and of all the means by which they may be carried into execution, would partake of the prolixity of a legal code, and could scarcely be embraced by the human mind. It would probably never be understood by the public. Its nature, therefore, requires, that only its great outlines should be marked, its important objects designated, and the minor ingredients which compose those objects be deduced from the nature of the objects themselves. That this idea was entertained by the framers of the American constitution, is not only to be inferred from the nature of the instrument, but from the language. Why else were some of the limitations, found in the ninth section of the 1st article, introduced?* It is also, in some degree, warranted by their having omitted to use any restrictive term which might prevent its receiving a fair and just interpretation. In consideration of this question, then, we must never forget, that it is *a constitution* we are expounding.

Although, among the enumerated powers of government, we do not find the word "bank" or "incorporation," we find the great powers to lay and collect taxes; to borrow money; to regulate commerce; to declare and conduct a war; and to raise and support armies and navies. The sword and the purse, all the external relations, and no inconsiderable portion of the industry of the

---

* Article I, Section 9, follows the provision enumerating the national government's powers and is a broad list of specific prohibitions that restrain the national government, including the inability to levy taxes or duties on articles from any state or to give preferential treatment to the ports of one state at the expense of another.

nation, are entrusted to its government. It can never be pretended that these vast powers draw after them others of inferior importance, merely because they are inferior. Such an idea can never be advanced. But it may with great reason be contended, that a government, entrusted with such ample powers, on the due execution of which the happiness and prosperity of the nation so vitally depends, must also be entrusted with ample means for their execution. The power being given, it is the interest of the nation to facilitate its execution. It can never be their interest, and cannot be presumed to have been their intention, to clog and embarrass its execution by withholding the most appropriate means. Throughout this vast republic, from the St. Croix to the Gulf of Mexico, from the Atlantic to the Pacific, revenue is to be collected and expended, armies are to be marched and supported. The exigencies of the nation may require that the treasure raised in the north should be transported to the south, *that* raised in the east conveyed to the west, or that this order should be reversed. Is that construction of the constitution to be preferred which would render these operations difficult, hazardous, and expensive? Can we adopt that construction, (unless the words imperiously require it), which would impute to the framers of that instrument, when granting these powers for the public good, the intention of impeding their exercise by withholding a choice of means? If, indeed, such be the mandate of the constitution, we have only to obey; but that instrument does not profess to enumerate the means by which the powers it confers may be executed; nor does it prohibit the creation of a corporation, if the existence of such a being be essential to the beneficial exercise of those powers. It is, then, the subject of fair inquiry, how far such means may be employed. . . .

But the constitution of the United States has not left the right of Congress to employ the necessary means, for the execution of the powers conferred on the government, to general reasoning. To its enumeration of powers is added that of making "all laws which shall be necessary and proper, for carrying into execution the foregoing powers, and all other powers vested by this constitution, in the government of the United States, or in any department thereof." . . .

We admit, as all must admit, that the powers of the government are limited, and that its limits are not to be transcended. But we think the sound construction of the constitution must allow to the national legislature that discretion, with respect to the means by which the powers it confers are to be carried into execution, which will enable that body to perform the high duties assigned to it, in the manner most beneficial to the people. Let the end be legitimate, let it be within the scope of the constitution, and all means which are appropriate, which are plainly adapted to that end, which are not prohibited, but consist with the letter and spirit of the constitution, are constitutional. . . .

It being the opinion of the Court, that the act incorporating the bank is constitutional; and that the power of establishing a branch in the State of Maryland might be properly exercised by the bank itself, we proceed to inquire—

Whether the State of Maryland may, without violating the constitution, tax that branch?

That the power of taxation is one of vital importance; that it is retained by the States; that it is not abridged by the grant of a similar power to the government of the Union; that it is to be concurrently exercised by the two governments: are truths which have never been denied. But, such is the paramount character of the constitution, that its capacity to withdraw any subject from the action of even this power, is admitted. The States are expressly forbidden to lay any duties on imports or exports, except what may be absolutely necessary for executing their inspection laws. If the obligation of this prohibition must be conceded—if it may restrain a State from the exercise of its taxing power on imports and exports; the same paramount character would seem to restrain, as it certainly may restrain, a State from such other exercise of this power, as is in its nature incompatible with, and repugnant to, the constitutional laws of the Union. A law, absolutely repugnant to another, as entirely repeals that other as if express terms of repeal were used.

On this ground the counsel for the bank place its claim to be exempted from the power of a State to tax its operations. There is no express provision for the case, but the claim has been sustained on a principle which so entirely pervades the constitution, is so intermixed with the materials which compose it, so interwoven with its web, so blended with its texture, as to be incapable of being separated from it, without rending it into shreds.

This great principle is, that the constitution and the laws made in pursuance thereof are supreme; that they control the constitution and laws of the respective States, and cannot be controlled by them. From this, which may be almost termed an axiom, other propositions are deduced as corollaries, on the truth or error of which, and on their application to this case, the cause has been supposed to depend. These are, 1st. that a power to create implies a power to preserve. 2nd. That a power to destroy, if wielded by a different hand, is hostile to, and incompatible with these powers to create and to preserve. 3d. That where this repugnancy exists, that authority which is supreme must control, not yield to that over which it is supreme.

These propositions, as abstract truths, would, perhaps, never be controverted. Their application to this case, however, has been denied; and, both in maintaining the affirmative and the negative, a splendor of eloquence, and strength of argument, seldom, if ever, surpassed, have been displayed.

The power of Congress to create, and of course to continue, the bank, was the subject of the preceding part of this opinion; and is no longer to be considered as questionable.

That the power of taxing it by the States may be exercised so as to destroy it, is too obvious to be denied. . . .

The Court has bestowed on this subject its most deliberate consideration. The result is a conviction that the States have no power, by taxation or otherwise, to retard, impede, burden, or in any manner control, the operations of the constitutional laws enacted by Congress to carry into execution the powers vested in the general government. This is, we think, the unavoidable consequence of that supremacy which the constitution has declared.

We are unanimously of opinion, that the law passed by the legislature of Maryland, imposing a tax on the Bank of the United States, is unconstitutional and void. . . .

Questions for Discussion

1. Why did the Court believe that the national government possessed powers beyond those enumerated in the Constitution?
2. Does Marshall's view in this case seem consistent with the view of national-state relations expressed by James Madison in *The Federalist*, No. 39?

 2.3

The Devil in Devolution

John D. Donahue

In the contemporary era, public support for transferring power from the government in Washington to the states is nearly at consensus levels. Polls regularly show that respondents overwhelmingly trust their state government to do a better job of "running things" than the federal government. Both major political parties and their leading candidates for office have strongly endorsed the concept of "devolution," the return of power and responsibility to state and local governments by the federal government. In the 1990s a number of federally dominated programs, welfare being the most prominent example, underwent major changes in the direction of increasing the role of the states in priority setting, funding discretion, and administration.

In this selection, John Donahue raises a number of concerns about devolutionary trends. He argues that "state borders are becoming more, not less, permeable," and that devolution eventually leads to destructive state rivalries. In

---

John D. Donahue is a professor at Harvard University's John F. Kennedy School of Government.

Donahue's view, the collective good of the nation suffers a "tragedy of the commons" as interstate rivalries create temptations for states to pursue their narrow interests by passing on significant policy costs to other states. From Donahue's perspective, devolution leads to the fragmentation of authority and makes success in addressing such issues less likely.

The shift in government's center of gravity away from Washington and toward the states—a transition propelled by both popular sentiment and budget imperatives, and blessed by leaders in both major parties—reflects an uncommon pause in an endless American argument over the balance between nation and state. That argument got underway when the Framers gathered in Philadelphia to launch a second attempt at nationhood, after less than a decade's dismal experience under the feeble Articles of Confederation. The Constitution they crafted was a compromise between those who wanted to strengthen the ties among essentially autonomous states, and those who sought to establish a new nation to supersede the states as the locus of the commonwealth. While anchoring the broad contours of state and federal roles, the Framers left it to their successors to adjust the balance to fit the circumstances of the world to come and the priorities of future generations.

This moment of consensus in favor of letting Washington fade while the states take the lead is badly timed. The public sector's current trajectory—the devolution of welfare and other programs, legislative and judicial action circumscribing Washington's authority, and the federal government's retreat to a domestic role largely defined by writing checks to entitlement claimants, creditors, and state and local governments—would make sense if economic and cultural ties reaching across state lines were *weakening* over time. But state borders are becoming more, not less, permeable.

From a vantage point three-fifths of the way between James Madison's day and our own, Woodrow Wilson wrote that the "common interests of a nation brought together in thought and interest and action by the telegraph and the telephone, as well as by the rushing mails which every express train carries, have a scope and variety, an infinite multiplication and intricate interlacing, of which a simpler day can have had no conception." Issues in which other states' citizens have no stakes, and hence no valid claim to a voice, are becoming rarer still in an age of air freight, interlinked computers, nonstop currency trading, and site-shopping global corporations. . . .

The concept of "the commons" can help to cast in a sharper light the perils of fragmented decision-making on issues of national consequence. In a much-noted 1968 article in *Science*, biologist Garrett Hardin invoked the parable of a herdsman pondering how many cattle to graze on the village commons. Self-interest will lead the herdsman to increase the size of his herd even if the commons is already overburdened, since he alone benefits from raising an extra animal, but shares the consequent damage to the common pasture. As each farmer follows the same logic, overgrazing wrecks the commons.

Where the nation as a whole is a commons, whether as an economic reality or as a political ideal, and states take action that ignores or narrowly exploits that fact, the frequent result is the kind of "tragedy" that Hardin's metaphor predicts: Collective value is squandered in the name of a constricted definition of gain. States win advantages that seem worthwhile only because other states bear much of the costs. America's most urgent public challenges—shoring up the economic underpinnings of an imperiled middle-class culture; developing and deploying productive workplace skills; orchestrating Americans' engagement with increasingly global capital—involve the stewardship of common interests. The fragmentation of authority makes success less likely. The phenomenon is by no means limited to contemporary economic issues, and a smattering of examples from other times and other policy agendas illustrate the theme.

Faith and Credit

In the late 1700s, states reluctant to raise taxes instead paid public debt with paper money, with progressively little gold or silver behind it. Even states like Georgia, Delaware, and New Jersey that exercised some restraint in issuing paper money saw merchants lose confidence in their currencies, as the flood of bad money debased the reputation of American money in general. Half a century later defaults and debt repudiations by Pennsylvania, Arkansas, Florida, Illinois, and a few other states—which for the states concerned were unfortunate, but apparently preferable to the alternative of paying what they owed—polluted the common American resource of creditworthiness, and for a time froze even solvent states and the federal government out of international credit markets.

Presidential primaries, which are run state by state, provide another example. Each state prefers to be first in line to hold its primary (or at least early in the queue). In recent presidential election seasons—and especially the 1996 Republican primaries—states have wrecked the common resource of a deliberative primary process in a rational (but nonetheless tragic) pursuit of parochial advantage. California's primary in June 1992 had come too late to matter; anxious to avoid another episode of irrelevance four years later, it staked out March 26 for its vote. But several other states, whose *own* votes would be rendered superfluous once California's crowd of delegates was selected, rescheduled their primaries in response. A spiral of competitive rescheduling led to ugly squabbles as Delaware and Louisiana crowded New Hampshire's traditional first-in-the-nation franchise; a mass of state primaries ended up bunched right behind New Hampshire, and a grotesquely compressed primary season ensued. The outcome was clear by the first days of March, and California's primary—although held two months earlier than it had been in 1992—was just as irrelevant. Most voters perceived the 1996 primary season as a brief spasm of televised name-calling. Even supporters of the eventual nominee felt that Senator Dole, and the voters, had been ill served by the process. . . .

The Constitution's "full faith and credit" clause, a court case in Hawaii, and the quadrennial uptick in political tawdriness brought an unusual sort of commons problem to center stage in 1996. The issue was whether the definition of "marriage" should be broadened to include same-sex unions. A handful of Hawaiian same-sex couples had asserted the right to have their relationships reckoned under state law as no different from heterosexual marriages, invoking provisions in the state constitution that bar sex discrimination in almost any form (including, the plaintiffs argued, restrictions on the gender of one's spouse). When a shift in the composition of Hawaii's supreme court made a seemingly lost cause suddenly viable, it dawned on advocates and opponents alike that if Hawaii legitimated same-sex marriage, those unions would have to be recognized nationwide. If any homosexual couple—at least those able to afford two tickets to Hawaii—could bypass more restrictive laws in their home states, the rapid result could be a national redefinition of what marriage means, without anyone outside Hawaii having any voice in the outcome.

National opponents of gay marriage staged a preemptive strike in the form of the Defense of Marriage Act, requiring the federal government to counter heterodoxy in Hawaii or anywhere else by declaring a *national* definition of marriage—one man, one woman, and that's that. Beyond excluding same-sex spouses from receiving benefits under any federal program, the act gave states the right to refuse recognition to other states' marriages. The Defense of Marriage Act raced through Congress and President Clinton quickly signed it (albeit without ceremony and literally in the middle of the night). Annoyed at being forced to alienate his gay supporters in order to stay wrapped in the family-values mantle, Clinton charged, no doubt correctly, that the bill's authors were driven by the partisan spirit of the election year. But whatever their motivations—and however one feels about same-sex marriage—they had a point: The definition of marriage in the United States should be settled by national deliberation.

There is an interesting historical irony here, however. Not so long ago, divorce was only a little more common, and only a little less out of the mainstream, than homosexual unions seem today. While the causes for its increase are many and complex, the pace was set in part by states' calculations of parochial advantage. Around the turn of the century legislators in several Western states—notably Nevada—passed liberal divorce legislation in part to encourage economic development. Unhappy couples facing onerous divorce laws in their home state could head West for a few weeks or months. There they could dissolve their union, while solidifying the local economy, in some striving desert town. Other states might have resisted the trend to more lenient divorce laws. But any couple—at least any able to afford a ticket to Reno—could bypass their home-state restrictions. If a legislature held the line it would only be subjecting its citizens to extra expense while sending money out of state.

The wholesale liberalization of American divorce laws is often seen as a mistake—if not from the perspective of men who can cast off unwanted obligations with minimal bother, at least from the perspective of women and, especially, young children who all too often are left economically stranded. Which raises a question: If states should be free to refuse recognition to marriages made elsewhere, on the grounds that another state's definition of marriage offends local morals, should they also be able to refuse to recognize out-of-state divorces? Suppose that Vermont, say, passed legislation toughening divorce laws and declaring Vermont marriages immune to dissolution by another state's laws. If the legislation survived constitutional challenge (which is doubtful, as it is for the Defense of Marriage Act's comparable provisions) there would be some definite advantages: More traditional states could wall themselves off as enclaves against unwelcome national trends; a potential spouse could signal the depth of his or her commitment by proposing a Vermont wedding. On the other hand, the United States would become a little bit less of a nation.

In one of the less glorious episodes in American history, this country attempted to define human slavery as an issue each state could settle on its own, according to its own economic and ethical lights. Northern states, however, eventually proved unwilling to accept the proposition that the moral commons could be so neatly subdivided. The Fugitive Slave Act required antislavery states to make room in their moral world for slaveholders to transport their "property" for use anywhere in the nation. The repercussions ultimately led to attempted secession, and then to the national abolition of slavery. The meaning of marriage may be another moral issue so basic that it must be dealt with through a national debate, protracted and painful as that will doubtless turn out to be.

Environmental Regulation

Antipollution law is perhaps the most obvious application of the "commons" metaphor to policymaking in a federal system. If a state maintains a lax regime of environmental laws it spares its own citizens, businesses, and government agencies from economic burdens. The "benefits" of environmental recklessness, in other words, are collected in-state. Part of the pollution consequently dumped into the air or water, however, drifts away to do its damage elsewhere in the nation. If states held all authority over environmental rule-making, the predictable result would be feeble regulations against any kinds of pollution where in-state costs and benefits of control are seriously out of balance. Even in states whose citizens valued the environment—even if the citizens of *all* states were willing to accept substantial economic costs in the name of cleaner air and water—constituents and representatives would calculate that their sacrifice could not on its own stem the tide and reluctantly settle for weaker rules than they would otherwise prefer.

A state contemplating tough antipollution rules might calculate that its citizens will pay for environmental improvements that will be enjoyed, in part, by others. Even worse, by imposing higher costs on business than do other states, it risks repelling investment, and thus losing jobs and tax revenues to states with weak environmental laws. Congress explicitly invoked the specter of a "race for the bottom"—competitive loosening of environmental laws in order to lure business—to justify federal standards that would "preclude efforts on the part of states to compete with each other in trying to attract new plants." In a series of legislative changes starting in the early 1970s, the major choices about how aggressively to act against pollution were moved to the federal government. While aspects of enforcement remained state responsibilities—introducing another level of complications that continues to plague environmental policy—the trade-off between environmental and economic values moved much closer to a single national standard.

National regulation in a diverse economy does have a downside. States differ in their environmental problems, and in the priorities of their citizens. Requiring all states to accept the same balance between environmental and economic values imposes some real costs and generates real political friction. Yet even if the tilt toward national authority is, on balance, the correct approach to environmental regulation, there is reason to doubt we got all the details right. Moreover, logic suggests that the federal role should be stronger for forms of pollution that readily cross state borders, and weaker for pollution that stays put. But federal authority is actually weaker under the Clean Air Act and the Clean Water Act than under the "Superfund" law covering hazardous waste. Toxic waste sites are undeniably nasty things. But most of them are situated within a single state, and stay there. . . .

Legalized Gambling

There has never been a time in America when a person determined to gamble could not find some action. Nor is *legal* gambling, for that matter, anything new. The Continental Congress fed and armed Washington's army, in part, with revenues from a lottery, and state-sanctioned games of chance financed the early growth of Harvard and other colleges. For much of this century, however, gambling has operated in the economic shadows. Except for the exotic enclave of Nevada, government's stance toward gambling ranged, until recently, from vigilant hostility to narrowly circumscribed tolerance.

This has changed with an astonishing speed and completeness. In 1988 Nevada and New Jersey were alone in allowing casino gambling. Eight years later there were around 500 casinos operating in 27 states, and some form of gambling was legal in all but two states. The total annual amount wagered legally in the United States is about $500 billion. (For a sense of scale, consider that America's entire annual output is in the range of $7,000 billion.)

Gambling brings some obvious benefits to the state that runs the lottery or hosts the casinos. It can generate relatively high-paying jobs even for workers without much training. It yields welcome revenues for the state treasury. (States took in $27 billion from lotteries in 1994, and had $9.8 billion in revenues left over after paying off winners and covering administrative costs. In 1994, taxes paid by casinos alone yielded $1.4 billion for states and localities.) Legalized gambling can also produce political benefits, most directly the rich lodes of campaign contributions available from a highly profitable industry that is so intensely dependent on political favor.

Yet there are costs as well. Some people will always gamble whether it is legal or not, but many more do so only when the law allows. Access to legal opportunities for gambling has been found to increase the number of people who develop a gambling problem. The consequences range from mild economic inconvenience to bankruptcy, embezzlement, divorce, and suicide. In 1995—ten years after their state launched a lottery, and four years after the first legal riverboat casino opened—nine out of ten Iowans indulged in gambling. One in twenty reported having a gambling problem, and Iowa social-service agencies were coping with a surge of collateral family and financial damage.

But shouldn't we leave it to officials in each state to tally up the expected costs and benefits and make decisions that sum to the right national policy? The logic of the commons makes this less than likely. If a state loosens its own restrictions on gambling, it gains the benefits in jobs, tax revenues, and political favor. It also suffers costs—but not *all* the costs. When citizens of *other* states buy the lottery tickets and visit the casinos, they leave their money behind when they return home, but take their gambling-related problems back with them. States that still ban gambling suffer much of the damage from the national trend toward legalization, but without sharing in the benefits.

Iowa, in fact, had maintained stringent antigambling laws until the mid-1980s. But as a growing number of Iowans played lotteries in neighboring states it became harder to resist proposals to revitalize a battered economy through riverboat casinos aimed at attracting out-of-state gamblers, especially from the prosperous, casino-free Chicago area. At first, Chicagoans did come, by the busload. But Illinois legislators, seeing gambling dollars heading down the interstate to Iowa, opted to allow riverboat gambling in their state, too. Iowa's initial liberalization law had tried to lower the risk of problem gambling by limiting the size of any one bet and the amount any person could gamble away in a single day. But when Illinois, Mississippi, and Louisiana introduced riverboats *without* any limits, Iowa lifted its own restrictions. In a similar way, after Montana allowed slot machines in taverns in 1985 neighboring South Dakota called and raised, allowing slot machines in bars *and* convenience stores.

By 1996 the only two states with no legal gambling at all were Utah, whose Mormon culture was uniquely resistant to the national trend, and Hawaii, where it is a good deal harder than in most other states for citizens to escape local restrictions by doing their gambling in the state next door. The federal government's absolute deference to the separate states began to bend that same year with legislation establishing a commission to examine the broader national impacts of gambling. A Nevada congresswoman denounced the bill as "the nose under the tent of Federal interference with the right of states to regulate gambling." She was entirely correct. But it is questionable whether exclusive state control over so massive a change in the legal economy's scope, with such sweeping implications for our culture, ever made much sense.

Not every issue, to be sure, can be cast as a commons problem. And even where state officials *are* tempted to pursue narrow agendas at the expense of national interests, it is not automatically true that the shared loss exceeds the advantages of state autonomy, or that an acceptable way can be found of safeguarding common interests without straining the framework of our federal system. There are two basic strategies for overcoming the confusion of incentives that trigger the tragedy of the commons. One is to fragment the commons into private holdings where property rights are unambiguous. The other is to maintain a polity that commands both the capacity and the legitimacy to give force to common interests. The debate over the future of America's federal-state balance can be seen, in a sense, as pivoting on this strategic choice. Devolution seeks to simplify incentives by subdividing the commons into separate plots. Federal reform requires accepting the challenge of balancing multiple interests within the national commonwealth. . . .

Questions for Discussion

1. What is the "tragedy of the commons"? Give some examples of how the concept is relevant to federal/state relations.
2. How would defenders of states' rights refute the arguments that Donahue puts forth? Are there any negative consequences to regulating at the national level a diverse economy and culture?

2.4

American Federalism—Half-Full or Half-Empty?

Martha Derthick

During the Clinton years, national policy initiatives, such as welfare reform, as well as a number of high profile Supreme Court decisions, seemed to provide evidence of a distinct trend toward devolution in the federal system. Politicians of both parties appeared to agree rhetorically that government closest to the people is best, and the Rehnquist Court developed a firm reputation as a strong defender of states' rights throughout the 1990s.

In this selection, Martha Derthick challenges the existence of a devolutionary trend, noting that "American federalism was born in ambiguity, it institutionalizes ambiguity in our form of government, and changes in it tend to be ambiguous." Consequently, one often finds individual policy spheres in which there is evidence of both centralization and decentralization. One such area is criminal justice, where the police and prosecutorial power largely remain in the hands of state and local officials, while federal criminal law has grown explosively to include even such matters as car jacking and disrupting a rodeo.

Derthick also suggests that the role education played in the 2000 Bush-Gore presidential race may indicate that both the public's and the politicians' commitment to devolution may be waning. Education has traditionally been a state and local function, yet it was a central issue in the campaign agendas of both candidates. From Derthick's perspective, any discernable trend in American federalism is more murky than clear.

L ast August [1999] the *Wall Street Journal* noted that some taxpayers were claiming that they did not have to pay federal income tax because they were residents of a state, not the United States. A few weeks earlier the *New York Times* carried a story describing Vice President Albert Gore's plan to have detailed positions on a wide range of issues in his quest for the Democratic presidential nomination in 2000. At the top of his list was education, a function not long ago considered a preserve of state and local governments.

Martha Derthick is professor of government and foreign affairs emeritus at the University of Virginia. She is the editor of *Dilemmas of Scale in America's Federal Democracy* (Cambridge, 1999).

Gore's "blizzard of positions" included preschool for all children, a ban on gang-style clothing, teacher testing, "second-chance" schools for trouble-prone students, back-to-school parent-teacher meetings where a strict discipline code would be signed, and "character education" courses in the schools. Gore proposed to amend the Family and Medical Leave Act to permit parents to attend the parent-teacher meetings during working hours.

As these contrasting conceptions suggest, American federalism is a highly protean form, long on change and confusion, short on fixed, generally accepted principles. In the event, a tax court judge fined the taxpayers who claimed not to be citizens of the United States. And the *Times* reporter hinted that many actions Gore planned to "require" would need local school board cooperation to take effect.

As the 20th century ends, public commentators often suggest that this is a time of decentralization in the federal system. The view derives mainly from a series of Supreme Court decisions that have sought to rehabilitate the states in constitutional doctrine and from passage of a welfare reform act in 1996 that office-holders and analysts alike interpreted as radically devolutionary.

But matters are more complicated than that. American federalism was born in ambiguity, it institutionalizes ambiguity in our form of government, and changes in it tend to be ambiguous too.

To sort out what is happening, I will distinguish among three spheres of activity: constitutional interpretation by the Supreme Court; electoral politics; and the everyday work of government as manifested in policies and programs.

The Supreme Court

A narrow majority of the Rehnquist Court led by the chief justice attaches importance to preserving federalism. To that end, it has made a series of daring and controversial decisions that purport to limit the powers of Congress or secure constitutional prerogatives of the states.

In *Printz* v. *U.S.* (1997) the Court invalidated a provision of the Brady Handgun Violence Prevention Act that required local law enforcement officers to conduct background checks on all gun purchasers. The Court objected that the provision impermissibly violated the Tenth Amendment by commandeering the state government to carry out a federal law. An earlier opinion, *New York* v. *U.S.* (1992), had begun to lay the ground for the anticommandeering principle. In another leading case, *U.S.* v. *Lopez* (1995), the Court held that Congress had exceeded its commerce clause power by prohibiting guns in school zones. Still other decisions signaled a retreat from federal judicial supervision of school desegregation, prison administration, and the judgments of state courts. Another line of cases has secured the state governments' immunity from certain classes of suits under federal law.

Some analysts profess to see a revolutionary development here, but qualifications are in order. The Court decides many cases in which it does not give primacy to federalism, as for example a 7–2 ruling in 1999 that state welfare programs may not restrict new residents to the welfare benefits they would have received in the states from which they moved. This ruling struck down a California law and by implication a provision of federal law that had authorized it. Moreover, the majority that has decided the leading federalism cases is narrow (often 5–4) and tenuous, inasmuch as it includes some of the oldest members of the Court. . . .

If this is a revolution, it is one that may not last.

Electoral Politics

Speaker Thomas P. O'Neill's* famous aphorism that "all politics is local" applied to virtually all structural aspects of U.S. electoral politics for a very long time. Determining electoral districts and voter qualifications, mobilizing voters, and financing campaigns were the province mainly of state laws and customs and were locally rooted well into this century. But that has ceased to be true under the impact of 20th-century constitutional amendments extending the electorate, as well as federal statutes and judicial decisions governing apportionment and voting rights. Federal supervision now extends even to such matters as ward-based versus at-large elections in local governments. And changes in technology and in social and economic structures mean that candidates for congressional seats or even lesser offices do not depend exclusively on funds raised from local constituencies. Candidates may get help from party committees and interest groups organized on a national scale.

Nationalization of electoral practices proceeds apace at century's end. The Motor Voter Act of 1993 requires states to allow all eligible citizens to register to vote when they apply for or renew a driver's license. It also requires states to allow mail-in registration forms at agencies that supply public assistance, such as welfare checks or help for the disabled. The costs are borne by the states.

Nevertheless, one hesitates to insist that our electoral processes are being comprehensively nationalized at a time when governors seem to have gained an advantage in access to the presidency, growing, arguably, out of the public's now chronic distrust of the national government. Of the four last presidents in this century, three were governors before they were elected, and in the run-up to the 2000 election, a governor, George W. Bush of Texas, has secured a large and early advantage over other Republican candidates. He owes his success partly to other

---

* Democratic Congressman Thomas (Tip) O'Neill from Massachusetts was Speaker of the U.S. House of Representatives from 1976 to 1987.

Republican governors—of whom there were 32 after the election of 1998—who have backed him under the lead of Michigan's John Engler. . . .

Policies and Programs

It is necessary to be selective because there are so many policies and programs. I will concentrate on three sets—welfare, schools, and criminal justice—that have traditionally been regarded as quite decentralized. Indeed, for decades they constituted the bedrock of local government activity.

The welfare reform legislation of 1996 is everyone's leading example of decentralization in action. The law converted what had been an open-ended matching grant, with federal funds tied to the number of cases, to a fixed-sum ("block") grant and explicitly ended individuals' entitlements to welfare. States gained freedom to design their own programs, a change already largely effectuated by White House decisions during the Reagan, Bush, and Clinton administrations to grant waivers of certain federal requirements to individual states. The decentralization of program authority in this case was an important change in intergovernmental relations. Still, its significance must be put in perspective.

Whatever may have happened with welfare in 1996, income support, which is the core function of the modern welfare state, has been largely federalized in the United States in the six decades since 1935. Social Security, Supplemental Security Income (SSI), and food stamps accounted for $431 billion in federal spending in 1998, compared with $22 billion for welfare, now known as TANF (or Temporary Assistance for Needy Families). I pass over the earned income tax credit, weighing in at a volume comparable to that for welfare, a use of federal tax law for income support that would take us too far afield here.

Welfare could be decentralized in 1996 in large part because, unlike income support for the aged and the disabled, it had never been fully centralized. The main change in 1996 was a national policy change that strongly discouraged dependency and certain behavior, especially out-of-wedlock pregnancies and lack of child support from fathers, that had come to be associated with welfare. To carry out this policy change, the new law imposed some stringent federal requirements, such as time limits for receipt of welfare, on the states. Surprisingly, a liberal president and conservative members of the new Republican majority in Congress coalesced in support of legislation, but the national coalition was so frail and incomplete that it became necessary to lodge discretion in the states to achieve a result.

That is one of the traditional functions of American federalism: in the absence of agreement at the national level, discretion can be left to the states. Typically, through *inaction* by Congress, matters are left with the states, which have initial jurisdiction. . . .

Elementary and secondary education, far from being off-limits to national politicians as a local matter, has risen to the top of their rhetorical agenda. It took a year for Congress to reauthorize the Elementary and Secondary Education Act in 1993–94. The resulting law consumed fourteen titles and 1,200 pages, covering subjects as wide-ranging as academic standards, racial desegregation, language assessments, migrant education, teacher training, math and science equipment, libraries, hate-crime prevention, vouchers, school prayer, sex education, gay rights, gun control, the handicapped, English as a second language, telecommunications, pornography, single-sex schools, national tests, home schooling, drugs, smoking—and more. The level of detail was minute. Any state receiving federal funds had to require that any student who brought a gun to school would be expelled for at least a year. Local officials could, however, modify the requirement on a case-by-case basis. School districts also had to refer offenders to local law enforcement officials. Developmentally disabled students were subject to the expulsion rule, but if school officials established that their behavior was related to their disability, the students could be placed in an alternative educational setting for up to forty-five days instead.

In 1999, when the act was again up for reauthorization, Congress by wide margins enacted "Ed-Flex," the Educational Flexibility Partnership Demonstration Act, which authorized the Secretary of Education to implement a nationwide program under which state educational agencies could apply for waivers of certain federal rules. To be eligible for Ed-Flex, states had to develop educational content and performance standards and procedures for holding districts and schools accountable for meeting educational goals. One could point to this law, of course, as an example of decentralization; members of Congress naturally did so. But in education as in welfare, the subject of waivers would never have arisen had not a vast body of law and regulation developed from which relief had to be sought.

In criminal justice, it remains true that most police and prosecutors are state and local officials. Ninety-five percent of prosecutions are handled by state and local governments. Yet federal criminal law has grown explosively as Congress has taken stands against such offenses as carjacking and church burning, disrupting a rodeo and damaging a livestock facility. . . .

The "Mores" of Intergovernmental Relations

In everyday affairs, how do we and our officials think and talk about governments in the federal system? Without having any evidence to support my point, I would argue that citizens and journalists routinely refer to "the government" as if there were only one—the Big One. That this is a country of many governments, though a patent fact, is nonetheless a fact that it takes a pedant or a lawyer to insist on.

Moreover, we are now accustomed to reading that Washington is giving orders to the states, or at least exhorting them to act in regard to one or another matter in which they have been found deficient. Some sample headlines from end-of-century stories in the *New York Times* would appear very odd to a student of American government who had gone to sleep in, say, 1955 and just awakened: "Clinton to Require State Efforts to Cut Drug Use in Prisons" (January 12, 1998); "White House Plans Medicaid Coverage of Viagra by States" (May 28, 1998); "Clinton to Chide States for Failing to Cover Children" (August 8, 1999). None of this is to say that the states promptly act on orders or admonitions from Washington, only that Washington is accustomed to giving them, without pausing to question the appropriateness of doing so—as is evident from an executive order on federalism that the Clinton administration issued, suspended when state officials angrily protested, and then issued in much revised form.

The offending order, issued in May 1998, contained a set of criteria for policymaking by federal agencies that was broad and inclusive enough invariably to justify federal government action: "(1) When the matter to be addressed by federal action occurs interstate as opposed to being contained within one State's boundaries. (2) When the source of the matter to be addressed occurs in a State different from the State (or States) where a significant amount of the harm occurs. (3) When there is a need for uniform national standards. (4) When decentralization increases the costs of government thus imposing additional burdens on the taxpayer. (5) When States have not adequately protected individual rights and liberties. (6) When States would be reluctant to impose necessary regulations because of fears that regulated business activity will relocate to other States. . . ." Only the most obtuse and indolent federal administrator could not have put this list to use.

The revised executive order, issued following consultation with state officials, was completely different. The section on policymaking criteria called for "strict adherence to constitutional principles," avoiding limits on policymaking discretion of the states except with constitutional and statutory authority, granting "maximum administrative discretion" to the states, encouraging states to "develop their own policies to achieve program objectives," where possible deferring to the states to "establish standards," consulting with appropriate state and local officials "as to the need for national standards," and consulting with them in developing national standards when such were found to be necessary.

It is hard to imagine a more-complete about-face. It is also hard to know how to interpret the event. One can cite the original order as evidence of the imperious attitudes that high federal officials actually bring to intergovernmental relations, or one can cite the revision as evidence of the continuing power of the states. In studying American federalism, the analyst is forever asking whether the glass is half-empty or half-full. That is the appropriate question as the century turns, and the answers are to be found more in the day-to-day operations of intergovernmental relations than in either Supreme Court decisions or executive orders. It requires a blind eye to call ours an era of devolution. But even with two sharp eyes, it is hard to detect a plain answer. Everywhere one looks, the answer remains murky and many-sided.

Questions for Discussion

1. What evidence does Derthick present to challenge the claim that devolution is a strong trend in American federalism? What arguments could you make to undercut her position?
2. The conduct of elections has traditionally been a state and local function, but concerns about the arbitrary design and counting of ballots in the 2000 presidential election, especially in Florida, have suggested to some that the federal government must play a new role in ensuring more uniformity in electoral procedures. What arguments would you raise to support both sides of the issue? What would your position on the issue be?

 Chapter 3

CIVIL LIBERTIES AND CIVIL RIGHTS

Abortion. Prayer in public schools. Libel and slander. School integration and vouchers. Affirmative action and racial quotas. The right to legal counsel. These often-emotional issues strike at the core of the relationship between the citizen and the state. The framers understood the central position of individual rights, seeing them as inalienable—that is, as God-given, neither handed down nor taken away by rulers or the government as a whole. Still, the government serves as the chief agency for protecting individual rights, even though it can effectively deny them as well (for example, through the long history of legal segregation). The framers and subsequent generations of policymakers have thus performed a pair of balancing acts with civil liberties and civil rights issues.

First, they have strived to balance the rights of individuals with the needs of the community at large. On many occasions, the individual and the community are best served by the same policy. For example, the court decision in *Gideon* v. *Wainwright* that guarantees indigents the right to counsel was a victory both for individual poor people and for society as a whole. Frequently, however, the interests of the community and the individual are, or appear to be, at odds. Does the right to freedom of speech and assembly extend to Nazis who wish to march through a predominantly Jewish community like Skokie, Illinois? The list of troubling and important questions in this area is endless and has produced a river of cases for the Supreme Court to wade through.

The second balance policymakers must maintain lies in the relative amounts of power accorded the government and its citizens. The government stands as the ultimate protector of individual liberties, such as the Constitution's enumerated rights of speech, religion, petition, and so forth. At the same time, the government can adopt policies and procedures that deny rights. The actions of an overzealous FBI or CIA have infringed on privacy rights, and many legislative initiatives have overstepped the bounds of propriety in seeking to regulate political organizations and speech. The Supreme Court's willingness to curb the government's assertion of power has varied. The Supreme Court of the 1990s was probably more likely to decide in favor of the government—whether national, state, or local—than it had been at any time since Earl Warren became chief justice in 1953.

What makes the study of civil rights and civil liberties so fascinating is the simultaneous timelessness and immediacy of the issues. For example, the notion of freedom of speech is as important today as it was in the eighteenth century, and contemporary controversies place basic issues, such as the potential defamation of a public figure, in new contexts. Likewise, civil rights and civil liberties issues hold our interest because their implications are extensive. Millions of individuals are directly affected by the Supreme Court's ruling in abortion or desegregation cases.

Although the legislative and executive branches play important roles in making and implementing rights policies, it is the judiciary that stands at center stage in this arena. At first such a responsibility may seem incongruous, since the courts are insulated from the influence of most citizens. In the end, however, this very independence from the popular will and the daily intrigues of politics is what renders the judicial branch, especially in its upper reaches, well suited to consider questions of rights. Protecting rights is frequently an unpopular business. In the 1940s and 1950s, for instance, Congress shied away from legislation that challenged racial separation, and the Supreme Court ruled on a series of desegregation cases, culminating in *Brown* v. *Board of Education.*

The direction of the Court is influenced by precedent and societal context as well as by individual appointments. Although the membership of the Court during the last twenty-five years has become more conservative, its decisions have not dramatically turned away from the expansive civil liberties positions under Chief Justice Earl Warren (1953–1969). For example, the Burger (1969–1986) and Rehnquist (from 1986) Courts have gradually expanded the flexibility of the police in carrying out searches and seizures. But their decisions have not overturned any of the key Warren Court precedents, such as *Mapp* v. *Ohio* (1961), which limited the use of evidence from an illegal search, or *Miranda* v. *Arizona* (1966), which guaranteed that the accused be made aware of their right to counsel and protection from self-incrimination. Still, the increasing willingness of the Rehnquist Court of the 1990s to limit or overturn previous decisions may indicate that some fundamental changes (such as overturning *Roe* v. *Wade*) remain possible, though unlikely.

The following selections show the variety of civil rights and civil liberties issues. The first two indicate the conflict over the possibility of limiting free speech. In *Near* v. *Minnesota* (1931), the Supreme Court refused to bar the publication of an irresponsible newspaper that had mounted vicious anti-Semitic attacks on Minneapolis public officials. This decision reflects the Court's great reluctance to order the prior restraint of any publication, even the most despicable. The *Near* decision was notable not for its immediate impact, which was next to nothing, but for the precedent it set. In 1971, the Court ruled in *New York Times* v. *United States* that the government could not suppress the publication of the Pentagon Papers, a highly critical history of U.S. involvement in Vietnam. The Defense Department had commissioned the extensive study and distributed it internally (though not widely). As Fred Friendly notes (3.2), the justices relied heavily on *Near* in their reasoning. That obscure Minnesota case thus had a major impact on an issue of great national importance.

Another area of civil liberties is the so-called right to privacy. Unlike enumerated rights, which protect speech, religion, assembly, and so on, the right to privacy is not acknowledged in the Constitution. Such a right has evolved, however, becoming explicit in *Griswold* v. *Connecticut* (1965). The *Griswold* ruling was a focal point in the 1987 confirmation hearings of Robert Bork, President Reagan's unsuccessful nominee for a Supreme Court seat.

Moreover, the 1973 *Roe* v. *Wade* abortion decision relied heavily on the "right of privacy" that Griswold began to establish. More generally, as Jeffrey Rosen (3.4) observes, privacy has become an issue that transcends legal rights. In an excerpt from his book *The Unwanted Gaze,* Rosen argues that the virtues of privacy go far beyond its constitutional significance.

This chapter's final two selections address one's right to protection under the law. *Gideon* v. *Wainright* culminates decades of incremental change in guaranteeing the right to counsel for accused felons. In the mid-1960s, the *Miranda* ruling (requiring that suspects be apprised of their rights) expanded the rights of accused felons. Alexander Nguyen addresses the continuing significance of *Miranda* as of 2000, both as a modest protection for the accused and as a hot-button issue for law-and-order conservatives. As with abortion rights, affirmative action, and separation of church and state, the rights of the accused remain contested as we begin the 21st century.

Near v. Minnesota (1931)

Among the rights guaranteed in the Constitution, perhaps the most fundamental is the freedom of expression. Without unfettered speech and a free press, the idea of democracy loses its meaning. Freedom of expression issues emerge in many forms, including controversies over libel, obscenity, and political speech. Even a very large number of articles could not capture the range of questions that courts regularly face in deciding freedom of expression cases.

In *Near v. Minnesota,* the central question revolves around prior restraint of the press. In 1931, the Supreme Court ruled 5 to 4 that Minnesota could not muzzle the publisher of a newspaper that was attacking various Minneapolis public officials. Although any public official who is the subject of a "malicious, scandalous, and defamatory" article can sue for libel, the state could not halt publication of a newspaper merely because it expected that paper to defame public officials.

Mr. Chief Justice Hughes delivered the opinion of the Court. . . .

Under this statute, [section one, clause (b)], the County Attorney of Hennepin County brought this action to enjoin the publication of what was described as a "malicious, scandalous and defamatory newspaper, magazine and periodical," known as "The Saturday Press," published by the defendants in the city of Minneapolis. The complaint alleged that the defendants, on September 24, 1927, and on eight subsequent dates in October and November, 1927, published and circulated editions of that periodical which were "largely devoted to malicious, scandalous and defamatory articles" concerning Charles G. Davis, Frank W. Brunskill, the *Minneapolis Tribune,* the *Minneapolis Journal,* Melvin C. Passolt, George E. Leach, the Jewish Race, the members of the Grand Jury of Hennepin County impaneled in November 1927, and then holding office, and other persons, as more fully appeared in exhibits annexed to the complaint, consisting of copies of the articles described and constituting 327 pages of the record. While the complaint did not so allege, it appears from the briefs of both parties that Charles G. Davis was a special law enforcement officer employed by a civic organization, that George E. Leach was Mayor of Minneapolis, that Frank W. Brunskill was its Chief of Police, and that Floyd B. Olson (the relator in this action) was County Attorney.

Without attempting to summarize the contents of the voluminous exhibits attached to the complaint, we deem it sufficient to say that the articles charged in substance that a Jewish gangster was in control of gambling, bootlegging and racketeering in Minneapolis, and that law enforcing officers and agencies were not energetically performing their duties. Most of the charges were directed against the Chief of Police; he was charged with gross neglect of duty, illicit relations with gangsters, and with participation in graft. The County Attorney was charged with knowing the existing conditions and with failure to take adequate measures to remedy them. The Mayor was accused of inefficiency and dereliction. One member of the grand jury was stated to be in sympathy with the gangsters. A special grand jury and a special prosecutor were demanded to deal with the situation in general, and, in particular, to investigate an attempt to assassinate one Guilford, one of the original defendants, who, it appears from the articles, was shot by gangsters after the first issue of the periodical had been published. There is no question but that the articles made serious accusations against the public officers named and others in connection with the prevalence of crimes and the failure to expose and punish them. . . .

If we cut through mere details of procedure, the operation and effect of the statute in substance is that public authorities may bring the owner or publisher of a newspaper or periodical before a judge upon a charge of conducting a business of publishing scandalous and defamatory matter—in particular that the matter consists of charges against public officers of official dereliction—and unless the owner or publisher is able and disposed to bring competent evidence to satisfy the judge that the charges are true and are published with good motives and for justifiable ends, his newspaper or periodical is suppressed and further publication is made punishable as a contempt. This is of the essence of censorship.

The question is whether a statute authorizing such proceedings in restraint of publication is consistent with the conception of the liberty of the press as historically conceived and guaranteed. In determining the extent of the constitutional protection, it has been generally, if not universally, considered that it is the chief purpose of the guaranty to prevent previous restraints upon publication. The struggle in England, directed against the legislative power of the licenser, resulted in renunciation of the censorship of the press. The liberty deemed to be established was thus described by Blackstone:* "The liberty of the press is indeed essential to the nature of a free state; but this consists in laying no *previous* restraints upon publications, and not in freedom from censure for criminal matter when published. Every freeman has an undoubted right to lay what sentiments he pleases before the public; to forbid this, is to destroy the freedom of the press; but if he publishes what is improper, mischievous or illegal, he must take the consequence of his own temerity." . . . The distinction was early pointed out

---

* Sir William Blackstone (1723–1780) was an English jurist and legal scholar whose writings served as the core of legal education in the United States during the nineteenth century.

between the extent of the freedom with respect to censorship under our constitutional system and that enjoyed in England. Here, as Madison said, "the great and essential rights of the people are secured against legislative as well as against executive ambition. They are secured, not by laws paramount to prerogative, but by constitutions paramount to laws. This security of the freedom of the press requires that it should be exempt not only from previous restraint by the Executive, as in Great Britain, but from legislative restraint also." . . .

The objection has . . . been made that the principle as to immunity from previous restraint is stated too broadly, if every such restraint is deemed to be prohibited. That is undoubtedly true; the protection even as to previous restraint is not absolutely unlimited. But the limitation has been recognized only in exceptional cases: "When a nation is at war many things that might be said in time of peace are such a hindrance to its effort that their utterance will not be endured so long as men fight and that no Court could regard them as protected by any constitutional right." . . . No one would question but that a government might prevent actual obstruction to its recruiting service or the publication of the sailing dates of transports or the number and location of troops. On similar grounds, the primary requirements of decency may be enforced against obscene publications. The security of the community life may be protected against incitements to acts of violence and the overthrow by force of orderly government. The constitutional guaranty of free speech does not "protect a man from an injunction against uttering words that may have all the effect of force. . . ." These limitations are not applicable here. Nor are we now concerned with questions as to the extent of authority to prevent publications in order to protect private rights according to the principles governing the exercise of the jurisdiction of courts of equity.

The exceptional nature of its limitations places in a strong light the general conception that liberty of the press, historically considered and taken up by the Federal Constitution, has meant, principally although not exclusively, immunity from previous restraints or censorship. The conception of the liberty of the press in this country had broadened with the exigencies of the colonial period and with the efforts to secure freedom from oppressive administration. That liberty was especially cherished for the immunity it afforded from previous restraint of the publication of censure of public officers and charges of official misconduct. . . . Madison, who was the leading spirit in the preparation of the First Amendment of the Federal Constitution, thus described the practice and sentiment which led to the guaranties of liberty of the press in state constitutions:[1]

"In every State, probably, in the Union, the press has exerted a freedom in canvassing the merits and measures of public men of every description which has not been confined to the strict limits of the common law. On this footing the freedom of the press has stood; on this footing it yet stands. . . . Some degree of abuse is inseparable from the proper use of everything, and in no instance is this more true than in that of the press. It has accordingly been decided by the practice of the States, that it is better to leave a few of its noxious branches to their luxuriant growth, than, by pruning them away, to injure the vigour of those yielding the proper fruits. And can the wisdom of this policy be doubted by any who reflect that to the press alone, chequered as it is with abuses, the world is indebted for all the triumphs which have been gained by reason and humanity over error and oppression; who reflect that to the same beneficent source the United States owe much of the lights which conducted them to the ranks of a free and independent nation, and which have improved their political system into a shape so auspicious to their happiness? Had 'Sedition Acts,' forbidding every publication that might bring the constituted agents into contempt or disrepute, or that might excite the hatred of the people against the authors of unjust or pernicious measures, been uniformly enforced against the press, might not the United States have been languishing at this day under the infirmities of a sickly Confederation?* Might they not, possibly, be miserable colonies, groaning under a foreign yoke?"

The fact that for approximately one hundred and fifty years there has been almost an entire absence of attempts to impose previous restraints upon publications relating to the malfeasance of public officers is significant of the deep-seated conviction that such restraints would violate constitutional right. Public officers, whose character and conduct remain open to debate and free discussion in the press, find their remedies for false accusations in actions under libel laws providing for redress and punishment, and not in proceedings to restrain the publication of newspapers and periodicals. The general principle that the constitutional guaranty of the liberty of the press gives immunity from previous restraints has been approved in many decisions under the provisions of state constitutions.

The importance of this immunity has not lessened. While reckless assaults upon public men . . . exert a baleful influence and deserve the severest condemnation in public opinion, it cannot be said that this abuse is greater, and it is believed to be less, than that which characterized the period in which our institutions took shape. Meanwhile, the administration of government has become more complex, the opportunities for malfeasance and corruption have multiplied, crime has grown to most serious proportions, and the danger of its protection by unfaithful officials and of the impairment of the fundamental security of life and property by criminal alliances and official neglect, emphasizes the primary need of a vigilant and courageous press, especially in great cities. The fact that the liberty of the press may be abused by miscreant purveyors of scandal does not make any the less necessary the immunity of the press from previous restraint in dealing with official misconduct. Subsequent punishment

---

* The fear of such legislation was scarcely idle. In 1798 Congress passed the Alien and Sedition Acts, which provided for indicting those who conspired against the administration or who spoke or wrote "with intent to defame" the government. The Sedition Act was enforced against a few individuals before being repealed during the Jefferson administration.

for such abuses as may exist is the appropriate remedy, consistent with constitutional privilege.

In attempted justification of the statute, it is said that it deals not with publication *per se*, but with the "business" of publishing defamation. If, however, the publisher has a constitutional right to publish, without previous restraint, an edition of his newspaper charging official derelictions, it cannot be denied that he may publish subsequent editions for the same purpose. He does not lose his right by exercising it. If his right exists, it may be exercised in publishing nine editions, as in this case, as well as in one edition. If previous restraint is permissible, it may be imposed at once; indeed, the wrong may be as serious in one publication as in several. Characterizing the publication as a business, and the business as a nuisance, does not permit an invasion of the constitutional immunity against restraint. Similarly, it does not matter that the newspaper or periodical is found to be "largely" or "chiefly" devoted to the publication of such derelictions. If the publisher has a right, without previous restraint, to publish them, his right cannot be deemed to be dependent upon his publishing something else, more or less, with the matter to which objection is made.

Nor can it be said that the constitutional freedom from previous restraint is lost because charges are made of derelictions which constitute crimes. With the multiplying provisions of penal codes, and of municipal charters and ordinances carrying penal sanctions, the conduct of public officers is very largely within the purview of criminal statutes. The freedom of the press from previous restraint has never been regarded as limited to such animadversions as lay outside the range of penal enactments. Historically, there is no such limitation; it is inconsistent with the reason which underlies the privilege, as the privilege so limited would be of slight value for the purposes for which it came to be established.

The statute in question cannot be justified by reason of the fact that the publisher is permitted to show, before injunction issues, that the matter published is true and is published with good motives and for justifiable ends. If such a statute, authorizing suppression and injunction on such a basis, is constitutionally valid, it would be equally permissible for the legislature to provide that at any time the publisher of any newspaper could be brought before a court, or even an administrative officer (as the constitutional protection may not be regarded as resting on mere procedural details) and required to produce proof of the truth of his publication, or of what he intended to publish, and of his motives, or stand enjoined. If this can be done, the legislature may provide machinery for determining in the complete exercise of its discretion what are justifiable ends and restrain publication accordingly. And it would be but a step to a complete system of censorship. The recognition of authority to impose previous restraint upon publication in order to protect the community against the circulation of charges of misconduct, and especially of official misconduct, necessarily would carry with it the admission of the authority of the censor against which the constitutional barrier was erected. The preliminary freedom, by virtue of the very reason for its existence, does not depend, as this Court has said, on proof of truth. . . .

Equally unavailing is the insistence that the statute is designed to prevent the circulation of scandal which tends to disturb the public peace and to provoke assaults and the commission of crime. Charges of reprehensible conduct, and in particular of official malfeasance, unquestionably create a public scandal, but the theory of the constitutional guaranty is that even a more serious public evil would be caused by authority to prevent publication. "To prohibit the intent to excite those unfavorable sentiments against those who administer the Government, is equivalent to a prohibition of the actual excitement of them; and to prohibit the actual excitement of them is equivalent to a prohibition of discussions having that tendency and effect; which, again, is equivalent to a protection of those who administer the Government, if they should at any time deserve the contempt or hatred of the people, against being exposed to it by free animadversions on their characters and conduct."[2] There is nothing new in the fact that charges of reprehensible conduct may create resentment and the disposition to resort to violent means of redress, but this well-understood tendency did not alter the determination to protect the press against censorship and restraint upon publication. As was said in *New Yorker Staats-Zeitung* v. *Nolan* . . . : "If the township may prevent the circulation of a newspaper for no reason other than that some of its inhabitants may violently disagree with it, and resent its circulation by resorting to physical violence, there is no limit to what may be prohibited." The danger of violent reactions becomes greater with effective organization of defiant groups resenting exposure, and if this consideration warranted legislative interference with the initial freedom of publication, the constitutional protection would be reduced to a mere form of words.

For these reasons we hold the statute, so far as it authorized the proceedings in this action under clause (b) of section one, to be an infringement of the liberty of the press guaranteed by the Fourteenth Amendment. We should add that this decision rests upon the operation and effect of the statute, without regard to the question of the truth of the charges contained in the particular periodical.* The fact that the public officers named in this case, and those associated with the charges of official dereliction, may be deemed to be impeccable, cannot affect the conclusion that the statute imposes an unconstitutional restraint upon publication.

Notes

1. Report on the Virginia Resolutions, Madison's Works, vol. iv, p. 544.
2. Madison, *op. cit.*, p. 549.

---

* Note the strength of this declaration. The falsity of a statement does not constitute adequate grounds for imposing prior restraint.

Questions for Discussion

1. Why should public figures be treated differently when libel or slander is alleged? Is it possible to libel someone as public as the president?
2. In what instances might prior restraint of a publication be appropriate? In wartime? In the case of a consistently obscene magazine?

 3.2

From the *Saturday Press* to the *New York Times*

Fred Friendly

Fred Friendly notes the importance of the *Near* decision in the Pentagon Papers case of 1971. In this instance the publisher was not a purveyor of sensational accusations but the *New York Times* and the *Washington Post,* which were printing long extracts of the Pentagon's classified history of American involvement in Vietnam. The only common thread between the Pentagon Papers case (*New York Times Co.* v. *United States*) and *Near* was the issue of prior restraint. But that thread held fast, demonstrating the importance of maintaining freedom of speech both in distasteful circumstances (*Near*) and when the national interest is at stake.

Although his name is hardly a household word, the ghost of Jay M. Near still stalks most U.S. courtrooms. There exists no plaque that bears his name, and even Colonel McCormick's marble memorial to Chief Justice Hughes's opinion omits the name of the case.* Near is truly the unknown soldier in the continuing struggle between the powers of government and the power of the press to publish the news.

The late Fred Friendly, formerly president of CBS News (1964–1966), was the Edward R. Murrow Professor of Journalism at Columbia University.

* Robert R. McCormick was an owner and publisher of the *Chicago Tribune* who attacked a host of public officials and took on various crusades.

Near v. *Minnesota* placed freedom of the press "in the least favorable light"; as Minnesota and New York newspapers and lawyers viewed the litigation, it was the worst possible case. But perhaps it is just because Near's cause did not at first appear to be significant, except to Colonel McCormick and Roger Baldwin,* that it created such sturdy law. So indestructible has it proved that its storied progeny, the Pentagon Papers case, was able to survive the political firestorms of 1971. If "great cases like hard cases make bad law," as the [Justice Oliver Wendell] Holmes proverb warns, it may follow that since few knew or cared about Near's cause, freedom of the press was transformed successfully from an eighteenth- and nineteenth-century ideal into a twentieth-century constitutional bulwark.

By his admonition, Holmes meant that volatile national confrontations which appeal to prejudices and distort judgment can be counterproductive in shaping the law of the future. Such emotional conflicts as slavery, as in the Dred Scott decision, and minimum-wage laws, as in *Adkins*, Holmes suggested seventy-seven years ago, "exercise a kind of hydraulic pressure which makes what previously was clear seem doubtful, and before which even well-settled principles of law will bend." In 1931 an American public plagued by economic panic, unemployment, Prohibition and the likes of Al Capone cared little about the civil rights of a scandalmonger from Minnesota. To paraphrase Holmes, Near's case embodied all the underwhelming interests required to shape the grand law of the future. His success was based not in frenzied national debate, but in quirks-of-fate delays in the Minnesota courts, the deaths of two conservative Justices, and Hoover's subsequent appointments.† It was the new Chief Justice who made the difference, not simply because he added one more vote to Near's side, but because of his unexpected passion for the First Amendment and his intellectual capacity to lead others, especially Justice Roberts.

The precedent of *Near* v. *Minnesota* has withstood onslaughts from Presidents, legislatures and even the judiciary itself in its attempts to enforce basic rights which seemed to clash with the First Amendment. It demonstrated the latent strengths for an amendment which had gone untested for 150 years. That five-to-four decision achieved far more than simply asserting Near's rights. . . . It marked the beginning of a concerted process "to plug the holes punched in the Bill of Rights," and what [Baltimore *Sun* writer George] Mencken had called in 1926 "the most noble opportunity that the Supreme Court, in all its history, ever faced." . . .

There have been hundreds of other press cases before the Court since 1931— some won, some lost. Perhaps the seminal judgment was the 1964 decision in *New York Times Co.* v. *Sullivan*, which prevented Southern courts from using the law of libel to thwart national news coverage of the civil rights battle. Although

---

* Roger Baldwin founded the American Civil Liberties Union.

† Justices William H. Taft and Edward T. Sanford died. President Herbert Hoover appointed Charles E. Hughes and Owen J. Roberts to replace them.

not a prior-restraint case, *Sullivan* freed the press from the threat of chilling damages in reporting the conduct of public officials in Alabama in the explosive sixties. Associate Justice William Brennan's majority opinion established that officials, and later public figures, could not recover libel damages for reports concerning their official actions without proving "malice," that is, deliberate lying or "reckless disregard for the truth."

But *Near's* ultimate legacy was finally realized forty years later, almost to the day, in the clash between the power of the presidency of the United States and two powerful newspapers, the *New York Times* and the *Washington Post*. Its official name was *New York Times Co.* v. *United States*, but it is remembered as the Pentagon Papers case. It began when the *New York Times* obtained a forty-seven-volume secret history of the Vietnam war from Daniel Ellsberg, a former analyst of the Rand Corporation; it ended with a major victory for the press in the Supreme Court. On June 13, 1971, the *New York Times* began publishing its synopsis and analysis of the secret documents, and two days later the Nixon Administration began legal efforts to restrain it. Later that week the government also sought to enjoin the *Washington Post* from publishing the same classified material. In a "frenzied train of events," as one Justice described it, the cases bobbed back and forth between district and appeals courts until, eleven days later, the Supreme Court agreed to try to untangle the conflicting and confusing opinions.

What dominated all the arguments in all briefs and opinions, from district court to Supreme Court, was the theory of no previous restraint, codified by Blackstone and incorporated by Madison, but made concrete in *Near*.

The Court met hastily on Saturday morning, June 25, and five days later announced its six-to-three decision. Leaning heavily on *Near v. Minnesota*, the Court held that the heavy burden of justifying the imposition of prior restraint had not been met by the government. It required nine opinions for the Supreme Court to explain its votes, and *Near* was cited ten times.

Justice William O. Douglas, in an opinion joined by Justice Hugo Black, quoted long passages from Chief Justice Hughes's majority opinion in *Near*. Believing that the government had no power to punish or restrain "material that is embarrassing to the powers-that-be," Douglas and Black reiterated Hughes's opinion: "The fact that liberty of the press may be abused . . . does not make any less necessary the immunity of the press." But it was Douglas' concluding statement that emphasized the tremendous strength of *Near*: "The stays in these cases that have been in effect for more than a week constitute a flouting of the principles of the First Amendment as interpreted in *Near v. Minnesota*."

Justice Black's language, in an opinion joined by Justice Douglas, also echoed some of the discussion during oral arguments in *Near*:

> Both the history and language of the First Amendment support the view that the press must be left free to publish news, whatever the source, without censorship, injunctions or prior restraints . . . Only a free and unrestrained press can effectively expose deception

in government . . . [T]he *New York Times*, the *Washington Post*, and other newspapers should be commended for serving the purpose that the Founding Fathers saw so clearly. In revealing the workings of government that led to the Vietnam War, the newspapers did precisely what the founders hoped and trusted they would do.

Even in the dissents in the Pentagon Papers case, *Near* was ubiquitous. Chief Justice Warren Burger, Justice John Harlan and Justice Harry Blackmun in their dissenting opinions also cited Hughes's exceptions to the prohibitions against prior restraint such as interfering with recruiting during wartime and publishing troopship sailing dates. As in *Near*, the Court's judgment in the Pentagon Papers case did not establish the absolutism of the First Amendment (as some journalists still contend) against *all* prior restraints. Justice Byron White wrote: "I do not say that in no circumstances would the First Amendment permit an injunction against publishing information about government plans and operations."

Although it was the judgment of the divided Court that lifted the prior restraint on the *New York Times*, the *Washington Post* and twenty other newspapers, which were prepared to publish sections of the Pentagon Papers, five sentences by District Court Judge Murray Gurfein endure. It is the kind of quotation Colonel McCormick might have had chiseled in his hall:

> The security of the Nation is not at the ramparts alone. Security also lies in the value of our free institutions. A cantankerous press, an obstinate press, a ubiquitous press must be suffered by those in authority in order to preserve the even greater values of freedom of expression and the right of the people to know . . . These are troubled times. There is no greater safety valve for discontent and cynicism about the affairs of Government than freedom of expression in any form.

. . . *Near* was a perilously close case, but "a morsel of genuine history," as Jefferson described such events, "a thing so rare as to be always valuable." . . .

Questions for Discussion

1. In light of the ruling in *New York Times Co.* v. *United States*, can you imagine any circumstances that would justify prior restraint of the press?
2. Does libel law adequately guard against an irresponsible and overaggressive press, or should there be other safeguards, such as an independent review board?

▨ 3.3

Griswold v. Connecticut (1965)

Since the 1960s, one of the most interesting and controversial fields of constitutional law has involved the alleged right of privacy. The Constitution nowhere explicitly spells out any such right, yet preserving privacy is of paramount concern in an increasingly intrusive society.

One key case (not presented here) is *Roe* v. *Wade* (1973), which declared abortion laws in almost all states unconstitutional. Justice Harry A. Blackmun held that the constitutional right to privacy allowed women to determine whether to go ahead with an abortion, although the rights of the mother were to be balanced against the potential right to life of the fetus (which was not a person in a constitutional sense). *Roe* v. *Wade* set off almost ceaseless attempts by pro-life activists to ban abortions. It also became a turning point in the Senate's defeat of Ronald Reagan's Supreme Court nominee, Appeals Court Judge Robert Bork, in 1987.

Griswold v. *Connecticut* (1965) laid the groundwork for *Roe* by giving the right of privacy formal constitutional protection. The decision grew from a challenge to Connecticut's restrictive but rarely enforced birth control laws. Estelle Griswold, executive director of the Planned Parenthood League of Connecticut, was convicted of dispensing birth control information to married people. The Supreme Court overturned the lower court's decision.

M r. Justice Douglas delivered the opinion of the Court. . . .
Coming to the merits, we are met with a wide range of questions that implicate the Due Process Clause of the Fourteenth Amendment. Overtones of some arguments suggest that *Lockner* v. *State of New York* . . . should be our guide. But we decline that invitation. . . . We do not sit as super-legislature to determine the wisdom, need, and propriety of laws that touch economic problems, business affairs, or social conditions. This law, however, operates directly on an intimate relation of husband and wife and their physician's role in one aspect of that relation.

The association of people is not mentioned in the Constitution nor in the Bill of Rights. The right to educate a child in a school of the parents' choice—whether public or private or parochial—is also not mentioned. Nor is the right to study any particular subject or any foreign language. Yet the First Amendment has been construed to include certain of those rights.

By *Pierce* v. *Society of Sisters* . . . , the right to educate one's children as one chooses is made applicable to the States by the force of the First and Fourteenth Amendments. By *Meyer* v. *State of Nebraska* . . . , the same dignity is given the right to study the German language in a private school. In other words, the State may not, consistently with the spirit of the First Amendment, contract the spectrum of available knowledge. The right of freedom of speech and press includes not only the right to utter or to print, but the right to distribute, the right to receive, the right to read (*Martin* v. *City of Struthers* . . .) and freedom of inquiry, freedom of thought, and freedom to teach (see *Wieman* v. *Updegraff* . . .)—indeed the freedom of the entire university community. . . . Without those peripheral rights the specific rights would be less secure. And so we reaffirm the principle of the *Pierce* and the *Meyer* cases.

In *NAACP* v. *State of Alabama* . . . we protected the "freedom to associate and privacy in one's associations," noting that freedom of association was a peripheral First Amendment right. Disclosure of membership lists of a constitutionally valid association, we held, was invalid "as entailing the likelihood of a substantial restraint upon the exercise by petitioner's members of their right to freedom of association." In other words, the First Amendment has a penumbra where privacy is protected from governmental intrusion.* In like context, we have protected forms of "association" that are not political in the customary sense but pertain to the social, legal, and economic benefit of the members. In *Schware* v. *Board of Bar Examiners*, . . . we held it not permissible to bar a lawyer from practice, because he had once been a member of the Communist Party. The man's "association with that Party" was not shown to be "anything more than a political faith in a political party" and was not action of a kind proving bad moral character.

Those cases involved more than the "right of assembly"—a right that extends to all irrespective of their race or ideology. The right of "association," like the right of belief is more than the right to attend a meeting; it includes the right to express one's attitudes or philosophies by membership in a group or by affiliation with it or by other lawful means. Association in that context is a form of expression of opinion; and while it is not expressly included in the First Amendment its existence is necessary in making the express guarantees fully meaningful.

The foregoing cases suggest that specific guarantees in the Bill of Rights have penumbras, formed by emanations from those guarantees that help give them life and substance. Various guarantees create zones of privacy. The right of association contained in the penumbra of the First Amendment is one, as we have seen. The Third Amendment in its prohibition against the quartering of soldiers "in any

---

* Justice William O. Douglas developed the analogy to a penumbra, "the partial shadow surrounding a complete shadow (as in an eclipse)." Douglas found a right to privacy in the "penumbras" of the First, Third, Fourth, Fifth, and Ninth Amendments. Most scholars of the Constitution agree that some right to privacy does exist, but the extension of that right is open to debate.

house" in time of peace without the consent of the owner is another facet of that privacy. The Fourth Amendment explicitly affirms the "right of the people to be secure in their persons, houses, papers, and effects, against unreasonable searches and seizures." The Fifth Amendment in its Self-Incrimination Clause enables the citizen to create a zone of privacy which government may not force him to surrender to his detriment. The Ninth Amendment provides: "The enumeration in the Constitution, of certain rights, shall not be construed to deny or disparage others retained by the people."

The Fourth and Fifth Amendments were described in *Boyd* v. *United States* . . . as protection against all governmental invasions "of the sanctity of a man's home and the privacies of life." We recently referred in *Mapp* v. *Ohio* . . . to the Fourth Amendment as creating a "right to privacy, no less important than any other right carefully and particularly reserved to the people." . . .

The present case, then, concerns a relationship lying within the zone of privacy created by several fundamental constitutional guarantees. And it concerns a law which, in forbidding the use of contraceptives rather than regulating their manufacture or sale, seeks to achieve its goals by means having a maximum destructive impact upon that relationship. Such a law cannot stand in light of the familiar principle, so often applied by this Court, that a "governmental purpose to control or prevent activities constitutionally subject to state regulation may not be achieved by means which sweep unnecessarily broadly and thereby invade the area of protected freedoms." *NAACP* v. *Alabama*. . . . Would we allow the police to search the sacred precincts of marital bedrooms for telltale signs of the use of contraceptives? The very idea is repulsive to the notions of privacy surrounding the marriage relationship.

We deal with a right to privacy older than the Bill of Rights—older than our political parties, older than our school system. Marriage is a coming together for better or for worse, hopefully enduring, and intimate to the degree of being sacred. It is an association that promotes a way of life, not causes; a harmony in living, not political faiths; a bilateral loyalty, not commercial or social projects. Yet it is an association for as noble a purpose as any involved in our prior decisions.

Mr. Justice Goldberg, whom the Chief Justice and Mr. Justice Brennan join, concurring:

I agree with the Court that Connecticut's birth-control law unconstitutionally intrudes upon the right of marital privacy, and I join in its opinion and judgment. Although I have not accepted the view that "due process" as used in the Fourteenth Amendment includes all of the first eight Amendments . . . I do agree that the concept of liberty protects those personal rights that are fundamental, and is not confined to the specific terms of the Bill of Rights. My conclusion that the concept of liberty is not so restricted and that it embraces the right of marital privacy though that right is not mentioned explicitly in the Constitution is supported both by numerous decisions of this Court, referred to in the Court's opinion, and by the language and history of the Ninth Amendment. In reaching the conclusion that the right of marital privacy is protected, as being within the protected penumbra of specific guarantees of the Bill of Rights, the Court refers to the Ninth Amendment. I add these words to emphasize the relevance of that Amendment to the Court's holding. . . . The Framers did not intend that the first eight amendments be construed to exhaust the basic and fundamental rights which the Constitution guaranteed to the people.

While this Court has had little occasion to interpret the Ninth Amendment "[i]t cannot be presumed that any clause in the constitution is intended to be without effect." *Marbury* v. *Madison.* . . . In interpreting the Constitution, "real effect should be given to all the words it uses." *Myers* v. *United States.* . . . The Ninth Amendment to the Constitution may be regarded by some as a recent discovery but since 1791 it has been a basic part of the Constitution which we are sworn to uphold. To hold that a right so basic and fundamental and so deep-rooted in our society as the right of privacy in marriage may be infringed because that right is not guaranteed in so many words by the first eight amendments to the Constitution is to ignore the Ninth Amendment and to give it no effect whatsoever. Moreover, a judicial construction that this fundamental right is not protected by the Constitution because it is not mentioned in explicit terms by one of the first eight amendments or elsewhere in the Constitution would violate the Ninth Amendment, which specifically states that "[t]he enumeration in the Constitution, of certain rights shall not be *construed* to deny or disparage others retained by the people." (Emphasis added.) . . . [T]he Ninth Amendment simply lends strong support to the view that the "liberty" protected by the Fifth and Fourteenth Amendments from infringement by the Federal Government or the States is not restricted to rights specifically mentioned in the first eight amendments. . . .

In sum, I believe that the right of privacy in the marital relation is fundamental and basic—a personal right "retained by the people" within the meaning of the Ninth Amendment. Connecticut cannot constitutionally abridge this fundamental right, which is protected by the Fourteenth Amendment from infringement by the States. I agree with the Court that petitioners' convictions must therefore be reversed.

Mr. Justice Black, with whom Mr. Justice Stewart joins, dissenting: . . .

The Court talks about a constitutional "right of privacy" as though there is some constitutional provision or provisions forbidding any law ever to be passed which might abridge the "privacy" of individuals. But there is not. . . .

One of the most effective ways of diluting or expanding a constitutionally guaranteed right is to substitute for the crucial word or words of a constitutional guarantee another word or words, more or less flexible and more or less restricted in meaning. This fact is well illustrated by the use of the term "right of privacy" as a comprehensive substitute for the Fourth Amendment's guarantee against "unreasonable searches and seizures." "Privacy" is a broad, abstract and ambiguous concept which can easily be shrunken in meaning but which can also, on the other hand, easily be interpreted as a constitutional ban against many things other than searches and seizures. I have expressed the view many times that First Amendment freedoms, for example, have suffered from a failure of the courts to stick to the simple language of the First Amendment in construing it, instead of invoking multitudes of words substituted for those the Framers used. For these reasons I get nowhere in this case by talk about a constitutional "right of privacy" as an emanation from one or more constitutional provisions. I like my privacy as well as the next one, but I am nevertheless compelled to admit that government has a right to invade it unless prohibited by some specific constitutional provision. For these reasons I cannot agree with the Court's judgment and the reasons it gives for holding this Connecticut law unconstitutional. . . .

My Brother Goldberg has adopted the recent discovery that the Ninth Amendment as well as the Due Process Clause can be used by this Court as authority to strike down all state legislation which this Court thinks violates "fundamental principles of liberty and justice," or is contrary to the "traditions and [collective] conscience of our people." He also states, without proof satisfactory to me, that in making decisions on this basis judges will not consider "their personal and private notions." One may ask how they can avoid considering them. Our Court certainly has no machinery with which to take a Gallup Poll. And the scientific miracles of this age have not yet produced a gadget which the Court can use to determine what traditions are rooted in the "[collective] conscience of our people." Moreover, one would certainly have to look far beyond the language of the Ninth Amendment to find that the Framers vested in this Court any such awesome veto powers over lawmaking, either by the States or by the Congress. Nor does anything in the history of the Amendment offer any support for such a shocking doctrine. The whole history of the adoption of the Constitution and Bill of Rights points the other way, and the very material quoted by my Brother Goldberg shows that the Ninth Amendment was intended to protect against the idea that "by enumerating particular exceptions to the grant of power" to the Federal Government, "those rights which were not singled out, were intended to be assigned into the hands of the General Government [the United States], and were consequently insecure." That Amendment was passed, not to broaden the powers of this Court or any other department of "the General Government," but, as every student of history knows, to assure the people that the Constitution in all its provisions was intended to limit the Federal Government to the powers granted expressly or by necessary implication. If any broad, unlimited power to hold laws unconstitutional because they offend what this Court conceives to be the "[collective] conscience of our people" is vested in this Court by the Ninth Amendment, the Fourteenth Amendment, or any other provision of the Constitution, it was not given by the Framers, but rather has been bestowed on the

Court by the Court. This fact is perhaps responsible for the peculiar phenomenon that for a period of a century and a half no serious suggestion was ever made that the Ninth Amendment, enacted to protect state powers against federal invasion, could be used as a weapon of federal power to prevent state legislatures from passing laws they consider appropriate to govern local affairs. Use of any such broad, unbounded judicial authority would make of this Court's members a day-to-day constitutional convention. . . .

Questions for Discussion

1. Can a right be fundamental yet not enumerated in the Constitution?
2. Should the state ever have an interest in the relationships and actions between consenting adults? In what instances?

 3.4

Why Privacy Matters

Jeffrey Rosen

If *Griswold* (3.3) opened the door for a broad judicial claim of "the right of privacy," and if *Roe* v. *Wade* built on Griswold's important, if shaky, foundation, what is there left to say about privacy? Plenty. After all, in a society that may provide everyone, in Andy Warhol's phrase, with his or her "fifteen minutes of fame," we honor celebrity, whatever its source. Moreover, with credit cards, e-mail, and omnipresent video cameras, we leave our mark everywhere with little forethought. Privacy may be a constitutional right, but we surrender it every day.

Jeffrey Rosen, a legal scholar and journalist, examined the implications of reducing privacy in his book, *The Unwanted Gaze: The Destruction of Privacy in America.* This selection, excerpted from that book, builds a case for enhancing privacy, not so much as a legal doctrine, but as a condition of a civil society that

---

Jeffrey Rosen is an associate professor at George Washington University Law school and legal affairs editor of the *New Republic*.

encourages individuals to retain the space that the Court, in *Griswold,* considered fundamental.

At the beginning of the 21st century, America is, more than ever, a culture of exhibitionism that also claims to be a culture concerned about privacy. Citizens cheerfully watch Big Brother TV, or set up Web cams in their bedrooms, even as they tell pollsters that privacy is one of the most important political issues facing the country today. The impulses toward exposure and concealment conflict with each other, obviously, but they also complement each other. "People worry about, and debate, ways to protect and preserve zones of intimacy and seclusion in a world with satellite eyes," as the legal historian Lawrence Friedman has observed. That debate—which often amounts to an alarmist muddle—has become a defining feature of life in what Friedman has called a horizontal society, in which identity is peculiarly open and authority is increasingly based on celebrity rather than on traditional notions of hierarchy.

In a horizontal society, being famous is a surer way of achieving status and authority than conforming to preordained social roles, and therefore the distinction between fame and infamy is elusive. Getting on television is itself a form of authority, regardless of whether one is there for behaving well or behaving badly. Those who exercise power in a horizontal society become celebrities, and celebrities, unlike the powerful in traditional societies, must surrender a great deal of their privacy. They must convey the impression of being accessible and familiar rather than remote and daunting, and they achieve this illusion by their willingness to share certain intimate details of their personal lives with faceless cameras.

A self-possessed private citizen has an inviolate personality, protected by boundaries of reserve that cannot be penetrated readily by strangers. A celebrity, by contrast, has an interactive personality: People feel free to approach a man like Sam Donaldson on the street. But the feelings of intimacy that celebrity generates are either misleading—we don't really know a television celebrity, even though he appears every night in our living room—or a sign of self-violation: When a celebrity leads so much of his life in public that nothing is held back for his genuine intimates, he becomes a buffoonish self-caricature, almost literally a talking head, devoid of the individuality, texture, and depth that characterize a genuinely self-possessed personality.

The culture of celebrity shows us the nature of the challenge to privacy that changes in law and technology are exacerbating at the dawn of the 21st century. When we think we know Sam Donaldson, it is because we have confused information with knowledge—we have formed an idea about him on the strength of isolated pieces of information. In an age when thinking, writing, reading, and gossip increasingly take place online, and when all kinds of disaggregated personal information is widely recorded and permanently retrievable in cyberspace, private citizens run the risk of being treated like celebrities in the worst sense, defined by characteristics that have been wrenched out of context, or reduced to a set of inadequate data points.

If I buy a home in Washington, D.C., for example, the purchase price is recorded online, and if I teach at a state university, my salary, too, may be available. And if, in a moment of youthful enthusiasm, I once posted intemperate comments to an Internet newsgroup, those comments are likely to be recorded on a Web service such as Dejanews, where anyone can retrieve them years later simply by typing my name into a popular search engine. In certain social circles, it is not uncommon for prospective romantic partners to perform Internet background checks on each other, and it's not unheard of for former partners to post reports in cyberspace about each other's performance.

In the past, these bits of information were strictly the stuff of gossip, and its subjects enjoyed a certain protection from easy judgments. When intimate personal information circulates among a small group of people who know us well, its significance can be weighed against other things they know about us. But when information is separated from its original context and revealed to strangers, we are vulnerable to being misjudged on the basis of our most embarrassing, and therefore most memorable, tastes and preferences. In a world where people are bombarded with information, they form impressions quickly, based on sound bites, and those impressions are likely to misrepresent our complicated and often contradictory characters.

Privacy protects us from being judged out of context in a world of short attention spans. Genuine knowledge of another person is the culmination of a slow process of mutual revelation. It requires the gradual setting aside of social masks and the incremental building of trust, which leads to the exchange of personal disclosures. It cannot be rushed, which is why, after intemperate self-revelation in the heat of passion, one may feel something close to self-betrayal. True knowledge of other people, in all their complexity, can be achieved with only a handful of intimate friends, lovers, or family members. To flourish, the intimate relationships on which true knowledge of others depends need time and private space—sanctuary from the gaze of the crowd, where mutual self-disclosure, measured and gradual, is possible.

In the vertical society of the 18th century, before the onset of modernity, notions of private property were a safeguard to privacy. If you wanted to read my diary, you had to break into my house, and if you broke into my house, I could sue you for trespass. The framers of the Fourth Amendment to the Constitution considered the search for a private diary without the permission of its author the paradigmatic example of an unconstitutional search. By the end of the 19th century, Louis D. Brandeis, the future Supreme Court justice, and Samuel D. Warren, his former law partner, worried that changes in technology as well as law were altering the nature of privacy, What had been seen as a physical threat now looked like a more insidious danger. "Instantaneous photographs and newspaper enterprise have invaded the sacred precincts of private and domestic life," they lamented in the most famous essay on privacy ever written. In that 1890 article they invoked the right to an "inviolate personality" to constrain the press.

But technological and legal change continued apace as the 20th century unfolded, eroding the protections for privacy to an extent that only became clear during President Bill Clinton's impeachment. The Supreme Court invoked a constitutional right to privacy in *Roe* v. *Wade* (1973), but the Court relied upon an amorphous vision of privacy—it was really a misnomer for the freedom to make intimate decisions about reproduction. Meanwhile, the Court neglected a more focused vision of privacy that has to do with our ability to control the conditions under which we make different aspects of ourselves accessible to others. Thus it was during the 1970s and 1980s that the long-standing principle that private diaries couldn't be subpoenaed as "mere evidence" in civil or white-collar criminal cases was quietly allowed to wither away.

And it was during the 1980s and 1990s that the Supreme Court's vague definition of sexual harassment (in addition to sexual extortion, the Court recognized a more ambiguous category known as "hostile environment" harassment) paved the way for increased monitoring of private speech and conduct. The Lewinsky investigation showed just how completely the legal climate had been transformed. Monica Lewinsky's own fate revealed the personal price, and pointed up the central value of privacy that had been lost. "It was such a violation," she complained to her biographer, recalling the experience of having her bookstore receipts subpoenaed and drafts of love letters retrieved from her computer. "It seemed that everyone in America had rights except for Monica Lewinsky. I felt like I wasn't a citizen of this country anymore."

Much has been made of the fact that transactions in cyberspace tend to generate detailed electronic footprints that expose our tastes and preferences to the operators of Web sites, who can then sell the information to private marketers. But to the frustration of professional privacy advocates, Americans don't always seem terribly concerned about the commercial exploitation of clickstream data. It is personal misinterpretation, as Lewinsky's ordeal so forcibly reminded us, that is the deeper threat. What individuals want in an exhibitionist society is not the right to be left alone, but the right to control the conditions of their own exposure. And that is what the new technology, along with legal developments, is making so difficult.

Defenders of transparency argue that more information, rather than less, is our best protection against misjudgment. We might think differently about a Charles Schwab employee who ordered *Memoirs of a Geisha* from Amazon.com if we knew that she also listened to the Doors and subscribed to *Popular Mechanics*. But even if we saw the logs of everything she had read and downloaded for a week, we would not come close to knowing who she really was. Instead, we would misjudge her in all sorts of new ways. If complete logs of every citizen's reading habits were available on the Internet, the limits of the average attention span would guarantee that no one's logs were read from beginning to end. Overwhelmed by information, citizens would click to a more interesting Web site. When attention spans are so short, privacy protects citizens from the misjudgments that can result from the exposure of both too much information and too little.

Defenders of transparency, however, question the social value of privacy. Richard Posner, the federal appeals court judge, argues that privacy can be inefficient and contribute to social fraud and misrepresentation, because it allows people to conceal true but embarrassing information about themselves from other people in order to gain unfair social or economic advantage. Philosopher Richard Wasserstrom suggests that our insistence on leading dual lives—one public, the other private—can amount to a kind of deception and hypocrisy; if we were less embarrassed by sexual and other private activities that have traditionally been associated with shame, we would have less to fear from disclosure because we would have nothing to hide. David Brin argues in the same vein in *The Transparent Society* (1998), and quotes John Perry Barlow, former lyricist for the Grateful Dead, now an advocate on cyberspace issues: "I have no secrets myself, and I think that everybody would be a lot happier and safer if they just let everything be known. Then nobody could use anything against them."

These defenders of transparency are confusing secrecy with privacy. But secrecy is only a small dimension of privacy if privacy is defined as the ability to control the conditions under which personal information is disclosed to others. Even those who claim that society would be better off if people were less embarrassed about discussing their sexual activities in public manage to feel annoyed and invaded when they are solicited by telemarketers during dinner. Moreover, the defenders of transparency have adopted a view of human personality as essentially unitary and integrated. They see social masks as a way of misrepresenting the true self. But that view of personality is simplistic and misleading. Instead of behaving as a single character, people display different characters in different contexts. I may (and do) wear different public masks when interacting with my students, my close friends, my family, and my dry cleaner. Far from being inauthentic, each of those masks helps me to act in a manner that suits different social settings. If the masks were to be violently torn away, what would be exposed would not be my true self but the spectacle of a wounded and defenseless man, as the ordeal of Clarence Thomas* shows.

If this "dramaturgical" view of character is correct, and if privacy is defined broadly as the ability to protect ourselves from being judged out of context, then there are clear political, social, and personal costs attached to the changes in the architecture of privacy. First, let's consider the political costs. The philosopher Judith Shklar gave a helpful example of the political value of privacy when she argued that, in a democracy, we don't need to know someone's title to avoid

---

* The 1991 Senate confirmation process for Supreme Court nominee Clarence Thomas was conducted amid charges of sexual harassment brought by Anita Hill, his former subordinate at the Equal Employment Opportunity Commission. Highly personal information about Thomas was made public in the course of his Judiciary Committee hearings. The Senate confirmed him by a 52–48 vote.

giving offense. The democratic honorifics *Mr.* and *Ms.* suggest that all citizens are entitled to equal respect, without revealing their rank or family background or professional accomplishments. Democracy is a space where citizens and strangers can interact without putting all their cards on the table—and privacy allows citizens who disagree profoundly to debate matters of common concern without confronting their irreconcilable differences.

There are also social costs of privacy's erosion. The heightened surveillance and monitoring that government officials experience in the political sphere are increasingly common in private workplaces as well, with similarly inhibiting effects on creativity and even productivity. Several surveys of monitoring in the workplace have suggested that electronically monitored workers experience higher levels of depression, tension, and anxiety, and lower levels of productivity, than those who are not monitored. It makes sense that people behave differently when they fear their conversations may be monitored. As the philosopher Stanley Benn noted, the knowledge that you are being observed changes your consciousness of yourself and your surroundings; even if the topic of conversation is not inherently private, your opinions and actions suddenly become candidates for a third party's approval or contempt. Uncertain as to when electronic monitoring may take place, employees will be more guarded and less spontaneous, and the increased formality of conversation and e-mail makes communication less efficient. In certain occupations, moreover, individuals will exaggerate the risks of public exposure: How many ambitious lawyers and law professors have changed their e-mailing habits in anticipation of U.S. Senate confirmation hearings that may never materialize?

Finally, there are the personal costs of the erosion of privacy. Privacy is important not only, or even primarily, to protect individual autonomy but also to allow individuals to form intimate relationships. In one of the most thoughtful essays on the subject, the Harvard University legal philosopher Charles Fried has written that, without a commitment to privacy, "respect, love, friendship, and trust" are "simply inconceivable." Friendship and romantic love can't be achieved without intimacy, and intimacy, in turn, depends on the selective and voluntary disclosure of personal information that we don't share with everyone else. In her story "The Other Two," Edith Wharton coolly describes a twice-divorced woman who finds herself serving tea to all three of her husbands at the same time. "She was 'as easy as an old shoe'—a shoe that too many feet had worn," Wharton writes. "Her elasticity was the result of tension in too many different directions. Alice Haskett—Alice Varick—Alice Waythorn—she had been each in turn, and had left hanging to each name a little of her privacy, a little of her personality, a little of the inmost self where the unknown god abides."

Properly shielded, friendships and loving relationships provide us with opportunities to share confidences and test ideas because we trust that our confidences won't be betrayed. ("A friend," said Emerson, "is someone before . . . [whom] I can think aloud.") To the degree that jokes, rough drafts, and written confidences can be wrenched out of context and subjected to public scrutiny, it is less likely that those confidences will be shared in the first place. Friendship, of course, will survive the new technologies of monitoring and surveillance. If I fear that my e-mail to my friends may be misinterpreted, I will take care to talk to my friends over the telephone or in person. But instead of behaving like citizens in totalitarian societies, and passively adjusting our behavior to the specter of surveillance, we should think more creatively about ways of preserving private spaces and sanctuaries in which intimate relationships can flourish.

There is also an important case for privacy that has to do with the development of human individuality. "Without privacy there is no individuality," Leontine Young noted in *Life among the Giants* (1966). "There are only types. Who can know what he thinks and feels if he never has the opportunity to be alone with his thoughts and feelings?" Studies of creativity show that the most creative thought takes place during periods of daydreaming and seclusion, when individuals allow ideas and impressions to run freely through their minds, in a process that can be impeded by the presence of others.

We are trained in this country to think of all concealment as a form of hypocrisy. But we are beginning to learn how much may be lost in a culture of transparency: the capacity for creativity and eccentricity, for the development of self and soul, for understanding, friendship, even love. There are dangers to pathological lying, but there are dangers as well to pathological truth telling. Privacy is a form of moral opacity, and opacity has its value. We need more shades and more blinds and more virtual curtains. Someday, perhaps, we will look back with nostalgia on a society that still believed opacity was possible—and was shocked to discover what happens when it is not.

Questions for Discussion

1. How does Rosen's approach to privacy differ from the reasoning in *Griswold*?
2. How might a "right of privacy" be applied to the circulation of personal information? More generally, can technology render privacy an impossibility?

3.5

Gideon v. Wainwright (1963)

Clarence Gideon, an indigent, was accused of breaking and entering a poolroom, a felony under Florida law. He proclaimed his innocence and requested that he be provided with a lawyer. The trial judge refused this request, Gideon was found guilty, and he was sentenced to a five-year term in the state penitentiary. In a handwritten statement Gideon appealed his case to the Supreme Court, which took the case and appointed Abe Fortas, a prominent Washington attorney and later Supreme Court justice, to represent him.

The Supreme Court had frequently ruled in specific circumstances that the Sixth Amendment guaranteed a right to counsel and that this right was incorporated by the Fourteenth Amendment and was thus applicable to the states. Still, before *Gideon* v. *Wainwright* (1963), the Court had not ruled that there was any general right to counsel. Indeed, the governing rule was that of *Betts* v. *Brady,* a 1942 decision that the right to counsel was not a "fundamental" right. The Court's reconsideration of the Betts rule after only twenty-one years was unusual.

After the decision in this case, Gideon was retried in Florida, with counsel, and found innocent. Subsequently, thousands of prisoners in Florida and elsewhere won their release on the grounds that they had not been represented by counsel at their trials.

Mr. Justice Black delivered the opinion of the Court. . . .

. . . Since 1942, when *Betts* v. *Brady* . . . was decided by a divided Court, the problem of a defendant's federal constitutional right to counsel in a state court has been a continuing source of controversy and litigation in both state and federal courts. To give this problem another review here, we granted certiorari. Since Gideon was proceeding *in forma pauperis*, we appointed counsel to represent him and requested both sides to discuss in their briefs and oral arguments the following: "Should this Court's holding in *Betts* v. *Brady* be reconsidered?" . . .

We think the Court in *Betts* had ample precedent for acknowledging that those guarantees of the Bill of Rights which are fundamental safeguards of liberty immune from federal abridgment are equally protected against state invasion by the Due Process Clause of the Fourteenth Amendment. This same principle was recognized, explained, and applied in *Powell* v. *Alabama* . . . , a case upholding the right of counsel, where the Court held that despite sweeping language to the contrary in *Hurtado* v. *California* . . . , the Fourteenth Amendment "embraced" those " 'fundamental principles of liberty and justice which lie at the base of all our civil and political institutions,' " even though they had been "specifically dealt with in another part of the federal Constitution." . . . In many cases other than *Powell* and *Betts*, this Court has looked to the fundamental nature of original Bill of Rights guarantees to decide whether the Fourteenth Amendment makes them obligatory on the States. . . .

We accept *Betts* v. *Brady*'s assumption, based as it was on our prior cases, that a provision of the Bill of Rights which is "fundamental and essential to a fair trial" is made obligatory upon the States by the Fourteenth Amendment. We think the Court in *Betts* was wrong, however, in concluding that the Sixth Amendment's guarantee of counsel is not one of these fundamental rights. Ten years before *Betts* v. *Brady*, this Court, after full consideration of all the historical data examined in *Betts*, had unequivocally declared that "the right to the aid of counsel is of this fundamental character." *Powell* v. *Alabama*. . . . While the Court at the close of its *Powell* opinion did by its language, as this Court frequently does, limit its holding to the particular facts and circumstances of that case, its conclusions about the fundamental nature of the right to counsel are unmistakable. . . .

In light of . . . many other prior decisions of this Court, it is not surprising that the *Betts* Court, when faced with the contention that "one charged with crime, who is unable to obtain counsel, must be furnished counsel by the State," conceded that "[e]xpressions in the opinions of this court lend color to the argument. . . ." The fact is that in deciding as it did—that "appointment of counsel is not a fundamental right, essential to a fair trial"—the Court in *Betts* v. *Brady* made an abrupt break with its own well-considered precedents. In returning to these old precedents, sounder we believe than the new, we but restore constitutional principles established to achieve a fair system of justice. Not only these precedents but also reason and reflection require us to recognize that in our adversary system of criminal justice, any person haled into court, who is too poor to hire a lawyer, cannot be assured a fair trial unless counsel is provided for him. This seems to us to be an obvious truth. Governments, both state and federal, quite properly spend vast sums of money to establish machinery to try defendants accused of crime. Lawyers to prosecute are everywhere deemed essential to protect the public's interest in an orderly society. Similarly, there are few defendants charged with crime, few indeed, who fail to hire the best lawyers they can get to prepare and present their defenses. That government hires lawyers to prosecute and defendants who have the money hire lawyers to defend are the strongest indications of the widespread belief that lawyers in criminal courts are necessities, not luxuries. The right of one charged with crime to counsel may not be deemed fundamental and essential to fair trials in some countries, but it is in ours. From the very beginning, our state and national constitutions and laws have laid great emphasis on procedural and substantive safeguards designed to assure fair trials before impartial tribunals in which every defendant stands equal before the law. This noble ideal cannot be realized if the poor man charged with crime has to face his accusers without a lawyer to assist him. . . .The Court in *Betts* v. *Brady* departed from the sound wisdom upon which the Court's holding in *Powell* v. *Alabama* rested. Florida, supported by two other states, has asked that *Betts* v. *Brady* be left intact. Twenty-two States, as friends of the Court,* argue that *Betts* was "an anachronism when handed down" and that it should now be overruled. We agree.

The judgment is reversed and the cause is remanded to the Supreme Court of Florida for further action not inconsistent with this opinion.

Mr. Justice Harlan, concurring:

I agree that *Betts* v. *Brady* should be overruled, but consider it entitled to a more respectful burial than has been accorded, at least on the part of those of us who were not on the Court when that case was decided.

I cannot subscribe to the view that *Betts* v. *Brady* represented "an abrupt break with its own well-considered precedents." In 1932, in *Powell* v. *Alabama* . . . , a capital case, this Court declared that under the particular facts there presented— "the ignorance and illiteracy of the defendants, their youth, the circumstances of public hostility . . . and above all that they stood in deadly peril of their lives"—the state court had a duty to assign counsel for the trial as a necessary requisite of due process of law. It is evident that these limiting facts were not added to the opinion as an afterthought; they were repeatedly emphasized, and were clearly regarded as important to the result.

Thus when this Court, a decade later, decided *Betts* v. *Brady*, it did no more than to admit of the possible existence of special circumstances in noncapital as well as capital trials, while at the same time insisting that such circumstances be shown in order to establish a denial of due process. The right to appointed counsel had been recognized as being considerably broader in federal prosecutions, see *Johnson* v. *Zerbst* . . . , but to have imposed these requirements on the States would indeed have been "an abrupt break" with the almost immediate past. The declaration that the right to appointed counsel in state prosecutions, as established in *Powell* v. *Alabama*, was not limited to capital cases was in truth not a departure from, but an extension of, existing precedent.

The principles declared in *Powell* and in *Betts*, however, have had a troubled journey throughout the years that have followed first the one case and then the other. Even by the time of the *Betts* decision, dictum in at least one of the Court's opinions had indicated that there was an absolute right to the services of counsel in the trial of state capital cases. Such dicta continued to appear in subsequent

---

* Various organizations and individuals, such as interest groups or state attorneys general, offer *amicus curiae* (friend of the court) briefs on major cases. Since the 1950s, *amicus* briefs as practiced by groups such as the National Association for the Advancement of Colored People (NAACP) and the American Civil Liberties Union (ACLU) have become a major tool for promoting social change.

decisions and any lingering doubts were finally eliminated by the holding of *Hamilton* v. *Alabama.* . . .

In noncapital cases, the "special circumstances" rule has continued to exist in form while its substance has been substantially and steadily eroded. In the first decade after *Betts,* there were cases in which the Court found special circumstances to be lacking, but usually by a sharply divided vote. However, no such decision has been cited to us, and I have found none, after *Quicksall* v. *Michigan* . . . , decided in 1950. At the same time, there have been not a few cases in which special circumstances were found in little or nothing more than the "complexity" of the legal questions presented, although those questions were often of only routine difficulty. The Court has come to recognize, in other words, that the mere existence of serious criminal charge constituted in itself special circumstances requiring the services of counsel at trial. In truth the *Betts* v. *Brady* rule is no longer a reality.

This evolution, however, appears not to have been fully recognized by many state courts, in this instance charged with the front-line responsibility for the enforcement of constitutional rights. To continue a rule which is honored by this Court only with lip service is not a healthy thing and in the long run will do disservice to the federal system.

The special circumstances rule has been formally abandoned in capital cases, and the time has now come when it should be similarly abandoned in noncapital cases, at least as to offenses which, as the one involved here, carry the possibility of a substantial prison sentence. (Whether the rule should extend to *all* criminal cases need not now be decided.) This indeed does no more than to make explicit something that has long since been foreshadowed in our decisions. . . .

Questions for Discussion

1. At what point does having access to counsel become a constitutional right? Is it a right for any felony? What about for a serious misdemeanor?
2. *Gideon* paved the way for the *Miranda* case, which required the police to inform a suspect of his or her constitutional rights, including the right to counsel. Should the police be able to question a suspect without counsel present?
3. Has *Gideon* completely closed the gap between the wealthy and the poor when it comes to obtaining adequate counsel?

3.6

The Assault

Alexander Nguyen

If 1963's *Gideon* decision (3.5) guaranteed the accused the right to a lawyer, the Supreme Court's 1966 *Miranda* ruling invested more meaning in that right by requiring police to warn suspects of their constitutional rights against self-incrimination. Since then, police (both in real life and on television) have ritualistically informed criminal suspects of their "Miranda rights" before they are questioned. Over the years, some legal scholars and some law-enforcement personnel have argued that they have been handicapped by not being able to use confessions made without a Miranda warning. Indeed, Alexander Nguyen leads off the following article with an example in which a confessed murderer walked free.

How to balance an individual's rights with the well-being of the community remains a difficult task. Most police professionals and legal scholars have concluded that requiring a warning against self-incrimination has not crippled either police or prosecutors. Nguyen, writing in 2000 as the Supreme Court was about to reconsider the *Miranda* ruling, argues that even current practices may lead to abuses and that the Miranda warning at least offer some modest protection against self-incrimination at very little cost to society at large.

Benbrook Lake near Fort Worth, Texas, is the kind of place where fishermen catch sandbass and lovers wake up to a tequila sunrise. But on a December day in 1983, violence came to Benbrook Lake in the person of Ronnie Dale Gaspard. He was affiliated with the Bandidos, a motorcycle gang whose members snorted methamphetamine off the tips of knife blades, and he was going there to settle a score. Which is why he was in a car and not on his bike. Which is also why he had been drinking a large amount of whiskey.

Gaspard was giving a ride to 23-year-old Denise Sanders. As they approached the lake, Gaspard stopped the car. Sanders stepped outside, clueless. A year or so prior, she had testified against the Bandidos, sending some of them to jail for drug trafficking. She shouldn't have done that, Gaspard thought, before he got out of his car and shot her in the head.

Alexander Nguyen was a writing fellow at The American Prospect when he wrote this article.

It wasn't long before police seized Gaspard and charged him with the murder. And then something happened that is the stuff of bad television drama. The police read Gaspard his Miranda rights. "You have the right to remain silent. . . . You have the right to an attorney. . . ." Gaspard asked for a lawyer but then confessed before the lawyer arrived. When these events later came to light in court, a judge suppressed Gaspard's confession, noting that it had been taken improperly after the accused had requested an attorney—a violation of Miranda procedures. Gaspard walked out free, smirking. "Nothing ever bothered me as much as seeing that guy walk out of the courthouse," the assistant district attorney was quoted as saying. "But there's nothing I can do. He is off and free."

Cases like this are rare, but they pack an emotional punch. Conservatives have argued for years that Miranda rights are an example of the way the criminal justice system bends too far to protect the guilty. The requirement to give the Miranda warning at just the right time, in just the right way, conservatives argue, has restricted law enforcement officers, has discouraged confessions, and has sometimes freed guilty criminals based on "technicalities."

"Miranda stands out as the single most damaging blow inflicted on law enforcement's ability to fight crime in roughly the last half-century," according to Paul Cassell, a law professor at the University of Utah who has emerged as the leading opponent of the Miranda doctrine. In a case last year before the conservative Fourth Circuit Court of Appeals, Cassell argued that if a confession can be shown to have been voluntarily given, it shouldn't matter whether there was a Miranda violation. Ruling in *Dickerson v. United States*, the court agreed. The justices decided that Miranda merely helps protect the constitutional right to avoid self-incrimination, but that there is no constitutional right to be informed in a strictly prescribed way of the right to remain silent and to have an attorney present. The U.S. Supreme Court agreed to review the case*. . . . At stake, criminal justice observers say, is a method of handling the rights of the accused that has become widely accepted in the law enforcement community, though not always followed to the letter since the Supreme Court made its original Miranda ruling more than three decades ago.

Ernesto Miranda's Confession

In its 1966 *Miranda v. Arizona* decision, the Supreme Court examined Ernesto Miranda's confession to kidnapping and sexually assaulting a mentally retarded woman. It turned out that police had failed to verbally inform him of his right

---

* The Supreme Court upheld the Miranda ruling by a 7–2 margin in June, 2000. Writing for the majority, Chief Justice William Rehnquist declared, "Miranda has become embedded by routine police practice to the point where the warnings have become part of our national culture. . . . Miranda announced a constitutional rule that Congress may not supersede legislatively. We decline to overrule Miranda ourselves."

not to talk and to have an attorney present at questioning. Therefore, Miranda's confession was inadmissible evidence. Unless police could back up suspects' statements with a signed form showing that the suspect had "voluntarily, knowingly, and intelligently" waived his constitutional right not to incriminate himself, the Court reasoned, such statements would not be allowable.

The Miranda ruling—along with other landmark Warren Court decisions, such as *Mapp v. Ohio* (forbidding admission of illegally obtained evidence) and *Gideon v. Wainwright* (providing attorneys for indigent criminal defendants)—changed the rules of the game in significant ways. The decisions ensured a fairer balance between individual rights and the state's interest in criminal prosecution. For the most part, supporters of those decisions say, the new rules stopped the infamous "third degree" by police during interrogations—physical coercion in the form of beating suspects with a rubber hose, for example, or plunging a suspect's head into a toilet. Occasional cases of brutal police interrogations still make the news, but police investigations on the whole are more professional and physical abuse has declined, longtime observers say.

According to conservatives, though, there have been unintended consequences, such as giving people like Ronnie Gaspard an undeserved break. Cassell has argued that as many as 28,000 violent criminals may be let off the hook each year because of the Miranda rules—an astounding claim.

Could Miranda have such a sweeping effect? Critics dispute Cassell's findings, noting that he derives them from the "crime clearance rate"—the rate at which police solve crimes. Cassell calculated that early in the 1960s police solved about 55 to 60 percent of criminal cases. By the end of the decade, the rate had fallen to 45 percent. He attributes that change entirely to Miranda. "But that's junk science of the silliest sort," says Stephen Schulhofer, a law professor at the University of Chicago, who believes that police solved crimes at a lower rate because crime soared during the 1960s while funding for police departments nationwide stagnated. Tracking "clearance capacity"—the number of police officers assigned per 100 violent crimes reported—Schulhofer reported that in 1960, 115 officers were assigned per 100 felonies, but only 51 were in 1968. "I don't think there's any mystery," says Schulhofer, about why the crime clearance rate dropped. In the 1990s, it should be noted, violent crimes fell to the lowest levels since 1973, when the Department of Justice first started recording the statistics. That doesn't speak to how many people are let off on "technicalities," but it casts some doubt on the claim that Miranda has significantly undermined law enforcement.

In fact, the law enforcement community does not uniformly view Miranda procedures as an impediment. Many police authorities say the Miranda rules are a useful tool in professional police work because they force police and prosecutors to gather scientific and forensic evidence to build a solid case. And studies suggest there has not been a decline in the rate at which the accused make confessions; it continues to hover at roughly 64 percent, which is what it was in the pre-Miranda era.

Having a prosecution blocked—as Ronnie Gaspard's was—because of a Miranda violation is so unusual that many people with long careers in law enforcement have never seen it happen. "How many cases were thrown out because of Miranda?" says Sergeant Norberto Huertas, a 22-year veteran of the Hartford Police Department in Connecticut. "None that I can think of." "How many times have I been able to suppress a confession because of Miranda?" says Page Kelley, a Cambridge, Massachusetts, public defender in her 14th year. Kelley rolls her eyes. "None." According to a 1987 Chicago survey, suppression motions succeeded in less than 1 percent of criminal cases—about four cases out of 10,000.

One of the reasons police and prosecutors have learned to live with Miranda is that the rules have not radically changed law enforcement. "The majority of suspects waive their rights," says Lieutenant James Blanchette of the Hartford Police Department. "Surprising, isn't it?" The usual procedure works like this: A suspect is apprehended, informed of his rights, and then invited to talk things over. If he is willing to talk, he is given a waiver form. Signing on the line at the bottom, he attests that he is aware of his rights and is speaking voluntarily. Various studies, including one by Cassell himself, have found that suspects waive their rights at an overwhelming rate—80 to 90 percent of the time.

So while the Supreme Court looks at the question this spring of whether police departments should be held to strict Miranda procedures, there are other equally important and crucially related questions: Are Miranda rules working well enough? Are they serving their original goal of providing fairness to suspects who may be ignorant of their rights, primarily the indigent or the illiterate? Is the brick wall that conservatives see blocking police work in actual practice a minor speed bump?

Going Through the Motions

At the Middlesex Superior Court in Cambridge, Massachusetts, Frank Ward seems to know everybody. He high-fives the bailiff. He asks prosecutors if they saw *The Practice* on TV last night. He discusses his current cases, which would normally be a breach of attorney-client privilege, if Ward were a lawyer. But he is a client, having been arrested for petty offenses ranging from larceny to drug use. By his own estimate, police have read him his Miranda rights more than 30 times, and by his own appraisal, the warnings don't do much. "Miranda is a big joke," he says. "It doesn't protect you from anything. It doesn't help or hurt you."

Ward says that officers usually usher him, handcuffed, into the booking room at the police station where another officer will read him his rights through a plexiglass window. "When they read it, you just nod and acknowledge it," he says. "They'll say, 'Do you understand?' And then you say, 'Yeah.' And then you sign the form."

Suspects waive their Miranda rights at a high rate because cops for the most part have turned them into a bureaucratic formality, according to George

Thomas, a law professor at Rutgers University. "Police have learned to be very clever about giving warnings. They make them seem routine. They'll say, 'What's your name, what's your address, how old are you, and by the way, you have these rights.'"

Police usually inform suspects of the rights by reading from a wallet-sized card they carry. The training manual of the Boston Police Department tells its officers that Miranda rights "can be administered in a variety of ways." Police can give a detailed explanation if they are so inclined. "The better practice," according to the manual, "is recitation by the officer, who reads the warnings from his card." Simply reading the rights abides by the letter of Miranda, but not its spirit, since police officers should also be prepared to explain the rights to suspects, according to Dennis Roberts, a criminal-defense lawyer in Oakland, California. "I make cops do it in court," he says. "They schlepp it out, it's usually dog-eared, and then they read it in a monotone; they have no idea what they're saying. It's a talismanic incantation of the words."

According to Richard Leo, a professor at the University of California, Irvine, who studies criminal interrogations, police have developed sophisticated and deceptive tactics that allow them to bait suspects into waiving their Miranda rights. "Criminal Interrogation and Confessions," the leading training manual for police interrogations, recommends, for example, that interrogators stand in front of the suspect while holding a thick folder as a prop. While talking, the interrogator "should finger through the case folder to create the impression that it contains material of an incriminating nature about the suspect." In this manner, police not only downplay the significance of Miranda rights; they have developed subtle tactics that make a waiver seem advantageous to a suspect.

Techniques such as the following are fairly typical. In a 1996 case in Sacramento, California, police took Kentrick McCoy into custody, photographed him, and then started to interview him.

> INTERROGATOR: I also need to know the real truth because I'm not sure she's telling us the whole story.
> SUSPECT: What, what is she trying to say?
> INTERROGATOR: Well, she's alleging that you pointed the gun at her.
> SUSPECT: Uh-huh [negative]. Nah-uh.
> INTERROGATOR: Alright, before we, before we do that, I, like I said I know there's more to the story than she's telling us. But—
> SUSPECT: I don't even know her, you know what I'm saying—
> INTERROGATOR: Whoa, whoa, whoa. I can't take your statement until we get through that Miranda issue.
> SUSPECT: Oh.
> INTERROGATOR: You can't tell me anything until we get through that.

"There's a lot of ways to get around Miranda," a homicide detective told *The Washington Post* in 1998. "Most guys know how to get somebody to waive their rights."

But even if police read the rights quickly or in a perfunctory manner, prosecutors and police officers have said—and the courts have generally agreed—that there is nothing puzzling about the right to remain silent. Except for rare cases (for example, 11-year-old defendant Nathaniel Abraham, asked by Ed Bradley on *60 Minutes* if he understood his Miranda rights, said, "No, no. I didn't understand. He had some white piece of paper and he's reading my rights"), the presumption—one supported by the cultural ubiquity of Miranda warnings on cop shows on television—remains that suspects already know their rights and that reading them is generally enough. "Ninety-one percent of all 13-year-olds can already recite Miranda," said Richard Moran, a professor of sociology at Mount Holyoke College, in a radio interview last June.

"Think about it," says Roberts, the criminal-defense attorney. "You're the DA, and someone says he didn't understand his rights. All you have to do is say, 'You said the confession was involuntarily given. Well, you know what a lawyer is, don't you? You understand what rights are, don't you? You know what that means; you went to third grade. Yeah, and you saw *Perry Mason* or *Ally McBeal*, right?' It's not that hard to establish."

So, if suspects understand their right to silence, why do so many go on to sign waiver forms and make confessions without the advice of a lawyer?

Understanding Your Rights

In its original Miranda ruling, the Supreme Court argued that "in-custody interrogation . . . contains inherently compelling pressures which work to undermine the individual's will to resist and to compel him to speak where he would not otherwise do so freely." By telling suspects about their constitutional rights, the Court hoped to neutralize the psychological homefield advantage of the police over the lone suspect inside the interrogation room. This was to ensure that statements would truly be voluntary and, by extension, not violate the Fifth Amendment.

Yet the tactics police departments have developed are so effective that police have even been able to extract false confessions from innocent suspects—a baffling phenomenon, but evidence that interrogations have continued to be psychologically compelling. This may be because Miranda never really addressed the most important of the "inherently compelling pressures" of police interrogations: the belief that if suspects keep quiet, they will look guilty. The root of this problem may be in the actual wording of Miranda itself. The warnings indicate the consequences of talking to the police ("Anything you say may be used against you in a court of law"). But they do not indicate the consequences of refusing to answer questions—which, in theory, should be nothing other than the continued presumption of innocence. It may be ignorance of this fact that causes suspects to waive their rights at such a high rate.

"If you have the right to remain silent, that means that there will be no adverse consequences if you don't talk," says Carol Steiker, a criminal-law professor at Harvard Law School. "But cops don't say that if you invoke Miranda, nothing bad will happen to you—but that's what it means to have a right." In fact, a suspect's refusal to speak after being read his rights cannot even be brought up at a later trial, says Anson Kaye, press secretary at the Middlesex district attorney's office in Massachusetts. In this sense, the problem with Miranda is not that suspects do not understand what it means to remain silent. It is that they do not understand the concept of *rights*. "[If you don't talk], they'll just make stuff up," says one criminal defendant interviewed for this story, who asked to remain anonymous. "They'll lie on your report, so it's on your behalf to just talk to them. Then they'll say you cooperated."

The original Miranda decision stated that warnings were needed "to make [the suspect] aware not only of the privilege, but also of the consequences of forgoing it. It is only through an awareness of these consequences that there can be any assurance of real understanding and intelligent exercise of the privilege." But how can a waiver be intelligently made if Miranda does not fully inform the suspects of the consequences of remaining silent and leaves instead the impression that silence is equivalent to guilt?

"If I were to tinker with Miranda," says Geoffrey Packard, a public defender in Cambridge, Massachusetts, "I would say, anything you say can be used against you. However, if you choose not to, that fact will not be used against you."

Miranda rights were intended to promote fair and equitable treatment for suspects who are not necessarily aware of their rights or are reluctant to exercise them. "Poor people are not going to say, 'Leave me alone, or I'll call my lawyer,'" says Packard. But they have imperfectly fulfilled their mandate by allowing police to downplay the significance of the rights they recite, or to make it seem in the suspect's interest to waive them. "I'm talking about the Mirandas of the world, the Hispanics, the blacks, the people in the ghettos and the barrios who don't know about their rights," said Harvard Law Professor Alan Dershowitz several years ago in a PBS interview. "We're not talking there about coercion necessarily. We're talking about fooling somebody into giving up a right that the Constitution gives them."

Whether it is a matter of "fooling" suspects or not, the Supreme Court has in the past recognized that there is a higher standard required by police than "going through the motions." Ernesto Miranda's own signed confession, after all, contained a typewritten paragraph saying that his statement had been made voluntarily and that he had full knowledge of his constitutional rights. But the Supreme Court ruled that because his rights hadn't been verbally explained to him, he hadn't been truly informed: "The mere fact that he signed a statement which contained a typed-in clause stating that he had 'full knowledge' of his 'legal rights' does not approach the knowing and intelligent waiver required to relinquish constitution rights." . . . The Supreme Court . . . might well ask if the Miranda warnings themselves, as they are used in actual day-to-day practice, have succeeded in giving suspects the full knowledge of the rights they are so often asked to sign away.

Questions for Discussion

1. Why do most police officers and prosecutors support the *Miranda* rule? Why is the *Miranda* procedure still an issue, thirty-five years after the Supreme Court handed down its initial ruling?
2. From your experience in watching shows like *Law and Order* on television, do you think that the *Miranda* warning makes any difference to an accused criminal? To the police officer?

Chapter 4

PUBLIC OPINION

At base, politics is the relationship between those who govern and those who are governed. Public opinion plays a crucial role in this relationship. Governments—even totalitarian states—must take into account the attitudes and perspectives of the public, because without the people's support no government can endure.

In modern democracies, the idea that governments should consider the wishes of the governed can be traced to the late seventeenth and eighteenth centuries, particularly to the egalitarian and majoritarian ideas of John Locke and Thomas Jefferson. Governing authority had previously been based on an aristocratic ideology that defended social and legal inequality as a proper and permanent fact of life. The various classes had fixed places in society, and the ruling class devised elaborate justifications for the exclusion of others from politics. But the dissemination of radically different social ideas, plus changes in economic circumstances, broadened the base of political participation. What the growing middle class thought became important, and in the early 1800s the term *public opinion* became commonplace.

In countries that boast democratic forms of government, like the United States, it appears virtually mandatory that the "will of the people" prevail. The difficulty is in determining what the will of the people is—or indeed, whether it exists. "To speak with precision of public opinion," wrote political scientist V. O. Key, "is a task not unlike coming to grips with the Holy Ghost," partly because the distinction between "public" and "private" opinion is not easy to make and is constantly changing. For example, thirty-five years ago cigarette smoking was a private matter, unregulated by government and absent from the agenda of political debate. By the 1970s, however, when smoking had been identified as a major public health hazard, advertising by tobacco companies was severely curtailed and movements to ban smoking in all public places were afoot. Today smoking is a public matter, and interest groups on both sides of the issue are involved in legislative deliberations. Questions about smoking now are a routine component of national public opinion polls.

The meaning of *opinion* is similarly vague. Opinions, beliefs, and attitudes are often treated as if they were the same, but scholars increasingly make distinctions among these terms. One social scientist, Bernard Hennessy, defines opinions as "immediate orientations toward contemporary controversial political objects," whereas attitudes are "more diffused and enduring orientations toward political objects not necessarily controversial at the moment."

For most purposes, however, it is preferable to think of public opinion in the broadest sense—in Key's definition, as "those opinions held by private persons which governments find it prudent to heed." Public opinion may be expressed in a letter (or many letters) to an elected official or to the editor of a newspaper, turnout at a protest march, the statements of a special interest group, the results of an election, or the findings of survey research. Often public opinion is gathered by impressions—legislators' sense of their districts, what their political intimates tell them, or the number of interest group representatives they see or hear. More and more often, however, public opinion is being derived scientifically from efforts to poll citizens.

Survey research is now a major element of political life, and citizens are constantly bombarded with poll results. Besides independent polling concerns such as the Gallup Organization, which periodically release information concerning public attitudes, the three major television networks have joined with major newspapers to create polling groups. Other efforts abound, and it seems fair to say that polling has become a major way of interpreting public opinion at the state and local as well as national level. Virtually all issues on the public agenda have generated public opinion data.

As opinion-gathering devices, polls are powerful vehicles for those who believe in majoritarian democracy. Unlike other methods of discovering public opinion, polls can represent the entire public, not just those elements with political resources or well-organized interest groups. Polls can be superior even to elections, because they report what everyone thinks rather than only what those who bother to vote think. Since poll results can make politicians aware of citizens' wishes, polls have the capacity to make government more responsible.

But not everyone believes poll-measured public opinion serves democratic ideals well. Often polls solicit opinions (and get them) on subjects on which little or no real opinion exists, such as on foreign policy. Not all polls are accurate, but their scientific aura lends them some credibility. Because all opinions count equally, polls tend to underrepresent intense opinion and give extra influence to the apathetic. Critics tend to believe that polls actually inhibit responsible government by forcing politicians to respond to public wishes that may be ill informed. Political leaders, in their quest for office, may follow poll results even when the long-term interests of the public are not well served.

Overall, both defenders and critics of opinion polls can point to convincing evidence for their views. Politicians probably are somewhat constrained by poll data and are restrained from taking action of which the public would disapprove. Programs such as Social Security, for example, are retained in their current form largely because the public strongly supports them. But it is also true that consistent, overwhelming majorities in the polls do not necessarily dictate public policy. This can be seen in the case of gun control; as early as 1938 the national polls showed that over 80 percent of the public favored hand-gun registration, but the organized efforts of the National Rifle Association have thwarted the passage of such a law.

The selections in this chapter were chosen to explain public opinion through the instrument of political polling. In the first selection, Benjamin Ginsberg criticizes polling as an instrument for assessing public opinion and suggests that the character of public opinion has changed because of its widespread use. The second selection, by Molly Sonner and Clyde Wilcox, examines the pattern of public opinion during the Monica Lewinsky scandal that so gripped the nation during President Clinton's last term. The conflict of values among the public, so evident during the Lewinsky scandal, is explored in greater depth in the Broder and Morin selection, especially the competing tension between the longing for moral values and resistance to imposing standards on others that affects much of today's political culture. In the final selection, Dana Milbank goes behind the scenes to examine how tracking polls are conducted during the last few weeks of a presidential election. Such polls often become the driving force behind both news coverage of the campaigns and strategic decisions by the candidates themselves.

Polling and the Transformation of Public Opinion

Benjamin Ginsberg

Public opinion is usually seen as flowing from citizens to public officials. Polling represents an important way for the public to make its wishes and preferences known to decision makers. The increasing use of polls to assess public opinion seems to enhance citizen influence, giving elected officials more to go on as they attempt to respond to their constituents' demands and concerns.

But polls are more than neutral indicators of the public's preferences. According to Benjamin Ginsberg, polling has fundamentally altered the character of public opinion and the relationship between citizens and their government. In his view, polling has made contemporary public opinion less likely to constrain authorities and possibly more subject to government manipulation and control. Rather than responding to public opinion, government may create, distort, or modify it. Ginsberg also believes that public opinion polling has weakened the impact of certain groups and their leaders in politics, particularly organized labor and working-class interests. In the past, these groups were closely linked with mass public opinion.

♦ ♦ ♦ **M**uch of the prominence of opinion polling as a civic institution derives from the significance that present-day political ideologies ascribe to the will of the people. Polls purport to provide reliable, scientifically derived information about the public's desires, fears, and beliefs, and so to give concrete expression to the conception of a popular will. The availability of accurate information certainly is no guarantee that governments will actually pay heed to popular opinions. Yet many students and practitioners of survey research have always believed that an accurate picture of the public's views might at least increase the chance that governments' actions would be informed by and responsive to popular sentiment.

Unfortunately, however, polls do more than simply measure and record the natural or spontaneous manifestation of popular belief. The data reported by opinion polls are actually the product of an interplay between opinion and the

Benjamin Ginsberg is a professor of political science at Johns Hopkins University.

survey instrument. As they measure, the polls interact with opinion, producing changes in the character and identity of the views receiving public expression. The changes induced by polling, in turn, have the most profound implications for the relationship between public opinion and government. In essence, polling has contributed to the domestication of opinion by helping to transform it from a politically potent, often disruptive force into a more docile, plebiscitary phenomenon.

Publicizing Opinion

Poll results and public opinion are terms that are used almost synonymously. As one indication of the extent to which public opinion is now identified with the polls, a sophisticated new national magazine entitled *Public Opinion* matter-of-factly devotes virtually all its attention to the presentation and discussion of survey data.

Yet, in spite of this general tendency to equate public opinion with survey results, polling is obviously not the only possible source of knowledge about the public's attitudes. Means of ascertaining public opinion certainly existed prior to the development of modern survey techniques. Statements from local notables and interest group spokespersons, letters to the press and to public officials, and sometimes demonstrations, protests, and riots provided indications of the populace's views long before the invention of the sample survey. Governments certainly took note of all these symptoms of the public's mood. As corporate executive and political commentator Chester Barnard once noted, prior to the availability of polling, legislators "read the local newspapers, toured their districts and talked with voters, received letters from the home state, and entertained delegations which claimed to speak for large and important blocks of voters."[1]

Obviously, these alternative modes of assessing public sentiment continue to be available. But it is significant that whenever poll results differ from the interpretation of public opinion offered by some other source, almost invariably the polls are presumed to be correct. The labor leader whose account of the views of the rank and file differs from the findings of a poll is automatically assumed to have misrepresented or misperceived membership opinion. Politicians who dare to quarrel with polls' negative assessments of their popularity or that of their programs are immediately derided by the press.

This presumption in favor of opinion polls stems from both their scientific and their representative character. Survey research is modeled after the methodology of the natural sciences and at least conveys an impression of technical sophistication and scientific objectivity. . . .

At the same time, polls can also claim to offer a more representative view of popular sentiment than any alternative source of information. Group spokesmen sometimes speak only for themselves. The distribution of opinion reflected by letters to newspapers and public officials is notoriously biased. Demonstrators and rioters, however sincere, are seldom more than a tiny and unrepresentative segment of the populace. Polls, by contrast, at least attempt to take equal account of all relevant individuals. And, indeed, by offering a representative view of public opinion, polls have often served as antidotes for false spokesmen and as guides to popular concerns that might never have been mentioned by individuals writing letters to legislators or newspaper editors.

Nevertheless, polling does more than just offer a scientifically derived and representative account of popular sentiment. The substitution of polling for other means of gauging the public's views also has the effect of changing several of the key characteristics of public opinion. Critics of survey research have often noted that polling can affect both the beliefs of individuals asked to respond to survey questions and the attitudes of those who subsequently read a survey's results. However, the most important aspect of polls is not their capacity to change individuals' beliefs. Rather the major impact of polling is the way polls cumulate and translate individuals' private beliefs into collective public opinions. . . .

Four fundamental changes in the character of public opinion can be traced directly to the introduction of survey research. First, polling alters both what is expressed and what is perceived as the opinion of the mass public by transforming public opinion from a voluntary to an externally subsidized matter. Second, polling modifies the manner in which opinion is publicly presented by transforming public opinion from a behavioral to an attitudinal phenomenon. Third, polling changes the origin of information about public beliefs by transforming public opinion from a property of groups to an attribute of individuals. Finally, polling partially removes individuals' control over their own public expressions of opinion by transforming public opinion from a spontaneous assertion to a constrained response.

. . . These four transformations have contributed markedly to the domestication or pacification of public opinion. Polling has rendered public opinion less dangerous, less disruptive, more permissive, and, perhaps, more amenable to governmental control.

From Voluntarism to Subsidy

In the absence of polling, the cost and effort required to organize and publicly communicate an opinion are normally borne by one or more of the individuals holding the opinion. Someone wishing to express a view about civil rights, for example, might write a letter, deliver a speech, contribute to an organization, or join a protest march. A wealthy individual might employ a public relations expert; a politically astute individual might assert that he or she represented the views of many others. But whatever the means, the organization and public communication of opinion would entail a voluntary expenditure of funds, effort, or time by the opinion holder. Polls, by contrast, organize and publicize opinion without requiring initiative or action on the part of individuals. With the exception of the small sample asked to submit to an interview, the individuals whose opinions are expressed through polls need take no action whatsoever. Polls underwrite or subsidize the costs of eliciting, organizing, and publicly expressing opinion.

This displacement of costs from the opinion holder to the polling agency has important consequences for the character of the opinions likely to receive public expression. In general, the willingness of individuals to bear the cost of publicly asserting their views is closely tied to the intensity with which they hold those views. Other things being equal, individuals with strong feelings about any given matter are more likely to invest whatever time and effort are needed to make their feelings known than are persons with less intense views. One seldom hears, for example, of a march on Washington by groups professing not to care much about abortion. As this example suggests, moreover, individuals with strongly held views are also more likely than their less zealous fellow citizens to be found at the extremes of opinion on any given question. Thus as long as the costs of asserting opinions are borne by opinion holders themselves, those with relatively extreme viewpoints are also disproportionately likely to bring their views to the public forum.

Polls weaken this relationship between the public expression of opinion and the intensity or extremity of opinion. The assertion of an opinion through a poll requires little effort. As a result, the beliefs of those who care relatively little or even hardly at all are as likely to be publicized as the opinions of those who care a great deal about the matter in question. The upshot is that the distribution of public opinion reported by polls generally differs considerably from the distribution that emerges from forms of public communication initiated by citizens. Political scientists Aage Clausen, Philip E. Converse, Warren E. Miller, and others have shown that the public opinion reported by surveys is, on the aggregate, both less intense and less extreme than the public opinion that would be defined by voluntary modes of popular expression. Similarly, poll respondents typically include a much larger proportion of individuals who "don't know," "don't care," or exhibit some other form of relative detachment from the debate on major public issues than the population of activists willing to express their views through voluntary or spontaneous means.

. . . Polls, in effect, submerge individuals with strongly held views in a more apathetic mass public. The data reported by polls are likely to suggest to public officials that they are working in a more permissive climate of opinion than might have been thought on the basis of alternative indicators of the popular mood. A government wishing to maintain some semblance of responsiveness to public opinion would typically find it less difficult to comply with the preferences reported by polls than to obey the opinion that might be inferred from letters, strikes, or protests. Indeed, relative to these other modes of public expression, polled opinion could be characterized as a collective statement of permission.

Certainly, even in the era of polling, voluntary expressions of public opinion can still count heavily. In recent years, for example, members of Congress were impressed by calls, letters, and telegrams from constituents—and threats from contributors—regarding President Reagan's various tax reform proposals. Groups like the National Rifle Association are masters in the use of this type of campaign. Nevertheless, contradiction by polls tends to reduce the weight and credibility of other sources of public opinion, an effect that can actually help governments to resist the pressure of constituent opinion. Constituency polls, for example, are often used by legislators as a basis for resisting the demands of political activists and pressure groups in their districts. . . .

The relatively permissive character of polled opinion can provide a government faced with demonstrations, protests, and other manifestations of public hostility a basis for claiming that its policies are compatible with true public opinion and opposed only by an unrepresentative group of activist malcontents.

A good illustration of how polls can play this role is the case of the "silent majority" on whose behalf Richard Nixon claimed to govern.* The silent majority was the Nixon administration's answer to the protestors, demonstrators, rioters, and other critics who demanded major changes in American foreign and domestic policies. Administration spokespersons frequently cited poll data, often drawing on Richard Scammon and Ben Wattenberg's influential treatise, *The Real Majority*, to question the popular standing of the activist opposition. According to the administration's interpretation, its activist opponents did not represent the views of the vast majority of "silent" Americans who could be found in the polls but not on picket lines or marches, or in civil disturbances.

Undoubtedly a majority of Americans were less than sympathetic to the protestors. But from the administration's perspective, the real virtue of the silent majority was precisely its silence. Many of those Americans who remained silent did so because they lacked strong opinions on the political issues of the day. The use of polls to identify a "silent majority" was a means of diluting the political weight and undermining the credibility of those members of the public with the strongest views while constructing a permissive majority of "silent" Americans. . . .

Another illustration of the permissive character of polled opinion is Lyndon Johnson's reaction to public opinion surveys about the Vietnam War. Johnson constantly referred to the polls in his attempt to convince friends, visitors, colleagues, and most of all himself that the public supported his war policies. Indeed, Johnson's eventual realization that public opinion had turned against his administration weighed heavily in his decision not to seek another term in office. The significance of this case is that polls permitted a president who was apparently actually concerned with his administration's responsiveness to public opinion to believe that he was doing what the people wanted. The polls appeared to

---

* Members of the "silent majority" were those respondents in the national public opinion polls who disapproved of the protests and demonstrations against the Vietnam War. They made up an overwhelming majority of the electorate, but their disapproval of the protesters deflected attention from the fact that many of them did not approve of government policy on the war.

indicate that despite the contrary assertions of protesters, demonstrators, and rioters, public opinion did not really demand an end to the war. After all, it was not until late in Johnson's term that a majority of those polled disapproved of his policies. In effect, the polls permitted a public official who had some actual desire to be responsive to public opinion to more easily convince himself that he had been.

From Behavior to Attitude

Prior to the advent of polling, public opinion could often only be inferred from political behavior. Before the availability of voter survey data, for example, analysts typically sought to deduce electoral opinion from voting patterns, attributing candidates' electoral fortunes to whatever characteristics of the public mood could be derived from election returns. Often population movements served as the bases for conclusions about public preferences. Even in recent years the movement of white urbanites to the metropolitan fringe, dubbed "white flight," has been seen as a key indicator of white attitudes toward racial integration. Especially in the case of the least articulate segments of the population, governments before the advent of polls often had little or no knowledge of the public mood until opinion manifested itself in some form of behavior. Generally this meant violent or disruptive activity.

In the modern era public opinion is synonymous with polls. But certainly through the nineteenth century, public opinion was usually equated with riots, strikes, demonstrations, and boycotts. Nineteenth-century public sentiment could sometimes reveal itself through the most curious forms of behavior. In London during the 1830s, for example, a favorite mechanism for the expression of popular opinion was the "illumination." In an "illumination" those espousing a particular point of view placed lanterns or candles in their windows. Often mobs went from house to house demanding that the occupants "illuminate." Householders who declined might have their windows smashed and dwelling sacked. On April 27, 1831, a large mob formed to demand electoral reform. According to a contemporary account:

> On that evening, the illumination was pretty general. . . . The mobs did a great deal of mischief. A numerous rabble proceeded along the Strand, destroying all windows that were not lighted. . . . In St. James' Square they broke the windows in the houses of the Bishop of London, the Marquis of Cleveland and Lord Grantham. The Bishop of Winchester and Mr. W. W. Wynn, seeing the mob approach, placed candles in their windows, which thus escaped. The mob then proceeded to St. James Street where they broke the windows of Crockford's, Jordon's, the Guards, and other Club houses. They next went to the Duke of Wellington's residence in Piccadilly, and discharged a shower of stones which broke several windows. The Duke's servants fired out of the windows over their heads to frighten them, but without effect. The policemen then informed the

mob that the corpse of the Duchess of Wellington was on the premises, which arrested further violence against Apsley House.[2]

. . . The advent of polling transformed public opinion from a behavioral to an attitudinal phenomenon. Polls elicit, organize, and publicize opinion without requiring any action on the part of the opinion holder. Of course, public presentation of an opinion via polls by no means precludes its subsequent expression through behavior. Nevertheless, polling does permit any interested party an opportunity to assess the state of the public's mood without having to wait for some behavioral manifestation. From the perspective of political elites, the obvious virtue of polls is that they make it possible to recognize and deal with popular attitudes—even the attitudes of the most inarticulate segments of the populace—before they materialize in some unpleasant, disruptive, or threatening form of political action. In democracies, of course, the most routine behavioral threat posed by public opinion is hostile action in the voting booth, and polling has become one of the chief means of democratic political elites to attempt to anticipate and avert the electorate's displeasure. But in both democratic and dictatorial contexts, governments have also employed polling extensively to help forestall the possibility of popular disobedience and unrest.

In recent years, for example, many Eastern European regimes have instituted survey programs. Polling has been used, in part, to forewarn the leadership of potential sources of popular disaffection, hostility, or antigovernment activities. As sociologist Bogdan Osolnik observed, in Eastern Europe opinion research provides "a warning that some attitudes which political actors consider to be generally accepted . . . have not yet been adopted by public opinion." Such "misunderstandings," says Osolnik, "can be extremely harmful—and dangerous."[3] Polling allows the regime an opportunity to resolve these potential "misunderstandings" before they pose a serious threat.

As early as the 1950s, to cite one concrete case, the Polish government obtained extensive survey data indicating that strong religious sentiment was widespread among the young. The regime became quite concerned with the implications of the continuing hold of "unorthodox ritualistic attitudes" on the generation that was expected to possess the strongest commitment to socialism. In response to its survey findings, the government embarked on a major program of antireligious and ideological indoctrination aimed at young people. . . .

Gestapo chief Heinrich Himmler is reputed to have carefully studied polls of German attitudes toward the Nazi regime and its policies. Apparently, whenever he noted that some of those surveyed failed to respond with the appropriate opinions, he demanded to know their names.

In the United States, polling has typically been used as an adjunct to policy implementation. Polling can provide administrators with some idea of what citizens are and are not likely to tolerate and, thus, help them to avoid popular disobedience and resistance. As early as the 1930s, federal agencies began to poll extensively. During that decade the United States Department of Agriculture established a Division of Program Surveys to undertake studies of attitudes toward federal farm programs. At the same time, extensive use was made of surveys by the Works Progress Administration, the Social Security Administration, and the Public Health Service. . . .

Nor is polling by U.S. governmental agencies confined to the domestic policy arena. Various units of the State Department and other foreign policy agencies have engaged in extensive polling abroad to assess the likely response of citizens of other nations to American foreign policy initiatives aimed at them. During the era of American involvement in Vietnam, both the Defense Department and the Agency for International Development sponsored extensive polling in that country to examine the effects of existing and proposed American programs. Similarly, polling was conducted in Cuba and the Dominican Republic to assess likely popular reaction to contemplated American intervention. A good deal of polling has also been sponsored in Europe by American governmental agencies concerned with European reactions to American propaganda appeals. . . .

Let me emphasize again that even the most extensive and skillful use of polling does not ensure that public opinion will manifest itself only attitudinally. Behavioral expressions of opinion in the form of protests, riots, strikes, and so on are common enough even in the era of survey research. . . .

In some instances, of course, the knowledge of popular attitudes gleaned from polls may convince those in power simply to bow to the popular will before it is too late. Such a response would certainly be consistent with the hopes expressed by polling advocates. Yet often enough the effect of polling is to lessen the threat or pressure that public opinion is likely to impose on administrators and policy makers. By converting opinion from a behavioral to an attitudinal phenomenon, polling is, in effect, also transforming public opinion into a less immediately threatening and dangerous phenomenon.

Polls can, however, also give a government a better opportunity to manipulate and modify public opinion and thus to avoid accommodation to citizens' preferences. One interesting recent example of this process is the activity of the 1965 American "Riot Commission." Charged with the task of preventing repetitions of the riots that rocked American cities during the 1960s, the National Advisory Commission on Civil Disorders sponsored and reviewed a large number of surveys of black attitudes on a variety of political, social, and economic questions. These surveys allowed the commission to identify a number of attitudes held by blacks that were said to have contributed to their disruptive behavior. As a result of its surveys, the commission was able to suggest several programs that might modify these attitudes and thus prevent further disorder. Significantly enough, the Riot Commission's report did not call for changes in the institutions and policies about which blacks had been violently expressing their views. The effect of polling was, in essence, to help the government find a way to *not* accommodate the opinions blacks had expressed in the streets of the urban ghettos of the United States.

From Group to Individual

Mass behavior was not the sole source of information about popular opinion prior to the advent of polling. Reports on the public's mood could usually also be obtained from the activists, leaders, or notables of the nation's organized and communal groups. Public officials or others interested in the views of working people, for example, would typically consult trade union officers. Similarly, anyone concerned with the attitudes of, say, farmers would turn to the heads of farm organizations. Of course, interest-group leaders, party leaders, and social notables seldom waited to be asked. These worthies would—and still do—voluntarily step forward to offer their impressions of membership opinion. While such impressions might not always be fully accurate, certainly group, party, and communal leaders often do have better opportunities to meet with and listen to their adherents than would be available to outsiders. Before the invention of polling these leaders quite probably possessed the most reliable data available on their followers' views. In the absence of contradictory evidence, at least, the claims of these leaders to have special knowledge of some portion of public opinion were strong enough to help give them a good deal of influence in national affairs. . . .

The advent of polling transformed public opinion from a property of groups to an attribute of individuals. Opinion surveys can elicit the views of individual citizens directly, allowing governments to bypass putative spokespersons for public opinion. Polls have never fully supplanted communal and interest-group leaders as sources of information about popular attitudes. Yet they do lessen the need for such intermediaries by permitting whatever agencies or organizations interested in learning the public's views to establish their own links with opinion holders. At the same time, polling often undermines the claims of group leaders and activists to speak for membership opinion. Frequently enough, polls seem to uncover discrepancies between the claims of leaders or self-appointed spokespersons on the one hand, and the opinions of the mass publics whose views these activists claim to reflect on the other. For example, during the 1960s and 1970s opponents of the American antiwar movement often took heart from poll data apparently indicating that youthful antiwar protesters who claimed to speak for "young people" really did not. Some poll data, at least, suggested that on the average individuals under thirty years of age were even more "hawkish" than respondents over the age of fifty.

This conversion of public opinion from a property of groups and their leaders to a more direct presentation of popular preferences has several consequences. On the one hand, polls undoubtedly provide a somewhat more representative picture of the public's views than would usually be obtained from group leaders and notables, who sometimes carelessly or deliberately misrepresent their adherents' opinions. Even with the best of intentions, the leaders of a group may be insufficiently sensitive to the inevitable disparity of viewpoints between activists and ordinary citizens and simply assume that their followers' views are merely echoes of their own. Polling can be a useful antidote to inaccuracy as well as to mendacity.

At the same time, however, by undermining the capacity of groups, interests, parties, and the like to speak for public opinion, polling can also diminish the effectiveness of public opinion as a force in political affairs. In essence, polling intervenes between opinion and its organized or collective expression. Though they may sometimes distort member opinion, organized groups, interests, and parties remain the most effective mechanisms through which opinion can be made to have an impact on government and politics. Polls' transformation of public opinion into an attribute of individuals increases the accuracy but very likely reduces the general efficacy with which mass opinion is publicly asserted.

Consider the role of labor unions during the Nixon era. Many of the Nixon administration's policies—wage and price controls in particular—were strongly opposed by organized labor. Yet polls constantly undercut the capacity of labor leaders to oppose the programs or to threaten electoral reprisals against legislators who supported it. Poll data seemed generally to suggest that Nixon was personally popular with union members and that most of the rank and file had no strong views on the programs that troubled the unions' leadership. As a result, the administration came to feel that it was reasonably safe to ignore the importunities of organized labor on a host of public issues. By enhancing the visibility of the opinions of ordinary workers, the polls surely drew a more representative picture of working-class opinion than had been offered by union officials. Yet the real cost of this more fully representative account of workers' views was, in a sense, a diminution of organized labor's influence over policy. . . .

Historically, the introduction of polling was, in fact, most damaging to the political fortunes of the groups that represented the interests and aspirations of the working classes. Polling erodes one of the major competitive advantages that has traditionally been available to lower-class groups and parties—a knowledge of mass public opinion superior to that of their middle- and upper-class opponents. The inability of bourgeois politicians to understand or sympathize with the needs of ordinary people is, of course, the point of one of the favorite morality tales of American political folklore, the misadventures of the "silk-stocking" candidate. To cite just one example, during the New York City mayoral race of 1894, the Committee of Seventy, a group that included the city's socially most prominent citizens, argued vehemently for improvements in the city's baths and lavatories, "to promote cleanliness and increased public comfort." The committee's members seemed undisturbed by the fact that the city and nation in 1894 were in the grip of a severe economic downturn accompanied by unusually high unemployment and considerable distress and misery among the working classes. The Committee of Seventy did not receive the thanks of many working-class New Yorkers for its firm stand on the lavatory issue.

Simply as a matter of social proximity, working-class parties or associations may have better access to mass opinion than is readily available to their rivals from the upper end of the social spectrum. As one Chicago precinct captain told University of Chicago political scientist Harold Gosnell during the 1930s, " . . . you think you can come in here and help the poor. You can't even talk to them on their own level, because you're better, you're from the University. I never graduated from high school, and I'm one of them."

Even more important than social proximity, however, is the matter of organization. In general, groups and parties that appeal mainly to working-class constituencies rely more heavily than their middle- and upper-class rivals on organizational strength and coherence. Organization has typically been the strategy of groups that must cumulate the collective energies of large numbers of individuals to counter their opponents' superior material means or institutional standing. In the course of both American and European political history, for example, disciplined and coherent party organizations were generally developed first by groups representing the working classes. . . .

What is important here is that their relatively coherent and disciplined mass organizations gave parties of the left a more accurate and extensive view of the public's mood than could normally be acquired by their less well organized opponents. . . . In the United States, the urban political machines that mobilized working-class constituencies employed armies of precinct workers and canvassers who were responsible for learning the preferences, wants, and needs of each and every voter living within an assigned precinct or election district. A Chicago machine precinct captain interviewed by Gosnell, for example, "thought that the main thing was to meet and talk to the voters on a man-to-man basis. . . . It did not matter where the voters were met—in the ball park, on the rinks, at dances, or at the bar. The main thing was to meet them." Through its extensive precinct organization, the urban machine developed a capacity to understand the moods and thus to anticipate and influence the actions of hundreds of thousands of voters.

The advent of polling eroded the advantage that social proximity and organization had given working-class parties in the competition for mass electoral support. Of course, any sort of political group can use an opinion survey. Polls are especially useful to carpetbaggers of all political stripes as a means of scouting what may be new and foreign territory. . . .*

In the United States, where systematic political polling was initiated during the second half of the nineteenth century, most of the early polls were sponsored by newspapers and magazines affiliated with conservative causes and middle- and upper-class political factions. Thus the conservative *Chicago Tribune* was a major

---

* The term *carpetbagger* originally was applied to northerners who moved to the South to make money during Reconstruction, after the Civil War. Hostile southerners believed these individuals stuffed everything they owned into a suitcase, or carpetbag. Today the term is used to describe any opportunistic people who try to exert power or influence in places where they do not belong.

promoter of the polls during this period. Prior to the critical election of 1896, the *Tribune* polled some 14,000 factory workers and purported to show that 80 percent favored McKinley over William Jennings Bryan. Many of the newspapers and periodicals that made extensive use of political polling at that time were linked with either the Mugwumps or the Prohibitionists—precisely the two political groupings whose members might be least expected to have much firsthand knowledge of the preferences of common folk.* During the 1896 campaign the Mugwump *Chicago Record* spent more than $60,000 to mail post-card ballots to a random sample of one voter in eight in twelve midwestern states. An additional 328,000 ballots went to all registered voters in Chicago. The Democrats feared that the *Record* poll was a Republican trick and urged their supporters not to participate. . . .

This affiliation of many of the major polls with groups on the political right continued through the early years of the twentieth century. The Hearst newspapers, for example, polled extensively. *Fortune* magazine published widely read polls. The *Literary Digest*, which sponsored a famous presidential poll, was affiliated with the Prohibitionists. The clientele of most of the major pre–World War II pollsters—George Gallup, Elmo Roper, and Claude Robinson, for example—was heavily Republican, reflecting both the personal predilections of the pollsters and relative capacities of Democrats and Republicans of the period to understand public opinion without the aid of complex statistical analysis. In recent years the use of political polling has become virtually universal. Nevertheless, the polling efforts and uses of other forms of modern political technology by groups on the political right have been far more elaborate and extensive than those of other political factions. . . .

At the present time, polling is used by parties and candidates of every political stripe in the United States and all the European democracies. Opinion surveys are hardly a monopoly of the political right. Yet the fact remains that in the absence of polling, parties and groups representing the working classes would normally reap the political advantage of a superior knowledge of public opinion. The irony of polling is that the development of scientific means of measuring public opinion had its most negative effect on precisely those groups whose political fortunes were historically most closely linked with mass public opinion.

---

* *Mugwump,* an Indian word meaning "chief," was used to label Republicans who refused to support James Blaine, the Republican presidential nominee in 1884, because they believed him to be opposed to many governmental reforms. Many came from wealthy, elitist backgrounds and were critical of patronage politics and political machines. Because the Mugwumps voted for Democrat Grover Cleveland, the term is sometimes used to describe individuals who leave their party when they are not pleased with a nominee. Prohibitionists were interested in banning the legal sale and consumption of alcohol. Because drinking was often associated with urban ethnic groups, Prohibitionists were considered to be hostile to lower- and working-class interests.

From Assertion to Response

In the absence of polling, individuals typically choose for themselves the subjects of any public assertions they might care to make. Those persons or groups willing to expend the funds, effort, or time needed to acquire a public platform normally also select the agenda or topics on which their views will be aired. The individual writing an angry letter to a newspaper or legislator generally singles out the object of his or her scorn. The organizers of a protest march typically define the aim of their own wrath. . . .

The introduction of opinion surveys certainly did not foreclose opportunities for individuals to proffer opinions on topics of their own choosing. Indeed, in the United States a multitude of organizations, groups, and individuals are continually stepping forward to present the most extraordinary notions. Nevertheless, polls elicit subjects' views on questions that have been selected by an external agency—the survey's sponsors—rather than by the respondents themselves. Polling thus erodes individuals' control over the agenda of their own expressions of opinion. . . .

The most obvious consequence of this change is that polling can create a misleading picture of the agenda of public concerns, for what appears significant to the agencies sponsoring polls may be quite different from the concerns of the general public. Discrepancies between the polls' agenda and the general public's interests were especially acute during the political and social turmoil of the late 1960s and early 1970s. Though, as we saw, polling was used by the government during this period to help curb disorder, the major commercial polls took little interest in the issues that aroused so much public concern. The year 1970, for example, was marked by racial strife and antiwar protest in the United States. At least fifty-four major antiwar protests and some forty major instances of racial violence occurred. Yet the 1970 national Gallup Poll devoted only 5 percent of its questions to American policy in Vietnam and only two of 162 questions to domestic race relations. Similarly, in 1971, despite the occurrence of some thirty-five major cases of racial unrest and twenty-six major episodes of student violence or protest, the national Gallup Poll that year devoted only two of its 194 questions to race relations and asked no questions at all about student protest. By contrast, that year's poll asked forty-two political "horse race" questions, concerning citizens' candidate preferences and electoral expectations, as well as eleven questions relating to presidential popularity. An observer attempting to gauge the public's interests from poll data might have concluded that Americans cared only about election forecasts and official popularity and were blithely unconcerned with the matters that were actually rending the social fabric of the era. . . .

Given the commercial character of the polling industry, differences between the polls' concerns and those of the general public are probably inevitable. Polls generally raise questions that are of interest to clients and purchasers of poll data—newspapers, political candidates, governmental agencies, business corporations, and so on. Questions of no immediate relevance to government, business, or politicians will not easily find their way into the surveys. This is particularly true of issues such as the validity of the capitalist economic system or the legitimacy of governmental authority, issues that business and government usually prefer not to see raised at all, much less at their own expense. Because they seldom pose questions about the foundations of the existing order, while constantly asking respondents to choose from among the alternatives defined by that order—candidates and consumer products, for example—polls may help to narrow the focus of public discussion and to reinforce the limits on what the public perceives to be realistic political and social possibilities.

But whatever the particular changes polling may help to produce in the focus of public discourse, the broader problem is that polling fundamentally alters the character of the public agenda of opinion. So long as groups and individuals typically present their opinions on topics of their own choosing, the agenda of opinion is likely to consist of citizens' own needs, hopes, and aspirations. Opinions elicited by polls, on the other hand, mainly concern matters of interest to government, business, or other poll sponsors. Typically, poll questions have as their ultimate purpose some form of exhortation. Businesses poll to help persuade customers to purchase their wares. Candidates poll as part of the process of convincing voters to support them. Governments poll as part of the process of inducing citizens to obey. . . .

In essence, rather than offer governments the opinions that citizens want them to learn, polls tell governments—or other sponsors—what they would like to learn about citizens' opinions. The end result is to change the public expression of opinion from an assertion of demand to a step in the process of persuasion.

Making Opinion Safer for Government

Taken together, the changes produced by polling contribute to the transformation of public opinion from an unpredictable, extreme, and often dangerous force into a more docile expression of public sentiment. Opinion stated through polls imposes less pressure and makes fewer demands on government than would more spontaneous or natural assertions of popular sentiment. Though opinion may be expressed more democratically via polls than through alternative means, polling can give public opinion a plebiscitary character—robbing opinion of precisely those features that might maximize its impact on government and policy.

Notes

1. Chester F. Barnard, "Public Opinion in a Democracy" (Herbert L. Baker Foundation, Princeton University, Princeton, N.J., 1939, pamphlet), 13.

2. Allan Silver, "The Demand for Order in Civil Society," in *The Police*, ed. David Bordua (New York: Wiley, 1967), 17–18.
3. Bogdan Osolnik, "Socialist Public Opinion," *Socialist Thought and Practice* 20 (October 1955): 120.

Questions for Discussion

1. How have the widespread use and acceptability of polls changed the character of public opinion? What are the consequences of such changes for democratic government?
2. Why might governments engage in polling?
3. How has the rise of polling affected interest-group politics? Which groups and elements in society have gained or lost?

 4.2

Forgiving and Forgetting: Public Support for Bill Clinton During the Lewinsky Scandal

Molly W. Sonner and Clyde Wilcox

In January of 1998, a news organization broke the story that President Bill Clinton had been sexually involved with Monica Lewinsky, a young White House intern. After first denying the charges, the president was later forced to acknowledge his guilt of having "an improper sexual relationship" with Lewinsky, creating a scandal that gripped the attention of the nation for more than a year. Eventually the House of Representatives impeached the president, who then faced a trial in the Senate.

To the surprise of many, after an initial drop in his job-approval ratings, Clinton's support in the polls remained strong throughout the ordeal. Public opinion was undoubtedly a key factor in Clinton's decision to fight his impeachment and the Senate's eventual vote for acquittal.

In this piece, Molly Sonner and Clyde Wilcox attempt to disentangle the complexity of public opinion surrounding the Clinton-Lewinsky scandal. They find

Molly W. Sonner is a research assistant at the Pew Research Center. Clyde Wilcox is Professor of Political Science at Georgetown University.

a variety of factors—ranging from a strong economy to Clinton's communication skills to widespread dislike of those most vigorously trying to bring down his presidency—converged to enable Clinton to survive.

I n January 1999, President Bill Clinton was, paradoxically, the most publicly shamed president of modern time and one of the most popular. He had admitted having an improper sexual relationship with a young White House intern. He had been impeached by the House of Representatives for allegedly lying about that relationship to a grand jury and for trying to obstruct the investigation of that affair. The media were full of the story, comedians quipped about some of the racier details of the affair, and the Internet hummed with Clinton jokes. Most importantly, the Senate was conducting a trial to determine if he should be removed from office—only the second such trial in the nation's history.

At the same time, Clinton was more popular than any contemporary president had ever been in the beginning of the sixth year of his presidency. Indeed, from the spring of 1998 through the end of the impeachment trial, the public remained remarkably stable in its support of Clinton and its belief that he should not be removed from office. The public wavered in its support for Clinton only once, immediately after the scandal broke in January 1998. Throughout the rest of the year, the public came to grips with the reality that the president had indeed had sexual relations with Lewinsky, and that he had testified in a misleading manner about that affair. Americans were forced to choose between their strong approval of Clinton's performance as president and their belief that this behavior was sufficiently immoral to remove him from office. Overwhelmingly, the public chose to support Clinton and oppose the notion that the charges justified his removal.

Clinton's resilient popularity presents a puzzle: Why, in the midst of a tawdry scandal, were his approval ratings so high? In this article we examine public opinion of Clinton and consider a series of explanations for his continued popularity.

The Public Stands by Its Man: Popular Response to the Clinton Crisis over Time

When the story broke on Wednesday, January 21, 1998, news organizations rushed to take the public pulse, conducting a flurry of overnight and two-day polls that showed Americans becoming less supportive of the president. Throughout the rest of the week and into the weekend, Clinton's job approval rating began to falter, dropping to 51 percent from 60 percent in one ABC News/*Washington Post* poll.

As Clinton responded to the charges with steely silence, the public expressed doubts about his innocence. Most Americans believed he had an affair with the young intern, and substantial numbers thought he was guilty of asking her to lie under oath, as well. After several days of all-Monica, all-the-time news, Americans began to question Clinton's fitness for office. A solid majority thought that he should resign if he lied under oath or if he encouraged Ms. Lewinsky to lie. If he was unwilling to take such action himself, just over half the respondents to an ABC News/*Washington Post* poll on January 25 said that his perjury should result in his impeachment.

Clinton's job performance wasn't the only indicator to take a hit, his personal ratings tumbled as well. According to an ABC News poll conducted on January 26, Americans were divided 51 percent to 41 percent on whether Clinton had the honesty and integrity to serve effectively as president and only 33 percent of those responding to a Gallup poll said that the phrase "honest and trustworthy" applied to him, a drop of 16 percentage points since February 1997.

Finally, amid eroding public support and a relentless barrage of punditry declaring the presidency in crisis, Bill and Hillary Clinton started to fight back (Zaller 1998). Clinton issued a forceful denial and the first lady defended her husband, appearing on NBC's *Today Show* and blaming the accusations on a vast "right wing conspiracy." Then Clinton delivered a skillful State of the Union Address to cheering crowds of Democratic supporters in Congress. With 36.5 million houses tuned in ("Clinton's Troubles" 1998), he reminded Americans of their current economic prosperity, offered them popular programs for the future, and ignored the lingering scandal.

The public responded as the White House hoped. Clinton's job approval ratings rebounded, Americans became more skeptical of his guilt, and support for impeachment dropped. By the end of the week, most polls indicated that Clinton's job performance was at the highest point in his presidency, hovering around 70 percent. An ABC News poll found the percent of Americans who believed he had the honesty and integrity to serve as president back up to 59 from its earlier low of 51. A survey by Gallup showed 43 percent of the public very confident in Clinton's abilities to carry out his duties as president, up from 29 percent who felt this way before the speech.

Americans did not simply react to the president playing the role of rhetorical leader; some found his strong denial of an illicit relationship convincing. In the days following his statement, Americans were less likely to think Clinton had sexual relations of any kind with Lewinsky, less inclined to think he lied about the affair under oath, and significantly less apt to believe that he encouraged Lewinsky to lie about it.[1]

An increasing number of Americans also supported the continuation of the Clinton presidency. Prior to the State of the Union address, almost two-thirds of Americans said that Clinton should resign if he lied under oath or if he encouraged Lewinsky to do so. Following his speech, support for resignation if either of these charges proved true fell to just over 50 percent. Even fewer Americans wanted Clinton to be impeached.

Many analysts argued that once the public was forced to confront Clinton's guilt, they would turn on Clinton. Instead, the public came increasingly to believe that even if the allegations were true, they did not justify removing the president. As the scandal progressed, a pattern set in. With each new revelation, Americans became more convinced of Clinton's guilt, and less supportive of his removal—and his popularity remained steady throughout.

By July, the public had simultaneously reached two strong judgments: that Clinton had lied under oath, and that he should remain in office. In a Pew Center survey, 66 percent of those asked said Clinton probably lied under oath about his relationship with Lewinsky; in February, only 52 percent had thought so. Almost half (48 percent) thought he probably pressured Lewinsky to lie, up from 40 percent who saw him as guilty of this in February. At the same time, just 31 percent of the public supported impeachment and removal from office if Clinton lied under oath; in February, fully half of respondents wanted him ousted for perjury. And only 41 percent supported impeachment for suborning perjury, down from 48 percent in February. The public had come to the conclusion that an immoral president who was doing a good job should be allowed to stay in office.

Throughout Clinton's trial in the Senate, public support for his job performance and opposition toward his impeachment remained unchanged. His approval ratings stayed in the low to mid-60s; support for his removal never rose above 35 percent. When the Senate voted for acquittal, 63 percent of those polled voiced their approval of this decision.

Explaining Clinton's Popularity

In light of its widespread disapproval of Clinton's conduct with Lewinsky, and the majority sentiment that he lacked critical moral judgment, why did the public continue to support Clinton? The available data do not permit a definitive explanation, but we believe that five factors helped to boost Clinton's popularity.

Let the Good Times Roll   One of the strongest predictors of aggregate presidential popularity is the performance of the economy. Simply put, presidents are generally popular when the economy is strong, and are much less so when the economy is weak.

Throughout the course of the scandal, the strong economy—considerably stronger than when Clinton took office in 1993—shielded Clinton from public criticism. Most Americans enjoyed slightly higher incomes, lower mortgage payments, considerably higher values for their mutual funds and retirement savings, greater job security, and more buying power. Moreover, Americans were able to feel confident and secure for the first time in many years. During the late

1980s and early 1990s, many Americans believed that their children would experience a lower standard of living than they had enjoyed. By 1999, the public was much more optimistic about the future.

Americans knew that Bill Clinton was not personally responsible for all of these positive trends, but they could remember when times had been worse and when they had held little hope that times would ever get better. With most trends tilting in a positive direction, they were loath to rock the boat.

Talking the Talk Clinton's support was also buoyed by his popular positions on public issues. Although his first term was marked by several ill-fated liberal policies, such as gays in military and massive health care reform, he responded to the 1994 GOP takeover of Congress by moving to the center, both in rhetoric and policy.

Clinton staked out rhetorical positions on issues such as school uniforms, discipline in the classroom, and an end to social promotion. He endorsed personal responsibility, hard work, and playing by the rules. He pushed welfare reform, a balanced budget, more police on the beat, fewer appeals from death-row inmates, and trade agreements with Canada and Mexico.

In late January 1999, as the Senate discussed his removal from office, Clinton delivered a masterly State of the Union speech in which he addressed all the major issues on the public agenda. He called for devoting most of the budget surplus to saving Social Security and Medicare. His education program combined an end to social promotion and the provision of report cards for schools with plans to hire more teachers and reduce class sizes. He challenged Congress to boost the minimum wage, expand child-care tax credits, and extend the Family and Medical Leave Act.

Clinton's selective embrace of both liberal and conservative policies clearly helped him maintain high job approval ratings in the midst of personal scandal. Indeed, in Pew polls taken over the course of the scandal, two-thirds of the public repeatedly said they didn't like Clinton as a person and over 60 percent consistently said they liked his policies. In February 1999, 54 percent of the respondents said they wanted the next president to pursue policies similar to those Clinton endorsed.

There's Something About Bill Presidential personalities are one of the great intangibles of politics—easy to talk about but difficult to measure. There is a consensus among political observers, however, that Bill Clinton is an extremely talented politician who communicates well with the American public. His ability to "feel the pain" of the average American has been the subject of much ridicule, yet his ability to project empathy helped him establish a rapport with the American public that earned him a cushion of goodwill. One *Washington Post* poll taken in September 1998, showed that while only slightly more than one in five respondents thought Clinton was honest and trustworthy nearly three in five thought he understood their problems.

In some ways, Clinton's connection with the American public is reminiscent of Ronald Reagan's. Reagan was and Clinton is a skilled communicator, but both men's relationship with the public goes deeper than that. Both come from modest backgrounds and made good by their skills and hard work. Both were able to make rhetorical use of their roots and convey that they remembered where they came from. Voters believed that Reagan shared their values and they forgave his inattention to detail. Similarly, they sensed Clinton's connection with average Americans and forgave him for the excesses in his personal life.

With Enemies Like These   Political judgments are necessarily comparisons. If the president were weakened and unable to conduct the nation's business, the congressional Republicans would dominate the policy agenda. Clinton benefitted from widespread public dislike of his enemies and skepticism of their motives.

Clinton's nemesis was Kenneth Starr, whose handling of the investigation—holding Lewinsky without her lawyer being present, forcing her mother to testify against her, allegedly allowing leaks from his office to the press—undermined his legitimacy in the eyes of the public. By the fall of 1998, according to a *Newsweek* poll, fully 58 percent of Americans disapproved of Starr's methods. They believed that he was more interested in removing the president than in finding the truth and that he had included licentious details of Clinton's sexual encounter with Lewinsky in his report to Congress in order to embarrass the president.

The House GOP leadership was no more sympathetic and it was a commonly-held perception that the case against the president was no more than a personal political vendetta. The angry rhetoric of Bob Barr (R-GA) and Tom DeLay (R-TX) made it clear that many Republicans truly hated Clinton, and news reports suggested that Judiciary Committee Chairman Henry Hyde (R-IL) personally disliked the president as well. A CBS News poll, taken in late July 1998, found 60 percent of the public characterizing the investigation as a partisan affair.

Not only were Clinton's antagonists unpopular, but there were no likable characters in the entire drama. Despite Lewinsky's youth, few Americans sympathized with her or saw her as a victim. News of Lewinsky's previous affair with a married man, reports of her claim to a friend that she was bringing her "presidential kneepads" to Washington, and, perhaps, a double standard about sexual affairs led many Americans to view Lewinsky unfavorably. Linda Tripp was seen by most Americans as mean-spirited, not driven by patriotism as she claimed. Paula Jones was widely viewed as motivated by a desire for financial gain and as a pawn in the hands of Republican activists.

In March 1998, in the midst of the investigation, a Pew poll showed that 62 percent of respondents had a favorable impression of Clinton, 36 percent were favorable toward Gingrich, 22 percent toward Starr, 17 percent toward Lewinsky, 10 percent toward Tripp, and 17 percent toward Paula Jones. Had the story had a clear, likable victim, or had the prosecutors and House GOP leadership seemed more balanced and judicious, it is possible they could have chipped away at Clinton's approval ratings.

When They Say It Isn't About Sex . . . It's About Sex   The public came to view this scandal, at its heart, as a man lying about an extramarital affair. Although surveys consistently show that substantial majorities of Americans disapprove of extramarital affairs, other surveys show that many engage in them, and many more contemplate them. Almost all Americans who have affairs lie about them, and those who contemplate them realize that they would lie about them. Thus, unlike lying about politics or the conduct of government, lying about sex is something that most Americans can understand and imagine themselves doing.

For many Americans, Clinton's affair with Lewinsky was a private matter of importance only to them and Hillary Clinton. In an ABC News poll conducted in mid-August 1998, two-thirds of those asked said that the affair had nothing to do with Clinton's job as president. Similarly, a CBS survey taken at the same time reported that 64 percent saw the matter as private. By defining this issue as personal, many Americans could condemn the behavior while supporting the president's policies.

Americans also believe that many public officials have sexual affairs and lie about them, a belief that was confirmed by a spate of confessions by Republicans of their own sexual escapades. Most dramatically, House speaker-elect Bob Livingstone (R-LA) admitted to marital infidelity, renounced his elected position, and resigned from Congress.

Americans would prefer that their politicians not lie to them. Overall, however, they think that it would be easier to simply not invade their privacy. One Pew poll taken in December 1998 found that, by a margin of 60 percent to 34 percent, Americans believe that the best way to avoid scandals like this in the future is to make sure a president's private life remains private, rather than to elect a president with high moral character.

Future Implications of the Crisis

In early 1999, there was scattered anecdotal evidence that the public was truly angry about the Republican focus on the Clinton-Lewinsky affair and their seemingly relentless pursuit of the president. It is possible that the public disgust with the proceedings will allow the Democrats to reap benefits at the polls in the 2000 presidential and congressional elections.

In politics, however, two years is an eternity. It is likely that the public's anger will dissipate over time and as other issues become more salient. The lasting impact of the impeachment hearings on public opinion depends on events that occur throughout 1999 and 2000 that either keep the impeachment process in the public mind or distract the public's memory.

The greatest political casualty of the impeachment process may not be either Clinton himself or the men and women who fought for his removal but the man who has patiently served under him for six years: Vice President Gore. Early horse-race polls pitting the vice president against likely GOP nominee George W. Bush show Gore trailing by margins as great as 10 percentage points.

Moreover, pollsters argue that Gore's weak showing is due, in part, to "Clinton fatigue"—public weariness of all the scandals surfacing during Clinton's time in the White House. Gore must now walk the fine line between accepting credit for the accomplishments of Clinton's policies and distancing himself from Clinton personally. Most Americans could make these distinctions about his boss; it remains to be seen if they'll grant him the same leeway.

Note

1. Unless otherwise noted, surveys used in this analysis were conducted by The Pew Research Center for The People & The Press between January 1998 and February 1999. Copies of the survey results are available from their Web site (www.people-press.org).

Questions for Discussion

1. What factors contributed to President Clinton's survival in office after his sexual involvement with Monica Lewinsky was revealed? In your view, should he have remained in office?
2. Sonner and Wilcox speculate that then-Vice President Al Gore would be the greatest "political casualty" of the attempt to remove President Clinton from office, suggesting Gore had to walk a fine line between accepting credit for Clinton's political accomplishments and distancing himself from Clinton's personal problems. Do you think the results of the 2000 presidential election confirm their speculation?

▓▓▓ 4.3

A Question of Values: The Split over Bill Clinton's Impeachment Has Its Roots in the 1960s

David S. Broder and Richard Morin

While President Clinton's job-approval rating remained high throughout the Monica Lewinsky scandal, and nearly two-thirds of the electorate approved of the Senate's decision not to remove him from office, public opinion on the issue nevertheless revealed a deep split in society over cultural and moral values. The electorate was divided roughly in half between those who thought the president was responsible for setting a moral example for the country and those who believed that a president's personal life was unimportant as long as he was doing a good job running the country. The public reaction to the scandal has engendered a heated debate among social commentators over the role of moral and ethical standards in the nation's political and social life.

In this piece, journalists David Broder and Richard Morin attempt to uncover where the divisions on moral and ethical values are. They believe that the public verdict in the Clinton matter would have been far different had the scandal occurred thirty years earlier, and that unresolved differences in values between generations are at the heart of today's political divisions. At base, the Clinton scandal confronted citizens with "choices between deeply held moral standards and an abhorrence of judging others' behavior." Such choices made many uncomfortable and are likely to remain unresolved.

T he sharply divided public reaction to the impeachment of President Clinton has provided a dramatic showcase of a struggle for American values that goes back to the 1960s and remains unresolved today.

As an emblematic figure from that troubled decade, polls and analysts say, Clinton confronts his fellow citizens with choices between deeply held moral standards and an abhorrence of judging others' behavior, a conflict the baby boomers have stirred all their adult lives.

David S. Broder is a *Washington Post* political correspondent. Richard Morin is the *Washington Post* Polling Director.

But few issues are more revealing than Clinton's impeachment when it comes to highlighting how values have changed over the past 30 years. Almost without exception, experts interviewed said the public verdict in his case is far different than it would have been in the late '60s because the values environment has changed.

That conflict over the social order is notably less violent than it was in 1968, when the assassinations of Martin Luther King Jr. and Robert F. Kennedy, anti-Vietnam War demonstrations, urban riots, and violent clashes between police and protesters at the Democratic National Convention scarred the nation's consciousness. But 1998, with a bitter, year-long battle in the courts and Congress climaxing in the first presidential impeachment in 130 years, has left deep divisions across social, political and generational lines.

They begin, according to the Post/Kaiser/Harvard survey,* with a near-even split between those (50 percent) who think a president "has a greater responsibility than leaders of other organizations to set the moral tone for the country" and those (48 percent) who say, "As long as he does a good job running the country, a president's personal life is not important."

Reflecting the partisanship engendered by the long investigation of Clinton's relationship with Monica S. Lewinsky, most Republicans demand a moral example and most Democrats reject it.

But sociologists and other students of American life interviewed in late December said the divisions go much deeper and have their roots in long-standing controversy generated not just by Clinton but by his baby boom generation.

While most Americans want Clinton to finish his term, and prefer censure as an alternative, few believe he is a good role model. Seven in 10 Americans—including a majority of baby boomers—said in the survey that Clinton does not have high personal moral or ethical standards. Six in 10—again including a majority of baby boomers—also said his standards are no better or worse than "most people of his generation."

The public sees a nation that lacks agreed-upon ethical guidelines for itself. More than six out of 10 said the country "was greatly divided when it comes to the most important values," rather than being in agreement. Ironically, on this one question there was unity. Republicans and Democrats, men and women, young and old all said they see a society split on moral and ethical issues.

With some exceptions, the experts tend to agree. Some describe it as a battle of extremes—the Puritanism of the Religious Right vs. the permissiveness of the aging children of the '60s. Others see the acceptance of Clinton's actions as proof that Americans are utterly cynical about their political leaders, mute spectators at a television drama they despise but cannot escape.

---

* The Post/Kaiser/Harvard survey, a collaborative effort of the *Washington Post,* the Henry J. Kaiser Family Foundation, and Harvard University, was conducted in the fall of 1998. It aimed to assess levels of toleration among the American public.

Some say it is a symptom of national ambivalence, of individuals longing for moral values but resistant to imposing their standards on others. And the more hopeful say the preference for censuring the president—rather than absolving him or removing him—is a healthy effort at synthesizing those opposing tendencies.

A few optimists say the upshot of all the discussion will be a standard for future presidents that is both more demanding and more realistic.

Few of the scholars are comfortable with the status quo, however.

"No analysis can absolve the people themselves of responsibility for the quandary we appear to be in," says Don Eberly, director of the Civil Society Project in Harrisburg, Pa. "Nonjudgmentalism, the trump card of moral debate, seems to have gained strength among the people, especially in the sexual realm, and this clearly does not bode well for America."

Over the last 30 years, polling shows the proportion of people saying they think their fellow citizens generally are as honest and moral as they used to be has fallen significantly. In a 1952 survey, as many answered yes as said no. In 1965, there were three yeses for every four noes. But this year there were almost three noes (71 percent) for every yes (26 percent).

In the same period, trust in government also has declined radically. In 1968, 61 percent said they trusted the government in Washington to do the right thing most or all the time; in 1998, only 33 percent felt that way.

Pollster Dan Yankelovich writes that "the transformation in values from the mid-'60s to the late-'70s confronts us with one of the sharpest discontinuities in our cultural history." In that period's "radical extension of individualism . . . from the political domain to personal lifestyles," he notes, the concepts of duty, social conformity, respectability and sexual morality were devalued, in favor of expressiveness and pleasure seeking.

This was a time in which Bill Clinton, moving through his twenties at Georgetown, Oxford and Yale, rejected military service, and experimented with marijuana. But in general, according to his biographer, Washington Post reporter David Maraniss, Clinton followed "a moderate course during an increasingly immoderate period." The stamp of that period remained on Clinton, in at least two areas: the evasiveness that characterized his dealings with the "threat" of military service and the permissiveness he allowed in his sexual life.

In judging Clinton's morals to be typical of his generation—only 7 percent thought them better, 27 percent worse—most of those surveyed made it clear they disapproved of them.

Yankelovich argues that in the 1990s, "a shift is now occurring toward a perception of the self as a moral actor with obligations and concerns as well as rights . . . we are beginning to measure a shift back toward absolute as distinct from relative values." That theme of individual responsibility is one Clinton has emphasized in his speeches, if not always in his actions.

From this perspective, the divided public verdict on the Clinton case represents not just a legal argument about the standards for impeachment and removal of a president, or a partisan battle between Republicans and Democrats, but also an unresolved debate about fundamental values.

At the extremes, the conflict amounts almost to the "culture war" some trace directly back to the 1960s. Randy Tate of the Christian Coalition and William J. Bennett, former Education secretary, have accused Clinton of subverting standards of honesty and decency so blatantly that he cannot be allowed to remain in office. Harvard professor Alan Dershowitz and many Democrats in the House have accused Clinton's opponents—notably independent counsel Kenneth W, Starr—of practicing "sexual McCarthyism," trampling civil liberties and invading people's privacy.

Alan Wolfe, a Boston University sociologist, argued in his book, "One Nation, After All," that the "culture war" is confined to political elites, and that most individuals struggle to balance their yearning for clear standards against their discomfort with passing judgment on others.

Wolfe said in an interview that he sees exactly that happening in the Clinton case—"even though people are torn, they are looking to find a way to negotiate through these competing impulses." Wolfe says he thought last January, when Lewinsky first became a household name, that "people would forgive adultery but lying in public would not pass. But people realized that the lying and the adultery were part of the same thing. I don't agree, but I recognize the wisdom in making that connection."

Others see the conflict in starker—and more worrisome—terms. David Blankenhorn, president of the Institute of American Values in New York, says the reaction to Clinton demonstrates that "many middle-class Americans obey an 11th Commandment: Thou shalt not judge. They view morality as a private matter. What I find troublesome is that . . . apart from treason, there is nothing worse than a democratic leader engaging in ongoing public lying. And yet a substantial number of Americans, have accepted this. . . . Remove ethics, and it makes this a society where politics trumps everything else."

Several observers traced this back to the 1960s. Christopher Gates, president of the Denver-based National Civic League, says that Pollster George Gallup Jr. "says the '60s and '70s were the time when our country fell apart and the bonds began to dissolve. You had a war between the generations, a war between the genders, you had Vietnam, break-ins, resignations, pardons. You had a huge dissolution of trust. And we have gone from a time when we presumed good intentions on the part of our leaders to the presumption of bad intentions."

Blankenhorn suggests that as a result of that legacy, "Clinton is in many ways the beneficiary of people's very low expectations of politicians and government."

But Georgia Sorenson, director of the center for political leadership and participation of the University of Maryland, points out that "participation has been deteriorating since the '60s, and it makes it hard for any person to lead now, no matter how committed."

Michael Sandel, director of the Harvard Institute for Policy Studies, says the consequences go further. "We've witnessed a politics of scandal, sensation and spectacle that has turned the president into another figure in the celebrity culture," he says. "The majesty and dignity of the presidency have been stripped away, but paradoxically that hasn't destroyed the popularity of this president. As citizens, we have become just spectators, even voyeurs. . . . We've told the pollsters we want the whole issue to be over, and yet we can't bring ourselves to change the channel. . . . It reflects a cynicism beyond mistrust. It reflects a view that government really doesn't matter, except as it provides occasional spectacular entertainment. It is not good news for democracy."

The Post/Kaiser/Harvard survey attempted to test Sandel's thesis by asking how many respondents had contacted their members of Congress about the impeachment issue. About one out of nine—11 percent—claimed to have done so. Among the vast majority who did not, the main reasons were that they didn't think it would make a difference (53 percent) or the issue wasn't important enough for them to get involved (21 percent).

But other experts interviewed are not nearly so concerned about public indifference or a decline in trust or an erosion of values. And there was some support for their views in the survey. About half those interviewed (48 percent) said they thought their representative in Congress had paid at least "a fair amount of attention" to opinions in their district, while only a third (35 percent) thought their elected officials largely ignored their constituents.

Charles Quigley, executive director of the Center for Civic Education in Calabasas, Calif., says, "What the Clinton thing says to me is that the majority are making subtle, sophisticated distinctions. They condemn what he did, but they want proportionality in punishment. They're questioning not only Clinton's values but those of the people who have gone after him."

Michael Josephson, president of the Josephson Institute of Ethics in Marina del Ray, Calif., and David Mathews, president of the Charles F. Kettering Foundation in Dayton, Ohio, say the partisanship of the House impeachment proceedings sent a worrisome signal to people. "Everyone thinks it is [political] positioning," Josephson says. "Otherwise, why would Republicans and Democrats come out so differently?"

"But," Mathews adds, "they have deep feelings about accountability and taking responsibility, not just by the president but by everyone. And when they see it disappearing, it scares them."

That may be true, but Wolfe and Eberly say politicians are not seen as the ones to lead a values revival. "When government becomes involved in moral matters, Americans are no longer sure they can trust it," Wolfe wrote in "One Nation, After All."

Eberly says: "The people just don't see the answer to our moral condition coming predominantly from lawmakers. . . . Americans tend to be generous toward sinners and hard on hypocrites, and the working assumption of many Americans is that most politicians fall into the latter category. While the American people strongly disapproved of Clinton's behavior, they grew steadily more unwilling to approve of action against him as it became clear that Congress would serve as judge and jury."

When asked what will be important to them in the presidential election of 2000, more of those surveyed in the Post/Kaiser/Harvard poll said the candidates' stands on issues than the combined total for those naming personal morals and ethics and broad principles and values.

On the other hand, looking to the future, a majority of Americans—55 percent—said in the survey they fear this society will become too accepting of behaviors that are bad for people, while 38 percent said their greatest worry was that the country would become too intolerant of actions that pose no such threat.

The survey indicates the divisions that have marked the past 30 years are likely to continue into the next generation.

Although more young people between 18 and 34 say they are more pessimistic about the threat of moral decline than their parents and grandparents, they are also more conflicted over values. They, more than their elders, express the greatest tolerance toward divorce, adultery and casual drug use. While many young Americans say that values are important to their politics, young adults are the least likely to agree that a president has a special obligation to "set an example with his personal life."

Questions for Discussion

1. What factors have caused the country to become so politically divided on moral and ethical issues? Is the division likely to be resolved in the near future?
2. One of the survey questions asks, "Which of following worries you more about the future: That the country will become too tolerant of behaviors that are bad for society, or that the country will become too intolerant of behaviors that do not do any real harm to society?" How would you answer this question? What arguments would you make to defend your position?

4.4

I Hear America Ringing

Dana Milbank

Polling to assess public opinion during a presidential election has become commonplace in recent decades, influencing both candidate behavior and coverage of the campaign, and as a consequence, potentially affecting the outcome of the election itself. Especially important during the last few weeks of a campaign have been the national tracking polls, typically conducted daily, which attempt to measure very short-run changes in support for presidential contenders.

In this selection, journalist Dana Milbank takes us behind the scenes of Zogby International, whose polls are regarded as among the most accurate, the results of which are used by Reuters News Service and MSNBC and are widely disseminated across the nation. Milbank concludes that surveying the American public on a daily basis is both complicated and hectic, a mixture of objective systematic procedures and pollster hunches. He emphasizes that polls are often poor predictors, and have the potential to be overinterpreted by media sources.

G enesee Street, running south from downtown, becomes a Religion Row. There's the steeple of First Presbyterian Church and the yellow-brick Temple Beth El on your left. On the right, you'll pass Saviour Lutheran Church. Then, just before the Church of our Lady of Lourdes and the Church of the Nazarene, right next to the AMF Pin-o-Rama bowling alley, is a Cathedral of our Civic Religion.

This is the headquarters of Zogby International, pollsters.

In this election season, the operation is a frenzied factory of public opinion, tracking every hiccup and sigh in the presidential race. Callers begin at 9 a.m. and end at midnight, when number-crunchers figure out who's winning and release the Reuters/MSNBC/Zogby daily tracking poll to the breathless media.

In politics this year, polling is everything. The results of these surveys drive the candidates' moves and the press coverage, which may, in turn, influence the election's outcome. For this reason, I have made a pilgrimage here to worship at the altar of public opinion.

Dana Milbank is a *Washington Post* staff writer.

The dinner hour is approaching. I put on my headset and push the button that tells the computer to dial a number. I call Washington state—no answer. I call Colorado—answering machine. I call Kansas—no reply. I call Michigan, where a man shouts "No!" and hangs up. I click "refusal—hostile" on my computer, and forge on.

My success doesn't improve much over the next hour. I get busy tones in Ohio and Kansas, disconnected numbers in Montana and Illinois, no answer in Virginia, Kentucky, Maine, Oklahoma and Massachusetts, a fax machine and a call-waiting "privacy manager" in Ohio, and a tree and shrub service in Upstate New York. In New York City, a woman advises me, "Sweetheart, you're in the middle of our dinner," and another hangs up on me. A Virginia man, shouting over a crying baby, exclaims "Excuse me? Nah!" Click. A California woman asks me, "No habla español?" A New Jersey woman informs me: "I'm one of Jehovah's Witnesses and there are certain things we don't do."

My hour of calling produces only one hit in 25 attempts: a 51-year-old woman in Cincinnati who is for Bush. The results of my piece of the tracking poll:

Bush: 100 percent

Everyone else: 0 percent

Margin of error: ±98 percent

Apparently, I'm not cut out for this. "You did a couple of things we would yell at our interviewers for," explains Steve McLaughlin, my tutor. "You've got to read your script word for word," he tells me.

But perhaps I shouldn't feel bad. With all the busy signals and disconnected numbers, it takes Zogby callers nearly 6,000 calls to get 400 complete responses. Only 35 percent of people reached by phone answer pollsters' questions, a number that has declined from 65 percent 15 years ago. Answering machines, caller ID, and telemarketers, poisoning the well have made poll-taking difficult. Even among those reached, it becomes immediately obvious that a large number of our countrymen have only the vaguest notion that there's an election happening.

But such cynicism is not necessarily warranted. Though large numbers of Americans are ill-informed, ill-mannered and ill-prepared to choose a leader, when you add them up, something magical happens. Individuals are transformed into a wise and noble creature: the American electorate. The polls, in their aggregate, invariably show a temperate and thoughtful nation. It would make de Tocqueville smile.

"There's a collective wisdom that emerges," says John Zogby, who started his firm in the 1980s. "When it all adds up there's a clear message. The community is never stupid."

Still, Zogby is the first to acknowledge polling's shortcomings. The polls, particularly daily ones, are just snapshots. "We're not predicting," Zogby says. "You can't read too much into the day-to-day change or try to read causality into it."

But the press tends to look for some fault in the declining candidate to justify a poll drop. The explosion of cable and Internet news outlets, which commission polls and hype the results, exacerbates the problem. "Having it govern the way a campaign gets covered is dangerous," Zogby says. "It becomes a tremendous disservice."

Another caveat: While polls are good at measuring trends, the numbers tend to reflect the pollsters' hunches as much as the respondents' answers. The raw numbers in a poll are meaningless until "weighted" (certain categories of voters are over- or under-emphasized) to mirror the population and to reflect the pollster's guess about who will vote. Most poll watchers don't realize that a Bush lead in raw numbers can become a Gore lead in weighted numbers.

"Twenty percent of this business is art, 80 percent is science," Zogby says. "Ultimately, you have to make a call about who's going to turn out to vote." Pollsters adjust their responses by gender, race, religion, age, region and income. The time of day a call is made, the response rate, how the questions are phrased and ordered, the suggestiveness of the questioner, and how a pollster defines a "likely voter" and "undecided" can all alter the results. Zogby controversially also weighs party identification, which he gauges through a series of questions.

Some other pollsters think Zogby favors Republicans (he says he's a Democrat and works for both sides). But Zogby has a good record among the three major public tracking polls. In 1996, he got Clinton's eight-point victory exactly right. Lately, his tracking poll has had a smoother pattern than the Gallup tracking poll (which recently galloped 18 points in a couple of days) and has been more consistent with larger polls than the Voter.com/Battleground tracking poll.

Zogby's calling center is a collection of 94 cubicles in a decrepit, dank office building abandoned by the phone company. The callers, whose pay starts at $6.25 an hour, are a mixture of students, retirees, immigrants from Eastern Europe and part-timers with day jobs. The place smells of pizza or whatever else is in the break area, which also includes a snack machine that sells Chicken Cordon Bleu. One woman's lapdog naps on the floor of her cubicle as she makes calls.

"Hello, my name is Fanny and I'm doing a poll of U.S. voters for Reuters News Agency and Zogby International," says Fanny George, a retired nurse. She calls numbers that pop up on her screen courtesy of the "computer-aided telephone interview," or CATI system, pronounced "Katie." CATI sends Fanny plenty of duds: no answer, a law office, a couple of refusals. But George, an expert caller with a grandmother's gentle voice, completes interviews at the clip of three per hour. Each one requires her to give voters choices for president that most have never heard of: Harry Browne, John Hagelin, Howard Phillips and David McReynolds.

As night approaches, there are 50 callers in the room, and a round of "Very likely? Somewhat likely? Unlikely" rises from din. The callers struggle with a confounded electorate. Mark Carchedi interviews a woman who can't understand what he means when he asks how likely she is to vote. Later comes the man who agrees to offer his phone number in case a reporter wants to ask about the poll. "Your area code?" Carchedi asks. The respondent doesn't respond. "What's your area code?" Nothing. "Sir, do you have an area code? . . . *Area code! . . . What's your area code?* . . . If somebody's calling you long-distance, what do they dial?" Carchedi finally procures the desired digits.

Callers here have heard it all: Many get obscenities and propositions, one polled Rodney Dangerfield, one respondent believed he was Jesus, another one put her dog on the phone, and one woman asked to describe her status as "married wanting to get divorced."

By 9 p.m., Frank Calaprice, a night supervisor, has begun to keep careful track of the tracking poll. He has met his quota of 93 responses from Zone 1 (Eastern) and must get 11 more in Zone 2 (Midwest) and 13 more in Zone 3 (South) by 10 p.m., when he turns his attentions to Zone 4 (California). He watches the tally on his computer, shifting callers from other Zogby polls as needed. He completes his last call in Zone 3 at 9:58, with two minutes to spare.

"It's very nerve-racking," Calaprice says. At 10 p.m., he begins to work on getting 26 more responses from the West Coast. By 11 p.m., he has 10 to go. He could add callers and finish the whole thing in five minutes, but he's been instructed that this could skew results. "I know there's a logic to everything they. do," he says. "I just don't personally know what it is."

"I'm going in," says Joe Mazloom.

It's midnight, and Mazloom, a wild-haired young man wearing bluejeans and a T-shirt, enters the response database and commands his computer to "export off CATI system." After a brief scare before midnight—several West Coast respondents don't respond because of the baseball playoffs—Calaprice has reached his 400-call quota, and it's time to crunch numbers.

In his office, next to the Cordon Bleu snack machine, Mazloom hits a few buttons and pulls up the day's raw numbers: Bush leads Gore by 44.6 percent to 40.1 percent overall, and 49.1 percent to 42.9 percent in a hypothetical two-way matchup. That gives an unweighted three-day average of 44.2 for Bush and 42.8 for Gore, and a three-day average in the two-way race of 47.3 for Bush and 45.1 for Gore.

Now the fun begins. Mazloom begins to balance the day's sample so it conforms with Zogby's hunches (based on exit polls from previous elections) about which type of people will show up on election days. Republicans, men and Jews are overrepresented in the day's sample, while African Americans and young voters must be doubled. Mazloom whips through spreadsheets, hitting buttons, adjusting regions, typing incomprehensible numbers (1071 0.805, 499 0.483). After several runs, the sample is weighted: slightly more women and Democrats, a quarter Catholic, more than a quarter elderly, and four-fifths white.

The weighted results invert the findings: Now Gore leads in the three-day average, 45.0 to 41.0; in the two-way race, Gore leads 47.5 to 44.5. The inversion, Mazloom says, comes mostly from the weighting for party identification.

Mazloom sends the results to a bleary-eyed Alan Crockett, Zogby's press man, waiting in his office to write the 2 a.m. press release. "The midnights are killing my social life," he says. Crockett slaps on the 3 percent margin of error and fields a call from Zogby, who dictates the day's headline and a quote. "RACE NOW JUST A 4-POINT LEAD," the release says. "Make no mistake about it, this is a very tight race."

By daybreak, political reporters everywhere will be using the results to do just what Zogby warned against: to find a reason why one candidate is doing badly and the other is doing well.

Questions for Discussion

1. What are some of the major problems pollsters face in conducting accurate tracking polls? What kinds of things can be done to better guarantee accuracy?
2. Why is pollster Zogby worried about the misuse of polling results? All things considered, in your view does the availability of tracking polls, such as the one described in this article, have a positive or negative influence on our electoral politics?

 Chapter 5

PARTICIPATION

In a democracy, political participation may take many forms, ranging from efforts by citizens merely to inform themselves about politics to running for and holding public office. Some citizens may even attempt to bypass more conventional modes of participation altogether by engaging in political protest marches or acts of civil disobedience—the nonviolent violation of laws that they believe to be unjust. For most citizens, however, political participation centers around the act of voting in an election.

Participation in free elections provides citizens with many benefits. When people believe they can communicate their needs and wants to those who govern, government becomes both stable and legitimate. Elections teach civic virtues and give citizens a sense of responsibility and personal satisfaction.

The key role of elections, however, is to provide a check on power. As James Madison wrote in *The Federalist,* No. 51, "If Angels were to govern men, neither external nor internal controls on the government would be necessary," but in the absence of heavenly guidance government must be restrained, and "a dependence on the people is, no doubt, the primary control" (see selection 1.5). The ballot box offers the public a way to control those who govern, since people seeking election must further citizens' interests to achieve public office. The public does not rule, but it influences those who do.

Although most Americans probably would be hard-pressed to give a sophisticated answer to the question "Why vote?", most firmly believe that democracy is "rule by the people" and that the cornerstone of popular democracy is free elections. Students are taught that everyone "ought to vote," and voting for the first time is a political rite of passage that serves as a powerful symbol of adulthood and allegiance to the American system. Many Americans hold the view that anyone who doesn't vote has forfeited the right to criticize the government.

In spite of these beliefs and feelings, however, many citizens do not participate in contemporary elections, a fact that could challenge the validity of popular democracy. The United States ranks near the bottom of Western democracies in voter turnout. Furthermore, current turnout rates do not compare favorably with those of past elections. For example, in presidential elections in the last half of the 1800s, about 75 percent of eligible voters turned out (nearly 82 percent in the election of 1876), whereas in recent elections only slightly more than 50 percent voted. Turnout rates in off-year state and local elections are often less than 30 percent. President Reagan, who beat President Carter by an overwhelming margin in 1980, was elected by just a little more than 27 percent of the eligible voters in that year.

Comparisons of our own past with that of other nations are fraught with difficulties. A century ago, the electorate included neither women nor blacks. Ballots were not secret, and there were few registration barriers to restrict participation by white males. This created a strong incentive for political parties to mobilize voters, sometimes by herding citizens to the polls and giving them ballots containing only one party's candidates. The eastern cities in particular were dominated by political machines. Consequently, some of the high turnout figures undoubtedly resulted from political corruption.

Some countries impose a fine for not voting—a policy that would raise turnout rates in the United States but would be interpreted as undemocratic by most Americans. Many Western democracies calculate turnout as the percentage of those on the electoral rolls who actually participate in an election, whereas in the United States turnout is calculated by dividing the number who vote by the total potential electorate—all persons of voting age, as determined by the U.S. Bureau of the Census. If this method were applied by other countries, U.S. voting rates would differ little from those of Canada, Great Britain, and Japan.

Surprisingly, voter turnout in the United States has constantly declined since the 1960 presidential election. This period has been marked by rising educational levels, increasingly prominent issues, and the removal of many voting barriers, such as poll taxes and registration and residency requirements. In addition, tremendous amounts of political information have been provided by the mass media, and campaigns have grown enormously in terms of cost and candidate exposure. Newspapers often chastise citizens for being lazy and uninterested in exercising their right to vote, but explanations for the turnout decline are much more complex.

One widely held belief is that, beginning in the mid-1960s, citizens developed mistrust of government officials and a diminished sense that their participation would make a difference. In 1966, about a quarter of the public believed the "people running the country don't care what happens to people like me." By 1977, 60 percent felt this way. By 1978, only 30 percent of Americans believed they could trust the government in Washington "to do what's right." In 1958, a similar poll revealed that 55 percent trusted the government.

Such disillusionment grew from the social disruptions of the 1960s, the assassinations of John F. Kennedy, Robert Kennedy, and Martin Luther King, Jr., the unpopular Vietnam War, the Watergate scandal, and the subsequent resignation of President Nixon. Huge increases in consumer prices in the 1970s and the perceived ineffectiveness of the Carter administration in dealing with the energy crisis and with the Iranian hostage situation also contributed to citizens' perception that leaders were neither trustworthy nor competent. Some scholars suggest that television played a role, too. According to the theory of "video malaise," TV tends to overwhelm viewers with the complexities of political controversies, which convinces the public that individuals are politically ineffective and that problems may be too difficult to solve. Further, the tone of the TV medium has been generally critical of authorities, highlighting the human weaknesses and mistakes of political leaders. Many voters thus question the worthwhileness of political participation.

A second widely accepted explanation for decreasing turnout relies on demographic factors. The arrival of the baby boomers at voting age during the mid-1960s, and constitutional changes that enfranchised eighteen- to twenty-year-olds, dramatically expanded the potential electorate between 1960 and 1972. Young voters made up an increasingly high proportion of the total electorate in the 1960s, 1970s, and early 1980s, yet this group participated less than older Americans did. Few saw politics as relevant to their lives. First-time eligible voters have had the lowest participation rates of any age group, perhaps because politics has to compete with schooling, social events, and courtship.

In the first selection, Micah Sifry challenges the notion that apathy is largely responsible for low voter turnout. He argues that party candidates with a populist or progressive message have the potential to greatly enlarge the active electorate. The second selection deals with the role of the citizen in contemporary politics. Michael Schudson argues that our current concept of citizenship, based on the Progressive model, needs revision. He asserts that we need a new concept of citizenship, one that makes demands on us but is not burdened with impossible expectations. The final selection, by Robert Putnam, posits a linkage between the broad involvement of citizens in the associational life of their community and the health of American democracy. Putnam is dismayed by the decline of "social capital" that seems to characterize American politics over the past quarter of a century.

Finding the Lost Voters

Micah L. Sifry

Few subjects engender more heated discussion during and after an election than the nation's low voter-turnout rate. For those who believe that citizen participation in elections is fundamental to American democracy, the 2000 presidential election was especially frustrating. Although voter registration barriers had been virtually eliminated and party and candidate expenditures set records in an effort to reach voters in one of the closest presidential contests in recent memory, barely half of the age-eligible voters went to the polls.

In this selection, Micah Sifry suggests that growing alienation from the major parties lies at the heart of why many people choose not to participate in elections. Besides the rise in the number of registered independents, who tend to vote less than partisans, poll data indicates that roughly a third of nonvoters aren't apathetic about voting, but are unhappy with the choices typically offered by Republicans and Democrats. Sifry believes the best way to enlarge the active electoral would be for parties to choose candidates committed to running progressive and populist campaigns, appealing to "potential voters" rather than solely concentrating on turning out "likely voters."

Al Garcia is one frustrated Democratic campaign manager. A criminal defense lawyer by trade and a 20-year veteran of Minnesota politics, he ran two candidates for the state assembly in 1998. Both were in Anoka County, ground zero of the Jesse Ventura vote.* One candidate, Jerry Newton, a decorated Vietnam veteran and small-business owner, fiscally conservative but very supportive of public schools and the environment, lost badly to a far-right pro-lifer as the voters who turned out for Ventura voted for Republican state representatives down the ballot. Garcia's other candidate, Luanne Koskinen, an incumbent with strong labor backing, barely held onto her office. Garcia's problems were hardly unique: Ventura voters across the state ended up costing Democrats control of the state assembly.

Micah Sifry is a senior analyst for Public Campaign, a public-interest group focusing upon campaign finance.

* Jesse Ventura, a former professional wrestler, was elected in 1998 as governor of Minnesota running on the Reform Party ticket.

Over lunch last winter at Billie's, a popular Anoka County restaurant, Garcia delivered his postmortem: Democrats had gotten whipped because they hadn't reached out to new voters—and there had been a lot of them. . . .

And why had his candidates fared so poorly? "We were too focused on the regular voters," Garcia said. "If you hadn't voted in two out of the last four elections, you didn't get anything from Luanne or Jerry." Targeting likely voters, of course, is standard practice in most campaigns these days. But Garcia said he'd known that strategy wouldn't be enough.

"I could sense it coming," he said. "My wife told me early on that she would support Ventura, and she hates politics. All my legal clients were supporting Jesse, from the first-time DWI offenders to the major dope dealers! And he was pulling at me, in my gut. I'm a blue-collar guy who grew up in north Minneapolis. My dad's a dockworker, my mother's a waitress. Like the folks in Anoka. And he was saying things that average people could connect with."

Garcia said he'd wanted his candidates to do the same thing. "The number-one issues in Anoka are taxes, wages, and traffic. That's what we wanted to focus on." But he'd been hamstrung by a centralized campaign effort run out of the House Democratic Caucus. "They had a $15,000 mail program—half of our budget— that we were forced to buy into or lose our field worker and party funds. Six out of the nine pieces they mailed were on education, even though we said that wasn't our top concern. And they mailed to too small a target group, and they wouldn't let us change it."

Campaigns at all levels of American politics these days are focused narrowly on "likely voters," people who vote regularly. Eric Johnson, campaign manager to Hubert "Skip" Humphrey, the losing Democratic candidate for governor, admitted as much after the election. "We didn't see Ventura coming because our polling screened out unlikely voters," he told *The Wall Street Journal*. All four of Minnesota's major polling organizations also failed to predict Ventura's victory because they factored out these voters.

The assumption governing the typical political campaign is that the American electorate is a stable, predictable mass—or, worse, that they're apathetic and easily manipulated. Ventura's victory is just the latest and loudest explosion of that piece of conventional wisdom.

Indeed, politicians are making a huge mistake when they focus only on "likely voters." A large subset of the "unlikely voters" filtered out by pollsters and left out of campaign targeting efforts might be better described as *discouraged* voters— potential participants who have been turned off or pushed out by an increasingly money-driven and manipulative electoral process.

Many of these citizens, people who are disproportionately downscale and correspondingly attracted to working-class issues and symbols, can be remotivated to turn out. A central question is whether more Democrats will take their campaigns to these voters or, by failing to do so, will continue to create opportunities for outsiders ranging from Jesse Ventura to Bernie Sanders to Patrick Buchanan.

Apathy or Independence?

Public trust in government has been declining steadily over the past four decades. The authoritative surveys conducted biennially since the 1950s by the University of Michigan's National Election Studies (NES) have found that large majorities of Americans, across all demographic groups, don't believe "you can trust the government in Washington to do what is right just about always [or] most of the time." Similarly, most people think "the government is pretty much run by a few big interests looking out for themselves." According to the NES, the percentage agreeing that "people like me don't have any say about what the government does" rose from 31 percent in 1952 to 53 percent in 1996. This is a strong statement of disaffection.

But some Americans still feel better represented than others. People are more likely to believe that they "don't have any say" if they are black rather than white, are poor rather than well-off, have a limited education compared to a college diploma or postgraduate degree, or work in blue-collar jobs rather than white-collar or professional fields. For example, 62 percent of people with a high school diploma said they don't have any say in what government does, compared to 40 percent of those with more education. And about 56 percent of those in the bottom two-thirds of the national income distribution felt left out, compared to 38 percent in the top twentieth.

A similar pattern applies to how Americans think about the major political parties. In general, polls find that between 50 and 60 percent of the population believes there are "important differences in what the Republicans and Democrats stand for." But in 1996, while most people in the top income brackets believed that there were significant differences between the parties, 50 percent of people in the bottom sixth of income distribution thought there was no difference. Similarly, 59 percent of those with less than a high school education and 40 percent of those with a high school diploma said there was no difference between the parties, compared to just 25 percent of those with at least some college education. Overall, blue-collar workers were almost twice as likely as professionals to believe party distinctions were meaningless.

Among active voters, the trend is away from the major parties and toward independence. From 1990 to 1998, while the number of voters registered as independent or third-party increased approximately 57 percent, the number of registered Republicans dropped by almost 5 percent and the number of Democrats by almost 14 percent, according to data collected from state agencies by the Committee for the Study of the American Electorate. Voters' political preferences—a looser definition than party registration—showed the same trend. The proportion of people identifying themselves as independents increased from 23 percent in 1952 to an average of 35 percent in the 1990s, according to the NES. Independent voters are somewhat more likely to be of lower income, education, age, and occupational status than hard-core party partisans (though this variation is tempered by the strong Democratic loyalties of many blacks). And 41 percent of people under the age of 29 self-identify as independents, according to a 1999 Gallup poll.

Independents are the most volatile of active voters, with a marked tendency to support candidates who come from "outside the box." All the exit polls going back to George Wallace's 1968 presidential candidacy show that voters who identify themselves as independents are about twice as likely as other voters to support third-party candidates. In Minnesota in 1998, Ventura won with 37 percent overall, but got 52 percent of independents.

As the National Voter Registration Act of 1993 (known as the motor-voter law) brings more voters onto the registration rolls, this trend toward electoral volatility seems likely to strengthen. In Florida, the numbers of registered Republicans, Democrats, and nonaffiliates/third-party registrants each rose by about 500,000 in the first two years of the law's implementation. Since 1996, however, the number of major party registrants has declined slightly, while the number of non-major party registrants has risen another 250,000. The same thing has happened in California, where the number of major party registrants has held steady since 1996, while the number of non-major party registrants has risen about 300,000.

Of course, rising voter alienation and disaffection from the two major parties does not prove that a different kind of political engagement is possible. After all, as measures of political alienation have risen, turnout in national and state elections has declined. But are citizens really just signaling their apathy when they fail to vote? Or are they more specifically alienated from the Democratic and Republican establishments and their candidates? In fact, a significant number of nonvoters look a lot like politically active independent voters.

It is difficult to find data that distinguishes those abstainers who are principled or angry and those who are merely indifferent, but it does exist. In May of 1996, the League of Women Voters released a poll that showed nonvoters were no more distrustful of the federal government than regular voters. Active voters were, however, far more likely to see significant differences between the parties on major issues, to believe that elections mattered and that their votes made a difference. The poll also suggested that efforts to mobilize voters were highly important: About three-quarters of voters said they had been contacted by a candidate or party, compared with less than half of the nonvoters.

But this says little about the actual political preferences of nonvoters. More answers can be found in two little-noticed surveys, one conducted in the summer of 1983 by ABC News, and the second done after the election of 1996 by Republican pollster Kellyanne Fitzpatrick. ABC News polled more than 2,500 voting-age Americans and then compared highly likely voters (people who were registered to vote who said they always vote) with very unlikely voters (people who were not registered to vote and gave little inclination that they were planning to vote in the next election). The Fitzpatrick poll compared a sample of 800 voters with one of 400 nonvoters. Together, the two surveys reveal some telling points.

First, about a third of nonvoters aren't apathetic. Rather, they're angry and feel shut out by the choices offered. When asked by ABC why they didn't vote in the 1980 presidential election, 36 percent of the nonvoters gave a political reason such as "None of the candidates appealed to me." Thirty-eight percent of the nonvoters in the Fitzpatrick poll didn't vote in 1996 because they "did not care for any of the candidates" or were "fed up with the political system" or "did not feel like candidates were interested in people like me."

Second, nonvoters tilt toward liberalism. In the ABC News poll, 60 percent of the nonvoters who said they had voted in 1980 recalled choosing either Jimmy Carter or John Anderson;* only 30 percent said they had voted for Ronald Reagan. Considering that after an election, voters tend to "recall" voting for the winner, this is a striking finding. Sixty-seven percent of nonvoters said they had voted for the Democratic candidate for the House of Representatives, compared to 52 percent of regular voters. In the Fitzpatrick poll, just 38 percent of nonvoters identified as conservatives, compared to 48 percent of the voting public. And while 17 percent of voters called themselves liberals, 22 percent of nonvoters chose that label. (A *New York Times*/CBS News poll found that those who were not planning to vote in the 1998 election preferred Democrats for Congress by 49 percent to 27 percent; likely voters, on the other hand, were evenly split between Republicans and Democrats.)

How To Reach Discouraged Voters

"Low turnout is the compound consequence of legal and procedural barriers intertwined with the parties' reluctance to mobilize many voters, especially working-class and minority voters," says Frances Fox Piven, who along with her husband Richard Cloward wrote *Why Americans Don't Vote* and built the movement that passed the motor-voter law. "I've come to the conclusion that party competition takes the form of demobilizing, not mobilizing, voters, because new voters threaten incumbents, raise new issues, or create the incentive to raise new issues," she adds. "You need mavericks, outsiders to try to mobilize new voters— nobody else wants to take the risk."

"Nonvoters matter a lot," agrees pollster Stanley Greenberg, "though most candidates act as if they don't. . . . There's no question that you can change the shape and size of the electorate, though that is more true for presidential elections than for individual, even statewide, campaigns." For example, turnout increased by 5.5 percent in the three-way presidential race of 1992. "There's reason to believe that the populist economic issues that Clinton was raising and the independent-libertarian issues that Perot was raising were at work there," Green-

---

* John Anderson, a Republican congressman who failed to receive his party's nomination for president, ran in the 1980 general election as an Independent. He received 6.7 percent of the votes cast.

berg argues. "By comparison, in 1994, conservative definitions of the issues brought in more rural, conservative portions of the electorate while the health care reform failure led many noncollege women to drop out." Pollster John Zogby agrees: "If there's a strong independent candidate in the race, you begin to see the numbers of undecided voters in those groups who often don't vote—younger voters, registered independents—start to decline in our surveys, a sign they are planning to vote."

Representative Jesse Jackson, Jr., points to his father's 1984 and 1988 campaigns as proof that discouraged voters can be effectively mobilized. Indeed, the number of Democratic primary voters rose from 18 million in 1984 to nearly 23 million in 1988, with Reverend Jackson's total share rising by 3.4 million. "If you're able to tap into the people who aren't consciously involved in politics or following it," the younger Jackson says, "and show how everything they do has something to do with politics—that shirt they wear, the stop sign, the taxes they pay, the schools they attend, the police officer on their street . . . you can inspire them and give them reason to participate."

It takes a certain kind of candidate, message, and campaign to reach these voters. "You're not going to be able to cater to traditional economic forces that have significant influence," says Jackson. "You have to have some relationship to them, but you can't be seen as beholden to them. You have to be seen as a real American; you have to be someone who can look the press right in the face and tell them exactly how it is. You have to be Beattyite, almost Bulworthian."

Not many American politicians are trying to run this kind of campaign or can convincingly pull it off. However, there are a number of successful examples that predate Jesse Ventura. What seems to matter most is that the candidate have a populist message and style—someone who wants to empower ordinary people versus the establishment, who is blue collar as opposed to buttoned-down, who favors effective government on behalf of the interests of average working people, and who supports sweeping efforts to clean up politics and reform the electoral process itself.

Those were Paul Wellstone's attributes in 1990, when he came from nowhere—he had been a college professor and progressive activist—to win the Minnesota Senate race. Not only did Wellstone draw more votes than the Democratic candidate in the previous Senate contest; more voters came out in 1990 than did in 1988, a presidential election year. (According to Francis Fox Piven, Wellstone attributed his victory in part to the increased number of poorer voters on the rolls, thanks to the earlier passage of a state-level, agency-based voter registration system.) Something similar happened in 1998 with Iowan Tom Vilsack, who waged a successful underdog run for governor and raised the Democratic vote total nearly 20 percent over the previous gubernatorial race. And activists in Washington State argue that their 1998 ballot initiative to raise the state minimum wage to the highest level in the country had a similar effect—drawing more votes than any other item or candidate on the ballot and bringing in enough new voters to swing control of both houses of the state legislature back to the Democratic column.

In 1990, Bernie Sanders, the former socialist mayor of Burlington, won Vermont's lone seat in Congress as an independent. He ran on issues like national health care, tax fairness, environmental activism, addressing the needs of the poor, and involving working people in the political process. In his first try for Congress in 1988, he came close, drawing 37.5 percent of the vote. Two years later, he won a solid victory with 56 percent of the vote. In both races, the total vote was way up—13 percent higher—compared to the previous election cycle.

And while Sanders did well in his breakthrough victory in 1990 with the college-educated, alternative life-style types who have moved up to Vermont in the past generation, his strongest support actually came from the poor conservative hill towns and farm communities of the state's "Northeast Kingdom." For example, Sanders's strongest showing statewide came in the county of Orleans, where he pulled 62 percent of the vote. A rural county on the border of Canada that voted solidly for George Bush in 1988, Orleans had a median household income in 1990 of $22,800, about $7,000 less than the state average. Only 14.2 percent of Orleans's residents were college graduates. The standard of living was low, with homes worth on average just $66,500, compared to $95,600 statewide. Nearly 15 percent of Orleans's residents were living under the official poverty line, 4 percent more than in the rest of the state.

And then there is Jesse Ventura, a socially liberal, fiscally conservative, pro-campaign finance reform, anti-establishment candidate with a working-class style, who hit discouraged voters—as well as disaffected Democrats and Republicans—on the bull's-eye. His campaign deliberately targeted "unlikely voters" by focusing his public appearances in an "Independent Belt" of bedroom communities to the north and west of Minnesota's Twin Cities, and by placing his offbeat TV ads not on the nightly news shows but on FOX programs like *The Simpsons* and *The X-Files*, and on cable TV wrestling programs. Helped by same-day voter registration, his candidacy drastically boosted turnout, and most of those new voters pulled his lever. He won a near-majority of 18- to 44-year-olds, the heart of political independents.

In several other ways, Ventura's vote corresponded with those groups least satisfied with the existing political choices. Far more self-identified liberals than conservatives voted for him. Women voted for him almost as much as men. In the high-income professional suburbs, Ventura did poorly. In the less affluent suburbs, he did very well. Turnout in many of these blue-collar districts was over 70 percent, with as many as 20 percent of the total registering on Election Day. Many rank-and-file union members swung to Ventura as well. "I could tell going into the election," said Doug Williams, head of an electrical workers' union. "I was getting requests for information on him from my members. People were wearing his T-shirts and bumper stickers—people who hadn't really participated before."

People think Ventura won because he was a celebrity. But his early name recognition in Minnesota, while high for a third-party candidate, only gave him a chance to get the voters' attention. It's what he said and how he said it that made him a contender. "The voters saw Jesse as someone who's an outsider who's going to change things," says Ed Gross, who worked on voter targeting for the Ventura campaign. "Watching the TV debates, they saw two 'suits' and one 'nonsuit'—and most of them don't wear suits. Not only that, one of the 'suits' had worked for the other, and they both were owned by big money."

Gross recognized the dynamic from the 1990 and 1996 Wellstone campaigns for Senate, on which he had also worked. "I told Ventura, in a lot of ways, to the voters, you are a Wellstone. And voters went for Wellstone because they want to have a connection. They've felt disconnected for a long time. They want to feel like the guy up there knows how they live." In the end, they latched onto Ventura with enthusiasm. And the strength of his campaign—which succeeded in a state with one of the lowest unemployment rates in the country—stands as a warning to both of the major parties: This could happen to you.

Raising Turnout, Reviving Politics

As the barriers to voter registration have fallen with the gradual implementation of motor-voter, the pool of potential voters has grown. According to the Federal Election Commission, the total number of registered voters rose from 129 million in 1994 to 151 million in 1998, an increase of 8 percent of the total voting-age population. But politicians haven't caught on. "Candidates aren't yet campaigning to those voters," says Linda Davidoff, the former executive director of Human SERVE, the nonprofit organization set up by Piven and Cloward to spearhead the motor-voter drive. "[But] motor-voter is laying the groundwork for poorer people to participate differently. There's an enormous opportunity here for candidates who get the picture and campaign to the potential voter," she says.

Jesse Jackson, Jr., is one politician who understands very well the new potential of reaching out to discouraged voters. One of the keys to his first race, in which he beat a veteran Democratic legislator backed by the Daley political machine in a special election to fill Mel Reynolds's seat, was his energetic campaign to register young voters. "He set up voter registration tables during local college registration," says Frank Watkins, his press secretary, "and we kept a record of those people and sent them a personal letter just before the election." Jackson registered about 6,500 new voters—5,000 of whom lived in his district. It's likely that many of them made up his winning margin of 6,000 votes.

Despite Jackson's evident success and personal energy (even though he's in a safe district, he's continued to work to turn out more voters, winning more votes than almost any other member of Congress), there's been little interest from the Democratic Party establishment in helping him spread his message of increasing political participation. "We went to the DNC and showed them how we did it,"

Watkins says, "and they sat there and looked at us like we were crazy. They'd rather focus on raising more and more money to spend on advertising to fewer and fewer people."

Obviously, going after the discouraged voters involves taking some risks, and it may be especially hard to do so in states that close their registration rolls weeks before Election Day. And there is a deeper challenge: convincing these citizens that voting really can matter again. Noting that outward expressions of populist anger seem to have declined in recent years, pollster John Zogby points to despair about politics as the explanation. "In one of my focus groups, a guy in Cleveland said, 'I'm now in the third of a series of lousy jobs. I lost my good job in '85. I was angry before. But now it's not going to happen. Government can't do anything. And my vote doesn't matter at all.' He had downsized his expectations," Zogby concludes. Piven agrees: "The sense that politics is so corrupt, combined with neoliberal rhetoric that argues that government can't do anything, tends to demobilize people."

The ultimate challenge then for anyone seeking to connect with discouraged voters is to restore their hope while not denying that they have good reason to be cynical. What is fascinating and exciting about each of the handful of populist victories of the last decade—by Jackson, Sanders, Wellstone, and Ventura—is that in every case, their success raised expectations about politics across the country. Hope, it seems, can be contagious; we need to keep it alive.

Questions for Discussion

1. Why does Micah Sifry believe so few people choose to vote in American elections, despite massive campaign efforts by competing candidates? What other factors do you believe play a role in the nation's poor record for voter turnout?

2. Sifry argues that voter turnout would increase if party candidates ran progressive and populist campaigns. Is it likely that parties in the future will take his advice? Do you have any additional suggestions that might help to increase voter participation?

5.2

Voting Rites: Why We Need a New Concept of Citizenship

Michael Schudson

In the face of voting turnout far less than that found in other countries or even in our own country's early history, a common response of political observers such as the mass media is to chastise the electorate for its failure to exercise the most basic of all citizen responsibilities. According to the common wisdom, well supported by public opinion surveys, many American voters are uninformed, disengaged from politics, and participate at a level that, in the eyes of many, is an embarrassment to a country that prides itself on "rule by the people."

In this provocative essay, Michael Schudson suggests that the lack of electoral participation "may not be individual failure so much as our contemporary conception of how democratic citizenship ought to work." He finds that the Progressive ideal of citizenship, with its expectations that each citizen possess a high level of political information and pay constant attention to public affairs, sets an unrealistic standard in the contemporary political world.

In Schudson's view, citizens flourish in an environment that encourages worthwhile citizenship activities in the broadest sense, and we should be intent on creating such an environment, not on turning every voter into an expert.

I f recent trends hold up, only about one of every three eligible voters will show up at the polls this fall. Inevitably, many will conclude that Americans have once again failed as citizens. The problem, however, may not be individual failure so much as our contemporary conception of how democratic citizenship ought to work. Nothing puts that conception into clearer perspective than changes in the act of voting over the past 200 years.

Imagine yourself a voter in the world of colonial Virginia where George Washington, Patrick Henry, and Thomas Jefferson learned their politics. As a matter of law, you must be a white male owning at least a modest amount of property. Your journey to vote may take several hours since there is probably only one polling place in the county. As you approach the courthouse, you see the

Michael Schudson is professor of communication and sociology at the University of California, San Diego.

sheriff supervising the election. Two candidates for office stand before you, both of them members of prominent local families. You watch the most prominent members of the community, the leading landowner and clergyman, cast their votes, and you know whom they have supported because they announce their votes in loud, clear voices. You do the same and then step over to the candidate for whom you have voted, and he treats you to a glass of rum punch. Your vote has been an act of restating and reaffirming the social hierarchy of a community where no one but a local notable would think of standing for office.

Now imagine you are in eighteenth century Massachusetts rather than Virginia. The model of voting is different, as you elect town selectmen and representatives at a town meeting. But, like Virginia, the New England model reflects an organic view that the polity has a single common good and that the leaders of locally prominent, wealthy, and well established families can be trusted to represent it. Dissent and conflict are no more acceptable in New England than in Virginia.

Move the clock ahead to the nineteenth century, as mass political parties cultivate a new democratic order. Now there is much more bustle around the polling place. The area is crowded with the banners and torches of rival parties. Election day is not set off from other days but is the culmination of a campaign of several months. You must still be a white male but not necessarily of property. During the campaign, you have marched in torchlight processions in military uniform with a club of like-minded men from your party. They may accompany you to the polls. If you were not active in the campaign, you may be roused on election day by a party worker to escort you on foot or by carriage. On the road, you may encounter clubs or groups from rival parties, and it would not be unusual if fisticuffs or even guns were to dissuade you from casting a ballot after all.

If you do proceed to the ballot box, you may step more lively with the encouragement of a dollar or two from the party—less a bribe than an acknowledgment that voting is a service to your party. A party worker hands you a colored ballot with the printed names of the party's candidates. You may also receive a slightly smaller ballot with the same names on it that can be surreptitiously placed inside the other so that you can cast two ballots rather than one. You are willing to do so not out of a strong sense that your party offers better public policies but because your party is your party, just as, in our own day, your high school is your high school. In any event, parties tend to be more devoted to distributing offices than to advocating policies.

Now turn to the early twentieth century as Progressive era reforms cleanse voting of what made it both compelling and, by our standards, corrupt. Reformers find the emphasis in campaigns on spectacle rather than substance much too emotional. They pioneer what they term an "educational campaign" that stresses the distribution of pamphlets on the issues rather than parades of solidarity. They pass legislation to ensure a secret ballot. They enact voter registration statutes. They help create an atmosphere in which it becomes more common for traditionally loyal party newspapers to "bolt" from party-endorsed candidates. They insist on official state ballots rather than party ballots and in some states develop state-approved voter information booklets rather than leaving education up to the parties themselves. At the same time, civil service reform limits the rewards parties can distribute to loyal partisans.

The world we experience today at the polls has been handed down to us from these reforms. What does voting look like and feel like today?

I asked my students at the University of California, San Diego to write about their experience of voting in 1992. Many of them had never voted before; hardly any had voted in a presidential election. It is something they looked forward to doing, especially those who supported Clinton. Still, some students felt a letdown in the act of voting:

> As I punched in the holes on my voting card, a slight sense of disappointment clouded my otherwise cheerful mood. First of all, the building behind Revelle Bargain Books was not what I had always imagined as a polling place. How could a location this close to the all-you-can-eat cafeteria be the site of a vote to choose the leader of our nation? Second, I could not understand why there were no curtains around my booth. As a child I can always remember crawling under curtains in voting booths to spy on my parents. Why couldn't I have those curtains to hide all of my important, private decisions?

Or listen to this student, a Filipino-American who voted for Bush:

> The more I tried to be aware of the political goings-on, through television mainly, the more I became aggravated with the whole situation. Perot represented the evil of a one-man monopoly, while Clinton was a man who knew how to manipulate an audience and use the media. In addition, Hillary reminded me of the stories and comments my parents made about Imelda Marcos. Taxes came to mind every time I considered Bush, but I decided he might be the best qualified candidate.
>
> My Dad was an influential part of my decision to go; not because he urged me to do so, but so that after the election I would finally be able to tell him that I voted.
>
> Needless to say, no one at the polling site seemed to talk politics, at least not when I was there. The silence did not bother me, though, since I am definitely not confident enough to talk politics to anyone outside of my family!

Or this immigrant Russian:

> My Mom went to vote with me that day (at the polling place in a neighbor's garage). The night before, I had marked my mother's sample ballot with circles around "yes" and "no" on particular propositions and checked the boxes next to "Feinstein" and "Boxer" so she would not forget. The sample ballot is very convenient. The propositions are especially grueling to read. They disguise themselves in legal/state jargon and refuse to give way to meaning.
>
> I felt distantly connected to other voters in other garages who would be making the same vote for change as I would. Nevertheless, I went through my ballot, standing in that cardboard cubicle, in a very ordinary way, feeling that I was, most likely, insignificant and that my views would find no representation. I remember guessing on some local offices, like county supervisor, and trying not to pick a "Christian right" candidate.

The individuality and jealously guarded privacy of voting today contrasts dramatically with the *viva voce* process of eighteenth century Virginia or the colorful party ticket voting of the nineteenth century. So do the indecision and uncertainty. The students felt inadequate to the election—and why not? The list of propositions and complex voter information pamphlets in California were overwhelming. My voter information pamphlet for the June 1994 primary ran forty-eight pages—and that was just for city and county offices and referenda. For state offices and ballot measures, a separate publication ran sixty-four pages. The obscurity of many candidates and issues encouraged mass pre-election mailings of leaflet slates of candidates produced by profit-making organizations with no connection to political parties. I received, for instance, "Voter Information Guide for Democrats" and "Crime Fighters '94" produced by "Democratic Choice '94." The weary voter had to read the fine print to learn that neither slate was endorsed by the Democratic party.

Whatever else we learn from elections, we are tutored in a sense of helplessness and fundamental inadequacy to the task of citizenship. We are told to be informed but discover that the information required to cast an informed vote is beyond our capacities. We are reminded that the United States has the lowest voter turnout of any democracy but rarely told that we have more elections for more levels of government with more elective offices at each level than any other country in the world. . . .

The Burden of Progressivism

We need a new concept of citizenship, one that asks something from us but is not burdened with the impossible expectations of the Progressive model. Contrast what we implicitly expect of ourselves today and what Thomas Jefferson hoped for citizens 200 years ago. In the preamble of Bill 79 to establish universal elementary instruction in Virginia, Jefferson observed that the people normally elect men of standing in the community. The community needs especially to educate these leaders. As for the citizenry at large, Jefferson sought to inculcate through the study of history knowledge that "they may be enabled to know ambition under all its shapes, and prompt to exert their natural powers to defeat its purposes." That was the whole of the citizen's job—watchfulness to defeat ambition.

Citizens were decidedly not to undertake their own evaluation of issues before the legislature. That was the job of representatives. The Founding Fathers assumed that voters would and should choose representatives on the basis of character, not issues. Representatives would have enough in common with the people they represented to keep their "interests" in mind. For the Founding Fathers, elected representatives—not parties, not interest groups, not newspapers, not citizens in the streets—were to make policy.

We have come to ask more of citizens. Today's dominant views about citizenship come from the Progressives' rationalist and ardently individualist worldview. The Progressive impulse was educational—to bring science to politics and professional management to cities, to substitute pamphlets for parades and parlors for streets. The practice of citizenship, at least in campaigning and voting, became privatized, more effortful, more cognitive, and a lot less fun.

In the eighteenth and nineteenth centuries, there was no concern about the people who did not vote. Political science and public discourse began to worry about nonvoters only after World War I when voting rates had declined to a low not reached again until the 1970s. . . .

The Progressive ideal requires citizens to possess a huge fund of political information and a ceaseless attentiveness to public issues. This could never be. Even at the Constitutional convention of 1787 a delegate observed that people grew "listless" with frequent elections. Fifty years later Tocqueville lamented, "Even when one has won the confidence of a democratic nation, it is a hard matter to attract its attention." . . .

. . . Perhaps television or party decline exacerbates it. But public inattention has been a fact of political life, with only momentary escapes, through our history. If this is so, what is a reasonable expectation for citizens, a reasonable standard of citizen competence?

A Practical Citizenship

Under democratic government, as the Founding Fathers constituted it, the representatives of the people could carry on the business of governing without individual citizens becoming experts on the questions of policy placed before the Congress. . . .

Citizens are not to be created one by one, pouring into each of them enough newspapers, information, or virtuous resolve for them to judge each issue and each candidate rationally. That is where the Progressive vision went wrong. Citizens flourish in an environment that supports worthwhile citizenship activities. We should be intent on creating such an environment, not on turning every voter into an expert.

If, like the Progressives, we take citizenship to be a function of the individual, we are bound to be discouraged. A classical model of citizenship asks that people seek the good of the general, the public. But this is either utopian—people just do not pay that kind of attention—or else undesirable because it honors public life to the exclusion of work-a-day labor or inner spiritual pursuits. A more Lockean, modern, realistic version is that citizens should be moved in public life by self-interest and so should acquire a fair understanding of their own interests and which public policies best serve them. But people's knowledge of public affairs fails even by this standard. Even self-interest in politics is a surprisingly weak reed since the gratifications of private life—getting home on time rather than stopping at the polls to vote, spending seven or eight dollars for a movie rather than for a campaign contribution—are more visible and immediate than the marginal contribution one might make to determining policy by voting, signing a petition, or writing a letter.

How low can we go? We can seek to build a political system where individuals will perform the right actions for their own or the public's interest without knowing much at all. People will do the right thing in general ignorance. User-friendly technology works this way; almost anyone can drive a car while knowing scarcely anything about what makes it run.

In *The Reasoning Voter*, Samuel Popkin suggests we are pretty close to this user-friendly politics already. Relatively little of what voters know, Popkin argues, comes to them as abstract political intelligence. They make intelligent voting decisions based only in small measure on their attending to campaign issues. People have little of the propositional knowledge that models of citizenship demand, but they have more background knowledge than they may realize. They know about economic issues because they have savings accounts, home mortgages, or mutual funds. They have views about health care reform because they know someone personally who has been denied health insurance because of a pre-existing condition. They have enough "by-product information" from daily life to make the broad, either-or choice of a presidential candidate in ways consistent with their own interests and views. . . .

In elections for school boards and other local contests, however, where public information about candidates is more limited and there are often no party labels (again, thanks to Progressive reforms), voters may find themselves in the polling booth without a clue about whom to support. . . .

The Citizens' Trustees

Citizens have to find trustees for their citizenship. Identifying adequate trustees and holding them responsible, I submit, is where we should focus attention. There are three main sets of trustees: politicians, lobbyists, and journalists. Elected officials are our primary trustees. Their obligation is to act with the public in view. They act not so much in response to deliberative public opinion—which rarely exists—but in anticipation of future reward or punishment at the polls. The politicians may not always perceive public opinion accurately. They may not judge well just how much they can lead and shape and how much they must follow and bow to public sentiment. But the motivational structure of elective office demands that they must always be sensitive on this point.

Lobbyists are a second set of trustees. If you believe in the individual's right to bear arms unrestrained by federal legislation, send your annual dues to the National Rifle Association. If you believe that the environment needs aggressive protection, send your dues to an environmental action group. If you do not know what you believe—and this is the common condition for most people on most issues before the nation—you will do better at expressing your will if you at least know that you tend to favor one party over another. Partisanship is a still useful cue. . . .

Two mechanisms keep politician-trustees responsible. The first is the election, fallible as it is. If the representative does not satisfy the citizens, they have a regularly scheduled opportunity to throw the bum out. The second constraint on the politician is the party system. Of course, the party is a more effective discipline on wayward politicians in strong parliamentary systems than in the United States. Here parties are relatively weak, and entrepreneurial politicians relatively independent of them. Still, a politician's party affiliation is a check on his or her policy views and a useful piece of information for voters.

The demands citizens make on lobbyists are much narrower than those placed on politicians—lobbyists are expected to be advocates rather than judges, suppliers of information and resources to sympathetic politicians rather than builders of politically viable solutions to public problems. They are the instructed agents of their organizations rather than Burkean independent-minded representatives. As individuals, they are easy to hold responsible. The question of responsibility with lobbyists is how to hold the whole system responsible since the balance of lobbying power tilts heavily toward the richest and most powerful groups in society. If the system works, it facilitates expression for intensely felt interests from the far corners of the country; if it works badly, it twists and clogs up the primary system of political representation.

The usual answer is to seek to limit the influence of lobbies through campaign finance reform and other restrictions on lobbying activities. An alternative approach seeks to grant lobbyists more authority rather than less influence. Instead of closing down access where the rich and powerful have the resources to guarantee their over-representation, can entree be opened in settings where a broad array of interest groups are assured a voice? In decision making in some federal administrative agencies, interest groups have been granted quasi-public standing. The Negotiated Rulemaking Act of 1990 enables agencies like the Environmental Protection Agency and the Occupational Safety and Health Administration to create committees of private organizations to write regulatory rules.

For instance, EPA arranged for the Sierra Club and the Natural Resources Defense Council to sit down with the American Petroleum Institute and the National Petroleum Refiners Association to work out rules to carry out the Clean Air Act. Millions of Americans belong to organizations that employ paid lobbyists; the lobbies are not about to disappear nor should they. But controlling them may be a delicate balance of restraining some kinds of influence while orchestrating other public opportunities for special interests to take on responsibility for governing.

The third set of trustees—the media—is the most difficult to hold accountable. The market mechanism does not serve well here. People buy a newspaper or watch a television network for many purposes besides gathering political information. The quality or quantity of political intelligence does not correlate well with the rise and fall of newspaper circulations or television news ratings.

There are, as the French press critic Claude-Jean Bertrand suggests, a variety of "media accountability systems"—nongovernmental mechanisms to keep the news media responsible to public interests and opinions. These include codes of ethics, in-house critics, media reporters, and ombudsmen, as well as liaison committees that news institutions have sometimes established with social groups they may report on or clash with. There are also letters to the editor, journalism reviews, journalism schools, awards for good news coverage, and libel suits or the threat of libel. . . .

The Overworked Citizen

William James said nearly a century ago that our moral destiny turns on "the power of voluntarily attending." But, he added, though crucial to our individual and collective destinies, attention tends to be "brief and fitful." This is the substantial underlying reality of political life that any efforts at enlarging citizenship must confront. Can we have a democracy if most people are not paying attention most of the time? The answer is that this is the only kind of democracy we will ever have. Our ways of organizing and evoking that brief and fitful attention are different but not necessarily any worse from those in our past.

One response could be to harness the rare moments of attentiveness. Social movements and the occasional closely fought, morally urgent election have sometimes done that. When political scientists have looked at intensively fought senatorial campaigns, for instance, and compared them to run-of-the-mill campaigns, they find much more information in the news media about candidates' policy positions, increased knowledge among voters about those positions, and apparently increased inclination of voters to make decisions on the issues. At the level of presidential politics and occasionally in senatorial or gubernatorial politics, there is enough information available for voter rationality to have a chance; but for other offices, . . . our elections say much more about the supply of candidates than the demands of voters.

An alternate response would be to build a society that makes more of situations that build citizenship without taxing attentiveness. In an environment that supports worthwhile citizenship activity, there is intrinsic reward for doing the right thing. If we interpret citizenship activity to mean taking unpaid and uncoerced responsibility for the welfare of strangers or the community at large, examples of good citizenship abound. I think of the people who serve as "room parents" in the schools or coach Little League. Why do they do it? Their own children would do just as well if someone else took on the job. Coaching Little League or serving in the Parent-Teachers Association are activities or practices rather than cognitive efforts; they are social and integrated into community life. They make citizenship itself into a "by-product" effect. Their success suggests that citizenship may be harder to instill when it involves burdens beyond daily life than to engineer it as an everyday social activity. The volunteers may not enjoy every minute, but they find intrinsic social reward in having friends, neighbors, and strangers praise and admire them.

Our common language for a better public life seems impoverished. We think of politicians with distrust rather than thinking of ways to enforce their trustworthiness. We think of lobbyists with disdain instead of thinking of ways to recognize and harness their virtues. We think of journalists alternately as heroes or scoundrels. And we think of our own citizenship too often with either guilt at our ignorance and lack of participation or with a moral pat on the back for having sacrificed more than our neighbors. We must think more about building a democratic environment that will make us smarter as a people than we are as individuals.

Questions for Discussion

1. What does Schudson mean by "the burden of Progressivism"? Does the Progressive model of citizenship seem unrealistic when applied to today's voters? Have you personally experienced the "burden of Progressivism"?
2. What components does Schudson believe should underlie a new concept of citizenship? In your view, how practical is Schudson's viewpoint?

Bowling Alone: America's Declining Social Capital

Robert D. Putnam

Political behavior is learned behavior. Although individual freedoms and rights provide the fundamental underpinnings of the nation, citizens learning by experience to act collectively in pursuit of shared goals has long been thought crucial to the success of American democracy. Over 150 years ago, Alexis de Tocqueville in *Democracy in America* acknowledged the critical role played by associational life in supporting democratic values.

In this selection, Robert Putnam questions whether the United States has retained the characteristics of civil society. He suggests that there is an important linkage between "citizen engagement" in community affairs and government performance. Civic engagement refers to people's associational connections to the life of their communities in the broadest sense, from going to church to participating in a bowling league to becoming involved in a political group. Experience in a wide array of such activities develops what Putnam calls "social capital": "features of social organization such as networks, norms, and social trust that facilitate coordination and cooperation for mutual benefit."

M any students of the new democracies that have emerged over the past decade and a half have emphasized the importance of a strong and active civil society to the consolidation of democracy. Especially with regard to the postcommunist countries, scholars and democratic activists alike have lamented the absence or obliteration of traditions of independent civic engagement and a widespread tendency toward passive reliance on the state. To those concerned with the weakness of civil societies in the developing or post-communist world, the advanced Western democracies and above all the United States have typically been taken as models to be emulated. There is striking evidence, however, that the vibrancy of American civil society has notably declined over the past several decades.

Robert D. Putnam is Clarence Dillon Professor of International Affairs and Director, Center for International Affairs, Harvard University.

Ever since the publication of Alexis de Tocqueville's *Democracy in America*, the United States has played a central role in systematic studies of the links between democracy and civil society. Although this is in part because trends in American life are often regarded as harbingers of social modernization, it is also because America has traditionally been considered unusually "civic" (a reputation that, as we shall later see, has not been entirely unjustified).

When Tocqueville visited the United States in the 1830s, it was the Americans' propensity for civic association that most impressed him as the key to their unprecedented ability to make democracy work. "Americans of all ages, all stations in life, and all types of disposition," he observed, "are forever forming associations. There are not only commercial and industrial associations in which all take part, but others of a thousand different types—religious, moral, serious, futile, very general and very limited, immensely large and very minute. . . . Nothing, in my view, deserves more attention than the intellectual and moral associations in America."[1]

Recently, American social scientists of a neo-Tocquevillean bent have unearthed a wide range of empirical evidence that the quality of public life and the performance of social institutions (and not only in America) are indeed powerfully influenced by norms and networks of civic engagement. Researchers in such fields as education, urban poverty, unemployment, the control of crime and drug abuse, and even health have discovered that successful outcomes are more likely in civically engaged communities. Similarly, research on the varying economic attainments of different ethnic groups in the United States has demonstrated the importance of social bonds within each group. These results are consistent with research in a wide range of settings that demonstrates the vital importance of social networks for job placement and many other economic outcomes. . . .

No doubt the mechanisms through which civic engagement and social connectedness produce such results—better schools, faster economic development, lower crime, and more effective government—are multiple and complex. . . . Social scientists in several fields have recently suggested a common framework for understanding these phenomena, a framework that rests on the concept of *social capital*.[2] By analogy with notions of physical capital and human capital—tools and training that enhance individual productivity—"social capital" refers to features of social organization such as networks, norms, and social trust that facilitate coordination and cooperation for mutual benefit.

For a variety of reasons, life is easier in a community blessed with a substantial stock of social capital. In the first place, networks of civic engagement foster sturdy norms of generalized reciprocity and encourage the emergence of social trust. Such networks facilitate coordination and communication, amplify reputations, and thus allow dilemmas of collective action to be resolved. When economic and political negotiation is embedded in dense networks of social interaction, incentives for opportunism are reduced. At the same time, networks of civic engagement embody past success at collaboration, which can serve as a cultural template for future collaboration. Finally, dense networks of interaction probably broaden the participants' sense of self, developing the "I" into the "we," or (in the language of rational-choice theorists) enhancing the participants' "taste" for collective benefits. . . .

Whatever Happened to Civic Engagement?

We begin with familiar evidence on changing patterns of political participation, not least because it is immediately relevant to issues of democracy in the narrow sense. Consider the well-known decline in turnout in national elections over the last three decades. From a relative high point in the early 1960s, voter turnout had by 1990 declined by nearly a quarter; tens of millions of Americans had forsaken their parents' habitual readiness to engage in the simplest act of citizenship. Broadly similar trends also characterize participation in state and local elections.

It is not just the voting booth that has been increasingly deserted by Americans. A series of identical questions posed by the Roper Organization to national samples ten times each year over the last two decades reveals that since 1973 the number of Americans who report that "in the past year" they have "attended a public meeting on town or school affairs" has fallen by more than a third (from 22 percent in 1973 to 13 percent in 1993). Similar (or even greater) relative declines are evident in responses to questions about attending a political rally or speech, serving on a committee of some local organization, and working for a political party. By almost every measure, Americans' direct engagement in politics and government has fallen steadily and sharply over the last generation, despite the fact that average levels of education—the best individual-level predictor of political participation—have risen sharply throughout this period. Every year over the last decade or two, millions more have withdrawn from the affairs of their communities.

Not coincidentally, Americans have also disengaged psychologically from politics and government over this era. The proportion of Americans who reply that they "trust the government in Washington" only "some of the time" or "almost never" has risen steadily from 30 percent in 1966 to 75 percent in 1992.

These trends are well known, of course, and taken by themselves would seem amenable to a strictly political explanation. Perhaps the long litany of political tragedies and scandals since the 1960s (assassinations, Vietnam, Watergate, Irangate, and so on) has triggered an understandable disgust for politics and government among Americans, and that in turn has motivated their withdrawal. I do not doubt that this common interpretation has some merit, but its limitations become plain when we examine trends in civic engagement of a wider sort.

Our survey of organizational membership among Americans can usefully begin with a glance at the aggregate results of the General Social Survey, a scientifically conducted, national-sample survey that has been repeated 14 times over the last two decades. Church-related groups constitute the most common type of organization joined by Americans; they are especially popular with women. Other types of organizations frequently joined by women include school-service groups (mostly parent-teacher associations), sports groups, professional societies, and literary societies. Among men, sports clubs, labor unions, professional societies, fraternal groups, veterans' groups, and service clubs are all relatively popular.

Religious affiliation is by far the most common associational membership among Americans. Indeed, by many measures America continues to be (even more than in Tocqueville's time) an astonishingly "churched" society. For example, the United States has more houses of worship per capita than any other nation on Earth. Yet religious sentiment in America seems to be becoming somewhat less tied to institutions and more self-defined.

How have these complex crosscurrents played out over the last three or four decades in terms of Americans' engagement with organized religion? The general pattern is clear: The 1960s witnessed a significant drop in reported weekly churchgoing—from roughly 48 percent in the late 1950s to roughly 41 percent in the early 1970s. Since then, it has stagnated or (according to some surveys) declined still further. Meanwhile, data from the General Social Survey show a modest decline in membership in all "church-related groups" over the last 20 years. It would seem, then, that net participation by Americans, both in religious services and in church-related groups, has declined modestly (by perhaps a sixth) since the 1960s.

For many years, labor unions provided one of the most common organizational affiliations among American workers. Yet union membership has been falling for nearly four decades, with the steepest decline occurring between 1975 and 1985. Since the mid-1950s, when union membership peaked, the unionized portion of the nonagricultural work force in America has dropped by more than half, falling from 32.5 percent in 1953 to 15.8 percent in 1992. By now, virtually all of the explosive growth in union membership that was associated with the New Deal has been erased. The solidarity of union halls is now mostly a fading memory of aging men.

The parent-teacher association (PTA) has been an especially important form of civic engagement in twentieth-century America because parental involvement in the educational process represents a particularly productive form of social capital. It is, therefore, dismaying to discover that participation in parent-teacher organizations has dropped drastically over the last generation, from more than 12 million in 1964 to barely 5 million in 1982 before recovering to approximately 7 million now.

Next, we turn to evidence on membership in (and volunteering for) civic and fraternal organizations. These data show some striking patterns. First, membership in traditional women's groups has declined more or less steadily since the mid-1960s. For example, membership in the national Federation of Women's Clubs is down by more than half (59 percent) since 1964, while membership in the League of Women Voters (LWV) is off 42 percent since 1969.[3]

Similar reductions are apparent in the numbers of volunteers for mainline civic organizations, such as the Boy Scouts (off by 26 percent since 1970) and the Red Cross (off by 61 percent since 1970). But what about the possibility that volunteers have simply switched their loyalties to other organizations? Evidence on "regular" (as opposed to occasional or "drop-by") volunteering is available from the Labor Department's Current Population Surveys of 1974 and 1989. These estimates suggest that serious volunteering declined by roughly one-sixth over these 15 years, from 24 percent of adults in 1974 to 20 percent in 1989. The multitudes of Red Cross aides and Boy Scout troop leaders now missing in action have apparently not been offset by equal numbers of new recruits elsewhere.

Fraternal organizations have also witnessed a substantial drop in membership during the 1980s and 1990s. Membership is down significantly in such groups as the Lions (off 12 percent since 1983), the Elks (off 18 percent since 1979), the Shriners (off 27 percent since 1979), the Jaycees (off 44 percent since 1979), and the Masons (down 39 percent since 1959). . . .

The most whimsical yet discomfiting bit of evidence of social disengagement in contemporary America that I have discovered is this: more Americans are bowling today than ever before, but bowling in organized leagues has plummeted in the last decade or so. Between 1980 and 1993 the total number of bowlers in America increased by 10 percent, while league bowling decreased by 40 percent. (Lest this be thought a wholly trivial example, I should note that nearly 80 million Americans went bowling at least once during 1993, *nearly a third more than voted in the 1994 congressional elections* and roughly the same number as claim to attend church regularly. Even after the 1980s' plunge in league bowling, nearly 3 percent of American adults regularly bowl in leagues.) The rise of solo bowling threatens the livelihood of bowling-lane proprietors because those who bowl as members of leagues consume three times as much beer and pizza as solo bowlers, and the money in bowling is in the beer and pizza, not the balls and shoes. The broader social significance, however, lies in the social interaction and even occasionally civic conversations over beer and pizza that solo bowlers forgo. Whether or not bowling beats balloting in the eyes of most Americans, bowling teams illustrate yet another vanishing form of social capital.

Countertrends

At this point, however, we must confront a serious counterargument. Perhaps the traditional forms of civic organization whose decay we have been tracing have been replaced by vibrant new organizations. For example, national environmental organizations (like the Sierra Club) and feminist groups (like the National Organization for Women) grew rapidly during the 1970s and 1980s and now count hundreds of thousands of dues-paying members. An even more dramatic example is the American Association of Retired Persons (AARP), which grew exponentially from 400,000 card-carrying members in 1960 to 33 million in 1993, becoming (after the Catholic Church) the largest private organization in the world. The national administrators of these organizations are among the most feared lobbyists in Washington, in large part because of their massive mailing lists of presumably loyal members.

These new mass-membership organizations are plainly of great political importance. From the point of view of social connectedness, however, they are sufficiently different from classic "secondary associations" that we need to invent a new label—perhaps "tertiary associations." For the vast majority of their members, the only act of membership consists in writing a check for dues or perhaps occasionally reading a newsletter. Few ever attend any meetings of such organizations, and most are unlikely ever (knowingly) to encounter any other member. The bond between any two members of the Sierra Club is less like the bond between any two members of a gardening club and more like the bond between any two Red Sox fans (or perhaps any two devoted Honda owners): they root for the same team and they share some of the same interests, but they are unaware of each other's existence. Their ties, in short, are to common symbols, common leaders, and perhaps common ideals, but not to one another. The theory of social capital argues that associational membership should, for example, increase social trust, but this prediction is much less straightforward with regard to membership in tertiary associations. From the point of view of social connectedness, the Environmental Defense Fund and a bowling league are just not in the same category.

If the growth of tertiary organizations represents one potential (but probably not real) counterexample to my thesis, a second countertrend is represented by the growing prominence of nonprofit organizations, especially nonprofit service agencies. This so-called third sector includes everything from Oxfam and the Metropolitan Museum of Art to the Ford Foundation and the Mayo Clinic. In other words, although most secondary associations are nonprofits, most nonprofit agencies are not secondary associations. To identify trends in the size of the nonprofit sector with trends in social connectedness would be another fundamental conceptual mistake.[4]

A third potential countertrend is much more relevant to an assessment of social capital and civic engagement. Some able researchers have argued that the last few decades have witnessed a rapid expansion in "support groups" of various sorts. Robert Wuthnow reports that fully 40 percent of all Americans claim to be "currently involved in [a] small group that meets regularly and provides support or caring for those who participate in it."[5] Many of these groups are religiously affiliated, but many others are not. For example, nearly 5 percent of Wuthnow's national sample claim to participate regularly in a "self-help" group, such as Alcoholics Anonymous, and nearly as many say they belong to book-discussion groups and hobby clubs.

The groups described by Wuthnow's respondents unquestionably represent an important form of social capital, and they need to be accounted for in any serious reckoning of trends in social connectedness. On the other hand, they do not typically play the same role as traditional civic associations. As Wuthnow emphasizes,

> Small groups may not be fostering community as effectively as many of their proponents would like. Some small groups merely provide occasions for individuals to focus on themselves in the presence of others. The social contract binding members together asserts only the weakest of obligations. Come if you have time. Talk if you feel like it. Respect everyone's opinion. Never criticize. Leave quietly if you become dissatisfied. . . . We can imagine that [these small groups] really substitute for families, neighborhoods, and broader community attachments that may demand lifelong commitments, when, in fact, they do not.[6]

All three of these potential countertrends—tertiary organizations, nonprofit organizations, and support groups—need somehow to be weighed against the erosion of conventional civic organizations. One way of doing so is to consult the General Social Survey.

Within all educational categories, total associational membership declined significantly between 1967 and 1993. Among the college-educated, the average number of group memberships per person fell from 2.8 to 2.0 (a 26-percent decline); among high-school graduates, the number fell from 1.8 to 1.2 (32 percent); and among those with fewer than 12 years of education, the number fell from 1.4 to 1.1 (25 percent). In other words, at *all* educational (and hence social) levels of American society, and counting *all* sorts of group memberships, *the average number of associational memberships has fallen by about a fourth over the last quarter-century*. Without controls for educational levels, the trend is not nearly so clear, but the central point is this: *more Americans than ever before are in social circumstances that foster associational involvement (higher education, middle age, and so on), but nevertheless aggregate associational membership appears to be stagnant or declining.*

Broken down by type of group, the downward trend is most marked for church-related groups, for labor unions, for fraternal and veterans' organizations, and for school-service groups. Conversely, membership in professional associations has risen over these years, although less than might have been predicted, given sharply rising educational and occupational levels. Essentially the same trends are evident for both men and women in the sample. In short, the available survey evidence confirms our earlier conclusion: American social capital in the form of civic associations has significantly eroded over the last generation.

Good Neighborliness and Social Trust

I noted earlier that most readily available quantitative evidence on trends in social connectedness involves formal settings, such as the voting booth, the union hall, or the PTA. One glaring exception is so widely discussed as to require little comment here: the most fundamental form of social capital is the family, and the massive evidence of the loosening of bonds within the family (both extended and nuclear) is well known. This trend, of course, is quite consistent with—and may help to explain—our theme of social decapitalization.

A second aspect of informal social capital on which we happen to have reasonably reliable time-series data involves neighborliness. In each General Social Survey since 1974 respondents have been asked, "How often do you spend a social evening with a neighbor?" The proportion of Americans who socialize with their neighbors more than once a year has slowly but steadily declined over the last two decades, from 72 percent in 1974 to 61 percent in 1993. (On the other hand, socializing with "friends who do not live in your neighborhood" appears to be on the increase, a trend that may reflect the growth of workplace-based social connections.)

Americans are also less trusting. The proportion of Americans saying that most people can be trusted fell by more than a third between 1960, when 58 percent chose that alternative, and 1993, when only 37 percent did. The same trend is apparent in all educational groups; indeed, because social trust is also correlated with education and because educational levels have risen sharply, the overall decrease in social trust is even more apparent if we control for education.

Our discussion of trends in social connectedness and civic engagement has tacitly assumed that all the forms of social capital that we have discussed are themselves coherently correlated across individuals. This is in fact true. Members of associations are much more likely than nonmembers to participate in politics, to spend time with neighbors, to express social trust, and so on. . . .

Why Is U.S. Social Capital Eroding?

As we have seen, something has happened in America in the last two or three decades to diminish civic engagement and social connectedness. What could that "something" be? Here are several possible explanations, along with some initial evidence on each.

The Movement of Women into the Labor Force   Over these same two or three decades, many millions of American women have moved out of the home into paid employment. This is the primary, though not the sole, reason why the weekly working hours of the average American have increased significantly during these years. It seems highly plausible that this social revolution should have reduced the time and energy available for building social capital. For certain organizations, such as the PTA, the League of Women Voters, the Federation of Women's Clubs, and the Red Cross, this is almost certainly an important part of the story. The sharpest decline in women's civic participation seems to have come in the 1970s; membership in such "women's" organizations as these has been virtually halved since the late 1960s. By contrast, most of the decline in participation in men's organizations occurred about ten years later; the total decline to date has been approximately 25 percent for the typical organization. On the other hand, the survey data imply that the aggregate declines for men are virtually as great as those for women. It is logically possible, of course, that the male declines might represent the knock-on effect of women's liberation, as dishwashing crowded out the lodge, but time-budget studies suggest that most husbands of working wives have assumed only a minor part of the housework. In short, something besides the women's revolution seems to lie behind the erosion of social capital.

Mobility: The "Re-potting" Hypothesis Numerous studies of organizational involvement have shown that residential stability and such related phenomena as homeownership are clearly associated with greater civic engagement. Mobility, like frequent re-potting of plants, tends to disrupt root systems, and it takes time for an uprooted individual to put down new roots. It seems plausible that the automobile, suburbanization, and the movement to the Sun Belt have reduced the social rootedness of the average American, but one fundamental difficulty with this hypothesis is apparent: the best evidence shows that residential stability and homeownership in America have risen modestly since 1965, and are surely higher now than during the 1950s, when civic engagement and social connectedness by our measures was definitely higher.

Other Demographic Transformations A range of additional changes have transformed the American family since the 1960s—fewer marriages, more divorces, fewer children, lower real wages, and so on. Each of these changes might account for some of the slackening of civic engagement, since married, middle-class parents are generally more socially involved than other people. Moreover, the changes in scale that have swept over the American economy in these years—illustrated by the replacement of the corner grocery by the supermarket and now perhaps of the supermarket by electronic shopping at home, or the replacement of community-based enterprises by outposts of distant multinational firms—may perhaps have undermined the material and even physical basis for civic engagement.

The Technological Transformation of Leisure There is reason to believe that deep-seated technological trends are radically "privatizing" or "individualizing" our use of leisure time and thus disrupting many opportunities for social-capital formation. The most obvious and probably the most powerful instrument of this revolution is television. Time-budget studies in the 1960s showed that the growth in time spent watching television dwarfed all other changes in the way Americans passed their days and nights. Television has made our communities (or, rather, what we experience as our communities) wider and shallower. In the language of economics, electronic technology enables individual tastes to be satisfied more fully, but at the cost of the positive social externalities associated with more primitive forms of entertainment. The same logic applies to the replacement of vaudeville by the movies and now of movies by the VCR. The new "virtual reality" helmets that we will soon don to be entertained in total isolation are merely the latest extension of this trend. Is technology thus driving a wedge between our individual interests and our collective interests? It is a question that seems worth exploring more systematically.

What Is to Be Done?

The last refuge of a social-scientific scoundrel is to call for more research. Nevertheless, I cannot forbear from suggesting some further lines of inquiry.

♦ . . . What types of organizations and networks most effectively embody—or generate—social capital, in the sense of mutual reciprocity, the resolution of dilemmas of collective action, and the broadening of social identities? . . .

♦ Another set of important issues involves macrosociological crosscurrents that might intersect with the trends described here. What will be the impact, for example, of electronic networks on social capital? My hunch is that meeting in an electronic forum is not the equivalent of meeting in a bowling alley—or even in a saloon—but hard empirical research is needed. What about the development of social capital in the workplace? . . .

♦ A rounded assessment of changes in American social capital over the last quarter-century needs to count the costs as well as the benefits of community engagement. We must not romanticize small-town, middle-class civic life in the America of the 1950s. In addition to the deleterious trends emphasized in this essay, recent decades have witnessed a substantial decline in intolerance and probably also in overt discrimination, and those beneficent trends may be related in complex ways to the erosion of traditional social capital. . . .

♦ Finally, and perhaps most urgently, we need to explore creatively how public policy impinges on (or might impinge on) social-capital formation. In some well-known instances, public policy has destroyed highly effective social networks and norms. American slum-clearance policy of the 1950s and 1960s, for example, renovated physical capital, but at a very high cost to existing social capital. The consolidation of country post offices and small school districts has promised administrative and financial efficiencies, but full-cost accounting for the effects of these policies on social capital might produce a more negative verdict. On the other hand, such past initiatives as the county agricultural-agent system, community colleges, and tax deductions for charitable contributions illustrate that government can encourage social-capital formation. Even a recent proposal in San Luis Obispo, California, to require that all new houses have front porches illustrates the power of government to influence where and how networks are formed.

The concept of "civil society" has played a central role in the recent global debate about the preconditions for democracy and democratization. In the newer democracies this phrase has properly focused attention on the need to foster a vibrant civic life in soils traditionally inhospitable to self-government. In the established democracies, ironically, growing numbers of citizens are questioning the effectiveness of their public institutions at the very moment when liberal democracy has swept the battlefield, both ideologically and geopolitically. In America, at least, there is reason to suspect that this democratic disarray may be linked to a broad and continuing erosion of civic engagement that began a quarter-century ago. . . . High on America's agenda should be the question of how to reverse these adverse trends in social connectedness, thus restoring civic engagement and civic trust.

Notes

1. Alexis de Tocqueville, *Democracy in America*, ed. J. P. Maier, trans. George Lawrence (Garden City, N.Y.: Anchor Books, 1969), 513–17.
2. James S. Coleman deserves primary credit for developing the "social capital" theoretical framework. See his "Social Capital in the Creation of Human Capital," *American Journal of Sociology* (Supplement) 94 (1988): S95–S120, as well as his *The Foundations of Social Theory* (Cambridge: Harvard University Press, 1990), 300–21. See also Mark Granovetter, "Economic Action and Social Structure: The Problem of Embeddedness," *American Journal of Sociology* 91 (1985): 481–510; Glenn C. Loury, "Why Should We Care About Group Inequality?" *Social Philosophy and Policy* 5 (1987): 249–71; and Robert D. Putnam, "The Prosperous Community: Social Capital and Public Life," *American Prospect* 13 (1993): 35–42. To my knowledge, the first scholar to use the term "social capital" in its current sense was Jane Jacobs, in *The Death and Life of Great American Cities* (New York: Random House, 1961), 138.
3. Data for the LWV are available over a longer time span and show an interesting pattern: a sharp slump during the Depression, a strong and sustained rise after World War II that more than tripled membership between 1945 and 1969, and then the post-1969 decline, which has already erased virtually all the postwar gains and continues still. This same historical pattern applies to those men's fraternal organizations for which comparable data are available—steady increases for the first seven decades of the century, interrupted only by the Great Depression, followed by a collapse in the 1970s and 1980s that has already wiped out most of the postwar expansion and continues apace.
4. Cf. Lester M. Salamon, "The Rise of the Nonprofit Sector," *Foreign Affairs* 73 (July–August 1994): 109–22. See also Salamon, "Partners in Public Service: The Scope and Theory of Government-Nonprofit Relations," in Walter W. Powell, ed., *The Nonprofit Sector: A Research Handbook* (New Haven: Yale University Press, 1987), 99–117. Salamon's empirical evidence does not sustain his broad claims about a global "associational revolution" comparable in significance to the rise of the nation-state several centuries ago.
5. Robert Wuthnow, *Sharing the Journey: Support Groups and America's New Quest for Community* (New York: The Free Press, 1994), 45.
6. Ibid., 3–6.

Questions for Discussion

1. What is "social capital" and how is it linked to politics? What indicators suggest that social capital is in decline in the United States?
2. What explanations for the decline in social capital does Putnam put forth? Does he offer any suggestions for reversing this undesirable trend? Does the rise in the use of the Internet bode well for the growth of social capital?

# Chapter 6

POLITICAL PARTIES

The word *party* is not mentioned in the U.S. Constitution. The nation's founders, suspicious of special interests, viewed parties as devices to organize factions— "to put in the place of the delegated will of the nation the will of party," as George Washington put it. Yet within a generation of the nation's founding, parties had emerged as instruments for structuring political conflict and encouraging mass participation.

In retrospect, the development of political parties seems almost inevitable. The United States has always harbored a diverse political culture, and the practical necessity of governing demands that majorities be forged among contending interests. Political parties evolved as the only solution to the problem of reconciling individual diversity with majority rule.

The American political party functions as an intermediary between the public and the government. A party can combine citizens' demands into a manageable number of issues, thus enabling the system to focus on society's most crucial problems. The party performs its mediating function primarily through coalition building—in the words of journalist David Broder, "the process of constructing majorities from the broad sentiments and interests that can be found to bridge the narrower needs and hopes of separate individuals and communities."

For example, Franklin Roosevelt's New Deal, forged in the 1930s in the face of deep economic depression, brought about a Democratic coalition that essentially dominated national policymaking for thirty years. Generally speaking, socioeconomic divisions shaped politics in the 1930s. Less affluent citizens tended to support the Roosevelt administration's provisions for social and economic security and government regulation of private enterprise. Those who were better off usually took the opposite position. By and large, the New Deal coalition came to represent northern urban workers, immigrants and ethnic minorities, blacks, Catholics, Jews, and many southerners.

Such coalition building has contributed greatly to the stability of American political life, but the parties also serve as the major vehicle for political change. Political coalitions are never permanent. Old issues are dealt with or decrease in importance, while new issues move onto the agenda. New voters enter the electorate, older ones die, and the economic and social circumstances of groups and regions change.

Confronted with a new political environment, parties may realign—rearrange the bases of their coalitions to reflect new issues and public concerns. Critical realignments usually occur in the midst of an economic crisis such as a depression. Such an event causes sharp and durable changes in voter perceptions and identities because of the parties' differing positions on how to handle the situation. Scholars have concluded that party realignment has taken place a number of times since the early 1800s as the party system has adjusted to the changing issues in politics.

There is a general consensus among political observers that the American party system today is again in the midst of change, but there is little consensus as to its direction. Throughout the system's first 150 years, political realignment took place roughly every thirty-two to thirty-six years, but after the transforming election of 1932, the "expected" rearrangement did not occur by the early 1970s. New Deal political issues had faded in importance by the late 1960s, yet neither party appeared able or willing to build stable coalitions around the new issues.

Civil rights and the Vietnam War deeply divided the dominant Democrats in the 1960s, and divisions among constituent elements intensified in the 1970s as the governing system addressed such questions as women's rights, affirmative action, and consumer and environmental protection. As the party's agenda moved from guaranteeing equality of opportunity to pushing for equality of circumstance, the old coalition became impossible to sustain. Similarly, the Republican party, though experiencing a variety of successes (especially at the presidential level), did not develop a stable electoral and governing coalition. During the Nixon years, the Watergate scandal stopped what many viewed as a long-term shift in the balance of power toward the Republican party. Ronald Reagan's popularity caused some voters to shift party allegiance and may have enticed increasing numbers of young voters to identify with the Republican party, but economic, cultural, and social divisions among Republicans remained a barrier to coalition unity.

The lack of a critical realignment by the party system has caused some political analysts to claim that the system is undergoing "dealignment"—the movement of voters away from both parties. This viewpoint holds that "candidate politics" is more prevalent than "party politics." Some observers even suggest that party politics is not possible in the age of high technology, mass media dominance, and a highly educated electorate that engages in split-ticket voting. Those who believe in dealignment point to the decline of the importance of party identification in voting, to the growth of independence among older voters, and to the nonalignment of young voters entering the electorate. They also note the great stress on the American political system over the past forty years. The Vietnam War, the energy crisis, the hyperinflation of the 1970s, and scandals in the highest places in government during the Reagan and Clinton administrations have heightened citizen awareness of political affairs and increased mistrust of public officials and political institutions, including parties.

Much of the decline in the importance of parties has been blamed on their inability to perform their traditional functions in the electoral process. For example, post-1968 reforms in both parties (but particularly in the Democratic party) mean that delegates to presidential nomination conventions are selected largely in primaries rather than in caucuses and state conventions, thus increasing the number of narrow-issue activists and decreasing the number of elected officials and party professionals. Some believe the parties have lost their ability to set the political agenda in the nomination process as well. Candidates no longer have to spend years working within the party hierarchy to become contenders; today fresh faces quickly emerge, thanks to the role played by the media, particularly television, in determining who is or is not a "serious" candidate.

Changes in campaigning and finances have also reduced the parties' traditional role in campaign organization. Campaigns are now largely run by candidate organizations rather than by the parties. The ever-increasing importance of money and the growth of political action committees (PACs) since the Campaign Reform Acts of 1971 and 1974 (which mandated financial reporting by candidate committees) have enabled individuals to rely less on traditional party sources of funds and more on funds made available by special interests. Not surprisingly, those interests play a major role in recruiting candidates, setting issue agendas, and, in some cases, actually mobilizing voters.

Campaigns have also become more oriented toward the media than toward personal contact with voters in recent decades, and independent political consultants are now more likely than party professionals to run campaigns. Candidates for most national or statewide offices routinely place their campaigns in the hands of a comprehensive political consulting firm, which is charged with raising funds, polling, advertising, and designing campaign strategy. One consequence is that officeholders now owe little allegiance either to party organizations or to party leaders; they are elected by their own efforts and are accountable to no one but themselves.

In spite of these trends, some political scientists assert that the two major parties are adjusting to the challenge of PAC politics, high technology, and mass media and are staging a resurgence, especially at the national level. Both have taken advantage of the PAC phenomenon by forming loose alliances with some prominent groups. In their emerging role as brokers, the national parties assist PACs in directing contributions to particular campaigns. Likewise, they aid candidates by soliciting contributions from PACs. In addition, the national parties provide professional assistance to candidates in the form of direct mail and polling services. The growing use of "soft money" by parties over the past decade suggests a stronger role for parties in campaigns in the future.

The readings that follow address various aspects of the changing party system. All three reflect the uncertainty many observers feel in assessing the contributions of contemporary political parties. In the first selection, Kay Lawson, a proponent of what she calls "real" political parties, argues that contemporary parties have been captured by elites and no longer operate as vehicles of influence for the masses. In her view, citizens need once again to take control of political parties if democracy is to succeed. In the second selection, Everett Carll Ladd takes issue with those who believe that "stronger" political parties are desirable in American politics. He is convinced parties remain a substantial presence in American political life, especially in Congress, and thus there is little public support for further increasing their influence. The final selection, by John Kenneth White and Daniel M. Shea, documents the resurgence of the national party organizations in political campaigns. Money is the key as both parties have adapted creatively to campaign finance regulations to again become a major force in elections.

▨ 6.1

Why We Still Need Real Political Parties

Kay Lawson

While all elected federal officials and almost all state officials continue to run for office under party labels, the role of parties in the process is much smaller than it was earlier in the nation's history. Most political scientists believe that we have moved from an era of "party politics" to an era of "candidate politics" characterized by a heightened role for the media, interest groups, and professional campaign operatives and consultants. Parties have not disappeared, but they are only one interest active in contemporary electoral politics and probably not the most important one.

In this selection, Kay Lawson argues that the development of political parties "made democracy possible" in the United States and the functions they performed for citizens at an earlier time are just as relevant today. In her view, today's parties have become captured by elites and other insiders, and the citizenry no longer views them as valuable institutions to solve social and economic problems. "Real" political parties are needed, she says—parties controlled by a broad base of citizens, concerned with aggregating interests and addressing policy issues, and able to hold public officials accountable to the party faithful. A strong advocate of party renewal, Lawson believes that only citizen activity within parties can restore parties to "democratic usefulness."

What Is a "Real Political Party"?

Scholars have as many definitions of party as there are parties. Some have gone so far as to declare that any organization that calls itself a party is a party.[1] Others argue that no clear definition is possible, that mere interest groups can slip in and out of partyhood with such ease and frequency that there is no good way to tell them apart. . . . For still others, myself among them, the line is very clear: A party is an organization that nominates candidates to stand for election to public office. Any group that does this becomes, unambiguously, a party. When it stops nominating candidates, it stops being a party.

Kay Lawson is a professor of political science at San Francisco State University. This article was written in 1993.

However, this simple and, I think, useful definition is not what I mean here by the term "real political party." Here, I use the word "real" in the good, strong, popular sense of "the very epitome of what the thing ought to be." The term implies not only an ideal but also a set of qualities upon which there is reasonably wide agreement.

Reasonably wide agreement, not unanimity. For some, I acknowledge, the very notion of an "ideal" political party is an oxymoron. We have become so accustomed to disliking our parties that we can no longer imagine what one we might admire would resemble.[2] Nevertheless, the idea of a "real" political party sets our tribal memories astir. Wasn't there a time . . . didn't Van Buren say . . . what was it that Lincoln suggested . . . I seem to recall that during the Great Depression Roosevelt. . . .[3]

Existentialists all, we define the good by the act that is pleasing to ourselves. A party is judged by the acts it performs. Realists all, we recognize that no organization acts unselfishly. Parties are organizations for acquiring control over powerful offices of government, and they act accordingly. Even when they have no hope of placing their own members in such control, they seek to influence the behavior of those who win elections. However, citizens all, we nevertheless look for parties whose selfish acts at the same time serve our own larger social purposes. Parties that work only for themselves may be real enough in their own evaluations, and in those of scholars intent on studying them regardless of their social usefulness—but they are not sufficiently real to the citizens who need them to do more.

It is no wonder, then, that parties in the United States today have little or no reality for most American citizens. Elite organizations that work only for themselves and fellow elites, they appear to most voters to serve no larger societal functions, or else to serve them so poorly that they no longer merit support. If forced by an inquiring pollster to think about them, we rank political parties at the bottom of any list of public institutions; and normally we don't pay them any attention at all. For that matter, we choose our candidates on the basis of incumbency, media personality, or issue stance rather than on what party labels they wear.[4]

What could political parties do in order to become real again? (The cynic interrupts, and offers to answer for the citizen trapped in a seemingly endless recession: "Get me a job.") And, indeed, the idea of Tammany as a "real political party" has its appeal.* William Riordon, in his widely read and humorous interviews of New York District Leader George Washington Plunkitt, taught many of us to think of the machine boss, even when motivated by the basest greed

---

* Tammany was a political society that was formed after the American Revolution and dominated New York City politics until well into the twentieth century. Though originally interested in political reform and helping the mass of citizens, by the mid-to-late nineteenth century the organization had been corrupted by its leadership and today is pointed to as a symbol of all that is associated with political machines and boss politics.

and engaged in the rawest expropriation of public moneys, as somehow a rather appealing figure, the "realistic" agent of a personalized democracy.[5] The voter gets a low-paying job, the boss gets the vote and with it access to all that power can buy. Textbook after textbook has accepted the idea that the machine, actually an instrument of oppressive criminality, was a useful if makeshift means of assimilating new citizens into "democracy" and that our most reasonable response to it might well be one of nostalgia for the good old days when that's how politics was done. (The careful scholarship of David Mayhew, who notes that very few cities ever actually had machines of any kind, has largely been ignored.)[6] Nevertheless, the facts are that the United States never had extensive machine politics, and that what it did have, none of us should reasonably want back. Parties that buy our votes with one-on-one material payoffs are not viable alternatives today, and cannot be the real political parties we seek.

The functions of real political parties go back longer in time than to turn-of-the-century machinations. They go back to the very origins of parties themselves. The modern political party came into being as a way to solve the problems raised for candidates by an expanding suffrage. As soon as it became impossible for the candidates to secure election—or reelection—by personally persuading the few persons of one's own elevated class who had the vote, some kind of vote-gathering organization became necessary. Furthermore, that organization had to find grounds on which to appeal to a larger and more economically heterogeneous electorate (racial and sexual heterogeneity came later, much later). In other words, it needed candidates *and* issues that would have a wider appeal. The originators of party naively believed that voters would follow their lead only for good reason. They lacked the mass communication technology and skills for persuading voters that bad reasons—or no reasons at all—could make a fair substitute. Although their own motive, the conquest of power, was the same as any party politician's today, they had a different view of what would motivate the voter: They believed they had to either buy the vote (a practice that began long before Tammany but became less and less feasible the more suffrage expanded) or offer to use that power on behalf of the voters' own interests. Parties became the agencies that made democracy possible because they believed their own fortunes depended on playing the democratic game with some minimal level of rectitude.

In the beginning, then (and it was a beginning that lasted well into the twentieth century), parties were organizations that did not seek to motivate voters solely through materialistic horsetrading; nor did they have the capacity to do so, lacking today's sloganistic media blitz. Instead, parties promised to perform specific functions—and voters who took the job seriously evaluated them on the basis of the quality of that performance. These functions, all of which made pragmatic good sense to vote-seeking organizations with limited funds and skills but all of which were also of great use to budding democracies, were the following:

First, parties *aggregated interests, formulated issues, and proposed programs*. They discovered the concerns of a significant body of voters, worked out necessary compromises, and wrote platforms incorporating this work.

Second, parties *recruited and trained candidates* who would support their programs. Training actually came first; working for and in the party was the best way to learn the delicate arts of competitive politics as well as to demonstrate one's aptitude for public office.

Third, parties *structured the vote*. It was they who gave life and meaning to elections. They did so by making their own nominations and allowing those selected to wear the label of the party—a label that had a consistent meaning, or at least one that changed only gradually over time. They did so by conducting campaigns for their candidates, raising the necessary funds, training volunteers, and canvassing door to door. They helped with registration and they got out the vote. In fact, their constant preparations gave substance to the coming election—specifically, by helping citizens decide to vote, and how.

Fourth, parties *provided a means of holding elected officials accountable*. If elected officials did not carry out the party's program, or the party's program once carried out did not produce the desired results, voters had the option of looking elsewhere—and activists had the option of choosing other candidates. For the voters who were not active party members, this function was performed by the parties together, not one by one: It was in their diversity, in the choice that they collectively made possible, that the noninvolved voters' hope of holding elected officials accountable lay. Those with the time and interest could, however, join and become active in a particular party, and there combine with like-minded others to utilize the organization as an instrument of accountability.

The Perversion of Parties

Do not American parties perform the same four functions today? Is it not, indeed, upon them that we depend for the performance of these tasks? The answers are: no and no, with one minor exception.

Although it makes sense when speaking of "real political parties" to begin with interest aggregation, because that is where the political process ideally begins and rebegins, in order to understand what has happened to our parties today we need to consider first how candidates are recruited—because that is where the political process begins today.

American parties today do not look for candidates to support their programs. Instead, they accept as their candidates whoever has been able to rally the strength to extract the nominations. A party's nomination is no longer its own to bestow. Primary elections ensure that the candidate who can gather the most funds and/or the candidate who is an incumbent running for reelection (and normally the two attributes are found in combination) will normally win the party's nomination without any help from the party whatsoever—and, indeed sometimes against the wishes of the party's active membership and leaders. Furthermore, in the vast majority of American elections, political parties are prevented from presenting candidates at all: More than 85 percent of municipal elections are, by law, nonpartisan. (There are, of course, vastly more city elections than state and national elections—some 19,000 per year in California, for example.) In these elections, the parties may not even make nominations; and in some states, they do not even have the right to endorse or repudiate any of the self-nominated candidates for city office.[7]

It is also less and less likely today that the candidates will have learned the art of politics by taking an active part in party life. Party activism is now rewarded, if at all, more by the opportunities it provides to have firsthand contact with candidates than by any chance to become one. Would-be candidates spend their time more effectively working with wealthy and powerful nonparty persons or groups than by bothering with intraparty activism. It is true that the candidate, having gained the nomination, may well benefit from training in a party-sponsored school for candidates; but that, of course, is a clear case of putting the cart before the horse (in this case, a horse that is already off and running). Today's parties do not perform the second function on our list.

And because they do not perform the second, they do not perform the first. Parties do not aggregate interests, formulate issues, and then propose programs that take stands on those issues that will appeal to a significant body of voters. The situation may look like that, at least in elections at the level of state and nation, but that is not what is going on. At the level of the states, where platforms are often written separately from the conventions, an effort may or may not be made to find out and aggregate the points of view of party members or the public; but even if made, that effort will almost always be limited to issues that have already been determined to be "important"—because either powerful interests or the media (normally both, the second in this case responding to the former) have declared them so and, furthermore, have determined the terms of the debate to be held on them. Ideas that might be excellent and clearly consistent with the party's broad philosophy of government (if one may still be discerned), but that seem likely to lower the income of a bloc of major contributors if ever implemented, are unlikely to gain a fair hearing. The same may be said for those ideas that might require extensive voter education. Proposals explaining a political agenda in detail, even when every detail is easy to understand, are similarly excluded. As the purpose is always to take as many of the votes of the massive number of nonpartisans as well as of the other party's putative supporters as possible, in addition to those of one's own supporters, the rush to the center would break the back—or at least the patience—of any animal more sensitive to strain than the American electorate. The final result would be an excellent document, entirely lacking in controversy, almost impossible to implement, and eminently unread.

At any rate, it doesn't matter. The program that *will* eventually matter, at least a little bit, will not be the party's program; it will be the program of the candidate, which may or may not agree with that of the party. As we have already seen, getting the nomination does not depend on concurrence with the party program (an absence of linkage that is true at the national level as well), although the attention given the national party's platform is considerably greater and is part of the work of the nominating convention. "Do you agree with the platform?" a reporter asked President Jimmy Carter after the 1980 Democratic convention. "I agree with most of it," the party's nominee affably replied. How nice someone thought to ask.

With the third function, we come to our minor exceptions. Today's political parties do perform some part of the job of structuring the vote. They do not do so, however, via the meaningfulness of the party label. Inasmuch as they no longer control their own nominations, their labels are now associated only with the transient programs of those who have become their candidates, programs as deliberately substanceless as their own. However, both our major parties have become particularly adept at fund-raising (each in its own way), and even if they have lost control over the choice of candidates for whom the money is being raised, they can sometimes play favorites to useful effect. They help with the task of canvassing, if not door to door, at least sometimes phone to phone. They work very hard indeed on voter registration and getting out the vote. They do all this guided not by their own programs or their own convictions but by the wishes of the candidates and by the candidates' and their own powerful professional advisers, political consultants whose concern for electoral victory far outweighs any passing dreams of principled formulation of issues with distinctive substantive content—and very often has little to do with issues at all. But our parties do help structure the vote. Even though today they share that role more than ever with the media, with the candidates' personal organizations, and with independently spending Political Action Committees . . . it must be granted that they are reasonably efficient electoral machines.[8]

As for the fourth function, surely little need be said. The only force that holds U.S. elected officials accountable is the force that is needed to open a wallet. Parties' wallets are now worth opening, but parties themselves have nothing substantive to which to hold the successful bearers of their name accountable. Candidates are chosen and elected whose loyalty to—or even familiarity with—the party platform is minimal at best. The ability of presidents to distance themselves from their own parties is obvious, but we sometimes imagine we see a measure of party discipline in Congress. To persuade ourselves of this, however, we must consent to a very diluted idea of what constitutes a party. Once inside Congress, those miscellaneous victors who succeeded in wresting the label away from one party or the other and using it to win public office may dutifully call themselves "Democrats" or "Republicans" and may even sometimes cobble together a program of sorts; but that program need have little in common with the program of the party organization that exists outside Congress. Furthermore, the other determinants of congressional votes—constituency pressure, personal friendships, personal convictions, and, above all, campaign donor pressure—are at least as likely to prevail should differences arise.

The Ever-Swifter Descent of the Parties—and Their Complicity Therewith

Because our parties no longer perform most of the functions a democratic society requires from its parties, their place in the affections of the American people drops lower and lower. This is apparent when any question about them is put to the people directly. Their dissatisfaction with the parties is not compensated for by a conviction that other institutions are working well: as is apparent not only in opinion polls regarding those institutions, but also in the increased demand for alternative democratic reforms in the political process, and in the decreasing interest of the public at large in any form of political activity whatsoever. Yet the parties themselves appear unconcerned about this decline, even to the point of deliberately fostering it—a phenomenon that is not so surprising as it may seem at first. Let us look at each of these factors in turn.

The first significant study of the declining popularity of the parties was made by Jack Dennis in 1975.[9] Bringing together his own work with that of others, Dennis pointed out such discoveries as the following:

- More than 66 percent of Americans thought that party labels should not be on the ballot.
- Eighty-five percent said that parties create conflict.
- Seventy-eight percent believed that parties confused rather than clarified the issues of the day.
- Only 26 percent believed that parties knew how to make the government responsible to citizens.
- Only 32 percent believed that parties did what they promised.
- Only 35 percent believed that parties wanted to know what citizens thought.
- Only 40 percent thought it mattered whether one party or another won an election.

In the seventeen years since Dennis published his study, the situation has not improved. Howard Reiter combined his own calculations with those of other authors to show that between 1974 and 1980 the number of those who believed that "parties help government pay attention to what people think" had fallen by four percentage points, to 18 percent, whereas the number who believed that "parties are only interested in people's votes, but not in their opinions," had risen during the same period by one point to 59 percent.[10] More recent figures confirm the pattern: Asked to give a letter grade to the performance of the two parties in the 1988 presidential campaign, a national sample gave both parties an average grade of C.[11] Other studies suggest that any improvement made by the parties in distinguishing themselves from each other in the voters' minds (a form of improvement that some studies suggested did take place to some extent during the Reagan years) had largely disappeared by 1990 and 1991, when a full 25 percent saw no difference between the parties in "keeping the country prosperous," 30 percent saw none in their ability to keep the nation out of war, and, most significant of all, 41 percent saw none in their ability to handle "the nation's most important problem" (whatever that might have been in their own minds).[12]

Dissatisfaction with the parties cannot be dismissed on the grounds that Americans are satisfied in general with their political system, even if they think the parties are largely worthless. The continuing decline in voter turnout is one index, and it is worthwhile to note not only that voting in presidential elections has dropped to the 50 percent level but also that a mere 33 percent of the voting-age population voted in the midterm elections of 1990 . . .

Yet another index of dissatisfaction is the growing interest in alternative means of democratizing our political system. There is now remarkably strong support for the devices of direct democracy, despite growing awareness of their deficiencies as a means of basing public policy on public will.[13] Asked "Should we trust our elected officials to make public decisions on all issues, or should the voters have a direct say on some issues?" a national sample favored giving voters a direct say by 76 percent (only 18 percent were opposed; 6 percent did not know). More specifically, a strong majority (57 percent) supported the idea of a national initiative—that is, a constitutional amendment permitting citizens to gather signatures for a proposed law to be placed on the ballot at the succeeding general election and to become law if a majority approved. Only one-fourth were opposed (18 percent were not sure). Fully two-thirds said they believed the Constitution should be changed to permit the recall of members of Congress, whereas 55 percent specified that it should allow recall of the president.[14]

Support for other reforms is also indicative of popular distress with the performance of our weak-partied political system. Term limits have been adopted in California to ensure that state legislators will not serve more than two consecutive terms in office, and the idea has recently been proposed for members of Congress as well. And the proposals for reforming campaign finance appear as endless as the resistance of the legislators whose votes would be needed for their success—but whose pockets always need more relining than the reforms would be likely to permit.

Yet there is little if any evidence that the parties are interested in making changes that would put themselves back in the ring as leading agencies in the democratic process. Another illustration from California is particularly apt. Parties are as weak in California as they are anywhere in the nation, and weaker than in most states.[15] Voting rates have been dropping, and ardent efforts by both parties to increase registration have had little payoff in terms of turnout. Recently, a body of antiparty law was successfully challenged as unconstitutional by a multipartisan reform group, the Committee for Party Renewal. The 1988 ruling of the U.S. Supreme Court in the case *Eu v. San Francisco County Democrats* gave the parties of California the right both to issue endorsements in primary elections and to set their own rules and regulations on important matters hitherto closely controlled by law. California's parties now have unambiguous opportunities to strengthen their ability to carry out several of the key functions identified earlier, becoming more responsive to their membership in the endorsement of candidates, in the writing of the state party platform, in the selection of delegates to the party's national convention, and in all party activities.

However, both major state parties have been extremely reluctant to take advantage of these opportunities. The Republicans have made no changes whatsoever, and the Democrats have instituted a method of endorsing primary contestants that greatly advantages incumbents and keeps final control at the highest echelons of the party. Neither party has made any other changes in internal rules that could be termed party-strengthening. The Democratic party rejected by a 2 to 1 vote a proposal to change to a mixed-delegate-selection system that would have had the undeniably party-building effect of giving California Democrats a strong say in the party's selection of its presidential candidate. (Half of California's delegates would have been picked in March caucuses—rather than all, as at present, at a June primary that takes place well after the national nominee has been clearly identified in other, earlier primaries.) The national Democratic party actively campaigned, along with the present state party leadership, for the rejection of this plan, even while acknowledging that the proposal did not contradict national party rules and that the state party did have the right to make the change if it wished. The opponents of the plan argued that it would be too expensive and time consuming, although evidence presented from other states suggested that the cost would have been minimal and that the party-building effects would have justified the time required. But what the plan *would* have done is give local party activists a much stronger say in candidate selection.[16]

A further example from California of a party insisting on maintaining its own weakness is the refusal (at present writing) of the state Democratic party to support a second lawsuit that, if successful, will give California's parties the right to issue endorsements in local elections. This despite the fact that nothing contributes more to the weakness of parties—or is more patently unconstitutional—than refusing them their First Amendment right of free speech in local elections, as is presently the law in California.[17]

Why should the parties in the nation's most populous state—or in any state—be so eager to maintain themselves as agencies incapable of performing the functions of responsive intermediary between people and the state? The answer is not hard to find. Our current parties are not impersonal organizations; they are elite organizations operating on behalf of themselves and fellow elites. As such, they seek power; and our electoral system gives that power not to those who win the support of a majority of the electorate but to those who win a plurality of the vote. So long as victory is won, by however small a percentage of the potential electorate, the fewer who take part in politics the better for the parties. With the advent of mass communication, the parties do not need mass participation to win and do not want it. It is helpful to have a stable and docile work force that can be convoked when needed to carry out, for no pay, the tedious jobs of registration and getting out the vote. But beyond that it is very difficult to know what to do with activists, especially those who are concerned about social problems. It is hard to keep them from expecting to play a role in issue formulation and candidate recruitment, and hard to keep them from figuring out ways to hold representatives accountable to a broader public than that represented by the most powerful PACs. The tears our parties' leaders occasionally weep, over declining public support and loss of membership, should suggest to us that donkey and elephant might both well be replaced by crocodile.

Why We Still Need Real Parties

If the political parties of the United States have degenerated into mere fund-raising electoral machines working on behalf of candidates who represent ever more narrow interests, with no need for or interest in serving as responsive intermediaries between people and the state, and if the general public is at the same time contemptuous and disinterested, is there any point in trying to change the situation, and if so, how?

The first question is easier to answer than the second. The point in trying to do something to change the parties is that the status quo provides us with a set of conditions that should be intolerable to any citizenry committed to its own democratic governance. The parties have become the tool—and merely one among many that are stronger—of persons much more interested in taking power for personal advantage than in resolving the problems from which we as a nation suffer. . . .

Furthermore, the continuing inability of our political system to treat . . . problems effectively is rife with the danger that democracy itself will be cast casually aside by those who do continue to vote, and who are clearly becoming ever more prepared to accept any form of leadership that seems to promise succor. We have already gone a very long way in that direction by so drastically over-extending the powers of the presidency in recent years. Lacking the methods and arenas that real parties might provide us for articulating our problems, for exploring practicable political solutions, and for placing men and women in office who are dedicated to enacting those solutions, we now sign over all power to those we do not know and who do not know us; we call them "leaders" and keep them in office so faithfully that it is no wonder they lose all interest in knowing what precisely we would have them do.

Sometimes, of course, we become so overwhelmed by the immensity of a particular problem that we feel we must "do something." But normally we can think of nothing better to do than write a check on behalf of the appropriate single interest group that, even if it works hard on the problem in question (an assumption that is not always well founded), is very likely to do so by refusing the degree of compromise with other interests that is essential to produce a national agenda composed of interconnected and harmonized policies moving steadily in a consistent direction. Yes, we still need real political parties. Is there any way, however, to get them? Certainly there is little point in asking them to please reform themselves. Citizens must use the weapons they have at their command, to serve their own purposes. And what weapons are those? We have, above all, the possibility of using our intelligences to recognize not only the seriousness of the situation but also our own responsibility for effecting change. We have the vote, and we might learn to use it—and to withhold it—more wisely, refusing to support any party that does not offer to take at least a few steps in the direction of responsible performance of the functions that parties have always been expected to perform in democracies. Voting for a minor party that has no chance of victory can send a stronger message for change to the major parties than accepting, year after year, the dreary burden of deciding which of two barely distinguishable evils is the lesser.

However, these are weak arms against the arsenals accumulated by the major parties over the years in the battle for power. The real weapons are inside the major parties. All we really have to do is go in and take them. Thus far the major parties have contented themselves with merely discouraging our participation; they have not closed their gates altogether. They are open to us, and if we dared to enter them as citizens bent on restoring them to democratic usefulness, we could no doubt succeed in turning them back into agents of our will. Such an effort is within the realm of the possible, and given our current predicament, may be the only way to recreate our democracy. . . .

Notes

1. Thomas Hodgkin, *African Political Parties* (London: Penguin, 1961), p. 16.
2. The American habit of disliking parties began even before the institution had been well established. "There is nothing," said our first vice-president, John Adams, "I dread so much as the division of the Republic into two great parties, each under its leader. . . . This . . . is to be feared as the greatest political evil under the Constitution.
3. For what Van Buren said, see Richard Hofstadter, *The Idea of a Party System* (Berkeley: University of California Press, 1969), pp. 223–231.
4. As of the midterm elections of 1990, incumbency reelection rates had reached 96.9 percent in the Senate and 96.0 percent in the House. Only fifteen House incumbents and one incumbent Senator were defeated for reelection. See *Congressional Quarterly Almanac*, 1990, pp. 903–906.
5. William T. Riordon, *Plunkitt of Tammany Hall* (New York: E. P. Dutton, 1963).
6. David Mayhew, *Placing Parties in American Politics: Organization, Electoral Settings, and Government Activity in the Twentieth Century* (Princeton, N.J.: Princeton University Press, 1986).
7. In one of the more recent examples, a Superior Court judge in San Francisco issued a restraining order on November 27, 1991, against the Democratic Party of San Francisco, barring it from endorsing Mayor Art Agnos for reelection. See Richard Winger, "Democratic Party Muzzled," *Ballot Access News* (newsletter privately published in San Francisco), December 9, 1991, p. 3.

8. For figures on PAC independent expenditures, see *Statistical Abstract of the United States 1990* (U.S. Department of Commerce: Bureau of the Census, 1990), p. 267.

9. Jack Dennis, "Trends in Public Support for the American Party System, *British Journal of Political Science* 5 (April 1975): 187–230.

10. Howard Reiter, Parties and Elections in Corporate America (New York: St. Martin's, 1987); Warren E. Miller, Arthur H. Miller, and Edward J. Schneider, *American National Election Studies Data Sourcebook, 1952–1978* (Cambridge, Mass.: Harvard University Press, 1980). It should be noted that, with regard to believing that the parties care about people's opinions, the 1980 figure was actually an improvement over that of 1978—62 percent.

11. *The People, The Press and Politics 1990* (Los Angeles: Times-Mirror Center for the People and the Press), November 16, 1990.

12. *Gallup Poll Monthly*, September 1990, no. 300, p. 32, and May 1991, no. 308, p. 36.

13. Thomas E. Cronin, *Direct Democracy: The Politics of Initiative, Referendum, and Recall* (Cambridge, Mass.: Harvard University Press, 1989).

14. Ibid., pp. 80, 174, and 132.

15. Kay Lawson, "How State Laws Undermine Parties," in A. James Reichley, ed., *Elections American Style* (Washington, D.C.: Brookings Institution, 1987).

16. Kay Lawson, "Questions Raised by Recent Attempts at Local Party Reform," paper presented at the Workshop on Political Organizations and Parties, Annual Meeting of the American Political Science Association, Washington, D.C., August 28, 1991.

17. Winger, "Democratic Party Muzzled," p. 3.

Questions for Discussion

1. Why does the author believe that contemporary American parties have ceased to be "real" political parties? What functions should parties perform in a political system?

2. Why does Lawson believe that there is "little if any evidence that parties are interested in making changes that would put themselves back in the ring as leading agencies in the democratic process"? What does she believe must be done for parties to again become important political institutions?

6.2

Of Political Parties Great and Strong

Everett Carll Ladd

The overwhelming majority of scholars who study political parties ascribe to the view, outlined in the preceding selection, that strong political parties are essential for American democracy to work well. They agree that only coherent parties, controlled by informed citizens working within them, acting in programmatic ways, can provide the glue to overcome the inherent difficulties in the separation of governmental powers. Such "responsible" parties, they maintain, would lead to an improvement in governmental performance, as well as restore citizens' confidence in the political system.

In this article, Everett Carll Ladd dissents from the prevailing view. He believes that the argument for stronger parties "is at its base an argument for a larger government," resting more on normative assumptions about the role of government than on democratic necessities. Those who want strong parties, he says, also prefer "positive" government—one aggressive in enacting and expanding programs. But the assumed relationship between strong parties and sounder policy is difficult to empirically confirm. Further, the American public is ambivalent about government's proper role and is quite comfortable with divided government.

Ladd believes that the nation currently has a "mixed" party system—a relatively strong party presence in government coupled with a weakened party role within the electorate. In his view, those advocating stronger parties fail to understand the primary source of voter complaints—"partisan unresponsiveness and politics too dominated by institutions inside the Beltway"—and he sees little support among the public for increasing the strength of political parties.

For most of this century political science orthodoxy has held that American political parties need strengthening, to the end of improving the quality of the nation's democracy. For the last 20 years, the Committee for Party

---

The late Everett Carll Ladd was professor of political science and director of the Institute for Social Inquiry at the University of Connecticut and executive director of the Roper Center for Public Opinion Research.

Renewal* has carried high the torch for stronger parties with this message embodied in its statement of principles: "Parties are indispensable to the realization of democracy. The stakes are no less than that."

The committee believes that party organization must be revitalized and refurbished, that political parties need to be more coherent and programmatic participators in government, and that the ties of individual voters to parties need to be made deeper and more evidently influential in voting decisions. In this view, a bigger party presence is the *sine qua non* of improving governmental performance and thus of restoring citizen confidence in the political system.

My own dissatisfaction with this view has been rising steadily. Over the years I have come to realize that the argument for stronger parties is at its base an argument for a larger government. It rests on a bundle of normative assumptions about what government should do, not on inherent democratic requirements. It goes hand in hand with arguments that the United States needs more government to solve problems, that the checks and balances system has been a terrible barrier to getting needed programs enacted, and finally that, in general, the good society requires a big polity. . . . This is not to say that parties are unneeded as representative institutions or that their continued weakening is desirable. Parties are needed. However, much of the contemporary unease with politics and government does not result from a diminished party role; indeed, a strengthening of parties might well exacerbate present discontent.

Tocqueville and "Great Parties"

Political scientists advocating stronger parties have often found comfort in the commentary of Alexis de Tocqueville.† Tocqueville did not deal with the strength of voter ties to parties or the internal discipline of parties in government. But he did seem to come down on the side of an enlarged party presence in his discussion of "large" or "great" and "minor" or "small" parties. "The political parties that I style great," he wrote in the first volume of *Democracy in America,* "are those which cling to principles rather than to their consequences; to general and not to special cases; to ideas and not to men. These parties are usually distinguished by nobler features, more generous passions, more genuine convictions, and a more

---

* The Committee for Party Renewal represents a group of mostly political scientists and some journalists who are advocates for strengthening the organizational capacities of American political parties. Among the major reforms they advocate is increasing the party role in the nomination process for president and developing closer ties between elected public officials and the party organization.

† Alexis de Tocqueville was a Frenchman who came to the United States in 1831, originally to study the prison system. He traveled widely on his visit and later wrote *Democracy in America,* a penetrating analysis of the effect of popular government and egalitarianism on the social and political life of the world's only democracy then in existence.

bold and open conduct than the others. In them private interest, which always plays the chief part in political passions, is more studiously veiled under the pretext of the public good. . . ." Large parties, then, are ones with a larger reach in ideas and principles, which contend with one another to determine the fundamental direction of a polity. The Washington-Adams-Hamilton Federalists were in Tocqueville's view a great party, as were Jefferson's Republicans.

In contrast, the America of Andrew Jackson's presidency, which Tocqueville visited, had, in the Frenchman's view, only "small" parties. "[I]t happens that when a calm state succeeds a violent revolution," he wrote, "great men seem suddenly to disappear and the powers of the human mind to lie concealed." He paints a rather despairing picture of small parties. Thus, they "are generally deficient in political good faith. As they are not sustained or dignified by lofty purposes, they ostensibly display the selfishness of their character in their actions. They glow with a factitious zeal; their language is vehement, but their conduct is timid and irresolute. The means which they employ are as wretched as the end at which they aim."

It's easy to see what Tocqueville had in mind by these references. The party activity he witnessed in the 1830s often seemed petty. It involved a highly developed interest in patronage, but often failed to aim for loftier goals. It was a time of consummate party "wheeler-dealers." "Party bosses" made their appearance on our political stage then. The reach of the conflict between the "Jackson men" and the "Adams men" seemed to Tocqueville petty in comparison to the struggle between the Federalists and the Antifederalists over the institutional future of the American Revolution—and so, of course, it was.

But great intuitive thinker that he was, Tocqueville recognized a flaw in his own reasoning and preferences, which led him to qualify his initial distinction. "Society is convulsed by great parties," he continued, [but] "it is only agitated by minor ones; it is torn by the former, by the latter it is [only] degraded. . . . America has had great parties, but has them no longer: and if her happiness is thereby considerably increased, her morality has suffered."

Narrow, often self-serving patronage parties are not an ideal many of us wish to defend, and Tocqueville certainly did not defend them. Still, he felt compelled to argue that the absence of great parties in the United States of the 1830s meant that the nation's "happiness is thereby considerably increased." And, seeing much to commend in the earlier American experience with great parties he felt obliged to observe nonetheless that society in general "is convulsed" by them. Whatever was he talking about?

Just this. There is real splendor in seeing a party of large reach and high principle do battle in a time of great transition in a polity. The spectacle is all the more attractive, naturally, if that truly great party wins. Tocqueville's European experience made him keenly aware, of course, that it was by no means certain it would win.

Beyond this, nineteenth-century liberal that he was, Tocqueville recognized that having people consumed by politics is not a proper goal for the polity in the

long run. There will be times when they must be so absorbed, and one de-
voutly hoped the parties of that day would serve them well in their search for
better government. But much of the time a more prosaic existence has its
attractions. . . .

From Great Parties to Strong Parties . . . and Strong Government

It is not by chance that the United States, where political parties are institution-
ally weaker than in any other industrial democracy, is also the country where the
reach of the national government—though it has expanded greatly in recent
decades—is still the most restricted. More collectivist, less individualist political
outlooks encourage the formation of stronger, more elite-directed parties, and
such parties are in turn powerful instruments for state action. . . . But on the
whole, one wants strong parties in order to advance "positive" government—to
enact and enlarge programs. E. E. Schattschneider made the point clearly in his
classic *The Struggle for Party Government* in 1948:

"As a nation we have had little opportunity to prepare ourselves for the
realization that it is now necessary for the government to act as it has never acted
before. . . . The essence of the governmental crisis consists of a deficiency of the
power to create, adopt, and execute a comprehensive plan of action in advance
of a predictable catastrophe in time to prevent and minimize it. . . . The central
difficulty of the whole system—the difficulty which causes all of the difficulties—
is the fact the government characteristically suffers from a deficiency of the power
to govern."

. . . Whether strong parties tend to advance sounder policy is, admittedly, a huge
and complex empirical question. But until it is seen as an empirical question,
treatment of it cannot advance much beyond the position—"Well, that's what I
want anyway!" I find nothing in the canon of American political science that
gives more empirical weight to the critics of the present workings of the separation of powers than to the proponents. Evidence seems at least as strong for the
argument that America's system of separated power, relatively uncurbed by strong
and disciplined parties, has improved public policy by helping to slow the rush of
government expansion and lessen the likelihood of ill-considered, precipitant
actions.

Questioning the Ideal of "Maximalist Politics"

The idea that "more politics" is more or less automatically desirable is deeply
entrenched in contemporary political commentary—in the writings of political
scientists, journalists, and other analysts. We see this in the literature on nonvoting. With some notable exceptions, much of the work on voter turnout sees low
turnout as a huge problem, as a failure of democracy.

One may advocate efforts to promote vigorous citizenship—including encouraging voting—without subscribing to the argument that the relatively low turnout in the United States . . . is on its face evidence of a grievous weakness in our democratic life. But many have argued that it does indicate just that. Thus Arthur T. Hadley wrote, "America's present problem . . . is an apathetic, cross-pressured society with strong feelings of political impotence, where more and more people find their lives out of control, believe in luck, and refrain from voting. . . . For us, now, an increase in voting is a sign of political health." Gary R. Orren argues that "if the health of a democracy can be measured by the level of popular participation in its electoral system, ours is ailing."

The argument is riddled with flaws. Consider, for example, Hadley's view that America is beset by an increasingly widespread decline of social obligation and participation—a surge in the number of "refrainers." This is simply not true. Voter turnout *has* declined from the 1960 level—the highest in this century. . . . But outside of voting, the data do not support an argument that participation is in decline. A study done in 1990 under the direction of Sidney Verba, Kay L. Schlozman, Henry R. Brady, and Norman H. Nie, showed once again a populace that is highly participatory in most areas of political activity (such as contributing money to political organizations, getting in contact with government officials, and the like) and even more so in nonpolitical public affairs (from a vast variety of organizational memberships to charitable giving and voluntary action).

Similarly, new findings in the United States and in Western Europe show that (1) charitable giving and voluntary action levels are increasing, not decreasing, in the United States, and (2) the levels dwarf those in Western Europe. . . .

Some factors that encourage high turnout are surely undesirable. Extreme fear can be a powerful incentive to vote—so as to prevent the feared outcome. Columnist George F. Will has reminded us that in the two presidential ballots conducted in Germany in 1932, 86 and 84 percent of the electorate cast ballots. In 1933, 89 percent voted in the assembly election in which the Nazis triumphed. Will asked: "Did the high 1933 turnout make the Nazi regime especially legitimate? Were the 1932 turnouts a sign of the health of the Weimar Republic?" His answer is the right one: "The turnouts reflected the unhealthy stakes of politics then: elections determined which mobs ruled the streets and who went to concentration camps." Americans are less inclined to fear massive upheaval or a dramatic discontinuity resulting from any particular election. In this environment, some people who are less interested in politics apparently feel a degree of security sufficient to permit them not to vote. . . .

The American ideological tradition has from the country's forming insisted on the need for a large public sector and a relatively small state. Properly construed, "public sector" refers to matters of common concern and action. The public sector hardly need be just governmental. The American idea has been that our common or public concerns as a people require vigorous activity outside the sphere of government. Tocqueville remarked on this at length a century and a half ago. He noted, for example, the extraordinary interest-group activity on behalf of all kinds of issues and objectives. "The political associations that exist in the United States," he wrote, "are only a single feature in the midst of the immense assemblage of associations in that country. . . . The Americans make associations to give entertainments, to found seminaries, to build inns, to construct churches, to diffuse books, to send missionaries to the antipodes; in this manner they found hospitals, prisons, and schools. . . . Wherever at the head of some new undertaking you see the government in France, or a man of rank in England, in the United States you will be sure to find an association."

In the first volume of *Democracy*, Tocqueville had given the classic statement of the fact that—far from holding back collective energy and participation—American individualism was its very source: "In the United States associations are established to promote the public safety, commerce, industry, morality, and religion. There is no end which the human will despairs of attaining through the combined power of individuals united into a society."

Today's Publics Assess Government

Over the last several decades, Americans have been expressing increasingly ambivalent feelings about the scope of government and the quality of governmental performance.

On the one hand, we have remained—despite our complaints about government's record—an optimistic people who believe that problems are something to be solved, not endured. Thus, in an age of considerable national affluence, we have fairly high expectations with regard to action in areas as wide-ranging as the environment, crime, schools, health care, and poverty. We want action in these areas and usually see governmental action as one part of the necessary response.

On the other hand, all kinds of indicators reveal doubts about the wisdom of continuing to expand government's reach. Ever since the passage of Proposition 13 in California in 1978,* tax protests have been a common part of the American political experience, and a highly democratic one at that. That is, the strongest insistence that tax hikes be curbed has often come from the lower half of the income spectrum, not from the upper half. In general, at the same time we are endorsing major interventions by government, we are calling government too big, too inefficient, too intrusive. Given the choice between government that does more and costs more, and that which does less and costs less, we are indicating a strong preference for the latter.

---

* Proposition 13 was a ballot initiative designed to amend the California state constitution. It was approved by the state's voters in 1978. By rolling back property tax rates then in existence and setting a ceiling on future rates, the referendum limited the ability of localities to use the property tax to raise revenues. The success of the referendum became a national symbol of the ability of citizens to directly limit government spending.

Many Americans are evidently angry about the performance of the country's political institutions. Consider, for example, judgments about Congress. Surveys from the 1940s through the 1960s consistently showed the national legislature getting pretty good marks. When Gallup asked in 1958 whether Congress was doing a good or poor job, it found only 12 percent saying poor. In a June 1970 survey, Gallup showed its respondents a card on which there were 10 boxes, numbered from +5 (for institutions "you like very much") down to –5 ("dislike very much"). Only 3 percent assigned Congress to the –4 and –5 boxes, and only 10 percent gave it a negative rating of any kind. Thirty-six percent gave it either a +4 or a +5. Things are surely different now. A number of survey organizations regularly ask their respondents whether they approve or disapprove of the way Congress is doing its job. The proportions bounce around, depending on the overall national mood and the latest headlines on congressional doings. But with a few brief exceptions, . . . the proportion saying they approve Congress's performance has remained in the range of one-fourth to one-third of the public. . . .

Today Americans' complaints about governmental performance are generally sweeping. The expectations of government from this highly ambivalent and conflicted public seems reasonably well heeded by the current system. Looking at the almost $1.5 trillion federal budget enacted for FY '94, it's hard to make the case that governmental action has been throttled. At the same time, a public that is dubious about government's performance and about the wisdom of expanding state action further may be well served by a system that puts substantial checks and limits on the development of new programs.

The founders of the American system sought to establish and sustain a type of government at once energetic and limited. This admixture of seeming opposites is in a sense jarring, but it has received the continuing support of much of the populace. The levels of government today are far higher than they were in the past, but the same admixture pertains. The American system continues to produce government that is extraordinarily energetic and highly constrained.

Knowing What's Best

If Americans are ambivalent about government's proper role and reluctant to issue the call, "Charge!" and if they show no signs of wanting to strengthen political parties, why should we urge upon them steps toward a stronger and "more responsible" party system? The only defensible answer would be: because, though much of the public doesn't know it, the absence of a stronger party system is a major reason why so many people are so dissatisfied with governmental performance. Is that answer valid?

One reason to doubt its validity is the fact that dissatisfaction with government's performance is evident in nearly all of the world's industrial democracies, not just the United States. Indeed, the United States does not rank at all high comparatively on many of these measures. If many countries with strong party systems manifest as much or more dissatisfaction with governmental institutions and performance as the United States does, the idea that strengthening our party system is likely to contribute to increased satisfaction and confidence is dubious. Admittedly, it does not necessarily reject such strengthening, since many other factors can shape confidence levels.

Today, majorities of record or near-record proportions are expressing dissatisfaction with or pessimism about their country's political and economic performance and their own personal prospects. In France, for example, a country with strong and disciplined political parties, economic pessimism is rampant, and the entire political class has come under intense criticism. The ruling Socialists were dealt a massive defeat in the 1993 elections for the National Assembly. With only a couple of exceptions, politicians of all the parties got low marks. In Great Britain, Prime Minister John Major has some of the lowest approval ratings of any British prime minister. Labour fares better, but its showing in the recent local elections where the Liberal Democrats bested it reveals a real lack of enthusiasm for the country's other major party.*

The argument on behalf of stronger parties needs to be examined in three distinct arenas—party organization, party in government, and party in the electorate. The case for stronger parties in the first two seems very weak. What's more, the argument runs in precisely the opposite direction from that which the public says it wants. The public's criticism, as seen clearly in survey data, is that politics is too much captured by political insiders—for example, by the elected Democratic and Republican politicians in the national legislature—and in general that "the system" is too insulated from meaningful day-to-day popular control. The call is somehow to check and limit the political class.

The last thing this public wants is stronger party organization and stronger party apparatus in government. Its present discontents push it in a direction similar to that pursued by the Progressive Movement early in this century. The Progressives believed that the principal institutions of American representative democracy—political parties, legislatures, city councils, and the like—had been captured by "the interests," were riddled with corruption, and often had been wrested from popular control. Muckraking journalists,† among them Ida M. Tarbell and Lincoln Steffens, graphically portrayed the venality and unresponsiveness that they saw as all too common in the nation's political life.

Many in the Progressive Movement concluded that the only way to cure these ills was to give individual citizens new authority to override and control repre-

---

* In May 1997 Labour party candidates won a majority in parliamentary elections, and Labour's Tony Blair became prime minister.

† Muckrakers is the label given to a group of early-twentieth-century writers who were instrumental in exposing political and business corruption during the period. Writing typically in a crusading style, the muckraking authors contributed to arousing public concern, which in a number of cases led to efforts to correct the exposed problems.

sentative institutions. They backed and saw enacted a host of "direct democracy" reforms: the direct primary to take nominations away from party "bosses"; initiatives and referenda, to allow the people to make laws directly; the recall, to permit voters to "kick the bums out" when they were performing badly, even before their regular terms were up. The success that the reformers had makes clear that they tapped a deep lode of resentment.

Today public frustrations resemble those of the Progressive Era and probably surpass anything between that era and our own. As in the Progressive Era, dissatisfaction gets expressed in increased backing for direct democracy. The American political culture is strongly individualistic, and we are always sympathetic to the idea of direct citizenry intervention above and beyond elections. But when things are seen going poorly in terms of the institutions' performance, direct democracy's appeal gets a special boost.

Many of the innovations of the Progressive Era, such as referenda and primaries, are in wide use today. And the public would now extend them further. But today's direct democracy agenda finds other expressions. Backing for term limits is one. Support for the Perot movement is another.

Appropriate Individualism

Political science has long favored a strengthening of parties, as opposed to more direct democracy, to deal with governmental unresponsiveness and increase popular control. The public plainly doesn't agree. Some might dismiss its evident disagreement with anything that smacks of augmenting the party apparatus and control as simply the unthinking response of a highly individualist culture. The culture is highly individualist. And that's not going to change, so practical politics suggests that improvements be made within its dictates. But beyond this, if Americans are at times excessively obedient to individualist assertions, it's not at all clear that they are wrong on the proper role of party organization and party machinery in government. Party leaders *are* political insiders. As modern government has mushroomed, the political class *has* become more insulated. Finding ways to check it further might permit ordinary voters to intervene more effectively and extensively in setting public policy.

The United States may not be beset by the old-fashioned venality and corruption that the Progressives faced, but the primary representative institutions often seem worlds apart from the general public, responding to insider agendas. Politics as usual inside the Beltway is highly insulated and in a sense isolated. The interests that dominate "Beltway politics" differ from those that the Progressives battled, but they may be no less insensitive to popular calls for change. The old Progressive answer of extending direct citizen authority and intervention deserves careful reconsideration as a partial answer to present-day insufficiencies and shortcomings in representative democracy.

Appropriate Party Bolstering

The one area where a strong case can be made for modest steps to strengthen the party presence involves the electorate. One of the most unusual features of the contemporary party system is the frequency with which split results are attained—for example, the Republicans winning the presidency pretty regularly, but not controlling both houses of Congress since 1954.* This condition seems to have two quite different sources—one involving something that much of the public intends, but the other quite unintentional and indeed fundamentally unwanted.

The intended dimension, what I call cognitive Madisonianism, starts from the fact that Americans have historically been less troubled than their counterparts in other democracies about divided control. It accords with the general thrust and biases of separation of powers. Into this, however, it seems that something new has been added. The high measure of ambivalence that so many citizens have about government's role, and from this the doubts they entertain about both political parties, seems to be well served by electoral outcomes that frequently give each of the major parties a piece of the action.

Today's public wants somewhat contradictory things of the modern state. And it sees the Democrats and Republicans as differing significantly on the issue of government's role. Cognitive Madisonianism insists that the two parties' competing views on government's proper role be pitted one against another, as when a Republican executive pushes one way and a Democratic legislature the other. The empirical work needed to explore cognitive Madisonianism satisfactorily has not been done—despite extensive surveys on related topics. We do know that high degrees of ambivalence concerning government's role have been present over the last 25 years, but survey data show nothing comparable for earlier periods, and large segments of the public express broad approval of divided government.

Those who see evidence of cognitive Madisonianism in two-tier voting must acknowledge nonetheless that more is at work. Even in the face of pronounced voter dissatisfaction with Congress, for example, historically unprecedented majorities of incumbents of both parties have been winning reelection, and House of Representative incumbents typically win by big margins. Underlying this development are several notable features of contemporary electioneering: (1) incumbents generally enjoy huge advantages in campaign contributions, and (2) they also enjoy a big advantage in government-provided resources—notably in the very large staffs given members through the "reforms" of the late 1960s and early 1970s. House members' staff was tripled, and many members have put a large bloc of their new assistants to work back in their districts—little electoral

---

* In 1994 the Republicans won majorities in both Houses of Congress. Although a reversal of tradition, this still resulted in "divided government," since Democrat Bill Clinton had been elected president in 1992.

machines available to them year-round at public expense. Finally, whereas in races for governor and U.S. senator, as well as for president, many voters know something substantial about the candidates' policy stands and records, they usually don't have much information of this kind on House members. They are likely, though, to have some vaguely favorable image of him or her, while having no impression at all of the challenger.

Getting voters to pay a bit more attention to party labels is the one thing that could upset this present dynamic. A voter might not know anything about a member of Congress's voting record, but still vote against him or her in favor of a challenger who is less known because the voter wanted to change party control, to give the "outs" a chance. There is abundant evidence that this is exactly what has happened historically. But over the last quarter-century, as incumbents have gained election resources far greater than ever before, the proportion of voters bound by significant "party awareness" has declined precipitously. "Vote for the person, not the party," is in many ways laudable. It conforms entirely to the American individualist tradition of democratic governance. Nonetheless, it sometimes works poorly, especially when large numbers of voters know little of consequence about the person. What's more, the person in Congress usually votes with his party these days. The pronounced decline of "party thinking" leaves many voters ill-equipped to express effectively the dissatisfaction they clearly feel. Voters don't like important aspects of legislative performance, for example, but voting "for the person" denies them a means of doing much to address their dissatisfaction. . . .

A Substantial Party Presence

More than three decades ago, political scientist and historian Clinton Rossiter wrote eloquently on the virtues of a "mixed" party system, one that gives a large role to the institutional parties and at the same time to individual voters. The current assumption in political science, though, is that the mixed system is no more because the party presence has declined so markedly. This is an excessive response to current trends and an unbalanced reading of them. Some developments have reduced the party presence. The media, for example, play a much larger role in political communication generally and in the process of candidate choice than ever before—mostly at the parties' expense.

But at the same time, in other areas we have actually moved toward stronger and in a way more disciplined political parties. The vehicle of the new "discipline" isn't institutional sanctions—party leaders being able to "punish" recalcitrant members—but rather growing ideological homogeneity within each of the two major parties. . . .

In recent years, . . . there has been a powerful movement toward greater "discipline," through the vehicle of internal philosophical agreement. Congressional Democrats today are much more coherently a liberal party, and congressional Republicans much more a conservative one than ever before. We can see this from the splendid roll-call analysis done regularly by political scientist William Schneider and his colleagues at *National Journal*. In their January 1991 report, for example, Richard E. Cohen and William Schneider noted that "bipartisanship was a rare commodity on key congressional votes in 1990. And divisions within each party narrowed, according to *National Journal*'s annual congressional vote ratings. . . . Southern Democrats and eastern Republicans, the traditional centers of ideological moderation in both the House and Senate, moved further apart in 1990. Their shifts (the southern Democrats to the Left and the eastern Republicans to the Right) were another sign of the increased partisanship [i.e., united parties arrayed against each other] in both chambers." The 1994 report by Cohen and Schneider reiterated similar findings and gave powerful evidence on the newfound responsibility of both congressional parties.

A Final Word

. . . the present party system contains its own distinctive strengths as well as new elements of weakness. The parties are much more programmatically coherent and internally disciplined by ideological agreement. . . . They present far clearer choices for all who care to pay attention. Advocates of stronger and more responsible parties have for the most part failed to call attention to the marked party strengthening evident in the data on the new internal coherence of the congressional Republican and Democratic parties.

The United States needs a mixed system, and it has one. Parties have been weakened in some regards but strengthened in others. They remain a substantial presence in American political life. They remain about as much of a presence as the public wants or will abide. And it is far from clear that groups such as the Committee on Party Renewal, which seek a general strengthening of parties in the electorate, as organizations, and in government, address the principal source of voter complaint—partisan unresponsiveness and a politics too dominated by institutions inside the Beltway.

Questions for Discussion

1. What, according to Ladd, is the relationship between strong political parties and an activist government?
2. What evidence does Ladd present to defend his view that the public does not want stronger political parties?
3. What does Ladd mean by "cognitive Madisonianism"? Why does he believe the public actually likes divided government? Do you agree?

6.3

Creative Party Finances in the Information Age

John Kenneth White and Daniel M. Shea

Many political observers believe that political parties have been in long-term decline, most notably regarding the electoral process. The decline is particularly evident during political campaigns, as the party organization's once near-monopoly on mobilizing voters is now shared with the media, political consultants, and interest groups. Since 1974, direct party spending on behalf of candidates has been limited, and responsibility for campaign fund-raising and for reporting to the Federal Election Commission lies squarely in the hands of each candidate's campaign committee.

But parties have learned to play a substantial role in campaigns and elections. Indeed, parties may not so much be in decline but in the midst of adapting to a new electoral role. Today's national party organizations have emerged as major providers of services to their candidates, ranging from offering fund-raising and survey-research help to running advertisements that support campaign efforts.

In this selection,* John Kenneth White and Daniel Shea discuss how both major parties have successfully adapted to the challenge posed by the trend toward candidate-centered electoral politics, in which money plays a crucial factor. According to White and Shea, parties have shown a "bold willingness to test the limits of campaign finance regulations," through such "creative" devices as issue advocacy, independent expenditures, soft money, state transfers, and bundling. The authors, however, worry about whether the new national party activities are healthy for American democracy.

T he organizational response by parties to the movement away from party brand loyalty has been greater services to candidates. Without money, party organizations could not help their clients, especially with the new tools of the Information Age, like survey research and television advertisements. It is not a coincidence that the drive to amass larger

---

John Kenneth White is Professor of Political Science at the Catholic University of America. Daniel M. Shea is Professor of Political Science at Allegheny College.

* Taken from John Kenneth White and Daniel M. Shea, "Creative Party Finances in the Information Age," in *New Party Politics: From Jefferson to Hamilton to the Information Age* (Boston: Bedford St. Martins, 2000), 222–236.

war chests began at precisely the time the national party committees adopted their professional, service-oriented outlook. By the end of the 1980s, both national parties had honed sophisticated fund-raising techniques, and they were working.

Party coffers swelled. In the mid-1970s, the Republicans collected roughly $40 million per election cycle. The Democrats lagged behind, bringing in approximately $18 million in receipts. By the late 1980s, these figures had jumped to well over $300 million and nearly $100 million, respectively. Within a decade these numbers had doubled again, and by 1996 the GOP raised over $416 million, with the Democrats compiling $221 million. Table 6.1 charts the receipts of Republicans and Democrats during the last two decades.

Two things make this growth particularly impressive. First, party fund-raising has been successful in spite of FECA regulations designed to reduce the flow of big money in elections. Second, and much related, these figures do not include an entire category of receipts, comprising hundreds of millions per election, dubbed "soft money." Soft money refers to funds raised outside the restraints of federal laws, but spent on activities to influence federal elections. An important distinction was made in a 1979 FECA ruling that permitted a portion of money raised for party building to be set aside in a special account. For example, money raised by the DNC to register voters in a given state or to run commercials designed to get out the vote can be stored in a special "non-federal" or soft money account. Hard money, on the other hand, refers to party money raised specifically for federal election campaigns. It is given to candidates either as a direct contribution or as a coordinated expenditure.

Several forces have contributed to the unprecedented fund-raising bonanza. Competition for control of the House of Representatives became a reality in the early 1990s. During the prior three decades, the Democratic lock on the House

Table 6.1
National Party Hard Money Receipts 1980 through 1998 (in millions of dollars)*

Party	1980	1982	1984	1986	1988
Democrats	$32	$39	$98	$65	$127
Republicans	$168	$215	$297	$255	$263

Party	1990	1992	1994	1996	1998
Democrats	$87	$178	$140	$222	$160
Republicans	$205	$267	$246	$416	$285

* Federal (hard dollars) only.
Source: Federal Election Commission New Release, April 9, 1999.

seemed impenetrable. But as GOP gains continued to mount, especially in the South, both parties realized a change was possible. The "earthquake of 1994" was actually quite predictable. As the uncertainty of the Democrats' hold on the House grew, so too did party spending on these races (see "The Parties Speak: Ten Myths about Money in Politics"). From 1986 to 1994, the amount of money spent by Democrats on congressional races more than tripled—from $6.4 million to nearly $22 million. The rate of growth for the GOP was a bit slower, perhaps because they were already spending heavily on these races, but even so went from just under $17 million in 1986 to $21.4 million a decade later. Of course, greater spending means a greater emphasis on raising funds.

Once the Republicans took control of the House in 1994, the ability for the parties to raise money from access-seeking groups and individuals was much simpler. The GOP found themselves in the unique position of being able to recast the direction of government, a prospect that excited many groups in their coalition and struck fear among those aligned with the Democrats. It is likely that this uncertainty compelled influence-seekers to hedge their bets, as best they could, and give lavishly to both parties (or anyone else who would/could take it, for that matter). This uncertainty factor was played out in other ways, at both the congressional and presidential election levels.

Finally, both parties demonstrated a bold willingness to test the limits of campaign finance regulations. The real story of party finances in the 1990s is one of clever ways of subverting and stretching FECA limits, including issue advocacy, independent expenditures, soft money, state transfers, and bundling.

Issue Advocacy

At Bill Clinton's urging, the DNC implemented an aggressive fund-raising plan and engineered a novel way of spending money. From July 1995 until election day 1996, the DNC bombarded the television airwaves with thousands of commercials. These spots cost $34 million, none of which was drawn from Clinton's campaign committee accounts.

How was this possible? As already noted, provisions of the Federal Election Commission stipulate that any money spent by a party "for the purpose of influencing" a candidate's chance in an election are considered a qualified expense, and therefore subject to limits. Such restrictions were upheld in *Buckley* v. *Valeo*.* The Court noted, however, that limits can be applied only to expenditures that expressly advocate the election or defeat of a candidate. Put differently, if an advertisement does not contain the magic words, like "vote for candidate

---

* *Buckley* v. *Valeo* was a U.S. Supreme Court case that upheld most of the provisions of the Federal Election Campaign Act of 1974, including limitations on party expenditures in campaigns. Prior to the act, party expenditures were not limited by law.

X" or "vote against candidate Y," it cannot be considered a campaign advertisement and therefore is not subject to limitations.

The DNC picked up on this loophole and ran with it. They crafted a series of issue advocacy spots that steered clear of expressly advocating Bill Clinton's reelection. This did not mean that the actor in the commercials could not be the president himself. Quite the contrary, the advertisements showed a hard-working Clinton in the serenity of the Oval Office acting as a barrier against "radical Republicanism." Voters in a dozen key states saw these DNC advertisements about once every three days for a year-and-a-half. To them, the ads were simply pro-Clinton commercials, but to the operatives at the DNC they were issue ads, protected by the First Amendment. The scheme worked. The Republicans eventually caught on to the issue advocacy scam and spent approximately $20 million. As noted by one party finance scholar, "this innovative form of party spending essentially rendered the contributions and spending limits of the FEC meaningless."[1] Table 6.2 notes two television commercials that were dubbed "issue ads." To most observers, they implied a good deal more than a discussion about public policy.

A study conducted by Paul Herrnson and Diana Dwyre examined the differences between television advertisements directly sponsored by candidates and those sponsored by the parties considered issue advocacy. Pundits have argued that the difference between the two is artificial, based on a poor understanding of campaign communications. The courts have found some sort of difference, they argue, where none exists. By examining a 1996 U.S. Senate race in careful detail, Herrnson and Dwyre conclude that the critics are essentially correct: There are more similarities than differences between candidate ads and party ads. The only real difference they find is that party-sponsored commercials tend to be more negative. They conclude by suggesting that the shift to party-based independent expenditures and issue ads has the potential to change the nature of congressional elections.[2]

By 1998, both parties had stepped-up their issue advocacy spending. The tack was still rather new, but national party operatives from both sides of the aisle seemed willing to learn. The Republicans orchestrated an aggressive fund-raising scheme called "operation breakout." The goal was to raise upwards of $20 million, divided equally between soft money expenditures and issue advocacy.

Independent Expenditures

But there is more to the story of innovative finance in the 1990s than issue advocacy. A second line of assault has been independent expenditures. In June of 1996, the Supreme Court issued a ruling in *Colorado Republican Federal Campaign Committee* v. *Federal Elections Commission*, a case that involved a decade-old complaint. In 1984, Democratic Representative Tim Wirth had thrown his hat

Table 6.2

When a Campaign Ad Is Not a Campaign Ad: Issue Advocacy Spots from the 1996 Election*

#1. Clinton Spot: "Finish" (released May 6, 1996)

Announcer:
> Head Start, Student Loans, Toxic Cleanup, Extra Police, Anti-Drug Programs.
> Dole-Gingrich want them cut. Now they're safe.
> Protected in the '96 budget because the President stood firm.
> Dole-Gingrich? Deadlock. Gridlock. Shutdowns.

The President's plan? Finish the job. Balance the budget. Reform welfare. Cut taxes. Protect Medicare.
> President Clinton says, get it done.
> Meet our challenges. Protect our values.

#2. Dole Spot: "More" (released June 20, 1996)

Announcer:
> Did you know there are over five million illegal immigrants in the United States?
> And that you spend five and one-half billion dollars a year to support them with welfare, food stamps, and other services?
> Under President Clinton, spending on illegals has gone up. While wages for the typical worker has gone down.
> And when efforts are made to stop giving benefits to illegal immigrants, Bill Clinton opposed them.
> Tell President Clinton to stop giving benefits to illegals, and end wasteful Washington spending.

---

* Both of these television advertisements were declared issue advocacy, and therefore not subject to federal spending restrictions.

Source: Brooks Jackson, "Financing the 1996 Campaign: The Law of the Jungle," in Larry J. Sabato, ed., *Toward the Millennium: The Elections of 1996* (Needham Heights, Mass.: Allyn & Bacon, 1997), 237.

---

in the ring for the U.S. Senate, but before any Republican candidate had done the same, the Colorado Republican Party launched a series of television ads attacking Wirth. The Federal Election Commission ruled that this expenditure, totaling a mere $15,000, should be counted against the party's spending limits that are applied to all senatorial campaigns. The Colorado Republicans disagreed, arguing their ad campaign was an independent expenditure—a form of speech protected under *Buckley*.

The Court sided with the Colorado Republicans, but the decision was far from unanimous. Four fragmented opinions were handed down, with three justices writing the plurality opinion. It was agreed that restrictions on "independent" advertisements are constitutionally protected, especially for political parties. Building upon this decision, and the fact that four of the other justices (in two separate opinions) were willing to strike down restrictions on party spending coordinated with the candidates, both parties pushed the envelope and began independent expenditure campaigns. In 1996, it was limited mostly to U.S. Senate races, with the amount totaling just over $11 million. (The Republicans were the most aggressive in this regard.) At first glance this amount might appear insignificant; yet considering that no party funds were spent in this way prior to 1996, this tactic marked yet another clever innovation—and provided a blueprint for future party spending. Moreover, the *Colorado* decision assured operatives in both parties that their issue advocacy programs would receive a friendly hearing in the courts if push came to shove.

Hard and Soft Money

Hard money refers to contributions to particular candidates that are subject to federal and state limits. Once these contributions are made, the party relinquishes control of the funds to the candidate. In 1998, congressional candidates could receive a $10,000 hard money contribution from their national party committees for a total contribution limit of $30,000 per election cycle. There is an additional $17,000 limit for Senate candidates shared by the national committee and the senate campaign committee. State parties can give up to $5,000 per Senate candidate each election.

Related to hard money contributions, parties can use *coordinated expenditures* to help candidates. Here, both the party and the candidate share control of the funds. Several common coordinated expenses including polling, direct mail, get-out-the-vote drives, and the production of radio and television commercials. In 1998, national parties were allowed to spend a maximum of $32,550 in coordinated expenditures per race. State party committees were limited to the same amount, and were allowed to transfer their spending limits to the national party through what is dubbed *agency agreements*. In effect, these agreements allow the national parties to double their spending limits. Coordinated expenditure limits for Senate races vary by population, ranging from just under $62,000 to a high of $1.5 million.

Both hard money and coordinated expenditures are fully disclosed. Table 6.3 highlights both of these more traditional forms of party giving, spanning from 1980 to 1998. The table suggests party giving is significant. There are fluctuations, based on whether it is a presidential election year, but on the whole both parties afford congressional candidates a great deal of help. There has been a shift away from direct contributions. Given that the national party committees have become more centralized and professional (i.e., more Hamiltonian), it makes sense that they would be anxious to play a role in how their money is spent. The

Table 6.3
National Party Committee Hard Money and Coordinated Expenditures, 1980–1998 (in millions of dollars)

Party	1980	1982	1984	1986	1988	1990	1992	1994	1996	1998
Democrats										
DNC										
Direct contributions	.78	.21	1.5	.03	.19	.06	<.01	.09	.03	<.01
Coordinated expenditures	7.8	.24	4.2	.51	11.2	.15	13.1	.38	7.0	6.0
DSCC										
Direct contributions	.95	.90	.66	.86	.60	.53	.69	.59	.56	.30
Coordinated expenditures	1.2	3.2	6.2	9.1	8.5	5.6	13.1	13.5	8.7	<.01
DCCC										
Direct contributions	1.2	.95	1.2	.91	.92	.56	.97	1.1	1.1	.43
Coordinated expenditures	.68	.34	1.8	2.3	3.3	3.6	4.8	8.1	5.9	2.9
Totals	11.3	5.8	15.5	13.6	24.8	10.5	32.6	23.7	23.2	9.7
Republicans										
RNC										
Direct contributions	1.6	2.8	1.3	.52	.45	.32	.91	.60	.50	.44
Coordinated expenditures	10.6	.39	10.7	<.01	11.4	.06	13.1	5.18	23.7	3.9
NRSC										
Direct contributions	.82	.94	.88	.94	1.0	.87	.80	.69	.72	.28
Coordinated expenditures	9.9	14.7	10.6	14.8	14.1	9.6	19.1	12.0	.32	.04
NRCC										
Direct contributions	3.9	4.3	4.1	2.5	2.1	1.2	.85	.87	1.3	.78
Coordinated expenditures	2.4	8.5	9.8	6.1	5.6	3.5	6.0	4.3	7.6	5.1
Total	29.4	31.6	37.4	62.2	34.9	15.5	40.8	23.6	34.1	10.5

Source: Federal Election Commission data.

Table 6.4

National Party Soft-Money Activity in the 1990s (receipts in millions of dollars)*

Party	1992	1994	1996	1998
DNC	36.4	48.3	103.3	56.9
DCCC	.51	5.6	11.3	16.8
DSCC	.66	.41	14.6	25.9
Total	42.1	54.1	127.1	92.8
RNC	41.8	49.3	114.6	74.8
NRCC	7.1	8.1	18.9	26.9
NRSC	10.5	6.1	27.7	37.9
Total	57.8	57.7	146.6	131.6

* Disbursements were nearly identical.
Source: Federal Elections Commission press release, April 9, 1999.

table underscores the import role that "hill committees"* now play in congressional elections. A few decades ago these units were minor players, but today they provide massive sums. The role of the National Republican Senatorial Committee (NRSC) and the NRCC in the early 1990s is most impressive. Between 1990 and 1994, the NRSC spent well over $40 million in direct contributions and coordinated expenditures. Finally, by comparing this table to Table 6.4, we find that the most significant growth in party involvement in congressional campaigning is not direct contributions or coordinated expenditures, but rather in soft money expenditures. Although reported contributions have remained somewhat level over the last two decades, soft money disbursements have shot up.

Collecting and disbursing soft money has become a full-time occupation for both national party committees and the hill committees. The soft money strategy is where the national party committees raise massive sums of money, but instead of spending it on behalf of a particular candidate, which would be subject to federal limits, they give it to state party committees or spend it on general party-building activities. There are a number of common soft money activities, including joint fund-raising costs, voter mobilization programs, administrative costs shared with state party organizations, and voter registration drives. In 1992, about 20 percent of soft money was transferred directly to state party organiza-

---

* *Hill committees* refers to the four party committees in the U.S. Senate and House of Representatives that raise and disburse funds to elect and re-elect members of their respective parties. The Democratic Congressional Campaign Committee (DCCC), and the Democratic Senatorial Campaign Committee (DSCC) and the National Republican Congressional Committee (NRCC) and the National Republican Senatorial Committee (NRSC) have emerged as major forces in campaign fundraising over the past two decades.

Table 6.5

Top Ten Soft Money Donors to the National Party Committees for the 1996 Election Cycle

Republican Donors	Amount	Democratic Donors	Amount
Philip Morris	$2,185,118	Jos. E. Seagram & Sons	$1,155,000
RJR Nabisco	$995,175	Walt Disney Co.	$866,800
Atlantic Richfield	$702,921	Communications Workers of America	$770,750
Jos. E. Seagram & Sons	$646,600	Food and Commercial Workers Union	$573,050
American Financial Corp.	$562,000	MCI	$536,136
AT&T	$549,590	Dream Works SKG	$525,000
Brown and Williamson	$515,000	Integrated Health Services	$524,000
U.S. Tobacco	$502,403	Assn. of Trial Lawyers	$515,000
Mariam Cannon Hayes	$500,000	Goldman, Sachs & Co.	$510,000

Source: Brooks Jackson, "Financing the 1996 Campaign: The Law of the Jungle," in Larry J. Sabato, ed., *Toward the Millennium: The Elections of 1996* (Needham Heights, Mass.: Allyn & Bacon, 1997), 245.

tions. By 1996, this increased to about 50 percent, probably due to the large number of joint television campaigns in target states. As noted in Table 6.4, the national parties collected and disbursed nearly $300 million in soft money in 1996—a whopping 200 percent increase over 1992, the previous presidential election year. There is also a near doubling of off-year soft money collection between 1994 and 1998.*

Soft money has also become the means by which fat cat contributors can channel money into the process. There are limits on the amount of money an individual, corporation, labor union, or interest group can give to candidates, but no restrictions on how much they can give to a national party committee. It has become the loophole of choice. In 1998, George Bush and the GOP organized what they dubbed "Team 100," a group where membership was limited to those who had donated at least $100,000 to the party. The Democrats actually outraised the Republicans that year in soft money. Just after the 1994 election, the GOP announced that it had received a $2.5 million donation from Amway Corporation. In 1996, the tobacco manufacturer Philip Morris contributed over $2 million to the Republicans and Seagrams liquor gave over $1 million to the Democrats. That year, some 303 contributors gave at least $100,000. Table 6.5 notes the top ten soft money contributors to both parties in the 1996 election.

---

* Parties raised more than $457 million in soft money donations in the 2000 election cycle. Republicans took in $239 million of such contributions, whereas Democrats garnered $218 million.

Transfers to State Party Committees

Federal laws require disclosure of soft money contributions, so we know who is giving these large sums to the parties at the national level. Several states, however, have limited reporting requirements and many have none at all. It is increasingly common to have large contributors send their checks to state party committees; the money is then used to support a specific candidate or transferred to the national party committees. A similar trick is for the national party committees to send money to the state committees, where it is then channeled back to the national party as a hard money contribution. Generally, the state committee is allowed to skim some of the funds for their trouble. In 1997, the DNC approached several state committees with a scheme for trading soft for hard dollars; they were offering a 10 percent commission, and there were many takers. Between January 1997 and April 1998, the DNC sent soft money contributions ranging from $11,000 to $172,000 to several states, and within days received back from these state hard dollar contributions—minus the commissions, of course.

The outcome of this activity has allowed the state party committees to play an increasing role in congressional elections. Their coffers are swelling and candidates are now expecting help from these organizations—a drastic change from the 1970s. On the other hand, money transferring is just another example of how the party system has become top-down . . . State and local committees have more resources than in the past, but have also lost autonomy to the national parties. State party leaders are increasingly frustrated by the strings attached to these deals, but go along with them because of the money involved.

Bundling

The parties, along with scores of favor-seeking interest groups, have devised a tool recently dubbed "bundling." This practice entails collecting checks made payable to a specific candidate by an intermediate agent, such as a party operative. These checks are individually within the legal limit (under $1,000 for an individual contribution and $5,000 for a PAC contribution), but combined to allow the party to contribute an immense "bundle of joy" to needy candidates. Of course, it also allows the party to receive credit for its efforts from the candidate.

Funding Nominating Conventions

Finally, the parties have discovered yet another finance regulation loophole, this one related to the funding of their presidential nominating conventions. In 1996, both parties received $12.4 million in public funds to pay for their conventions. According to FECA rules, the only other money that the parties can receive would be gifts from companies with a local business connection in the city where the convention is being held—"host committees." Not a single *Fortune 500* company is located in San Diego, the site of the GOP convention in 1996, but the party took the position that any business selling its products in the city had a "local connection." Philip Morris, Time Warner, Microsoft and AT&T gave the party millions for the event. Amway Corporation, the same company that gave the Republicans $2.5 million in 1994, gave another $1.3 million for the convention in 1996. As for the Democrats, the Chicago Committee raised just under $21 million from private donors. Many corporations gave to both conventions. As noted by Brooks Jackson, a CNN correspondent, "The post-Watergate limits broke down in spectacular fashion. . . . Both parties consumed record amounts of money even though the conventions had long since lost their original function: choosing a candidate.[3]

. . . the tale of party money in American elections is long, convoluted, and ever-changing. Certainly the variations during the 1990s are enough to make one's head spin. Each election, it seems that new court decisions, FECA rulings, and strategic approaches push parties and candidates down new fund-raising paths. Not long ago coordinated expenditures were voguish; today it seems that issue advocacy and soft money are on top.

Since the 1960s, the means by which parties and candidates could reach out to voters has been revolutionized. Not long ago legions of party activists hit the streets to rally support for their ticket, but today television commercials do the same in a fraction of the time. Computerized mailing lists have replaced literature drops, sophisticated telemarketing operations have taken over for the local phone bank, and satellite teleconferencing has replaced smoke-filled rooms. The Internet is also bursting onto the campaign scene. . . .

This chapter has also underscored that America's parties have demonstrated an ability to adapt and refine their role to changing environmental constraints— this time to new technologies, federal regulations, and the spiraling cost of elections. Both parties have devised new ways of squeezing the fat from the frying pan. With immense war chests, the parties are today key players in the election process. This is true at all levels of government, but especially so at the national level.

What is perhaps most surprising about this turn is that it has occurred even though average voters seem increasingly frustrated with partisan politics. Candidates need money and the parties are now in a position to help. But this does not mean that the voters have been lured back into the system. Although issue advocacy, independent expenditures, transfers, bundling, and soft money have given party organizations renewed energy, these activities have worsened the public's skepticism about the party system. Most see the proliferation of border-line fund-raising as a pestilence. Calls for reform, this time directed at party-based loopholes like soft money, are growing. It is likely that the parties will continue to fall back on the Court's interpretation of money and free speech in *Buckley*, but this does not mean that the public will be onboard. From their perspective, it is all a scam.

The best way to characterize the turn parties have taken with regard to raising and disbursing funds, then, is to return to our models of party politics. Without question, the focus that the national party committees place on raising ever-larger sums has led to a professionalization and centralization of the party system. Neighborhood-based electioneering, where activists visit their neighbors and rally support for a ticket, is gone—or at the very least fading fast. The Jeffersonian model has been replaced nearly overnight with electronic communications, campaign consultants, and aggressive national party committees. The party system has also maintained its tight connection to wealthy individuals and affluent groups. One might even suggest that the fat cat-party connection is as strong in the Information Age as at any point in our nation's history. How one interprets this development depends greatly on one's outlook about the proper course of party politics and the role of the average citizen in democracy. . . .

Notes

1. Anthony Corrado, "Financing the 1996 Elections," in Gerald M. Pomper, ed., *The Election of 1996* (Chatham, NJ: Chatham House, 1997), 148.
2. Paul S. Herrnson and Diana Dwyre, "Party Issue Advocacy in Congressional Election Campaigns," in John C. Green and Daniel M. Shea, eds., *The State of the Parties 3rd ed.* (Lanham, Md.: Rowman and Littlefield, 1999), 86–104.
3. Brooks Jackson, "Financing the 1996 Campaign: The Law of the Jungle," in Larry J. Sabato, ed., *Toward the Millennium: The Elections of 1996* (Needham Heights, Mass.: 1997), 240–241.

Questions for Discussion

1. Despite federal election laws that greatly limit direct contributions by parties to candidates, how have the two major parties managed to play a major financial role in electoral campaigns?
2. Recent proposals in Congress have attempted to either ban or limit "soft money" contributions to the parties. What arguments might support such proposals? What arguments might oppose them?

 Chapter 7

CAMPAIGNS AND ELECTIONS

Few aspects of American politics have changed as much in recent decades as the ways in which candidates campaign for national office. A half century ago, electioneering was dominated by political parties, which were the main means of communication between candidates and voters. Party parades, mailings, rallies, and door-to-door canvassing were the essential ingredients of campaigns. Party affiliation, based on strong bonds of ethnic, class, regional, or religious identity, was the key factor in determining how voters cast their ballots. Ticket splitters who voted for a president from one party and Senate or House members from another were a small minority.

Today's campaigns are candidate centered. An individual politician's campaign organization raises funds, mobilizes activists, advertises on television, conducts sophisticated direct-mail operations, and polls voters, all largely independent of party organization. Political consultants, pollsters, and outside strategists have replaced the party bosses as central figures in campaigns. Candidates' issue positions and personal attractiveness have challenged party loyalties as key factors in voters' decisions. Split-ticket voting is now quite common.

The new style of campaigning is especially apparent in presidential elections. Prior to the 1970s, candidates were nominated by party professionals who were usually chosen through state conventions or caucuses tightly controlled by the party organization. The eventual nominee typically had worked his way up the party hierarchy over a long period, had served in a number of elected positions in government, and was able to put together a coalition of state party delegations to win the nomination. Once such a person was nominated, the presidential campaign was usually run by the national party organization. Between 1952 and 1968, for example, at least one of the party campaigns was run by the national committee staff in each election; in 1956 and 1964, both campaigns were run by the national party organizations.

The contemporary route to the presidency is quite different. Nominations are often won or lost on the basis of the personal appeal of candidates on television and their ability to put together effective campaign organizations. Traditional party factors are far less influential, as candidates with commanding media presence can gain recognition and stature almost overnight. Having held elected political office is now no longer a prerequisite to becoming a serious candidate, as demonstrated by the campaigns of television evangelist Pat Robertson and preacher/ activist Jesse Jackson in 1988. Moreover, the nominating delegates are often amateurs in politics, motivated more by issues than by party loyalty. After the nomination, the presidential campaign is run by the candidate's organization rather than by the national party. (Since 1972, no general election campaign has been run by either the Republican or the Democratic national committee staffs.)

A number of factors have contributed to the new style of campaign politics. Some reflect social changes, such as rising levels of education, which have created an electorate far more independent and unwilling to follow party labels blindly. Others have resulted from reforms in the political parties, especially the Democratic party, which are now far more open and democratic. New people have the opportunity to enter politics despite little partisan background. Perhaps most important has been the emergence of television as the primary political communications medium and of technological improvements in direct-mail techniques, polling, and other practices.

In general, there has been a shift in the nature of key campaign resources. The skill and labor of party functionaries, who are often volunteers, are less important; financial resources, so necessary in purchasing the services and skills of the new campaign operatives, consultants, pollsters, and media specialists, have become crucial. Expensive campaign travel by jet is now the norm, and the cost of network television advertising is exorbitant.

Not surprisingly, the costs of running national campaigns have risen tremendously. The 2000 presidential election campaign was by far the most expensive in history. According to Federal Election Commission data, George W. Bush raised more than $191 million in private funds for his campaign, and his Democratic counterpart Al Gore was the recipient of more than $132 million of such funds. In addition, each of the major party candidates received more than $67 million in federal funds. Even third party efforts can be expensive. Reform Party candidate Pat Buchanan, who received less than one percent of the vote on election day, spent more than $44 million on his campaign.

Senate and House races have been affected by the new style of campaigning as well. Senate contests are often highly competitive, typically attracting wealthy, prominent challengers and inspiring huge expenditures of funds, particularly for television advertising. Senate races that cost between $10 million and $20 million are common. In a 1996 U.S. Senate race in California, the two candidates together spent more than $45 million. Four years later, the New York U.S. Senate contest between Democrat Hillary Clinton and Republican Rick Lazio cost nearly $93 million all told. In the 2000 U.S. Senate race in New Jersey, Democrat John Corzine spent more than $60 million of his own money to win the seat!

House races are far less competitive than their Senate counterparts. Challengers are often relatively unknown, and they find it difficult to get funding and free media attention. Incumbents, in contrast, stay in the public eye through their work in Congress and their actions to help constituents. Also, their large victory margins in elections attract contributions for future campaigns. Despite the fact that incumbent safety in the House appears to be greater than at any time in history, House elections have not escaped huge campaign expenditures. According to Federal Election Commission figures, in 1974 the average House incumbent spent about $56,000, the average challenger $40,000. By 1992 incumbents were outspending challengers on the average of three and a half to one, with the average incumbent spending over $560,000. In 2000, Democratic incumbents averaged $673,000 in their races; Republican incumbents, $775,000. Open-seat congressional contests are especially expensive. In 2000, Democrats spent on average just under $1 million contesting such seats; Republicans spent more than $1.25 million.

The selections in this chapter focus on campaigning in the 2000 elections and assess the meaning of the parity between the parties, which was reflected in the tight presidential and congressional races. In the first selection Burt Solomon raises the question of whether the close balance between the parties in 2000 reflects party parity or intense party divisiveness. In his view, the clear regional strength of the parties may mask a pattern of less one-party voting within many states. The final two selections deal with contemporary campaigns. Alan Ehrenhalt looks at the increasing impact of interest groups in Wisconsin elections, especially the role played by independent expenditures and issue advocacy ads. He views with alarm a situation in which campaign agendas are increasingly set by interest groups, to the detriment of candidates. In the final selection, Robert Dreyfuss looks at the role GOTV (get-out-the-vote) efforts played in the 2000 election. He makes a compelling case that even in the age of campaigning through the media, person-to-person contact with potential voters has a role in modern campaigns.

7.1

Presidency—Disunity for All

Burt Solomon

The meaning of the 2000 election has been much debated. Although the distinct regional differences in the close vote are evident, and on the surface suggest a generally polarized nation, there is some question about whether the election was divisive or just evenly divided. Nationwide party parity may not be the same as intense party divisiveness.

In this selection, Burt Solomon argues that the clear regional strength of the parties may mask what is a pattern of increasingly less homogeneous party voting patterns within individual states, even states long considered to be solidly in the camp of one of the major parties. States like West Virginia, Oregon, New Hampshire and Florida—traditionally one-party states—proved to be very competitive in the 2000 elections. Solomon also finds the nation made up more of independent, centrist voters than of intense partisan ideologues, who tend to dominate the rhetoric of political campaigns. Traditional partisan cleavages based on such factors as income or rural-urban divisions seem not as sharp as they had previously appeared, and residential mobility patterns have contributed to decreasing state distinctiveness.

Jim Pierce is a retired AFL-CIO organizer who has run the Democratic party's get-out-the-vote effort in Charlotte, N.C., for the past 40 years. This time around, it was a cinch. Volunteers deluged local party officials with calls, and, after 150 had phoned, he called a meeting so he could look them over. "I was amazed," he said. The 120 who showed up for coffee and Danish in early September were predominantly young, white professionals—bank managers, insurance company executives, software engineers. "I [did] know five of them," Pierce recalled. "All the rest were completely new." By Election Day, 1,200 volunteers had signed up—and Pierce intends to keep in touch.

> The volunteers came within 4 percentage points of delivering a victory for Al Gore, the Democratic presidential nominee, in Charlotte and surrounding Mecklenburg County, the most populous jurisdiction in a decidedly Republican state. Pierce, 75, is optimistic

Bert Solomon is a correspondent for *National Journal.*

about what lies ahead for Democrats in the booming metropolitan area, with a population of more than 1.3 million and climbing fast. These newcomers (including maybe
60,000 or 70,000 Hispanics, drawn mainly by construction jobs) will make the county
reliably Democratic inside of a decade, he figured. "It nearly is, now."

It isn't only Charlotte that is changing. "The way Mecklenburg thinks is the
way the rest of the state is beginning to think," as North Carolina's economy
shifts from textiles and tobacco to high technology and high finance, and as
teenagers leave for college and return with new ways of thinking, Pierce observed.
Year by year, a once-provincial state is becoming more like the rest of the
country—more urban and suburban, more diverse and more politically divided.

The U.S. Supreme Court, like the Florida Supreme Court—and like the
electorate—was sharply divided in determining whether Gore or George W. Bush
will rest his hand on a Bible at the West Front of the Capitol on Jan. 20. The
nation's Justices, in splitting 5–4 in the matter of *Bush* vs. *Gore* and offering up a
tangle of dissenting opinions, showed themselves no more sure of their principles
than the voters have been. The correlation between the August jurists' presumed
political sentiments and their legal conclusions was either a remarkable coincidence or uncomfortable evidence that nobody in government will bother anymore to rise above their personal preferences in pursuit of the greater good.

Though when you think about it, why should the nation's highest courts be any
purer in spirit, or less divided in political outlook, than the public is? More than
ever, as the early-1900s columnist Finley Peter Dunne's character Mr. Dooley
once explained, the high Court is only following the muddled election returns.
The astonishingly close election on Nov. 7 between Vice President Gore and
Gov. George W. Bush of Texas suggested that the dead-even divisions evident on
the bench have been spreading into almost every corner of the country. The
nominees' respective voters, while obviously divided in political partiality, are
increasingly scrambled when it comes to geography.

Charlotte and North Carolina, for instance, are hardly alone in shedding some
of their parochialism and are starting to look—politically and maybe culturally,
too—more like the rest of America. In a way, this is the most interesting—and
potentially far-reaching—manifestation of the 50–50 electorate that the voters
revealed themselves to be last month. The mobility and ease with which Americans move around the country, especially in a period when prosperity, or the hope
for it, makes those moves affordable and advisable, means that regional divisions
are becoming less important. With so many people moving, and the Internet
economy exposing more and more Americans to the same stream of information,
people are taking their values—and their divisions—with them to all parts of the
country.

That helps explain why so many states in Election 2000 were in play. First and
foremost, Florida—the nation's fourth-most-populous and demographically odd-
est state—can no longer be counted as a Republican bastion. Other states,
ordinarily ensconced in a partisan camp, weren't. Reliably Democratic West

Virginia went for Bush, and Oregon almost did. New Hampshire, traditionally Republican, came within 1.3 percentage points of voting for Gore. "A lot of the 'Live Free or Die' associations that people had with New Hampshire have changed in the last four years," explained Gov. Jeanne Shaheen, a Democrat who just won a third term.

From coast to coast, places that used to be one of a kind are becoming more and more like everywhere else. In this whirl of a world, people of contradictory backgrounds increasingly mix, and they can't help but gradually be influenced by one another's attitudes. In the Pennsylvania countryside, the Amish farmer in his horse-drawn buggy goes home down the same lane as the suburban Philadelphian in his Lexus; in Montana, a militiaman may build a house for a civilization-weary Hollywood screenwriter. During the presidential campaign, Gore vilified Houston for its polluted air, yet he defeated the Texas governor in the state's biggest city, where Bush's parents live and vote. Compared with a quarter-century ago, "Texas is much more diverse, much more heterogeneous," said Texas A&M rural sociologist Steve H. Murdock, who is the state government's top demographer. "We're seeing a real melting pot." He described a sort of "blending and homogenization" that is under way not only between urban and rural sections of particular states, but also between states.

Think of demographic swirls in a marble-cake country. In an age of mobile workers and telecommuters, people of every description are moving just about everywhere, carrying their cultural and political viewpoints with them. "For the first time in a hundred years, we really do have national parties," said Charles S. Bullock, a University of Georgia expert on elections. Not since then, arguably, has the political control of the nation been so genuinely up for grabs.

The Parties at Parity

Never before in American history have all three national elections wound up dead even. Besides the virtual tie in the race for the White House, voters nationwide also divided evenly in casting ballots for the House of Representatives (candidates of each party drew 49 percent) and for the Senate (50 percent to 48 percent, in Republicans' favor), according to exit polls. . . .

The state races finished dead even, too. The votes cast nationwide in the 11 gubernatorial elections split 50 percent to 49 percent, for the GOP. When the new state legislatures meet, Republicans will control 17 of them and the Democrats, 16; the parties will share control in 16 others. (Nebraska's unicameral Legislature is nonpartisan, though Republican in spirit.) At least four legislative chambers will, like the U.S. Senate, have a precisely divided membership—the Washington State House of Representatives and the state Senates in Arizona, Maine, and South Carolina.

The election "was an accurate reflection of the underlying partisan division in the United States," said Gary Jacobson, a political scientist at the University of California (San Diego). He sees the major parties as having reached parity in 1984 or 1985, as President Reagan's political success attracted the loyalty of new voters who took the places of dying New Deal-era Democrats and—probably more crucial—prompted many conservative Democrats to start thinking of themselves as Republicans, especially across the South. More than a century after the end of the Civil War, history let go, and the Solid South crumpled. In the states of the old Confederacy, Republicans now hold 71 of the 125 House seats and 13 of the 22 Senate seats.

Even before Republicans drove conservative Democrats out of office in the South, Democrats were doing the same to liberal Republicans in the North. The unorthodox result: ideologically coherent political parties. . . .

The parity in party strength caught up with Congress in 1994, by Jacobson's account, in the wake of the early Clinton Administration's permissive cultural tone and its failed, big-government approach to health care. Then, last month, in a largely passionless, party-line election, the 50–50 partisan split spread up and down the ballot. The Democrats, Jacobson figured, still lead the Republicans in self-identified voters by 4 to 5 percentage points (instead of 8 to 9 points, as before Reagan), but the Republicans are a little more likely to vote and to support their party's candidates. Only 8 percent of Republicans voted for Gore last month, while 11 percent of Democrats backed Bush. "There is no majority party in the U.S.," said Merle Black, a political scientist at Emory University, and there hasn't been since at least 1994.

The dominant trend, in fact, has been the relative decline of both parties, compared with the growing ranks of political independents. Ordinarily, independent voters go to the polls and cast the bulk of their ballots for a particular candidate—the victor. This Nov. 7, in the absence of urgent issues and in the presence of less-than-stellar nominees, they didn't. Neither Bush nor Gore succeeded in wowing the public: As voters left the polls, 55 percent confessed to reservations about the ballot they had just cast. Neither would-be President provided any political coattails for the benefit of candidates listed lower on the ballot. "A return to normalcy," said Michael W. Traugott, a political scientist at the University of Michigan and an administrator of the venerable National Election Studies, which has been surveying voters for five decades.

Nor is parity expected to go away anytime soon. "We've probably hit an equilibrium for now," said John R. Petrocik, a specialist in political parties at the University of Missouri (Columbia). How long will it last? Until something happens. . . .

The nation has gone through periods of parity before. From 1876 to 1892, no presidential candidate gained as much as 51 percent of the popular vote. Yet some things got done—civil service reform, antitrust legislation, regulation of the railroads, and action on tariffs. In the realigning election of 1896, the Democrats shifted to the left, toward the vigorous populism of William Jennings Bryan, and away from the gold-standard centrism of Grover Cleveland—"the Clinton of his time," said James E. Campbell, a State University of New York (Buffalo) expert on elections. By believing in something too strongly, the Democrats did themselves in and enabled the Republicans to regain political control.

A Cultural Divide

The ebbs and flows in sentiment that have created the nation's politically delicate balance are more complicated still. For one thing, the Republicans may have gained ground in recent years because of "the incredible percentage of dual-income couples," who may be "inclined to have a more conservative view of the world," suggested Peter A. Morrison, a demographer at the RAND think tank. Even so, a family's political views, at least in these best-of-all-possible times, seem to depend less than they once did on economic class.

Karl Marx, perusing the exit polls, would have gagged at the specter of self-described upper-class voters who preferred left-of-center Gore (by 56 percent to 39 percent) and working-class voters who backed Gore tepidly (50 percent to 46 percent). The corps of political scientists who predicted this fall that Gore would win comfortably because of an unusually enduring prosperity has had to eat crow. . . .

"The relationship between income and politics has changed—it's not as dramatic," concluded John C. Green, a political scientist at the University of Akron. "Cultural factors are much more relevant."

The exit polls left little doubt: Voting was a cultural act. The more often that voters attend religious services, the likelier they were to stab a chad for Bush; the correlation was nearly a straight line. The 48 percent of voters who have a gun at home decisively (61 percent to 36 percent) favored Bush; almost as eagerly, the unarmed 52 percent voted for Gore.

"Do you hunt?" asked John Morgan Sr., a demographer who works for the Republican National Committee. He described the 50–50 split in the electorate as basically a cultural struggle between the city and the country—polarized between liberal and conservative. In recent years, almost every religious denomination has undergone a civil war of sorts. Why not in politics, too? "It's more of a cultural divide than a political divide," said Michael Bowers, a political scientist at the University of Nevada (Las Vegas).

Although the country overall seems to be moving toward a balanced middle, it's not true everywhere. Some states are becoming politically more one-sided. In California, the fast-growing population of minority groups has made that vast state increasingly Democratic. That's why Sen. Dianne Feinstein, D-Calif, romped to re-election on the strength of her showing in minority communities. But she fared far less well among white voters, drawing only the same proportion as did Maria Cantwell, a Democrat in neighboring Washington, who squeaked into the Senate.

Utah is another state that, despite many new residents, is becoming more, well, Utahan. Because of a certain self-selection by choosy migrants, the newcomers to Utah's Interstate 15 corridor of high-tech development are just as conservative as the natives. "It looks like we would be more Democratic because of them, but we are not," bemoaned Meghan Holbrook, who chairs the Democratic Party in the Republican-dominated state. Similarly, in South Carolina, newcomers helped lead the already-conservative state into the Republican fold. . . .

But to say that some states are siding with one partisan camp over the other isn't as simple as it sounds. The migrants to South Carolina, said Freymeyer, tend to be more liberal on social issues involving race or sex than do the longtime residents. These newcomers had a hand this year in pushing the Legislature to remove the Confederate flag from atop the Statehouse because it had become an embarrassment to a commerce-minded state. In this state that was the first to secede from the Union in the Civil War, Freymeyer reported, Southern accents aren't heard as much anymore on city streets.

So, was the election divisive, or just evenly divided? For a minority of voters, the divisions are profound. Cultural and political polarization, such as between gun-toting churchgoers and secular environmentalists, is nothing new. Still, political scientists say that no more than a third of the electorate feels polarized. Green counts only 15 percent on each side as strong partisans. The National Election Studies survey in 1998 measured strong Democrats at 19 percent of the populace and strong Republicans at 10 percent. Morris P. Fiorina, a political scientist at the Hoover Institution on War, Revolution, and Peace, noted that roughly one-tenth of the public favors a ban on abortion, with exceptions only when the mother's life is at stake, and about the same percentage agrees to third-trimester abortions for any reason—everyone else is somewhere in between.

For the rest of the population, the divisions aren't that deep—"not especially deep in terms of everybody's lives," Green specified. Bush and Gore, he said, snarled at each other over policy disputes, but "they agreed more than they disagreed" during the campaign, and their differences don't reflect deep social animosities. "The vast bulk of the country," Fiorina said, "is not that committed, one way or the other." Between the passionate extremes lies the muddled middle, which is believed to be growing in size—and in political weight.

Here's some negative evidence: How often have citizens climbed the barricades—literal or metaphorical—in the nerve-racking weeks since Nov. 7 to insist on Bush or Gore as a humbled nation's 43rd President? Even as the culture is increasingly heterogeneous, the divisions seem to be getting less sharp.

There are good demographic reasons why this is so. "Today, virtually all suburbanites are suburban by birth, whether they've moved from Maryland to Virginia or from Maryland to California," said Larry Long, a veteran demographer at the Census Bureau. "There is a certain evening-out across the country." These days, gun owners and pacifists, churchgoers and atheists, live next door to one another—or even in the same household. Diversity—you can't get away from it anymore.

Add this to Americans' native pragmatism and to the calming effects of peace and prosperity, and you have a saving grace at this potentially dangerous political time: Most people simply don't care very much.

More Like America

Teenagers in every cranny of America watch "Friends" and MTV. A national culture has intruded everywhere. George Ritzer, a sociologist at the University of Maryland, has written about "the McDonaldization of society." As Freymeyer at Presbyterian College put it, "Even people in the middle of nowhere in Idaho have the same cultural influences as people in New York City."

And there's more: people keep moving. The census data is subtle, but clear: In 30 states, a rising proportion of inhabitants were born somewhere other than the state in which they now reside.

Consider Florida. A scant 30.5 percent of Floridians in 1990 were natives of the Sunshine State, down from 31.2 percent in 1980. (The figures for 2000 won't be available for at least a year.) Only Nevada was home to a greater proportion of outsiders.

This isn't a surprise to anyone who has watched TV news of late. The shouts and squawks at the county canvassing centers have come in a multitude of discordant accents. Florida isn't a Southern state anymore. Indeed, what Florida is, never stops changing. "The whole election in Florida was upside down," exclaimed Jim Kane, the editor in chief of Florida Voter Poll, a bimonthly newsletter based in Fort Lauderdale. According to exit polls, Bush narrowly defeated Gore among elderly voters, evidently because of what Kane describes as a wave of younger, more conservative retirees from the Midwest who are replacing the earlier, Depression-scarred arrivals from the Northeast. Florida's younger voters broke disproportionately Democratic, in part because a smaller share of the Hispanic vote is made up of Republican-leaning Cuban-Americans and a larger share is composed of Puerto Ricans and other Democratic-inclined blocs. "The Democratic Party in Florida has gotten new life out of this election," Kane reported.

The political parties in Florida are "extraordinarily competitive," said Steve C. Craig, a University of Florida expert on the state's political behavior. And they're increasingly centrist. A decade ago, Republicans ran as unapologetic conservatives—until Jeb Bush lost his first gubernatorial race running that way in 1994 and found electoral redemption four years later as a born-again moderate. This year, conservative Rep. Bill McCollum, R-Fla., tried a similar tack in his race for the Senate, but fell short.

The identical, politically telling dynamic was evident last month also in New Hampshire. Former Sen. Gordon Humphrey, who served two terms (1979–91) as a staunchly conservative Republican, posed as a moderate in running for governor against Shaheen, who had decimated true-blue conservatives in her two previous races. Many newcomers had never heard of Humphrey, and Shaheen spent a lot of campaign money to tell them what she wanted them to think of him. And she won, even though she had refused to take the pledge—de rigueur in traditionally penny-pinching New Hampshire—against imposing an income tax or a sales tax. (Only Alaska and New Hampshire still have neither.) This made Shaheen the first anti-antitax governor in the Granite State's modern political history.

"The state has changed," said Joan Greene, who runs a market research firm in Nashua. A state rife with abandoned factories and textile mills has become the eighth-most-affluent state in a wealthy nation. It has undergone a gentrification, courtesy of an influx of people from Massachusetts and other Northeastern states, drawn by New Hampshire's low taxes, quaint feel, and high-tech development. More than 1,000 software companies have started up, mainly in southern New Hampshire and along the state's 18-mile shoreline, which boosters have dubbed the "e-coast." The proportion of residents who are natives sank from 49 percent in 1980 to 44 percent in 1990. Thomas J. Duffy, an expert on demographics in the state's planning office, guesses that it will tumble to between 40 percent and 42 percent for 2000. New Hampshire "has to be different, with this influx," he said.

Different from the way New Hampshire was, that is—and more like America now is. In the ages of its inhabitants and in the kinds of jobs they hold, Duffy said, New Hampshire is no longer very different from the rest of the country. Yankee accents are still common in the backwoods north country, but not so much in the state's traffic-snarled south. Gov. Shaheen says the new New Hampshirites are more moderate on social issues than the natives. The state has become one of 10 in the nation to extend its antidiscrimination statute to cover gays and lesbians.

New Hampshire is still a Republican state, but not like it was, and it may not be Republican forever. In an issue-less election, the GOP can count on 54 percent to 55 percent of the votes, a share 4 or 5 percentage points lower than a decade or two ago, said Richard F. Winters, a political scientist at Dartmouth College. The implication, he added, is that a decade from now, the strength of the parties in New Hampshire will be even.

A comparable convergence is taking place all over the country:

> In Georgia, the explosive growth of the Atlanta metropolitan area has ushered in what Merle Black described as "two competitive minority parties." Georgians voted decisively for Bush (by 12 percentage points), but even more decisively (by 18 points) for Sen. Zell Miller, a populist Democrat, who won even in suburban Cobb County, ordinarily a Republican bastion.

In Nevada, a torrent of new and politically unpredictable residents has thrown the state into a partisan impasse. Statewide, registered Republicans outnumber Democrats by a trifling 838 (out of 732,024, combined). "This will be a battleground state for a long time," said Ryan Erwin, the executive director of Nevada's GOP.

In West Virginia, a Democratic electorate bolted to Bush, scared by Gore's enthusiasm for gun control and his environmental reluctance about coal mining. At the same time, West Virginians replaced their Republican governor with a Democrat and gave more votes than ever before (and an eighth term in office) to Robert C. Byrd, the Senate's senior Democrat.

Even Texas, with its mythic culture and its 10-gallon pride, is unmistakably edging toward the political mainstream. The Lone Star State's population is growing fast, by a fifth during the 1990s. Roughly half of the increase of 3 million people has been among Hispanics, many of whom need health insurance and other benefits. Over time, Democratic-leaning Hispanics are expected to grow in political strength. They "will gradually break down more of the state's resistance to a meaningful safety net," . . .

As Hispanics have spread all over Texas, and as Southern Baptists have congregated in the suburbs, some of the state's customary voting patterns have broken down. Notably, the political distance between the countryside and the metropolitan areas is shrinking. Rural Texans remain a little more conservative, but the stark differences are gone.

A fading in the traditional political distinctions between urban and rural citizens isn't peculiar to Texas. Kenneth M. Johnson, a demographer at Loyola University in Chicago, said that in urban and rural areas he sees a convergence in fertility patterns and, interestingly, in the speed at which new technology is introduced. Planners at a rural telephone company, for example, "were clearly stunned" when they discovered that their customers were lagging city folks in buying cell phones and ordering call-waiting by a mere six months, instead of the two or more years that were the typical delays in rural areas for getting telephones, televisions, or microwave ovens.

Paradoxically, we have become a 50–50 nation even as our popular culture, our corporate culture, and our sources of information and recreation have become increasingly standardized. It is a paradox, however, that may not last. An increasingly common culture and the increasing homogeneity of America's diversity could affect politics for years to come: Just about every place, at least now and again, is in play.

When Texas demographer Steve Murdock drove across dusty Texas recently, he met the face of the future in the unlikeliest of settings: At a Dairy Queen, he listened to some old men deep in conversation about what they had found the previous evening on the Internet. How long will it be until they start thinking less like Texans and more like citizens of a wider world, or until their children or their grandchildren do?

Questions for Discussion

1. Burt Solomon suggests that the regional distinctiveness in partisan voting patterns may play less of a role in the nation's future politics than it has in our immediate past. What factors led him to that conclusion? What will it mean for political campaigning in the future?
2. Solomon argues that the 2000 election was characterized by a close partisan division in the vote, but it was not an especially divisive election? Do you agree or disagree?
3. The author makes the case that even though the nation is becoming more culturally heterogeneous, political divisions seem to be getting less sharp. How can such an apparent paradox be explained?

 7.2

Political Pawns

Alan Ehrenhalt

The role of money in campaigns has always been a bone of contention, and periodically the nation hears the cries of those interested in reforming the system. Generally speaking, despite the enactment of laws designed to limit both contributions and candidate spending, most observers believe that such legal efforts have largely been unsuccessful. Supreme Court rulings treating campaign contributions as a form of protected "free speech" have thus far been an insurmountable barrier to limiting the role of money in politics. And individuals, parties, and interest groups have become quite innovative in finding ways to circumvent the existing intentions of campaign finance regulation.

In this piece, Alan Ehrenhalt examines how a number of interest groups have used independent expenditures and issue advocacy advertisements to affect the nature of campaigning for public office in Wisconsin, a state with rather stringent campaign finance laws. He argues that such activities have created a situation in which campaign agendas are increasingly set by interest groups, to the detriment

Alan Ehrenhalt is executive editor of *Governing*.

of candidates. And he worries that money in the electoral process has affected the nature of the policymaking process in the state as well.

___

One morning in the fall of 1998, Judy Robson woke up to the sound of a radio ad talking about the special needs of older people. "Maybe it's for Geritol," she remembers thinking. But it turned out to be a testimonial—for somebody living in her hometown of Beloit, Wisconsin. This person sounded like a saint—willing to go to any length to make the lives of senior citizens a little brighter. "Who could that be?" she mused.

Then she found out. "Judy Robson," the announcer intoned. "She has given a lifetime of service for the community. Taking care of people, keeping them healthy."

To the unpretentious Robson, it was more than a little embarrassing—it was bizarre. "Where on earth is this coming from?" Robson asked herself. It took her only a few seconds to figure it out. The testimonial was coming from the Wisconsin Education Association Council. Robson was running for the state Senate in a close race, and the teachers' union badly wanted her to win so that the Senate would stay in Democratic hands. They had launched a series of independent expenditure ads* that made her sound like Mother Teresa. But they didn't tell her about the ads because that might have been considered collusion—a felony under state law.

As the campaign proceeded, Judy Robson encountered a new batch of ads that were equally surprising but much less flattering. One of them showed her next to a lava lamp, and suggested that Robson, a student activist 30 years ago, was still somehow a representative of the counterculture. It said she had "never met a tax she didn't think was groovy."

As negative ads go these days, that's a pretty mild specimen. Even so, Robson was eager to find out where it came from. She knew the ad was placed by Wisconsin Manufacturers and Commerce, so probably it was initiated by one of the WMC's member companies. But the manufacturers don't disclose the original sources of their campaign money, and the courts say they don't have to. The anti-Robson ads were labeled "issue advocacy,"† aimed at informing the public. They did not expressly endorse or oppose any contestant for office, and thus could not be regulated as a campaign expense.

___

* *Independent expenditures* reflect communications with the public that directly advocate either the defeat or the election of a specific candidate (and use the words *vote for* or *vote against*). Such communications must not be coordinated with a particular candidate. Disclosure of independent expenditures is required, but there are no limits to the amount of spending.

† *Issue advocacy* involves communication purposely to address a particular policy issue or idea. Such ads may address candidates indirectly but must not advocate either their election or their defeat. Issue advocacy ads are not subject to either spending limits or disclosure laws.

It may seem a little odd for a TV "issue ad" denouncing a candidate in the middle of a close state Senate contest to be called anything but an obvious campaign gimmick. But almost everything about Wisconsin politics is a little strange these days. You run for office, your friends bombard the air waves with testimonials, and you're the last one to hear them. Your enemies heap piles of abuse on you—and there's no way you can be sure who's behind it. If you happen to be running for the legislature in a marginal district, there's a good chance you'll end up feeling like a pawn in someone else's very expensive game.

Nothing that's happening in Wisconsin politics is exactly unique to that state. Both independent expenditures and so-called issue advocacy are creatures of the U.S. Supreme Court, which held in 1976, in *Buckley* v. *Valeo*, that they are entitled to the full protection of free speech under the First Amendment. A whole series of subsequent decisions, at the federal level and in more than a dozen state courts, have reinforced that view.

Both forms of spending were used heavily in the 1996 presidential and congressional elections, and even more heavily in 1998, when more than $300 million is estimated to have been spent nationally on issue advocacy commercials alone. By mid-March of this year, the Annenberg Public Policy Center reported recently, issue ad spending throughout the country was already over the $100 million mark, headed for record-breaking levels as the campaign season proceeds.

As the dollars have mounted, Congress has begun to take an interest in the issue ad problem: The Senate passed legislation in June to require disclosure for some of the groups financing the ads, and the House plans to vote on a similar measure. But it's not clear that any substantive reform of federal law will take place this year—and even if it does, the escalation of issue ad politics at the state level seems likely to continue.

Nowhere has a state political system been transformed by these expenditures the way Wisconsin's has. And it has all happened disconcertingly fast. Five years ago, issue ads had never even been used in legislative campaigns there. Candidates raised most of the money and made the important strategic decisions. Today, hardly anyone is surprised when a close campaign for the state Senate costs a million dollars—and most of the funds are raised and spent, and crucial decisions made, without the candidate knowing a thing about it. The bulk of the money comes from Wisconsin, but a significant portion comes from outside the state.

Wisconsin politics is now dominated by two big interest group clusters. One centers around the WMC, with the Farm Bureau, Realtors and builders as allies. The other has WEAC at the center, and trial lawyers and the state AFL-CIO in supporting roles.

Among members of the legislature, the most common lament is that "we have lost control of our campaigns." It pervades both chambers and cuts across party lines. "Our campaigns have been hijacked," Judy Robson says. "You have your message, you have your strategy, and then bing—these ads come in and they've taken over your campaign." Republican Dale Schultz, one of Robson's Senate colleagues, agrees. "What we're seeing," he says, "is the steady erosion of the political process. Candidates are about one election away from being totally irrelevant."

Of all places, one might reasonably ask, why is this happening in Wisconsin—the home of political reform and progressive governors, and one of the most scandal-free states in American politics?

It is happening for a few simple reasons. One is the close balance in the legislature. For most of the past decade, the Senate has been a seat or two away from switching party control; the Assembly has been just a few seats away. Were either institution overwhelmingly Republican or overwhelmingly Democratic, no major interest group would be investing huge sums in its elections. But as things stand, a handful of marginal districts each year determine who gets the gavel the following January—and the right to set the agenda.

From the perspective of the manufacturers, the difference is between a legislature eager to provide tax relief and one determined to impose onerous new corporate burdens. From the point of view of the Wisconsin Education Association, it is the difference between an institution friendly to teachers and labor causes, and one that sees unions as a malevolent force in the state's affairs. The opportunity to tip that balance is too tempting to resist.

A second reason is that Wisconsin, unlike many large states (including neighboring Illinois), prohibits direct corporate contributions to political campaigns. So business has to find other ways to make its presence felt in the political process. The court decisions establishing unregulated "issue advocacy," with no need for disclosure, have turned out to be the perfect vehicle.

Then there is the failure of public financing. Wisconsin actually had one of the early systems of public financing for legislative campaigns, and it worked reasonably well for a while. But it was not indexed for inflation, and by the 1990s, the fund simply was not providing subsidies large enough to persuade candidates in competitive districts to accept it. So it is essentially useless.

Finally, and inescapably, there is the presence of WEAC—the Wisconsin Education Association Council. Teachers are a major political force in dozens of states around the country, but they may be strongest of all in Wisconsin. WEAC was instrumental in the Democratic takeover of both chambers in 1974—creating majorities that lasted nearly two decades. In the 1980s, as partisan competition grew more intense, it was the teachers who provided the dollars and organizational help to keep Democratic strength intact.

That's also when the teachers began experimenting with independent expenditures, running TV and radio ads in support of their favored candidates. These came with full disclosure of the source. There was no reason for WEAC not to reveal the source of the money, because everyone already knew: The source was the dollar a month that the group automatically collected from the dues of the union's 90,000 members. Republicans complained, but did little to challenge this arrangement.

As late as 1995, few on either side saw anything momentous in this independent spending. And no one at all realized the potential importance of issue advocacy. "I'd never even heard of the concept," says James Buchen, the manufacturers' lobbyist and chief campaign tactician.

Then came one dramatic special election—a recall election for the state Senate, with Republicans holding a 17–16 lead. There was outside involvement on both sides, but it was the Sierra Club, to the surprise of many, that tried something genuinely new: issue ads, rather than conventional independent expenditures. They were a transparent attempt to influence the outcome, but they were done with precision. There was no outright support or opposition expressed toward any candidate, and thus no need for messy disclosure. And the ads did influence the outcome. The Republican incumbent was recalled, the Democrats took back the Senate, and the state's political process was on its way to what has become issue advocacy addiction.

By 1998, it was obvious that the rules of the game had changed. That fall, with the legislature again on the line, the state began to see elections in which the efforts of outside interests substantially exceeded those of the candidates.

A prime example was the 27th District, in the Madison suburbs, held for years by a Democrat who chose to give it up. Republicans felt that they could win it, and that winning would guarantee them control of the chamber.

The race began as an evenly matched contest between Democrat Jon Erpenbach, a relative political newcomer, and GOP nominee Nancy Mistele, a longtime school board member. But by Labor Day, it was a fight to the death between the teachers and the manufacturers.

"The campaign was totally out of my control," Erpenbach says. "It's almost like I was a golfer with some sponsor's patch on my sleeve. 'Jon Erpenbach brought to you by the WEAC.' People would come up to me and say, 'Oh, you're the teachers' guy.'"

In one TV ad, a citizen complained that "the Madison teachers' union and Jon Erpenbach say Wisconsin needs higher property taxes. I say higher taxes may cost me my home." In other ads, the WMC and the WEAC essentially took the opportunity to attack each other, with the candidates scarcely mentioned. "I was a bit player," Erpenbach says ruefully.

When the votes were counted, Erpenbach and his sponsors had narrowly won. All told, the campaign cost well over $1 million. Erpenbach himself raised $181,000—no small sum in a Senate district—and Mistele about $300,000. But the teachers and the manufacturers together spent $650,000 on broadcast advertising alone. "WEAC and WMC," says one Madison campaign veteran, "were like two giants battling on the plains of Israel. I think they balanced each other off. There was no David."

The 2000 campaign has already begun, and the Wisconsin Senate is once again in play, with Democrats clinging to a 17–16 advantage. It is widely assumed that the Erpenbach syndrome of 1998 will return in an even more massive way. "It's going to be a bloodbath," says Michael McCabe, who leads a reform group called the Wisconsin Democracy Campaign. "Many more groups are going to be committed with issue advocacy. . . . There are a lot of people starting to say that this is madness."

If so, much of it will be played out in the rural northwest corner of the state, in the 10th Senate District. Democrat Alice Clausing is the vulnerable incumbent. The manufacturers are bent on defeating her; the other side seems equally determined to save her.

The only way to advertise on television in the 10th is to buy time on Minneapolis stations. If one side goes that route, the other will follow, and total spending could far exceed that of the Erpenbach-Mistele showdown in 1998. Clausing is certain of one thing: "This," she says, "will be the campaign that swings public sentiment in favor of campaign finance reform."

In many ways, the whole thing resembles an arms race, and that is how many of the participants characterize it. "For us," says John Stocks of the WEAC, "it's a function of what WMC decides to do. We are prepared to play the role of the equalizer if necessary." The WMC sees it a little differently. The Democrats, says James Buchen, "want to have WEAC alone on the playing field. Until we came along, they had it to themselves. If anything, we've leveled the playing field."

Buchen makes an argument that the legislators themselves never make. He says the autonomy of the candidates is not necessarily equivalent to the public good. "It's interesting," he says, "that the candidates think the campaigns belong to them. Politicians have deceived themselves that they are the source of honest truth and discussion in elections. Everybody has an ownership interest in the campaign. If we don't come in and talk about taxes and hold their feet to the fire, they may not talk about it at all."

Brady Williamson, a Madison lawyer who argued the case for unrestrained issue advocacy before the state Supreme Court, admits that "perhaps the process is being 'taken away' from the candidates. But it was never the candidates' exclusive franchise. . . . The framers wanted a system in which there were many voices." . . .

There are those who insist that, for all the money spent by interest groups, the return on investment has been meager. Both the teachers and manufacturers have taken aim at several vulnerable incumbents in the past two election cycles, but with just one exception, the incumbents have survived. . . .

What the money unmistakably does, however, is set the agenda. "You'll get a lot of debate over how effective these ads are," says McCabe. "But there's no question that they shape the whole debate." He's right. Visit any district where WEAC and WMC are at each other's throats, and you'll find that the predominant issues by far are taxes and education. Anything else the candidates might want to emphasize is likely to be drowned out. Nobody disputes that taxes and schools are important subjects. But making them the only subjects is worrisome.

Just as troubling is the question of what the big-money campaigns have done to the legislature itself. Five years ago, veteran observers will tell you, the Wisconsin Assembly and Senate were competitive but reasonably well-mannered institutions, with a substantial amount of cooperation among individual members across the aisle.

In the wake of the changes in the campaign system, the sessions have degenerated into bitter struggles between two highly partisan and combative teams, each built around a set of interest groups, each maneuvering to protect itself politically and gain advantage in the next round of elections that will decide control. "It has changed the whole nature of lawmaking and public policy," . . .

Not that the legislative result of the past few years has tilted much to either side. What it has mainly tilted toward is stalemate—budgets approved weeks or months behind schedule, tedious and angry debates over minor matters, and virtually none of the ambitious public policy experimentation that Wisconsin has traditionally been noted for. . . .

About the only players who can be said to have benefited from these changes are the top leaders. As recently as the mid-1990s, Wisconsin's legislature seemed to be evolving, like those in most other states, toward a system in which individual members possessed considerable autonomy and the leadership had relatively few weapons with which to keep them in line.

The new campaign system has changed those relationships in a way nobody expected. With more partisanship have come tighter discipline and more control by the two top leaders . . . They are the ones who find the candidates in the swing districts, raise money for them, work out strategy and message for the party as a whole and coordinate tactics with the major interest groups, to the extent that can be done within the confines of the law. Most of the disclosed money from political action committees goes to the leadership, not to the individual candidates. The leaders largely determine how it will be spent.

"The members are much more beholden to legislative leaders than I've seen in 20 years," says lobbyist Michael McCabe. "It's been such a dramatic shift in such a short time. It doesn't seem to mesh with the state's political culture."

Moreover, there are those who wonder whether it is only a matter of time before even the leadership is forced to yield some of its clout to the interest groups that are financing the whole operation. . . .

In short, Wisconsin politics is a mess, and it's not difficult to envision it getting even worse over the next few years. Unless, of course, the legislature finds a way to halt the arms race. No matter how the elections come out this fall, efforts will be made next year to do that. The issue of campaign finance has already been guaranteed a place on the 2001 agenda. But the obstacles that stand in the way of a solution are formidable.

One approach would be to craft a law stating that a specified kind of issue advocacy—say, a broadcast in the month prior to an election, and featuring the name and/or likeness of a candidate—is, in fact, a campaign ad and subject to disclosure. . . . Some experts believe it could survive a court challenge; others do not. If such a law survived, it might reduce drastically the number of issue ads. But the manufacturers and their business allies would be certain to fight it, because it would dismantle their favorite weapon without inconveniencing the other side at all.

The business coalition believes that the real culprit is the automatic dues deduction that finances the WEAC independent expenditures. Take the deduction away, they say, and the WEAC commercials would disappear. Then there would be no need for the manufacturers to retaliate. But like the disclosure option, this approach is destabilizing—it would penalize one side while leaving the other unaffected.

Another answer might be to grant any candidate matching money to respond to issue ads attacking him. . . .

Then there is the possibility of reviving the moribund public financing system. The public financing option, after failing to attract much support nationwide for most of the 1990s, is making a small comeback. This year, for the first time, Maine is trying a system of public funding for legislative campaigns, Vermont and Hawaii are launching them, and a Massachusetts law is scheduled to take effect in 2002. All provide full public financing to candidates who agree to refuse private contributions and abide by spending limits.

Wisconsin actually has had a public financing law for more than 20 years. All it has to do is put some money into the program. But that will not be politically easy. Having had access to massive infusions of campaign money for nearly a decade now, politicians may find it difficult to scale back to an operation built on meager public subsidies. . . .

On the other hand, there are those who believe that if the campaigns this fall are disturbing enough, the time will be ripe to entertain politically risky proposals. "We're near a breaking point," argues McCabe. "After a very ugly 2000, the calls for reform will be that much more intense."

What he is banking on is that come next spring, the loudest voices for change won't be from reform-minded lobbyists like him, but from legislators who finally realize that the current system is squeezing them out of power. "The key," says Jon Erpenbach, "is this: You have to put control in the hands of the candidates. . . ."

Questions for Discussion

1. What are some of the negative effects of independent spending and issue advocacy by interest groups in the electoral and governing processes in the state of Wisconsin? Are there any positive effects?

2. What are the political and legal barriers to restricting either independent expenditures or issue ads?

7.3

Rousing the Democratic Base

Robert Dreyfuss

With the ever-increasing role played by the "air war" of impersonal radio and television advertising in modern campaigns, it is easy to overlook the fact that even today, elections are often determined by the far less visible "ground war" of a campaign. Get-out-the-vote (GOTV) efforts, especially those involving personal contact, can be highly effective. In an era characterized by overall low voter turnout, a group that can mobilize its members and adherents to vote at rates higher than the general population is especially valuable to political parties and their candidates. For example, Republican-oriented groups, such as the Christian Right and the NRA, deserve much of the credit for the Republicans' capturing the House and Senate during the 1990s.

In this selection, Robert Dreyfuss discusses the efforts by two Democrat-oriented groups in 2000—the AFL-CIO and the NAACP—to increase the turnout among targeted populations. In an era when some believe "parties have become shells to move money," grassroots efforts by interest groups in many parts of the country have supplanted previous efforts by state and local party organizations. Efforts by the two groups probably contributed to 2000 Democratic candidate Al Gore's winning such swing states as Pennsylvania and Michigan and making the election in Florida, early on considered a solid Bush state, so close.

I f Al Gore finds himself standing across from Chief Justice Rehnquist, taking the oath of office in January, it would be fitting if Paul Lemmon were holding the Bible. As Pennsylvania state director for the national AFL-CIO, it's Lemmon's job to make sure that the state's 23 crucial electoral votes end up in Gore's column. Raised by Italian immigrants in the gritty coal and industrial heart of southwestern Pennsylvania, Lemmon is a longtime union official and organizer, first with the United Mine Workers and then with the AFL-CIO's national headquarters. In 1996 Lemmon oversaw the labor federation's voter mobilization efforts in 13 midwestern states, and earlier this year, he worked the Iowa caucuses. "Now," he says, "they've brought me back to Pennsylvania."

Robert Dreyfuss is a freelance journalist based in Alexandria, Virginia, specializing in politics and national security issues.

That's a state where labor's turnout is likely to determine who wins. In 1996 voters from union households in Pennsylvania made up 29 percent of all voters and handed the state to Bill Clinton. According to the AFL-CIO, Clinton lost among nonunion voters in several industrial states in 1996, including Pennsylvania and Ohio, but he won those states by carrying huge majorities of union voters. In an attempt to guarantee a repeat, Lemmon is coordinating a statewide voter education and get-out-the-vote (GOTV) drive aimed at turning out union voters at a rate 15 to 20 percent higher than the public at large. Using a strategy that was field-tested in 1996 and 1998, Lemmon's statewide team is organizing a systematic, member-to-member political education campaign centered on in-depth discussion of issues, not merely on candidates. Rather than telling members which way to vote, the AFL-CIO's effort is aimed at giving union members a conscious appreciation of labor's political muscle. "It's a matter of exciting them about feeling the power they have in the process," Lemmon says. "People realize that labor unions are back."

Labor's GOTV effort is taking place against the backdrop of a decades-long decline in voter turnout. Four years ago, for the first time in post–World War II history, less than half of America's voting-age population trooped to the polls to vote in a presidential election. This year, with less-than-inspiring candidates put forward by the two major parties and third-party candidates who have failed to create much excitement, there are preliminary indications that even more voters may stay home.

The causes of this decline are myriad—from post-Watergate and post-Vietnam disaffection to the deteriorating conduct of political campaigns, to the Twee-dledee-Tweedledum nature of many races, to the erosion of political and social institutions. The two parties barely make a pretense any longer of maintaining grass-roots, precinct-by-precinct organizations. They rely instead on television and on sophisticated, computer-driven targeting of so-called "persuadables." By going after the elusive swing voter, often no more than a tiny segment of the voting population, the parties—and their pollsters, consultants, and direct mail gurus—have abandoned likely nonvoters and the unregistered.

With nonvoting being systemic, short of a revolution in the political culture there is little chance that anything—least of all, voter registration and GOTV—will have more than marginal impact on overall turnout. Yet that very fact means that organizations that can mobilize people to vote are golden. The AFL-CIO, having proven in recent years that it can deliver millions of voters to polling places on election day, is far and away the most effective—and, to the Republican Party's chagrin, the vast majority of those votes go to Democrats. This year the AFL-CIO's effort is being complemented by a parallel campaign launched by the NAACP, whose members and supporters cast their votes for Democrats in an even more lopsided fashion. Should Gore win, or should the Democrats win back control of Congress, the grass-roots power of the AFL-CIO and the NAACP will be the reason why. That's especially true now that the two main Republican-oriented grass-roots groups are, for different reasons, hobbled.

The Christian Coalition, weakened and in disarray, wields a mere fraction of the power it did a decade ago, and the National Rifle Association may find itself matched tit for tat by a host of gun control groups in the all-important suburbs.

In Pennsylvania, Lemmon and his colleagues from the state AFL-CIO—including about 100 rank-and-file activists and staff—divided the state into five geographic zones and began meeting in August with every local union president in the state, seeking to identify a network of activists, first within each local, then at each workplace, and finally inside each shift change. Since the organizing is based on the principle that workers are most receptive to messages from other workers who speak their language, public-sector workers are being recruited to carry the message to other public-sector workers; ditto for private-sector unions and for the building trades. Then workers and their families are reached through continual workplace contacts, home visits, phone calls, and mail.

"It's got to be multiple hits," says Lemmon, adding that the goal is to ensure that every union member is contacted between eight and 13 times by November.

The key to the state is Philadelphia, a Democratic stronghold, according to Joe Rauscher, president of the Central Labor Council in Philadelphia. Every weekend during September and October, up to 600 rank-and-file union members have volunteered to do member-to-member walking tours. "We get people from UFCW to talk to other UFCW members, and so on," he says, referring to the United Food and Commercial Workers, which has 23,000 members in Philadelphia. The goal of the effort in the city is to deliver a 300,000-vote plurality for Gore, one-third higher than the 225,000 votes by which Clinton carried Philly in 1996, says Rauscher.

Pat Gillespie, business manager for the AFL-CIO Building Trades Council in Philadelphia, acknowledges that the apathy and disinterest plaguing the public at large have an impact on labor, too, noting the energy it takes to get people registered and get them to the polls. "We're dunning them, but it's a hard sell," says Gillespie. Yet he says that the 70,000 unionists in eastern Pennsylvania who belong to the 42 building trades locals—electricians, laborers, bricklayers, carpenters, sheet metal workers, and so on—will turn out almost en bloc. "A number of unions will get close to 90 percent turnout," he says. "But they work it."

The mastermind of organized labor's election drive this year is Steve Rosenthal, political director of the AFL-CIO. From his office on the seventh floor of the federation's national headquarters, he enjoys a spectacular view of the White House, just over the treetops of Lafayette Square. Rosenthal appears to be in a good mood, and no wonder: After some fragmentation, most of the AFL-CIO's constituent unions have come together to endorse Gore, including the Teamsters and the United Auto Workers, both major players in the battleground states of the Midwest. Across a conference table, surrounded by shelves filled with hard hats and union caps side by side with binders and stacks of folders, the fast-talking, New York-accented Rosenthal reels off statistics to show labor's expected clout in November.

"Everywhere we've run The Program—that's what we call it, The Program—there's been a higher turnout of union voters," he says. Example: In Iowa, during the Democratic caucuses in January, voters from union households made up 35 percent of caucus-goers in areas where labor focused its efforts, and less than 10 percent in areas where they did not. "It works," he says. "We've set up in a few states little controlled experiments like that. You can look at place after place where we've done this stuff."

What the AFL-CIO is doing this year is a nationwide extension of the approach it used experimentally in 1996 in places such as Wisconsin and southern California. That year, the AFL-CIO spent as much as $35 million, most of it going to expensive (and largely ineffective) television advertisements. But in some regions, organized labor opted for an on-the-ground, issues-based campaign. In those areas, rather than a flurry of last-minute, pre-election activity, organizers emphasized the use of union volunteers to make phone calls and knock on the doors of fellow union members far in advance of election day. Instead of just trying to get members to vote for the union-endorsed candidate, organizers stressed issues of concern to union members: right-to-work laws, minimum wage, workplace safety, job training assistance, Social Security, and efforts to restrict political activity by unions under the rubric of "paycheck protection." Partly as a result, says Rosenthal, union voters made up 23 percent of the electorate in 1996, compared to about 14 percent in 1994. And while Bill Clinton and Bob Dole split the nonunion vote, union voters went for Clinton 64 to 28.

In 1998 the AFL-CIO used the program more widely. Where it was utilized, fully three-quarters of union members ended up voting for the union-endorsed candidate—yet only about one in 10 union members were reached. This year the federation is involved in a much more aggressive organizing effort, launched in March 1999. "It's the earliest we've ever started," says Rosenthal, who adds that the AFL-CIO is targeting 25 states and 71 congressional districts with an all-out campaign. Upwards of 500 organizers have been trained at AFL-CIO headquarters and then dispatched to targeted areas. "Basically, it's a throwback to what we were doing in the 1930s and '40s, when we were at our peak," he says. "It is a culture change."

Parallel with the AFL-CIO's Labor 2000 effort, the NAACP launched its own unprecedented GOTV effort in July by creating the National Voter Fund, an issues-oriented advocacy group that plans to spend $9 million to maximize African-American turnout. Targeting 40 congressional districts and more than a dozen key states, including Pennsylvania, Ohio, Michigan, Illinois, Wisconsin, and Missouri, the fund operates independently but draws on the resources of 2,200 NAACP chapters across the country, along with thousands of black churches and community organizations.

Although the NAACP has long conducted voter-registration campaigns—and, this year, having already registered 2.8 million people, is well on the way toward its goal of four million—the Voter Fund is something of a culture change as well. For the first time, according to veteran organizer Heather Booth, the fund's director, the NAACP has a sister organization able to directly target its resources on specific electoral races and to use sophisticated, computer-based techniques to match voter files to the NAACP's membership lists. "Our goal," says Booth, "is to identify people who can become neighbor-to-neighbor, community-to-community leaders [and] who can build local, on-the-ground operations."

In Philadelphia the NAACP's Voter Fund is mobilizing the city's 280,000 African-American voters, registering voters at supermarkets, shopping centers, transit centers, community colleges, high schools, and churches. Like the AFL-CIO's campaign, the Voter Fund is concentrating on issues, using its member activists to talk to other members and potential new voters about bread-and-butter concerns and key civil rights issues such as affirmative action. And, organizers say, it's more than registration, with machinery being put into place to maintain contact with voters right through election day. Like labor, NAACP organizers will sustain repeated "touches" to voters and potential voters, through phone banks, direct mail, community forums, a motorcade, and extensive use of well-known African-American performers and radio personalities. Perhaps most important, a network of 30 black churches in Philadelphia—and 170 more in surrounding areas—is working closely with the NAACP, organizing GOTV sermons and events on the first two Sundays of October. "We know which ministers are fairly civic-minded," says J. Whyatt Mondesire, president of the NAACP in Philadelphia.

To call the African-American vote crucial for Democrats is an understatement. According to David Bositis of the Joint Center for Political and Economic Studies, in 1996 Clinton lost among white voters 43 to 46, while blacks split 84 to 12 for Clinton. "There's a great deal of uncertainty when you mobilize a white voter to the polls," says Bositis. "With blacks, that's not the case."

And this year, black voters are concentrated in states that are up for grabs in the presidential contest, including the band of states from New Jersey to Missouri and key southern states like Florida and Georgia. The NAACP's National Voter Fund seeks to improve on 1998, when, in several states, black voters turned out at a higher percentage than did white voters. In Michigan blacks were 13 percent of the voting-age population—but comprised 19 percent of the overall vote, splitting 70 to 27 for the Democrats.

Of course, there is enormous overlap between organized labor and the African-American community, especially in cities like Philadelphia. And no one knows that better than Janet Ryder, statewide political director of the 38,000-member American Federation of Teachers (AFT) and vice president of the city's Central Labor Council. A veteran organizer, with nearly two decades in the political trenches, Ryder is not only spearheading the turnout drive among teachers, but she is working alongside the NAACP to bring registration and GOTV into Philadelphia's high schools. Together, the AFT and NAACP identified 18 high schools, developed lists of students eligible to vote, and scheduled assemblies with NAACP representatives. "We hype 'em up!" says Ryder.

Overall, of course, voters this year are anything but hyped up. With the exception of a boomlet of interest around Senator John McCain's quixotic challenge to Governor Bush, voter interest in politics has flagged throughout the year. In mid-September, the Voter Involvement Index maintained by the Joan Shorenstein Center on the Press, Politics and Public Policy languished at 25 percent, reflecting the number of voters who have paid attention to the campaign. Data collected by the Pew Research Center for The People & The Press showed that just 34 percent of Americans showed interest in the two parties' conventions, compared to 44 percent in 1996 and 53 percent in 1992—a lack of interest reflected in record-low viewership of the convention broadcasts. The Pew Research Center found that a big reason for the low voter interest was that nearly half of registered voters felt that "things will be pretty much the same for me" regardless of who wins the election.

"What we know is that voter turnout will be low," says Curtis Gans, director of the Committee for the Study of the American Electorate (CSAE). "We have a continuing decline of youth interest, which is filtering its way up the electorate." Despite the occurrence of competitive primaries in both parties, primary turnout through August was, at 17.7 percent, the second lowest since 1960, according to a CSAE study—and no higher than in 1996, when President Clinton's nomination was uncontested. This decline was in spite of heralded reforms meant to encourage participation, including simplified registration procedures, early voting, easier absentee voting, mail ballots, and, in Arizona, experimental Internet voting. . . .*

Especially glaring is the abdication of the two political parties in maintaining a grass-roots infrastructure. "The political parties are fictions three years out of four," says Lee Sigelman, professor of political science at George Washington University. "There has been a withering away of big-city political machines, in particular." . . .

In Pennsylvania—where turnout has fallen from 68 percent in 1964 to 49 percent in 1996—labor's organizers are well aware of the decline of the Democratic Party. When it comes to field organization and GOTV efforts, the party is nonexistent across much of the state, says Paul Lemmon. "Probably with the exception of Philadelphia, there is no party structure in Pennsylvania," he says. Even in Philadelphia, once notorious for its well-organized wards, "the labor movement basically is the party," says Joe Rauscher. He says that the party is

---

* Turnout in the 2000 election was just over 50 percent of age-eligible voters.

gradually allowing the ward system to atrophy, leaving committee spots unfilled and failing to groom people for party positions like ward leader.

Even more blunt is Steve Rosenthal. "The parties have become shells to move money," he says. "It used to be that the party had someone on your block, in your workplace, in your district, reminding you to go out and vote. That doesn't exist anymore." Still, Rosenthal says that as the number of voters shrinks, labor can augment its clout. "As everybody else stays home, we become more important."

Though the AFL-CIO, the NAACP's Voter Fund, and just about everyone is making use of vastly improved databases and technology to target voters, the parties and campaigns are using them to communicate only with the most reliable voters and with carefully defined segments of undecided voters. Republicans, especially, lacking the foot soldiers who turn out to support Democrats, spend vast amounts on direct mail, phone calls, and paid canvassers—now aided by an almost military-like precision provided by private data firms. The Pennsylvania GOP has a "comprehensive turnout operation" that includes hundreds of grass-roots workers in all 67 counties, says Lauren Cotter Brobson, state party communications director, disputing charges that the parties have allowed their grass-roots organizations to evaporate. Still, the state GOP relies more heavily on GeoVoter, a Wisconsin-based voter targeting company. "It's an extremely powerful tool," she says.

GeoVoter uses patented software to merge information about voters from dozens of disparate files—from registration lists to voting records, to census data specific for tiny slivers of geography, to magazine subscriptions lists—then blends in the results of millions of telephone surveys about individual voter attitudes on issues like taxes, abortion, and guns. Then all of that information is organized into a computerized display of a neighborhood: Click on a voter's name, and a detailed profile of that voter's household is instantly available. GeoVoter is only one of dozens of such firms. Collectively, their information can be used to mobilize small segments of the electorate—or, in conjunction with negative mailings, to suppress turnout from unwanted voters likely to back one's opponent.

Advances in technology have lowered its price, so that even candidates with small purses can make use of it. Jerry Dorchuck, chairman and CEO of Philadelphia-based PMI/Automated TeleSystems, offers a highly sophisticated system that can send voice-mail messages in the candidate's own voice to voters' homes for a minuscule eight cents a call, or less. "We just took a contract to make one million calls in Pennsylvania for $50,000," he says, or five cents a call. His system can also ask voters to respond to queries about opinions, interests, and concerns—then instantly tabulate those results and dispatch a direct mail piece to that voter on precisely his or her chief concern. "We e-mail the information right into the mail house, which then coordinates with the campaign manager," he says.

Such new technologies will have an enormous impact on the outcome of this year's election, and their power is likely only to grow in the future. But there is no real substitute for on-the-ground armies, like those being organized by the AFL-CIO and the NAACP, which can mobilize voters for specific issues and candidates. . . .

[T]he AFL-CIO's GOTV team isn't taking any chances. "When you're out there at 5:00 A.M, at the plant gate, you're sending a message that this is important," says Lemmon. And on election day, his organization will mount an old-fashioned knock-and-drag operation—watching the polls, seeing who's voted, and knocking on nonvoters' doors to get them out to vote.

Questions for Discussion

1. Why are grassroots GOTV campaigns typically more effective than mass-communications efforts on television in increasing voter turnout?
2. Why are many GOTV efforts now typically in the hands of interest groups rather than political parties?

 Chapter 8

THE MASS MEDIA

Information is the lifeblood of a democratic system, and the communication of information is essential to democratic politics. Citizens need trustworthy, diverse, and objective information to perform their electoral role adequately. Decision makers need reliable information about the values, preferences, and opinions of citizens to respond intelligently to them. The mass media play a crucial role in the relationship between citizens and their government. Yet their potential impact on political life leaves many people feeling ambivalent.

On the one hand, the mass media have the potential to help the nation realize its democratic possibilities. They can expand the range of public debate and broaden the attentive audience, which creates an informed public. If they perform as a watchdog over elected officials, political accountability can be greatly improved.

On the other hand, the mass media's potential to propagandize and to manipulate the public could undermine the democratic process. In *Politics in the Media Age,* Ronald Berkman and Laura W. Kitch point out that even in the nineteenth century some people were worried that "by seeking the sensational and simplifying political matters," the mass media could "divert the attention of the masses, arouse irrational passions, and lower the level of political debate." In this century, government management of the news during both world wars exposed the danger that entire populations could be swayed. Government regulation of radio and television in our own period, as well as control over many of the sources of the news, raises concerns that the mass media are at best dependent on, and at worst captives of, the very institutions they scrutinize. The increasing concentration of media ownership, particularly in the past decade, suggests that diverse political information is hard to come by.

It is not surprising that media critics are found at both ends of the political spectrum. Social conservatives claim that violence and sexually suggestive material on television have undermined the American family and contributed to a decline in morals. Social liberals assert that television's depiction of women and minorities perpetuates unflattering stereotypes and limits social progress. Economic conservatives worry that the media's focus on business abuses and tight-fisted bankers will undermine the capitalist system. Economic liberals

241

bemoan the fact that the media can never be a force for economic justice and equality because they draw their revenue from commercial sources.

Of course, when our nation was founded there was no such thing as the mass media. The newspapers that existed were partisan forums, directed toward narrow groups of elite supporters. Not until the Jacksonian era of the late 1820s and 1830s did American politics develop its mass character and the first mass circulation newspapers came into being.

Today the mass media are a fact of life. Most of what we know about politics and government comes from the media. A. C. Nielsen reports that 98 percent of American families own at least one television set and that the nation has more radios than people. Few of us acquire political information from other people; instead, strangers decide what information most of us receive.

Television is particularly pervasive. By the time the average American reaches eighteen years of age, he or she has probably spent more time in front of a TV set than in a classroom (roughly 15,000 hours). Television is highly credible because it utilizes both sight and sound. Although television is primarily an entertainment medium, many programs have either explicit or implicit political content. News programs and documentaries are obviously political, and entertainment shows that deal with, say, the police or education have some underlying orientation toward the institution in question. Even a show such as "Sesame Street" reveals strong values about politically relevant subjects such as race relations. Advertisements too are full of politically relevant content, particularly in the stereotypes they convey.

Because there are so many potential influences on political behavior and values, it is difficult to assess what effect such factors have. The mass media's impact is often inferred from their content, but the relationship is difficult to pin down. The one apparent truism is that the media exert the least influence when they attempt to affect people's views and preferences directly, especially through such devices as political endorsements. In 1936, for example, Republican Alf Landon was endorsed by over 80 percent of the daily newspapers in the country, but Democrat Franklin Roosevelt achieved one of the biggest electoral landslides in U.S. history.

Media impact appears to be strongest in ambiguous, unstructured situations in which individuals have little prior information. Because most people know little about most political subjects, the media can set agendas, not so much by telling the public what to think as by telling it whom and what to think about. A good example is the presidential nomination process. By focusing citizens' attention on the actions of certain individuals and particular issues, the media can confer status (one candidate is "the strong frontrunner") and create disadvantage (another candidate "has little experience"). Audiences learn not only what the campaign issues are but how much importance to attach to them.

Research on the subject has yielded mixed results, suggesting the media are neither as benign as their supporters have argued nor as damaging as many critics have claimed. We need to distinguish among the various types of media and to specify the conditions under which they do influence political orientations and behavior. Their effect will remain a controversial subject, as the selections in this chapter exemplify.

In the first selection, Joshua Meyrowitz makes a strong case that the electronic media have greatly affected our perceptions of political leadership, making it difficult for Americans to find leaders they respect and trust. The second essay deals with bias in the news. Thomas Patterson suggests that today's media are characterized less by an ideological bias than by an "antipolitics" bias. He contends that the new bias has evolved as the descriptive style of reporting has given way to a more interpretive style, giving journalists unprecedented control over content. In the final selection, Scott Stossel looks at the problems television news had on election night 2000, when all three networks improperly declared a winner of the presidential election, only to rescind their calls later.

8.1

Lowering the Political Hero to Our Level

Joshua Meyrowitz

Image has always been important in politics. Whether an individual is viewed as honest or untrustworthy, hard-working or lazy, tough or mean, has much to do with that person's political success. Moreover, the use of the electronic media, particularly television, has dramatically altered how the public views political figures and has especially affected the image of elected leadership.

According to Joshua Meyrowitz, before the invention of the electronic media, the public held political leaders in awe. Politicians' images were based on mystification and careful management of public impressions. Political figures operated at a great distance from the public, who had limited access to them.

Radio and television, however, "reveal too much and too often." Television in particular appears to make politicians available for public inspection. This clouds the distinction between politicians' "onstage" and "backstage" behavior. Their human frailties are highlighted, as TV cameras show them sweating or reacting with anger or tears. National politicians no longer have the opportunity to test their presentations. They appear to the whole nation at the same time, and so they are more likely to make mistakes. Ill-chosen words or the inevitable inconsistencies that arise during a campaign are exaggerated, and call into question a politician's honesty and competence.

In the end, "the familiarity fostered by electronic media all too easily breeds contempt." According to Meyrowitz, mystification is necessary for an image of strong leadership, yet disclosure eliminates mystery. As a result, few contemporary political leaders are universally revered in their own lifetime.

A ll our recent Presidents have been plagued with problems of "credibility." Lyndon Johnson abdicated his office; Richard Nixon left the presidency in disgrace; Gerald Ford's "appointment" to the presidency was later rejected by the electorate; Jimmy Carter suffered a landslide defeat after being strongly challenged within his own party; and even the comparatively popular

Joshua Meyrowitz is a professor of communication at the University of New Hampshire.

Ronald Reagan has followed his predecessors in the now familiar roller coaster ride in the polls.*

We seem to be having difficulty finding leaders who have charisma and style and who are also competent and trustworthy. In the wish to keep at least one recent leader in high esteem, many people have chosen to forget that in his thousand days in office, John Kennedy faced many crises of credibility and accusations of "news management."

During the 1990 campaign, *Newsweek* analyzed recent political polls and concluded that "perhaps the most telling political finding of all is the high degree of disenchantment voters feel about most of the major candidates."[1] Of course, every horse race has its winner, and no matter how uninspiring the field of candidates, people will always have their favorites. The obsession with poll percentage points and the concern over who wins and who loses, however, tend to obscure the more fundamental issue of the decline in the image of leaders in general.

There are at least two ways to study the image and rhetoric of the presidency. One is to examine the content and form of speeches and actions; in other words, to look at specific strategies, choices, and decisions. Another method is to examine the situations within which Presidents perform their roles. This second method requires a shift in focus away from the specific rhetorical strategies of individual politicians and toward the general environment that surrounds the presidency and is therefore shared by all who seek that office.

This [article] employs the latter method to reinterpret the causes of the political woes of some of our recent national politicians and to shed some light on our leadership problem in general. I suggest that the decline in presidential image may have surprisingly little to do with a simple lack of potentially great leaders, and much to do with a specific communication environment—a communication environment that undermines the politician's ability to behave like, and therefore be perceived as, the traditional "great leader."

The Merging of Political Arenas and Styles

Before the widespread use of electronic media, the towns and cities of the country served as backstage areas of rehearsal for national political figures. By the time William Jennings Bryan delivered his powerful "cross of gold" speech to win the nomination for President at the 1896 Democratic convention, for example, he had already practiced the speech many times in different parts of the country.

The legendary oratory of Bryan and the treasured images of many of our other political heroes were made possible by their ability to practice and modify their

---

* Ronald Reagan, especially after 1982 and before 1987, enjoyed levels of public regard that were exceptional among recent presidents and presidential contenders.

public performances. Early mistakes could be limited to small forums, minor changes could be tested, and speeches and presentations could be honed to perfection. Politicians could thrill many different crowds on different days with a single well-turned phrase. Bryan, for example, was very fond of his closing line in the 1896 speech ("You shall not press down upon the brow of labor this crown of thorns, you shall not crucify mankind upon a cross of gold")—so fond, in fact, that he had used it many times in other speeches and debates. In his memoirs, Bryan noted his early realization of the line's "fitness for the conclusion of a climax," and after using it in smaller public arenas, he "laid it away for a proper occasion."[2]

Today, through radio and television, the national politician often faces a single audience. Wherever the politician speaks, he or she addresses people all over the country. Major speeches, therefore, cannot be tested in advance. Because they can be presented only once, they tend to be relatively coarse and undramatic. Inspiring lines either are consumed quickly or they become impotent clichés.

Nineteenth century America provided multiple political arenas in which politicians could perfect the form and the substance of their main ideas. They could also buttress their central platforms with slightly different promises to different audiences. Today, because politicians address so many different types of people simultaneously, they have great difficulty speaking in specifics. And any slip of the tongue is amplified in significance because of the millions of people who have witnessed it. Those who analyze changing rhetorical styles without taking such situational changes into account overlook a major political variable.

Many Americans are still hoping for the emergence of an old-style, dynamic "great leader." Yet electronic media of communication are making it almost impossible to find one. There is no lack of potential leaders, but rather an overabundance of information about them. The great leader image depends on mystification and careful management of public impressions. Through television, we see too much of our politicians, and they are losing control over their images and performances. As a result, our political leaders are being stripped of their aura and are being brought closer to the level of the average person.

The impact of electronic media on the staging of politics can best be understood by analyzing it in relation to the staging requirements of *any* social role. . . . Regardless of competence, regardless of desire, there is a limit to how long any person can play out an idealized conception of a social role. All people must eat, sleep, and go to the bathroom. All people need time to think about their social behavior, prepare for social encounters, and rest from them. Further, we all play different roles in different situations. One man, for example, may be a father, a son, a husband, an old college roommate, and a boss. He may also be President of the United States. He needs to emphasize different aspects of his personality in order to function in each of these roles. The performance of social roles, therefore, is in many ways like a multistage drama. The strength and clarity of a particular onstage, or "front region," performance depend on isolating the audience from the backstage, or "back region." Rehearsals, relaxations, and behaviors from other onstage roles must be kept out of the limelight. The need to shield backstage behaviors is especially acute in the performance of roles that rely heavily on mystification and on an aura of greatness—roles such as those performed by national political leaders.

Yet electronic media of communication have been eroding barriers between the politician's traditional back and front regions. The camera eye and the microphone ear have been probing many aspects of the national politician's behavior and transmitting this information to 225 million Americans. By revealing to its audience both traditionally onstage and traditionally backstage activities, television could be said to provide a "sidestage," or "middle region," view of public figures. We watch politicians move from backstage to onstage to backstage. We see politicians address crowds of well-wishers, then greet their families "in private." We join candidates as they speak with their advisors, and we sit behind them as they watch conventions on television. We see candidates address many different types of audiences in many different settings.

By definition, the "private" behaviors now exposed are no longer true back region activities precisely because they are exposed to the public. But neither are they merely traditional front region performances. The traditional balance between rehearsal and performance has been upset. Through electronic coverage, politicians' freedom to isolate themselves from their audiences is being limited. In the process, politicians are not only losing aspects of their privacy—a complaint we often hear—but, more important, they are simultaneously losing their ability to play many facets of the high and mighty roles of traditional leaders. For when actors lose parts of their rehearsal time, their performances naturally move toward the extemporaneous.

The sidestage perspective offered by television makes normal differences in behavior appear to be evidence of inconsistency or dishonesty. We all behave differently in different situations, depending on who is there and who is not. Yet when television news programs edit together videotape sequences that show a politician saying and doing different things in different places and before different audiences, the politician may appear, at best, indecisive and, at worst, dishonest.

The reconfiguration of the stage of politics demands a drive toward consistency in all exposed spheres. To be carried off smoothly, the new political performance requires a new "middle region" role: behavior that lacks the extreme formality of former front region behavior and also lacks the extreme informality of traditional back region behavior. Wise politicians make the most of the new situation. They try to expose selected, positive aspects of their back regions in order to ingratiate themselves with the public. Yet there is a difference between *coping* with the new situation and truly *controlling* it. Regardless of how well individual politicians adjust to the new exposure, the overall image of leaders changes in the process. The new political performance remains a performance, but its style is markedly changed.

Mystification and awe are supported by distance and limited access. Our new media reveal too much and too often for traditional notions of political leadership to prevail. The television camera invades politicians' personal spheres like a spy in back regions. It watches them sweat, sees them grimace at their own ill-phrased remarks. It coolly records them as they succumb to emotions. The camera minimizes the distance between audience and performer. The speaker's platform once raised a politician up and away from the people—both literally and symbolically. The camera now brings the politician close for the people's inspection. And in this sense, it lowers politicians to the level of their audience. The camera brings a rich range of expressive information to the audience; it highlights politicians' mortality and mutes abstract and conceptual rhetoric. While verbal rhetoric can transcend humanity and reach for the divine, intimate expressive information often exposes human frailty. No wonder old style politicians, who continue to assume the grand postures of another era, now seem like clowns or crooks. The personal close-up view forces many politicians to pretend to be less than they would like to be (and, thereby, in a social sense, they actually become less).

Some people were privy to a sort of "middle region" for politicians before television. Through consistent physical proximity, for example, many reporters would see politicians in a multiplicity of front region roles and a smattering of back region activities. Yet, the relationship between politicians and some journalists was itself a personal back region interaction that was distinguished from press accounts to the public. Before television, most of the news stories released were not records of this personal back region relationship or even of a "middle region." The politician could always distinguish for the press what was "on" the record, what was "off" the record, what should be paraphrased, and what must be attributed to "a high government official." Thus, even when the journalists and the politicians were intimates, the news releases were usually impersonal social communications. Print media can "report on" what happens in one place and bring the report to another place. But the report is by no means a "presentation" of the actual place-bound experience. The print reporters who interviewed Theodore Roosevelt while he was being shaved, for example, did not have an experience "equivalent" to the resulting news reports. Because private interactions with reporters were once distinct from the public communications released in newspapers, much of a politician's "personality" was well hidden from the average citizen.

Private press-politician interactions continue to take place, but electronic media have created new political situations that change the overall "distance" between politician and voter. With electronic coverage, politicians lose a great deal of control over their messages and performances. When they ask that the television camera or tape recorder be turned off, the politicians appear to have something to hide. When the camera or microphone is on, politicians can no longer separate their interaction with the press from their interaction with the public. The camera unthinkingly records the flash of anger and the shiver in the cold; it determinedly shadows our leaders as they trip over words or down stairs.

And, unlike the testimony of journalists or of other witnesses, words and actions recorded on electronic tape are impossible to deny. Thus, while politicians try hard to structure the *content* of the media coverage, the *form* of the coverage itself is changing the nature of political image. The revealing nature of television's presentational information cannot be fully counteracted by manipulation, practice, and high-paid consultants. Even a staged media event is often more personally revealing than a transcript of an informal speech or interview. When in 1977, President Carter allowed NBC cameras into the White House for a day, the result may not have been what he intended. As *The New York Times* reported:

> Mr. Carter is a master of controlled images, and he is obviously primed for the occasion. When he isn't flashing his warm smile, he is being soothingly cool under pressure. But the camera ferrets out that telltale tick, that comforting indication of ordinary humanity. It finds his fingers nervously caressing a paperclip or playing with a pen. It captures the almost imperceptible tightening of facial muscles when the President is given an unflattering newspaper story about one of his sons.[3]

Some politicians, of course, have better "media images" than others, but few can manipulate their images as easily as politicians could in a print era. The nature and the extent of this loss of control become even clearer when back and front regions are not viewed as mutually exclusive categories. Most actions encompass both types of behavior. In many situations, for example, an individual can play a front region role while simultaneously giving off covert back region cues to "teammates" (facial expressions, "code" remarks, fingers crossed behind the back, etc.). . . . Because expressions are constant and personal, an individual's exuding of expressions is a type of ongoing back region activity that was once accessible only to those in close physical proximity. Thus, the degree of control over access to back regions is not simply binary—access/no access—but infinitely variable. Any medium of communication can be analyzed in relation to those personal characteristics it transmits and those it restricts.

Print, for example, conveys words but no intonations or facial gestures; radio sends intonations along with the words but provides no visual information; television transmits the full audio/visual spectrum of verbal, vocal, and gestural. In this sense, the trend from print to radio to television represents a shrinking shield for back region activities and an increase in the energy required to manage impressions. Further, Albert Mehrabian's formula for relative message impact—7% verbal, 38% vocal, and 55% facial and postural—suggests that the trend in media development not only leads to revealing more, but to revealing more of more. From the portrait to the photograph to the movie to the video close-up, media have been providing a closer, more replicative, more immediate, and, therefore, less idealized image of the leader. "Greatness" is an abstraction, and it fades as the image of distant leaders comes to resemble an encounter with an intimate acquaintance.

As cameras continue to get lighter and smaller, and as microphones and lenses become more sensitive, the distinctions between public and private contexts continue to erode. It is no longer necessary for politicians to stop what they are doing in order to pose for a picture or to step up to a microphone. As a result, it is increasingly difficult for politicians to distinguish between the ways in which they behave in "real situations" and the ways in which they present themselves for the media. The new public image of politicians, therefore, has many of the characteristics of the former backstage of political life, and many once informal interactions among politicians and their families, staff, reporters, and constituents have become more stiff and formal as they are exposed to national audiences. . . .

Most politicians, even Presidents, continue to maintain a truly private backstage area, but that area is being pushed further and further into the background, and it continues to shrink both spatially and temporally.

Writing and print not only hide general back region actions and behaviors, they also conceal the act of producing "images" and messages. Presidents once had the time to prepare speeches carefully. Even seemingly "spontaneous" messages were prepared in advance, often with the help of advisors, counselors, and family members. Delays, indecision, and the pondering of alternative solutions in response to problems were hidden in the invisible backstage area created by the inherent slowness of older media. Before the invention of the telegraph, for example, a President never needed to be awakened in the middle of the night to respond to a crisis. A few hours' delay meant little.

Electronic media, however, leave little secret time for preparations and response. Because messages *can* be sent instantly across the nation and the world, any delay in hearing from a President is apparent. And in televised press conferences, even a few seconds of thought by a politician may be seen as a sign of indecisiveness, weakness, or senility. More and more, therefore, the public messages conveyed by officials are, in fact, spontaneous.

Politicians find it more difficult to hide their need for time and for advice in the preparation of public statements. They must either reveal the decision process (by turning to advisors or by saying that they need more time to study the issue) or they must present very informal, off-the-cuff comments that naturally lack the craftsmanship of prepared texts. The new media demand that the politician walk and talk steadily and unthinkingly along a performance tightrope. On either side is danger: A few seconds of silence or a slip of the tongue can lead to a fall in the polls.

The changing arenas of politics affect not only the perceptions of audiences but also the response of politicians to their own performances. In face-to-face behavior, we must get a sense of ourselves from the ongoing response of others. We can never see ourselves quite the way others see us. On videotape, however, politicians are able to see exactly the same image of themselves as is seen by the public. In live interactions, a speaker's nervousness and mistakes are usually politely ignored by audiences and therefore often soon forgotten by the speaker too. With television, politicians acquire permanent records of themselves sweating, stammering, or anxiously licking their lips. Television, therefore, has the power to increase a politician's self-doubt and lower self-esteem.

Highly replicative media are demystifying leaders not only for their own time, but for history as well. Few leaders are universally revered in their own lifetime. But less replicative media allowed, at least, for greater idealization of leaders after they died. Idiosyncrasies and physical flaws were interred with a President's bones, their good deeds and their accomplishments lived after them. Once a President died, all that remained were flattering painted portraits and the written texts of speeches. An unusual speaking style or an unattractive facial expression was soon forgotten.

If Lincoln had been passed down to us only through painted portraits, perhaps his homeliness would have faded further with time. The rest of the Lincoln legend, however, including Lincoln's image as a dynamic speaker, continues to be preserved by the *lack* of recordings of his unusually high, thin voice, which rose even higher when he was nervous. Similarly, Thomas Jefferson's slight speech impediment is rarely mentioned. Through new media, however, the idiosyncrasies of Presidents are preserved and passed down to the next generation. Instead of inheriting only summaries and recollections, future generations will judge the styles of former Presidents for themselves. They will see Gerald Ford lose his balance, Carter sweating under pressure, and Reagan dozing during an audience with the Pope. Presidential mispronunciations, hesitations, perspiration, and physical and verbal clumsiness are now being preserved for all time.

Expressions are part of the shared repertoire of all people. When under control and exposed briefly, expressive messages show the "humanity" of the "great leader." But when they are flowing freely and constantly, expressive messages suggest that those we look up to may, after all, be no different from ourselves. The more intense our search for evidence of greatness, the more it eludes us.

There is a demand today for two things: fully open, accessible administrations and strong, powerful leaders. Rarely do we consider that these two demands may, unfortunately, be incompatible. We want to spy on our leaders, yet we want them to inspire us. We cannot have both disclosure *and* the mystification necessary for an image of greatness. The post-Watergate fascination with uncovering cover-ups has not been accompanied by a sophisticated notion of what will inevitably be found in the closets of all leaders. The familiarity fostered by electronic media all too easily breeds contempt.

Notes

1. David M. Alpern, "A Newsweek Poll on the Issues," *Newsweek*, 3 March 1980, 29.
2. William Jennings Bryan and Mary Baird Bryan, *The Memoirs of William Jennings Bryan, Vol. 1,* Reprint of 1925 edition (Port Washington, New York: Kennikat, 1971), 103.
3. John J. O'Connor, "TV: A Full Day at the White House," *The New York Times,* 14 April 1977.

Questions for Discussion

1. Why does the author believe that "old style" political heroes are no longer possible?
2. It has been said that American voters prefer a "candidate of the people but not like the people." What does this mean? Would Meyrowitz agree with this assertion?

 8.2

Bad News, Bad Governance

Thomas E. Patterson

Do the media cover politics in a biased manner? Both Republicans and Democrats constantly accuse the press of negative coverage and bias in reporting. Supporters and detractors of presidents are particularly adamant in their criticisms of the press. For example, Republicans consistently criticize the press for alleged favorable coverage of President Clinton, but the president and his supporters are just as vigorous in condemning the press for focusing on the president's failings rather than what the White House views as the substantial accomplishments of the administration.

In this selection, Thomas Patterson asserts that real media bias is found along neither an ideological nor a partisan dimension but rather in the "antipolitics" bias of the news media. Patterson believes that there has been a revolution in news reporting in recent decades, as descriptive journalism has given way to an interpretive style that inevitably focuses on the negative in politics. Reporters have developed a jaded opinion of politicians of all persuasions, and during the 1990s both parties' elected officials were covered in a negative manner. In Patterson's view, the new interpretive style of reporting "elevates the journalist's voice above that of the newsmaker" and cannot be justified either by the journalists' political or policy expertise or by their position in the political system.

Patterson believes the media need to rethink their current model of reporting. What is needed is a more balanced portrayal of the workings of the political

Thomas E. Patterson is the Benjamin Bradlee Professor of Press and Politics at Harvard University's John F. Kennedy School of Government.

system. Journalism needs to move away from its interpretive style, since journalists are not an appropriate vehicle for the articulation of values that are at stake in political conflict. Political leaders must be given more opportunities to make their claims without media interpretation.

The first 100 days of the 104th Congress were historic, but one would never have guessed that from the tone of the news coverage. Although the initiatives in the Republicans' Contract with America* moved rapidly through the House of Representatives, statements about the House from network reporters and their sources were 65 percent negative and only 35 percent positive. The Senate coverage was even harsher: 71 percent negative to 29 percent positive. Each of the GOP's top congressional leaders, Newt Gingrich, Robert Dole, and Richard Armey, was portrayed negatively, and their combined coverage was more than 60 percent unfavorable. Nor was the blistering attack on Congress and its leaders confined to network television. According to the Center for Media and Public Affairs, coverage of the early weeks of the 104th Congress in major newspapers was nearly as negative.[1]

Why did the press treat the Republican Congress so harshly? Some would attribute it to the alleged liberal bias of the news media. According to this theory, the national press "tends to be strongly biased in favor of the Democratic-liberal-left axis of opinion and strongly biased against the Republican-conservative-right axis of opinion."[2]

The problem with this thesis is that it often does not fit the facts: during the first 100 days of the 104th Congress, congressional Democrats actually received worse coverage than congressional Republicans: 82 percent negative coverage versus 68 percent negative. Democrats received substantially less attention from the press than the Republicans did but were more soundly criticized when their activities were reported.[3]

The inadequacy of the liberal-bias theory of national news coverage is also apparent in the media's treatment of Bill Clinton's presidency. Although Clinton is the first Democratic president in 12 years, he did not even get the honeymoon period that newly elected presidents might expect from the press. Clinton's coverage was only 43 percent positive during his first two months on the job. Six

---

* The Contract with America was a pledge signed on the steps of the U.S. Capitol by 300 Republicans running for the House of Representatives in September 1994. In the pledge were a series of proposals that later became the basis for the Republicans' House legislative agenda in the 104th Congress. Included were such items as structural changes in the way the House was governed internally, as well as policy changes such as constitutional amendments to balance the budget and to impose congressional term limits, reductions of welfare benefits, the easing of regulations on business, and major cuts in taxes.

months into his presidency, Clinton's numbers were worse—only 34 percent of news evaluations were positive, while 66 percent were negative. . . .

In the media's view, Clinton did almost everything wrong during his inaugural year. In the spring, for example, a series of failed nominations, including those of Lani Guinier and Zoe Baird, and personal controversies, such as the president's $200 haircut, led reporters to speak of "amateur hour" at the White House. Said ABC's John McWethy, "The Clinton administration has repeatedly bungled high-profile nominations with the president looking indecisive, his staff incompetent." Newsweek's Joe Klein told CBS's Dan Rather, "He got away from the values that made him seem like one of us—a guy who'd ride the bus. Now he's a guy who takes the plane and gets his hair cut for $200."[4]

Antipolitics: The Real Bias of the News Media

The liberal-bias theory fails because it ignores the checks and balances within the news system. Although journalists are disproportionally liberal and Democratic in their personal beliefs,[5] the norms of their profession include a commitment to the balanced treatment of the two political parties, a code that is enforced by the layer of editors who oversee the work of reporters.

The norms of objectivity do not, however, include a restraint on skepticism. Reporters have a jaded opinion of politicians, whether liberal or conservative, and of the political process within which they operate. More than anything else, it is this derisive attitude that accounts for the news media's rough treatment of Clinton and the Republican Congress.

The absence of effective restraints on this attitude is reflected in the fact that political leaders and institutions are likely to be criticized almost regardless of what they do. The Democratic-controlled 103d Congress (1993–94) was derided by the press as a do-nothing legislature that would not tackle the budget deficit, welfare, and political reform issues. The New York Times labeled the 103d Congress as the least productive and most factitious in memory.[6] An analysis by the Center for Media and Public Affairs found that television coverage of the 103d Congress was 64 percent negative.[7] . . .

President Clinton's first year in office also provides an instructive study in the press's tendency to criticize irrespective of the situation. No news theme was more persistent than the notion that Clinton was reneging on his policy commitments. This theme surfaced in the first weeks of his presidency, when Clinton broke a campaign promise to open the nation's shores to the Haitian boat people and sought a compromise with Congress for a new policy on gays in the military. Compromises over tax increases and spending cuts in pursuit of a deficit-reduction policy kept the theme alive into the summer. In the fall, the theme appeared during the kickoff of the health care debate, when Clinton expressed a willingness to include the plans of others as long as they accepted his basic positions on universal coverage and cost containment. The Center for Media and Public Affairs' analysis indicates that more than 60 percent of news references to Clinton's handling of domestic policy issues were negative in tone. These criticisms were voiced through the statements of reporters, Clinton's partisan opponents, and ordinary people. On the *NBC Evening News* of 19 July, for example, a gay ex-Marine criticized the "don't ask, don't tell" compromise policy: "I think it's a cop-out from what he planned to do. It's just a cheap imitation."[8]

Some of this criticism was right on target, but much of it was undeserved. The fact is that Clinton kept far more campaign promises than he broke. Among the promises kept were a tax increase on higher incomes, an end to the ban on abortion counseling in family-planning clinics, a family-leave program, banking reform, NAFTA, a college-loan program, the Brady bill, and a youth training program. Clinton also proposed numerous programs that were still working their way through Congress as 1993 ended. . . .

Clinton's reward? A slew of bad news. Small wonder that in a year-end interview with *Rolling Stone* magazine, Clinton exploded at the claim that he had not honored his policy commitments: "I have fought more damn battles here than any President in 20 years with the possible exception of Reagan's first budget, and not gotten one damn bit of credit from the knee-jerk liberal press. I am damn sick and tired of it."[9] Clinton had a legitimate beef, but he misjudged the cause of his bad press: it was not the press's "knee-jerk liberalism" but its ingrained cynicism.

Journalists Unleashed: The Rise of Interpretive Journalism

The political scientist Austin Ranney has traced the press's antipolitics bias to the Progressive movement, the turn-of-the-century reform effort that sought to curb political power through such devices as the initiative, the referendum, the recall, and the direct primary.[10]

The Progressive spirit was expressed through a form of muckraking journalism that attacked concentrations of power in any form, political or economic. Muckraking was eventually quieted by the excesses of its practitioners and by the emerging rules of objective journalism, which held that reporters should refrain from expressing their opinions in news stories.

Straightforward reporting became the dominant style. The journalist's guidelines were the five Ws: who said what, where, when, and why. The focus was the facts of an event rather than the underlying political situation. Since the facts were often based on what politicians had said or done, they greatly influenced the tone of the coverage. A standard formula for a news story was a descriptive account of what politicians said and to whom they said it. News accounts did not ordinarily delve into why they said it, for that would venture into the realm of subjectivity. At the very least, journalists took pains to separate the facts of an event from their interpretations of it.

Today, facts and interpretation are freely intermixed in news reporting. Interpretation provides the theme, and the facts illuminate it. The theme is primary; the facts are illustrative. As a result, events are compressed and joined together within a common theme. Reporters question politicians' actions and commonly attribute strategic intentions to them, giving politicians less of a chance to speak for themselves.[11]

Interpretive reporting is nearly as old as journalism itself but has only recently become the dominant model of news coverage. When the television networks in the 1960s changed from a 15-minute format to a 30-minute format and began to generate most of their own news, they increasingly relied upon an interpretive style of reporting.[12] The inverted-pyramid form of the traditional newspaper story is less well suited to television. This form trails off as it proceeds from the most salient fact of an event to the least important, allowing the newspaper editor to cut the story almost anywhere in order to fit it into the available space. The reader's eye anticipates the concluding line. On television, however, this form gives the appearance of a news story that has been abruptly terminated, ending with a whimper rather than a bang. Accordingly, network executives devised a punchier, more thematic style of reporting built around story lines rather than facts. NBC's Reuven Frank instructed his correspondents: "Every news story should, without any sacrifice of probity or responsibility, display the attributes of fiction, of drama. It should have structure and conflict, problem and denouement, rising action and falling action, a beginning, a middle and an end."[13]

Newspapers pursued the interpretive style less as an attempt to imitate television than as an effort to establish a separate niche in the news market. Unable to compete with television as a source of fast-breaking news, the newspapers migrated toward reports designed to explain or embellish the previous day's events. The extent to which this interpretive form of reporting has taken over newspaper coverage is evident in the *New York Times*. Between 1960 and 1992, the proportion of interpretive reports on its front page increased tenfold, from 8 percent to 80 percent.[14]

The interpretive style empowers journalists by giving them more control over the news message. Whereas descriptive reporting is driven by the facts, the interpretive form is driven by the theme around which the story is built. . . .

The interpretive style elevates the journalist's voice above that of the news maker. As the narrator, the journalist is always at the center of the story, so much so that during network coverage of the 1992 general election, for example, journalists spoke six minutes for every minute that the candidates were shown speaking. A viewer who watched the network news every night of the general election would have heard less from the mouths of Clinton, Bush, and Ross Perot than from viewing a single presidential debate.[15] . . .

Cynicism Unleashed: Vietnam, Watergate, and the Rise of Attack Journalism

At nearly the same time that interpretive journalism was working its way into the news system, the Vietnam and Watergate issues soured the relationship between journalists and politicians. The deceptions perpetuated by the Johnson and Nixon administrations convinced reporters that they had failed in their duty to the nation by taking political leaders at their word.

Although politicians such as William Fulbright, Eugene McCarthy, Sam Ervin, and Howard Baker played a pivotal role in the downfall of Johnson and Nixon, journalists saw themselves as the real heroes. "The press won on Watergate," declared Ben Bradlee, executive editor of the *Washington Post*.[16] The *New York Times*'s James Reston said much the same thing about Vietnam: "Maybe historians will agree that the reporters and the cameras were decisive in the end. They brought the issue of the war to the people, before the Congress and the courts, and forced the withdrawal of American power from Vietnam."[17]

Many in the press went a step further and concluded that all politicians were suspect. Two presidents had lied, therefore no politician could be taken at his word.[18] It was a comfortable assumption for a press with a watchdog philosophy. "Our habits of mind," the *Washington Post*'s Paul Taylor observes, "are shaped by what Lionel Trilling once described as the 'adversary culture.' . . . We are progressive reformers, deeply skeptical of all the major institutions of society except our own."[19]

Even as late as the early 1970s, however, the old rules of journalism maintained a powerful hold on reporters. The press attacked Johnson and Nixon, but only when the charges could be substantiated. Thus the Watergate story developed slowly, gathering strength only as incriminating facts and credible allegations came increasingly to light.

The press was unable to sustain this exacting type of scrutiny, however. Investigative journalism requires an amount of time and knowledge that journalists do not routinely possess. It ordinarily takes a great deal of effort to determine the validity of a politician's claim or to uncover the full range of motives behind it. The pressures of the 24-hour news cycle make it nearly impossible for journalists to engage in this type of reporting on a regular basis. . . .

By the 1980s, attack journalism had come to include reporters as direct participants; they regularly worked their own criticisms into their interpretive reports. These attacks are circumscribed in that journalists seldom contest the values inherent in political conflict, but they constantly question politicians' motives, methods, and effectiveness. This type of reporting looks like watchdog journalism but is not. It is ideological in its premise: politicians are assumed to act out of self-interest rather than also from political conviction. Journalists routinely claim that politicians make promises they do not intend to keep or could not keep even if they tried. Most bad-press stories criticize politicians for shifting their positions, waffling on tough issues, posturing, or pandering to whichever group they happen to be facing.[20]

The evidence, however, shows otherwise. Four major scholarly studies have systematically compared what presidential candidates said on the campaign trail and what they did in office when elected. Each of these studies reached the same conclusion: presidents fulfill the promises they made as candidates. For example, political scientist Gerald Pomper's exhaustive study of party platforms in nine presidential elections found that the victorious candidates, once in office, tried to fulfill nearly all of their policy commitments and succeeded in achieving most of them. When presidents fail to deliver on a promise, it is usually because Congress refuses to act or because conditions have changed dramatically.[21] . . .

Furthermore, contrary to what the press may imply, the play of politics is not in itself dishonorable. Press accounts of the Clinton presidency and the Contract with America made it appear as if negotiation and deals violate a sacred bond. Each compromise was reported as a headlong retreat from principle. This perspective is as unfair as it is silly. Officeholders are rarely in a position to act decisively on their own. The president and members of Congress are separately elected and share power. For a president or members of Congress to adhere rigidly to their positions is to invite deadlock and risk failure. Compromise in a system of checks and balances is not perfidy; it is the intended outcome of this constitutional arrangement.

Bad News and the Public's Trust in Leaders and Institutions

In the 1960 presidential race, 75 percent of the news coverage received by Kennedy and Nixon was positive in tone. Only 25 percent was negative. When Clinton, Bush, and Perot ran in 1992, more than 60 percent of their coverage was negative in tone.[22]

This difference is not a simple reflection of the difference between Kennedy and Nixon, on the one hand, and Clinton, Bush, and Perot, on the other. Between 1960 and 1992, the tone of election coverage became steadily more negative regardless of who was running. Candidates of the 1960s received more favorable coverage than those of the 1970s, who in turn received more favorable coverage than candidates of the 1980s. Since 1980, more than half of all news coverage of presidential candidates has been negative in tone.[23] The increase in interpretive journalism and in press cynicism has meant that those who run for the presidency can expect rough treatment by the press.

This type of coverage has a decisive impact on voters' perceptions of the candidates. By the time the 1992 race had narrowed to Clinton, Bush, and Perot, polls indicated that most voters were unhappy with the candidates; all three had high negative ratings, and more than half of those surveyed said they wished they had other candidates from which to select. . . .

The electorate's disenchantment is without precedent. The Gallup organization first asked voters their opinions of the presidential candidates in 1936. Through the 1960s, Barry Goldwater in 1964 was the only candidate with an overall negative rating with the voters. Since then, most candidates have had a negative rating. This trend coincides exactly with the trend in the press's portrayal of the candidates.[24]

The same pattern holds true for Congress and the presidency. Since the late 1980s, news coverage of these institutions has been highly negative in tone. It is hardly surprising that the public's perception of Congress and the president during this period has been largely unfavorable. The press's bad-news tendency is not the only reason why voters' impressions of politics and politicians have been so negative in recent elections, but it is a major factor. . . .

The public has few psychological defenses against the news media's claim that political leaders are self-interested and inept. Unlike messages that attempt to change issue attitudes (such as editorials that take a position on abortion policy), the claim that an officeholder has a devious motive or lacks ability does not contradict any deeply held belief. Moreover, the message appears to be factual rather than what it really is, mere opinion. Like the proverbial Monday morning quarterback, journalists claim to have all the answers and talk as if the best course of action was evident from the start—that is, to all except those in charge of running the show. . . .

Of course, politics is sometimes plagued by officeholders' deceit and myopia, and the media should inform the public about that. But the press has gone way beyond that point, and the effect is to rob political leaders of the public confidence that is required to govern effectively. Leaders must have substantial latitude if they are to pursue policies that will serve the public interest in the long run. The discontinuous, fluid, and transient form of politics that the press generates works against such leadership. It is a politics of shifting standards and fleeting controversies, spurring citizens to demand immediate solutions to stubborn problems, which in turn encourages politicians to pursue short-term and ultimately self-limiting policies and strategies.

The presidency is particularly affected by a hypercritical press. Much of the president's authority derives not from constitutional grants of power but from the public force that is inherent in the president's position as the only official chosen by the whole nation. When the president's public approval ratings are high, Congress is more responsive to presidential leadership. When approval ratings are low or in decline, which has now become the norm, congressional resistance intensifies.

Government itself has also been weakened by the media's antipolitics message. It is ironic that journalists, who tend to have liberal beliefs, have become the unwitting handmaiden of the conservatives. Right-wing attacks on government activism gain power when the public believes that government is ineffective and run by inept and self-serving officials. Opinion polls during the 1994 campaign indicated a majority of Americans believed, contrary to fact, that under Clinton the economy had receded, the budget deficit had increased, and tax rates on lower-income Americans had been raised. . . .

Back to Basics: Improving the News

The news media have little justification for their arrogant portrayal of politics. They ought to be more humble, for they fail to meet fully the two standards that apply to those who exercise power in a democratic system: accountability and representation.

In the case of elected officials, accountability is obtained through party competition and the ballot. Every politician has felt the sting of partisan rebuke, and thousands of them have lost their jobs through defeat at the polls. The public has no comparable hold over journalists, and there is very little accountability within the press itself. The unwritten rule is that journalists do not attack other journalists. Rarely does a major news organization sharply criticize the reporting practices of a competitor.

The U.S. news media have resisted formal efforts at self-regulation. In 1973, with the sponsorship of major foundations, a National News Council was established for the purpose of handling complaints about the news practices of the major U.S. newspapers and broadcast networks. Similar councils have been important in some European countries in correcting press abuses, but the U.S. council was disbanded after a decade of ineffectiveness. Several leading news organizations, including the *New York Times*, refused to participate in the council's proceedings or heed its findings.

Accountability is also not obtained through journalists' claim to professional standards. In fact, journalism is not a full-fledged profession. Unlike medicine, law, and other such professions, there is no body of knowledge in journalism against which a practitioner's actions can be measured. Medical malpractice is defined by careless or willful departures from scientifically or clinically verified practices. "Journalistic malpractice" is nearly an oxymoron. There are many good journalists who prize accuracy and thoroughness in their reporting, but even they embrace assumptions about political behavior that are half-truths at best.

Walter Lippmann was right in arguing that news and truth coincide only at a few points and that all else in the news is opinion.[25] Consider journalists' claim to know the motives, supposedly self-serving, behind the actions of political leaders. The attribution of motives is risky business under the best of circumstances. The person engaged in a behavior often cannot untangle the complex web of motives behind it. How then can the journalist, viewing politicians from the outside, know that their promises are calculated deceptions? . . .

The power of the media needs to be contained not only due to a lack of accountability but also because the press excludes itself from the politics of representation. Politics is essentially a process for the mobilization of bias—that is, it involves the representation of particular values and interests. Candidates, officeholders, parties, and groups are in the business of representation. But what interests do journalists represent? CBS News executive Richard Salant once said that his reporters covered stories "from nobody's point of view."[26] What he was saying in effect was that journalists do not consistently represent the political concerns of any group in particular.

The news, at best, is a workable compromise between the economic need of news organizations to attract and hold their audiences and the polity's need for a public forum. Interpretive journalism rests on the fiction that journalists can adequately supply the second of these needs. Except when fulfilling a genuine watchdog role, journalists are not an appropriate vehicle for the articulation of the values at stake in political conflict. Their interest is the riveting news report. National issues are nearly always secondary to a good story, which is why Newt Gingrich's personal foibles received as much coverage as his policy positions during the first hundred days of the 104th Congress.[27]

If the news is to better serve a representational function, the political leaders who are the carriers of policy messages must be given more opportunities to make their claims. There is no justification for election coverage that allots six minutes to the journalist for every minute that a candidate speaks. The trend toward interpretive reporting has diminished the voices of those who are involved in the representation of values. . . .

Notes

1. "No Newt Is Good Newt," *Media Monitor* (Center for Media and Public Affairs), pp. 2–5 (Mar.–Apr. 1995).
2. Edith Efron, *The News Twisters* (Los Angeles: Nash, 1971), p. 47.
3. "No Newt Is Good Newt," p. 2.
4. "The Honeymoon That Wasn't," *Media Monitor* (Center for Media and Public Affairs), pp. 2–3 (Sept.–Oct. 1993).
5. David H. Weaver and G. Cleveland Wilhoit, *The American Journalist*, 2d ed. (Bloomington: Indiana University Press, 1986), p. 29; S. Robert Lichter and Stanley Rothman, "Media and Business Elites," *Public Opinion*, p. 42 (Oct.–Nov. 1981).
6. "Congress's Sour Finish," *New York Times*, 8 Oct. 1994.
7. "No Newt Is Good Newt," p. 2.
8. "The Honeymoon That Wasn't," p. 4.
9. Thomas E. Patterson, *Out of Order* (New York: Vintage, 1994), p. 245.
10. Austin Ranney, *Channels of Power* (New York: Basic Books, 1983), pp. 52–55.
11. Kristi Andersen and Stuart J. Thorson, "Public Discourse or Strategic Game? Changes in Our Conception of Elections," *Studies in American Political Development*, 3:273 (1989).
12. Paul Weaver, "Is Television News Biased?" *Public Interest*, 27:69 (1972).
13. Quoted in Michael Robinson and Margaret Sheehan, *Over the Wire and on TV* (New York: Russell Sage Foundation, 1983), p. 226.
14. Patterson, *Out of Order*, p. 82.
15. "Clinton's the One," *Media Monitor* (Center for Media and Public Affairs), p. 2 (Nov. 1992).
16. Quoted in Max Kampelman, "The Power of the Press," *Policy Review*, 7:18 (Fall 1978).

17. James Reston, "End of the Tunnel," *New York Times*, 30 Apr. 1975.

18. See, for example, Kampelman, "Power of the Press," pp. 7–41; Irving Kristol, "Crisis over Journalism," in *Press, Politics, and Popular Government*, ed. George Will (Washington, DC: American Enterprise Institute, 1972), p. 50.

19. Paul Taylor, *See How They Run* (New York: Knopf, 1990), p. 23.

20. Michael Robinson, "Improving Election Information in the Media" (Paper delivered at Voting for Democracy Forum, Washington, DC, Sept. 1983), p. 2.

21. Gerald Pomper with Susan Lederman, *Elections in America* (New York: Dodd, Mead, 1976), chap. 8. See also Michael G. Krukones, *Promises and Performance: Presidential Campaigns as Policy Predictors* (Lanham, MD: University Press of America, 1984); Ian Budge and Richard I. Hofferbert, "Mandates and Policy Outputs: U.S. Party Platforms and Federal Expenditures," *American Political Science Review*, 84:111–32 (1990); Jeff Fishel, *Presidents and Promises* (Washington, DC: Congressional Quarterly Press, 1985), pp. 38, 42–43.

22. Patterson, *Out of Order*, p. 20.

23. Ibid.

24. Ibid., p. 23.

25. Walter Lippmann, *Public Opinion* (1922; reprint ed., New York: Free Press, 1965), p. 229.

26. Quoted in Edward Jay Epstein, *News from Nowhere* (New York: Random House, 1973), p. ix.

27. "No Newt Is Good Newt," p. 2.

Questions for Discussion

1. What explanations does Patterson offer for the increasingly negative press coverage of politicians? What suggestions does he offer that might lead to more balanced coverage?

2. Why does Patterson find the liberal-bias theory of national news coverage so unconvincing? Do you agree?

8.3

Echo Chamber of Horrors

Scott Stossel

Election-night television coverage of the presidential contest has always had its share of criticism, ranging from the alleged bias of reporters and commentators to charges that projecting winners early in the evening before all states had concluded their voting could suppress voter turnout. Criticism after the coverage on election night 2000 was even more serious as the national news networks faced the embarrassing situation of calling a national winner, only to later rescind their call. Even the two presidential candidates, who apparently got their results from national television like the rest of the U.S. public, were confused. In fact, Democratic candidate Al Gore phoned Republican contender George W. Bush twice the morning after the election, once to concede and later to retract his concession. The election was not settled until weeks later, ultimately by a Supreme Court decision that halted the recount of votes in Florida.

In this selection, Scott Stossel examines how television news could be so wrong about something as important as a presidential election. He finds that the primary cause is related to structural changes in the news business. Today's networks are owned and operated by huge conglomerates that are less interested in news as a public service than with boosting ratings and profits. Network news divisions are underfunded, yet television news teams face tremendous pressure to be first in reporting a top news story. This can often lead to "speculation-as-news," which sometimes has disastrous consequences.

> *Let's get one thing straight right from the get-go. We would rather be last in reporting returns than be wrong. . . . If we say somebody has carried a state, you can pretty much take it to the bank, book it that that's true.*
> —DAN RATHER, CBS News, early evening, November 7

> *We've always said, you know, this is not an exact science. It's an imperfect art at best. And one of the things I think we could do better is to underscore more often with people that while we believe we were right in making these calls . . . they can be wrong.*
> —DAN RATHER on CNN's Reliable Sources, November 11

Scott Stossel is executive editor of *The American Prospect.*

It is not long past 4:00 A.M, Eastern Standard Time, on the morning of November 8, and Brit Hume and the rest of the Fox News commentators have lapsed into silence for what seems like a full 20 seconds, an eternity in television time. A quiet moment of contrition, perhaps, for the series of prognosticatory debacles that has preceded? A humble recognition of the fact that by this point—with the presidency effectively having been granted to and rescinded from each candidate over the course of six hours—there is nothing left to say?

If only.

No, the Fox News folks are quiet because they are watching CNN. Fox is at this moment broadcasting live video from War Memorial Plaza in Nashville, where thousands of Al Gore supporters stand in the rain, waiting for the vice president to appear and bring dramatic closure to the evening. People have been watching the stage with an acute sense of anticipation for hours, enduring a cold drizzle that, as the night drags on, has begun to feel unhappily appropriate. By this time in the morning, they—along with the millions of us watching television at home—have been subjected to a full range of results and emotions. Florida, and with it the election, has been given to them (7:49 P.M.), taken away from them (9:54 P.M.), given to George W. Bush (2:16 A.M.), and taken away from him (3:50 A.M.). Special graphics saying "George Bush, President-elect" and "George Bush, 43rd President" have appeared and then vanished. The vice president, the networks report, has called the governor to concede (2:30 A.M.) and then unconcede (3:45 A.M.). The crowd on War Memorial Plaza—and the viewers at home—are dazed and stupefied.

This is also a fair description of the network news anchors. Peter Jennings and Tom Brokaw appear pained and enervated; Dan Rather, though apologetic, seems oddly energized, growing loopier as the hour grows later. "We've lived by the crystal ball; we're eating so much broken glass. We're in critical condition," he says. "We don't just have egg on our face; we have an omelet," Brokaw says. "If you're disgusted with us, frankly, I don't blame you," says Rather. Jennings, glancing despairingly around the studio for direction that is not forthcoming, admits he honestly doesn't know what to do next. It's not just Jennings: No one does.

This may be the best explanation for how it is that at this moment, circa 4:00 A.M. on November 8, the Fox News team (Brit Hume, *The Weekly Standard*'s Fred Barnes and Bill Kristol, and National Public Radio's Mara Liasson) has come to be watching CNN. As Hume comments in his desultory way on the scene in Nashville, he stops to survey the live video feed and then to listen to what sound like official announcements in the background. Except it turns out that these announcements are emanating from the giant video screen overhanging the plaza like a JumboTron at a rock concert: CNN correspondent John King is describing in authoritative tones what he knows about what is happening at the War Memorial, which is effectively nothing. Yet Hume and gang, apparently mesmerized by the prospect of some real information—is Gore about to appear?—strain to listen. And 10, 15—could it even have been 20?—seconds pass without comment from the Fox studio. All that can be heard are the murmur of the crowd and the strains of CNN. Mara Liasson finally breaks in with an embarrassed, "Well, enough of that. Our coverage is better than that," and Hume quickly concurs with a chuckle.

What makes this tableau even more weirdly postmodern is that the people on the plaza are gleaning most of their information from the television networks, which are being broadcast on the large screen looming over the crowd. (A similar screen is set up by the capitol building in Austin, where throngs of Bush supporters are gathered.) And what the networks are broadcasting, of course, is the scene at Nashville's War Memorial Plaza—so what the people on the plaza are seeing on the network broadcasts is . . . themselves, watching themselves watching themselves (and so on) on the huge TV above. Which means, in effect, that they are gleaning information from themselves—except, of course, they don't know anything. It makes your head spin.

This moment is as emblematic of the evening's TV follies as any: Network A publicly reduced to watching Network B for information while Network B, in turn, watches itself. Can there be any more apt a symbol for the infinite feedback loop that television news has become? (Actually, maybe so: At one point, CNN's Judy Woodruff asks correspondent John King, "What's that noise in the background?" King, grinning sheepishly, responds, "Um, that's me. They've got CNN broadcasting on the big screen, so there's an echo." As you hear King's words reverberating a split second later in the background, the crowd on the plaza breaks into laughter and applause.)

TOM BROKAW: *Doris, Doris, Doris . . .*
DORIS KEARNS GOODWIN, historian-turned-TV analyst: *Uh oh, something has happened.*
                                                    —NBC News, November 8, 2:18 A.M.

There is no underestimating the psychological impact of the unanimous network calls for Bush. For anyone born since 1940—and for pretty much everyone else, too—television is truth. Yes, everyone knows that advertisements are full of distortions and exaggerations, that pundits are full of hot air, that sitcoms and dramas and even "reality TV" are not real. But in a matter as weighty as this, the presidency of the United States, television is simply not wrong. Television, for most of us, is reality.

Even presidents and would-be presidents get their reality from TV, which is why Gore conceded in response to the 2:16 A.M. network call. When Tom Brokaw said, "George Bush is the president-elect of the United States," television was not just reporting an external reality. It was declaring reality. Hundreds of thousands of votes remained to be counted in Florida and elsewhere. But with the network calls for Bush, the election was—as the mammoth TV screen outside the capitol in Austin blared while displaying a video montage of George W. at work and play—signed, sealed, delivered to the Texas governor. This despite the fact that, based on the vote count then current, he hadn't actually won.

Television cannot be blamed for butterfly ballots, hanging chads, or the oddity of the Florida vote count's falling within the statistical margin of error, but it can be blamed for the erroneous impression that the election was won by Bush and then stolen by Gore. Bush may yet, through courts and counts, legitimately win this election. But if he doesn't, there will be the lingering feeling that his rightful election-night victory was yanked away from him unfairly. And depending on the outcome, Gore will look like either a sore loser or an illegitimate winner. While it is demonstrably false that a Bush victory was clear on the morning of November 8, the power of television is such that the impression many people had on Wednesday morning was that a victory by Bush (the television said he won!) was stolen by Gore. This is not a trivial misunderstanding; the media, through faulty news coverage, may have robbed a Gore presidency of whatever fragile legitimacy it might have had. And having declared Bush the winner, the networks had, however subconsciously, a stake in continuing to depict Gore as a sore loser.

The networks giveth and the networks taketh away.
                                        —TOM BROKAW, NBC News, late evening, November 7

How could the networks (all of them!) have screwed up something so important (twice!) as a presidential election call, briefly coronating the wrong candidate?

For a satisfactory answer to this question, we have to go back to 1934, when passage of the Federal Communications Act established licensed broadcasters' responsibility to serve "the public interest, convenience, and necessity." The act was supposed to ensure that, since the government was basically giving away part of the public domain, the commercial licensees would produce at least some programming that served the public interest and not just a broadcaster's bottom line.

At the dawn of television, news rarely made money, and it wasn't expected to do so. Though the very first television news show—*Camel Newsreel Theatre,* which premiered in 1948 on NBC—was designed as a fundamentally commercial enterprise (its sponsorship contract stipulated that there must always be a Camel cigarette burning visibly in an ashtray on the news desk), subsequent news programs like *The Huntley-Brinkley Report* (which premiered in 1956) and the *CBS Evening News with Walter Cronkite* (which premiered in 1963) were aimed at generating prestige but not necessarily profits for the networks. Broadcasters could generate quality news programming and serve the public interest without being overly concerned with commercial imperatives.

CBS's *60 Minutes* changed that. Premiering in 1968, *60 Minutes* was almost a decade old before it became the ratings hit that it remains today. But when it did, as one of its creators, Don Hewitt, said years later, "it single-handedly ruined television." Before 60 *Minutes*, news shows were seen as a public service; after its great success, they were seen as potential profit centers.

For a few years, news divisions managed to hold the line, albeit feebly, against eroding quality, even in the new profit-maximizing environment. The legacy of network news was still a proud one, and the diversity of ownership produced healthy competition among network news divisions for talent and stories. But as conglomerates came into power—like General Electric (which bought NBC), a product manufacturer and defense subcontractor; Westinghouse (which bought CBS), a manufacturer and defense contractor with insurance and banking interests; and Disney, a media-entertainment complex (which bought ABC)—the emphasis on the bottom line intensified. News division budgets were sometimes cut deeply.

After the dismal 1988 election (Michael Dukakis versus George H. W. Bush) drew poor ratings, the corporate bosses at GE and Westinghouse pointed to the $17 million it cost to do polling and data collection for each of the news divisions and asked whether that figure couldn't be reduced. Until this point, each network had its own armada of statisticians, pollsters, and political scientists, who would collect data in the field and oversee the decision-making process on election night, making sure calls were made accurately and not prematurely. In this way, each network served as a check and balance on all the others: As soon as, say, ABC had declared so-and-so the winner in Florida, then NBC and CBS would be checking their own, independently collected numbers to see whether they felt comfortable following suit. Yes, the networks competed hard to be first; but they were very careful because if they were wrong they would be shown up quickly.

But in 1990, under pressure from corporate headquarters, the Big Three networks joined with CNN and the Associated Press to establish the Voter News Service (VNS). The VNS pooled survey and polling data for all the news organizations, saving them each up to $10 million per election. This also had the advantage of relieving the individual networks of the responsibility to make election projections. Instead, VNS would make the call on a given state or election and then make that call available to all the networks and news services at the same time. But while this saved money, it removed the system of checks in place under the old regime, since VNS had become the sole source of data.

Compounding this problem, ABC News decided in 1994 to set up, more or less clandestinely, its own decision desk to interpret and extrapolate from VNS data. Drawing on VNS data but making its own predictions, ABC successfully called George Pataki's gubernatorial defeat of Mario Cuomo in New York, Chuck Robb's senatorial defeat of Oliver North in Virginia, and George W. Bush's defeat of Ann Richards in Texas before VNS did—and therefore before any of the other networks did. It was, according to Richard Morin, director of polling for *The Washington Post*, "the polling equivalent of Pearl Harbor." By 1996 all the networks had their own decision desks for processing VNS data.

This has brought us to the current arrangement—the worst of all possible worlds. With everyone drawing on the same VNS data pool, there's no opportunity for independent corroboration (or disputing) of results. Yet with each network hoping to have its predictions be the first, there's enormous competitive pressure to make calls prematurely, before VNS has called an election or a state. This is why we had the spectacle on election night of states and congressional elections being pulled back and forth willy-nilly. And it's why we are now treated to the bizarre spectacle of networks crowing not about who was right first but who was wrong last. (We also get to see network executives trying to hide behind VNS—as if VNS were other than a creation of the networks!)

This is where we appear to be, folks. The CBS New—News has now, for the second time tonight, pulled back Florida.
                                               —DAN RATHER, around 3:50 A.M., November 8

The most malodorous product of this execrable system in the 2000 election was the botched Florida call. When Florida was declared the first time, all the networks and VNS gave the state to Gore at about the same time. They also all retracted around the same time, within a 20-minute period. But here's a telling point, little noted in press reports to date: VNS never called Florida for Bush. The numbers it was producing around 2:15 A.M. were trending that way, but not definitively enough for them to make the call. It was reportedly Fox decision desk staffer John Ellis—who, as has widely been reported (originally by Jane Mayer in *The New Yorker*), is a first cousin of George W. and Jeb Bush and had been on the phone with them all night—who called Florida, and thus the election, for Bush that night. The other networks, under pressure from their corporate chieftains not to get badly beaten by the upstart Fox, quickly followed suit over the next two minutes. It's impossible to put too fine a point on this: The outcome of a very close presidential election was nearly decided by George Bush's first cousin—who had quit his job as a columnist for *The Boston Globe* because, he said, his loyalty to his cousin would trump his commitment to objective journalism. If that doesn't indicate a problem with the system as currently constituted, what does?

The problems afflicting television news (PBS's *NewsHour with Jim Lehrer* is an admirable exception to most of what follows here) go broader and deeper than incorrect election calls, serious as those may be. The list of negative indicators is long and familiar. The evening network news audience has dropped from 40 million to 20 million over the past 10 years, with viewers defecting to CNN or the Internet or simply tuning out. In the 1960s, the average candidate sound bite on television was 45 seconds; today it's less than eight seconds. According to the *Hess Report*, a project of the Brookings Institution funded by Pew Charitable Trusts, nightly news shows are devoting less and less time to campaign coverage. The last eight weeks of this election (before November 7, that is) saw 670 fewer minutes of coverage than the comparable period in 1992. And the percentage of that time dedicated to "horse race coverage," as opposed to exploration of substantive policy issues, keeps increasing; it comprised 71 percent of all campaign coverage between Labor Day and the end of October this year. Horse race coverage bleeds quickly into wanton speculation. CNN may have been the first network to institutionalize speculation-as-news—the art of reporting on something not just as or after it happens, but before. Now all of the networks have caught on.

The most urgent challenge of all may be how to minimize what I'll call the Ellis effect: the danger that TV media will cross the line from reporting an event to affecting it. To some extent, there's an inevitable Heisenberg principle at work in all reporting. No media rendering of events is completely transparent, and such basic decisions as what to cover and how to cover it can always have an impact on an audience's perception of reality, which may then affect how the audience reacts to it. But surely there is something to be done about the more tangible problems of "changing" reality by making erroneous election calls, or of suppressing turnout by making early (even if correct) election calls. Republican Congressmen Billy Tauzin of Louisiana, Christopher Cox of California, and Cliff Stearns of Florida held a press conference on November 17 to demand hearings on the effects of early calls by the networks, especially in Democratic states. While Tauzin was engaging in partisan gamesmanship, this is a bipartisan complaint.

Other than momentary embarrassment, the networks have suffered no ill effects from their dreadful election-night performance. Quite the opposite. At 11:00 P.M. on November 7, CNN had nearly eight million viewers, its highest total since the day of the Columbine murders. For the three days after the election, the cable networks CNN, MSNBC, and Fox News drew ratings 500 percent greater than their average third-quarter numbers. And the total election-night audience for broadcast and cable combined was 61.6 million viewers, a 70 percent increase from 1996, when Bill Clinton clobbered Bob Dole. In fact, while ratings were higher in the 1960 and 1976 elections because the overall U.S. population was smaller, the 2000 election drew more households than any election in television history. What's more, advertisers are banging down the door to buy slots on the election-controversy broadcasts. Larry Goodman, CNN's president of ad sales and marketing, has reported that clients have come to him saying, "Get me on the air and keep me on the air for as long as this thing stays hot." And trade publications report that some networks are selling special "breaking news" packages to advertisers. It is clear that, given the perverse logic of the news industry whereby bad news is good for ratings and profits, the networks can financially afford to address some of their problems.

A straightforward solution to the Heisenberg-Ellis problem would be a proscription on calling elections before all votes are cast. Legislators on both sides of the aisle have expressed an interest in some kind of regulation along this line, and a recent Pew Research Center poll found that 87 percent of respondents thought networks should wait until all votes are counted before announcing election results.

An easy remedy for the problem of VNS being the lone data source is to establish competitors who will also collect exit poll data and early returns. The hard part is finding the funding to bankroll such competitors. (Currently, the *Los*

Angeles Times has the only other national-election-data service.) But this remedy addresses the most extreme symptom of the debasement of public-service programming by television.

Curtis Gans of the Committee for the Study of the American Electorate proposes a regulation that correlates the size of a local broadcaster's market share with the size of its mandated public-service obligation, as a way of ensuring that primary election debates, for example, get more television coverage. Robert Lichter, head of the Center for Media and Public Affairs, proposes outlawing paid campaign commercials outright and replacing them with free prime-time slots (in chunks of 15 minutes and longer) to candidates from parties who have polled more than 5 percent in the previous election.

But such proposals seem, one way or another, politically unrealistic: too utopian, too naive about the broadcasters' lobbying clout, too cavalier about abrogating the First Amendment. What's more, an occupational flaw of the civic-minded media critic is the chronic underestimation of the human appetite for fluff over substance. An effective reform plan must take this foible into account. More important, such a plan must one way or another win network news divisions enough distance from commercial demands that they have the freedom and the resources necessary to produce good news programming.

I said earlier that the most apt symbols of the election-night follies were those that signified the closed-loop nature of the network news media. But perhaps a still better symbol of television news today is George Stephanopoulos's beard. As November 7 turned to November 8, viewers could watch as the ABC commentator's beard grew visibly darker—remarkably so, like something in a time-lapse photography series.

What the gradual darkening of George's beard suggests to me—he stayed on the air for 14 hours straight—is that the relationship between time and the news has changed. No longer, the former Clinton aide's face seemed to be saying, is the news a fixed point in time. News, in other words, used to be presented for the most part in discrete increments, with the arrival of the morning and evening newspapers or the broadcast of the nightly news. News was not simply information, an endless supply of data, but, rather, perspective, something you could take the time to digest. Of course, in reality, events never stopped long enough for the morning paper or the evening newscast to fix them in place; after all, the conceit that we ever knew the "latest" from Israel or Tallahassee just because we read the morning paper was always arrogant. And the new, continuous-flow definition of news more nearly approximates the flow of life itself. Still, news in the days when the news cycle remained a once-per-24-hour-period proposition was certainly different—not to say better—in that it gave more time both to viewers and to news broadcasters, who could produce real stories, place them in their proper context, and explain them, rather than simply provide running commentary on a live video feed. What we see when we watch CNN or MSNBC, or news on the networks that is constantly "breaking" (as with O.J. or impeachment or Jon Benet or, now, the 2000 election) is not news in the classic sense but, as media expert

Bob Lichter has put it, the "news-gathering process. You're watching reporters gathering items. Some turn out to be right; some turn out to be wrong; some are propaganda spinning from the campaigns." We would do well to remember this.

Questions for Discussion

1. What factors led all of the national news networks to mistakenly declare a winner of the 2000 presidential election? What might be done to avoid such confusion in the future?
2. Stossel argues that the fundamental nature of television reporting of political events has been altered in recent years, and these changes have had negative consequences. According to the author, what are the sources of the problem? How might the problem be corrected?

 Chapter 9

Interest Groups

The United States has always been a nation of joiners, and more interest groups are active in our governmental affairs than in any other nation. Still, Americans have never been comfortable with special-interest politics. Ever since James Madison first warned of the "mischiefs of faction" in *The Federalist,* No. 10 (the first selection in this chapter), citizens, politicians, and scholars have debated the role of special interests in policymaking.

The conflict between special interests and the public interest has been especially evident when the government has seemed to be functioning ineffectively. During the Progressive era, for example, the influence of railroads, oil companies, and insurance firms drew the attention of scholars and the popular press; consequently, regulation of lobbyists became a major aim of the reformers. During the New Deal, in contrast, relatively little attention was paid to special interests. The dominant view of scholars during and after that period was pluralism—the belief that competition among groups is healthy for democracy.

By the 1960s, however, it had become obvious that such competition was highly distorted; some special interests almost always lost in the political process, and others—especially those with money, access, or inside information—usually won. The interest group universe had a blatant representational bias, as well; some interests, such as business, were well represented in the process, whereas others (minorities, the poor, and consumers) were seriously underrepresented.

Renewed attention to the role of interest groups grew stronger in the 1970s and 1980s. The tremendous expansion in the number of interest groups, the decline of political parties, and the heightened visibility of interest groups in the electoral and policymaking processes appeared to parallel government's inability to deal with economic and social problems. From the inability of Congress and the president to work together during the Carter years to the $200 billion deficits and influence-peddling scandals of the Reagan presidency, interest groups have been accused of being at the heart of the problem of contemporary government.

Depending on one's perspective, the United States is either blessed or cursed with many special interests. The constitutional guarantees of free speech, free association, and petition are basic to group formation. Because political organizations often parallel government structure, federalism and the separation of powers have encouraged a multiplicity of groups as interests organize around various local, state, and national access points. Societal cleavages also help foster interest group development. Differences in economics, climate, culture, and tradition, and in racial, ethnic, and religious backgrounds, create ready-made interests within American life. Finally, our cultural values may well play a role. As Alexis de Tocqueville observed more than 150 years ago, values such as individuality and personal achievement underlie the propensity of citizens to join groups.

There is a difference, however, between the existence of special interests and the emergence of special interest groups—associations of individuals who share attitudes or goals and attempt to influence public policy. In a simple society there is little need for interest groups, because people have no political or economic reason to organize when they work only for their families. Not until the mid- to late-nineteenth century did interest groups start to appear regularly on the American political scene. As the nation became economically and socially complex, new interests were created and old ones redefined. Farming, for example, became specialized, commercialized, and dependent on other economic sectors. U.S. trade policies appeared to affect southern cotton farmers and midwestern grain producers, and it soon made sense for such people to organize.

Many political scientists argue that new interest groups are a natural consequence of a growing society. Groups develop both to improve individuals' positions or to protect existing advantages. For example, mobilization of business interests in the 1960s and 1970s often resulted from threats posed by consumer groups and environmentalists. The post–World War II era, especially since 1960, has witnessed a dramatic increase in the number of special interests that have organized for political purposes. New groups have crowded into areas such as business and agriculture, which already were well organized, but the most rapid expansion has taken place in areas that were poorly organized or not organized at all. Women, blacks, environmentalists, consumers, and other nonoccupational interests are now actively represented by groups.

Such changes have been so extensive that even the term *interest group* no longer seems appropriate. Much of the business lobbying in Washington, for example, is now done by representatives of individual companies as well as by "peak" associations, such as the National Association of Manufacturers, which represent groups of companies. Many institutions, even colleges and universities, have their own lobbyists. Some of the so-called groups operating in Washington are not mass membership organizations governed by a board of elected directors; one study of public interest groups discovered that 40 percent of the groups had fewer than one thousand members and 30 percent had no members at all. A large number of active groups are staff organizations, composed of a handful of individuals who are funded by foundation resources. Some are totally private concerns, like Ralph Nader's organization Public Citizen, which claims to lobby for all consumers.

Lobbying has become a growth industry. From 1975 to 1985, the number of registered lobbyists in Washington doubled; the number of attorneys more than tripled between 1973 and 1983, rising to more than 37,000. Washington now abounds with lobbying firms, which contract with companies and groups to represent their interests. Some have more than fifty clients, ranging from individual companies to entire nations. Some plan and manage political campaigns, as well as advise specialized interests.

New techniques of influence have also appeared as lobbyists have embraced technology. Orchestrated mass mailings to legislators or the president can be put in motion within minutes by some of the more sophisticated lobbies. The Campaign Finance Acts of 1971 and 1974 have made it possible for almost all groups to create political action committees (PACs) to coordinate financial contributions to candidates for public office. In 2000, over 4,500 PACs were registered. Soft-money contributions to the parties, which are outside of federal regulations, have given organized interests further political leverage.

To provide a sense of the controversy over interest groups and a flavor of today's environment, this chapter includes a diverse range of selections. *The Federalist,* No. 10; is a classic statement of the dilemma special interests posed to the framers, who sought to control the detrimental effects of factions, especially "majority factions." Jeffrey Birnbaum surveys the history of lobbying in America, focusing on some of the scandals that have given lobbyists an unsavory reputation. He suggests there is much improvement in how lobbyists conduct themselves today.

The final two selections look at the contemporary interest group universe and the influence of organized interests in both the electoral and policy processes. Theda Skocpol examines the factors underlying the decline of membership federations over the past half century and the recent proliferation of "associations without members" and attempts to assess the meaning of such trends for American democracy. In the final selection, Allan Cigler and Burdett Loomis argue that the scope of interest group activity at the beginning of the 21st century is much broader than in the past, as groups have come to dominate political communication in the nation. Politics, in the authors' view, has come to resemble marketing, in that well-funded organized interests have the advantage in this age of information.

9.1

The Federalist, No. 10

James Madison

There is an inherent tension in any democratic society. Liberty demands that citizens be allowed to pursue their special interests, even if those interests are offensive and selfish; yet the pursuit of special interests may conflict with the public interest. The nation's founders were well aware of this dilemma and directed many of their efforts toward constructing a government that respected personal freedom but was capable of acting for the collective good.

This paper is perhaps the best statement of what the founders thought about special interests or factions. At base they feared all special interests, especially "majority factions," which had the potential to tyrannize the system. Madison realized, however, that special interests "are sown in the nature of man" and any attempt to eliminate them would involve the destruction of liberty, a remedy "worse than the disease." Madison's solution was to limit the effects of factions by promoting competition among them and designing a government with an elaborate system of checks and balances to reduce the power of any single, strong group, whether made up of a majority or a minority of citizens.

Among the numerous advantages promised by a well constructed Union, none deserves to be more accurately developed than its tendency to break and control the violence of faction.* The friend of popular governments, never finds himself so much alarmed for their character and fate, as when he contemplates their propensity to this dangerous vice. He will not fail therefore to set a due value on any plan which, without violating the principles to which he is attached, provides a proper cure for it. The instability, injustice and confusion introduced into the public councils, have in truth been the mortal diseases under which popular governments have every where perished; as they continue to be the favorite and fruitful topics from which the adversaries to liberty derive their most specious declamations. The valuable improvements made by the

---

* Madison used the term *faction* to denote any special interest, including parties. Although interest groups did exist, they were not organized in the sense in which we think of them today. Interest "groups" representing special interests were not common until after the Civil War.

American Constitutions on the popular models, both ancient and modern, cannot certainly be too much admired; but it would be an unwarrantable partiality, to contend that they have as effectually obviated the danger on this side as was wished and expected. Complaints are every where heard from our most considerate and virtuous citizens, equally the friends of public and private faith, and of public and personal liberty; that our governments are too unstable; that the public good is disregarded in the conflicts of rival parties; and that measures are too often decided, not according to the rules of justice, and the rights of the minor party; but by the superior force of an interested and over-bearing majority. However anxiously we may wish that these complaints had no foundation, the evidence of known facts will not permit us to deny that they are in some degree true. It will be found indeed, on a candid review of our situation, that some of the distresses under which we labor, have been erroneously charged on the operation of our governments; but it will be found, at the same time, that other causes will not alone account for many of our heaviest misfortunes; and particulary for that prevailing and increasing distrust of public engagements, and alarm for private rights, which are echoed from one end of the continent to the other. These must be chiefly, if not wholly, effects of the unsteadiness and injustice, with which a factious spirit has tainted our public administrations.

By a faction I understand a number of citizens, whether amounting to a majority or minority of the whole, who are united and actuated by some common impulse of passion, or of interest, adverse to the rights of other citizens, or to the permanent and aggregate interests of the community.

There are two methods of curing the mischiefs of faction: the one, by removing its causes; the other, by controlling its effects.

There are again two methods of removing the causes of faction: the one by destroying the liberty which is essential to its existence; the other, by giving to every citizen the same opinions, the same passions, and the same interests.

It could never be more truly said than of the first remedy, that it is worse than the disease. Liberty is to faction, what air is to fire, an aliment without which it instantly expires. But it could not be a less folly to abolish liberty, which is essential to political life, because it nourishes faction, than it would be to wish the annihilation of air, which is essential to animal life, because it imparts to fire its destructive agency.

The second expedient is as impracticable, as the first would be unwise. As long as the reason of man continues fallible, and he is at liberty to exercise it, different opinions will be formed. As long as the connection subsists between his reason and his self-love, his opinions and his passions will have a reciprocal influence on each other; and the former will be objects to which the latter will attach themselves. The diversity in the faculties of men from which the rights of property originate, is not less an insuperable obstacle to a uniformity of interests. The protection of these faculties is the first object of Government. From the protection of different and unequal faculties of acquiring property, the possession of different degrees and kinds of property immediately results: and from the influence of these on the sentiments and views of the respective proprietors, ensues a division of the society into different interests and parties.

The latent causes of faction are thus sown in the nature of man; and we see them every where brought into different degrees of activity, according to the different circumstances of civil society. A zeal for different opinions concerning religion, concerning Government and many other points, as well of speculation as of practice; an attachment to different leaders ambitiously contending for pre-eminence and power; or to persons of other descriptions whose fortunes have been interesting to the human passions, have in turn divided mankind into parties, inflamed them with mutual animosity, and rendered them much more disposed to vex and oppress each other, than to co-operate for their common good. So strong is this propensity of mankind to fall into mutual animosities, that where no substantial occasion presents itself, the most frivolous and fanciful distinctions have been sufficient to kindle their unfriendly passions, and excite their most violent conflicts. But the most common and durable source of factions, have been the various and unequal distribution of property. Those who hold, and those who are without property, have ever formed distinct interests in society. Those who are creditors, and those who are debtors, fall under a like discrimination. A landed interest, a manufacturing interest, a mercantile interest, a monied interest, with many lesser interests, grow up of necessity in civilized nations, and divide them into different classes, actuated by different sentiments and views. The regulation of these various and interfering interests forms the principal task of modern Legislation, and involves the spirit of party and faction in the necessary and ordinary operations of Government.

No man is allowed to be a judge in his own cause; because his interest would certainly bias his judgment, and, not improbably, corrupt his integrity. With equal, nay with greater reason, a body of men, are unfit to be both judges and parties, at the same time; yet, what are many of the most important acts of legislation, but so many judicial determinations, not indeed concerning the rights of single persons, but concerning the rights of large bodies of citizens; and what are the different classes of legislators, but advocates and parties to the causes which they determine? Is a law proposed concerning private debts? It is a question to which the creditors are parties on one side, and the debtors on the other. Justice ought to hold the balance between them. Yet the parties are and must be themselves the judges; and the most numerous party, or, in other words, the most powerful faction must be expected to prevail. Shall domestic manufactures be encouraged, and in what degree, by restrictions on foreign manufactures? are questions which would be differently decided by the landed and the manufacturing classes; and probably by neither, with a sole regard to justice and the public good. . . .

It is in vain to say, that enlightened statesmen will be able to adjust these clashing interests, and render them all subservient to the public good. Enlightened statesmen will not always be at the helm: Nor, in many cases, can such an adjustment be made at all, without taking into view indirect and remote considerations, which will rarely prevail over the immediate interest which one party may find in disregarding the rights of another, or the good of the whole.

The inference to which we are brought, is, that the causes of faction cannot be removed; and that relief is only to be sought in the means of controlling its *effects*.

If a faction consists of less than a majority, relief is supplied by the republican principle, which enables the majority to defeat its sinister views by regular vote: It may clog the administration, it may convulse the society; but it will be unable to execute and mask its violence under the forms of the Constitution. When a majority is included in a faction, the form of popular government on the other hand enables it to sacrifice to its ruling passion or interest, both the public good and the rights of other citizens. To secure the public good, and private rights, against the danger of such a faction, and at the same time to preserve the spirit and the form of popular government, is then the great object to which our enquiries are directed: Let me add that it is the great desideratum, by which alone this form of government can be rescued from the opprobrium under which it has so long labored, and be recommended to the esteem and adoption of mankind.

By what means is this object attainable? Evidently by one of two only. Either the existence of the same passion or interest in a majority at the same time, must be prevented; or the majority, having such co-existent passion or interest, must be rendered, by their number and local situation, unable to concert and carry into effect schemes of oppression. If the impulse and the opportunity be suffered to coincide, we well know that neither moral nor religious motives can be relied on as an adequate control. They are not found to be such on the injustice and violence of individuals, and lose their efficacy in proportion to the number combined together; that is, in proportion as their efficacy becomes needful.

From this view of the subject, it may be concluded, that a pure Democracy, by which I mean, a Society, consisting of a small number of citizens, who assemble and administer the Government in person, can admit of no cure for the mischiefs of faction. A common passion or interest will, in almost every case, be felt by a majority of the whole; a communication and concert results from the form of Government itself; and there is nothing to check the inducements to sacrifice the weaker party, or an obnoxious individual. Hence it is, that such Democracies have ever been spectacles of turbulence and contention; have ever been found incompatible with personal security, or the rights of property; and have in general been as short in their lives, as they have been violent in their deaths. Theoretic politicians, who have patronized this species of Government, have erroneously supposed, that by reducing mankind to a perfect equality in their political rights, they would, at the same time, be perfectly equalized and assimilated in their possessions, their opinions, and their passions.

A Republic, by which I mean a Government in which the scheme of representation takes place, opens a different prospect, and promises the cure for which we are seeking. Let us examine the points in which it varies from pure Democracy, and we shall comprehend both the nature of the cure, and the efficacy which it must derive from the Union.

The two great points of difference between a Democracy and a Republic are, first, the delegation of the Government, in the latter, to a small number of citizens elected by the rest: secondly, the greater number of citizens, and greater sphere of country, over which the latter may be extended.

The effect of the first difference is, on the one hand to refine and enlarge the public views, by passing them through the medium of a chosen body of citizens, whose wisdom may best discern the true interest of their country, and whose patriotism and love of justice, will be least likely to sacrifice it to temporary or partial considerations. Under such a regulation, it may well happen that the public voice pronounced by the representatives of the people, will be more consonant to the public good, than if pronounced by the people themselves convened for the purpose. On the other hand, the effect may be inverted. Men of factious tempers, of local prejudices, or of sinister designs, may by intrigue, by corruption or by other means, first obtain the suffrages, and then betray the interests of the people. The question resulting is, whether small or extensive Republics are most favorable to the election of proper guardians of the public weal: and it is clearly decided in favor of the latter by two obvious considerations.

In the first place it is to be remarked that however small the Republic may be, the Representatives must be raised to a certain number, in order to guard against the cabals of a few; and that however large it may be, they must be limited to a certain number, in order to guard against the confusion of a multitude. Hence the number of Representatives in the two cases, not being in proportion to that of the Constituents, and being proportionally greatest in the small Republic, it follows, that if the proportion of fit characters, be not less, in the large than in the small Republic, the former will present a greater option, and consequently a greater probability of a fit choice.

In the next place, as each Representative will be chosen by a greater number of citizens in the large than in the small Republic, it will be more difficult for unworthy candidates to practise with success the vicious arts, by which elections are too often carried; and the suffrages of the people being more free, will be more likely to centre on men who possess the most attractive merit, and the most diffusive and established characters.

It must be confessed, that in this, as in most other cases, there is a mean, on both sides of which inconveniencies will be found to lie. By enlarging too much the number of electors, you render the representative too little acquainted with all their local circumstances and lesser interests; and by reducing it too much, you render him unduly attached to these, and too little fit to comprehend and pursue great and national objects. The Federal Constitution forms a happy combination in this respect; the great and aggregate interests being referred to the national, the local and particular, to the state legislatures.

The other point of difference is, the greater number of citizens and extent of territory which may be brought within the compass of Republican, than of Democratic Government; and it is this circumstance principally which renders factious combinations less to be dreaded in the former, than in the latter. The smaller the society, the fewer probably will be the distinct parties and interests composing it; the fewer the distinct parties and interests, the more frequently will a majority be found of the same party; and the smaller the number of individuals composing a majority, and the smaller the compass within which they are placed, the more easily will they concert and execute their plans of oppression. Extend the sphere, and you take in a greater variety of parties and interests; you make it less probable that a majority of the whole will have a common motive to invade the rights of other citizens; or if such a common motive exists, it will be more difficult for all who feel it to discover their own strength, and to act in unison with each other. . . .

Hence it clearly appears, that the same advantage, which a Republic has over a Democracy, in controlling the effects of faction, is enjoyed by a large over a small Republic—is enjoyed by the Union over the States composing it. Does this advantage consist in the substitution of Representatives, whose enlightened views and virtuous sentiments render them superior to local prejudices, and to schemes of injustice? It will not be denied, that the Representation of the Union will be most likely to possess these requisite endowments. Does it consist in the greater security afforded by a greater variety of parties, against the event of any one party being able to outnumber and oppress the rest? In an equal degree does the encreased variety of parties, comprised within the Union, encrease this security? Does it, in fine, consist in the greater obstacles opposed to the concern and accomplishment of the secret wishes of an unjust and interested majority? Here, again, the extent of the Union gives it the most palpable advantage.

The influence of factious leaders may kindle a flame within their particular States, but will be unable to spread a general conflagration through the other States: a religious sect, may degenerate into a political faction in a part of the Confederacy; but the variety of sects dispersed over the entire face of it, must secure the national Councils against any danger from that source: a rage for paper money, for an abolition of debts, for an equal division of property, or for any other improper or wicked project, will be less apt to pervade the whole body of the Union, than a particular member of it; in the same proportion as such a malady is more likely to taint a particular county or district, than an entire State.

In the extent and proper structure of the Union, therefore, we behold a Republican remedy for the diseases most incident to Republican Government. And according to the degree of pleasure and pride, we feel in being Republicans, ought to be our zeal in cherishing the spirit, and supporting the character of Federalists.

Questions for Discussion

1. What is Madison's view of human nature? What factors led him to this conclusion?
2. According to Madison, what are the differences between a democracy and a republic? Would Madison's view on the subject be "popular" today?

 9.2

Lobbyists—Why the Bad Rap?

Jeffrey H. Birnbaum

Lobbying activity has a long history in the United States, protected by constitutional provisions that give citizens "the right to petition the government for a redress of grievances." At the dawn of the republic this right was often expressed literally, as citizens signed and formally presented to elected representatives written petitions describing their problems. The petitioning process was all but forgotten shortly thereafter: Individuals quickly learned that traveling to Washington and dealing directly with public officials was a much more effective way to influence the new government on a range of concerns, from procuring jobs to policy. Today, it is estimated that roughly 80,000 lobbyists operate in Washington.

In this selection, Jeffrey Birnbaum surveys the colorful history of lobbying in the nation's capital. He finds that many incidents of unethical, if not illegal, behavior by special-interest representatives in D.C. have contributed to the unsavory stereotype of the Washington lobbyist. According to Birnbaum, well-financed American business and manufacturing interests have long used their resources to dictate public policy, their activities largely unregulated and undisclosed.

Birnbaum believes that the relationship between lobbyists and public officials has changed in recent decades, "representing a complex symbiosis of lobbyists and politicians." Lobbyists still seek influence, and money is still important, but blatant bribery by those seeking favors is now uncommon. More common are

Jeffrey H. Birnbaum is a senior correspondent for *Time* magazine. This essay is adapted from his book *The Lobbyists* (Times Books, 1992).

attempts to influence legislators through devices such as campaign contributions. And often it is the legislators rather than the lobbyists who initiate contact in attempts to raise money for their re-election campaigns. Lobbying techniques have changed as well. Grassroots lobbying, which involves mobilizing a legislator's home constituents, has emerged as one of the most effective ways for special interests to influence public policy.

I n the past 10 years, the number of lobbyists in Washington has, by some estimates, more than doubled. This modern army of 80,000 uses techniques that are as old as the republic, but its forces wield influence with a precision and sophistication that is purely high tech. Right behind the commanders are divisions of specialists: economists, lawyers, direct-mail producers and telephone salespeople, public relations experts, pollsters, and even accountants, all marching to the time-honored First Amendment–guaranteed beat of petitioning the government for redress of grievances. What follows is a look at the history of lobbying, which lobbyists themselves concede has not always been commendable. It explains in short why lobbying has a bad rap.

Booze, Broads, and Bribes

Lobbying in the early days of the republic was not performed with a great deal of finesse. The first attempt at mass pressure on the U.S. government—during a meeting of the First Continental Congress in Philadelphia in 1783—featured fixed bayonets. Several hundred soldiers from the local garrison felt they were due extra compensation and threatened the assembled legislators with their rifles. The Congress disagreed with them but boldly adjourned to meet again to consider the aggrieved soldiers' requests—at a safe distance, in Princeton, New Jersey. Business interests of the time used more subtle lobbying tactics. After the Continental Congress concluded its meetings each day, hogsheads of wine and port flowed without restraint at sumptuous meals. Wealthy merchants picked up the check.

Blatant bribery was swiftly added to the lobbyists' repertoire. One of the new Congress's major debates was whether to fund the national debt and to assume the debts of the states. Some historians believe that Rep. John Vining of Delaware sold his deciding vote to the money changers who stood to profit most from the action. Rumor had it that the bribe was 1,000 English guineas, but Sen. William Maclay of Pennsylvania wrote in his journal that Vining's vote was probably purchased for a "tenth part of the sum."

The word "lobbyist" comes from Britain, where the journalists who stood in lobbies of the House of Commons waiting to interview newsmakers were so dubbed. It was first used in America in 1829 during Andrew Jackson's presidency when privilege seekers in New York's capital, Albany, were referred to as lobby-agents. Three years later, the term was abbreviated to "lobbyist" and has been heard frequently ever since, mostly as an expression of reproach.

President Jackson was the first of many American presidents to rail against lobbyists and their business patrons. He sought to deflate financier Nicholas Biddle's power by withdrawing federal deposits from his Second Bank of the United States. But Biddle was not without supporters, notably the illustrious Daniel Webster, who would go on to become secretary of state. The ardency of Webster's convictions on the issue was bolstered not so much by principle as by cash. On December 21, 1833, Webster, then senator from Massachusetts, wrote to Biddle: "If it is wished that my relation to the bank should be continued, it may be well to send me the usual retainers." After an especially eloquent speech by Webster, Biddle paid him $10,000. Webster received in total $32,000 in what would be seen as bribes today but was then considered business as usual.

Lobbying flourished as America grew. Washington was swarming with so many big-business lobbyists by 1852 that future president James Buchanan wrote to his friend, future president Franklin Pierce, that "the host of contractors, speculators, stockjobbers, and lobby members which haunt the halls of Congress . . . are sufficient to alarm every friend of this country. Their progress must be arrested." The influence of business was so strong that at the close of one congressional session, Sen. J. S. Morrill sarcastically moved to appoint a committee to inquire if the president of the Pennsylvania Railroad, skulking in the outer lobby, wanted Congress to consider any further legislation before adjournment.

One of the most heavy-handed corporate lobbyists at the time was Samuel Colt, the famous gun manufacturer. Colt paid a "contingent fee" of $10,000 to one congressman and probably many others to refrain from attacking a patent-extension bill that would have helped his company's sales. To supplement the effort, Colt's high-living lobbyist, Alexander Hay, distributed beautifully deco-rated revolvers to lawmakers. Other more attractive gratuities were also dispensed: to wit, three young women known as Spiritualists, who, according to one account, were very active in "moving with the members" of Congress on Colt's behalf. Other women of less spiritual natures called "chicks" were also available upon request.

Washington was flooded with even more lobbyists in the wake of the financial panic of 1857. "Everywhere," wrote historian Roy Franklin Nichols, "there was importunity." The most underhanded lobbying battle raged between railroad and steamship companies as lobbyists for each side fought bitterly to reduce govern-ment subsidies to the other. Commodore Cornelius Vanderbilt himself led the steamship companies' campaign, often from the gaming tables of a night spot called Pendleton's Gambling House. Hapless lawmakers would fall into debt there and be forced to surrender their votes under threat of exposure or demand for payment. Other times, lawmakers would be allowed to win—as long as they agreed to vote the right way.

The 1850s' most powerful lobbyist was an imposing man named Thurlow Weed. His diverse background included working as a printer and newspaper editor, crusading against the perfidy of corporate power. But for the price of $5,000, Weed switched allegiances and began to lobby for lower duties on wool for the Bay State Mills of Lawrence, Massachusetts. His predecessor had come to Washington armed with facts and figures and was laughed out of town: Weed came armed with cold cash and stayed for years. Weed also has the distinction of being the first lobbyist to hire a journalist in a lobbying campaign, David M. Stone of New York's *Journal of Commerce*.

The Court Steps In

Washington got a new "King of the Lobby," Samuel Ward, after the Civil War. He reigned for 15 years as the undisputed master of dinner-table deceit. "The way to a man's 'Aye' is through his stomach," he said. Ward's pedigree was impeccable: he was the great-great-grandson of Richard Ward, a colonial governor; the great-grandson of Samuel Ward, one of the framers of the Constitution, and the great nephew of General Francis Marion, the famous "Swamp Fox" of the Revolutionary War. His father headed the New York banking firm of Prime, Ward and King, and his sister, Julia Ward Howe, wrote "The Battle Hymn of the Republic."

Washington suited Ward's penchant for living well, and he quickly proved he could charm the natives for profit. With his balding pate, sweeping mustache, and diamond-studded shirts, he was a striking figure, hosting dinners and breakfasts of ham boiled in champagne and seasoned with wisps of newly mown hay.

Ward's clients ran the gamut. He was hired for $12,000 plus dinner expenses by Hugh McCulloch, an Indiana banker who later became President Lincoln's treasury secretary, to "court, woo, and charm congressmen, especially Democrats prone to oppose the war." He was also associated with Joe Morrissey, the lottery boss. It seemed incongruous, but Morrissey retained Ward to promote a bill that would impose a tax on lotteries. Morrissey believed that he could afford the levy but that it would drive his less prosperous rivals out of business.

Ward could be quite conniving, despite his elegant manners. He once wrote to his friend, Henry Wadsworth Longfellow: "When I see you again I will tell you how a client, eager to prevent the arrival at a committee of a certain member before it should adjourn, offered me $5,000 to accomplish this purpose, which I did, by having [the congressman's] boots mislaid while I smoked a cigar and condoled with him until they could be found at 11:45. I had the satisfaction of a good laugh [and] a good fee in my pocket."

When a congressional committee questioned Ward about his activities, he deflected their inquiries with erudition and humor. "Talleyrand says that diplomacy is assisted by good dinners," he responded. "At good dinners people do not talk shop, but they give people a right, perhaps, to ask a gentleman a civil question and get a civil answer." Ward insisted that he refused to take on issues that were meritless, but he also conceded that "the profession of lobbying is not commendable," a characterization still echoing today.

Under the weak presidencies that followed the Civil War, lobbying reached new heights—and depths. Two of the most jarring events were the Crédit Mobilier scandal in 1872, in which millions of federal dollars earmarked for a transcontinental railroad were diverted into the pockets of representatives, senators, and even a future president, James Garfield; and Jay Gould and Jim Fisk's attempt to corner the gold market in 1869. This latter effort, which ultimately failed, implicated the president himself.

The Supreme Court heard a rare case in 1875 involving a lobbyist, *Trist* v. *Child*, during Ulysses Grant's troubled presidency. The High Court refused to uphold the lobbyist's claim for payment after he had fulfilled his part of a contract to influence legislation. The ruling denied the payment on the ground that such an undertaking was contrary to "sound policy and good morals." The opinion continued: "If any of the great corporations of the country were to hire adventurers who make market of themselves in this way, to propose passage of a general law with a view to promotion of their private interests, the moral sense of every right-minded man would instinctively denounce the employers and employed as steeped in corruption and employment as infamous. If the instances were numerous, open, and tolerated they would be regarded as a measure of decay of public morals and degeneracy of the time. No prophetic spirit would be needed to foretell the consequences near at hand." Notably absent from the learned decision was the simple, telling observation that lobbyists and lobbying had become so enmeshed in the fabric of the government that an aggrieved lobbyist did not hesitate to go to the highest court in the land for redress.

That same year, lobbying moved further into the modern age with the first recorded instance of grass-roots lobbying. Instead of simply relying on individual adventurers in Washington, business interests began to reach back to the states and districts of congressmen for constituents to support their causes. The bellowing of home-state voices became so loud that Rep. George Frisbie Hoar forced a resolution through his Judiciary Committee requiring for the first time public disclosure by lobbyists about their activities. Hoar said he offered the resolution because four people from different parts of the country representing an important corporation had accosted and tried to sway four of his committee members. The resolution went nowhere, but grass-roots lobbying became a standard tool of the lobbyists' trade.

The first president to seriously challenge the business lobby was Woodrow Wilson, who had prominently featured its villainy in his 1912 campaign. Wilson had studied lobbyists' impact in Washington as a Princeton professor and concluded that it was dangerous. In a scholarly paper, he noted that special interests could not buy an entire legislature but could purchase individual committees, which was where the real power resided anyway. Such observations became grist for his presidential campaign speeches: "The masters of the government of the

United States are the combined capitalists and manufacturers. It is written over every intimate page of the records of Congress; it is written all through the history of conferences at the White House. . . . The government of the United States is a foster child of the special interests. It is not allowed to have a will of its own."

Wilson told the lobbyists to get out of town when he took office in 1913, and for the most part, they did. A few diehards stayed, but according to Cordell Hull, they "became less pestiferous when they discovered just what our policy was and saw they could not influence us."

A story printed in the *New York World* by Martin M. Mulhall, the top lobbyist for the National Association of Manufacturers, soon demonstrated exactly why Wilson was so eager to banish lobbyists. Mulhall held no public title, but, as a powerful lobbyist, he had his own private office in the Capitol. He wrote that he paid the chief page of the House $50 a month and maintained a close association with Rep. John Dwight, the House minority leader, and with Rep. James T. McDermott, a Democrat from Chicago, whom he paid $1,500 to $2,000. These well-placed lawmakers gave him advance information about legislation and helped him dictate appointments to key committees.

Finis J. Garrett, a Tennessee Democrat and the House's minority leader, chaired a four-month inquiry into Mulhall's revelations that eventually censured McDermott. Garrett later proposed legislation that would require lobbyists to register with the clerk of the House and to disclose their employers. The bill passed the House but died in the Senate, not to become law, despite many intervening scandals, for another 33 years.

Lobbyists, scandals, and the harried congressional committees investigating them had all roared back by the 1920s. The Caraway Committee, launched in 1927 by Sen. Thaddeus Caraway (D-Ark.), rocked the city with the contention that most lobbying was simply fraud. Fully 90 percent of the nearly 400 lobbying groups listed in the Washington telephone directory were "fakes" whose primary aim was not to affect legislation but to bilk clients, said the committee.

At the end of the investigation, Caraway recommended yet another bill to register lobbyists. He wanted lobbying defined as "any effort in influencing Congress upon any matter coming before it, whether it be by distributing literature, appearing before committees of Congress, or seeking to interview members of either the House or Senate" and a lobbyist as "one who shall engage, for pay, to attempt to influence legislation or to prevent legislation by the national Congress." The Senate passed the stringent measure without dissent, but it died in the House because of lobbyists' pressure.

Former government and party officials began running on the cash-paved track of lobbying in the late 1920s and 1930s, setting a precedent that continues today. Women started to become full-fledged lobbyists during this time period, too. Mabel Walker Williebrandt, once assistant attorney general in charge of enforcing Prohibition laws, traded in her experience for bananas, oranges, apples, and cherries as counsel to Fruit Industries, Ltd. Quite simply, lobbying power resided with people who had personal connections to government.

According to journalist and lobbying historian Kenneth Crawford: "In the Hoover days, one who wanted to put on the fix saw James Francis Burke, secretary of the Republican National Committee; C. Bascom Slemp, who had been secretary to President Coolidge; or Edward Everett Gann, husband of the redoubtable social warrior, Dolly Gann, sister of Vice President Charles Curtis. Early in the Roosevelt administration, the men to get things done were Bruce Kremer, a friend of the attorney general; Robert Jackson of New Hampshire, long-time treasurer of the Democratic National Committee; Arthur Mullen, National Committeeman from Nebraska; and Joe Davies, later ambassador to Russia and Belgium."

Senator Hugo L. Black (D-Ala.) who was later a Supreme Court justice, introduced a bill to register and regulate lobbyists after a particularly egregious display of lobbying power in a debate over regulation of public utilities. This time, it passed both chambers of Congress—but it died in a House-Senate conference committee, thanks to the efforts of hundreds of lobbyists. Lobbyists didn't escape unscathed, however, and for the first time, utility lobbyists were required to make limited disclosure of their activities under terms of the final Public Utilities Holding Company Act.

Congress finally got around to regulating the business of lobbying as a whole in the 1930s and 1940s, starting with the vast and influential shipping industry. The Merchant Marine Act of 1936 required shipping agents to file disclosures with the Commerce Department before working to influence marine legislation or administrative decisions. Two years later, amid reports of Fascist and Nazi propaganda circulating in the United States, the Foreign Agents Registration Act was passed, requiring anyone who represented a foreign government or individual to register with the Justice Department.

In 1946, Congress passed the Federal Regulation of Lobbying Act as part of the Congressional Reorganization Act, requiring all lobbyists to register in Congress and report the amount and sources of their income from lobbying. There was no attempt to limit lobbying; that would violate the First Amendment's right to petition the government. It defined a lobbyist as a person or organization whose job is to influence the passage or defeat of legislation and who receives money for that purpose.

Like all previous lobbying strictures, the law was ignored at first. In 1950, spurred by complaints from President Harry Truman, a committee headed by Rep. Frank M. Buchanan, Democrat from Pennsylvania, investigated a wide range of lobbying abuses. The Congress of the time, the president complained, was "the most thoroughly surrounded . . . with lobbies in the whole history of this great country of ours. . . . There were more lobbyists in Washington, there was more money spent by lobbyists in Washington, than ever before." The committee requested detailed information about lobbying from 200 corporations, labor unions, and farm groups. The 152 organizations that replied said they had spent $32 million on lobbying from January 1, 1948, through May 31, 1950, and fewer than 50 of them had disclosed a single dime of it as required by the new lobbying law.

The Buchanan report also noted that lobbying had changed over the years. In effect, it said, lobbying had become less blatant and, in this view, more insidious. In 1948, there were 1,016 registered lobbyists. Two years later, the number had more than doubled to 2,047. Buchanan said the figures "reflect a significant picture of tremendous amounts of time and money being expended by pressure groups and pressure interests through the country in seeking to influence actions by Congress."

In the 1870s and 1880s, he continued, "lobbying meant direct, individual solicitation of legislators, with a strong presumption of corruption attached . . . [but] modern pressure on legislative bodies is rarely corrupt. . . . It is increasingly indirect, and [it is] largely the product of group rather than individual effort. . . . The printed word is much more extensively used by organizations as a means of pursuing legislative aims than personal contact with legislators by individual lobbyists."

The Buchanan Committee recommended strengthening the lobbying law, but no action was taken. Instead, in 1954, the Supreme Court weakened the already porous lobbying statute by exempting many types of lobbyists from the law's disclosure requirements. The Court decided that only those who solicited and collected money specifically with lobbying in mind need comply and that organizations need register only if they had lobbying as their "principal purpose" when they collected the funds. What's more, only direct contacts with legislators were considered lobbying; indirect pressure, such as the growing practice of grass-roots lobbying, was excluded.

A Complex Relationship

In the late 1940s and 1950s, it was "often hard to tell where the legislator [left] off and the lobbyist begins," according to lobbying expert James Deakin. Entire pieces of legislation were drafted by lobbyists. According to Rep. Arthur Klein, a Democratic member of the House Labor Committee, the primary author of the Taft-Hartley Act of 1947,* which restricted labor union activities, was neither Taft nor Hartley but William G. Ingles, a $24,000-a-year lawyer and highly

---

* The Taft-Hartley Act of 1947 was technically a series of amendments to the National Labor Relations (Wagner) Act of 1935, which many members of the business community felt was too pro-union. A major provision of the Taft-Hartley Act allowed states to pass right-to-work laws, which in effect banned "closed shop" requirements (which had made it mandatory for employers to hire only members of unions). Taft-Hartley also delineated various unfair labor practices by unions (the 1935 act only listed unfair labor practices by employers).

labor-dependent lobbyist for Allis-Chalmers, Fruehauf Trailer, J. I. Case, and Inland Steel.

The unprecedented expansion of government after the war was accompanied by a rapid growth in the number of lobbyists. Sensing their advantage, lawmakers began to play one off against the other. "Everything in Washington is a two-way street," Deakin wrote: "The legislators use the lobbyists as much as the lobbyists use them. A cocktail party—like an office conversation—may give the congressman information he needs. Or it may give him something he needs even more: cash. The Washington party has become an increasingly utilitarian institution. Invited to a reception, the lobbyist may find that he is giving more than he gets. The pressure boy is pressured. As he leaves, pleasantly oiled, his attention is directed to a hat in which he is expected to drop $50 or $100 for the congressman's campaign. . . . Washington is a very practical town, and money and votes mean more than liquor. In the final analysis, this is why bribes, blondes, and booze don't rank as high as they once did in the lobbyist's scheme of things. They just aren't as important to the congressman (to his political survival, which is his first law) as votes and money with which to get votes. The legislator may accept the lobbyist's entertainment, and gladly, but he is far more likely to do what the lobbyist wants if votes are involved."

The 1940s and 1950s were also the heyday of the brilliant, brash Thomas "the Cork" Corcoran, former law clerk to Oliver Wendell Holmes and President Franklin Roosevelt's chief legislative operative. Corcoran helped write much of the New Deal legislation, including the Securities and Exchange Act. He also supplied Roosevelt with the phrase, "This generation has a rendezvous with destiny." He made enemies when he tried to help Roosevelt pack the Supreme Court,* and he was blocked from the job he most coveted, becoming the U.S. solicitor general. He became instead a high-priced lobbyist for corporate interests, cementing what has since become a well-established route from White House adviser to Washington lobbyist.

Top executives of corporations were increasingly enlisted as lobbyists during the 1960s, but always under the strict guidance of their Washington consultants. Lobbying had come far since the early days of the republic, representing a complex symbiosis of lobbyists and politicians—but traditional, big-money lobbyists still wooed, and occasionally brought crashing down, lawmakers. The most famous victim of lawmakers' penchant for fancy living was Robert G. (Bobby) Baker, whose route from Pickens, South Carolina, to riches on the banks of the Potomac River was eased by lobbyists. Baker was secretary to the Democratic

---

* President Franklin Roosevelt, frustrated with the Supreme Court's reluctance to uphold major pieces of New Deal legislation, proposed a plan in 1937 to expand the size of the Court by appointing a new member for each sitting justice who had reached seventy years of age. If the plan had been approved, Roosevelt could have immediately appointed six justices, making the Court a fifteen-member body. Congress and the nation's press were strongly against the measure, viewing it as a thinly veiled attempt to "pack" the Court to create a liberal majority.

majority in the Senate. With a salary of $19,600 a year, he managed to accumulate assets of $2,166,886 in less than nine years.

Improper contacts with lobbyists also helped bring down Richard M. Nixon's presidency. Investigations revealed that a number of corporations violated the federal law that prohibits them from contributing to the campaigns of federal office seekers. Some of those funds found their way into the hands of the Republican operatives who broke into Democratic Party headquarters in Washington's Watergate complex on June 17, 1972.

Foreign interests have increasingly hired Washington lobbyists in recent years. This foreign money led to the 1976 Koreagate scandal. The *Washington Post* reported that South Korean agents gave between $500,000 and $1 million a year in cash and gifts to members of Congress to help maintain a "favorable legislative climate" for South Korea. The Koreans, led by businessman and socialite Tongsun Park, sought to bribe U.S. officials and buy influence among journalists, funneling illegal gifts to as many as 115 lawmakers. In 1978, the House voted to reprimand three California Democrats for their part in the scandal, and Richard T. Hanna, a former California congressman, was sentenced to prison.

Subtlety Wields Influence

During the 1980s, lobbying was rarely so heavyhanded, yet it became astonishingly effective. Communications techniques reached new heights of sophistication and complexity, and with them lobbyists were able to mobilize thousands of ordinary citizens for the first time. When Congress was considering increasing milk price supports in 1980, for example, lawmakers heard not just from lobbyists for the dairy farmers who wanted the subsidy hiked but also from thousands of worried managers of fast-food restaurants spurred on by an "action alert" newsletter distributed by the fast-food industry's trade association.

The break-up of American Telephone & Telegraph spurred one of the decade's biggest grass-roots lobbying efforts. Legislators heard from thousands of telephone company managers and employees; not only had AT&T put out an action alert but so had the Communications Workers of America, 90 percent of whose members were AT&T employees. At the same time, a coalition of AT&T competitors stirred up its own pressure in favor of the break-up, mailing 70,000 envelopes bearing an imitation of the Bell System logo and this attention-grabbing warning: "Notice of Telephone Rate Increase Enclosed." The letter inside warned the reader that unless the recipient helped lobby in favor of the break-up, telephone rates would double.

Individual corporations also began using their employees and suppliers as lobbyists, a method previously used with great success by labor unions. The National Association of Home Builders—the 125,000-member trade association of the housing industry—developed one of the most comprehensive electoral strategies ever devised in the corporate world. Its 250-page manual, "Blueprint for Victory: Homebuilder's Political Offensive," outlined all aspects of what it called its G. I. (Get Involved) Program. The manual detailed telephone or house-to-house canvassing techniques, how to organize a "Victory Caravan" to transport campaign volunteers, and many other strategies previously reserved for political movements.

The Old and the New

In the postwar era, presidents continued to bash lobbyists. Harry Truman, whose presidency has been much discussed this campaign year, used these words: "There are a great many organizations with lots of money who maintain lobbyists in Washington. I'd say 15 million people in the United States are represented by lobbyists," he said. "The other 150 million have only one man who is elected at large to represent them—that is the president of the United States."

John F. Kennedy also attacked lobbyists, telling an audience at Ohio's Wittenberg College in 1960, "The consumer is the only man in our economy without a high-powered lobbyist in Washington. I intend to be that lobbyist." Yet throughout his presidency, he maintained a close friendship with one of Washington's prominent lawyer-lobbyists, Clark Clifford, remarking jovially at one point that Clifford was not like other consultants who wanted rewards for their assistance to him. "You don't hear Clark clamoring," Kennedy said. "All he asked in return was that we advertise his law firm on the back of the one-dollar bills." That lighthearted quip told much about the power of lobbyists and the personal relationships that nurture the business.

Lobbyists remain an integral part of the Washington establishment, but the scandals of the past continue to stigmatize their standing. One lobbyist captured the feeling: "My mother has never introduced me as 'my son, the lobbyist.' My son, the Washington representative, maybe, or the legislative consultant. But never as the lobbyist. I can't say I blame her." This explains a paradox of Washington life. While lobbyists are highly compensated and influential, they occupy a kind of underclass in the nation's capital. They are frequently left standing in hallways and reception areas for hours at a time. Theirs are the first appointments canceled or postponed when legislators are pressed by other business calls. Their activity suffuses the culture of the city, but their status suffers from a long history of lobbying scandals.

Questions for Discussion

1. How has Washington lobbying changed since the early days of the republic? What forces have brought about such changes? Is the negative image of lobbyists still warranted?
2. Why is it so difficult to regulate lobbying activity?

9.3

Associations Without Members

Theda Skocpol

Over the past half century, the interest group universe has experienced profound change. The number of organized interests in American politics has grown tremendously, as virtually every interest imaginable is now represented by a formally organized group. New voices have been heard, and the expansion of representation has had many positive consequences, including the expansion of rights for various categories of citizens.

In this article, Theda Skocpol surveys the changes that have taken place in the style and substance of civic and association activities since the 1950s, and she speculates as to their consequences for a democratic polity. Particularly troublesome to Skocpol is the decline of "locally rooted and nationally active membership associations." Such groups have been replaced by "organizations without members," leadership-dominated advocacy groups with little democratic input. In Skocpol's view, the new groups are unable to mobilize mass support as well as the older membership organizations do, letting elites dominate policymaking and frustrating meaningful political reform.

In just a third of a century, Americans have dramatically changed their style of civic and political association. A civic world once centered in locally rooted and nationally active membership associations is a relic. Today, Americans volunteer for causes and projects, but only rarely as ongoing members. They send checks to service and advocacy groups run by professionals, often funded by foundations or professional fundraisers. Prime-time airways echo with debates among their spokespersons: the National Abortion Rights Action League debates the National Right to Life Committee; the Concord Coalition takes on the American Association of Retired Persons; and the Environmental Defense Fund counters business groups. Entertained or bemused, disengaged viewers watch as polarized advocates debate.

The largest membership groups of the 1950s were old-line and well-established, with founding dates ranging from 1733 for the Masons to 1939 for the Woman's Division of Christian Service (a Methodist women's association formed from

Theda Skocpol is professor of political science at Harvard University.

"missionary" societies with nineteenth-century roots). Like most large membership associations throughout American history, most 1950s associations recruited members across class lines. They held regular local meetings and convened periodic assemblies of elected leaders and delegates at the state, regional, or national levels. Engaged in multiple rather than narrowly specialized pursuits, many associations combined social or ritual activities with community service, mutual aid, and involvement in national affairs. Patriotism was a leitmotif; during and after World War II, a passionate and victorious national endeavor, these associations sharply expanded their memberships and renewed the vigor of their local and national activities.

To be sure, very large associations were not the only membership federations that mattered in postwar America. Also prominent were somewhat smaller, elite-dominated civic groups—including male service groups like Rotary, Lions, and Kiwanis, and longstanding female groups like the American Association of University Women and the League of Women Voters. Dozens of ethnically based fraternal and cultural associations flourished, as did African-American fraternal groups like the Prince Hall Masons and the Improved Benevolent and Protective Order of Elks of the World.

For many membership federations, this was a golden era of national as well as community impact. Popularly rooted membership federations rivaled professional and business associations for influence in policy debates. The AFL-CIO was in the thick of struggles about economic and social policies; the American Legion and the Veterans of Foreign Wars advanced veterans' programs; the American Farm Bureau Federation (AFBF) joined other farmers' associations to influence national and state agricultural policies; and the National Congress of Parents and Teachers (PTA) and the General Federation of Women's Clubs were influential on educational, health, and family issues. The results could be decisive, as exemplified by the pivotal role of the American Legion in drafting and lobbying for the GI Bill of 1944.

Then, suddenly, old-line membership federations seemed passé. Upheavals shook America during "the long 1960s," stretching from the mid-1950s through the mid-1970s. The southern Civil Rights movement challenged white racial domination and spurred legislation to enforce legal equality and voting rights for African Americans. Inspired by Civil Rights achievements, additional "rights" movements exploded, promoting equality for women, dignity for homosexuals, the unionization of farm workers, and the mobilization of other nonwhite ethnic minorities. Movements arose to oppose U.S. involvement in the war in Vietnam, champion a new environmentalism, and further other public causes. At the forefront of these groundswells were younger Americans, especially from the growing ranks of college students and university graduates.

The great social movements of the long 1960s were propelled by combinations of grassroots protest, activist radicalism, and professionally led efforts to lobby government and educate the public. Some older membership associations ended up participating and expanding their bases of support, yet the groups that sparked movements were more agile and flexibly structured than pre-existing membership federations.

The upheavals of the 1960s could have left behind a reconfigured civic world, in which some old-line membership associations had declined but others had reoriented and reenergized themselves. Within each great social movement, memberships could have consolidated and groups coalesced into new omnibus federations able to link the grass roots to state, regional, and national leaderships, allowing longstanding American civic traditions to continue in new ways.

But this is not what happened. Instead, the 1960s, 1970s, and 1980s brought extraordinary organizational proliferation and professionalization. At the national level alone, the *Encyclopedia of Associations* listed approximately 6,500 associations in 1958. This total grew by 1990 to almost 23,000. Within the expanding group universe, moreover, new kinds of associations came to the fore: relatively centralized and professionally led organizations focused on policy lobbying and public education.

Another wave of the advocacy explosion involved "public interest" or "citizens'" groups seeking to shape public opinion and influence legislation. Citizens' advocacy groups espouse "causes" ranging from environmental protection (for example, the Sierra Club and the Environmental Defense Fund), to the well-being of poor children (the Children's Defense Fund), to reforming politics (Common Cause) and cutting public entitlements (the Concord Coalition).

The Fortunes of Membership Associations

As the associational explosions of 1960 to 1990 took off, America's once large and confident membership federations were not only bypassed in national politics; they also dwindled as locally rooted participant groups. To be sure, some membership associations have been founded or expanded in recent decades. By far the largest is the American Association of Retired Persons (AARP), which now boasts more than 33 million adherents, about one-half of all Americans aged 50 or older. But AARP is not a democratically controlled organization. Launched in 1958 with backing from a teachers' retirement group and an insurance company, the AARP grew rapidly in the 1970s and 1980s by offering commercial discounts to members and establishing a Washington headquarters to monitor and lobby about federal legislation affecting seniors. The AARP has a legislative and policy staff of 165 people, 28 registered lobbyists, and more than 1,200 staff members in the field. After recent efforts to expand its regional and local infrastructure, the AARP involves about 5 to 10 percent of its members in (undemocratic) membership chapters. But for the most part, the AARP national office—covering an entire city block with its own zip code—deals with masses of individual adherents through the mail.

Four additional recently expanded membership associations use modern mass recruitment methods, yet are also rooted in local and state units. Interestingly, these groups are heavily involved in partisan electoral politics. Two recently launched groups are the National Right to Life Committee (founded in 1973) and the Christian Coalition (founded in 1989). They bridge from church congregations, through which they recruit members and activists, to the conservative wing of the Republican Party, through which they exercise political influence. Two old-line membership federations—the National Education Association (founded in 1857) and the National Rifle Association (founded in 1871)—experienced explosive growth after reorienting themselves to take part in partisan politics. The NRA expanded in the 1970s, when right-wing activists opposed to gun control changed what had traditionally been a network of marksmen's clubs into a conservative, Republican-leaning advocacy group fiercely opposed to gun control legislation. During the same period, the NEA burgeoned from a relatively elitist association of public educators into a quasi-union for public school teachers and a stalwart in local, state, and national Democratic Party politics.

Although they fall short of enrolling 1 percent of the adult population, some additional chapter-based membership associations were fueled by the social movements of the 1960s and 1970s. From 1960 to 1990, the Sierra Club (originally created in 1892) ballooned from some 15,000 members to 565,000 members meeting in 378 "local groups." And the National Audubon Society (founded in 1905) went from 30,000 members and 330 chapters in 1958 to about 600,000 members and more than 500 chapters in the 1990s. The National Organization for Women (NOW) reached 1,122 members and 14 chapters within a year of its founding in 1966, and spread across all 50 states with some 125,000 members meeting in 700 chapters by 1978. But notice that these "1960s" movement associations do not match the organizational scope of old-line membership federations. At its post–World War II high point in 1955, for example, the General Federation of Women's Clubs boasted more than 826,000 members meeting in 15,168 local clubs, themselves divided into representative networks within each of the 50 states plus the District of Columbia. By contrast, at its high point in 1993, NOW reported some 280,000 members and 800 chapters, with no intermediate tier of representative governance between the national center and local chapters. These membership associations certainly matter, but mainly as counterexamples to dominant associational trends—of organizations without members.

After nearly a century of civic life rooted in nation-spanning membership federations, why was America's associational universe so transformed? A variety of factors have contributed, including racial and gender change; shifts in the political opportunity structure; new techniques and models for building organizations; and recent transformations in U.S. class relations. Taken together, I suggest, these account for civic America's abrupt and momentous transition from membership to advocacy.

Society Decompartmentalized

Until recent times, most American membership associations enrolled business and professional people together with white-collar folks, farmers, and craft or industrial workers. There was a degree of fellowship across class lines—yet at the price of other kinds of exclusions. With only a few exceptions, old-line associations enrolled either men or women, not both together (although male-only fraternal and veterans' groups often had ties to ladies' auxiliaries). Racial separation was also the rule. Although African Americans did manage to create and greatly expand fraternal associations of their own, they unquestionably resented exclusion by the parallel white fraternals.

Given the pervasiveness of gender and racial separation in classic civic America, established voluntary associations were bound to be shaken after the 1950s. Moreover, changing gender roles and identities blended with other changing values to undercut not just membership appeals but long-standing routes to associational leadership. For example, values of patriotism, brotherhood, and sacrifice had been celebrated by all fraternal groups. During and after each war, the Masons, Knights of Pythias, Elks, Knights of Columbus, Moose, Eagles, and scores of other fraternal groups celebrated and memorialized the contributions of their soldier-members. So did women's auxiliaries, not to mention men's service clubs and trade union "brotherhoods." But "manly" ideals of military service faded after the early 1960s as America's bitter experiences during the war in Vietnam disrupted the intergenerational continuity of male identification with martial brotherliness.

In the past third of a century, female civic leadership has changed as much or more than male leadership. Historically, U.S. women's associations—ranging from female auxiliaries of male groups to independent groups like the General Federation of Women's Clubs, the PTA, and church-connected associations—benefited from the activism of educated wives and mothers. Although a tiny fraction of all U.S. females, higher-educated women were a surprisingly substantial and widespread presence—because the United States was a pioneer in the schooling of girls and the higher education of women. By 1880, some 40,000 American women constituted a third of all students in U.S. institutions of higher learning; women's share rose to nearly half at the early twentieth-century peak in 1920, when some 283,000 women were enrolled in institutions of higher learning. Many higher-educated women of the late 1800s and early 1900s married immediately and stayed out of the paid labor force. Others taught for a time in primary and secondary schools, then got married and stopped teaching (either voluntarily or because school systems would not employ married women). Former teachers accumulated in every community. With skills to make connections within and across communities—and some time on their hands as their children grew older—former teachers and other educated women became mainstays of classic U.S. voluntary life.

Of course, more American women than ever before are now college-educated. But contemporary educated women face new opportunities and constraints. Paid work and family responsibilities are no longer separate spheres, and the occupational structure is less sex-segregated at all levels. Today, even married women with children are very likely to be employed, at least part-time. Despite new time pressures, educated and employed women have certainly not dropped out of civic life. Women employed part-time are more likely to be members of groups or volunteers than housewives; and fully employed women are often drawn into associations or civic projects through work. Yet styles of civic involvement have changed—much to the disadvantage of broad-gauged associations trying to hold regular meetings.

The Lure of Washington, D.C.

The centralization of political change in Washington, D.C. also affected the associational universe. Consider the odyssey of civil rights lawyer Marian Wright Edelman. Fresh from grassroots struggles in Mississippi, she arrived in Washington, D.C. in the late 1960s to lobby for Mississippi's Head Start program. She soon realized that arguing on behalf of children might be the best way to influence legislation and sway public sympathy in favor of the poor, including African Americans. So between 1968 and 1973 Edelman obtained funding from major foundations and developed a new advocacy and policy research association, the Children's Defense Fund (CDF). With a skillful staff, a small national network of individual supporters, ties to social service agencies and foundations, and excellent relationships with the national media, the CDF has been a determined proponent of federal antipoverty programs ever since. The CDF has also worked with Democrats and other liberal advocacy groups to expand such efforts; and during periods of conservative Republican ascendancy, the CDF has been a fierce (if not always successful) defender of federal social programs.

Activists, in short, have gone where the action is. In this same period, congressional committees and their staffs subdivided and multiplied. During the later 1970s and 1980s, the process of group formation became self-reinforcing—not only because groups arose to counter other groups, but also because groups begot more groups. Because businesses and citizens use advocacy groups to influence government outside of parties and between elections, it is not surprising that the contemporary group explosion coincides with waning voter loyalty to the two major political parties. As late as the 1950s, U.S. political parties were networks of local and state organizations through which party officials often brokered nominations, cooperated with locally rooted membership associations, and some-

times directly mobilized voters. The party structure and the associational structure were mutually reinforcing.

Then, demographic shifts, reapportionment struggles, and the social upheavals
of the 1960s disrupted old party organizations; and changes in party rules led to
nomination elections that favored activists and candidate-centered efforts over
backroom brokering by party insiders. Such "reforms" were meant to enhance
grassroots participation, but in practice have furthered oligarchical ways of
running elections. No longer the preserve of party organizations, U.S. campaigns
are now managed by coteries of media consultants, pollsters, direct mail specialists, and—above all—fundraisers. In this revamped electoral arena, advocacy
groups have much to offer, hoping to get access to elected officials in return for
helping candidates. In low-turnout battles to win party nominations, even groups
with modest mail memberships may be able to field enough (paid or unpaid)
activists to make a difference. At all stages of the electoral process, advocacy
groups with or without members can provide endorsements that may be useful in
media or direct mail efforts. And PACs pushing business interests or public
interest causes can help candidates raise the huge amounts of money they need
to compete.

A New Model of Association-Building

Classic American association-builders took it for granted that the best way to
gain national influence, moral or political, was to knit together national, state,
and local groups that met regularly and engaged in a degree of representative
governance. Leaders who desired to speak on behalf of masses of Americans found
it natural to proceed by recruiting self-renewing mass memberships and spreading
a network of interactive groups. After the start-up phase, associational budgets
usually depended heavily on membership dues and on sales of newsletters or
supplies to members and local groups. Supporters had to be continuously recruited through social networks and person-to-person contacts. And if leverage
over government was desired, an association had to be able to influence legislators, citizens, and newspapers across many districts. For all of these reasons, classic
civic entrepreneurs with national ambitions moved quickly to recruit activists
and members in every state and across as many towns and cities as possible within
each state.

Today, nationally ambitious civic entrepreneurs proceed in quite different ways.
When Marian Wright Edelman launched a new advocacy and research group to
lobby for the needs of children and the poor, she turned to private foundations
for funding and then recruited an expert staff of researchers and lobbyists. In the
early 1970s, when John Gardner launched Common Cause as a "national citizens
lobby" demanding governmental reforms, he arranged for start-up contributions
from several wealthy friends, contacted reporters in the national media, and
purchased mailing lists to solicit masses of members giving modest monetary

contributions. Patron grants, direct mail techniques, and the capacity to convey images and messages through the mass media have changed the realities of organization building and maintenance.

The very model of civic effectiveness has been up-ended since the 1960s. No longer do civic entrepreneurs think of constructing vast federations and recruiting interactive citizen-members. When a new cause (or tactic) arises, activists envisage opening a national office and managing association-building as well as national projects from the center. Even a group aiming to speak for large numbers of Americans does not absolutely need members. And if mass adherents are recruited through the mail, why hold meetings? From a managerial point of view, interactions with groups of members may be downright inefficient. In the old-time membership federations, annual elections of leaders and a modicum of representative governance went hand in hand with membership dues and interactive meetings. But for the professional executives of today's advocacy organizations, direct mail members can be more appealing because, as Kenneth Godwin and Robert Cameron Mitchell explain, "they contribute without 'meddling'" and "do not take part in leadership selection or policy discussions." This does not mean the new advocacy groups are malevolent; they are just responding rationally to the environment in which they find themselves.

Associational Change and Democracy

This brings us, finally, to what may be the most civically consequential change in late-twentieth-century America: the rise of a very large, highly educated upper middle class in which "expert" professionals are prominent along with businesspeople and managers. When U.S. professionals were a tiny, geographically dispersed stratum, they understood themselves as "trustees of community," in the terminology of Stephen Brint. Working closely with and for nonprofessional fellow citizens in thousands of towns and cities, lawyers, doctors, ministers, and teachers once found it quite natural to join—and eventually help to lead—locally rooted, cross-class voluntary associations. But today's professionals are more likely to see themselves as expert individuals who can best contribute to national well-being by working with other specialists to tackle complex technical or social problems.

Cause-oriented advocacy groups offer busy, privileged Americans a rich menu of opportunities to, in effect, hire other professionals and managers to represent their values and interests in public life. Why should highly trained and economically well-off elites spend years working their way up the leadership ladders of traditional membership federations when they can take leading staff roles at the top, or express their preferences by writing a check?

If America has experienced a great civic transformation from membership to advocacy—so what? Most traditional associations were racially exclusive and gender segregated; and their policy efforts were not always broad-minded. More than a few observers suggest that recent civic reorganizations may be for the best. American public life has been rejuvenated, say the optimists, by social movements and advocacy groups fighting for social rights and an enlarged understanding of the public good.

Local community organizations, neighborhood groups, and grassroots protest movements nowadays tap popular energies and involve people otherwise left out of organized politics. And social interchanges live on in small support groups and occasional volunteering. According to the research of Robert Wuthnow, about 75 million men and women, a remarkable 40 percent of the adult population, report taking part in "a small group that meets regularly and provides caring and support for those who participate in it." Wuthnow estimates that there may be some 3 million such groups, including Bible study groups, 12-step self-help groups, book discussion clubs, singles groups, hobby groups, and disease support groups. Individuals find community, spiritual connection, introspection, and personal gratification in small support groups. Meanwhile, people reach out through volunteering. As many as half of all Americans give time to the community this way, their efforts often coordinated by paid social service professionals. Contemporary volunteering can be intermittent and flexibly structured, an intense one-shot effort or spending "an evening a week on an activity for a few months as time permits, rather than having to make a long-term commitment to an organization."

In the optimistic view, the good civic things Americans once did are still being done—in new ways and in new settings. But if we look at U.S. democracy in its entirety and bring issues of power and social leverage to the fore, then optimists are surely overlooking the downsides of our recently reorganized civic life. Too many valuable aspects of the old civic America are not being reproduced or reinvented in the new public world of memberless organizations.

Despite the multiplicity of voices raised within it, America's new civic universe is remarkably oligarchical. Because today's advocacy groups are staff-heavy and focused on lobbying, research, and media projects, they are managed from the top with few opportunities for member leverage from below. Even when they have hundreds of thousands of adherents, contemporary associations are heavily tilted toward upper-middle-class constituencies. Whether we are talking about memberless advocacy groups, advocacy groups with some chapters, mailing-list associations, or nonprofit institutions, it is hard to escape the conclusion that the wealthiest and best-educated Americans are much more privileged in the new civic world than their (less numerous) counterparts were in the pre-1960s civic world of cross-class membership federations.

Mostly, they involve people in "doing for" others—feeding the needy at a church soup kitchen; tutoring children at an after-school clinic; or guiding visitors at a museum exhibit—rather than in "doing with" fellow citizens. Important as such volunteering may be, it cannot substitute for the central citizenship functions that membership federations performed.

A top-heavy civic world not only encourages "doing for" rather than "doing with." It also distorts national politics and public policymaking. Imagine for a moment what might have happened if the GI Bill of 1944 had been debated and legislated in a civic world configured more like the one that prevailed during the 1993–1994 debates over the national health insurance proposal put forward by the first administration of President Bill Clinton. This is not an entirely fanciful comparison, because goals supported by the vast majority of Americans were at issue in both periods: in the 1940s, care and opportunity for millions of military veterans returning from World War II; in the 1990s, access for all Americans to a modicum of health insurance coverage. Back in the 1940s, moreover, there were elite actors—university presidents, liberal intellectuals, and conservative congressmen—who could have condemned the GI Bill to the same fate as the 1990s health security plan. University presidents and liberal New Dealers initially favored versions of the GI Bill that would have been bureaucratically complicated, niggardly with public expenditures, and extraordinarily limited in veterans' access to subsidized higher education.

But in the actual civic circumstances of the 1940s, elites did not retain control of public debates or legislative initiatives. Instead, a vast voluntary membership federation, the American Legion, stepped in and drafted a bill to guarantee every one of the returning veterans up to four years of post–high school education, along with family and employment benefits, business loans, and home mortgages. Not only did the Legion draft one of the most generous pieces of social legislation in American history, thousands of local Legion posts and dozens of state organizations mounted a massive public education and lobbying campaign to ensure that even conservative congressional representatives would vote for the new legislation.

Half a century later, the 1990s health security episode played out in a transformed civic universe dominated by advocacy groups, pollsters, and big-money media campaigns. Top-heavy advocacy groups did not mobilize mass support for a sensible reform plan. Hundreds of business and professional groups influenced the Clinton administration's complex policy schemes, and then used a combination of congressional lobbying and media campaigns to block new legislation. Both the artificial polarization and the elitism of today's organized civic universe may help to explain why increasing numbers of Americans are turned off by and pulling back from public life. Large majorities say that wealthy "special interests" dominate the federal government, and many Americans express cynicism about the chances for regular people to make a difference. People may be entertained by advocacy clashes on television, but they are also ignoring many public debates and withdrawing into privatism. Voting less and less, American citizens increasingly act—and claim to feel—like mere spectators in a polity where all the significant action seems to go on above their heads, with their views ignored by pundits and clashing partisans.

From the nineteenth through the mid-twentieth century, American democracy flourished within a unique matrix of state and society. Not only was America the world's first manhood democracy and the first nation in the world to establish mass public education. It also had a uniquely balanced civic life, in which markets expanded but could not subsume civil society, in which governments at multiple levels deliberately and indirectly encouraged federated voluntary associations. National elites had to pay attention to the values and interests of millions of ordinary Americans.

Over the past third of a century, the old civic America has been bypassed and shoved to the side by a gaggle of professionally dominated advocacy groups and nonprofit institutions rarely attached to memberships worthy of the name. Ideals of shared citizenship and possibilities for democratic leverage have been compromised in the process. Since the 1960s, many good things have happened in America. New voices are now heard, and there have been invaluable gains in equality and liberty. But vital links in the nation's associational life have frayed, and we may need to find creative ways to repair those links if America is to avoid becoming a country of detached spectators. There is no going back to the civic world we have lost. But we Americans can and should look for ways to recreate the best of our civic past in new forms suited to a renewed democratic future.

Questions for Discussion

1. What factors led to a decline in importance of membership federations in the nation's civic and political life? What kinds of organizations have taken their place?
2. Although Skocpol believes that the number of organized interests represented in the interest group universe over the past half century has grown, she also believes that the political system may be less democratic than it had previously been. How can such a paradox be explained?

9.4

From Big Bird to Bill Gates: Organized Interests and the Emergence of Hyperpolitics

Allan J. Cigler and Burdett A. Loomis

Not only have recent decades witnessed a proliferation of groups, but the scope of their political activity has increased as well. More groups than ever before are involved in more kinds of behaviors to influence policy and electoral outcomes. No longer are many groups satisfied to lobby just on issues of immediate concern or to play a secondary role in elections by contributing to candidates.

In this selection, Allan Cigler and Burdett Loomis argue that organized interests—especially moneyed interests—are involved in a permanent, ongoing campaign to influence political communication in the nation. According to the authors, politics has become an offshoot of marketing, where information is key. Most information is "interested," reflecting the underlying views of those who sponsor and disseminate it. In both the electoral and policymaking sides of American politics, information is shaped by organized interests that carry out expensive campaigns designed to dominate discourse on political matters. In the authors' view, we are in an era of "hyperpolitics," characterized by many voices being expressed, but with few guidelines to sort out their value.

I n 1995–1996, after gaining control of Congress, members of the new Republican majority set their sights on cutting all funds for television's Public Broadcasting Service (PBS), which they saw as representing both an inappropriate use of federal funds and a bastion of liberal thought. Given that federal spending on public broadcasting had been declining since the 1980s and that it could not lobby (at least formally) on its own behalf, PBS looked vulnerable, given the House Republicans' early success in 1995 in passing its Contract with America. But PBS did have an important, latent resource: the support of millions of individuals who watched public television, and especially those whose children had grown up with *Sesame Street*'s endearing characters.

PBS and its member stations were prohibited from lobbying, yet they did find ways to mobilize their viewers and subscribers to communicate with their repre-

Allan Cigler is Chancellor's Club Teaching Professor of Political Science at the University of Kansas. Burdett A. Loomis is a professor of political science at the University of Kansas.

sentatives in Congress. In that PBS supporters are widely distributed across the country and disproportionately well-educated, this group responded quickly and effectively to the congressional threats, as framed by PBS executives such as Paula Kerger of New York's WNET. Once the political conflict was defined in terms of increasingly unpopular Speaker Newt Gingrich (R-Ga.) against the always popular Big Bird, the battle was essentially over—and PBS survived, more or less intact. Indeed, in 1997 the Congress voted to appropriate $300 million for PBS in fiscal year 2000, an increase of $50 million above the 1999 spending level.

In 1988 Microsoft had no meaningful Washington presence, and Democrats controlled both houses of Congress. Ten years later Microsoft was discovered planning a huge (and surreptitious) public relations offensive to counter federal antitrust initiatives, to say nothing of burnishing the image of CEO Bill Gates. And Republicans were seeking to extend their four years of control on Capitol Hill, which might allow them to mount another attack on public broadcasting. Even more important than these major changes to the political landscape, however, has been the broad trend toward the politicization of almost all communication—ranging from television's *Ellen's* conversion from a situation comedy to an advocacy program for gay rights to the exponential increase in Internet usage. . . .

In this [essay] we will broach the argument that interests—especially moneyed interests—increasingly have come to dominate political communication in the United States. Both on the electoral and policymaking sides of American politics, information is shaped by expensive campaigns that seek to dominate the discourse on the major issues of the day. This does not mean that traditional electoral politics is unimportant, nor that honored lobbying tactics of access and personal relationships are insignificant. Far from it. Still, in a post-Cold War–post-civil rights era, the absence of overarching societal issues (with abortion as something of an exception) means that interests will compete aggressively in selling their version of public policy problems and solutions—solutions that may, as with telecommunications reform, greatly enrich specific private groups.

Politics more than ever has become an offshoot of marketing. In such a context, most information is "interested." That is, the information reflects, sometimes subtly, sometimes not, the underlying views of the interests who sponsor and disseminate it. Even science becomes adversarial, because, it seems, every side on an issue can purchase a study to support its point of view. Indeed, the tobacco discourse of the late 1990s is noteworthy because the industry finally retreated from some of its most ludicrous "scientific" claims that denied the carcinogenic and addictive elements of smoking. Most lessons of the past thirty years have schooled interests to construct a coherent story line and stick to it, on policies ranging from teenage pregnancy to international trade.

We will examine the changing roles of organized interests in electoral politics and policymaking. . . .

Groups, Parties, and Campaigns: A Blurring of Roles

The long-standing relationship between political parties and interest groups in elections has changed in recent decades. Rather than aggregating various mass interests, parties have developed some of the policy-advocating characteristics typically associated with more narrow interests. At the same time parties have become less important to mobilizing voters and running campaigns. Although the vast majority of interest groups still refrain from direct electoral involvement, more and more of them have assumed some of the activities usually associated with parties, such as recruiting candidates, organizing campaigns, and running advertisements. In some tight races, interest group voices have even drowned out those of the candidates.

The decline of parties in elections represents a long-term trend that began around the turn of the century, but a series of party and campaign reforms in the early 1970s were responsible for drastically altering party-interest group relations in the electoral process. The party reforms broke the state and local organizational control over party business, including the nomination process, and thus created opportunities for organized interest influence. The campaign finance changes of the early 1970s also offered advantages to interest groups. The growth of political action committees (PACs), the limitations on party spending, and the requirement that the individual campaign organization be the legal agent of the candidate all had the effect of decreasing an already diminished party role in providing campaign resources to candidates.

The parties did adapt to the interest group threat. By the mid-1980s the national parties were increasingly becoming service vendors to party candidates, successfully coping with the realities of modern, candidate-centered campaigns. PAC-party relations became less conflictual and more cooperative. Both parties embraced their emerging role as brokers by forming loose fund-raising alliances with many PACs and beginning to offer them regular assistance in directing contributions to particular campaigns, as well as aiding candidates in soliciting funds from potential donor PACs. The fear of some that organized interests (through PACs) would supplant parties in the electoral process never materialized.

The 1990s have witnessed another benchmark in relations between parties and organized interests, one that may presage an even more prominent role for *both* parties and organized interests in the electoral process, perhaps at the expense of candidate domination of campaign agendas. . . . [T]he candidate-centered system that has characterized electoral politics for more than half a century may face its most serious challenge to date.

There are a number of prominent features of the emerging system. Foremost is the huge escalation of organized interest money found in our most recent elections, much of it raised and spent outside of the controlling provisions of the Federal Election Campaign Act (FECA). Although some of the growth has been in PAC and independent spending . . . the most startling development has come in extensive soft money contributions by organized interests to the national political parties—money creatively spent by the parties beyond FECA restrictions. These contributions, in some instances more than $1 million, do not typically come from interest groups per se but most notably from individual corporations. The rise in importance of soft money to the parties may increase organized interest leverage on individual campaigns, as well as on the parties. In 1996, for example, the major parties succeeded in raising $285 million in soft money, but this achievement rendered them highly dependent on large contributions from affluent interests.

The overall number of organized interests offering financial support has expanded as well, with many new groups entering the fray. For example, the American Cancer Society, a venerable nonprofit organization, recently contributed $30,000 to the Democratic and Republican parties in order to gain "the same access" as others, according to its national vice president for federal and state affairs, who said, "We wanted to look like players and be players."[1] Although this action is subject to a court challenge, the tax-exempt society sees such gifts as appropriate because the funds were targeted to party annual conferences and dinners, not campaign activity.

Beyond soft money contributions, the direct campaign efforts mustered by some organized interests in the mid-1990s were of historical proportions. Organized labor spent $35 million in 1996 to reverse the 1994 Democratic loss of Congress; some of these funds went to train union activists to organize targeted congressional districts and to increase voter registration, but the bulk of the funds went to buy air time for 27,000 television commercials in forty congressional districts—almost 800 spots per district. In 1996 the National Rifle Association became active in more than 10,000 political races at local, state, and national levels despite running a deficit and cutting its staff.

Another distinguishing feature of the emerging system is the blurring of traditional party and interest group roles in campaigns. In 1996, for example, both national parties became *group patrons*, as they used some of their soft money to fund group electoral activity such as registration drives and telephone banks. Republicans contributed to a number of antitax and prolife groups, and Democrats channeled some of their funds to a variety of groups they believed would mobilize minority voters. In a very real sense, the parties were contracting out their voter mobilization function to various organized interests. Both parties, but the Republicans in particular, have also "created a dazzling galaxy of policy institutes, foundations and think tanks, each of which can raise money from private interests and which can aid the party and party candidates in a variety of ways."[2]

A number of organized interests have been increasing the level of their activities in what traditionally has be thought of as party arena. As James Guth and his associates put it, "In an era when party organizations have either atrophied or find it difficult to activate sympathetic voters, religious interest groups are an important new force. . . . Such groups have become significant electoral competitors (and often adjuncts) to party committees, candidate organizations, and other traditional interest groups." Thus, in 1996 religious grassroots contacts of potential voters compared "quite favorably" with voters' contacts by party organizations, political candidates, and business or labor groups. More than 54 million voter guides were distributed using church-based networks in 1996. In a number of states, Christian Right adherents have captured the formal Republican Party organization, and one estimate counted roughly 200,000 movement activists as involved in the 1996 elections at various levels.

Although many of the efforts of organized labor and the Christian Right have been coordinated with party or candidate efforts (most often unofficially, so campaign finance laws would not be violated), a lot of interest group electoral activity in the 1990s has been independent of candidate or party efforts. It is difficult at times to discern which organized interests were involved, because expenditures and disclosure are not regulated by current campaign finance laws. For example, at least $150 million was spent on issue advocacy campaigns in 1996. As long as the ads did not advocate voting for or defeating a specific candidate, interests could express their issue-based concerns in a thinly veiled attempt to support or oppose a given candidate. Well-known groups such as the AFL-CIO, the Sierra Club, the National Education Association, the National Abortion Rights Action League, and the National Federation of Independent Businesses were especially prominent. Some entities operated in the shadows. Triad Management, a political consulting firm, apparently channeled at least $3 million from conservative donors to purchase television ads in support of competitive-seat Republican candidates. Approximately twenty-five groups sponsored $100 million in issue advocacy ads in 1996, and they concentrated their efforts in fifty-four competitive House and Senate races. In some cases the amount spent on issue advocacy in a race has exceeded that spent by the candidates, raising concerns that the candidates themselves had lost control over the discourse of the campaign. That is precisely the point for some interest group leaders. As Paul Jacob, executive director of U.S. Term Limits, observed, "If politicians get to control the campaign, these issues [such as term limits] won't be talked about."[3]

Existing campaign finance laws have lost much of their meaning, and prospects for meaningful change are remote. As a consequence, neither parties nor interest groups are much constrained in their fund-raising and spending behavior. Parties have more money than ever before and can be expected to expand their efforts as well. Court rulings now permit parties to engage in independent spending in the same manner as interest groups, and using soft money for issue advocacy advertisements is in vogue.

The meaning of all this for American representative democracy is unclear. In many ways party-interest group relations have been functionally altered, especially in that the party now has an enhanced electoral role as a fund-raiser. But in the process of becoming a vendor engaged in modern candidate-centered elections, the party has surrendered some of its traditional functions of grassroots activism and voter mobilization, which have been largely left to those organized interests with adequate resources to perform them.

National parties look suspiciously like special interests themselves, with their primary concern being to raise campaign resources for their parties' officeholders seeking reelection (the party of the incumbents), with little advice from party activists. When incumbents are threatened, both national parties may even cooperate with each other, as they did in 1987 in the face of a public outcry over congressional pay raises (the party chairs agreed not to offer financial support to challengers of those incumbents who had made the pay raise a campaign issue).

An electoral system based largely on the ability of parties and their candidates to raise funds from organized interests, especially through large contributions, inevitably clashes with the dominant notion of parties as representatives of mass interests and potential counterweights to the excessive demands of particular interests. Rather, the parties may well have become, as political scientist Thomas Ferguson has theorized, not much more than investment vehicles for wealthy interests who can choose to invest directly in candidates, or broadly in parties, or specifically in issue advocacy advertisements.

Interests, Information, and Policies: Many Voices, Whose Tune?

If organized interests have changed their approaches to electoral politics, so too have they altered their strategies to affect governmental decisions. Although organized interests continue to lobby in time-honored ways within the corridors of Washington institutions, such as Congress and bureaucratic agencies, they have begun to spend more time shaping perceptions of problems and political agendas. In addition, they are devoting more and more attention to earlier stages of policy formulation, especially the fundamental defining and redefining of issues. Indeed, successfully defining conditions as problems (such as smog, learning disabilities, or global warming) often represents the single most important step in changing policies.

In the politics of problem definition, everyone can play by calling a press conference, releasing a study, going on a talk show, commissioning a poll, or buying an advertisement. There is no shortage in Washington either of well-defined problems or potential solutions, as the capital is awash in arguments and evidence that seek to define problems and set agendas. What is more difficult to understand very well is how certain definitions come to prevail within the context of political institutions that often, though not always, resist the consideration of new—or newly packaged—ideas.

As problem definition and agenda status become increasingly important elements of policymaking, organized interests have stepped up their attempts to expand, restrict, or redirect conflict on given issues. The public interest and environmental movements of the 1960s often led the way in understanding these elements of political life, leaving business to catch up in the 1970s and 1980s. Jeffrey Berry, a long-time student of public interest groups, has concluded that citizen groups have driven the policy agenda since the 1960s, thus forcing business interests to respond to sets of issues developed by groups such as Common Cause and environmental organizations.

Following on the heels of these agenda successes has been the institutionalization of interests within the government, especially when broad public concerns are at stake. For instance, many of the 1995 battles over the Contract with America* placed legislators in sharp conflict with programs supported by members of government agencies, such as the Environmental Protection Agency. Moreover, many interests have found homes *within* the Congress in the form of caucuses composed of sitting legislators.

And there's the rub. *As more interests seek to define problems and push agenda items, more messages emanate from more sources.* For threatened interests, whether corporate, environmental, or professional, the decision to socialize a conflict (and to expand the attentive audience) has no meaning unless it can be accomplished. Even Ralph Nader, the past master of using the press to expand the scope of conflict, has recently found it difficult to attract media attention. Some interests can cut through the cacophony of voices; in particular, those in E. E. Schattschneider's "heavenly chorus" of affluent groups can—at a price—get their message across by spending lavishly on public relations campaigns or by buying advertising time and space. In addition, if such messages are directed toward legislators who have received substantial campaign contributions from these same interests, they typically reach an audience already inclined toward receptivity.

The emphasis on problem definition looms large when major public policy issues are on the table and tremendous uncertainty exists. Lots of substantive interests are in play, many competing scenarios are put forward, legislative decisions are always contingent, and public policy outcomes are often filled with unanticipated consequences. . . .

In policy battles, the capacity to obtain information and control its dissemination is the most important political power of all. Political scientist James Thurber echoes Schattschneider in arguing that if participants cannot resolve conflict on their own turf, " 'outsiders' from other committees, agencies, bureaus, groups, the media, or the general public will take the issue away from them."[4] This scope-of-conflict perspective is extremely important to the dynamics of policy formulation, and it is also a source of the greatest type of uncertainty of all—conflict

---

* In September 1994, in the midst of the congressional campaign, more than 300 Republican candidates signed a pledge on the Capitol steps, called the Contract with America, promising to act swiftly on a set of wide-sweeping proposals to address what they believed were major political concerns. Among the issues to be dealt with were constitutional amendments imposing term limits on members of Congress and requiring a balanced budget, making major income tax cuts, cutting back the number of government regulations, and reducing welfare spending.

redefinition, as in changing a simple agricultural issue into a more complex environmental problem. . . .

Although some corporate interests (such as Microsoft, until the 1990s) have resisted involvement in Washington politics, there has been a surge of activity since the late 1970s. As Jeffrey Birnbaum has observed, the growth of corporate (and trade association) lobbying makes good economic sense: "[Even] in relatively small changes to larger pieces of legislation . . . big money is made and lost. Careful *investment* in a Washington lobbyist can yield enormous returns in the form of taxes avoided or regulations curbed—an odd negative sort of calculation, but one that forms the basis of the economics of lobbying."[5]

The nature of high-stakes decisions makes such investment almost mandatory, given the potential for tremendous gains and losses. In addition, the usual cost-benefit logic that applies to most managerial decisions—lobbying extensively versus building a new plant or embarking on an ambitious new research project—does not apply in high-stakes circumstances, because the potential benefits or costs are so great that virtually any expenditure can be justified, even if its chance to affect the outcome is minuscule. Indeed, spending on a host of tactics—from election contributions to insider access to public relations campaigns—may represent a strategy designed as much to protect lobbyists from criticism by their corporate or trade associations as to influence a given decision.

It may be a mistake to make too much of a distinction between an organized interest spending money in investing in candidates through contributions and providing information to elected officials with lobbying, advertising, or public relations campaigns. . . . Nevertheless, information exchanges between interest groups and legislators are distinct from the seeking of influence through contributions or favors. One scholar, Jack Wright, has noted that interests

> achieve influence in the legislative process not by applying electoral or financial pressure, but by developing expertise about politics and policy and by strategically sharing this expertise with legislators through normal lobbying activities. . . . [Organized interests] can and do exercise substantial influence even without making campaign contributions and . . . contributions and other material gifts or favors are not the primary sources of interest group influence in the legislative process.[6]

Even if information, and not favors or contributions, reflects the basis for interest group influence, does that mean that money is unimportant? Or that all information is equal? Hardly. Inevitably, some interests have much greater resources to develop information that shapes policy debates. . . .

Interests, Hyperpolitics, and the Permanent Campaign

At the turn of the twenty-first century, the outward appearance of the Washington lobbying community remains true to its manifestations in 1975 or 1985; the Gucci culture continues apace, with expensive suits and the constant buzz of the telephone call (cellular these days). In many ways, this appearance of stability is not deceptive at all. The big dogs of capital lobbying are still there—a Tommy Boggs or a Tom Korologos*—trading on personal ties, political acuity, and the ability to raise a quick $10,000 (maybe even $100,000) with a word in the right ear at the right time. Favors are granted, favors are returned, and the quality of their political intelligence remains top flight.

At the same time, things are not the same. Some of the changes are obvious: the ability to create all varieties of grassroots pressure, a tactic raised to art form by Jack Bonner's firm;[†] the promise and uncertainty of the Internet (a recent survey reported that 97 percent of all legislative staff used the Internet to gather information), and the rash of policy-oriented television advertisements that have followed in the wake of the series of "Harry and Louise" commercials used in the health care debate. Moreover, the assault of issue-advocacy advertising in the 1996 congressional campaigns (in the wake of liberating court decisions that weakened restrictions on spending for such ads) may have ushered in an era of interest group-dominated electioneering. In addition, the entry of highly sophisticated information industry players into the political process (for example, Microsoft, a host of Silicon Valley firms, to say nothing of content providers such as Disney, which now owns ABC) may well lead to the politicization of many decisions over both the channels and the content of communication.

In general, we see three major trends taking shape and complementing each other. First, more interests are engaged in more kinds of behaviors to influence policy outcomes. Interests monitor more actions than they once did, and stand ready to swing into action more quickly when a red flag is raised (often by a lobbyist on retainer). Given the high stakes of governmental decisions, whether in a House committee or an EPA bureau, the monitoring-action combination is a worthwhile investment.

Second, there is little distinction, for most practical purposes, between "outside" and "inside" lobbying. Most effective influence relies on both. To be sure, a key provision can still find its way into an omnibus bill without a ripple, but battles over most major issues are fought simultaneously on multiple fronts. A call or fax from a House member's most important banker or editor or university president can be prompted by a lobbyist at the first sign of a problem in a committee hearing or, more likely, a casual conversation. Jack Bonner and a

---

* Thomas Hale Boggs is the well-connected son of Hale Boggs, former Democratic House leader, and is the brother of ABC Commentator Cokie Roberts. Boggs has been a major presence in Washington politics since the 1970s, and his firm grosses more than $10 million a year in lobbying fees. Korologos is similar to Boggs, except with a Republican spin; working as a partner of Timmons and Company, he represents such powerful interests as Major League Baseball, Anheuser-Busch, and the NRA.

† Jack Bonner and his firm represent the new breed of all-encompassing lobbying firms operating in Washington. They have been particularly innovative and very successful in orchestrating grassroots campaigns that target key members of Congress for their clients.

dozen other constituent-lobbying experts can construct a set of grassroots (or elite "grasstops") entreaties within a few days, if not a few hours. And a media buyer can target any sample of legislators for advertisements that run in their districts, thus ensuring that they know that their constituents and key Washington interests are watching their every action on an important bill.

Related to the diminished distinction between Washington and constituency-based lobbying is the increasing joint emphases on lobbying in state capitals and Washington. In particular, the tobacco settlement activity and the intensive campaigns of Microsoft to ward off antitrust actions in the states demonstrate how national and state politics are linked in an age of devolution.

Third, and perhaps most dramatic, is the declining distinction between the politics of elections and the politics of policymaking. Of course, in a democracy these are inextricably linked, and PACs may have solidified these ties since the 1970s. But these linkages have become much stronger—in many ways reflecting the "permanent campaign" of presidential elections—politics that emerged in the 1970s and 1980s. Blumenthal sees this as combining "image-making with strategic calculation. Under the permanent campaign government is turned into the perpetual campaign."[7] In the 1990s, many interests have come to see the combination of electoral and policy politics in much the same light, with the issue advocacy ads of 1996 serving as the initial demonstration of this new era. In addition, many interests are now viewing the "campaign" idea as one that defines their broader lobbying strategies and blurring the lines between electoral campaigns and public relations efforts.

All three of these trends—a move toward more activities, a lessened distinction between inside and outside lobbying, and the adoption of campaign-based strategies—come together in a 1998 business community initiative on international trade. Based on an initiative from the Commerce Department (and the tacit backing of a cautious White House), corporate advocates of free trade have embarked on a series of campaigns to argue publicly on behalf of free trade. As the National Journal reported, "The patrons of these pro-trade campaigns are typically multinational businesses, trade associations, lobbying groups and Washington think tanks, all called to action by Congress's declining support for . . . trade liberalization."[8] Responding to the growing strength of the much less well-funded loose coalition of labor, human rights, consumers, and environmental groups, the protrade interests, although not abandoning their insider initiatives, have reacted to their opponents' success in expanding the scope of the conflict over trade to issues such as domestic jobs, human rights, and environmental quality. Consider, for example, the actions of Cargill, the huge, privately held agriculture and financial services conglomerate. Historically, the firm has sought influence in the quiet ways, scarcely causing a ripple in public perceptions. But in 1998 the corporation sent 750 sets of videotapes, fact sheets, and sample speeches to its domestic plants and offices, so that its employees could make public pitches in community after community about the domestic impact of trade, especially in rural areas.[9]

At the same time, one thirty-year-old trade coalition (the less than aptly named Emergency Committee for American Trade) is sponsoring a campaign based on Cargill's efforts, while the Business Roundtable, another veteran group of top corporate leaders, "is spending a million dollars [in 1998] to shore up support of free trade in the districts of a dozen congressmen."[10] The Chamber of Commerce and the National Association of Manufacturers have initiated similar efforts to offer their members information and analyses to buttress free trade arguments beyond the Beltway.

In addition, a host of think tanks, from the moderate Brookings Institution to the libertarian Cato Institute, have developed initiatives to provide higher quality information on the benefits of trade. On a related tack, the Washington-based Center for Strategic and International Studies has embarked on a pilot project in Tennessee to educate public officials, corporate leaders, academics, and students on the strategic importance of enhanced international trade.

The combination of many business organizations, the Commerce Department, a variety of think tanks, and congressional supporters illustrates the "campaign" nature of large-scale lobbying. The direction of influence is not clear, as business leaders respond to administration entreaties, but also hope to pressure the White House to support free trade aggressively. The lobbying is directed at community leaders and the public at large, but there is little capacity to measure its effectiveness. It does not seek, at least in 1998, to influence a particular piece of legislation. Rather, the campaign emphasizes an entire set of narratives on free trade that can be used by the executive branch, legislators, lobbyists, or grassroots advocates. . . .

Given such cacophony, coupled to high-stakes decisions, it is no wonder that those cultural icons Bill Gates and Big Bird have entered the political fray. Their respective interests, both economic and cultural, are great, and the costs of investing in lobbying, although substantial, pale before the potential benefits. But there is a cost to this extension of politics to much of our communication, what we choose to call *hyperpolitics*. If all information is seen as interested, as just one more story, then how do decision makers sort it all out? What voices cut through the "data smog" of a society that can cough up studies and stories at a moment's notice, and communicate them broadly or narrowly, as tactics suggest? Although some students of interest groups . . . see hopeful signs for a vigorous pluralism that accords major roles to consumers, public interest advocates, and environmentalists, we remain skeptical. The costs of lobbying in a hyperpolitics state are great, and the stakes are high. Money surely does not guarantee success, but the capacity to spend keeps well-heeled interests in the game, able to play the range of games that have come to define the politics of influence as we move further into the age of information.

Notes

1. Jonathan D. Salant, "Cancer Group Give to GOP, Democrats," *Kansas City Star*, March 30, 1998, A12.
2. Clyde Wilcox and Wesley Joe, "Dead Law: The Federal Election Finance Regulations, 1974–1996," *PS* 31 (March 1998): 15.
3. Donna Cassata, "Independent Groups' Ads Increasingly Steer Campaigns," *CQ Weekly*, May 2, 1998, 1114.
4. James Thurber, *Divided Democracy* (Washington, D.C.: CQ Press), 336.
5. Jeffrey Birnbaum, *The Lobbyists* (New York: Times Books, 1993), 4, emphasis added.
6. Wright, *Interest Groups and Congress*, 88.
7. Sidney Blumenthal, *The Permanent Campaign* (New York: Touchstone, 1982), 23.
8. Julie Kosterlitz, "Trade Crusade," *National Journal*, May 9, 1998, 1054. In addition to the specific citations noted here and later, the following paragraphs draw generally on this story.
9. Ibid., 1055.
10. Ibid.

Questions for Discussion

1. What do Cigler and Loomis mean by the term *hyperpolitics*? Why is it so difficult for public officials to make decisions in an environment characterized by hyperpolitics?
2. Cigler and Loomis argue that the traditional distinctions between political parties and interest groups no longer hold true in the contemporary political context. What factors have contributed to the "blurring of roles" between parties and interest groups? Is such a condition healthy for American democracy?

 Chapter 10

CONGRESS

Of the three branches of government, the legislature is invariably the most open to scrutiny and influence. Members of Congress are directly accountable to their constituents. Even in a security-conscious age of metal detectors and concrete barriers, the U.S. Congress remains easily accessible to citizens who seek to influence their representatives and senators or merely to observe them in action. Just as the growth of government has affected the presidency and, to a lesser extent, the Supreme Court (see Chapters 11 and 13), Congress has changed greatly in the post-World War II era, especially since the mid-1960s.

Some of these changes are straightforward. For example, in 1947 members of Congress employed 2,030 staff aides in their personal offices. In 1999 the total came to 7,282, despite some post-1994 cuts. Other developments have been more obscure, though no less important. The informal rules of legislative behavior have changed; today newcomers need not undergo a decade-long apprenticeship before wielding even a bit of power. Despite these and many other changes, however, contemporary legislators take on the same basic responsibilities as their predecessors: representing their constituents and making decisions about the major issues of the day.

Over the course of the American experience, Congress has received countless criticisms of its inefficiencies and its responsiveness to special interests. A bicameral (two-house) legislature is by nature difficult to control, even when a single political party holds majorities in both chambers. In addition, Congress often must face an executive branch whose interests run directly counter to its own. Differences in opinion between the two chambers or between Congress and the executive can and do produce deadlocks, especially when different parties control the different branches.

Similarly, the representative nature of Congress makes it an appropriate target for interest groups. Legislators run expensive reelection campaigns. These require substantial contributions, which frequently come from the growing number of political action committees that represent a wide range of groups. The structure of Congress allows interest groups easy access to a hundred subcommittees that deal with very specific issues ranging from oil exploration to air traffic control to military construction. The small membership and narrow focus of most House and Senate subcommittees provide attractive opportunities for a seemingly limitless number of lobbyists to influence public policies.

The selections in this chapter emphasize both continuity and change in congressional politics. They illustrate the rise of individualism on Capitol Hill. The days are gone when autocratic committee chairs could control the legislative agenda. To exercise real power as a committee chair in the House has ordinarily required at least twenty years' consecutive service on a given panel. This fact encouraged long careers and promoted the image of Congress as a body of tottering graybeards who relied on seniority and the power of their committee positions, rather than the strength of their ideas or intellect, to dominate the process.

By the early 1970s, however, congressional structure and personnel had undergone a dramatic transformation, especially in the House. After the 1982 elections, more than two-thirds of the 535 members of Congress (100 senators, 435 representatives) had arrived on Capitol Hill since 1974. Accompanying this upheaval in personnel was a series of reforms that greatly dispersed power within the Congress. The changes of the 1969–1975 period profoundly affected the House of Representatives. Committee chairs lost much of their authority, and the big winners were the rank-and-file House members, especially the majority Democrats. These representatives demonstrated their new clout in 1975 by voting within the Democratic Caucus to oust three senior committee chairs.

Political scientist Kenneth Shepsle, in the first selection, assesses these changes by first sketching the "textbook Congress" of the 1950s and then noting the various ways in which Congress has diverged from the conventional wisdom of that era. In particular, the decline of committees has led to more variability and uncertainty in congressional politics. The seeming equilibrium of the 1950s Congress has given way to a less predictable, less coherent legislative process within a fragmented House of Representatives. Changes in the way the House does business rest in large part on the replacement of veteran members with newcomers. Although this turnover slowed substantially during the 1980s as incumbents dominated electoral politics, 110 new representatives entered the House in the wake of the 1992 elections. Even more important was the group of 73 freshmen Republicans whose victories allowed the GOP to win control of the House in 1994.

Changes have affected the Senate less profoundly than they have the House, because the upper chamber has always relied on informal cooperation among its members. Nevertheless, some senators have become increasingly adept at tying the body into knots by relying on rules and traditions that evolved to protect minority rights. Senators such as Jesse Helms, Paul Wellstone, and Phil Gramm have acted to obstruct the regular flow of legislative business, acknowledging that in so doing they will win no popularity contests among their colleagues. Indeed, the obstructionism practiced by these and other senators has made leading the Senate a formidable—and perhaps impossible—task.

Historically, congressional politics has reflected continuing tensions between forces of centralization and decentralization. In the late 1970s, for example, decentralizing trends prevailed as subcommittees proliferated and individual legislators gained substantial personal resources, such as staff. Electoral competition for House seats has also declined, and most representatives are well insulated from any pressures that party leaders may seek to employ. Speakers Tip O'Neill, Jim Wright, and Thomas Foley instituted a strategy of "inclusive" leadership that gave large numbers of the majority Democrats an increased stake in the process. In addition, the memberships of the Democratic and the Republican parties in the House have become more homogeneous. As Republicans have gained increasing numbers of seats in the South, moderate-to-conservative southern Democrats have lost much of their power. And fewer moderate Republicans have won election, as conservatives have come to dominate their party.

These trends came together in 1994–1995, when Republicans captured control of the House for the first time since 1955. The House Republicans, led by Speaker Newt Gingrich and bolstered by seventy-three first-term insurgents, had to learn how to govern as a majority. Using the ten-point Contract with America as their script, the House acted on a host of major legislative initiatives in the first 100 (actually 93) days of the 104th Congress in early 1995 and subsequently confronted President Clinton on budget issues to the point of shutting down parts of the federal government in late 1995 and early 1996. The Republicans did learn that they needed support in the Senate and the White House to accomplish much of their agenda, and they did, eventually, "learn to legislate," and they have maintained their majority status through the 107th Congress (2001–2002).

After two centuries of development, Congress remains at the core of societal decision making. Its limitations are great, however, for almost all of its members are subject to re-election every two years and Congress is most effective when it enjoys strong executive direction. The closed congressional power system that existed in the early 1960s gave way to a much more open, democratic, decentralized system in the 1980s and 1990s. In neither era did Congress function as an efficient, completely representative body.

Indeed, committees often do remain important units within Congress, as Mark Murray demonstrates in his profile of House transportation chairman, Bud Shuster (R-Pa.). In general, however, the role of committees has declined, as Richard Cohen documents in his article. Moreover, in 2001 Republicans in the House complied with their self-imposed term limitations on committee chairs. Thirteen three-term chairmen were replaced—one further impact of the "Republican Revolution" fomented in 1994–1995.

Such actions demonstrate that Congress is not what it used to be. At the same time, the public at large neither understands or expresses much confidence in the contemporary Congress, regardless of its so-called reforms. In an eloquent essay, first delivered to members of the American Political Science Association, former Representative Lee Hamilton (D-Ind.) offers a detailed set of recommendations as to what professors might teach their students about Congress. Hamilton's essay stands as an extraordinarily cogent defense of the legislative branch and why it is important to understand how Congress operates.

10.1

The Changing Textbook Congress

Kenneth A. Shepsle

Ordinarily, it takes a while for political scientists to agree that a certain article is a "classic" piece of work. For Kenneth Shepsle's "The Changing Textbook Congress," however, the recognition came quickly and virtually universally. A most imaginative and provocative theorist, Shepsle places congressional developments of the 1960s through the 1980s in a context of an institution that has changed profoundly since scholars painted their definitive portrait of the Congress of the 1940s and 1950s.

One of Shepsle's chief interests is determining how institutional equilibrium, or balance among forces, is established. Committees dominated the earlier era's equilibrium, but since the 1960s committees have come under pressure from individual members, with their considerable staff and technology resources, and from party leaders, who have gained substantial powers through a series of reform efforts. Moreover, most House members must represent increasingly large and diverse districts, which makes coalition building all the more difficult.

Shepsle does not identify a clear contemporary equilibrium within Congress. With large numbers of power centers and stronger individual members, we may be entering an era marked more by uncertainty and fluidity than by a well-defined equilibrium.

When scholars talk about Congress to one another, their students, or the public, they often have a stylized version in mind, a textbook Congress characterized by a few main tendencies and described in broad terms. This is not to say that they are incapable of filling in fine-grained detail, making distinctions, or describing change. But at the core of their descriptions and distinctions are approximations, caricatures, and generalities. They are always incomplete and somewhat inaccurate, but still they consist of robust regularities. . . .

The textbook Congress I have in mind is the one that emerged from World War II and the Legislative Reorganization Act of 1946. Its main features per-

Kenneth A. Shepsle is professor of government at Harvard University.

sisted until the mid-1960s; its images remained in writings on Congress well into the 1970s. . . .

To illuminate the institutional dynamics of the past forty years, this chapter describes some early signs of change in the textbook Congress in the 1950s, suggests how events of the 1960s and 1970s disrupted the equilibrium, and looks at some of the emerging features of a new textbook Congress, though I am not convinced that a new equilibrium has yet been established. The story I develop here is not a historical tour d'horizon [overview]. Rather it addresses theoretical issues of institutional development involving the capacity of Congress and its members to represent their constituencies, to make national policy, and to balance the intrinsic tensions between these tasks. . . .

The Textbook Congress: The Late 1940s to the Mid-1960s

Any portrait of Congress after World War II must begin with the member and, in a popular phrase of the time, "his work as he sees it." Then, as now, legislators divided their time between Washington and home, the relative proportions slowly changing in favor of Washington during the 1950s. In Washington they divided their time between chamber, committee, and personal office; all three demands grew from the 1940s to the 1960s as chamber work load, committee activity, and constituency demands increased.

In 1947, just after passage of the Legislative Reorganization Act, the average House member had three staff assistants and the average senator six. Because even these modest averages would be the envy of a contemporary member of the British Parliament or of most state legislatures, they indicate that by midcentury the American national legislature was a highly professional place. Nevertheless, by the mid-1960s congressional staffs had swelled even further: a typical House member now had twelve assistants and a typical senator eighteen. Committee staffs, too, grew dramatically from an average of ten to nearly thirty in the House and from fifteen to more than thirty in the Senate. These numbers do not include the substantial staffs of the nearly 400 offices of institutional leaders, informal groups, and legislative support agencies.

Since most committee staffers during these twenty years were in fact under the control of committee chairmen, some of the more senior legislators came to head sizable organizations. Indeed, if most legislators in the Eightieth Congress (1947–8) could be said to have headed mom 'n pop businesses with a handful of clerks and assistants, by the mid-1960s they had come to oversee major modern enterprises with secretaries, receptionists, interns, and a variety of legislative, administrative, and political professionals (typically lawyers). A committee chair or ranking minority member, who might also head a couple of subcommittees or party committees, might have a staff exceeding one hundred.

This growth transformed legislative life and work. In the 1940s the House had its norms and the Senate its folkways, perhaps even an inner club.* Hard work, long apprenticeship, restrained participation of younger members, specialization (particularly in the House), courtesy, reciprocity, and institutional loyalty characterized daily life in each chamber. Even if these norms of behavior were only suggestions, frequent contact among colleagues made them a reality. Undoubtedly, members who were neighbors in the same office building, who shared a committee assignment, or who traveled back and forth to Washington from the same state or region came to know each other exceedingly well. But even more distant relationships were based on familiarity and frequent formal or informal meeting.

By the mid-1960s this had all changed. The rubbing of elbows was replaced by liaisons between legislative corporate enterprises, typically at the staff level. Surrounded or protected by a bevy of clerks and assistants, members met other members only occasionally and briefly on the chamber floor or in committee meetings. And many of the norms supporting work and specialization eroded.

With limited time and resources, legislators of the 1940s and 1950s concentrated on only a few activities. They simply did not have the staffs or money to be able to involve themselves in a wide range of policy issues, manage a network of ombudsman activities back home, raise campaign finances, or intercede broadly and frequently in the executive branch's administration of programs. Rather, they picked their spots selectively and depended on jurisdictional decentralization and reciprocity among committees to divide the legislative labor, on the legislative party for voting cues inside the chamber, and on local party organizations for campaign resources and electioneering.

During the 1960s, as congressional offices gained staff and funding, members began to take on many new activities. Larger staffs in district offices, trips home, and franking privileges enabled them to develop a personal presence before their constituencies. This permitted them to orchestrate electioneering, polling, voter mobilization, and campaign finance activities themselves. They grew less dependent on organizations outside their own enterprises—local parties, for example—which previously performed such functions. The geographic constituency had, of course, always been important, but it had often been mediated by party, both local and national. By the mid-1960s the members' relationships with their constituencies were growing increasingly unmediated (just as the relationships between members were growing increasingly mediated). They were constant presences in their districts, had begun to develop personal followings, and consequently achieved a certain independence from their parties (and hence some insulation from party fortunes). As members made more trips home and allocated more staff to district offices and more Washington staff to constituency service

---

* The consensus view of the Senate of this era emphasized its dominance by a core of generally senior senators, who came disproportionately but not exclusively from the South.

and constituency-oriented legislation, calculations of how they would present themselves to the folks back home and explain their Washington activities took on added importance. Constituents' needs (the geographic imperative) began to compete with party as a guide to behavior.

Personal and institutional arrangements in Washington also changed. In the 1950s members, especially in the House, limited themselves to work on a few issues, determined to a considerable extent by their places in the committee system. Most members were able to land assignments to committees that were directly relevant to their constituencies. Much of their time, energy, and limited staff resources were devoted to work inside these little legislatures. By partitioning policy into committee jurisdictions, and matching member interests with those jurisdictions, legislative arrangements permitted members to get the most out of their limited resources. Aside from those with institutional ambitions, who hoped one day to be appointed to the Appropriations, Rules, or Ways and Means committees (Appropriations, Finance, Foreign Relations, or Armed Services in the Senate), most members had only limited incentives to become actively involved in policy areas outside their own assignments and were content to serve on legislative committees that had jurisdiction over the issues of central importance to their constituents. Thus, with limited means and incentives, members sustained a system of deference and reciprocity as part of the 1950s equilibrium, especially in the House.

Because of the growth of resources within their own enterprises in the 1960s, members began to acquire enhanced in-house capabilities. Deference to expert committee judgments on policy outside the jurisdiction of committees on which a member served was no longer so necessary. Members could now afford to assign some of their staff to track developments in other policy areas. The charge to the staffer became "Find something of interest for the boss, something that will help the district." Members were also no longer so dependent on party signals; with greater resources they were better able to determine their interests. In short, greater resources led to vertical integration—the absorption into the member enterprise of activities formerly conducted outside it—and with that, to member independence. Consequently, the relationship in which jurisdiction constrained both interest and activism began to fray as the 1960s came to an end.

Incentives for members to break away from the institutional niches in which they found themselves also multiplied. In both the 1960s and the 1970s, reapportionments,* along with economic and demographic changes, produced congressional districts that were neither so purely rural nor so purely urban as they had been. Increasingly, the districts were mixed, often including a major city and a number of towns, as well as perhaps some rural areas. Member

---

* The Constitution mandates reapportionment of House seats among the states every ten years. This requirement became especially significant in the 1960s and 1970s as the Supreme Court interpreted the Constitution to mean that districts should be drawn as equally in population as possible.

interests began to reflect this heterogeneity. Issues were also evolving in ways that cut across existing interest-group configurations and committee jurisdictions. Except in a few cases, one or two major committee jurisdictions could no longer encompass the interests of a district. Members thus had to diversify their portfolios of legislative activities. And this meant less specialization, less deference, less reciprocity.

Thus the limited resources and truncated policy interests characteristic of House members and to a lesser extent members of the Senate in the 1940s and 1950s began to give way in the 1960s and 1970s. Increased member resources and more diverse constituencies provided both the means and the incentives for members to break out of a now restrictive division and specialization of labor. Geographic imperatives were beginning to supersede considerations of party and seniority to become the principal basis on which members defined their responsibilities and work habits. Geography was also beginning to threaten jurisdiction as the principal basis on which the House organized its business.

These changes were less dramatic in the Senate only because it had traditionally been a much less specialized institution. Resources were more plentiful and constituencies more heterogeneous than in the House. And because the Senate was smaller, members had to have more diverse activities and interests. Yet even in the Senate the pressure toward less specialization was growing. Entire states were becoming more heterogeneous as a result of the industrialization of the South, the switch to a service economy in the North, and the nationalization of financial matters (so that even South Dakota could become a center for credit activities). And senators, like their House counterparts, were expanding their enterprises. By the end of the period the Senate, though less dramatically than the House, was also a less specialized place.

The argument I am making here is that geography, jurisdiction, and party hang together in a sort of equilibrium. The 1940s and 1950s represented one such equilibrium in which local parties helped the members get elected and legislative parties loosely coordinated committee activity. But the division of labor and committee dominance of jurisdiction were the central features of the textbook Congress. Committees both accommodated member needs and controlled agendas and decisionmaking. This arrangement "advantaged senior members, committees, and the majority party, with the chairmen of the standing committees sitting at the intersection of these groups." More heterogeneous constituencies and increased member resources upset this textbook equilibrium. Members have adapted by voting themselves even more resources and expanding their activities. By the 1970s parties both inside and outside the legislature had become considerably more submissive holding companies for member enterprises than had earlier been the case. Committees, too, had changed character. . . .

Beginning with the 1958 elections, however, and continuing throughout the 1960s, a new breed of legislator was coming to Washington, one more committed to legislative activism and policy entrepreneurship than in the past, one beginning to reflect demographic changes, and, most important, one that found ways to stay in office. By the early 1970s these legislators had accumulated considerable seniority. Thus the old equilibrium was disrupted and the stage set for institutional developments that would strike at the heart of the textbook Congress.

The Changing Textbook Congress: The 1970s and 1980s

An idiosyncratic historical factor had an important bearing on the institutional reforms of the 1970s that undermined the textbook Congress. For much of the twentieth century the Democratic party in Congress spoke with a heavy southern accent. In 1948, for example, more than 53 percent of the Democrats in the House and nearly 56 percent of those in the Senate came from the eleven Confederate states and five border states (Kentucky, Maryland, Missouri, Oklahoma, and West Virginia). These states accounted for only a third of all House and Senate seats. Beginning with the 1958 landslide, however, this distribution changed. In 1960 the same sixteen states accounted for just under 50 percent of Democratically held House seats and 43 percent of Democratically held Senate seats. By 1982 the numbers had fallen to 40 percent and 39 percent, respectively, and have held at that level. . . . Increasingly, Democrats were winning and holding seats in the North and West and, to a somewhat lesser extent, Republicans were becoming competitive in the South.

The nationalization of the Democratic coalition in Congress, however, was reflected far more slowly at the top of the seniority ladder.* Although between 1955 and 1967 the proportion of southern Democrats (border states excluded) in the House had dropped from 43 percent to 35 percent (46 percent to 28 percent in the Senate), the proportion of House committee chairs held by southerners fell from 63 percent to 50 percent, and rose from 53 percent to 56 percent in the Senate. Southerners held two of the three exclusive committee chairs in the House and two of the four in the Senate in 1955; in 1967 they held all of them.

The tension between liberal rank-and-file legislators and conservative southern committee chairs was important in the 1960s but had few institutional repercussions. True, Judge Howard Smith (Democrat of Virginia), the tyrannical chairman of the House Rules Committee, lost in a classic power struggle with Speaker Rayburn in 1961. But the defeat should not be exaggerated. Committees and their chairs maintained both the power to propose legislation and the power to block it in their respective jurisdictions. In 1967 southern Democrats George H. Mahon of Texas, William M. Colmer of Mississippi, and Wilbur D. Mills of Arkansas chaired the Appropriations, Rules, and Ways and Means committees, respectively, in a manner not very different from that of the incumbents a decade

---

* *Seniority* means the number of consecutive terms a legislator has served on a committee. The most senior majority-party member would automatically become chair of the committee. This practice was modified but not eliminated in the 1970s.

earlier. Although the massive legislative productivity of the Eighty-ninth Congress (1965–66) did much to relieve this tension, it relieved it not so much by changing legislative institutions as by managing to mobilize very large liberal majorities. After the 1966 elections, and with the Vietnam War consuming more and more resources and attention, the Eighty-ninth Congress increasingly seemed like a brief interlude in the committee dominance that stretched back to World War II, if not earlier.

By the end of the 1960s a Democratic president had been chased from office, and the 1968 Democratic convention revealed the tensions created by the war in Vietnam and disagreements over a range of domestic issues. Despite a Democratic landslide in 1964, Republican gains for the decade amounted to thirty-eight seats in the House and eight in the Senate, further accentuating the liberal cast of the Democratic rank and file in Congress. As the 1970s opened, then, liberal Democratic majorities in each chamber confronted a conservative president [Richard Nixon], conservative Republican minorities in each chamber, and often conservative southern committee chairmen of their own party who together blocked many of their legislative initiatives. The liberals thus turned inward, using the Democratic Caucus to effect dramatic changes in institutional practices, especially in the House.

The Age of Reform   Despite the tensions it caused, the mature committee system had many advantages. The division of labor in the House not only allowed for decisions based on expertise, but perhaps more important, it sorted out and routinized congressional careers. Committees provided opportunities for political ambitions to be realized, and they did so in a manner that encouraged members to invest in committee careers. In an undifferentiated legislature, or in a committee-based legislature in which the durability of a committee career or the prospects for a committee leadership post depended on the wishes and whims of powerful party leaders (for example, the Speaker in the nineteenth century House), individual legislators have less incentive to invest effort in committee activities. Such investments are put at risk every time the political environment changes. Specialization and careerism are encouraged, however, when rewards depend primarily on individual effort (and luck), and not on the interventions and patronage of others. An important by-product is the encouragement given talented men and women to come to the legislature and to remain there. The slow predictability of career development under a seniority system may repel the impatient, but its inexorability places limits on risks by reducing a member's dependence on arbitrary power and unexpected events.

Even Voltaire's optimistic Dr. Pangloss, however, would recognize another side to this coin. When a committee system that links geography and jurisdiction through the assignment process is combined with an institutional bargain producing deference and reciprocity, it provides the foundation for the distributive politics of interest-group liberalism. But there are no guarantees of success. The legislative process is full of hurdles and veto groups, and occasionally they restrain legislative activism enough to stimulate a reaction. Thus in the 1950s, authorizing committees, frustrated by a stingy House Appropriations Committee, created entitlements as a means of circumventing the normal appropriations process. In the 1960s the Rules Committee became the major obstacle and it, too, was tamed. In the 1970s the Ways and Means Committee, which lacked an internal division of labor through subcommittees, bottled up many significant legislative proposals; it was dealt with by the Subcommittee Bill of Rights and the Committee Reform Amendments of 1974. The solution in the 1950s had no effect on legislative arrangements. The solution in the 1960s entailed modest structural reform that directly affected only one committee. In the 1970s, however, the committee system itself became the object of tinkering.

The decade of the 1970s was truly an age of legislative reform. In effect, it witnessed a representational revolt against a system that dramatically skewed rewards toward the old and senior who were often out of step with fellow partisans. It is a long story, admirably told in detail elsewhere. Here I shall focus on the way reforms enabled the rise of four power centers that competed, and continue to compete, with the standing committees for political influence.

First, full committees and their chairs steadily lost power to their subcommittees. At least since the Legislative Reorganization Act of 1946, subcommittees have been a significant structural element of the committee system in the House. However, until the 1970s they were principally a tool of senior committee members, especially committee chairmen, who typically determined subcommittee structure, named members, assigned bills, allocated staff resources, and orchestrated the timing and sequence in which the full committee would take up their proposals and forward them to the floor. Because the structures were determined idiosyncratically by individual chairmen, committees could be very different. Ways and Means had no subcommittees. Armed Services had numbered subcommittees with no fixed jurisdictions. Appropriations had rigidly arranged subcommittees. In almost all cases the chairman called the tune, despite an occasional committee revolt.

During the 1970s a series of reforms whittled away at the powers of the committee chairmen. In 1970 chairmen began to lose some control of their agendas. They could no longer refuse to call meetings; a committee majority could vote to meet anyway with the ranking majority member presiding. Once a rule had been granted for floor consideration of a bill, the chairman could not delay consideration for more than a week; after seven days, a committee majority could move floor consideration.

In 1973 the Democratic members of a House committee were designated as the committee caucus and empowered to choose subcommittee chairs and set subcommittee budgets. During the next two years, committees developed a procedure that allowed members, in order of committee seniority, to bid for subcommittee chairmanships. Also in 1973 the Democratic Caucus passed the Subcommittee Bill of Rights, which mandated that legislation be referred to subcommittees, that subcommittees have full control over their own agendas, and that they be provided with adequate staff and budget. In 1974 the Committee Reform Amendments required that full committees (Budget and Rules excepted) establish at least four subcommittees, an implicit strike against the undifferentiated structure of Ways and Means. In 1976 committee caucuses were given the authority to determine the number of subcommittees and their respective jurisdictions. Finally, in 1977 the selection procedure for committee chairs was changed, allowing the party caucus to elect them by secret ballot.

Full committees and their chairs thus had had their wings clipped. A chair was now beholden to the committee caucus, power had devolved upon subcommittees, and standing committees were rapidly becoming holding companies for their subunits.

Another center of power was created by the growth of member resources. Through House Resolution 5 and Senate Resolution 60, members were able to tap into committee and subcommittee budgets to hire staff to conduct their committee work. Additional resources were available for travel and office support. Budgets for congressional support agencies such as the General Accounting Office, the Congressional Research Service, and the Office of Technology Assessment, which individual members could employ for specific projects, also increased enormously. In short, member enterprises were becoming increasingly self-sufficient.

Committee power was also compromised by increased voting and amendment activity on the floor. The early 1970s marked the virtual end to anonymous floor votes. The secret ballot was never used in floor votes in the House, but voice votes, division votes, and unrecorded teller votes had allowed tallies to be detached from the identity of individual members. This changed as it became increasingly easy to demand a public roll call, a demand greatly facilitated by the advent of electronic voting in 1973. Roll call votes in turn stimulated amendment activity on the floor. In effect, full committees and their chairs, robbed of some of their control of agendas by subcommittees, were now robbed of more control by this change in floor procedure.

Floor activity was further stimulated by the declining frequency with which the Rules Committee was permitted to issue closed rules, which barred floor amendments to legislation. The specific occasion for this change was the debate on retaining the oil depletion allowance. Because this tax break was protected by the Ways and Means Committee, on which the oil-producing states were well represented, efforts to change the policy could only come about through floor amendments. But Ways and Means bills traditionally were protected by a closed rule. The Democratic Caucus devised a policy in which a caucus majority could instruct its members on the Rules Committee to vote specific amendments in order. Applying this strategy to the oil depletion allowance, the caucus in effect ended the tradition of closed-rule protection of committee bills. This encouraged floor amendments and at the same time reduced committee control over final legislation. It also encouraged committees to anticipate floor behavior more carefully when they marked up a bill.

Finally, committee dominance was challenged by the increased power of the Democratic Caucus and the Speaker. For all the delegation of committee operations to subcommittees and individual members, the changes in the congressional landscape were not all of one piece. In particular, before the 1970s the Democratic Caucus was a moribund organization primarily concerned with electing officers and attending to the final stages of committee assignments. After these activities were completed in the first few days of a new Congress, the caucus was rarely heard from. In the 1970s, however, as committees and chairmen were being undermined by subcommittees, there was a parallel movement to strengthen central party leadership and rank-and-file participation.

The first breach came in the seniority system. In 1971 the Democratic Caucus relieved its Committee on Committees—the Democratic members of the Ways and Means Committee—of having to rely on seniority in nominating committee chairs. This had the effect of putting sitting chairs on notice, although none was threatened at the time. In 1974 it became possible for a small number of caucus members to force individual votes on nominees for chairs and later to vote by secret ballot. In 1975 the caucus took upon itself the right to vote on subcommittee chairs of the Appropriations Committee. In that same year three incumbent chairmen were denied reelection to their posts (a fourth, Wilbur Mills, resigned under pressure).

Next came the democratizing reforms. Members were limited in the number of committee and subcommittee berths they could occupy and the number they could chair. As the constraints became more binding, it was necessary to move further down the ladder of seniority to fill positions. Power thus became more broadly distributed.

But perhaps the most significant reforms were those that strengthened the Speaker and made the position accountable to the caucus. In 1973 House party leaders (Speaker, majority leader, and whip) were included on the Committee on Committees, giving them an increased say in committee assignments. The caucus also established the Steering and Policy Committee with the Speaker as chair. In 1974 Democratic committee assignments were taken away from the party's complement on Ways and Means and given to the new committee. In addition, the Speaker was given the power to appoint and remove a majority of the members of the committee and the Democratic members of the Rules Committee. In 1974 the Speaker also was empowered to refer bills simultaneously or sequentially to several committees, to create ad hoc committees, and, in 1977, to set time limits for their deliberations. Finally, in 1977 Speaker Thomas P. O'Neill started employing task forces to develop and manage particular policy issues. These task forces overlapped but were not coincident with the committees of jurisdiction and, most significant, they were appointed by the Speaker.

The caucus itself became more powerful. As mentioned, caucus majorities could instruct the Rules Committee and elect committee chairs and Appropriations subcommittee chairs. Caucus meetings could be called easily, requiring only a small number of signatories to a request, so that party matters could be thoroughly aired. In effect, the caucus became a substitute arena for both the floor and the committee rooms in which issues could be joined and majorities mobilized.

The revolt of the 1970s thus strengthened four power centers. It liberated members and subcommittees, restored to the Speakership an authority it had not known since the days of Joe Cannon,* and invigorated the party caucus. Some of the reforms had a decentralizing effect, some a recentralizing effect. Standing committees and their chairs were caught in the middle. Geography and party benefited; the division-of-labor jurisdictions were its victims. . . .

A New Textbook Congress?

The textbook Congress of the 1940s and 1950s reflected an equilibrium of sorts among institutional structure, partisan alignments, and electoral forces. There was a "conspiracy" between jurisdiction and geography. Congressional institutions were organized around policy jurisdictions, and geographic forces were accommodated through an assignment process that ensured representatives would land berths on committees important to their constituents. Reciprocity and deference sealed the bargain. Committees controlled policy formation in their respective jurisdictions. Floor activity was generally dominated by members from the committee of jurisdiction. Members' resources were sufficiently modest that they were devoted chiefly to committee-related activities. Constituencies were sufficiently homogeneous that this limitation did not, for most members, impose much hardship. Coordination was accomplished by senior committee members, each minding his own store. This system was supported by a structure that rewarded specialization, hard work, and waiting one's turn in the queue. Parties hovered in the background as the institutional means for organizing each chamber and electing leaders. Occasionally they would serve to mobilize majorities for partisan objectives, but these occasions were rare. The parties, especially the Democrats, were heterogeneous holding companies, incapable of cohering around specific policy directions except under unusual circumstances and therefore unwilling to empower their respective leaders or caucuses.

Something happened in the 1960s. The election of an executive and a congressional majority from the same party certainly was one important feature. Policy

---

* Representative Joseph Cannon (R-Ill.) served as Speaker from 1903 to 1911. His power in this office was successfully challenged by a coalition of Democrats and dissident Republicans in 1910.

activism, restrained since the end of World War II, was encouraged. This exacerbated some divisions inside the Democratic coalition, leading to piecemeal institutional tinkering such as the expansion of the Rules Committee and the circumvention of the Appropriations Committee. At the same time the Voting Rights Act, occasioned by the temporarily oversized condition of the majority party in the Eighty-ninth Congress, set into motion political events that, together with demographic and economic trends, altered political alignments in the South. By the 1980s, Democrats from the North and the South were coming into greater agreement on matters of policy.

Thus the underlying conditions supporting the equilibrium among geographical, jurisdictional, and partisan imperatives were overwhelmed during the 1960s. The 1970s witnessed adjustments to these changed conditions that transformed the textbook Congress. Institutional reform was initiated by the Democratic Caucus. Demographic, generational, and political trends, frustrated by the inexorable workings of the seniority system, sought an alternative mode of expression. Majorities in the caucus remade the committee system. With this victimization came less emphasis on specialization, less deference toward committees as the floor became a genuine forum for policy formulation, and a general fraying of the division of labor.

One trend began with the Legislative Reorganization Act of 1946 itself. In the past forty years members have gradually acquired the resources to free themselves from other institutional players. The condition of the contemporary member of Congress has been described as "atomistic individualism" and the members themselves have been called "enterprises." The slow accretion of resources permitted members to respond to the changes in their home districts and encouraged them to cross the boundaries of specialization. These developments began to erode the reciprocity, deference, and division of labor that defined the textbook Congress.

The old equilibrium between geography and jurisdiction, with party hovering in the background, has changed. Geography (as represented by resource-rich member enterprises) has undermined the strictures of jurisdiction. But has the new order liberated party from its former holding-company status? In terms of political power the Democratic Caucus has reached new heights in the past decade. Party leaders have not had so many institutional tools and resources since the days of Boss Cannon. Committee leaders have never in the modern era been weaker or more beholden to party institutions. And, in terms of voting behavior, Democrats and Republicans have not exhibited as much internal cohesion in a good long while. Party, it would seem, is on the rise. But so, too, are the member enterprises.

What, then, has grown up in the vacuum created by the demise of the textbook Congress? I am not convinced that relationships have settled into a regular pattern in anything like the way they were institutionalized in the textbook Congress.

First, too many members of Congress remain too dissatisfied. The aggressive moves by Jim Wright* to redefine the Speaker's role are a partial response to this circumstance. Prospective changes in the Senate majority party leadership alignment in the 101st Congress convey a similar signal. The issue at stake is whether central party organs can credibly coordinate activities in Congress, thereby damping the centrifugal tendencies of resource-rich members, or whether leaders will remain, in one scholar's words, "janitors for an untidy chamber."

One possible equilibrium of a new textbook Congress, therefore, would have member enterprises balanced off against party leaders; committees and other manifestations of a specialized division of labor would be relegated to the background. Coordination, formerly achieved in a piecemeal, decentralized fashion by the committee system, would fall heavily on party leaders and their institutional allies, the Rules and Budget committees and the party caucuses. However, unless party leaders can construct a solution to the budgetary mess in Congress— a solution that will entail revising the budget process—the burden of coordination will be more than the leaders can bear. Government by continuing resolutions, reconciliation proposals, and other omnibus mechanisms forms an unstable fulcrum for institutional equilibrium.[†]

Second, any success from the continued strengthening of leadership resources and institutions is highly contingent on the support of the members. Strong leadership institutions have to be seen by the rank and file as solutions to institutional problems. This requires a consensus among majority party members both on the nature of the problems and the desirability of the solutions. A consensus of sorts has existed for several years: demographic and other trends have homogenized the priorities of Democrats; experience with the spate of reforms in the 1970s has convinced many that decentralized ways of doing things severely tax the capacity of Congress to act; and, since 1982, the Reagan presidency has provided a unifying target.

But what happens if the bases for consensus erode? A major issue—trade and currency problems, for instance, or war in Central America or the Middle East—could set region against region within the majority party and reverse the trend toward consensus. Alternatively, the election of a Democratic president could redefine the roles of legislative leaders, possibly pitting congressional and presidential factions against one another in a battle for partisan leadership.[‡] The

---

* Jim Wright was Speaker from 1987 to 1989.

[†] Reconciliation proposals and continuing resolutions are budget-related bills that often combine many subjects in a catch-all (or omnibus) piece of legislation. Control by committees or other specialized groupings is rendered difficult by such practices.

[‡] As of 1994, that had not happened much in the Clinton administration, although House Democratic Whip David Bonior did lead the opposition to the Clinton-backed North American Free Trade Agreement in 1993.

point here is that the equilibrium between strong leaders and strong members is vulnerable to perturbations in the circumstances supporting it.

. . . The member enterprises, however, will not go away. Members will never again be as specialized, as deferential, as willing "to go along to get along" as in the textbook Congress of the 1950s. For better or worse, we are stuck with full-service members of Congress. They are incredibly competent at representing the diverse interests that geographic representation has given them. But can they pass a bill or mobilize a coalition? Can they govern?

Questions for Discussion

1. How did the seniority system, which rewarded simple longevity rather than talent or political support, survive for so long? What are the advantages of promoting leaders based on seniority? The liabilities?
2. Why do you think legislators create strong "member enterprises"? Why might these undermine the committee system?

 10.2

Ten Things I Wish Political Scientists Would Teach About Congress

Lee H. Hamilton

For 34 years, Representative Lee H. Hamilton (D-Ind.) served with distinction in the U.S. House. He chaired the International Relations Committee, and he acted consistently to educate his constituents and the American public about the complexities of Congress. Since retiring in 1998, he has headed the Woodrow Wilson International Center for Scholars and Congressional Institute at Indiana University. He delivered the following remarks to more than a thousand attentive academics at the annual meeting of the American Political Science Association in 2000.

Although Hamilton's speech was warmly received, his thoughts are even more impressive and compelling in print. He implores political scientists to teach about the Congress that he knows—an imperfect but essential body that plays a crucial role in knitting the fabric of American politics. Although his remarks were directed at teachers, they were ultimately targeted toward students. Every student of American politics should seriously consider this thoughtful veteran legislator's arguments.

My purpose this afternoon is to offer some thoughts on the role that you, as political scientists, can play in improving public understanding of the U.S. Congress.

I do not know what each of you teaches about the Congress—but I do know—on the basis of several thousand public meetings over three decades—that the lack of public understanding about the institution is huge.

That lack of understanding among ordinary Americans concerns me deeply because it increases the public's suspicions and cynicism about the Congress, weakens the relationship between voters and their representatives, makes it harder for public officials to govern, and prevents our representative democracy from working the way it should. . . .

I believe you can improve public understanding of Congress by teaching several basic, and rather simple, lessons about this sometimes puzzling institution.

My concern here is not with *your* understanding of the Congress. In my experience, political scientists understand the institution very well. And I know that many of you are excellent teachers who teach many of the things that I will recommend—and much more.

The point I want to make is that you, as much as anyone, have the power to influence the way Americans view our political system. That is not an influence you, or anyone else, should take lightly, because the way Americans look at politics shapes the capacity of our government to meet the needs of the country. . . .

Ten Things to Teach About Congress

So, here are several basic lessons about Congress that I would like you to teach.

Lesson #1: Congress is the most important link between the American people and their national government. . . . Many Americans have little appreciation for the basic function and role of Congress in our political system. I want you to help them understand that Congress is the institution whose job it is to seek consensus out of the many and diverse views of the American people. I want you to explain that Congress performs the extraordinary task of legislating and overseeing the government in the interest of more than 275 million Americans.

For all its deficiencies—which I will get to later—Congress has three great strengths:

1. *Representative:* Congress is, by far, the most representative institution in the United States. We live in a complicated country of vast size and remarkable diversity. Our people are many; they're spread far and wide; and they represent a great variety of beliefs, religions, and ethnicities. It isn't easy for such a country to live together peacefully and productively. Although Congress does not perfectly mirror the demographics of the American people, it does help bind us together by representing the country's great diversity.

2. *Accessible:* Congress is also accessible—much more so than any other part of the federal government. Congress is the primary "listening post" of the people. If an ordinary American has a complaint or suggestion about the government, he cannot reach the President, or the Vice President, or a cabinet secretary—or even a deputy assistant secretary. He can reach his Representative or Senator.

3. *Deliberative:* And Congress is our nation's chief deliberative body. It is the place where the many views and interests of the American people on all manner of subjects get thrashed out. It remains the central forum for vigorous public debate, consensus building and decision making on the most important issues of the day.

Lesson #2: Congress has a major impact on people's everyday lives. . . . Many Americans believe Congress accomplishes little and is simply irrelevant to their daily lives. I'd like you to help correct that misperception. . . .

Not long before I left Congress, a group of constituents visiting my Indiana office told me that Congress was irrelevant. So I asked them a few questions. How had they gotten to my office? On the interstate highway, they said. Had any of them gone to the local university? Yes, they said, admitting they'd got some help from federal student loans. Did any of them have grandparents on Social Security and Medicare? Well sure, they replied, picking up on where I was headed. Their lives had been profoundly affected by Congress. They just hadn't focused on all of the connections before.

Americans pay more attention to Congress as they understand the impact congressional decisions have on the fabric of their lives. When Congress funds basic research in science, it's helping create the future cures for deadly diseases. When it raises the minimum wage, it's enabling people to rise out of poverty. When it protects national parks, it's preserving our natural heritage. . . .

It's remarkable how quickly we forget that Congress has been involved in some big things in recent years.

+ Erasing the federal deficit.
+ Overhauling the welfare and public housing systems.
+ Rewriting telecommunications laws.

♦ Approving billions to improve roads and bridges.
♦ Liberalizing international trade.

Although we may not all like what Congress did on each of these issues, after debating policy options and gauging public sentiment, it acted.

I'm amazed every year by the headlines that come out—especially in the summer—saying that Congress is drifting, or deadlocked, or dysfunctional, or dead in the water. This talk of a "do nothing" Congress is almost always misleading and off the mark.

Even when Congress is not producing blockbuster bills, Members are typically working on scores of other, less-publicized matters that sustain and improve the quality of life here and abroad. Every year, Congress passes appropriations bills that fund hundreds of billions of dollars worth of important federal programs. It also spends time overseeing those programs and laying the groundwork for future action on matters that take more than one Congress to resolve. The Clean Air Act and Immigration Reform Act, for instance, took multiple Congresses to complete due to their inherent complexity.

The pundits like to judge Congress midstream, during the middle of a session or when it is struggling to reach consensus on an issue. These judgments are usually premature. If we look at the record of Congress at the end of a session, we will usually find that it has accomplished more than we might have expected, and a lot more than was predicted by the pundits in August.

Lesson #3: *Congress was not designed to move quickly and efficiently.* . . . One of the most common complaints about the Congress is that it's always arguing and bickering. I must have heard the complaint a hundred times: "Why can't you guys ever agree? This perception is a major factor in the public's lack of confidence in the institution.

Why is it so difficult for Congress to reach agreement? Part of the answer involves politics. The struggle for partisan or personal advantage, particularly in an election year, can stall the work of Congress substantially.

But there is much more to it than that. Our system of government was intentionally set up with many checks and balances to prevent hasty action. Legislative dispute and delay, while frustrating, are not necessarily signs of democracy in decay.

The task of achieving consensus is made especially difficult today because the issues before Congress are so numerous, complex and technical, and they come at Members with staggering rapidity.

In the Federalist Papers, Madison wrote that a Member of Congress must understand just three issues: commerce, taxation and the militia. To a Member today, that observation is a bit quaint, to say the least.

Take the ten most difficult issues facing our country and you can be sure that Congress will take each of them up in some form over the coming year.

New, complex issues are constantly being added to the congressional docket. A few years ago, I sat down with the Speaker of the House to discuss what bills should be placed on the House calendar in the closing days of the session. The Speaker noted that most of the issues we were discussing would not even have been on the agenda 15 years earlier.

Many Americans think that reasonable people agree on the solutions to major national problems, and they see no good reason for Congress not to implement such a consensus. Yet the truth is there is far less consensus in the country than is often thought. Survey after survey shows that Americans don't even agree on what are the most important issues facing the country, let alone the best way to solve them.

People misunderstand Congress' role if they demand that Congress be a model of efficiency and quick action. Congress can work quickly if a broad consensus exists in the country. But such a consensus is rare—especially on the tough issues at the forefront of public life today. Usually, Congress must build a consensus. It cannot simply impose one on the American people.

The quest for consensus can be painfully slow, and even exasperating, but it is the only way to resolve disputes peacefully and produce policies that reflect the varied perspectives of our diverse citizenry.

Lesson #4: The legislative process is dynamic and complex. . . . When I visit with students in American government classes, I make a point of flipping through their textbooks to see the diagram illustrating "How a Bill Becomes a Law." The diagram usually explains that a piece of legislation, once introduced, moves through subcommittee and committee, then to the House and Senate floors, then to a House-Senate conference, and finally to the President for his signature or veto.

In a technical sense, of course, these diagrams are generally accurate. But my reaction to them is: "How boring! How sterile!" They fail to convey the challenge, the hard work, the excitement, the obstacles to overcome, the political pressures, the defeats suffered, and the victories achieved to enact legislation. They give a woefully incomplete picture of how complicated and untidy the legislative process can be, and they barely hint at the clash of interests and the multitude of difficult things a Member must do to shepherd an idea into law.

One of the most important and time-consuming aspects of the legislative process is conversation: the scores—even hundreds—of one-on-one talks that a skillful Member will have with colleagues to make the case for a particular bill, to learn what arguments opponents will use to try to block it, and to get a sense of what adjustments might be needed to move it along.

These conversations end up posing difficult dilemmas to a Member pushing a bill. For instance, should the Member alter the proposal to broaden its appeal, or keep the bill as it is and hope to defeat the opposition?

How should the Member use the media—to rally public support behind the measure, put pressure on opponents, and advance the legislation? Making news is now a key part of making law.

The increased size and scope of individual bills today makes the legislative process still more complicated. Almost half of the major bills are referred to more than one committee in each chamber. *Ad hoc* caucuses are sometimes created to address new concerns. As the number of actors involved proliferates, the possibilities for conflict over a bill increase.

All of this adds up to a process that is extremely dynamic, unpredictable and messy. There are ways for astute Members to get around nearly every stage in the traditional model of the process.*

As chair of the House Foreign Affairs Committee, I was sometimes surprised to see a bill that I had submitted to the Rules Committee† returned to me with many provisions I had never seen before—because the House leadership, or someone else, had intervened to alter it. That same bill might then be altered further before it moved to the floor.

Even for Members, it can be difficult to know when and where the key decisions on a bill will be made.

Lesson #5. *The country needs more politicians.* . . . Members of Congress are, first and foremost, politicians. Their number one objective is to get re-elected.

Yet the art of politics does not often get high praise these days. When the federal government was almost shut down a few years back, that was considered "politics." When Washington, D.C. was consumed by the impeachment of President Clinton, and the rest of the people's business had to take a back seat, that was attributed to "politics."

Showing skill as a "politician" has come to mean demonstrating the ability to raise campaign funds, to engage in the tit-for-tat exchange of negative advertising, to fudge your positions, or to jockey for public support based on polls and focus groups.

But the fact is that good politicians are vital to the success of our representative democracy. When I say "politician," I mean someone who knows how to practice the art of politics.

This art involves an assortment of important, but often underappreciated, skills. Good politicians must know how to listen—in order to find out what people want. They must be able to build support for their ideas with colleagues, constituents and key individuals. They must search for common ground across parties and among people with diverse interests. They must be able to compro-

---

* For an extended discourse on this development, see Barbara Sinclair's aptly titled *Unorthodox Lawmaking,* 2nd ed. (Washington: CQ Press, 2001).

† The Rules Committee, controlled by the majority party leadership, establishes the conditions for debate and passage of bills on the House floor.

mise while preserving core beliefs. And they must get results—achieving passage of legislation that meets people's needs.

To avoid coming apart at the seams, our country needs people who know how to practice the art of politics. That is what good politicians do: they make democratic government possible in a nation alive with competing factions.

Politicians may not be popular, but they are indispensable to making representative democracy work. That's why we need more politicians, not fewer.

Lesson #6: Members of Congress behave better than people think. . . . The perception that Members are corrupt, or immoral, or enriching themselves at the taxpayer's expense, takes a serious toll on our system of government.

Several years ago, I was watching the evening news on television when the anchorman announced the death of Wilbur Mills, the legendary former Chairman of the House Ways and Means Committee. There was a lot he could have said about Mills. He could have recounted the central role Mills played in creating Medicare, in shaping the Social Security system, or in drafting the tax code. But he didn't. Instead, he recalled how Mills' career had foundered after he'd been found early one morning with an Argentinean stripper named Fanne Foxe.

Now, one of the perks of being chairman of an influential committee in Congress, as I was at the time, is that you can pick up the phone and get through to television news anchors. Which I did. I chided him for summing up Mills' career with a scandal. Much to my surprise, he apologized.

The fact is, though, he wasn't doing anything unusual. Americans of all stripes like to dwell on misbehavior by members of Congress. People look at the latest scandal and assume they're seeing the real Congress. But they're not, not by a long shot.

Don't get me wrong. I'm not proposing my former colleagues for sainthood. But as the press lauds two vice presidential candidates—Republican Dick Cheney and Democrat Joe Lieberman—for their probity in Congress, we should remember that probity is the rule, not the exception.

Some Members, of course, do engage in improper conduct—and our system of financing elections degrades politician and donor alike—but my experience is that most Members are remarkable people who care deeply about our country and seek to better it through their public service. Most could make far more money on the outside, but choose to serve in Congress because they want to contribute to their country. . . .

When I entered the House, gifts and the use of campaign contributions for personal use were unrestricted; financial disclosure was not required of Members; there was no written code of conduct; and no standing House ethics committee existed to police the membership. All that has changed.

Certainly, Congress still has major strides to make in this area. . . . But the ethical climate at the Capitol is light years ahead of where it was a couple of decades ago. And, I might add, light years ahead of the common wisdom.

Lesson #7: Members of Congress do pay attention to their constituents. . . .
Often I hear that members of Congress only pay attention to power brokers and
big-time donors and don't care about ordinary citizens. That simply is not true.

Sometimes when I stood in front of a roomful of voters, I could feel a curtain
of doubt hanging between them and me: I took the positions I did, they believed,
because of this or that campaign contribution, not because I'd spent time studying
and weighing the merits of issues. They had given themselves over to cynicism,
and cynicism is the great enemy of democracy. It is very difficult for public
officials to govern when their character, values, and motives are always suspect.

Of course, Members of Congress are influenced by special interests—often too
much, in my view—but they are even more influenced by their constituents.

Members are—for the most part—very good politicians. They know what their
constituents think. They hold numerous public meetings, poll their districts
regularly, talk on the phone with constituents frequently, and answer hundreds of
letters and e-mail messages daily. They are constantly helping to solve constituents' problems.

Members really do believe that constituent views are important; during all my
years in Congress I never heard a Member say otherwise.

. . . In fact, . . . Members are sometimes too close to their constituents—particularly when they risk reflecting their constituents' views at the expense of their
own judgment. It was Lincoln who said that the art of democratic government is
to be out in front of your constituents, but not too far out in front.

Lesson #8: Citizens play an essential role in making Congress work. This
leads me to the next point I'd like you to emphasize in your teaching—that
citizens play an essential role in making Congress work.

The American people bear more responsibility for the success of our representative democracy than they realize. If people don't participate in the political
process, their views cannot be effectively represented. This is not just a matter of
voting. Our system depends upon open and trusting interaction between representatives and the people who elected them.

Let me give you an example of what I mean. Back in the late 1970s, I was
meeting with a group of constituents in Switzerland County, a deeply rural,
tobacco-growing county in the far southern corner of Indiana. It was not a place
I expected to come for enlightenment on international politics.

While talking with the group, though, the subject of the Panama Canal treaties
came up. This was well before the media had focused on the issue, but a man I'd
never met suddenly stood up and laid out the clearest, most evenly reasoned
argument for ratification that I ever did hear on the matter—even after the treaty
debate mushroomed into a raging national issue. I was flabbergasted, but took it
as a humbling reminder that as a Member of Congress, you can always find
constituents who can teach you a thing or two about an issue.

My constituent in Switzerland County understood that the relationship between a citizen and a representative requires more than a quick handshake, or a

vote, or a moment's pause to sign a computer-generated postcard. He understood that there must be a conversation, a process of mutual education, between citizens and representatives.

Many Americans have given up on the conversation. They must understand that they need to get involved if they want our system to improve.

They need to know that the nature of this relationship between the representative and the represented—and the honesty of the exchange between the two—shapes the strength of our representative democracy.

Lesson #9: Congress needs a lot of improvement. . . . I urge you to be unrelenting critics of the Congress—but in the context of everything else I've said so far.

I won't go into detail here because you are familiar with these problems.

- *Money chase:* The incessant money chase—to fund increasingly costly campaigns—diverts Members' attention from their important responsibilities and leads to a growing sense that access is bought and sold.
- *Perpetual campaign:* Many Members—especially Members of the House—operate today in a state of perpetual campaigning. Rather than trying to develop consensus and pass laws, they view the legislative session primarily as an opportunity to frame issues and position themselves for the next election.
- *Ease of re-election:* It is extremely difficult to defeat incumbents in Congress. Their financial advantages are great and they use the redistricting process to create districts that are heavily partisan in their favor. Less than 10 percent of congressional seats—perhaps as few as 12 seats—will be competitive in this November's election. Competitive elections in many House districts would do more to improve the Congress than any other single reform.
- *Partisanship:* Bitter partisanship and personal attacks have become all too common in Congress—poisoning the atmosphere and making it harder to meet the needs of the country.
- *Influence of special interests:* Special interest groups have too much influence over Congress. They play an important role by representing the views of different segments of the population, but they often have tunnel vision—advancing narrow interests at the expense of the national interest.
- *Weakening of committees:* The committee system has been eroded and is close to collapse. Authorizing committees may not even be needed anymore.* Legislation is regularly drafted in informal settings outside the authorizing committees and brought directly to the House or Senate floor. The result is that the main sources of policy expertise are excluded, deliberation is cut short,

---

* Historically, Congress first authorizes action through legislation; it then appropriates funds to pay for that legislation. In recent years, a good deal of legislation has been contained within appropriation bills.

and decisions are more tightly controlled by the congressional leadership. [See selection 10.]

♦ *Failure to think long-term:* Congress devotes too little attention to some of the country's major long-range challenges. How can we ensure that we have adequate food, energy, and water supplies well into the future? How do we maintain a prosperous and open economy? What domestic and international environmental challenges will we face? Congress spends so much of its time struggling to pass its basic spending bills that these kinds of long-term issues are simply set aside and not dealt with.

♦ *Decline in oversight:* Congress doesn't perform adequate oversight of government programs. Oversight of the implementation of laws is at the very core of good government. But congressional oversight has shifted away in recent years from the systematic review of programs to highly politicized investigations of individual public officials. These investigations reduce the time and political will available for rooting out flaws in public policy.

♦ *Scheduling practices:* Current scheduling practices make it difficult for Congress to carry out its responsibilities. Many Members are now in Washington only between Tuesday and Thursday, with the remaining time spent in their districts. The resulting two-and-a-half-to-three-day legislative workweek makes it impossible for Members to attend all of their committee meetings and other official business.

♦ *Appropriations process:* There is a severe lack of accountability in the appropriations process. Congress increasingly turns to omnibus legislation—combining hundreds of different provisions into one huge bill, tacking on unrelated riders and wasteful earmarks, and allowing only one up-or-down vote on the entire package. Not a single Member can know all that is in these bills—and most are familiar with only a small part of them. Simply put, they are abominations.

♦ *Restrictive rules:* The rules for the consideration of bills in the House are often too restrictive. Although there has been some improvement in the 106th Congress [1999–2000], the House leadership has tended over the years to design rules that sharply curtail debate, restrict the opportunity for the average Member to participate, and limit the amendments and policy options that can be considered.

♦ *Senate confirmation of appointments:* The Senate regularly fails to consider presidential nominations for key judicial posts and cabinet positions in a timely manner. Sometimes, senators hold up nominations by tying them to unrelated partisan demands. This practice blocks appointments that are critical for the effective functioning of our government.

♦ *Ceding too much power to the President:* Congress often weakens its own power by acting too timidly. Consider its record in foreign policy. It regularly fails to authorize the use of military force as it is mandated to do by law, and frequently passes the buck to the President by enacting sanctions legislation that only he can decide whether or not to enforce. When Congress fails to measure up to its constitutional responsibility, it cedes power to the President.

Congress must take its own reform seriously. It should work on reform every year—not every ten years, as has been its pattern.

Lesson #10: Our representative democracy works. . . . Our representative democracy works. It may be slow, messy, cumbersome, and even unresponsive at times, but it has many strengths, and continues to serve us well.

Some say our institutions of government—including the Congress—create more problems than they solve. In the past decade, we experienced an intensified assault on government from some quarters, and "government" and "Washington, D.C.," became bad words, symbols of the worst kind of corruption and waste. My hope is that we are now beginning to move away from that kind of extreme antigovernment rhetoric. The more positive tone of the present presidential campaign would suggest that we are.

Representative democracy, for all its faults, is our best hope for dealing with our nation's problems. It works through a process of deliberation, negotiation and compromise—in a word, the process of politics. Politics is the way we represent the will of the people in this country. At its best, our representative democracy gives a system whereby all of us have a voice in the process and a stake in the product.

I don't for a moment agree with those who think that our representative democracy has failed or that the future of the country is bleak.

Just consider the condition of America today. In general I think it is a better place than it was when I came to Congress some 35 years ago.

* The Cold War is over, and we are at peace.
* Our economy is thriving and is the envy of the world.
* We have greatly improved the lot of older Americans with programs like Social Security and Medicare.
* Women and minorities have had new doors opened to them as never before.
* The Internet has brought a world of knowledge to the most remote classrooms and homes.
* And, most of all, this is still a land of opportunity where everyone has a chance, not an equal chance unfortunately, but still a chance to become the best they can be.

Of course, our country still faces serious problems—from reducing economic inequality to improving access to health care to strengthening our schools—but overall we are doing quite well. . . .

Churchill's remark that "democracy is the worst system devised by the wit of man, except for all the others," still rings true.

I would hope that when each student leaves his class, he or she would appreciate that this representative democracy of ours works reasonably well.

Conclusion

I've spoken today about what I would like you to teach about the Congress. Most—perhaps all—of what I have said is elementary and obvious to you. But it is not obvious to ordinary Americans. They perceive only dimly what the Congress is all about.

I know some veteran political scientists, long since tenured, who still insist on teaching an introductory government course to freshmen. They appreciate that their most important duty is to teach their students to understand the political process and to be good citizens.

Your job—and mine, too—is to help Americans understand government—including the Congress—better. I do not know of anything more important for you and me to teach.

Questions for Discussion

1. Of Hamilton's ten items, which one do you see as most problematic? Which is most surprising?
2. Has your assessment of the Congress and its members become more positive after reading Hamilton's speech? Why or why not?

10.3

Going Nowhere: A Gridlocked Congress?

Sarah A. Binder

Until the 1950s and 1960s, the same party usually controlled both the executive and legislative branches of the national government. When government was divided, it was likely part of a transition from one party's dominance to that of the other. Since 1969, however, divided control of the Congress and the presidency has been the rule rather than the exception. And in the 1981–2000 period, only in 1993–1994 did one party (the Democrats) win control of both branches. Most scholars and journalists argue that divided government leads to gridlock and unresponsiveness. In 1990, however, David Mayhew published findings revealing that divided governments were just as productive as those controlled by a single party (he did not discuss the *contents* of the legislation in detail).

Subsequently, Sarah Binder examined the implications of divided control and found that it did make some differences in legislative productivity. Her careful research does not resolve the question of the ultimate impact of divided government, but in this brief *Brookings Review* article, she argues that divided government and other forces do contribute to so-called gridlock. Still, much of what we label gridlock is intrinsic to our system of extensive checks and balances.

Gridlock is not a modern legislative invention. Although the term is said to have entered the American political lexicon after the 1980 elections, Alexander Hamilton was complaining more than two centuries ago about the deadlock rooted in the design of the Continental Congress. In many ways, gridlock is endemic to our national politics, the natural consequence of separated institutions sharing and competing for power.

But even casual observers of Washington recognize tremendous variation in Congress's performance. At times, congressional prowess is stunning. The Great Society Congress under Lyndon Johnson, for example, enacted landmark health care, environment, civil rights, transportation, and education statutes (to name a few). At other times, gridlock prevails, as when, in 1992, congressional efforts

---

Sarah A. Binder is a fellow in the Brookings Governmental Studies program and assistant professor of political science at George Washington University. She is the author of *Minority Rights, Majority Rule: Partisanship and the Development of Congress* (Cambridge, 1997).

to cut the capital gains tax and to reform lobbying, campaign finance, banking, parental leave, and voter registration laws (to name a few) ended in deadlock.

What accounts for such uneven performance? Why is Congress sometimes remarkably successful and other times mired in stalemate? For all our attention to the minutiae of Congress, we know little about the dimensions and causes of gridlock. How much do we have? How often do we get it? What drives it up and down? Such questions are particularly acute today, as Democrats and Republicans trade barbs over the do-nothing 106th Congress. Despite the first budget surplus in 30 years, Congress and the president remain deadlocked over numerous high-profile issues (including Social Security, Medicare, managed health care, and campaign finance reform), and they show few prospects of acting on these and other salient issues before the 2000 elections.*

An Elusive Concept

Some argue that gridlock is simply a constant of American political life. James Madison bequeathed us a political system designed not to work, a government of sharply limited powers. But surely the framers (dissatisfied with their governing experiment after the Revolution and fearful of rebellious debtors in the states) sought a strong national government that could govern—deliberately and efficiently, albeit insulated from the passions of popular majorities. Gridlock may be a frequent *consequence* of the Constitution, but that does not mean the framers *preferred* it.

Others might object to labeling legislative inaction as "gridlock." If a government that "governs least governs best," then policy stability should be applauded, not derided as gridlock. But views about gridlock tend to vary with one's political circumstance. Former Senate Majority Leader Bob Dole put it best: "If you're against something, you'd better hope there's a little gridlock." Legislative action, after all, can produce either liberal or conservative policy change. "Gridlock" might simply be an unfortunate choice of words, a clumsy term for Washington's inability to broach and secure policy compromise (whether liberal or conservative in design). If so, understanding the causes of gridlock should interest any keen observer or participant in national politics, regardless of party or ideology.

Evaluating Gridlock

Getting a handle on gridlock is tricky. Typically, scholars assess Congress's productivity, counting up the number of important laws enacted each Congress. When output is low, we say that gridlock is high, and vice versa. But measuring

---

* In fact, none of these issues were resolved in the 106th Congress (1999–2000).

output without respect to the agenda of salient issues risks misstating the true level of gridlock. A Congress might produce little legislation because it is truly gridlocked. Or it might be unproductive because it faces a limited agenda. With little on its legislative plate, surely Congress should not be blamed for producing meager results. We can evaluate Congress's performance only if we have some idea of the size of the underlying policy agenda.

Gridlock is best viewed, then, as the share of salient issues on the nation's agenda left in limbo at the close of each Congress. Just what are the salient issues on the nation's agenda? The editorial page of the *New York Times* (the nation's paper of record) serves admirably as an indicator. Indeed, one can reconstruct the policy agenda for the past half-century of American politics by identifying all the legislative issues of each Congress discussed by the *Times* (whether in support or in opposition—to take into account the paper's often liberal political perspective). Salient issues are those addressed at least four times in a single Congress.

In terms of size, the agenda ranges as we might expect (table 1). It is smallest in the 1950s, in the quiescent years of the Eisenhower presidency. It jumps sharply under the activist administrations of JFK and LBJ in the 1960s and continues to rise steadily in the 1970s and 1980s. Only in recent years has the number of issues on the agenda declined, most likely reflecting the tightening of budgets and the associated dampening of legislative activism.

. . . Gridlock has led a rollercoaster existence over the past 50 years. Is Congress particularly gridlocked today? Critics who claim so are partially right. Gridlock

Table 1
Size of the Policy Agenda, 1947–96

Congress (Years)	Number of Issues on Agenda	Congress (Years)	Number of Issues on Agenda
80 (1947–48)	85	93 (1973–74)	133
81 (1949–50)	85	94 (1975–76)	138
82 (1951–52)	72	95 (1977–78)	150
83 (1953–54)	74	96 (1979–80)	144
84 (1955–56)	84	97 (1981–82)	127
85 (1957–58)	89	98 (1983–84)	138
86 (1959–60)	70	99 (1985–86)	160
87 (1961–62)	129	100 (1987–88)	140
88 (1963–64)	102	101 (1989–90)	147
89 (1965–66)	96	102 (1991–92)	126
90 (1967–68)	119	103 (1993–94)	94
91 (1969–70)	144	104 (1995–96)	118
92 (1971–72)	135		

has trended upward since 1947 and has been, on average, 25 points higher in the 1990s than it was in the 1940s. It peaked in the early 1990s, when George Bush faced a Democratic Congress. Fully 65 percent of the 23 most salient agenda issues remained unresolved when the 102nd Congress drew to a close in 1992. With the arrival of unified government under Bill Clinton and congressional Democrats after the 1992 elections, gridlock still remained at an historic high, with more than half of the 16 most visible issues left in limbo when the 103rd Congress adjourned.

But gridlock does not simply trend upward. From its unprecedented highs in the early 1990s, gridlock dropped 14 points in the 104th Congress (1995–96), reflecting election year compromises on reforming welfare, health care, immigration, and telecommunication laws, as well as increasing the minimum wage. Still, no recent Congress has matched the performance of the Kennedy–Johnson era, four years of legislative prowess in which the Democratic presidents and their Democratic Congresses stalemated on just roughly a quarter of the policy agenda (deadlocking on 14 of the 50 most salient issues across those four years).

The Usual Suspects

How do we account for such variation in Congress's performance? Pundits typically round up some usual suspects to explain unusually high levels of gridlock. Numerous explanations have been offered, for example, for the extreme gridlock that has stymied the current Congress. Among them are divided party control of government, the upcoming presidential election in 2000, the razor-thin majority in the House, and the meager safety cushion provided by a budget in the black for the first time in 30 years. All are plausible explanations for the current impasse in Washington. But how do these culprits stack up against the record of the past 50 years?

Arguments about the effects of divided government traditionally revolve around the importance of political parties for bridging our separated legislative and executive institutions. Unified party control is necessary, the argument goes, for ensuring that the two branches share common policy and electoral motivations. Under divided government, competing policy views and electoral incentives are said to make legislative compromise unlikely. Both parties seek policy outcomes that enhance their own electoral reputations, but neither side wants the other to reap electoral benefit from achieving its policy agenda.

If the traditional argument about divided government is correct, stalemate should be more prevalent in periods of split party control, less so under unified government. And, indeed, when control of Congress and the presidency has been divided between the parties, 43 percent of the agenda has ended in gridlock, whereas when party control is unified, only 38 percent of the agenda has been left undone. Still, given the pointed criticism perennially lodged against divided government, that mere 5 percentage point difference comes as something of a surprise—except to those who remember the "unified gridlock" of Clinton's first term, when Congress adjourned with much of the Democrats' agenda deadlocked.

What about the suggestion that stalemate is more likely in the run-up to a presidential election? At such times, the party out of power will have a strong incentive to block legislation in hopes of regaining the White House. Republican reluctance to negotiate over tax cuts in 1999 is a prime example of a party seeking to have an "issue" rather than a bill as a presidential election approaches. The logic is sound, the evidence mixed. Gridlock has increased, but only marginally, in the two-year periods leading up to presidential elections. After all, despite the fractious politics of 1995 and the approaching presidential election in 1996, Clinton and the Republican Congress managed to forge compromise on a number of salient issues—including welfare, telecommunications, immigration, health insurance, and lobbying reform. Similarly, the size of the House majority party has not had any systematic effect on the level of gridlock in recent decades.

Conventional wisdom also holds that gridlock is a function of tough fiscal times. When the budget is in surplus, legislative compromise should be easier—because politicians are theoretically no longer caught in a zero-sum game. Whether a coalition seeks higher spending or lower taxes, ample federal coffers can cover the side-payments necessary to forge a successful coalition. The argument rings true at the extremes. The deficit relative to outlays stood at nearly 20 percent during the 102nd Congress (1991–92), when gridlock peaked at over 65 percent. When the surplus relative to outlays reached 20 percent during the 80th Congress (1947–48), gridlock was a mere 26 percent. Viewed more broadly over the past half-century, however, the relationship between the two is less direct, though sunnier fiscal times are generally associated with lower levels of deadlock. Excess resources by themselves cannot wipe out gridlock, a finding confirmed by Congress's current predicament despite the emergent budget surplus.

Other Causes of Deadlock

To accurately map the dynamics of gridlock, we need to recognize the electoral and institutional contexts in which Congress labors. Perhaps the most striking feature of today's electoral environment is the disappearing political center. If we think of political moderates as those legislators who are closer to the midpoint of the two parties than to their own party's center, we can size up the reach of the political center over the past five decades. By this score, more than 30 percent of the members of Congress in the 1960s and 1970s were centrists; today, moderates make up less than 10 percent of the House and Senate.

The number of moderates is important because it affects the ease with which policy compromise is reached. When the two major parties are polarized—with few centrist legislators bridging the gap—parties have little incentive to agree and every incentive to distinguish their records and positions. As Congressman Barney Frank (D-MA) observed this past fall, "Right now, the differences between the two parties are so great, it doesn't make sense for us to compromise. We'll show where we stand, and let the people decide." As a result, the relationship between partisan polarization and legislative gridlock is direct, with stalemate more frequent as the political center shrinks.

Similarly, if the two chambers are ideologically akin to one another—as boll weevil House Democrats* and the Senate's Republican median were in the early 1980s—bicameral agreements should be easier to reach. With the House and Senate quite distant, the prospects for bicameral agreement recede. The fate of Newt Gingrich's Contract with America is a good case in point, as many of the measures triumphantly passed by House Republicans in 1995 were killed or ignored by the Republican Senate. Over the past half-century, bicameral differences have strongly shaped the incidence of gridlock, leaving the two tightly entwined at century's end.

Institutional rules also shape the behavior of legislators and policy outcomes. They are particularly important in assessing the conduct of the Senate, where the filibuster makes simple majorities powerless in the face of a determined minority. "Tit-for-tat" filibustering has compounded the problem, as control of the Senate has passed back and forth between Democrats and Republicans over the past two decades. Republican filibusters stymied much of Clinton's agenda under unified Democratic control in 1993 and 1994. Then, when Republicans regained control of the chamber in 1995, Democrats returned the favor by filibustering conservative initiatives. Even a minority of one can take the Senate hostage by placing a "hold"† on bills or nominations headed for the Senate floor until the senator's (often unrelated) policy or political demands are met. By empowering supermajorities in a political system that moves primarily by majority rule, the Senate makes its own contribution to gridlock.

Forever Gridlocked?

In many ways, Washington's proclivity for deadlock is preordained—a fact of life given the electoral and institutional worlds of Congress (table 2). Using the past half-century as our guide, we can expect divided party control of government to

---

* Boll weevils, named for a pernicious Southern insect, were conservative Southern Democrats, who exercised disproportionate power in Congress between the 1930s and the 1970s.

† An unofficial request to halt consideration of a proposal, at least temporarily.

Table 2
Contributors to Policy Gridlock, 1951–96

Independent Variable	Change in Independent Variable (From → To)	Simulated Change in Level of Gridlock
Divided government	unified → divided	+8%
Percentage of "centrists"	19% → 34%	−10%
Policy distance between House and Senate	.07 → .30	+13%
Filibuster threat	0 → 7.5	+6%
Budget situation (surplus/deficit as percentage of federal outlays)	−19% → −2%	−2%

Note: The simulated changes in gridlock are based on statistical estimates from a grouped logit model in which the level of gridlock is the dependent variable. Additional independent variables include a set of controls (not shown) for ideological diversity across members, time spent in the minority for each new majority party, and the public mood. Changes in gridlock are simulated by varying the values of each independent variable between the values in column 2 (i.e., one standard deviation below and above its mean value for continuous variables and between 0 and 1 for divided government). For parameter estimates and details on measurement, see Sarah A. Binder, "The Dynamics of Legislative Gridlock," *American Political Science Review*, vol. 93 (September 1999): 519–533.

increase the level of gridlock by roughly 8 percent. Given on average 25 salient issues on the agenda each Congress, the arrival of unified government should resolve on average only 2 additional issues. Incremental slips in the share of moderate legislators have similar effects, here increasing gridlock by roughly 10 percent or an additional 2 to 3 issues. When bicameral differences increase, gridlock also takes a marked step upward—here having the effect of stalemating 3 more legislative issues in the average Congress. In contrast, improved fiscal discipline only marginally affects the incidence of deadlock, with a large fall in the size of the deficit here reducing gridlock a mere 2 percent.

But neither institutional nor electoral features of Congress are immutable. True, we are likely stuck with a bicameral system, despite calls from Governor Jesse Ventura (Reform-MN) and others to consider the unicameral alternative. But the impact of the filibuster can be lessened by reforming Senate rules to make it easier to invoke cloture or by eliminating the noxious practice of anonymous holds. Elections, of course, are the ultimate recourse for voters dissatisfied by partisan polarization and the conduct of Congress. Nudging Congress back to the center by sending more centrist legislators to Washington would be one way to alleviate gridlock. Still, diagnosing the ills of a body politic is one thing; rousing the patient to seek treatment is another.

Questions for Discussion

1. Does a divided government necessarily guarantee "gridlock" in national policy making? Is George W. Bush, with a 50–50 Senate and a narrow Republican margin in the House, any better off than Bill Clinton, who faced a Republican Congress?
2. Can you make an argument that the Framers intentionally designed a governmental structure that was likely to produce gridlock?

 10.4

King of the Roads

Mark Murray

In the Congress of the 1950s, as described by Shepsle (10-1), committee chairmen in the Senate and especially the House were legitimately considered "barons" who dominated their policy jurisdictions. Seniority (consecutive terms on a committee) dictated who would become chairman, and southern Democrats tended to ascend to these positions in disproportionate numbers, largely because of the regional weakness of the Republican Party. By the 1990s, however, both congressional parties had limited the power of committee leaders. Among the Democrats, a few old-school barons remained, most notably Energy and Commerce's John Dingell and Ways and Means's Dan Rostenkowski. When Republicans won control of the House in 1994, Transportation Committee chairman Bud Shuster demonstrated that old-style power could still be exercised, despite the overall diminishment of committee authority.

In this *National Journal* article, Mark Murray illustrates how Shuster came to accumulate real power over a broad swath of policy. By rewarding his friends (and

---

Mark Murray is a reporter for the *National Journal*.

punishing his opponents), Shuster used his chairmanship to pass huge highway and airport construction bills in 1998 and 1999, respectively. Although he won re-election in 2000, Shuster resigned his seat in early 2001, largely because Republican rules required that he give up his chairmanship. The congressman might well have the last laugh: His son might win the nomination for a seat that is relatively safe for any Republican candidate.

When you drive on Interstate 99 through central Pennsylvania, the first things you notice are the gentle, tree-clad Allegheny Mountains that surround the highway. The view almost compels you to pull over, get out of the car, and take in the scenery.

But to an inside-the-beltway eye, there's something else striking about I-99: It's named, the Bud Shuster Highway. State officials named it after Shuster—the 14-term Republican congressman from Pennsylvania who chairs the powerful House Transportation and Infrastructure Committee—because he played a key role in securing $270 million over more than 20 years to transform an old two-lane road into this 58-mile, four-lane highway.* After all, the interstate was what the residents of this hardscrabble area wanted from the millionaire computer-business owner they sent to Congress in 1972. "When he was first elected to office, he came to the local business community and said, 'Where do you want me to place my emphasis in Washington?' " recalls local business leader Marty Marasco. "And, basically, they told him, 'Bud, we need highways, we need improved air accessibility, and we need infrastructure.' "

All agree that as a member of the House Transportation Committee, Shuster has delivered. In addition to the highway, he has helped central Pennsylvania win federal dollars for bridges, water and sewer projects, a bus-testing center, and airports. According to critics, these infrastructure improvements have been a little too much for this mostly rural district. Its largest city is Altoona, with a population of just over 51,000.

As you head north on picturesque I-99 near its midpoint in East Freedom, Pa., it's hard to miss another landmark bearing the Shuster name: the Shuster Chrysler dealership.

In 1990, Maurice Lawruk, an Altoona millionaire developer, became the guarantor of a $260,000 lease for Shuster Chrysler, which is headed by the Transportation Committee chairman's two sons, Robert and William. Lawruk also invested $30,000 in the dealership. But Lawruk, it seems, wasn't your typical business partner. As first reported by the Capitol Hill newspaper Roll Call, less than two years before Lawruk's involvement with Shuster Chrysler, Bud Shus-

---

* In 2000, Rep. Shuster won re-election, but he resigned his seat in 2001, largely because term limits on committee chairmen forced him out of his Transportation Committee position.

ter—along with the late Sen. H. John Heinz, III, R-Pa.—helped the businessman win a $3 million low-income housing contract with the Department of Housing and Urban Development.

Moreover, two months after Lawruk became the dealership's guarantor, Shuster intervened on Lawruk's behalf in a labor dispute the developer was having with the Bush Administration. Shuster again intervened for Lawruk the following year. In 1996, in a formal complaint to the House Standards of Official Conduct (Ethics) Committee, the Congressional Accountability Project (a Ralph Nader-affiliated organization) questioned whether Shuster should have assisted someone who had given him generous campaign donations and helped his family. This complaint, which contains several other charges involving Shuster's ties to special interests, is still pending before the Ethics Committee.*

Shuster, 68, has chaired the House Transportation Committee since the Republicans took over Congress in 1995. But due to the term limits that Newt Gingrich and his GOP revolutionaries imposed on House committee chairmen, this year is most likely Shuster's final one as full committee chairman. And nothing has symbolized his six-year tenure more than the Bud Shuster Highway and the car dealership that sits beside it.

As chairman, Shuster has had a hand in passing two of the most important and expensive pieces of legislation since the GOP takeover. In 1998, he helped to pave the way for a six-year, $218 billion highway and mass transit construction bill. This year, he helped to pass a $40 billion bill to fund airport construction projects. "When you build infrastructure, you create jobs," Shuster told National Journal. "You create economic prosperity."

Indeed, Shuster has chalked up a remarkable record. At a time when congressional rancor is the norm, he has made his committee the most bipartisan on Capitol Hill. As the power of committee chairmen has diminished, he has been able to frustrate, and often defeat, his party's leadership. And as critics have slapped Congress with the "Do-Nothing" label, Shuster's committee has been responsible for a flurry of legislative activity. Not surprisingly, his colleagues regard him as one of the last great chairmen on Capitol Hill. "He's probably one of a dying breed," said Rep. Ray LaHood, R-Ill., who sits on Shuster's panel.

But the car dealership stands as a reminder of Shuster's ties to special interests. In fact, a federal investigation into favors for property owners in Boston led to an indictment of and misdemeanor guilty plea from Ann Eppard, Shuster's former chief of staff, who's now one of Washington's most powerful lobbyists.

Shuster has also been attacked for being Washington's pork barrel king, and he's been accused of threatening to eliminate his opponents' transportation projects. Perhaps more than any other member since Dan Rostenkowski, D-Ill., who ruled the House Ways and Means Committee, Shuster represents the best and worst of Congress. And it's not surprising: To get legislation passed, members

---

* In 2000, Shuster received a "letter of reproval" from the Ethics Committee. This was widely viewed as a "slap on the wrist."

often have to twist arms, intimidate opponents, and win colleagues' support with pork barrel projects. To amass power and rank (not to mention win re-election), members have to raise considerable sums of campaign money, and fund raising often involves cozying up to lobbyists and returning favors to large donors. "The reality is, in this legislative system, the people are the combination of the good and bad," says Meredith McGehee of Common Cause, a liberal watchdog group.

But Fred Wertheimer, president of the campaign finance reform group Democracy 21, believes that the American political system should be better than that. "There obviously are better ways to do business than through the corrupt practices that benefit large donors at the expense of average citizens," he said. "I would give minimum weight that (Shuster) practices the best of politics and maximum weight that he practices the worst."

The Trust Fund Wars

Shuster's two great legislative triumphs as chairman have been the highway and aviation bills. More than anything else, they were battles over the heart and soul of the budget process.

In 1956, to help build the interstate highway system, the federal government created the Highway Trust Fund, which was to be financed by gasoline taxes. The logic was simple: Gasoline taxes that motorists paid would be dedicated to road construction and improvement.

But in the late 1960s, the Johnson Administration—in a move, some say, to help pay for the escalating war in Vietnam—decided to make the Highway Trust Fund and all other trust funds part of the unified federal budget. The change became effective in 1969. Consequently, cash reserves from gasoline taxes were used to make the federal budget bigger. So when Washington embarked on its budget-balancing crusade in the 1990s, trust fund dollars that weren't spent on highways went toward other discretionary spending.

Shuster recalls that when he wanted to join the Transportation Committee (then called the Public Works Committee) as a freshman in 1973, he had to first pass a trust fund litmus test from former Rep. William Harsha, R-Ohio, who was then the committee's ranking member. " 'Where do you stand on protecting the Highway Trust Fund?' " Shuster remembers Harsha asking. "And that was an easy one for me," Shuster says, "because I believe deeply in protecting the trust funds. . . . It's fraudulent (for the government) to take your gas tax money and not spend it for the purpose intended."

In his 1998 highway reauthorization bill, Shuster proposed taking the trust fund "off-budget" in order to pay for a massive increase in funding road improvements. "I am not a big spender. I am a fiscal conservative," he argued during the House debate over his bill. "But there is a fundamental difference between spending tax dollars to build assets and pouring money down a rat hole."

Shuster's quest wasn't easy, and it didn't succeed without compromises. Appropriations and Budget committee members have always resisted off-budget moves because such tactics reduce the amount of spending that these members control. Other opponents—including the Clinton Administration—objected to Shuster's bill because it would have significantly increased transportation spending, and that would have meant reducing spending on other programs. "Will education suffer? Will the environment suffer? Will housing suffer?" asked Rep. Michael N. Castle, R-Del., during the House floor debate.

But Shuster was able to strike a deal with his opponents, with considerable help from Sens. Christopher S. Bond, R-Mo.; Robert C. Byrd, D-W.Va.; Phil Gramm, R-Texas; and John W. Warner, R-Va. Under the compromise, the trust fund was to remain "on-budget," meaning that the money in it could still be used to prop up the federal budget. But a fire wall was erected around the trust fund. This ensured that the money couldn't be used on anything other than highways. The fire wall also eliminated appropriators' authority to limit highway spending. On June 9, 1998, President Clinton signed into law the $218 billion Transportation Equity Act for the 21st Century (TEA-21)—the largest public works bill in U.S. history.

That a Republican congressman would work to pass such a mammoth spending bill still infuriates fiscal conservatives. "That was the low point in the Republicans' control of Congress, because it established that it was business as usual," said Marshall Wittmann, a senior fellow in governmental studies at the conservative Hudson Institute.

The next year, 1999, Shuster once again frustrated fiscal conservatives—this time with his Aviation Investment and Reform Act for the 21st Century (AIR-21). As he did with the highway bill, Shuster proposed taking the aviation trust fund (which consists of revenues from taxes on airline tickets and aviation fuel) off-budget to finance increased spending for airport projects.

But the appropriators and budgeteers—particularly Senate Budget Committee Chairman Pete V. Domenici, R-N.M.—were determined not to give in to Shuster. "It stuck in their craw that he had beat them on the highway bill," an aviation lobbyist said. So for almost six months after the House and Senate had passed their respective aviation bills, Shuster wrangled with Domenici. Finally, Senate Majority Leader Trent Lott, R-Miss., stepped in and helped broker a compromise. "Trent was crucial in the Senate," Shuster admitted.

The deal that was struck, which President Clinton signed into law in April, resulted in a three-year, $40 billion bill. Under the agreement, Shuster wasn't able to take the aviation trust fund off-budget, nor did he get a fire wall that was similar to the highway compromise. And although the aviation deal promised a general-fund contribution for the Federal Aviation Administration's operations, the money would be subject to the annual appropriations process. The day the agreement was reached, Domenici's spokeswoman declared victory: "(Shuster) capitulated, so we're pretty happy."

Yet, as it turned out, Shuster got what he always wanted: a guarantee (through congressional points of order) that the money from the aviation trust fund would be dedicated exclusively to paying for significant increases in aviation infrastructure. "Shuster won on money, and Domenici won on process," one observer remarked after the deal was made. "Shuster's laughing all the way to the bank." . . .

Why did Shuster succeed in the trust fund wars when other chairmen had failed? Part of the answer is good timing. A key argument for keeping the transportation trust funds part of the unified budget was to keep the nation's soaring deficit under control, notes Stan Collender, a federal budget expert at Fleishman Hillard.* But in the era of budget surpluses, he says, "you take away that last remaining argument. Shuster was at the right place at the right time."

According to Shuster's friends and foes, another reason for his success is focus. Shuster has devoted most of his energies to unlocking the trust funds. In the battle over the aviation bill, Shuster simply cared about it more than Domenici and the other budget hawks did, notes Todd Hauptli, the senior vice president for legislative affairs at the American Association of Airport Executives and the Airports Council International. "He just made it clear from the beginning that he was not going to go away," Hauptli said. "The dirty little secret about Washington is, persistence pays off."

Shuster agrees that his focus on transportation has played a large role in his legislative triumphs, and it has since he came to Congress. "While I like to think I was the best freshman member of the Transportation Committee," he recalled, "I may well have been the worst member of the Education and Labor Committee because I simply didn't give time to it. I focused my time on the Transportation Committee."

Another reason for Shuster's success is the bipartisan nature of the committee. Shuster works very well with the committee's ranking member, Rep. James L. Oberstar, D-Minn.[†] "There is a great reservoir of trust between us that makes a whale of a difference in getting stuff done," Oberstar said.

When crafting any large piece of legislation, Shuster works to reach a deal with Oberstar, the subcommittee chairman who has jurisdiction over the bill, and the subcommittee's ranking member. Once the "Big Four" agree to the compromise, they vote together for and against amendments to the bill. They also try to keep contentious labor and environmental provisions out of the legislation. In addition, Shuster goes out of his way to work with other committee members, says William J. Hughes, a former committee staffer who now works in the Speaker's office. "He will accommodate members on the committee. . . . Because he has taken care of everyone else, if he can't work out a deal with you, you are going to be beat."

---

* A public relations and lobbying firm.

[†] A *ranking member* is the highest-ranking member of the committee's minority party.

Shuster's staff is regarded as one of the best on the Hill. In particular, observers have lauded the work of Chief of Staff Jack Schenendorf, who has worked on the Transportation Committee for more than 20 years. "I call him the half-million-dollar man," said former Shuster staffer Jeffrey P. Nelligan, who now works at the General Accounting Office. "Any lobbying association, any group would just give their eyeteeth to have that guy."

But critics point to another reason for Shuster's success: sheer strength. "He's not winning his debates on intellectual arguments. And he's not winning the debates on 'It's the right thing to do for America,'" said a senior Senate aide. "He's winning those debates on pure power. Bud Shuster's politics are about power, and he's good at it."

Much of Shuster's power comes from the size of his committee, which, at 75 members, is the biggest committee in the history of Congress. With Republicans having such a slim majority in the House, the chairman has been able to use this gigantic, bipartisan committee to have his way with the GOP leadership. "At any given time, on any given issue, Shuster can command at least 40 Republican votes," Hauptli said. "And as a result, Shuster's gotten the leadership to go along with him on issues that they might not otherwise be supportive of."

Shuster's power also resides in his ability to entice potential supporters with spending earmarks, which are more commonly known as pork barrel projects. The final highway bill contained almost 2,000 spending earmarks totaling $9 billion—between 4 percent and 5 percent of the $218 billion piece of legislation. (An analysis by Gannett News Service found that Pennsylvania benefited more from these earmarks than any other state. The state received 186 projects totaling $801 million.) "If we have to (round up) the tough votes to raise money, then it's not unreasonable for the members who are casting those votes . . . to be able to have a voice in how 5 percent of that money is spent," Shuster explained.

Critics have attacked Shuster's predilection for distributing pork. Rep. Tom Coburn, R-Okla., complained about Shuster's tactics during the 1998 highway bill debate. Coburn cited a voice mail left for one of his aides by a Shuster staffer as evidence: "'Matt, this is Darrell Wilson with the Transportation Committee. I'm calling about the (highway) bill. . . . We have a deal for you on the funding levels for that. I originally spoke with your office last September, and we said there was $10 million in this bill for your boss. Well, we are now upping that by $5 million . . . I just want to know where your boss wants to spend that money.'" Rep. John Shadegg, R-Ariz., who spoke after Coburn, said, "It is pure and simple bribery."

But Shuster stresses that earmarked projects still must be vetted by state transportation departments before they can proceed. He also points out that most highway dollars are distributed to the states, and that this process is just as political and suspect. "Angels in heaven don't decide where highways or airports are going to be built."

Shuster has also been criticized for taking pork away. For example, during the 1995 House debate over the Line-Item Veto* Act, former Rep. William H. Orton, D-Utah (who's currently running for governor of that state), had offered an amendment that would have made transportation projects subject to the line-item veto. On the floor, Orton made it clear that a member of Shuster's staff had threatened Orton not to offer the amendment. "The staff of the chairman, the gentleman from Pennsylvania, had let it be known that they are looking at transportation projects in my district, and if I offered the amendment, there will be retaliation," Orton said. The amendment was soundly defeated, 65–360.

As it turned out, a $1 billion highway project in Provo, Utah, lost its funding, but the money was eventually restored. "Members were scared to death with what Bud Shuster did to us," said a former Orton staffer. Furthermore, Reps. Pete Hoekstra, R-Mich., and Dan Miller, R-Fla., charged in 1998 that funding for their transportation projects had been significantly cut because they voted against the highway bill.

Shuster denies any acts of retaliation. "I have never threatened a single member," he said. "And I challenge the media and anybody else to name one person (that) I have ever threatened." Shuster admits, however, that his supporters tend to get more funding for their transportation projects than his opponents do. . . .

Questions for Discussion

1. Why was Rep. Shuster so powerful? Why did his colleagues allow him to become such a strong committee chairman?
2. What are the implications of Shuster's "pork barrel" spending for America's transportation needs? How else might Congress decide to distribute funds for roads, airports, and mass transportation?

---

* A bill that allowed presidents to veto particular spending lines in a budget. Signed by Bill Clinton, this legislation was later declared unconstitutional by the Supreme Court.

10.5

Crackup of the Committees

Richard Cohen

Committees have long enjoyed more power and independence in the American Congress than in any other legislative body in the world. They continue to hold this position, but the sweep of their power (and that of those who chair these committees) has diminished since the 1970s. Stronger party leaders, more assertive party caucuses, and independently powerful individual legislators have combined to rein in committee prerogatives. And Republicans in the House have further weakened their committee chairs by subjecting them to term limits of six years.

Richard Cohen briefly reviews the history of the committee system and examines the erosion of committee power over the past 25 years. Some representatives and senators may be nostalgic for the old days of powerful "barons," but most individual members and party leaders are satisfied with the changes, even if—as Cohen illustrates—there are some real costs to diminishing the authority of committees and their chairs.

From the scant handful of major bills passed by the House and the Senate this year, one unmistakable fact emerges: The congressional committees have lost their long-standing pre-eminence as the center of legislative ideas and debates.

During May and June [1999], for example, both the House and the Senate considered major gun control proposals that were not written or reviewed by either chamber's Judiciary Committee. Earlier this month, Senate Majority Leader Trent Lott, R-Miss., after bowing to Democratic demands for action on patients' rights, took the unusual step of selecting as the focus of the floor debate a bill crafted by key Democrats. Republicans offered an alternative measure that was initially prepared by a Senate GOP task force and was modified only slightly by the committee with jurisdiction. Meanwhile, key House committees are so splintered over their managed care legislation that Speaker J. Dennis Hastert, R-Ill., this week devided a plan to bypass them altogether.

Richard E. Cohen is a veteran prize-winning congressional reporter at the *National Journal*. He is author of several books, including *Rostenkowski* (Chicago: Ivan R. Dee, 1999), a biography of former Ways and Means Committee chairman Daniel Rostenkowski (D-Ill.).

Also both chambers have taken up major tax cuts that were cleared by the tax-writing committees, but were not really the handiwork of a majority of their members. The chairmen of the House Ways and Means and Senate Finance committees wrote their tax legislation in consultation chiefly with a handful of senior aides. The committees then spent only a few hours on token review of the major budgetary and tax-policy consequences and made modest changes before the full House and Senate advanced the bills with little debate and amid grumbling, even from some Republicans.

Publicly and privately, "there was virtually no discussion of the [tax] bill with members," complained moderate Rep. Michael N. Castle, R-Del., who forced last-minute changes in the House proposal. "Everything has been fed to everybody."

This ad hoc legislating flouts the textbook model for how Congress makes laws. As generations of high school students have learned in civics courses, legislation is supposed to result when thorough hearings are followed by a committee review of alternatives in an attempt to build consensus, and then by a second and third round of those same debates on the House and Senate floors. Such a framework was described more than a century ago by a respected political scientist who initially framed his ideas as a Princeton University undergraduate and later became President.

"Congress in session is Congress on public exhibition, whilst Congress in its committee rooms is Congress at work," wrote Woodrow Wilson in his classic 1885 study, *Congressional Government*. "Whatever is to be done must be done by, or through, the committee."

For most of the 20th century, Wilson's doctrine remained the rule on Capitol Hill. Small groups of members working in committees typically won deference for their expertise on particular policy matters. Generally, committee chairmen were recognized as first among equals. Their legislation was carefully crafted after extensive debate and deal-making and was rarely challenged on the House or Senate floor.

Over the past 30 years, however, committee power has eroded to the point where it now has largely collapsed. In many respects, this process has been both gradual and purposeful. It began during the era of Democratic control and has been greatly accelerated by both parties during the past decade. The death warrant for the old system came in 1995, when Newt Gingrich, R-Ga., assumed power as House Speaker. As part of his top-down management style, Gingrich circumvented and intentionally undermined the committee process by creating Republican task forces and demanding that they write legislation reflecting his own views.

With Gingrich gone, this legislative year began with promises that a more mature and steady Republican majority would pay greater homage to committee perquisites. Upon taking over as House Speaker in January [2000], Hastert embraced a return to the "regular order." More comfortable than Gingrich with the committee system, Hastert promised to give the panels free, or at least freer, rein to achieve his general goals.

To be sure, some of the same chairmen who meekly ducked decisions under Gingrich have sought to impose their own marks on legislation in Hastert's House. "There is a stronger sense that our members are charting their own course," said a veteran House GOP aide. But Hastert often has found that implementing his lofty goal of a return to legislating-as-usual hasn't worked out smoothly.

In the Senate, Lott, now in his fourth year as Majority Leader, seems more settled in his post and less inclined to create party task forces to guide the work of committee chairmen. Nevertheless, Senate committees, like their counterparts in the House, routinely find that they, too, suffer because of their own ineffectiveness or lack of deliberation—or simply are ignored by party leaders. In both chambers, this has been the case in recent months with the gun control, tax cut, and patients' rights legislation. A similar scenario is likely to develop this fall on campaign finance reform.

Democrats, for their part, have been eager to criticize the Republicans for their continued efforts to detour around the conventional committee process. "It's an everyday occurrence now for committees to lose control," said Rep. Martin Frost of Texas, the chairman of the House Democratic Caucus.

Even GOP allies see little prospect for resolving the problem. Committees "will become increasingly irrelevant from the standpoint of legislation," veteran conservative activist Gordon S. Jones wrote last September in *The World & I*, a magazine published by *The Washington Times*.

That judgment may sound radical, but it is really only what has been obvious for some time. Despite occasional bursts of nostalgia from chairmen seeking to reclaim what they view as their due prerogatives, the arrangements that Woodrow Wilson described are as dated as quill pens and snuffboxes. And as the century ends, the breakdown of the committee system has become a major factor in the chaos that pervades Capitol Hill. Congressional leaders repeatedly have encountered difficulties with party-driven legislation that was hastily brought to the House or Senate floor without a thorough vetting—or any attempts at bipartisan compromise—among the experts at the committee level.

Republican leaders, said Frost, "have danced on the edge several times and are flirting with disaster. You can't always cram for the final exam and get A's. Plus, their incompetence emboldens our side to go after them."

The increasing use of the filibuster in the Senate is one indicator that objectionable legislation is being scheduled more frequently for floor consideration, thus boosting combativeness. In a paper presented this month to a Capitol Hill conference on civility in the Senate, congressional scholar Barbara Sinclair, a political science professor at the University of California (Los Angeles), wrote that in the Senate during 1997–98, "half of all major measures ran into filibuster problems." During June, the Senate was hamstrung by simultaneous gridlock on managed care reform, appropriations, and steel-import legislation. . . .

Baronies under Siege

Democrats these days are well-positioned to criticize Republican operations, but they had plenty of their own problems in running the House and Senate committees while they held the majority. And the Democrats were responsible for major changes in the committee system that have had a lingering impact on the GOP-controlled Congress.

For most of the 20th century—following the Republicans' 1911 revolt against their domineering Speaker Joseph G. Cannon, who was called "czar"—the majority party in the House under both Democratic and GOP control gave the committees broad authority to dictate the agenda. The seeds for the destruction of that system were planted in the 1960s, when the mostly Southern and conservative Democratic committee chairmen in both the House and the Senate resisted large parts of President Kennedy's "New Frontier" program.

The views of most of these conservative Democratic chairmen ran counter to those of most of their party colleagues, who wanted to increase the role of the federal government on economic and social issues. But during the early 1960s, Democratic congressional leaders lacked the muscle to break the deadlocks that resulted.

The old-style Democratic committee barons changed course and went along with President Lyndon B. Johnson's "Great Society" initiative only when LBJ's huge election victory in 1964 allowed him to define the terms of debate the following year. Perhaps the best example occurred in 1965, when Wilbur D. Mills, D-Ark., the masterful consensus builder who chaired the Ways and Means Committee, abandoned his longtime opposition to government-sponsored medical care for the elderly and took the lead in painstakingly building a bipartisan coalition to enact what became the Medicare program. "Generally, the committee system accommodated change," Hofman said. "Committees knew where the wind was blowing."

Even in those days, however, the committee system hardly functioned perfectly. Segregationist Chairman James O. Eastland, D-Miss., and other Southern Democrats who controlled the Senate Judiciary Committee opposed civil rights legislation so ferociously that Democratic leaders were forced to take those bills directly to the Senate floor.

Eventually, President Johnson's popularity waned, and the coalition of Southerners and cautious Northern Democrats who took their cues from the big-city political machines regained control of the House and its committees. They engaged in a titanic struggle with liberal Democratic reformers who demanded a more activist federal government. The struggle continued until after the 1974 election, when the "Watergate babies" eliminated the final vestiges of the old system—including the iron-clad seniority rules, closed-door dealmaking, and Southern dominance among congressional Democrats. Another key step in 1974 was passage of the Congressional Budget Act, which created an annual budgeting process that supersedes the committees' role.

What followed was the democratization of the Democratic Caucus and of House committees: Subcommittee chairmen gained vast new influence; junior members won seats on the most powerful committees; party leaders—notably Speaker Thomas P. "Tip" O'Neill Jr., D-Mass.—became national figures.

With the introduction of C-SPAN coverage of the House in 1978, Hofman said, "members viewed themselves as much more independent, through the use of modern communications techniques." A prime early example was the move in 1982 by two young lawmakers—then-Sen. Bill Bradley, D-N.J., and Rep. Richard A. Gephardt, D-Mo.—to craft a massive tax reform plan and sell it to the nation. Slowly, reluctantly, the old-style committee chairmen accommodated themselves to the changes.

During the Reagan years of politically divided government, important legislation was written largely in informal settings outside of the committee process. This was the case with the crafting of Social Security reform in 1983 and the so-called Gramm-Rudman-Hollings deficit reduction scheme in 1985.

In 1994, the final year of the Democratic majority, the committee system collapsed under the combined weight of its own decrepitude and the Clinton Administration's legislative naivete. The Administration's insistent demand for action on a costly, indigestible plan for national health care coverage triggered the final, whimpering end: Neither House nor Senate committees were able to produce credible legislative proposals.

Transforming the Way Congress Works

When the Republicans took control of Congress in January 1995, armed with their ready-made legislative agenda, the Contract With America, the committees became all but superfluous. The document, signed by nearly all Republican House candidates in 1994, committed a Republican-controlled House to voting on 10 main planks and a variety of sub-topics, ranging from balancing the budget to congressional term limits.

What the committee chairmen may have thought about those goals simply did not matter. Gingrich was viewed by colleagues, and saw himself, as the political revolution's paramount leader. Members of the large and feisty GOP freshman class in each chamber emphasized that they would oppose a return of domineering committee chairmen of the type that had flourished during the era of Democratic control.

Especially in the House, Republicans "rightly sensed that their enemies were not just the Democrats' policies, but also their prevailing policy-making structures," wrote University of Maryland political scientist Roger H. Davidson . . .

In keeping with the Contract With America's promise to "transform the way Congress works," House Republicans during early 1995 approved significant procedural reforms to weaken the grip of committee chairmen, including a six-year term limit for full-committee and subcommittee chairmen.* (In the Senate, a similar six-year rule for committee chairmen, which has received less public attention, took effect in 1997.)

Other significant changes that weakened the power of House chairmen include the elimination of proxy voting in committees and the enhancement of the Speaker's authority to refer legislation to committees. In addition, Republicans cut committee staff positions by one-third in the House and by one-sixth in the Senate. They also eliminated three minor House committees and merged or eliminated several dozen House and Senate subcommittees.

"The corporate party leadership, and the Speaker in particular, gained substantial power at the expense of committees and committee chairs," notes Congressional scholar Christopher Deering . . .

During the Gingrich years, Republicans also moved away from the Democratic majority's practice of calling in federal agency officials for oversight hearings to pinpoint bureaucratic failures. Rather than focus on programmatic oversight, Republicans trained their committee guns on investigative oversight to uncover scandal, especially among Clinton administration officials. . . .

According to official records, the Democratic-controlled House committees issued reports on 55 federal programs and related matters in 1991–92, while the comparable total from the GOP majority in 1997–98 was a mere 14. Republicans concede that their cutback in committee staffing has left them with few aides experienced in conducting oversight. Indeed, the House Rules Committee recently has been working with the Congressional Research Service to assist Capitol Hill staffers in learning how to conduct program oversight.

The committees' supervisory role also has been diminished by the Clinton Administration's unusually aggressive efforts to deny or at least limit oversight. At a recent hearing of a House Rules subcommittee chaired by Rep. John Linder, R-Ga., five House GOP chairmen recounted their difficulties in securing information from the Clinton Administration.

"Trying to get the facts out of this Administration is some trick," said Judiciary Committee Chairman Henry J. Hyde, R-Ill., who voiced frustration with White House responses to his impeachment inquiry last fall. Linder said that the panel may seek a House rules change to improve compliance with committee inquiries.

The Bumpy Road to Regular Order

The regimen of the early Gingrich years gradually broke down following the unpopular federal government shutdowns during the winter of 1995–96, the House reprimand of the Speaker for ethics violations in early 1997, and an aborted coup attempt against him in mid-1997. These incidents crippled Ging-

---

*See selection 3.4 for an example of why this limitation has become so important.

rich, weakened his command of his leadership team, and gave committees an opportunity to regain legislative primacy.

Yet members still complain of an absence of true debate and thoughtfulness in most committee actions. "The deliberative process does not happen very often," said GOP Rep. Castle.

In recent years, a growing number of members seeking to learn about issues have often found committee hearings so stage-managed as to be useless, and these members have stopped relying on the committees as a source for education and deliberation. In one alternative approach, small groups of members get together and call experts to their offices for private discussions. Likewise, the failure of many committees to promote serious debates on issues has created pressure—especially in the clubbier Senate—for bipartisan closed-door meetings in party leaders' offices. . . .

At . . . times, committee chairmen have had problems when their views have run counter to a majority of their party. For instance, House Armed Services Committee Chairman Floyd Spence, R-S.C., sparked an uproar on July 1, when he made what is usually a routine motion on the House floor to send the defense authorization bill to a House-Senate conference committee. In doing so, Spence backed what appeared to be an innocuous effort by committee Democrats to "recognize the achievement of goals" by U.S. forces and the Clinton administration in the Kosovo conflict.

GOP hard-liners seized the opportunity to launch another rhetorical attack on Clinton's handling of the war, which had ended weeks earlier. Rep. Randy "Duke" Cunningham, R-Calif., termed the legislative commendations of the administration "sickening." Although the House—including Hastert and Spence—voted for the language, 261–162, most Republicans were opposed.

This incident underscores a larger point: Congress's entire debate on Kosovo this spring occurred largely outside of the committee process, again because of divisions among Republicans on the key panels and weak leadership by their chairmen, who couldn't settle differences. Debate resulted chiefly when GOP leaders called measures directly to the House or Senate floor. Rep. Tom Campbell, R-Calif., took the unusual route of filing proposals under the 1973 War Powers Resolution in what became a futile effort to force the House to take a position.

On gun control, which gained great urgency this spring following the high school massacre in Littleton, Colo., the key House committee of jurisdiction was also circumvented because of its inability to resolve splits among Republicans. In May—after Democrats forced the GOP to move the issue directly to the Senate floor, where Vice President Gore cast the tie-breaking vote to give his party a ringing victory—Hastert voiced support for some gun control steps.

Hyde favored action akin to the Senate-passed measure, but most of the predominantly Southern and Western Republicans on his panel strongly opposed new gun restrictions. The Judiciary Committee lost control of the issue, and

House Majority Whip Tom DeLay, R-Texas, worked with Dingell to produce a weak alternative; then the Rules Committee structured the House debate to permit votes on various alternatives. In the end, the House rejected the Dingell amendment and other gun control provisions, and instead approved several steps designed to address moral decay and to expand juvenile justice programs. Since then, procedural objections have delayed efforts to craft a limited House-Senate compromise.

After the House vote, DeLay proclaimed, "I think the process moved very well." Likewise, Rules Committee Chairman David Dreier, R-Calif., praised the GOP's handling of the issue and blamed the failure on Democratic partisanship. "It was a brilliant process," Dreier said in an interview. "It allowed the House to work its will. . . . I would have preferred a different outcome. But we still may get something in a conference committee."

The most successful House chairman under Republican rule has been Bud Shuster, R-Pa., the head of the Transportation and Infrastructure Committee, who has frequently defied party leaders by pressing for public works spending that far exceeds their budget plans. Shuster generally has prevailed because—unlike other House chairmen—he works assiduously to develop bipartisan consensus on his 75-member committee, and he is willing to challenge current GOP dogma. "He embarrasses the leadership, but I admire the ways he gets things done," said a victim of Shuster's exploits.

Even when House and Senate committees manage to handle their legislation in a relatively routine fashion, they often face setbacks later in the process at the hands of Republican leaders. For instance, in resolving differences between two competing bank reform proposals before House floor debate began, committee chairmen and other senior Republicans dropped controversial amendments—one, from the Banking and Financial Services Committee, to restrict redlining (refusal to do business in poor neighborhoods) by insurance companies; the other, from the Commerce Committee, to strengthen privacy of banking records.

Neither proposal was debated on the House floor, even though each was supported by committee majorities that included Democrats and some Republicans. "In each case, the Rules Committee dictated the winner," charged a Rules Committee Democratic aide. . . .

Floundering to Exert Control

Despite the setbacks that House and Senate committees have encountered, congressional Republican leaders contend that, with some exceptions, they have restored legislative power to the committees. The leaders also emphasize their continuing desire for a less active federal government and make clear that they would not sanction a return to the old system of omnipotent chairmen.

Republicans, to be sure, have been handicapped by the nearly hopeless dynamics of the 106th Congress.* They currently have only five-seat control in both the House and the Senate, and they must contend with a wounded Democratic President bent on reasserting his political primacy and leaving a legacy of peace and prosperity. Their dual challenge is keeping their diverse forces unified while confronting Democrats—especially in the House—who have become increasingly confident that they will regain control in next year's election. It is easy to see why Republican leaders, when confronted with difficult legislation, might surmise that the only way to exert control in the current climate is to move decisively, without waiting for often-wayward committees to work their will.

For their part, Gephardt and other Democrats have said that they will promote closer party coordination with the committees if they regain the majority. At the start, at least, the Democrats' desire to effectively manipulate the levers of power most likely would override some of their past excesses. But the prospect that most of the Democrats' House chairmen would be strong liberals could soon pose the same kinds of problems that Republicans have had since 1995.

Few in the House or Senate—or, for that matter, in the news media or academia—give much thought to the committee system's problems. With most lawmakers spending only three or four days a week in Washington and focusing mainly on the crisis of the week, they find little reward in thinking about seemingly intractable dilemmas. In the meantime, the problem deepens.

Questions for Discussion

1. If, as Cohen contends, committees are becoming less powerful, why was Rep. Bud Shuster (10.4) able to buck the trend? What makes Transportation different from a committee like House Banking or Senate Foreign Relations?
2. In 2001, House Republicans followed through on their promise to limit committee chairs to three two-year terms. As a result, thirteen of sixteen chairs were required to step down. To what extent does this buttress Cohen's argument about the "crackup of the committees?"

---

* This is the same margin that prevails in the 107th Congress (2001–2002).

 Chapter 11

THE PRESIDENCY

On the surface, the public knows far more about the president than it does about any other political figure. What the president does—whether traveling to a summit of world leaders or going to church—is news. One major trend in American politics has been for presidents to become increasingly public figures, to the point where the public often holds unrealistically high expectations for their performance. Yet we usually know relatively little about how the president makes decisions and even less about how the institution of the presidency operates on a day-to-day basis.

A generation ago, Alexander Bickel called the Supreme Court "the least dangerous branch" because of its inability to implement decisions. Today, we might consider the presidency the most dangerous branch, because the possibility of exercising immense power, especially in military matters and foreign policy, resides there. From the Korean War to the Persian Gulf conflict, presidents have demonstrated their dominance. In domestic policy, on the other hand, the president is far more constrained by Congress and, occasionally, by the courts. This continuing difference between the domestic and foreign/military policy arenas has been aptly labeled the "two presidencies" phenomenon by political scientist Aaron Wildavsky.

Indeed, the power of the president has long attracted the attention of presidential scholars. Without question the presidency has become much more powerful since Franklin Roosevelt recast its very nature in the 1930s. Even those presidents who have been most reluctant to increase the reach of the federal government, such as Dwight Eisenhower and Ronald Reagan, have sought to take advantage of the prerogatives of executive authority. At the same time, presidential power has waxed and waned in the modern era. In large part it is dependent on the president's relationship with the legislative branch and capacity to retain substantial support from the public.

The presidencies of Lyndon Johnson, Richard Nixon, Gerald Ford, and Jimmy Carter all demonstrated that Congress and the American people can impose major limitations on any president, even those, like Johnson and Nixon, who are eager to extend the limits of executive authority. Each of these presidencies was judged a failure, to a greater or lesser extent, by the public. These presidents were held accountable for actions and policies they could not completely control. As the presidency became more visible in the 1960s and 1970s, its occupants confronted an unwieldy Congress and an increasingly skeptical citizenry. Scholars, politicians, and journalists wondered whether the job had become impossible.

Then came the Reagan presidency. Its record will be the subject of debate for decades to come, but one thing is abundantly clear from the Reagan years: The presidency is not an unmanageable job. Reagan demonstrated that even without working congressional majorities in both houses, the president can act authoritatively and maintain relatively high popularity ratings well into a second term. George Bush, his successor, consistently received strong job approval ratings, especially in the wake of Operation Desert Storm in the Gulf War.

In the end, however, President Bush lost much of his support for taking a principled action—he endorsed a tax increase, in order to help balance the budget, thus contradicting his 1988 campaign pledge ("Read my lips . . .") of no new taxes. Most economists conclude that the 1990 budget agreement (see selection 14.4) eventually helped turn budget deficits into surpluses. But the economy's short-term performance, along with Bush's broken promise, led to his defeat in 1992 by Arkansas governor Bill Clinton.

As Clinton's presidency ended in January 2001, evaluating the state of the office was difficult. In many ways, Clinton had learned a great deal about serving effectively as president in an era of divided government and narrow partisan majorities. The public gave him considerable credit, and he departed the White House with a higher job-approval rating than the highly popular Reagan. At the same time, Clinton left only modest policy legacies, aside from the considerable accomplishment of serving during the great turnaround from huge deficits to large budget surpluses. Most analysts believe that Federal Reserve chairman Alan Greenspan was as much (if not more) responsible for the state of the economy as Clinton was. And in international relations, Clinton could genuinely claim credit for some major successes (expanded trade, intervention in Bosnia), but he created no general policy blueprint for how the United States might act as the sole remaining superpower. Finally, his moral failings led many Americans to distrust him and allowed his opponents to pursue him with an unrelenting vengeance throughout his presidency. At the beginning of the 21st century, the role of the president remained strangely undefined, in the realms of both domestic and foreign policymaking.

The following selections examine the modern presidency from both institutional and psychological perspectives. Richard E. Neustadt offers his now classic formulation of presidential influence: Presidents must protect their reputations and popularity as they seek to persuade legislators and even their own administrative appointees to support their policy initiatives. Political scientist Robert Dahl dissects the notion of the presidential mandate as an element in the "pseudo-democratization" of the American presidency. Indeed, Dahl sees the contemporary presidency as representing exactly what the framers sought to avoid: an executive who obtains office by pandering to an ill-informed and malleable public that is incapable of producing a meaningful mandate for action. This has become all the more significant as presidents have adopted polling and other campaign strategies to frame and deliver their messages.

If Neustadt and Dahl offer scholarly yet general assessments of the presidency, Evan Thomas and his *Newsweek* colleagues give us a detailed assessment of how and why President Clinton escaped impeachment. Similar to most other analyses of the Senate's impeachment trial, Thomas finds that Clinton was probably never in much danger of being convicted. He describes the House members who "managed" the prosecution as playing out a political string that began far earlier in the Clinton administration. The impeachment episode demonstrated the remarkable resilience of Bill Clinton, who delivered his annual state of the union message just as his impeachment trial was beginning—and won favorable reviews for a speech that was noteworthy as much for his having given it as for its content.

Moreover, during his eight years in office, Clinton learned skills that allowed him to maneuver much of his policy agenda into law. In fact, most presidents do accomplish a good deal of what they set out to do. Political reporter Carl Cannon, writing at the beginning of George W. Bush's term in office, assesses how well past presidents fulfill their promises. Drawing on numerous studies by presidential scholars, Cannon observes that even in periods of divided government the chief executive can get most of his proposals passed. The powers of setting an agenda and bargaining for its approval are substantial and well worth winning, if even by fewer than 1,000 votes in a single state.

11.1

The Power to Persuade

Richard E. Neustadt

The American president generally is regarded as the most powerful elected official in the world. Some of this power derives from the presidential power of command. The president can order a wide range of policies to be carried out, especially when dealing with foreign affairs or defense issues. At the same time, any chief executive must confront the numerous obstacles to exercising presidential authority. Some of these are constitutional, such as the independent power bases of the Congress and the Supreme Court. Others are less formal but no less restrictive; for example, the bureaucracy often serves as a brake on presidential initiatives (see Chapter 12).

In this selection, political scientist Richard E. Neustadt fleshes out the nature of presidential power as the power to persuade—a classic formulation on which a generation of scholars has built. Not only are presidents obliged to persuade Congress of the virtues of their proposals; they must also persuade their own administrations, and often their top aides, that their proposals have merit, even after they have won legislative approval. (Although Neustadt added three chapters to his book *Presidential Power* in 1980, this excerpt appeared in the original edition, published in 1960, and is replete with references to the Truman and Eisenhower administrations.)

T he limits on command suggest the structure of our government. The constitutional convention of 1787 is supposed to have created a government of "separated powers." It did nothing of the sort. Rather, it created a government of separated institutions *sharing* powers. "I am part of the legislative process," Eisenhower often said in 1959 as a reminder of his veto. Congress, the dispenser of authority and funds, is no less part of the administrative process. Federalism adds another set of separated institutions. The Bill of Rights adds others. Many public purposes can only be achieved by voluntary acts of private institutions; the press, for one, in Douglass Cater's phrase, is a "fourth branch of

---

Richard E. Neustadt is professor emeritus of government at Harvard University.

government." And with the coming of alliances abroad, the separate institutions of a London, or a Bonn, share in the making of American public policy.

What the Constitution separates our political parties do not combine. . . . The President and congressmen who bear one party's label are divided by dependence upon different sets of voters. The differences are sharpest at the stage of nomination. The White House has too small a share in nominating congressmen, and Congress has too little weight in nominating Presidents for party to erase their constitutional separation. Party links are stronger than is frequently supposed, but nominating processes assure the separation.

The separateness of institutions and the sharing of authority prescribe the terms on which a President persuades. When one man shares authority with another, but does not gain or lose his job upon the other's whim, his willingness to act upon the urging of the other turns on whether he conceives the action right for him.* The essence of a President's persuasive task is to convince such men that what the White House wants of them is what they ought to do for their sake and on their authority.

Persuasive power, thus defined, amounts to more than charm or reasoned argument. These have their uses for a President, but these are not the whole of his resources. . . . The status and authority inherent in his office reinforce his logic and his charm.

Status adds something to persuasiveness; authority adds still more. When Truman urged wage changes on his Secretary of Commerce while the latter was administering the steel mills, he and Secretary Sawyer were not just two men reasoning with one another.† Had they been so, Sawyer probably would never have agreed to act. Truman's status gave him special claims to Sawyer's loyalty, or at least attention. In [English political theorist] Walter Bagehot's charming phrase "no man can *argue* on his knees." Although there is no kneeling in this country, few men—and exceedingly few Cabinet officers—are immune to the impulse to say "yes" to the President of the United States. It grows harder to say "no" when they are seated in his oval office at the White House, or in his study on the second floor, where almost tangibly he partakes of the aura of his physical surroundings. . . .

A President's authority and status give him great advantages in dealing with the men he would persuade. Each "power" is a vantage point for him in the degree that other men have use for his authority. From the veto to appointments, from publicity to budgeting, and so down a long list, the White House now controls

---

* From the vantage point of the 1990s, Neustadt's language seems insensitive to gender. Remember, he wrote in 1960 when (1) there was little such sensitivity and (2) virtually all top-level appointees were men.

† In 1952, President Truman seized control of the steel industry to prevent a strike during the Korean War. The Supreme Court ruled his action unconstitutional.

the most encompassing array of vantage points in the American political system. With hardly an exception, the men who share in governing this country are aware that at some time, in some degree, the doing of *their* jobs, the furthering of *their* ambitions, may depend upon the President of the United States. Their need for presidential action, or their fear of it, is bound to be recurrent if not actually continuous. Their need or fear is his advantage.

A President's advantages are greater than mere listing of his "powers" might suggest. The men with whom he deals must deal with him until the last day of his term. Because they have continuing relationships with him, his future, while it lasts, supports his present influence. Even though there is no need or fear of him today, what he could do tomorrow may supply today's advantage. Continuing relationships may convert any "power," any aspect of his status, into vantage points in almost any case. When he induces other men to do what he wants done, a President can trade on their dependence now *and* later.

The President's advantages are checked by the advantages of others. Continuing relationships will pull in both directions. These are relationships of mutual dependence. A President depends upon the men he would persuade; he has to reckon with his need or fear of them. They too will possess status, or authority, or both, else they would be of little use to him. Their vantage points confront his own; their power tempers his.

Persuasion is a two-way street. Sawyer, it will be recalled, did not respond at once to Truman's plan for wage increases at the steel mills. On the contrary, the Secretary hesitated and delayed and only acquiesced when he was satisfied that publicly he would not bear the onus of decision. Sawyer had some points of vantage all his own from which to resist presidential pressure. If he had to reckon with coercive implications in the President's "situations of strength," so had Truman to be mindful of the implications underlying Sawyer's place as a department head, as steel administrator, and as a Cabinet spokesman for business. Loyalty is reciprocal. Having taken on a dirty job in the steel crisis, Sawyer had strong claims to loyal support. Besides, he had authority to do some things that the White House could ill afford. . . . He might have resigned in a huff (the removal power also works two ways). Or, . . . he might have declined to sign necessary orders. Or, he might have let it be known publicly that he deplored what he was told to do and protested its doing. By following any of these courses Sawyer almost surely would have strengthened the position of [steel] management, weakened the position of the White House, and embittered the union. But the whole purpose of a wage increase was to enhance White House persuasiveness in urging settlement upon union and companies alike. Although Sawyer's status and authority did not give him the power to prevent an increase outright, they gave him capability to undermine its purpose. . . .

The power to persuade is the power to bargain. Status and authority yield bargaining advantages. But in a government of "separated institutions sharing powers," they yield them to all sides. With the array of vantage points at his disposal, a President may be far more persuasive than his logic or his charm could make him. But outcomes are not guaranteed by his advantages. There remain the counter pressures those whom he would influence can bring to bear on him from vantage points at their disposal. Command has limited utility; persuasion becomes give-and-take. It is well that the White House holds the vantage points it does. In such a business any President may need them all—and more.

I

This view of power as akin to bargaining is one we commonly accept in the sphere of congressional relations. Every textbook states and every legislative session demonstrates that . . . a President will often be unable to obtain congressional action on his terms or even to halt action he opposes. The reverse is equally accepted: Congress often is frustrated by the President. Their formal powers are so intertwined that neither will accomplish very much, for very long, without the acquiescence of the other. By the same token, though, what one demands the other can resist. The stage is set for that great game, much like collective bargaining, in which each seeks to profit from the other's needs and fears. It is a game played catch-as-catch-can, case by case. And everybody knows the game, observers and participants alike. . . .

In only one sphere is the concept [of power as give-and-take] unfamiliar: the sphere of executive relations. Perhaps because of civics textbooks and teaching in our schools, Americans instinctively resist the view that power in this sphere resembles power in all others. Even Washington reporters, White House aides, and congressmen are not immune to the illusion that administrative agencies comprise a single structure, "the" Executive Branch, where presidential word is law, or ought to be. Yet . . . when a President seeks something from executive officials his persuasiveness is subject to the same sorts of limitations as in the case of congressmen, or governors, or national committeemen, or private citizens, or foreign governments. There are no generic differences, no differences in kind and only sometimes in degree. The incidents preceding the dismissal of [General Douglas] MacArthur* and the incidents surrounding seizure of the steel mills make it plain that here as elsewhere influence derives from bargaining advantages; power is a give-and-take.

Like our governmental structure as a whole, the executive establishment consists of separated institutions sharing powers. The President heads one of

---

* A strong-willed commander of U.N. and American forces in South Korea and a prospective Republican presidential nominee, General MacArthur repeatedly challenged President Truman over Korean War strategies. Truman ultimately removed him from his command. This action reinforced the president's role as commander-in-chief, although MacArthur received much popular and legislative support upon his return to the United States.

these; Cabinet officers, agency administrators, and military commanders head others. Below the departmental level, virtually independent bureau chiefs head many more. Under mid-century conditions, Federal operations spill across dividing lines on organization charts; almost every policy entangles many agencies; almost every program calls for interagency collaboration. Everything somehow involves the President. But operating agencies owe their existence least of all to one another—and only in some part to him. Each has a separate statutory base; each has its statutes to administer; each deals with a different set of subcommittees at the Capitol. Each has its own peculiar set of clients, friends, and enemies outside the formal government. Each has a different set of specialized careerists inside its own bailiwick. Our Constitution gives the President the "take-care" clause and the appointive power. Our statutes give him central budgeting and a degree of personnel control. All agency administrators are responsible to him. But they *also* are responsible to Congress, to their clients, to their staffs, and to themselves. In short, they have five masters. Only after all of those do they owe any loyalty to each other.

"The members of the Cabinet," Charles G. Dawes used to remark, "are a President's natural enemies." Dawes had been Harding's Budget Director, Coolidge's Vice-President, and Hoover's Ambassador to London; he also had been General Pershing's chief assistant for supply in the First World War. The words are highly colored, but Dawes knew whereof he spoke. The men who have to serve so many masters cannot help but be somewhat the "enemy" of any one of them. By the same token, any master wanting service is in some degree the "enemy" of such a servant. A President is likely to want loyal support but not to relish trouble on his doorstep. Yet the more his Cabinet members cleave to him, the more they may need help from him in fending off the wrath of rival masters. Help, though, is synonymous with trouble. Many a Cabinet officer, with loyalty ill-rewarded by his lights and help withheld, has come to view the White House as innately hostile to department heads. Dawes's dictum can be turned around.

A senior presidential aide remarked to me in Eisenhower's time: "If some of these Cabinet members would just take time out to stop and ask themselves, 'What would I want if I were President?', they wouldn't give him all the trouble he's been having." But even if they asked themselves the question, such officials often could not act upon the answer. Their personal attachment to the President is all too often overwhelmed by duty to their other masters. . . .

Some aides will have more vantage points than a selective memory. Sherman Adams, for example, as the Assistant to the President under Eisenhower, scarcely deserved the appelation "White House aide" in the meaning of the term before his time or as applied to other members of the Eisenhower entourage. Although Adams was by no means "chief of staff" in any sense so sweeping—or so simple—as press commentaries often took for granted, he apparently became no more dependent on the President than Eisenhower on him. "I need him," said the President when Adams turned out to have been remarkably imprudent in the

Goldfine case, and delegated to him even the decision on his own departure.*
This instance is extreme, but the tendency it illustrates is common enough. Any
aide who demonstrates to others that he has the President's consistent confidence
and a consistent part in presidential business will acquire so much business on his
own account that he becomes in some sense independent of his chief. Nothing
in the Constitution keeps a well-placed aide from converting status into power
of his own, usable in some degree even against the President—an outcome not
unknown in Truman's regime or, by all accounts, in Eisenhower's.

The more an officeholder's status and his "powers" stem from sources independent of the President, the stronger will be his potential pressure *on* the
President. Department heads in general have more bargaining power than do
most members of the White House staff; but bureau chiefs may have still more,
and specialists at upper levels of established career services may have almost
unlimited reserves of the enormous power which consists of sitting still. As
Franklin Roosevelt once remarked:

> The Treasury is so large and far-flung and ingrained in its practices that I find it almost
> impossible to get the action and results I want—even with Henry [Morgenthau] there.
> But the Treasury is not to be compared with the State Department. You should go
> through the experience of trying to get any changes in the thinking, policy, and action
> of the career diplomats and then you'd know what a real problem was. But the Treasury
> and the State Department put together are nothing compared with the Na-a-vy. The
> admirals are really something to cope with—and I should know. To change anything in
> the Na-a-vy is like punching a feather bed. You punch it with your right and you punch
> it with your left until you are finally exhausted, and then you find the damn bed just as
> it was before you started punching.[1]

. . . Real power is reciprocal and varies markedly with organization, subject
matter, personality, and situation. The mere fact that persuasion is directed at
executive officials signifies no necessary easing of his [the President's] way. Any
new congressman of the Administration's party, especially if narrowly elected,
may turn out more amenable (though less useful) to the President than any
seasoned bureau chief "downtown." *The probabilities of power do not derive from the
literary theory of the Constitution.*

II

There is a widely held belief in the United States that were it not for folly or for
knavery, a reasonable President would need no power other than the logic of his

---

* Businessman Bernard Goldfine gave Sherman Adams, Eisenhower's top aide, the gift of a
vicuna coat. When it became public, Adams's acceptance of the gift caused substantial embarrassment to the president, and Adams subsequently resigned.

argument. No less a personage than Eisenhower has subscribed to that belief in many a campaign speech and press-conference remark. But faulty reasoning and bad intentions do not cause all quarrels with Presidents. The best of reasoning and of intent cannot compose them all. For in the first place, what the President wants will rarely seem a trifle to the men he wants it from. And in the second place, they will be bound to judge it by the standard of their own responsibilities, not his. However logical his argument according to his lights, their judgment may not bring them to his view. . . . An able Eisenhower aide with long congressional experience remarked to me in 1958: "The people on the Hill don't do what they might *like* to do, they do what they think they *have* to do in their own interest as *they* see it. . . ." This states the case precisely.

The essence of a President's persuasive task with congressmen and everybody else, is *to induce them to believe that what he wants of them is what their own appraisal of their own responsibilities requires them to do in their interest, not his.* Because men may differ in their views on public policy, because differences in outlook stem from differences in duty—duty to one's office, one's constituents, oneself—that task is bound to be more like collective bargaining than like a reasoned argument among philosopher kings. Overtly or implicitly, hard bargaining has characterized all illustrations offered up to now. This is the reason why: persuasion deals in the coin of self-interest with men who have some freedom to reject what they find counterfeit.

III

A President draws influence from bargaining advantages. But does he always need them? . . . Suppose most players of the governmental game see policy objectives much alike, then can he not rely on logic (or on charm) to get him what he wants? The answer is that even then most outcomes turn on bargaining. The reason for this answer is a simple one: most men who share in governing have interests of their own beyond the realm of policy *objectives.* The sponsorship of policy, the form it takes, the conduct of it, and the credit for it separate their interest from the President's, despite agreement on the end in view. In political government, the means can matter quite as much as ends; they often matter more. And there are always differences of interest in the means. . . .

Adequate or not, a President's own choices are the only means *in his own hands* of guarding his own prospects for effective influence. He can draw power from continuing relationships in the degree that he can capitalize upon the needs of others for the Presidency's status and authority. He helps himself to do so, though, by nothing save ability to recognize the preconditions and the chance advantages and to proceed accordingly in the course of the choice-making that comes his way. To ask how he can guard prospective influence is thus to raise a further question: what helps him guard his power stakes in his own acts of choice?

Notes

1. Quoted in Marriner S. Eccles, *Beckoning Frontiers* (New York: Knopf, 1951), 336.

Questions for Discussion

1. Why must presidents be able to "persuade" their own administrative appointees?
2. Can presidents *increase* their ability to persuade? How? By making good choices?

 11.2

Myth of the Presidential Mandate

Robert A. Dahl

The term *mandate* appears frequently in discussions of presidential elections. Presidents claim mandates—often broadly defined—in the wake of their victories. The people, they say, have spoken. After all, among elected officials only the president has a national constituency. The problem comes in interpreting what the people have to say. Many potential voters do not cast their ballots; in recent presidential contests, these individuals constituted almost 50 percent of the potential electorate. Moreover, many reasons lie behind the millions of votes that support a given candidate.

Political scientist and democratic theorist Robert Dahl argues that not until Woodrow Wilson's presidency did chief executives begin to claim mandates for their policies and goals. Such claims have become commonplace, but Dahl casts substantial doubt on their validity. Even with sophisticated sample surveys, Dahl finds the complexities underlying mandates exceedingly difficult to fathom. In addition, presidents frequently win by less than a majority of the popular vote and often receive only a bit more than a quarter of the ballots of all those eligible to

---

Robert A. Dahl is professor emeritus of political science at Yale University.

vote. In sum, although presidents may be eager to claim mandates for their actions, in most instances these claims are self-serving rather than based on adequate criteria of clear relationships between the candidate and the electorate.

O n election night in 1980 the vice president–elect [George Bush] enthu-siastically informed the country that Ronald Reagan's triumph was

> . . . not simply a mandate for a change but a mandate for peace and freedom; a mandate for prosperity; a mandate for opportunity for all Americans regardless of race, sex, or creed; a mandate for leadership that is both strong and compassionate . . . a mandate to make government the servant of the people in the way our founding fathers intended; a mandate for hope; a mandate for hope for the fulfillment of the great dream that President-elect Reagan has worked for all his life.[1]

I suppose there are no limits to permissible exaggeration in the elation of victory, especially by a vice president elect. He may therefore be excused, I imagine, for failing to note, as did many others who made comments in a similar vein in the weeks and months that followed, that Reagan's lofty mandate was provided by 50.9 percent of the voters. A decade later it is much more evident, as it should have been then, that what was widely interpreted as Reagan's mandate, not only by supporters but by opponents, was more myth than reality.

In claiming that the outcome of the election provided a mandate to the president from the American people to bring about the policies, programs, emphases, and new directions uttered during the campaign by the winning candidate and his supporters, the vice president elect was like other commenta-tors echoing a familiar theory.

Origin and Development

A history of the theory of the presidential mandate has not been written, and I have no intention of supplying one here. However, if anyone could be said to have created the myth of the presidential mandate, surely it would be Andrew Jackson. Although he never used the word mandate, so far as I know, he was the first American president to claim not only that the president is uniquely repre-sentative of all the people, but that his election confers on him a mandate from the people in support of his policy. Jackson's claim was a fateful step in the democratization of the constitutional system of the United States—or rather what I prefer to call the pseudodemocratization of the presidency.

As Leonard White observed, it was Jackson's "settled conviction" that "the President was an immediate and direct representative of the people."[2] Presumably as a result of his defeat in 1824 in both the electoral college and the House of Representatives, in his first presidential message to Congress, in order that "as few impediments as possible should exist to the free operation of the public will," he proposed that the Constitution be amended to provide for the direct election of the president.[3]

> "To the people," he said, "belongs the right of electing their Chief Magistrate: it was never designed that their choice should, in any case, be defeated, either by the intervention of electoral colleges or by . . . the House of Representatives."[4]

His great issue of policy was the Bank of the United States, which he unwaveringly believed was harmful to the general good. Acting on this conviction, in 1832 he vetoed the bill to renew the bank's charter. Like his predecessors, he justified the veto as a protection against unconstitutional legislation; but unlike his predecessors in their comparatively infrequent use of the veto he also justified it as a defense of his or his party's policies.

Following his veto of the bank's charter, the bank became the main issue in the presidential election of 1832. As a consequence, Jackson's reelection was widely regarded, even among his opponents (in private, at least), as amounting to "something like a popular ratification" of his policy.[5] When in order to speed the demise of the bank Jackson found it necessary to fire his treasury secretary, he justified his action on the ground, among others, that "The President is the direct representative of the American people, but the Secretaries are not."[6]

Innovative though it was, Jackson's theory of the presidential mandate was less robust than it was to become in the hands of his successors. In 1848 James Polk explicitly formulated the claim in a defense of his use of the veto on matters of policy, that as a representative of the people the president was, if not more representative than the Congress, at any rate equally so.

> "The people, by the constitution, have commanded the President, as much as they have commanded the legislative branch of the Government, to execute their will. . . . The President represents in the executive department the whole people of the United States, as each member of the legislative department represents portions of them. . . ." The President is responsible "not only to an enlightened public opinion, but to the people of the whole Union, who elected him, as the representatives in the legislative branches are responsible to the people of particular States or districts. . . ."[7]

Notice that in Jackson's and Polk's views, the president, both constitutionally and as representative of the people, is on a par with Congress. They did not claim that in either respect the president is superior to Congress. It was Woodrow Wilson who took the further step in the evolution of the theory by asserting that in representing the people the president is not merely equal to Congress but actually superior to it.

Earlier Views Because the theory of the presidential mandate espoused by Jackson and Polk has become an integral part of our present-day conception of the presidency, it may be hard for us to grasp how sharply that notion veered off from the views of the earlier presidents.

As James Ceaser has shown, the Framers designed the presidential election process as a means of improving the chances of electing a *national* figure who would enjoy majority support. They hoped their contrivance would avoid not only the populistic competition among candidates dependent on "the popular arts," which they rightly believed would occur if the president were elected by the people, but also what they believed would necessarily be a factional choice if the president were chosen by the Congress, particularly by the House.[8]

In adopting the solution of an electoral college, however, the Framers seriously underestimated the extent to which the strong impulse toward democratization that was already clearly evident among Americans—particularly among their opponents, the anti-Federalists—would subvert and alter their carefully contrived constitutional structure. Since this is a theme I shall pick up later, I want now to mention only two such failures that bear closely on the theory of the presidential mandate. First, the Founders did not foresee the development of political parties nor comprehend how a two-party system might achieve their goal of insuring the election of a figure of national rather than merely local renown. Second, as Ceaser remarks, although the Founders recognized "the need for a popular judgment of the performance of an incumbent" and designed a method for selecting the president that would, as they thought, provide that opportunity, they "did not see elections as performing the role of instituting decisive changes in policy in response to popular demands."[9] In short, the theory of the presidential mandate not only cannot be found in the Framers' conception of the Constitution; almost certainly it violates that conception.

No president prior to Jackson challenged the view that Congress was the legitimate representative of the people. Even Thomas Jefferson, who adeptly employed the emerging role of party leader to gain congressional support for his policies and decisions,

> was more Whig than . . . the British Whigs themselves in subordinating [the executive power] to "the supreme legislative power." . . . The tone of his messages is uniformly deferential to Congress. His first one closes with these words: "Nothing shall be wanting on my part to inform, as far as in my power, the legislative judgment, nor to carry that judgment into faithful execution."[10]

James Madison, demonstrating that a great constitutional theorist and an adept leader in Congress could be decidedly less than a great president, deferred so greatly to Congress that in his communications to that body his extreme caution rendered him "almost unintelligible"[11]—a quality one would hardly expect from one who had been a master of lucid exposition at the Constitutional Convention. His successor, James Monroe, was so convinced that Congress should decide domestic issues without presidential influence that throughout the debates in Congress on "the greatest political issue of his day . . . the admission of Missouri and the status of slavery in Louisiana Territory," he remained utterly silent.[12]

Madison and Monroe serve not as examples of how presidents should behave but as evidence of how early presidents thought they should behave. Considering the constitutional views and the behavior of Jackson's predecessors, it is not hard to see why his opponents called themselves Whigs in order to emphasize his dereliction from the earlier and presumably constitutionally correct view of the presidency.

Woodrow Wilson The long and almost unbroken succession of mediocrities who succeeded to the presidency between Polk and Wilson for the most part subscribed to the Whig view of the office and seem to have laid no claim to a popular mandate for their policies—when they had any. Even Abraham Lincoln, in justifying the unprecedented scope of presidential power he believed he needed in order to meet secession and civil war, rested his case on constitutional grounds, and not as a mandate from the people.[13] Indeed, since he distinctly failed to gain a majority of votes in the election of 1860, any claim to a popular mandate would have been dubious at best. Like Lincoln, Theodore Roosevelt also had a rather unrestricted view of presidential power; he expressed the view then emerging among Progressives that chief executives were also representatives of the people. Yet the stewardship he claimed for the presidency was ostensibly drawn—rather freely drawn, I must say—from the Constitution, not from the mystique of the mandate.[14]

Woodrow Wilson, more as political scientist than as president, brought the mandate theory to what now appears to be its canonical form. His formulation was influenced by his admiration for the British system of cabinet government. In 1879, while still a senior at Princeton, he published an essay recommending the adoption of cabinet government in the United States.[15] He provided little indication as to how this change was to be brought about, however, and soon abandoned the idea without yet having found an alternative solution.[16] Nevertheless, he continued to contrast the American system of congressional government, in which Congress was all-powerful but lacked executive leadership, with British cabinet government, in which parliament, though all powerful, was firmly led by the prime minister and his cabinet. Since Americans were not likely to adopt the British cabinet system, however, he began to consider the alternative of more powerful presidential leadership.[17] In his *Congressional Government*, published in 1885, he acknowledged that "the representatives of the people are the proper ultimate authority in all matters of government, and that administration is merely the clerical part of government."[18] Congress is "unquestionably, the predominant and controlling force, the center and source of all motive and of all regulative power." Yet a discussion of policy that goes beyond "special pleas for special privilege" is simply impossible in the House, "a disintegrate mass of jarring elements," while the Senate is no more than "a small, select, and leisurely House of Representatives."[19]

By 1908, when *Constitutional Government in the United States* was published, Wilson had arrived at strong presidential leadership as a feasible solution. He faulted the earlier presidents who had adopted the Whig theory of the Constitution.

> . . . (T)he makers of the Constitution were not enacting Whig theory. . . . The President is at liberty, both in law and conscience, to be as big a man as he can. His capacity will set the limit; and if Congress be overborne by him, it will be no fault of the makers of the Constitution—it will be from no lack of constitutional powers on its part, but only because the President has the nation behind him, and Congress has not. He has no means of compelling Congress except through public opinion. . . . (T)he early Whig theory of political dynamics . . . is far from being a democratic theory. . . . It is particularly intended to prevent the will of the people as a whole from having at any moment an unobstructed sweep and ascendancy.

And he contrasted the president with Congress in terms that would become commonplace among later generations of commentators, including political scientists:

> Members of the House and Senate are representatives of localities, are voted for only by sections of voters, or by local bodies of electors like the members of the state legislatures.[20] There is no national party choice except that of President. No one else represents the people as a whole, exercising a national choice. . . . The nation as a whole has chosen him, and is conscious that it has no other political spokesman. His is the only national voice in affairs. . . . He is the representative of no constituency, but of the whole people. When he speaks in his true character, he speaks for no special interest. . . . (T)here is but one national voice in the country, and that is the voice of the President.[21]

Since Wilson, it has become commonplace for presidents and commentators alike to argue that by virtue of his election the president has received a mandate for his aims and policies from the people of the United States. The myth of the mandate is now a standard weapon in the arsenal of persuasive symbols all presidents exploit. For example, as the Watergate scandals emerged in mid-1973, Patrick Buchanan, then an aide in the Nixon White House, suggested that the president should accuse his accusers of "seeking to destroy the democratic mandate of 1972." Three weeks later in an address to the country Nixon said:

> Last November, the American people were given the clearest choice of this century. Your votes were a mandate, which I accepted, to complete the initiatives we began in my first term and to fulfill the promises I made for my second term.[22]

If the spurious nature of Nixon's claim now seems self-evident, the dubious grounds for virtually all such pretensions are perhaps less obvious.[23]

Critique of the Theory

What does a president's claim to a mandate amount to? The meaning of the term itself is not altogether clear.[24] Fortunately, however, in his excellent book *Interpreting Elections*, Stanley Kelley has "piece[d] together a coherent statement of the theory."

> Its first element is the belief that elections carry messages about problems, policies, and programs—messages plain to all and specific enough to be directive. . . . Second, the theory holds that certain of these messages must be treated as authoritative commands . . . either to the victorious candidate or to the candidate and his party. . . . To qualify as mandates, messages about policies and programs must reflect the *stable* views both of individual voters and of the electorate. . . . In the electorate as a whole, the numbers of those for or against a policy or program matter. To suggest that a mandate exists for a particular policy is to suggest that more than a bare majority of those voting are agreed upon it. The common view holds that landslide victories are more likely to involve mandates than are narrow ones. . . . The final element of the theory is a negative imperative: Governments should not undertake major innovations in policy or procedure, except in emergencies, unless the electorate has had an opportunity to consider them in an election and thus to express its views.[25]

To bring out the central problems more clearly, let me extract what might be called the primitive theory of the popular presidential mandate. According to this theory, a presidential election can accomplish four things. First, it confers constitutional and legal authority on the victor. Second, at the same time, it also conveys information. At a minimum it reveals the first preferences for president of a plurality of votes. Third, according to the primitive theory, the election, at least under the conditions Kelley describes, conveys further information: namely that a clear majority of voters prefer the winner because they prefer his policies and wish him to pursue his policies. Finally, because the president's policies reflect the wishes of a majority of voters, when conflicts over policy arise between president and Congress, the president's policies ought to prevail.

While we can readily accept the first two propositions, the third, which is pivotal to the theory, might be false. But if the third is false, then so is the fourth. So the question arises: Beyond revealing the first preferences of a plurality of voters, do presidential elections also reveal the additional information that a plurality (or a majority) of voters prefer the policies of the winner and wish the winner to pursue those policies?

In appraising the theory I want to distinguish between two different kinds of criticisms. First, some critics contend that even when the wishes of constituents can be known, they should not be regarded as in any way binding on a legislator. I have in mind, for example, Edmund Burke's famous argument that he would not sacrifice to public opinion his independent judgment of how well a policy would serve his constituents' interests, and the argument suggested by Hanna Pitkin that representatives bound by instructions would be prevented from entering into the compromises that legislation usually requires.[26]

Second, some critics, on the other hand, may hold that when the wishes of constituents on matters of policy can be clearly discerned, they ought to be given great and perhaps even decisive weight. But, these critics contend, constituents' wishes usually cannot be known, at least when the constituency is large and diverse, as in presidential elections. In expressing his doubts on the matter in 1913, A. Lawrence Lowell quoted Sir Henry Maine: "The devotee of democracy is much in the same position as the Greeks with their oracles. All agreed that the voice of an oracle was the voice of god, but everybody allowed that when he spoke he was not as intelligible as might be desired."[27]

It is exclusively the second kind of criticism that I want now to consider. Here again I am indebted to Stanley Kelley for his succinct summary of the main criticisms.

> Critics allege that 1) some particular claim of a mandate is unsupported by adequate evidence; 2) most claims of mandates are unsupported by adequate evidence; 3) most claims of mandates are politically self-serving; or 4) it is not possible in principle to make a valid claim of a mandate, since it is impossible to sort out voters' intentions.[28]

Kelley goes on to say that while the first three criticisms may well be valid, the fourth has been outdated by the sample survey,* which "has again given us the ability to discover the grounds of voters' choices." In effect, then, Kelley rejects the primitive theory and advances the possibility of a more sophisticated mandate theory according to which the information about policies is conveyed not by the election outcome but instead by opinion surveys. Thus the two functions are cleanly split: presidential elections are for electing a president, opinion surveys provide information about the opinions, attitudes, and judgments that account for the outcome.

However, I would propose a fifth proposition, which I believe is also implicit in Kelley's analysis:

> 5) While it may not be strictly impossible in principle to make a reasoned and well-grounded claim to a presidential mandate, to do so in practice requires a complex analysis that in the end may not yield much support for presidential claims.

But if we reject the primitive theory of the mandate and adopt the more sophisticated theory, then it follows that prior to the introduction of scientific sample surveys, no president could reasonably have defended his claim to a mandate. To put a precise date on the proposition, let me remind you that the first presidential election in which scientific surveys formed the basis of an extended and systematic analysis was 1940.[29]

I do not mean to say that no election before 1940 now permits us to draw the conclusion that a president's major policies were supported by a substantial majority of the electorate. But I do mean that for most presidential elections before 1940 a valid reconstruction of the policy views of the electorate is impossible or enormously difficult, even with the aid of aggregate data and other indirect indicators of voters' views. When we consider that presidents ordinarily asserted their claims soon after their elections, well before historians and social scientists could have sifted through reams of indirect evidence, then we must

---

* Sampling techniques allow a relatively small number of respondents (1,500 for a national sample) to accurately reflect the views of a much larger population (150 million adults).

conclude that before 1940 no contemporary claim to a presidential mandate could have been supported by the evidence available at the time.

While the absence of surveys undermines presidential claims to a mandate before 1940, the existence of surveys since then would not necessarily have supported such claims. Ignoring all other shortcomings of the early election studies, the analysis of the 1940 election I just mentioned was not published until 1948. While that interval between the election and the analysis may have set a record, the systematic analysis of survey evidence that is necessary (though perhaps not sufficient) to interpret what a presidential election means always comes well after presidents and commentators have already told the world, on wholly inadequate evidence, what the election means.[30] Perhaps the most famous voting study to date, *The American Voter*, which drew primarily on interviews conducted in 1952 and 1956, appeared in 1960.[31] The book by Stanley Kelley that I have drawn on so freely here, which interprets the elections of 1964, 1972, and 1980, appeared in 1983.

A backward glance quickly reveals how empty the claims to a presidential mandate have been in recent elections. Take 1960. If more than a bare majority is essential to a mandate, then surely Kennedy could have received no mandate, since he gained less than 50 percent of the total popular vote by the official count—just how much less by the unofficial count varies with the counter. Yet "on the day after election, and every day thereafter," Theodore Sorenson tells us, "he rejected the argument that the country had given him no mandate. Every election has a winner and a loser, he said in effect. There may be difficulties with the Congress, but a margin of only one vote would still be a mandate."[32]

By contrast, 1964 was a landslide election, as was 1972. From his analysis, however, Kelley concludes that "Johnson's and Nixon's specific claims of meaningful mandates do not stand up well when confronted by evidence." To be sure, in both elections some of the major policies of the winners were supported by large majorities among those to whom these issues were salient. Yet "none of these policies was cited by more than 21% of respondents as a reason to like Johnson, Nixon, or their parties."[33]

In 1968, Nixon gained office with only 43 percent of the popular vote. No mandate there. Likewise in 1976, Carter won with a bare 50.1 percent. Once again, no mandate there.

When Reagan won in 1980, thanks to the much higher quality of surveys undertaken by the media, a more sophisticated understanding of what that election meant no longer had to depend on the academic analyses that would only follow some years later. Nonetheless, many commentators, bemused as they so often are by the arithmetical peculiarities of the electoral college, immediately proclaimed both a landslide and a mandate for Reagan's policies. What they often failed to note was that Reagan gained just under 51 percent of the popular vote. Despite the claims of the vice president elect, surely we can find no mandate there. Our doubts are strengthened by the fact that in the elections to the House, Democratic candidates won just over 50 percent of the popular vote and a majority of seats. However, they lost control of the Senate. No Democratic mandate there, either.

These clear and immediate signs that the elections of 1980 failed to confer a mandate on the president or his Democratic opponents were, however, largely ignored. For it was so widely asserted as to be commonplace that Reagan's election reflected a profound shift of opinion away from New Deal programs and toward the new conservatism. However, from this analysis of the survey evidence, Kelley concludes that the commitment of voters to candidates was weak; a substantial proportion of Reagan voters were more interested in voting against Carter than for Reagan; and despite claims by journalists and others, the New Deal coalition did not really collapse. Nor was there any profound shift toward conservatism. "The evidence from press surveys . . . contradicts the claims that voters shifted toward conservatism and that this ideological shift elected Reagan." In any case, the relation between ideological location and policy preferences was "of a relatively modest magnitude."[34]

In winning by a landslide of popular votes in 1984, Reagan achieved one prerequisite to a mandate. Yet in that same election, Democratic candidates for the House won 52 percent of the popular votes. Two years earlier, they had won 55 percent of the votes. On the face of it, surely the 1984 elections gave no mandate to Reagan.

Before the end of 1986, when the Democrats had once again won a majority of popular votes in elections to the House and had also regained a majority of seats in the Senate, it should have been clear and it should be even clearer now that the major social and economic policies for which Reagan and his supporters had claimed a mandate have persistently failed to gain majority support. Indeed, the major domestic policies and programs established during the thirty years preceding Reagan in the White House have not been overturned in the grand revolution of policy that his election was supposed to have ushered in. For eight years, what Reagan and his supporters claimed as a mandate to reverse those policies was regularly rejected by means of the only legitimate and constitutional processes we Americans have for determining what the policies of the United States government should be.

What are we to make of this long history of unsupported claims to a presidential mandate? The myth of the mandate would be less important if it were not one element in the larger process of the pseudodemocratization of the presidency— the creation of a type of chief executive that in my view should have no proper place in a democratic republic.

Yet even if we consider it in isolation from the larger development of the presidency, the myth is harmful to American political life. By portraying the president as the only representative of the whole people and Congress as merely representing narrow, special, and parochial interests, the myth of the mandate elevates the president to an exalted position in our constitutional system at the expense of Congress. The myth of the mandate fosters the belief that the particular interests of the diverse human beings who form the citizen body in a large, complex, and pluralistic country like ours constitute no legitimate element in the general good. The myth confers on the aims of the groups who benefit from presidential policies an aura of national interest and public good to which they are no more entitled than the groups whose interests are reflected in the policies that gain support by congressional majorities. Because the myth is almost always employed to support deceptive, misleading, and manipulative interpretations, it is harmful to the political understanding of citizens.

It is, I imagine, now too deeply rooted in American political life and too useful a part of the political arsenal of presidents to be abandoned. Perhaps the most we can hope for is that commentators on public affairs in the media and in academic pursuits will dismiss claims to a presidential mandate with the scorn they usually deserve.

But if a presidential election does not confer a mandate on the victor, what does a presidential election mean, if anything at all? While a presidential election does not confer a popular mandate on the president—nor, for that matter, on congressional majorities—it confers the legitimate authority, right, and opportunity on a president to try to gain the adoption by constitutional means of the policies the president supports. In the same way, elections to Congress confer on a member the authority, right, and opportunity to try to gain the adoption by constitutional means of the policies he or she supports. Each may reasonably contend that a particular policy is in the public good or public interest and, moreover, is supported by a majority of citizens.

I do not say that whatever policy is finally adopted following discussion, debate, and constitutional processes necessarily reflects what a majority of citizens would prefer, or what would be in their interests, or what would be in the public good in any other sense. What I do say is that no elected leader, including the president, is uniquely privileged to say what an election means—nor to claim that the election has conferred on the president a mandate to enact the particular policies the president supports. . . .

Notes

1. Stanley Kelley, Jr., *Interpreting Elections* (Princeton, N.J.: Princeton University Press, 1983), 217.
2. Leonard D. White, *The Jacksonians: A Study in Administrative History, 1829–1861* (New York: Free Press, 1954), 23.
3. Quoted in ibid., 23.
4. Cited in James W. Ceaser, *Presidential Selection: Theory and Development* (Princeton, N.J.: Princeton University Press, 1979), 160, fn. 58.
5. White, *Jacksonians*, 23.
6. Ibid., 23.
7. Ibid., 24.
8. Although Madison and Hamilton opposed the contingent solution of a House election in the event that no candidate received a majority of electoral votes, Gouverneur Morris and James Wilson accepted it as not too great a concession. Ceaser, *Presidential Selection*, 80–81.
9. Ibid., 84.

10. Edward S. Corwin, *The President: Offices and Powers, 1789–1948,* 3rd ed. (New York: New York University Press, 1948), 20.

11. Wilfred E. Binkley, *President and Congress* (New York: Alfred A. Knopf, 1947), 56.

12. Leonard D. White, *The Jeffersonians: A Study in Administrative History, 1801–1829* (New York: Free Press, 1951), 31.

13. Lincoln drew primarily on the war power, which he created by uniting the president's constitutional obligation "to take care that the laws be faithfully executed" with his power as commander-in-chief. He interpreted the war power as a veritable cornucopia of implicit constitutional authority for the extraordinary emergency measures he undertook during an extraordinary national crisis. (Corwin, *The President,* 277ff.)

14. "Every executive officer, in particular the President, Roosevelt maintained, 'was a steward of the people bound actively and affirmatively to do all he could for the people. . . .' He held therefore that, unless specifically forbidden by the Constitution or by law, the President had 'to do anything that the needs of the nation demanded. . . .' 'Under this interpretation of executive power,' he recalled, 'I did and caused to be done many things not previously done. . . . I did not usurp power, but I did greatly broaden the use of executive power.' " See John Morton Blum, *The Republican Roosevelt* (New York: Atheneum, 1954), 108.

15. Woodrow Wilson, *Cabinet Government in the United States* (Stamford, Conn.: Overbrook Press, 1947), orig. publication in *International Review,* 1879.

16. "He seems not to have paid much attention to the practical question of how so radical an alteration was to be brought about. As far as I know, Wilson's only published words on how to initiate the English system are in the article, *Committee or Cabinet Government,* which appeared in the *Overland Monthly* for January, 1884." His solution was to amend Section 6 of Article I of the Constitution to permit members of Congress to hold offices as members of the Cabinet, and to extend the terms of the president and representatives. See Walter Lippmann, *Introduction to Congressional Government* (New York: Meridian Books, 1956), 14–15.

17. Wilson's unfavorable comparative judgment is particularly clear in *Congressional Government: A Study in American Politics* (New York: Meridian Books, 1956; reprint of 1885 ed.), 181. Just as Jackson had proposed the direct election of the president, in his first annual message Wilson proposed that a system of direct national primaries be adopted. See Ceaser, *Presidential Selection,* 173.

18. Wilson, *Congressional Government,* 181.

19. Ibid., 31, 72–73, 145.

20. The Seventeenth Amendment requiring a direct election of senators was not adopted until 1913.

21. Woodrow Wilson, *Constitutional Government in the United States* (New York: Columbia University Press, 1908), 67–68, 70, 202–203.

22. Kelley, *Interpreting Elections,* 99.

23. For other examples of claims to a presidential mandate resulting from the election, see William Safire, *Safire's Political Dictionary* (New York: Random House, 1978), 398; and Kelley, *Interpreting Elections,* 72–74, 126–129, 168.

24. See "mandate" in *Oxford English Dictionary* (Oxford, England: Oxford University Press, 1971, compact edition); Safire, *Political Dictionary,* 398; Jack C. Plano and Milton Greenberg, *The American Political Dictionary* (New York: Holt, Rinehart and Winston, 1979), 130; Julius Gould and William L. Kolb, *A Dictionary of the Social Sciences* (New York: The Free Press, 1964), 404; Jay M. Shafritz, *The Dorsey Dictionary of American Government and Politics* (Chicago: The Dorsey Press, 1988), 340.

25. Kelley, *Interpreting Elections,* 126–128.

26. Cited in ibid., 133.

27. Cited in ibid., 134.

28. Ibid., 136.

29. Paul F. Lazarsfeld, Bernard Berelson, and Hazel Gaudet, *The People's Choice* (New York: Columbia University Press, 1948).

30. The early election studies are summarized in Bernard R. Berelson and Paul F. Lazarsfeld, *Voting* (Chicago: University of Chicago Press, 1954), 331ff.

31. Angus Campbell et al., *The American Voter* (New York: Wiley, 1960).
32. Quoted in Safire, *Political Dictionary*, 398.
33. Kelley, *Interpreting Elections*, 139–140.
34. Ibid., 170–172, 174–181, 185, 187.

Questions for Discussion

1. What is a mandate? Why is it so important, or at least useful, for a president to make such a claim in establishing a set of policy priorities?
2. In what ways does the idea of a presidential mandate violate the assumptions of the Constitution's framers?
3. Did George W. Bush have any possible mandate after the 2000 election? Did he claim one?

 11.3

Why Clinton Won

Evan Thomas

Bill Clinton. Fiercely defended by some, like most African Americans, bitterly attacked by others, like religious conservatives, few Americans were neutral toward our first baby-boomer president. This dualism played out during the entire Clinton presidency, and in its aftermath. Given his superb political skills and broad understanding of a wide range of policies, even his harshest critics conceded that he had the tools to make a superb chief executive. At the same time, even his most fervent admirers found his personal choices and moral leadership to be suspect at best. Above all, Bill Clinton demonstrated that a public figure could survive, even prosper, amid continuing legal and political attacks. The culmination of these attacks came in his impeachment trial, conducted by the Senate in January and February 1999. By a narrow, highly partisan majority, the House of Representatives voted to impeach Clinton in December 1998, in the wake of an election in which Democrats had gained House seats, largely because the public

Evan Thomas is assistant managing editor of *Newsweek* and author of *Robert Kennedy: His Life*.

reacted negatively to partisan attacks during the fall campaign. The last act of the House in the 105th Congress placed impeachment first on the Senate's agenda for the 106th Congress.

In the following selection, veteran *Newsweek* writer Evan Thomas and a team of reporters piece together an account of how Clinton won acquittal and how the ordinarily contentious Senate worked to bring this political drama to a rapid (and foregone) conclusion. In the end, impeachment played out as a partisan episode that typified the acid politics of a divided government during the Clinton era. The Senate did find ways to mute its partisanship and to recognize that little value would come of a lengthy process that would be destructive for both the presidency and the Congress. What is left open, however, is the extent to which impeachment may be used in the future as one more weapon of partisan conflict.

On Jan. 5, two weeks after the House had impeached President Clinton, eight ranking senators—four Republicans and four Democrats—met privately in Senate Majority Leader Trent Lott's hideaway office on the third floor of the Capitol. The most senior senator, Strom Thurmond of South Carolina, had something he wanted to say. At 96, Thurmond does not speak up much these days, and when he does, his drawl can be hard to comprehend. But on this occasion he was perfectly clear about the prospects for convicting the president of high crimes and misdemeanors. "It takes two thirds to get rid of this fella," said Thurmond. "We don't have it. Let's get it over."

A simple, reasonable declaration of fact. But not much had been straightforward or rational about the Lewinsky scandal. Stunned by the vote to impeach in the House, the White House, said a top Clinton aide, viewed the Senate as a "barn full of hay"—ready to catch fire. Right-wing Republicans were demanding a show trial to expose Bill Clinton and, by extension, the moral relativism of the Democratic Party. Several of the House "managers" chosen to prosecute the president were feverishly scheming to dish new dirt into the record. The rules were archaic or unclear: the Senate had not tried a president for high crimes since 1868. The pundits were saying that anything could happen and network executives were hoping it would.

Like most climactic battles, however, this one was determined by careful groundwork. When the scandal broke last year, Clinton chose to go to war rather than sue for peace. "Well, we'll just have to win, then," he told his old adviser Dick Morris a year ago. The president's team cleverly demonized the prosecutor and played to public opinion, successfully arguing that this was about sex, not constitutional substance. And, as always, Clinton was unusually lucky—especially in his enemies. Still, it all could have spun out of Clinton's control. In the end the president was spared . . . by a mix of high-mindedness, backroom dealing and senatorial vanity. For some years now, Senate old-timers have been quietly muttering about a loss of civility and collegiality in their chamber. They blamed

TV cameras and an influx of bomb throwers from the House. To the traditional-
ists, the impeachment vote in the House was a spectacle not to be repeated. The
dignity of the upper house was at stake. The senators had read the polls and
weren't interested in rummaging through Clinton's sex life. The best strategy:
preserve institutional pride and get it over with fast.

At first, the president's worst nightmare was a Senate united—against him.
The White House plan—really, more a hope—was to keep the trial as partisan as
possible. A vote split along party lines would fall short of the two thirds necessary
to convict. It would make the trial look like pure politics, with the Republicans
in the role of witch hunters. The president was downcast, then, when the Senate
took its first vote on Jan. 8—deciding, 100–0, to set some ground rules. The vote
put off the hard decisions, like whether to call witnesses, but to Clinton it
demonstrated dangerous senatorial solidarity. "It was his lowest moment," said an
aide who worked closely with him.

The 13 House managers were just as unhappy about the 100–0 vote. "A group
hug," scoffed Congressman Chris Cannon of Utah, "a collective pant-wetting."
The day before the vote, Lott had announced that he wanted to pay a visit to the
managers. "This ain't good, guys," Rep. Lindsey Graham told his colleagues.
Senators almost never deign to visit the House. Lott was already suspect to the
House managers—a little too slick, too willing to make deals. He must be
bringing bad news, warned Graham. Sure enough, Lott told the managers that
the Senate would never permit a normal trial, though he blamed the Democrats.
After Lott left, three of the managers—Cannon, Graham and Jim Rogan—were
so angry they talked openly about quitting in protest. "I won't participate in any
sham trial," Rogan declared.*

In late December a few of the House managers had realized they would need to
resort to guerrilla warfare. Graham, a third-term congressman from South Carolina, jokingly remarked to a *Newsweek* reporter that he had begun to like
Congress when he realized it was a "street fight." Now, in order to shake up the
prissy senators, he wanted to portray Clinton as rough sex fiend and cover-up
artist. During the House impeachment proceedings, the Judiciary Committee
had paraded members into a secret evidence room. They were shown a report
from Ken Starr about a witness in the Paula Jones sexual-harassment case called
Jane Doe Five. About 20 years ago, Clinton had allegedly forced himself upon
Jane Doe Five. The evidence was murky: Jane Doe had broken down in tears
when questioned by Starr's investigators, who failed to ask follow-up questions.
Jane Doe Five was not part of the impeachment case sent over to the Senate.
Graham and others hoped, however, to get the press interested. They were glad
when NBC's Lisa Myers interviewed Jane Doe, and looked forward to an expose
on "Dateline." Graham, who calls himself "the Jane Doe guy," also went digging

---

* Rogan was the only House impeachment manager to come from a competitive seat. He waged
a vigorous re-election bid and never backed away from his impeachment positions, but he lost
his 2000 re-election bid in his California seat.

for other women. He says he called a *Newsweek* reporter at home because he had heard that the magazine was working on a story about Clinton and a former Miss America. Told no, he asked, "Got anything else coming?"

Clinton's legal team feared the House's fishing expedition. "We didn't know what was out there," said one of the president's lawyers. "That's when we started talking about putting on a real defense." Such a trial, this lawyer estimated, would last "a year and a half." He added, "We weren't bluffing." Some of the president's political advisers cringed at a long trial, but the president wanted an all-out defense "on the law and the facts," said the lawyer. "He believed he had done nothing wrong." Closely questioning his lawyers, Clinton was deeply involved in his own defense. So was the First Lady, though she never attended staff meetings; instead she communicated through aides and the president himself. Hillary's focus was entirely on the constitutional issues. It had been her idea to parade scholars before the House Judiciary Committee, and in the Senate trial she continued to offer arguments on the proper definition of "high crimes." She didn't want to get into the facts.

The White House was frustrated and a little rattled when the House managers put on their opening arguments in the second week of January. The Sunday TV shows credited the House team with making a strong case, especially on obstruction of justice. "It was full of sloppy lawyering," groused a member of the Clinton team. The White House set up a war room full of computers in the ceremonial office of the vice president in the Capitol. Searching through Monica's testimony on CD-ROM, the president's lawyers picked over the managers' case, finding holes and mistakes. Off in a corner sat a desk that had belonged to Richard Nixon, with holes carved out for his secret taping system. No one used the desk.

The president talked on the phone to a few Democratic senators most nights during the trial, but he was powerless to do anything about the senator he feared most: Robert Byrd of West Virginia. Any White House lobbying would be "jury tampering," Byrd warned before the trial began. Pompous and shrewd, Byrd declared that his loyalty was to the Bible and the Constitution, not the Democratic Party. He hinted broadly to senators that he might vote to convict. As ranking member of the Appropriations Committee, Byrd was a danger to the White House: he could use Senate pork to swing votes.

Senate Minority Leader Tom Daschle knew that he had to handle Byrd with extreme care. Daschle played to Byrd's ego, calling him every day and inviting him to address his colleagues on Senate history and custom. The Republicans, meanwhile, were courting Byrd, showering him with praise as "the conscience of the Senate." But House Manager Bob Barr had already offended Byrd's sense of institutional propriety: the hard-right Georgia congressman had publicly suggested that the Senate lacked "the attention span" to hold an impeachment trial. Going over to the Senate floor at the trial's outset, Barr tried to apologize to Byrd, and claims that Byrd forgave him. A Democratic senator who witnessed the exchange has a different recollection. Through thin lips, with eyes narrowed, Byrd told Barr, "I assure you I listened. I assure you I have a long memory."

On Jan. 22, as the trial ended its second week, Byrd happily surprised the Democrats and stunned the Republicans. He moved to dismiss the entire case. Though the motion failed along party lines, it showed that the Democrats were sticking together, and that Byrd, for the time being at least, was not a renegade. Byrd's motion was the turning point: the president was relieved; the House managers were crushed. "We had a huge head of momentum, but Byrd killed it," said a House manager. "He used his status as the patriarch in a baldly partisan fashion." Republican senators, meanwhile, were queasy about the managers' plan to introduce a host of witnesses. Sen. Slade Gorton of Washington approached a House manager on the Senate floor. "Oh, my God," Gorton exclaimed, "you can't possibly have more than three witnesses." Gorton was "all atwitter," gesticulating like the Mad Hatter in "Alice in Wonderland," said the disgruntled House manager. The encounter did not bode well; Gorton was seen as a stalking horse for Lott.

On Jan. 27, the Senate held the key vote on witnesses. Three was all the House got—not even live witnesses, but videotaped depositions. The vote broke along party lines, and the talking heads immediately proclaimed partisan warfare. They were wrong. Behind the scenes Daschle and Lott were forging an alliance of convenience. Lott and Daschle are opposites: Lott is a former Ole Miss cheer-leader, Daschle cerebral and introverted. Neither man really likes the other. They had squabbled so openly last year that Democrat Patrick Leahy of Vermont had pleaded with both men to make peace for the sake of the institution. But Lott and Daschle had a shared interest in a short, dignified impeachment trial: Daschle to save his president, Lott to try to rescue his party from deeper disaster. During the trial, they talked so often that Lott put a direct-dial button on his phone.*

Lott had to tread carefully with the 20-odd right-wing senators who kept talking about the party's "base"—the conservative true believers who turn out at election time. The "base," these senators argued, wanted to see a full-scale trial. Lott smiled and listened to the right-wingers, but he quietly did business with Daschle. He gave the Democratic leader a veto over calling more witnesses or expanding the scope of the trial. That meant no Jane Does. Over in the House, the managers privately grumbled that they had been sold out. Every day, as he met with his team, Judiciary chairman Henry Hyde staged an elaborate ritual of cutting the tip off his long, fat cigar. One day he mused aloud that he would like to do the same to the male organ of a certain senator. The press was also letting down the House diehards. NBC News had held the story by reporter Lisa Myers

---

* In 2001, Lott and Daschle negotiated an historic power-sharing arrangement in the wake of the 50–50 split produced by the 2000 elections. Again, it was a marriage of convenience that served both their purposes.

about Jane Doe Five. Congressman Cannon began brandishing a button that read FREE LISA MYERS.

Clinton's team was beginning to breathe easier. They knew the Republicans were divided. One GOPer was even secretly offering to help the White House . . . As it turned out, the White House didn't really need a spy: the senators were running to TV cameras to openly announce their stratagems. Indeed, Democrats and Republicans were spending so much time together in "green rooms" waiting to go on TV talk shows that they were beginning to bond across party lines. As Leahy was getting made up for one show, a Republican in the next chair teased him about using up all the makeup to cover his bald head. The two solons began discussing a deal to limit witnesses. After mingling for days in the Senate chamber, Republicans and Democrats began visiting each other's sanctums, the cloak rooms; the Democrats were not surprised to find that the Republicans had better food.

The last hope of the House managers was to make Monica Lewinsky turn on Bill Clinton, or at least seem pitiable. But the questioning by Rep. Ed Bryant of Tennessee was hapless. At their first, informal meeting on Jan. 24, Bryant had clumsily asked Lewinsky if she had voted for Clinton. Her lawyer stopped her from answering, while other lawyers in the room rolled their eyes. Bryant did no better in the formal deposition on Feb. 1. Few senators even bothered to view the whole deposition the next day when it was made available on videotape in a secure room on the fourth floor of the Capitol. One who did came out shaking his head. "Seems to me," drawled Fritz Hollings of South Carolina, "that *she* was deposing *him.*"

Things were going so well for the White House that spokesman Joe Lockhart felt compelled to declare a "gloat-free zone." That day Thurmond had voted against bringing in Lewinsky as a live witness with a loud "No!" The 96-year-old senator, an old ladies' man, had been flirting with White House lawyer Cheryl Mills, bringing her candy and fruit as she sat waiting for the trial to begin on the Senate floor. As the legal team met the next morning, one of the lawyers cracked, "Cheryl finally delivered Strom." The lawyers burst out laughing—and abruptly stopped. They remembered the injunction against gloating.

The last real threat to Clinton was the move by some Senate moderates to fashion a "finding of fact" that would condemn Clinton's behavior without removing him from office. The idea was touted by a pair of Maine Republicans, Susan Collins and Olympia Snowe. It had some commonsense appeal as a compromise. The White House hated the idea: Snowe and Collins, both moderates, couldn't be written off as right-wing nuts. They offered the dangerous temptation of bipartisanship. An impassioned speech by Snowe had persuaded wary Republicans to join with Democrats to start off the trial with a unanimous agreement. But this resolution wouldn't fly without at least some Democratic support. By now the Democrats were a united front in opposition to any Republican initiative.

All except Bob Byrd, that is. Byrd's fellow senators were having trouble figuring out the aging patriarch. Having moved to dismiss the case, he was now vaguely threatening to vote to convict. "Never underestimate Byrd's desire to be at the center of attention," said one Senate watcher in the White House. Last Friday, on the final day of the trial, Byrd was dead center. With five Republicans (all Northeastern moderates) voting to acquit, the Democrats had a shot at blocking even a simple majority to convict on both perjury and obstruction of justice. Byrd was the swing vote. In three days of closed-door deliberations, he waited until the very end to give his speech. Rambling on for 22 minutes, he accused the president of lying and committing high crimes—but didn't say how he was going to vote. Not until a few minutes before the vote did anxious White House lawyers learn Byrd's intentions. He would vote to acquit.

In the family quarters of the White House where he was pointedly not watching the vote, Clinton was "hugely relieved," said one of his lawyers. After five weeks and seemingly interminable speechifying, the impeachment trial was finally over. In the Senate chamber, the sergeant-of-arms escorted the House managers out the door, down the marble corridor and to the exact midpoint between the House and the Senate under the Capitol dome. As the embarrassed congressmen stepped across the border, the sergeant-of-arms gravely shook their hands. "Thank you for coming," he said. The House managers, for once, were speechless.

Questions for Discussion

1. What lessons do the Clinton impeachment proceedings teach us about the U.S. Senate in the context of relations with the presidency?
2. Was impeachment essentially a partisan undertaking, or was there real substance to the accusations? Did the Clinton impeachment experience make it more or less likely that the Congress will seriously consider impeachment in the future?

11.4

Promises, Promises

Carl M. Cannon

As a part of their campaigns and their power to set the policy agenda for the country, presidents make promises—lots of promises. That is scarcely remarkable. What is remarkable, however, is that most presidents fulfill about two-thirds of those promises. As citizens, we're generally skeptical, if not downright cynical, about politicians' ability to deliver on their promises. But deliver they do, sometimes by proposing legislation, sometimes by issuing executive orders, and sometimes by changing the ways in which laws are administered.

In this January 2001 piece from the *National Journal,* Carl Cannon examines Bill Clinton's record as a promise keeper in the context of other presidents' performance. This article demonstrates why capturing the presidency is so important. Even in difficult legislative circumstances (divided government, or a 50–50 Senate for George W. Bush), presidents most often find a way to keep their word.

"Politicians are the same all over," Nikita Khrushchev once said. "They promise to build a bridge, even where there is no river." The former Soviet premier's pithy critique certainly applies to American politicians. Even in a representative democracy, there is little punishment for promising voters the moon—or bridges to nowhere. Governors and members of Congress do it. So do mayors, legislators, and sheriffs. Dog catchers probably do it if they are running in contested elections.

There is one office, however, in which promises truly do matter: The presidency of the United States. The spotlight is simply too intense—it is kept shining on the White House by the media, the out-of-power party, and historians—for Presidents to ignore what they said during the campaign.

"There's a kind of a myth, that we all go around making promises we don't intend to keep," 1988 Democratic presidential nominee Michael Dukakis noted. "Nobody runs for the presidency if you don't feel awfully strongly about certain things."

Carl Cannon is a staff correspondent at *National Journal.*

Presidential scholars and political scientists say Dukakis is right. "By and large, Presidents do indeed keep their promises," says George C. Edwards III, director of the Center for Presidential Studies at Texas A&M University. "When Presidents don't keep their promises, it's not because it's inconvenient or they were insincere. It's because they had to bite the bullet."

Of the modern Presidents, no one kept more promises than the man leaving office this month after eight years in the White House. In other words, Nikita Khrushchev never met Bill Clinton.

"Clinton didn't get a lot of help from Congress—he did a lot of this on his own," says Rutgers University political scientist Gerald Pomper, a pioneer in charting modern presidential promises. "And he's doing it right up until the end. He's showing that there is an immense amount of power in the presidency—if you don't care about the political consequences."

As Pomper suggests, Clinton's record is all the more impressive when you consider the context of his Administration. Not only did Clinton contend with a restive Republican Congress for the last six years of his tenure, but also he was the first President in 130 years to be impeached. Further, Clinton came into office with no coattails and a mandate clouded by the fact that he had won with only 43 percent of the vote. He had no Washington experience and no real experience of working with Republicans in Arkansas. On top of all that, not since Jimmy Carter has a President made anything like the sheer number of promises Clinton made.

If Clinton is gilding the lily a bit with his recess appointments,* 11th-hour environmental executive orders, and last-ditch foreign policy initiatives and treaty signings, it's also true that keeping promises helps solidify a President's standing for posterity.

Woodrow Wilson's lofty reputation was forged, in part, during the very first month of his presidency, March 1913, when he called Congress back into session in order to keep a campaign promise to ease tariffs and expand free trade. By the end of 1914, Wilson had signed legislation on banking and currency reform and strengthening antitrust laws—these were the cornerstones of his "New Freedom" platform.

Earlier in this century, Presidents made far fewer promises. Compared with modern candidates, they barely campaigned. In 1928, when Republican Herbert Hoover ran against Democrat Al Smith, Hoover gave only seven speeches and offered few specifics other than his support for keeping Prohibition. Four years later, even in the face of the Great Depression, Democratic candidate Franklin D. Roosevelt, the man whom presidency scholars regard as being the first modern President, was stinting with his campaign promises. On April 7, 1932, in a radio

---

* A recess appointment is one made while the Senate is out of session. Appointees can serve without confirmation through the next session of Congress.

address from Albany, N.Y., Roosevelt vowed to "revise" the Hawley-Smoot tariff law, and on May 22, 1932, Roosevelt implied—but that was all—the need for public works projects.

In fact, FDR that year accepted the Democratic nomination in Chicago by scoffing at those who would promise too much. "Let it be from now on the task of our party to break foolish traditions," Roosevelt said. "We will break foolish traditions and leave it to the Republican leadership, far more skilled in that art, to break promises." FDR didn't always follow his own advice. At Pittsburgh's Forbes Field on Oct. 19, 1932, Roosevelt excoriated Hoover for deficit spending and promised that, as President, he would balance the federal budget and reduce "government operations" by 25 percent. (These were, indeed, "foolish" promises, and Roosevelt had the good sense to break them immediately after taking office. Four years later when he was headed back to western Pennsylvania for a speech, Roosevelt asked speechwriter Sam Rosenman what he should say about his earlier promise. "Deny you were ever in Pittsburgh," Rosenman quipped.)

In the past decade, the reputation of John F. Kennedy—a President that Khrushchev did know—has also been burnished, as it becomes clearer to political scientists that he kept many more promises than he was given credit for. JFK has generally been faulted for accomplishing too little in Congress during his famous Thousand Days. Throughout the 1960 campaign, Kennedy had promised to take strong action, in the form of executive orders, in the realm of civil rights. He'd do it, Kennedy vowed, "with a stroke of a pen." Instead, Kennedy put those issues on the back burner so that he could work with Southern conservatives—most of them Democrats—on more easily achievable goals, and hundreds of liberals mailed pens to the White House in protest.

In recent years, however, a form of re-revisionism has taken place as Pomper and other scholars have concluded that Kennedy was right in line with other Presidents in keeping his promises. In his 1991 book *Promises Kept: John F Kennedy's New Frontier*, UCLA political scientist Irving Bernstein argued that Kennedy was on the verge of winning sweeping legislative victories on civil rights, tax relief, aid to education, and Medicare when he was killed.

In a study of five Presidents from 1960–84, American University professor of government Jeff Fishel attempted to tally the precise percentage of specific promises kept by these leaders. According to Fishel's study, published in the 1985 book *Presidents and Promises*, the chief executives kept their promises about two-thirds of the time. Giving them credit for fulfilling promises or making concerted efforts to fulfill them, Fishel grades JFK out at 67 percent, followed by Carter at 65 percent, Reagan and LBJ at 63 percent, and Richard Nixon at 60 percent.

Fishel's work picked up where Pomper's left off, although the two scholars looked at promises a bit differently. In his own study of every President from Harry S. Truman to Gerald R. Ford, Pomper compared these Presidents' records with the stances made in their party platforms and found that each Administration made strong efforts to fulfill its platform. On average, each President was success-ful about 70 percent of the time. More recently, Pomper supervised two studies of the Clinton Administration and found that Clinton reached this figure as well.

"In just the first two years after the 1992 election, Clinton fulfilled 70 percent of the [Democratic] platform promises, and the same percentage in the two years after the 1996 election," Pomper said in an interview.

Likewise, an analysis by Knight Ridder Newspapers of Clinton's first term credited the President with keeping 106 of the 160 promises he made in 1992—a success rate of 66 percent. If he received credit for "trying hard" to keep his promises, this figure would increase to 81 percent. In 1996, Joe Lockhart, who was then a spokesman for the Clinton-Gore campaign, cited such studies when defending the campaign's slogan: "Promises made, promises kept."

Republican presidential nominee Bob Dole implicitly confirmed how salient this claim was to voters by challenging it directly. "Never has America seen a politician who brags so freely about promises he never kept, votes he hasn't earned, goals he never accomplished, or virtues he never displayed," Dole told audiences. "Would you buy a used campaign promise from this man?"

The answer was yes. But the primary reason Dole's line of attack didn't work was that it didn't ring true to voters.

The Clinton Record

It is certainly understandable that conservatives found it hard to believe that Clinton was actually a promise keeper—or that voters would see him that way. In their own dealings with Clinton on the budget and other matters, Republicans in Congress found him unreliable—and that was long before Monica Lewinsky and Clinton's tortured formulation about truth depending on what the meaning of the word is is. To Clinton critics, the indelible image was first provided by then-top White House aide George Stephanopoulos in a Feb. 15, 1996, *Larry King Live* interview. Rattling off a list of Clinton accomplishments, Stephanopou-los added, "He's kept the promises he meant to keep."

Conservatives pounced on this remark, but Stephanopoulos' comment was simply an unfortunate choice of words. Probably more instructive is the testi-mony of William Galston, a University of Maryland (College Park) professor who served as Clinton's White House domestic policy adviser. "From my very first day of work, I had posted on my office wall a list of presidential promises," Galston recalled. "I looked at it every morning to make sure I remembered what the President said we ought to be doing there."

During the issues-driven, three-man race of 1992, Clinton had offered the most detailed policy prescriptions for the budget—and for much else of what he said ailed America. He laid it all out in hundreds of campaign speeches and a 232-page campaign booklet, *Putting People First*. Clinton vowed to cut the projected annual federal deficit in half during his first term; raise taxes on the wealthiest Americans; increase assistance to the working poor under the Earned-Income Tax Credit program; spend more on worker retraining; support the North American Free Trade Agreement; bolster the federally guaranteed student loan program; and guarantee all Americans access to "quality, affordable" health care. In what was often his biggest applause line—and before Democratic audiences, no less— Clinton promised "to end welfare as we know it."

All these things, he insisted, would revitalize the slumbering American economy, which he predicted would respond by creating 8 million new jobs. It actually created nearly 11 million.

To fight crime, Clinton said, he'd push for a five-day waiting period for handgun purchases and put 100,000 new cops on the street. He promised advocates for the poor that he would make Head Start virtually an entitlement program, and he assured women's groups he'd sign the Family and Medical Leave Act, guaranteeing American workers two weeks of unpaid leave for births, adoptions, or family medical emergencies. Twice President Bush vetoed it; Clinton said signing it would be his first order of business, which it was—on his initial day in office.

Clinton also had promised feminists he'd rescind the executive orders signed by Bush relating to abortion, including the so-called gag rule, which was designed to prevent doctors in federally funded clinics from recommending abortions. He promised environmentalists and loggers he would personally forge a compromise on cutting timber in the Pacific Northwest. He assured good-government advocates he'd work for campaign finance reform. No issue was too detailed. To Irish-Americans, Clinton promised he'd grant Sinn Fein leader Gerry Adams a visa to visit America, and that he would go outside established U.S. precedents in working for peace in Northern Ireland. He assured African-American audiences that he would usher in a more humane approach to dealing with Haitian refugees. He told gay and lesbian groups at California fund-raisers he would work to lift the ban on gays in the military.

As President, Clinton fought for all these things except campaign finance reform. And he attained almost his entire agenda. He failed at health care, but not for lack of trying, and was widely criticized for the naive way he approached the gays-in-the-military issue. When he broke a promise, Clinton tended to do it spectacularly. He dropped campaign reform at the request of congressional Democrats, but then set all kinds of dubious records for raising the same "soft money" he had promised to outlaw.

Other times, he was virtually forced to keep his promises. A Republican Congress enacted welfare reform over Clinton's misgivings—he actually vetoed it twice. Likewise, balancing the budget wasn't his idea either. Clinton embraced it just before the GOP-controlled Congress foisted it on him. One could have other quibbles, too: The 100,000 cops came out being something closer to 60,000. But this is considered close enough in the field of presidential promises.

Broken Promises

In his research, Fishel divides presidential promises into three categories: specific promises, rhetorical promises, and those in the middle. An example of a specific promise is Jimmy Carter's 1976 vow to create an Education Department. A rhetorical promise is Reagan's expressed desire to go down in history as the President "who made Americans believe in themselves again." One in the middle might be Clinton's vow to run "the most ethical Administration in history."

Sometimes these different types of campaign promises conflict with one another. Clinton's rhetorical vow to make abortion "safe, legal, and rare" was on a collision course with his specific vows to the National Abortion and Reproductive Rights Action League to work to reduce various barriers to abortion. Clinton chose the specific promise over the rhetorical one. On only his second day in office, Clinton signed five executive orders favored by NARAL, including one overturning the gag rule.*

Ronald Reagan made specific promises that collided with one another. In 1980, he vowed to balance the budget, pass a huge tax cut, and spend vast resources building up the nation's military defense. The three promises proved, as many Democrats warned, to be mutually exclusive. The tax cut and the military buildup, which Reagan accomplished, put the federal budget even more wildly out of balance than it was before. Reagan's admirers give him vast reservoirs of credit for helping to end the Cold War, restoring Americans' sense of self-confidence, and igniting the economy. His detractors point out that he left behind a sea of red ink. Both are accurate.

The Reagan example also underscores another truth about promises. They are not all created equal. One doesn't have to be a presidential scholar to understand that Dwight D. Eisenhower's 1952 vow to go to Korea—ostensibly to find a way to end the Korean War—was more significant than, say, Clinton's 1992 promise to create a Technical Extension Service to the Small Business Administration. If the importance of the pledges is factored in, Washburn University political scientist Bob Beatty says, Reagan ranks ahead of Clinton, and even LBJ, when it comes to keeping his promises. Conversely, Carter doesn't get as much credit, even though he made hundreds of specific promises and followed through on the bulk of them.

"Jimmy Carter is a special case," Beatty says. "Carter did much of what he said he would do, most of which failed. He followed through on what he said he would do, but in doing so didn't accomplish what he'd hoped. In that sense, Carter gets an A for keeping his promises, but . . . many of those promises shouldn't have been kept."

------

* In January 2001 President George W. Bush made a similar move by signing an order preventing international organizations that received U.S. aid from funding abortions with any of their funds.

Perhaps there should be a fourth category of presidential promises: ones that should never have been made in the first place. Certainly, FDR's Pittsburgh pledge to balance the budget would fall into this category. So would Jimmy Carter's promise to bring U.S. troops home from Korea, a promise he backed away from later. The most famous might be George Bush's "Read my lips, no new taxes" pledge. The problem is that if he hadn't made that promise, Bush might never have been elected in the first place.

Promising Peace

It is a truism among presidential scholars that nothing in the world quite prepares a presidential candidate for actually serving in the Oval Office. It is for this reason that Presidents often find that the promises they made as candidates are unrealistic. Many of the fiscal and budgetary policies that their predecessors pursued look more logical when viewed from the perspective of the White House. Even more frequently, candidates learn that a foreign policy mess they vowed to avoid is, in fact, unavoidable. That is in part what Texas A&M scholar George Edwards means when he says Presidents have to "bite the bullet." Simply put, what a President finds he must do after taking office is to let the bullets fly.

Woodrow Wilson won his close re-election campaign of 1916 over Charles Evan Hughes on the slogan "He kept us out of war." This was certainly Wilson's intention; it was also good politics. As World War I ravaged Europe in 1916, Americans concluded that they wanted no part of it. Wilson had wanted no part of it from the start: In August of 1914, he had urged his countrymen not only to remain neutral, but also to be "impartial in thought as well as in action." After his re-election, Wilson tried to mediate peace terms between Germany and Great Britain. But the Germans, devastated by their losses of life in the field and mistrustful of Wilson, embarked on one last gambit—an escalation of their submarine warfare—that brought the United States into the conflict.

And so it went through much of the century on presidential promises of neutrality and peace.

In 1940, Roosevelt already knew that the United States would have to fight Germany—and perhaps Japan as well—but he kept this realization from the American people. On Oct. 30, 1940, slightly more than a week before Election Day, Roosevelt told a cheering crowd in Boston Garden, "I have said this before, but I'll say it again and again and again: Your boys are not going to be sent into any foreign wars." In truth, by that time, FDR was quietly preparing for just such a war—and actively trying to provoke the Germans into firing on U.S. destroyers in the North Atlantic.

History has a way of repeating itself. In 1964, President Johnson assured voters, "We are not about to send American boys nine or 10 thousand miles away from home to do what Asian boys ought to be doing themselves." But as other Democrats excoriated Republican nominee Barry Goldwater for saying that

America shouldn't be getting in Vietnam unless it intended to win there, Johnson was already planning a huge escalation. During the year, he quietly increased the number of U.S. military "advisers" in Vietnam from 16,000 to 25,000. Within a year of LBJ's landslide victory over Goldwater, this number was 180,000.

In 1968, Richard M. Nixon sought to defuse Vietnam as an issue by telling voters, "New leadership will end the war and win the peace in the Pacific." Those words were interpreted in the press as Nixon's "secret plan" to end the war in Vietnam. But Nixon had no real plan.

In all three of these cases, these Presidents were guilty of either wishful thinking or telling voters what they wanted to hear—or both. Eisenhower provided a contrast in 1952. With U.S. troops bogged down in a grim war of attrition in Korea, Ike told an audience in Detroit on Oct. 24, 1952, just two weeks before Election Day: "That job requires a personal trip to Korea. I shall make that trip. I shall go to Korea!"

It was, notes Eisenhower biographer Geoffrey Perret, more than a pledge to go and physically see the battlefield himself; it was an implicit promise that the soldier who had overseen the Normandy invasion would find a way to end the fighting in Korea. Eisenhower kept both of those promises—and was re-elected in 1956, despite the fact that the economy was in a recession.

"This was the five-star general, Eisenhower, winner of the war in Europe, talking," says presidential scholar David M. Abshire, who at the time was an Army lieutenant commanding a company in Korea. "He was saying, 'I'm going to go see for myself how we can wrap this up.'"

The perfect contrast is probably Bill Clinton, who came into office with no military or foreign policy experience. There was no war that Clinton needed to assure Americans he'd avoid. But he promised to link U.S. relations with China more closely to human rights; complained that Israel had been pressured by the U.S. to "make one-sided concessions"; and vowed not to normalize relations with Vietnam until a "full accounting" of all POWs and MIAs was made. As it turned out, Clinton temporized on all these issues, for some of the same reasons his predecessors had not kept their promises on foreign policy. Stephen Wayne, presidential scholar at Georgetown University, says that presidential promises, particularly those concerning foreign policy, are made "based on incomplete knowledge." In other words, the world never looks quite the same from inside the Oval Office as from outside.

After winning re-election in 1996, Clinton held a press conference in the East Room and was asked by a reporter about a specific campaign promise he'd made on the train on the way to the Democratic National Convention in Chicago— and then again at the convention itself—to do away with one of America's least popular taxes, the capital gains taxes people paid when they sold their own homes. Will it be in the budget you submit to Congress?

"The answer is yes, my homeowners' exemption, capital gains exemption, is in the budget," the President replied. Looking his questioner in the eye, he added: "*Everything* I talked about at Chicago is in the budget."

And so it was. The capital gains provision became law, as did numerous other 1996 campaign promises, including setting aside vast tracts of Western lands for environmental protection; increasing spending on elementary school reading programs; $1,500 tax credits for working-class American families' college expenses; and expansion of Medicare to cover more people. In fact, Clinton was well on his way to delivering on another round of promises the very week that his second term was derailed by the sex scandal that resulted in his impeachment and a lost year of his presidency.

Historians might note, approvingly, that Clinton and his allies fashioned an impeachment defense that rested, at least in part, on convincing a majority of the American people that whatever promises the President didn't keep in his personal life—and despite the dubious veracity of his testimony in the Paula Corbin Jones sexual harassment case—Clinton *had* kept his word to the American people on the policy issues that mattered to them. It's unlikely this approach would have worked if it didn't conform to Americans' impressions—or to reality.

Questions for Discussion

1. Is it surprising to you that most presidents keep most of their promises? Why? Does it matter that they do?
2. What is a presidential promise? What difficulties do reporters and political scientists face in defining a promise?

 Chapter 12

Bureaucracy

The terms *bureaucracy* and *bureaucrat* evoke negative images for most Americans. To many, *bureaucracy* is a synonym for red tape, rigidity, insensitivity, and long waiting lines, and *bureaucrat* suggests a faceless government drone sitting at a desk, pushing papers, and stamping forms. In fact, a bureaucracy is any complex organization that operates on the basis of a hierarchical authority structure with job specialization. Corporations are bureaucracies, as are educational institutions. The question is whether a bureaucracy complements democracy. On the one hand, it seems wise to have a government run by professionals whose jobs are not dependent on politics. But we seem to have created a class of government employees who are beyond the control of the voters.

In recent years, public officials and candidates for public office have nurtured the negative image of the public sector and those employed by it. Bureaucracy-bashing is good politics. Four recent presidents—Nixon, Carter, Reagan, and George W. Bush—were first elected during campaigns that made opposition to the Washington bureaucracy a central theme. Every election year congressional candidates remind the public that the federal government has paid $91 for three-cent screws or $511 for a sixty-cent lightbulb. Contempt for the Washington bureaucracy may have reached a zenith during the Reagan presidency. Attorney General Edwin Meese once came to a cabinet meeting carrying a chubby, faceless, large-bottomed doll and announced that it was a bureaucrat doll—you place it on a stack of papers and it just sits there.

According to one student of American bureaucracy, Barry D. Karl, "the growth of the bureaucratic state may be the single most unintended consequence of the Constitution of 1787." The Constitution says little about the administration of government. It gives the president the appointment power and the obligation "to take care that the laws [are] faithfully executed," which suggests that the framers were well aware of the administrative needs of the new nation. But belief in limited government and fear of centralized power led them to envision a minimal role for the new federal government.

Thus, the administrative apparatus during the first few presidencies was very small. The State Department had only nine employees at its beginning, and the War Department had fewer than one hundred employees until 1801, at the start of the Jefferson presidency. Compared to Western European countries, the

U.S. bureaucracy experienced a rather late development, well after the growth of mass democracy under Andrew Jackson in the 1830s. By 1861, on the eve of the Civil War, roughly 80 percent of all federal personnel still worked for the Post Office Department.

The Civil War was one of the most significant events in the growth of American bureaucracy. Mobilization for the war effort led to the creation of many new agencies and the hiring of a large number of public employees. The growth of a national economy and rapid industrialization after the war also had a profound effect on the size and functions of the federal government, which began to pay attention to particular constituencies. "Clientele" agencies such as the Department of Agriculture (1889) and the Department of Commerce and Labor (1903) were created to service increasingly organized interests.

This period also marked the beginning of the development of a professional bureaucratic class. Before 1883, all federal workers were patronage employees, appointed by the president. When presidencies changed hands, many government employees were out of a job. The assassination of President James A. Garfield in 1881 by an unsuccessful patronage applicant provided the impetus for passage of the Pendleton Act (1882), which established the civil service system. Only about 10 percent of government employees were initially covered by the act, but today more than 90 percent are; they receive their jobs on the basis of competitive merit, usually as the result of written examinations. Firing someone for political reasons is illegal.

The New Deal and mobilization for World War II gave the federal bureaucracy the basic form it has today. As the federal government took on an expanded social and economic role, myriad new agencies were created. Today there are more than a hundred federal government agencies, and the government employs almost 5 million people, 2.9 million of whom are civilians.

Despite the widely shared view that the federal bureaucracy has grown rapidly in recent decades, the number of federal employees has been relatively constant since 1945. Most of the growth in the public sector has been at the state and local levels. Nor do most federal bureaucrats work in or around the nation's capital. Only about 12 percent of federal employees work in Washington; 300,000, or 10 percent, work in California. Federal government employment as a percentage of the total work force decreased over the past two decades. "Big government" is more dollars and rules than it is huge numbers of federal bureaucrats.

Whatever the size of the bureaucracy, its nature poses a dilemma. We need a bureaucratic organization and professional administrators so that government can carry out its basic functions without political interference. But the growth of a professional bureaucratic class has been considered at odds with American political values. Use of the term *civil servant* is an insistence that government employees serve the public, not their employer or themselves. Although Americans want state services, the fear of strong central government and administrative tyranny remains.

Because the U.S. government is involved in so many activities, almost everyone can view some aspect of bureaucracy as illegitimate and threatening. Conservatives generally disapprove of government's redistribution of income and regulation of business, viewing it as intrusive and at odds with traditional free-market philosophy. Liberals are concerned about the bureaucracy's intelligence-gathering and domestic policing activities; the secrecy and potential violation of civil liberties raise concerns about "Big Brother" watching.

And the federal bureaucracy represents more than the passive administration of laws passed by the elected branches of government. Bureaucrats are given substantial authority: They issue rules, enforce compliance, allocate federal funds, and regulate economic activity. Because of their expertise, they often formulate policy, although the most successful bureaucratic policymakers work closely with Congress.

The American solution to the dilemma posed by the coexistence of bureaucracy and democracy is to keep the bureaucracy accountable through scrutiny by the other branches of government and by the nation's press. Congressional oversight of bureaucratic practices and spending, central direction in policymaking by the president and his staff, and judicial review of administrative processes and rule making are all important restraints on bureaucratic discretion.

The selections in this chapter are intended to convey a sense of the impact of the bureaucracy on American politics, the controversial nature of its activities, and the difficulties facing those who wish to reform it. Charles Peters discusses some of the problems inherent in large organizations and explains how they can lead to flawed bureaucratic decisions. James Q. Wilson focuses on the difficulties managers of public organizations confront because of their lack of control over agency revenues, productivity factors, and agency goals due to external political constraints.

The article by Nicholas Thompson and the one by Norm Ornstein and Tom Donilon address the issue of how government can attract talented individuals for public service. Thompson examines what incentives might attract younger people in an era when the private sector can offer not only better compensation, but also more compelling challenges. Ornstein and Donilon look at another aspect of recruitment—how to attract highly talented individuals to serve at the very top levels of government. Despite some serious efforts in 2000 and 2001 to make the appointment and confirmation process work more smoothly, a "confirmation clog" remains in the Senate (and, to an extent, within the executive branch) that discourages strong candidates from putting forth their names for top appointments. Although public service is often seen as attractive and challenging, government needs to find ways to make it easier and more productive for talented individuals to spend part of their careers in the public sector.

From Ouagadougou to Cape Canaveral: Why the Bad News Doesn't Travel Up

Charles Peters

On January 28, 1986, seven crew members of the space shuttle Challenger were killed in a midflight explosion. The tragedy was caused by the disintegration of a type of seal called an O-ring, which led to failure in the joint between segments of one of the eight solid booster rockets. It can be argued, however, that the fundamental reason for the shuttle disaster was a communication failure within the hierarchy of the National Aeronautics and Space Administration (NASA). Private engineers on the project were aware of a history of problems with the O-rings and had advised certain mid-level NASA officials not to launch under certain conditions. Had top-level officials known of the problems, the launch might not have taken place.

In this selection, Charles Peters suggests that it is extremely difficult for top managers in a large organization to be aware of problems at various levels of a bureaucratic hierarchy. Officials at NASA were under tremendous political pressure to launch the shuttle, so negative information was suppressed within the chain of command. Peters suggests that this problem is common and can be blamed for a number of the government's recent flawed decisions. The remedies, he suggests, are more direct government oversight and an active press.

Everyone is asking why the top NASA officials who decided to launch the fatal Challenger flight had not been told of the concerns of people down below, like Allan McDonald and the other worried engineers at Morton Thiokol.*

In the first issue of *The Washington Monthly*, Russell Baker and I wrote, "In any reasonably large government organization, there exists an elaborate system of information cutoffs, comparable to that by which city water systems shut off large

---

* Morton Thiokol is the private engineering company that was in charge of the design and construction of the space shuttle booster rocket.

Charles Peters is editor-in-chief of *The Washington Monthly*.

water-main breaks, closing down, first small feeder pipes, then larger and larger valves. The object is to prevent information, particularly of an unpleasant character, from rising to the top of the agency, where it may produce results unpleasant to the lower ranks.

"Thus, the executive at or near the top lives in constant danger of not knowing, until he reads it on Page One some morning, that his department is hip-deep in disaster."

This seemed to us to be a serious problem for government, not only because the people at the top didn't know but because the same system of cut-offs operated to keep Congress, the press, and the public in the dark. (Often it also would operate to keep in the dark people within the organization but outside the immediate chain of command—this happened with the astronauts, who were not told about the concern with the O-rings.)

I first became aware of this during the sixties, when I worked at the Peace Corps. Repeatedly I would find that a problem that was well-known by people at lower and middle levels of the organization, whose responsibility it was, would be unknown at the top of the chain of command or by anyone outside.

The most serious problems of the Peace Corps had their origins in Sargent Shriver's desire to get the organization moving.* He did not want it to become mired in feasibility studies, he wanted to get volunteers overseas and into action fast. To fulfill his wishes, corners were cut. Training was usually inadequate in language, culture, and technical skills. Volunteers were selected who were not suited to their assignments. For example, the country then known as Tanganyika asked for surveyors, and we sent them people whose only connection with surveying had been holding the rod and chain while the surveyor sighted through his gizmo. Worse, volunteers were sent to places where no job at all awaited them. These fictitious assignments were motivated sometimes by the host official's desire to please the brother-in-law of the president of the United States and sometimes by the official's ignorance of what was going on at the lower levels of his own bureaucracy.

But subordinates would not tell Shriver about the problems. There were two reasons for this. One was fear. They knew that he wanted action, not excuses, and they suspected that their careers would suffer if he heard too many of the latter. The other reason was that they felt it was their job to solve problems, not burden the boss with them. They and Shriver shared the view expressed by Deke Slayton, the former astronaut, when he was asked about the failure of middle-level managers to tell top NASA officials about the problems they were encountering. "You depend on managers to make a decision based on the information they have. If they had to transmit all the fine detail to the top people, it wouldn't get launched but once every ten years."

---

* Sargent Shriver—President Kennedy's brother-in-law—was the first director of the Peace Corps. The organization was set up to send American volunteers to help people in Third World countries. In 1972, Shriver was the Democratic vice-presidential candidate.

The point is not without merit. It is easy for large organizations to fall into "once every ten years" habits. Leaders who want to avoid that danger learn to set goals and communicate a sense of urgency about meeting them. But what many of them never learn is that once you set those goals you have to guard against the tendency of those down below to spare you not only "all the fine detail" but essential facts about significant problems.

For instance, when Jimmy Carter gave the Pentagon the goal of rescuing the Iranian hostages, he relied on the chain of command to tell him if there were any problems. So he did not find out until after the disaster at Desert One that the Delta Commandos thought the Marine pilots assigned to fly the helicopters were incompetent.*

In NASA's case chances have been taken with the shuttle from the beginning—the insulating thermal tiles had not gone through a reentry test before the first shuttle crew risked their lives to try them out—but in recent years the pressure to cut corners has increased markedly. Competition with the European Ariane rocket and the Reagan administration's desire to see agencies like NASA run as if they were private businesses have led to a speedup in the launch schedule, with a goal of 14 this year [1986] and 24 by 1988.

"The game NASA is playing is the maximum tonnage per year at the minimum costs possible," says Paul Cloutier, a professor of space physics. "Some high officials don't want to hear about problems," reports *Newsweek*, "especially if fixing them will cost money."

Under pressures like these, the NASA launch team watched Columbia, after seven delays, fall about a month behind schedule and then saw Challenger delayed, first by bad weather, then by damaged door handles, and then by bad weather again. Little wonder that [NASA's launch chief] Lawrence Mulloy, when he heard the warnings from the Thiokol engineers, burst out: "My God, Thiokol, when do you want me to launch? Next April?"

Mulloy may be one of the villains of this story, but it is important to realize that you need Lawrence Mulloys to get things done. It is also important to realize that, if you have a Lawrence Mulloy, you must protect yourself against what he might fail to do or what he might do wrong in his enthusiastic rush to get the job done.

And you can't just ask him if he has any doubts. If he's a gung-ho type, he's going to suppress the negatives. When Jimmy Carter asked General David Jones to check out the Iran rescue plan, Jones said to Colonel Beckwith: "Charlie, tell me what you really think about the mission. Be straight with me."

"Sir, we're going to do it!" Beckwith replied. "We want to do it, and we're ready."

---

* In the spring of 1980, President Carter made a decision to have a U.S. commando force attempt to rescue the American hostages held in Iran. A number of reasons have been suggested for the failure of the mission. The helicopters chosen for the mission evidently could not operate successfully in the sand and wind of the Iranian desert. One crashed on takeoff, killing a number of soldiers, and the mission was aborted.

John Kennedy received similar confident reports from the chain of command about the readiness of the CIA's Cuban Brigade to charge ashore at the Bay of Pigs and overthrow Fidel Castro. And Sargent Shriver had every reason to believe that the Peace Corps was getting off to a fabulous start, based on what his chain of command was telling him.

With Shriver, as with NASA's senior officials, the conviction that everything was A-OK was fortified by skillful public relations. Bill Moyers was only one of the geniuses involved in this side of the Peace Corps. At NASA, Julian Scheer began a tradition of inspired PR that endured until Challenger. These were men who could sell air conditioning in Murmansk. The trouble is they also sold their bosses the same air conditioning. Every organization has a tendency to believe its own PR—NASA's walls are lined with glamorizing posters and photographs of the shuttle and other space machines—and usually the top man is the most thoroughly seduced because, after all, it reflects the most glory on him.

Favorable publicity and how to get it is therefore the dominant subject of Washington staff meetings. The minutes of the Nuclear Regulatory Commission show that when the reactor was about to melt down at Three Mile Island, the commissioners were worried less about what to do to fix the reactor than they were about what they were going to say to the press.

One of the hottest rumors around Washington is that the White House had put pressure on NASA to launch so that the president could point with pride to the teacher in space during his State of the Union speech. The White House denies this story, and my sources tell me the denial is true. But NASA had—and this is fact, not rumor—put pressure on *itself* by asking the president to mention Christa McAuliffe. In a memorandum dated January 8, NASA proposed that the president say: "Tonight while I am speaking to you, a young elementary school teacher from Concord, New Hampshire, is taking us all on the ultimate field trip as she orbits the earth as the first citizen passenger on the space shuttle. Christa McAuliffe's journey is a prelude to the journeys of other Americans living and working together in a permanently manned space station in the mid-1990s. Mrs. McAuliffe's week in space is just one of the achievements in space we have planned for the coming year."

The flight was scheduled for January 23. It was postponed and postponed again. Now it was January 28, the morning of the day the speech was to be delivered, the last chance for the launch to take place in time to have it mentioned by the president. NASA officials must have feared they were about to lose a PR opportunity of stunning magnitude, an opportunity to impress not only the media and the public but the agency's two most important constituencies, the White House and the Congress. Wouldn't you feel pressure to get that launch off this morning so that the president could talk about it tonight?

NASA's sensitivity to the media in regard to the launch schedule was nothing short of unreal. Here is what Richard G. Smith, the director of the Kennedy Space Center, had to say about it after the disaster: "Every time there was a delay, the press would say, 'Look, there's another delay. . . . here's a bunch of idiots who can't even handle a launch schedule.' You think that doesn't have an impact? If you think it doesn't, you're stupid."

I do not recall seeing a single story like those Smith describes. Perhaps there were a few. The point, however, is to realize how large even a little bit of press criticism loomed in NASA's thinking.

Sargent Shriver liked good press as much as, if not more than, the next man. But he also had an instinct that the ultimate bad press would come if the world found out about your disaster before you had a chance to do something to prevent it. He and an assistant named William Haddad decided to make sure that Shriver got the bad news first. Who was going to find it out for them? Me.

It was July 1961. They decided to call me an evaluator and send me out to our domestic training programs and later overseas to find out what was really going on. My first stop was the University of California at Berkeley where our Ghana project was being trained. Fortunately, except for grossly inadequate language instruction, this program was excellent. But soon I began finding serious deficiencies in other training programs and in our projects abroad.

Shriver was not always delighted by these reports. Indeed, at one point I heard I was going to be fired. I liked my job, and I knew that the reports that I and the other evaluators who had joined me were writing were true. I didn't want to be fired. What could I do?

I knew he was planning to visit our projects in Africa. So I prepared a memorandum that contrasted what the chain of command was saying with what I and my associates were reporting. Shriver left for Africa. I heard nothing for several weeks. Then came a cable from Somalia: "Tell Peters his reports are right." I knew then that, however much Shriver wanted to hear the good news and get good publicity, he could take the bad news. The fact that he could take the bad news meant that the Peace Corps began to face its problems and do something about them before they became a scandal.

NASA did the opposite. A 1983 reorganization shifted the responsibility for monitoring flight safety from the chief engineer in Washington to the field. This may sound good. "We're not going to micromanage," said James M. Beggs, then the NASA administrator. But the catch is that if you decentralize, you must maintain the flow of information from the field to the top so that the organization's leader will know what those decentralized managers are doing. What NASA's reorganization did, according to safety engineers who talked to Mark Tapscott of the *Washington Times,* was to close off "an independent channel with authority to make things happen at the top."

I suspect what happened is that the top NASA administrators, who were pushing employees down below to dramatically increase the number of launches, either consciously or unconsciously did not want to be confronted with the dangers they were thereby risking.

This is what distinguishes the bad leaders from the good. The good leader, realizing that there is a natural human tendency to avoid bad news, traps himself into having to face it. He encourages whistleblowers instead of firing them. He visits the field himself and talks to the privates and lieutenants as well as the generals to find out the real problems. He can use others to do this for him, as Shriver used me. . . . But he must have some independent knowledge of what's going on down below in order to have a feel for whether the chain of command is giving him the straight dope.

What most often happens, of course, is that the boss, if he goes to the field at all, talks only to the colonels and generals. Sometimes he doesn't want to know what the privates know. He may be hoping that the lid can be kept on whatever problems are developing, at least until his watch is over, so that he won't be blamed when they finally surface. Or he may have a very good idea that bad things are being done and simply wants to retain "deniability," meaning that the deed cannot be traced to him. The story of Watergate is filled with "Don't tell me" and "I don't want to know."

When NASA's George Hardy told Thiokol engineers that he was appalled by their verbal recommendation that the launch be postponed and asked Thiokol to reconsider and make another recommendation, Thiokol, which Hardy well knew was worried about losing its shuttle contract, was in effect being told, "Don't tell me" or "Don't tell me officially so I won't have to pass bad news along and my bosses will have deniability."

In addition to the leader himself, others must be concerned with making him face the bad news. This includes subordinates. Their having the courage to speak out about what is wrong is crucial, and people like Bruce Cook of NASA and Allan McDonald of Thiokol deserve great credit for having done so. But it is a fact that none of the subordinates who knew the danger to the shuttle took the next step and resigned in protest so that the public could find out what was going on in time to prevent disaster. The almost universal tendency to place one's own career above one's moral responsibility to take a stand on matters like these has to be one of the most depressing facts about bureaucratic culture today.

Even when the issue was simply providing facts for an internal NASA investigation after the disaster, here is the state of mind Bruce Cook describes in a recent article in the *Washington Post*: "Another [NASA employee] told me to step away from his doorway while he searched for a document in his filing cabinet so that no one would see me in his office and suspect that he'd been the one I'd gotten it from."

It may be illuminating to note here that at the Peace Corps I found my most candid informants were the volunteers. They had no career stake in the organization—they were in for just two years—and thus had no reason to fear the results of their candor. Doesn't this suggest that we might be better off with more short-term employees in the government, people who are planning to leave anyway and thus have no hesitation to blow the whistle when necessary?

Certainly the process of getting bad news from the bottom to the top can be helped by institutionalizing it, as it was in the case of the Peace Corps Evaluation Division, and by hiring to perform it employees who have demonstrated courage and independence as well as the ability to elicit the truth and report it clearly.

Two other institutions that can help this process are the Congress and the White House. But the staff they have to perform this function is tiny. The White House depends on the OMB to tell it what the executive branch is doing. Before the Challenger exploded, the OMB had four examiners to cover science and space. The Senate subcommittee on Space, Science and Technology had a staff of three. Needless to say, they had not heard about the O-rings.

Another problem is lack of experience. Too few congressmen and too few of their staff have enough experience serving in the executive branch to have a sense of the right question to ask. OMB examiners usually come aboard straight from graduate school, totally innocent of practical experience in government.

The press shares this innocence. Only a handful of journalists have worked in the bureaucracy. Like the members of Congress, they treat policy formulation as the ultimate reality: Congress passed this bill today; the president signed that bill. That's what the TV reporters on the Capitol steps and the White House lawn tell us about. But suppose the legislation in question concerns coal mine safety. Nobody is going to know what it all adds up to until some members of Congress and some members of the press go down into the coal mine to find out if conditions actually are safer or if only more crazy regulations have been added.

Unfortunately, neither the congressmen nor the press display much enthusiasm for visits to the mines. Yet this is what I found to be the key to getting the real story about the Peace Corps. I had to go to Ouagadougou and talk to the volunteers at their sites before I could really know what the Peace Corps was doing and what its problems were. I wasn't going to find out by asking the public affairs office. . . .

Because the reporters don't know any better, they don't press the Congress to do any better. What journalists could do is make the public aware of how little attention Congress devotes to what is called "oversight," i.e., finding out what the programs it has authorized are actually doing. If the press would publicize the nonperformance of this function, it is at least possible that the public would begin to reward the congressmen who perform it consistently and punish those who ignore it by not reelecting them.

But the press will never do this until it gets itself out of Larry Speakes's office. Woodward and Bernstein didn't get the Watergate story by talking to Ron Ziegler,* or, for that matter, by using other reportorial techniques favored by the media elite, like questioning Richard Nixon at a press conference or interviewing other administration luminaries at fancy restaurants. They had to find lower-level sources like Hugh Sloan, just as the reporters who finally got the NASA story had to find the Richard Cooks and Allan McDonalds.

Eileen Shanahan, a former reporter for the *New York Times* and a former assistant secretary of HEW, recently wrote "of the many times I tried, during my

---

* Larry Speakes was Ronald Reagan's press secretary at the time this article was written. Ron Ziegler was President Nixon's press secretary. Bob Woodward and Carl Bernstein were the two *Washington Post* writers credited with unraveling the Watergate scandal.

tenure in the Department of Health, Education and Welfare, to interest distin-guished reporters from distinguished publications in the effort the department was making to find out whether its billion-dollar programs actually were reaching the intended beneficiaries and doing any good. Their eyes glazed over."

I have had a similar experience with reporters during my 25 years in Washing-ton. For most of that time they have seemed to think they knew everything about bureaucracy because they had read a Kafka novel and stood in line at the post office. In their ignorance, they adopted a kind of wise-guy, world-weary fatalism that said nothing could be done about bureaucratic problems. They had little or no sense about how to approach organizations with an anthropologist's feel for the interaction of attitudes, values, and institutional pressures.

There are a couple of reasons, however, to hope that the performance of the press will improve. The coverage of business news has become increasingly sophisticated about the way institutional pressures affect executive and corporate behavior, mainly because the comparison of our economy with Japan's made the importance of cultural factors so obvious. And on defense issues, visits to the field are increasingly common as reporters attempt to find out whether this or that weapon works.

But these are mere beachheads. They need to be radically expanded to include the coverage of all the institutions that affect our lives, especially government. This may seem unlikely, but if the press studies the Challenger case, I do not see how it can avoid perceiving the critical role bureaucratic pressure played in bringing about the disaster. What the press must then realize is that similar pressures vitally influence almost everything this government does, and that we will never understand why government fails until we understand those pressures and how human beings in public office react to them.*

Questions for Discussion

1. What factors operate within large organizations to prevent top leaders from learning about organizational difficulties? How might a leader of an organiza-tion overcome such factors?
2. According to the author, why don't congressional oversight and press scru-tiny of the bureaucracy uncover problems? How could such oversight be improved?

---

* In 1990, NASA experienced another public relations disaster when its $1.5 billion Hubble Space Telescope failed to focus clearly. NASA's investigating panel fixed the blame for the telescope flaw on the same management climate that led to the fatal explosion of the space shuttle Challenger in 1986. As in the shuttle case, the report indicated that engineers working on the telescope as far back as 1980 and 1981 were discouraged from bringing potential problems to the attention of their superiors.

12.2

Constraints on Public Managers

James Q. Wilson

Companies like AT&T or McDonald's rival in size and budget some of the largest government organizations and, on paper, are organized similarly, with a hierarchical authority structure and multiple layers of administration. They are bureaucracies in every sense of the term. Critics of government bureaucracy often point to the successes of such private sector organizations as efficient deliverers of services or products, in contrast to public bureaucracies that often are stereotyped as being bound by rules or red tape and staffed by unmotivated and unresponsive workers. Every election sees candidates committed to reforming government bureaucracies in an attempt to "run government more like a business."

Although government and private bureaucracies share many characteristics, they are different in fundamental ways, creating difficulties for those who aspire to make government agencies more like their private sector counterparts. In this selection, James Q. Wilson argues that all government agencies have certain characteristics that tend to make their management far more difficult than managing a business: "Government management tends to be driven by the *constraints* on the organization, not the *tasks* of the organization." Managerial control is particularly problematic because public managers have relatively little control over revenues, factors of production, and agency goals, which are "all vested to an important degree in entities external to the organization—legislatures, courts, politicians, and interest groups." One result is that public managers become "averse to any action that risks violating a significant constraint," rigidly interpreting rules and avoiding innovation.

By the time the office opens at 8:45 A.M., the line of people waiting to do business at the Registry of Motor Vehicles in Watertown, Massachusetts, often will be twenty-five deep. By midday, especially if it is near the end of the month, the line may extend clear around the building. Inside, motorists wait in slow-moving rows before poorly marked windows to get a driver's license or to register an automobile. When someone gets to the head of the line, he or she is

James Q. Wilson is professor of management and public policy at UCLA and past president of the American Political Science Association.

often told by the clerk that it is the wrong line: "Get an application over there and then come back," or "This is only for people getting a new license; if you want to replace one you lost, you have to go to the next window." The customers grumble impatiently. The clerks act harried and sometimes speak brusquely, even rudely. What seems to be a simple transaction may take 45 minutes or even longer. . . .

Not far away, people also wait in line at a McDonald's fast-food restaurant. There are several lines; each is short, each moves quickly. The menu is clearly displayed on attractive signs. The workers behind the counter are invariably polite. If someone's order cannot be filled immediately, he or she is asked to step aside for a moment while the food is prepared and then is brought back to the head of the line to receive the order. The atmosphere is friendly and good-natured. The room is immaculately clean.

Many people have noticed the difference between getting a driver's license and ordering a Big Mac. Most will explain it by saying that bureaucracies are different from businesses. "Bureaucracies" behave as they do because they are run by unqualified "bureaucrats" and are enmeshed in "rules" and "red tape."

But business firms are also bureaucracies, and McDonald's is a bureaucracy that regulates virtually every detail of its employees' behavior by a complex and all-encompassing set of rules. Its operations manual is six hundred pages long and weighs four pounds.[1] In it one learns that french fries are to be nine-thirty-seconds of an inch thick and that grill workers are to place hamburger patties on the grill from left to right, six to a row for six rows. They are then to flip the third row first, followed by the fourth, fifth, and sixth rows, and finally the first and second. The amount of sauce placed on each bun is precisely specified. Every window must be washed every day. Workers must get down on their hands and knees and pick up litter as soon as it appears. These and countless other rules designed to reduce the workers to interchangeable automata were inculcated in franchise managers at Hamburger University located in a $40 million facility. There are plenty of rules governing the Registry, but they are only a small fraction of the rules that govern every detail of every operation at McDonald's. Indeed, if the DMV manager tried to impose on his employees as demanding a set of rules as those that govern the McDonald's staff, they would probably rebel and he would lose his job.

It is just as hard to explain the differences between the two organizations by reference to the quality or compensation of their employees. The Registry workers are all adults, most with at least a high-school education; the McDonald's employees are mostly teenagers, many still in school. The Registry staff is well-paid compared to the McDonald's workers, most of whom receive only the minimum wage. . . .

Not only are the differences between the two organizations not to be explained by reference to "rules" or "red tape" or "incompetent workers," the differences call into question many of the most frequently mentioned complaints about how government agencies are supposed to behave. For example: "Government agencies are big spenders." The Watertown office of the Registry is in a modest building that can barely handle its clientele. The teletype machine used to check information submitted by people requesting a replacement license was antiquated and prone to errors. Three or four clerks often had to wait in line to use equipment described by the office manager as "personally signed by Thomas Edison." No computers or word processors were available to handle the preparation of licenses and registrations; any error made by a clerk while manually typing a form meant starting over again on another form.

Or: "Government agencies hire people regardless of whether they are really needed." Despite the fact that the citizens of Massachusetts probably have more contact with the Registry than with any other state agency, and despite the fact that these citizens complain more about Registry service than about that of any other bureau, the Watertown branch, like all Registry offices, was seriously understaffed. . . .

Or: "Government agencies are imperialistic, always grasping for new functions." But there is no record of the Registry doing much grasping, even though one could imagine a case being made that the state government could usefully create at Registry offices "one-stop" multi-service centers where people could not only get drivers' licenses but also pay taxes and parking fines, obtain information, and transact other official business. The Registry seemed content to provide one service.

In short, many of the popular stereotypes about government agencies and their members are either questionable or incomplete. To explain why government agencies behave as they do, it is not enough to know that they are "bureaucracies"—that is, it is not enough to know that they are big, or complex, or have rules. What is crucial is that they are *government* bureaucracies. . . . [N]ot all government bureaucracies behave the same way or suffer from the same problems. . . . But all government agencies have in common certain characteristics that tend to make their management far more difficult than managing a McDonald's. These common characteristics are the constraints of public agencies.

The key constraints are three in number. To a much greater extent than is true of private bureaucracies, government agencies (1) cannot lawfully retain and devote to the private benefit of their members the earnings of the organization, (2) cannot allocate the factors of production in accordance with the preferences of the organization's administrators, and (3) must serve goals not of the organization's own choosing. Control over revenues, productive factors, and agency goals is all vested to an important degree in entities external to the organization—legislatures, courts, politicians, and interest groups. Given this, agency managers must attend to the demands of these external entities. As a result, government management tends to be driven by the *constraints* on the organization, not the *tasks* of the organization. To say the same thing in other words, whereas business management focuses on the "bottom line" (that is, profits), government management focuses on the "top line" (that is, constraints). . . .

Revenues and Incentives

In the days leading up to September 30, the federal government is Cinderella, courted by legions of individuals and organizations eager to get grants and contracts from the unexpended funds still at the disposal of each agency. At midnight on September 30, the government's coach turns into a pumpkin. That is the moment—the end of the fiscal year—at which every agency, with a few exceptions, must return all unexpended funds to the Treasury Department. . . . Because of these fiscal rules agencies do not have a material incentive to economize: Why scrimp and save if you cannot keep the results of your frugality?

. . . When a private firm has a good year, many of its officers and workers may receive bonuses. Even if no bonus is paid, these employees may buy stock in the firm so that they can profit from any growth in earnings (and, if they sell the stock in a timely manner, profit from a drop in earnings). Should a public bureaucrat be discovered trying to do what private bureaucrats routinely do, he or she would be charged with corruption.

We take it for granted that bureaucrats should not profit from their offices and nod approvingly when a bureaucrat who has so benefited is indicted and put on trial. But why should we take this view? Once a very different view prevailed. In the seventeenth century, a French colonel would buy his commission from the king, take the king's money to run his regiment, and pocket the profit. At one time a European tax collector was paid by keeping a percentage of the taxes he collected. In this country, some prisons were once managed by giving the warden a sum of money based on how many prisoners were under his control and letting him keep the difference between what he received and what it cost him to feed the prisoners. Such behavior today would be grounds for criminal prosecution. Why? What has changed?

Mostly we the citizenry have changed. We are creatures of the Enlightenment: We believe that the nation ought not to be the property of the sovereign; that laws are intended to rationalize society and (if possible) perfect mankind; and that public service ought to be neutral and disinterested. We worry that a prison warden paid in the old way would have a strong incentive to starve his prisoners in order to maximize his income; that a regiment supported by a greedy colonel would not be properly equipped; and that a tax collector paid on a commission basis would extort excessive taxes from us. These changes reflect our desire to eliminate moral hazards—namely, creating incentives for people to act wrongly. But why should this desire rule out more carefully designed compensation plans that would pay government managers for achieving officially approved goals and would allow efficient agencies to keep any unspent part of their budget for use next year?

Part of the answer is obvious. Often we do not know whether a manager or an agency has achieved the goals we want because either the goals are vague or inconsistent, or their attainment cannot be observed, or both. Bureau chiefs in the Department of State would have to go on welfare if their pay depended on their ability to demonstrate convincingly that they had attained their bureaus' objectives.

But many government agencies have reasonably clear goals toward which progress can be measured. The Social Security Administration, the Postal Service, and the General Services Administration all come to mind. Why not let earnings depend importantly on performance? Why not let agencies keep excess revenues?

I am not entirely certain why this does not happen. To some degree it is because of a widespread cultural norm that people should not profit from public service. . . .

But in part it is because we know that even government agencies with clear goals and readily observable behavior only can be evaluated by making political (and thus conflict-ridden) judgments. If the Welfare Department delivers every benefit check within 24 hours after the application is received, Senator Smith may be pleased but Senator Jones will be irritated because this speedy delivery almost surely would require that the standards of eligibility be relaxed so that many ineligible clients would get money. There is no objective standard by which the tradeoff between speed and accuracy in the Welfare Department can be evaluated. . . .

The closest we can come to supplying a nonpolitical, nonarbitrary evaluation of an organization's performance is by its ability to earn from customers revenues in excess of costs. This is how business firms, private colleges, and most hospitals are evaluated. But government agencies cannot be evaluated by this market test because they either supply a service for which there are no willing customers (for example, prisons or the IRS) or are monopoly suppliers of a valued service (for example, the welfare department and the Registry of Motor Vehicles). Neither an organization with unwilling customers nor one with the exclusive right to serve such customers as exist can be evaluated by knowing how many customers they attract. When there is no external, nonpolitical evaluation of agency performance, there is no way to allow the agency to retain earnings that is not subject to agency manipulation. . . .

Critics of government agencies like to describe them as "bloated bureaucracies," defenders of them as "starved for funds." The truth is more complicated. Legislators judge government *programs* differently from how they judge government *bureaus*. Programs, such as Social Security, have constituencies that benefit from them. Constituencies press legislators for increases in program expenditures. If the constituencies are found in many districts, the pressures are felt by many legislators. These pressures ordinarily are not countered by those from any organized group that wants the benefits cut. Bureaucrats may or may not be constituencies. If they are few in number or concentrated in one legislative district they may have little political leverage with which to demand an increase in numbers or benefits. For example, expenditures on Social Security have grown steadily since the program began in 1935, but the offices, pay rates, and perquisites of Social Security administrators have not grown correspondingly.

If the bureaucrats are numerous, well-organized, and found in many districts (for example, letter carriers in the old Post Office Department or sanitation workers in New York City) they may have enough leverage to insure that their benefits increase faster than their workload. But even numerous and organized bureaucrats labor under a strategic disadvantage arising from the fact that legislators find it easier to constrain bureaucratic inputs than bureaucratic outputs. The reasons are partly conceptual, partly political. Conceptually, an office building or pay schedule is a tangible input, easily understood by all; "good health" or a "decent retirement" or an "educated child" are matters of opinion. Politically, legislators face more or less steady pressures to keep tax rates down while allowing program benefits to grow. The conceptual ambiguities combine neatly with the political realities: The rational course of action for a legislator is to appeal to taxpayers by ostentatiously constraining the budget for buildings, pay raises, and managerial benefits while appealing to program beneficiaries by loudly calling for more money to be spent on health, retirement, or education. (Witness the difficulty schoolteachers have in obtaining pay increases without threatening a strike, even at a time when expenditures on education are growing.) As a result, there are many lavish programs in this country administered by modestly paid bureaucrats working on out-of-date equipment in cramped offices.*

The inability of public managers to capture surplus revenues for their own use alters the pattern of incentives at work in government agencies. Beyond a certain point additional effort does not produce additional earnings. (In this country, Congress from time to time has authorized higher salaries for senior bureaucrats but then put a cap on actual payments to them so that the pay increases were never received. This was done to insure that no bureaucrat would earn more than members of Congress at a time when those members were unwilling to accept the political costs of raising their own salaries. As a result, the pay differential between the top bureaucratic rank and those just below it nearly vanished.) If political constraints reduce the marginal effect of money incentives, then the relative importance of other, nonmonetary incentives will increase. . . .

That bureaucratic performance in most government agencies cannot be linked to monetary benefits is not the whole explanation for the difference between public and private management. There are many examples of private organizations whose members cannot appropriate money surpluses for their own benefit. Private schools ordinarily are run on a nonprofit basis. Neither the headmaster nor the teachers share in the profit of these schools; indeed, most such schools earn no profit at all and instead struggle to keep afloat by soliciting contributions from friends and alumni. Nevertheless, the evidence is quite clear that on the

---

* Elsewhere, government officials may enjoy generous salaries and lavish offices. Indeed, in some underdeveloped nations, travelers see all about them signs of public munificence and private squalor. The two may be connected.

average, private schools, both secular and denominational, do a better job than public ones in educating children.[2]

Acquiring and Using the Factors of Production

A business firm acquires capital by retaining earnings, borrowing money, or selling shares of ownership; a government agency (with some exceptions) acquires capital by persuading a legislature to appropriate it. A business firm hires, promotes, demotes, and fires personnel with considerable though not perfect freedom; a federal government agency is told by Congress how many persons it can hire and at what rate of pay, by the Office of Personnel Management (OPM) what rules it must follow in selecting and assigning personnel, by the Office of Management and Budget (OMB) how many persons of each rank it may employ, by the Merit Systems Protection Board (MSPB) what procedures it must follow in demoting or discharging personnel, and by the courts whether it has faithfully followed the rules of Congress, OPM, OMB, and MSPB. A business firm purchases goods and services by internally defined procedures (including those that allow it to buy from someone other than the lowest bidder if a more expensive vendor seems more reliable), or to skip the bidding procedure altogether in favor of direct negotiations; a government agency must purchase much of what it uses by formally advertising for bids, accepting the lowest, and keeping the vendor at arm's length. When a business firm develops a good working relationship with a contractor, it often uses that vendor repeatedly without looking for a new one; when a government agency has a satisfactory relationship with a contractor, ordinarily it cannot use the vendor again without putting a new project out for a fresh set of bids. When a business firm finds that certain offices or factories are no longer economical it will close or combine them; when a government agency wishes to shut down a local office or military base often it must get the permission of the legislature (even when formal permission is not necessary, informal consultation is). When a business firm draws up its annual budget each expenditure item can be reviewed as a discretionary amount (except for legally mandated payments of taxes to government and interest to banks and bondholders); when a government agency makes up its budget many of the detailed expenditure items are mandated by the legislature.

All these complexities of doing business in or with the government are well-known to citizens and firms. These complexities in hiring, purchasing, contracting, and budgeting often are said to be the result of the "bureaucracy's love of red tape." But few, if any, of the rules producing this complexity would have been generated by the bureaucracy if left to its own devices, and many are as cordially disliked by the bureaucrats as by their clients. These rules have been imposed on the agencies by external actors, chiefly the legislature. They are not bureaucratic rules but *political* ones. In principle the legislature could allow the Social Security Administration, the Defense Department, or the New York City public school system to follow the same rules as IBM, General Electric, or Harvard University. In practice they could not. The reason is politics, or more precisely, democratic politics.

The differences are made clear in Steven Kelman's comparison of how government agencies and private firms buy computers. The agency officials he interviewed were much less satisfied with the quality of the computers and support services they purchased than were their private counterparts. The reason is that private firms are free to do what every householder does in buying a dishwasher or an automobile—look at the past performance of the people with whom he or she previously has done business and buy a new product based on these judgments. Contrary to what many people suppose, most firms buying a computer do not write up detailed specifications and then ask for bids, giving the contract to the lowest bidder who meets the specifications. Instead, they hold conversations with a computer manufacturer with whom they, or other firms like them, have had experience. In these discussions they develop a sense of their needs and form a judgment as to the quality and reliability of the people with whom they may do business. When the purchase is finally made, only one firm may be asked to bid, and then on the basis of jointly developed (and sometimes rather general) guidelines.

No government purchasing agent can afford to do business this way. He or she would be accused (by unsuccessful bidders and their congressional allies) of collusion, favoritism, and sweetheart deals. Instead, agencies must either ask for sealed bids or for competitive written responses to detailed (*very* detailed) "requests for proposals" (RFPs). The agencies will not be allowed to take into account past performance or intangible managerial qualities. As a result, the agencies must deny themselves the use of the most important information someone can have—judgment shaped by personal knowledge and past experience. Thus, the government often buys the wrong computers from unreliable suppliers.[3]

Constraints at Work: The Case of the Postal Service

From the founding of the republic until 1971 the Post Office Department was a cabinet agency wholly subordinate to the president and Congress. As such it received its funds from annual appropriations, its personnel from presidential appointments and civil service examinations, and its physical plant from detailed political decisions about the appropriate location of post offices. Postal rates were set by Congress after hearings, dominated by organized interests that mail in bulk (for example, direct-mail advertisers and magazine publishers) and influenced by an awareness of the harmful political effects of raising the rates for first-class letters mailed by individual citizens (most of whom voted). Congress responded to these pressures by keeping rates low. . . . The wages of postal employees were set with an eye on the political power of the unions representing those employees:

Congress rarely forgot that there were hundreds of organized letter carriers in every congressional district.

In 1971, the Post Office Department was transformed into the United States Postal Service (USPS), a semiautonomous government corporation. The USPS is headed by an eleven-member board of governors, nine appointed by the president and confirmed by the Senate; these nine then appoint a postmaster general and a deputy postmaster general. It derives its revenues entirely from the prices it charges and the money it borrows rather than from congressional appropriations (though subsidies still were paid to the USPS during a transition period). The postal rates are set not by Congress but by the USPS itself, guided by a legislative standard. . . . The USPS has its own personnel system, separate from that of the rest of the federal government, and bargains directly with its own unions.

Having loosened some of the constraints upon it, the Postal Service was able to do things that in the past it could do only with great difficulty if at all. . . . When it was still a regular government department, a small local post office could only be closed after a bitter fight with the member of Congress from the affected district. As a result, few were closed. After the reorganization, the number closed increased: Between 1976 and 1979, the USPS closed about twenty-four a year; between 1983 and 1986, it closed over two hundred a year.[4] . . . When the old Post Office, in the interest of cutting costs, tried to end the custom of delivering mail to each recipient's front door and instead proposed to deliver mail (at least in new suburban communities) either to the curbside or to "cluster boxes,"* intense pressure on Congress forced the department to abandon the idea. By 1978 the USPS had acquired enough autonomy to implement the idea despite continued congressional grumblings.[5] Because the USPS can raise its own capital by issuing bonds it has been able to forge ahead with the automation of mail-sorting procedures. It now has hundreds of sophisticated optical scanners and bar-code readers that enable employees to sort mail much faster than before. By 1986 optical character readers were processing 90 million pieces of mail a day. Finally, despite political objections, the USPS was slowly expanding the use of the nine-digit zip code.

In short, acquiring greater autonomy increased the ability of the Postal Service to acquire, allocate, and control the factors of production. More broadly, the whole tone of postal management changed. It began to adopt corporate-style management practices, complete with elaborate "mission statements," glossy annual reports, a tightened organizational structure, and an effort to decentralize some decisions to local managers.

Though Congress loosened the reins, it did not take them off. On many key issues the phrase *quasi-autonomous* meant hardly autonomous at all. Congress at

---

* A cluster box is a metal structure containing from twelve to one hundred mailboxes to which mail for a given neighborhood is delivered.

any time can amend the Postal Reorganization Act to limit the service's freedom of action; even the threat of such an amendment, made evident by committee hearings, often is enough to alter the service's programs. The nine-digit zip code was finally adopted but its implementation was delayed by Congress for over two years, thus impeding the efforts of the USPS to obtain voluntary compliance from the business community.

When the USPS, in a move designed to save over $400 million and thereby avoid a rate increase, announced in 1977 that it planned to eliminate Saturday mail deliveries, the service was able to produce public opinion data indicating that most people would prefer no Saturday delivery to higher postage rates. No matter. The House of Representatives by an overwhelming vote passed a resolution opposing the change, and the USPS backed down. It seems the employee unions feared that the elimination of Saturday deliveries would lead to laying off postal workers.[6]

Similarly, when the USPS in 1975–76 sought to close many rural post offices it had as an ally the General Accounting Office.* A GAO study suggested that twelve thousand such offices could be closed at a savings of $100 million per year without reducing service to any appreciable extent (many of the small offices served no more than a dozen families and were located within a few miles of other offices that could provide the same service more economically). The rural postmasters saw matters differently, and they found a sympathetic audience in Congress. Announcing that "the rural post office has always been a uniquely American institution" and that "service" is more important than "profit," senators and representatives joined in amending the Postal Reorganization Act to block such closings temporarily and inhibit them permanently.[7] As John Tierney notes, the year that the USPS timidly closed 72 of its 30,521 offices, the Great Atlantic and Pacific Tea Company closed 174 of its 1,634 stores, and "that was that.[8] . . ."

My argument is not that all the changes the USPS would like to make are desirable, or that every vestige of politics should be removed from its management. . . . Rather, it is that one cannot explain the behavior of government bureaucracies simply by reference to the fact that they are bureaucracies; the central fact is that they are *government* bureaucracies. Nor am I arguing that government (or more broadly, politics) is bad, only that it is inevitably (and to some extent desirably) sensitive to constituency demands. . . . For example, if Congress had been content to ask of the old Post Office Department that it deliver all first-class mail within three days at the lowest possible cost, it could have let the department arrange its delivery system, set its rates, locate its offices,

---

* The General Accounting Office (GAO), a research agency of Congress, has the broad mission of overseeing and investigating how executive branch agencies spend appropriated funds. Its activities, often controversial, range from investigating cost overruns in the Department of Defense to assessing the adequacy of environmental regulations. GAO typically initiates its activities at the request of congressional committee leaders.

and hire its personnel in whatever way it wished—provided that the mail got delivered within three days and at a price that did not lead mail users to abandon the Post Office in favor of a private delivery service. Managers then would be evaluated on the basis of how well they achieved these goals.

Of course, Congress had many goals, not just one: It wanted to please many different classes of mail users, satisfy constituency demands for having many small post offices rather than a few large ones, cope with union demands for wage increases, and respond to public criticism of mail service. Congress could not provide a consistent rank-ordering of these goals, which is to say that it could not decide on how much of one goal (e.g., keeping prices low) should be sacrificed to attain more of another goal (e.g., keeping rural post offices open). This inability to decide is not a reflection on the intelligence of Congress; rather, it is the inevitable consequence of Congress being a representative body whose individual members respond differently to different constituencies.

Neither Congress nor the postal authorities have ever supported an obvious method of allowing the customers to decide the matter for themselves—namely, by letting private firms compete with the Postal Service for the first-class mail business. For over a century the Post Office has had a legal monopoly on the regular delivery of first-class mail. It is a crime to establish any "private express for the conveyance of letters or packets . . . by regular trips or at stated periods over any post route."[9] This is justified by postal executives on the grounds that private competitors would skim away the most profitable business (for example, delivering business mail or utility bills in big cities), leaving the government with the most costly business (for example, delivering a Christmas card from Aunt Annie in Eudora, Kansas, to Uncle Matt in Wakefield, Massachusetts). In time the Post Office began to face competition anyway, from private parcel and express delivery services that did not deliver "by regular trips or at stated periods" (so as not to violate the private express statute) and from electronic mail and fund-transferring systems. But by then it had become USPS, giving it both greater latitude in and incentive for meeting that competition.

Faced with political superiors that find it conceptually easier and politically necessary to focus on inputs, agency managers also tend to focus on inputs. Nowhere is this more evident than in defense procurement programs. The Defense Department, through the Defense Logistics Agency (DLA), each year acquires food, fuel, clothing, and spare parts worth (in 1984) $15 billion, manages a supply system containing over two million items, and administers over $186 billion in government contracts.[10] Congress and the president repeatedly have made clear their desire that this system be run efficiently and make use of off-the-shelf, commercially available products (as opposed to more expensive, "made-to-order" items).[11] Periodically, however, the press reports scandals involving the purchase of $435 hammers and $700 toilet seats. Some of these stories are exaggerated,[12] but there is little doubt that waste and inefficiency occur. Congressional investigations are mounted and presidential commissions are appointed to find ways of solving these problems. Among the solutions offered are demands that tighter rules be imposed, more auditors be hired, and fuller reports be made.

Less dramatic but more common than the stories of scandals and overpriced hammers are the continuing demands of various constituencies for influence over the procurement process. Occasionally this takes the form of requests for special favors, such as preferentially awarding a contract to a politically favored firm. But just as important and more pervasive in their effects are the legal constraints placed on the procurement process to insure that contracts are awarded "fairly"— that is, in ways that allow equal access to the bidding process by all firms and special access by politically significant ones. For example, section 52 of the *Federal Acquisition Regulation* contains dozens of provisions governing the need to give special attention to suppliers that are small businesses (especially a "small disadvantaged business"), women-owned small businesses, handicapped workers, or disabled and Vietnam-era veterans, or are located in areas with a "labor surplus."*[13] Moreover, only materials produced in the United States can be acquired for public use unless, under the Buy American Act, the government certifies that the cost is "unreasonable" or finds that the supplies are not available in this country in sufficient quantity or adequate quality.[14]

The goal of "fairness" underlies almost every phase of the procurement process, not because the American government is committed heart and soul to fairness as an abstract social good but because if a procurement decision is questioned it is much easier to justify the decision if it can be shown that the decision was "fairly" made on the basis of "objective" criteria. Those criteria are spelled out in the *Federal Acquisition Regulation*, a complex document of over six thousand pages. The essential rules are that all potential suppliers must be offered an equal opportunity to bid on a contract; that the agency's procurement decision must be objectively justifiable on the basis of written specifications; that contracts awarded on the basis of sealed bids must go to the contractor offering the lowest price; and that unsuccessful bidders must be offered a chance to protest decisions with which they disagree.[15] . . .

To understand the bureaucratic significance of these rules, put yourself in the shoes of a Defense Logistics Agency manager. A decision you made is challenged because someone thinks that you gave a contract to an unqualified firm or purchased something of poor quality. What is your response—that in your

---

* For example, the law requires that a "fair proportion of the total purchases and contracts" shall be "placed with small-business enterprises" and that "small business concerns owned and controlled by socially and economically disadvantaged individuals, shall have the maximum practicable opportunity to participate in the performance of contracts let by any Federal agency" [15 *U.S. Code* 637(d)(l)]. In pursuance of this law, it is the government's policy "to place a fair proportion" of its acquisitions with small business concerns and small business disadvantaged concerns (*Federal Acquisition Regulation,* 19.201a). A "socially and economically disadvantaged individual" includes, but is not limited to, a black American, Hispanic American, Native American, Asian-Pacific American, or Asian-Indian American (ibid., 52.219.2).

judgment it was a good buy from a reliable firm? Such a remark is tantamount to inviting yourself to explain to a hostile congressional committee why you think your judgment is any good. A much safer response is "I followed the rules." . . .

If despite all your devotion to the rules Congress uncovers an especially blatant case of paying too much for too little (for example, a $3,000 coffeepot), the prudent response is to suggest that what is needed are more rules, more auditors, and more tightly constrained procedures. The consequence of this may be to prevent the buying of any more $3,000 coffeepots, or it may be to increase the complexity of the procurement process so that fewer good firms will submit bids to supply coffeepots, or it may be to increase the cost of monitoring that process so that the money saved by buying cheaper pots is lost by hiring more pot inspectors. . . .

Public Versus Private Management

The late Professor Wallace Sayre once said that public and private management is alike in all unimportant respects.[16] This view has been disputed vigorously by many people who are convinced that whatever problems beset government agencies also afflict private organizations. The clearest statement of that view can be found in John Kenneth Galbraith's *The New Industrial State*. Galbraith argues that large corporations, like public agencies, are dominated by "technostructures" that are governed by their own bureaucratic logic rather than by the dictates of the market. These corporations have insulated themselves from the market by their ability to control demand (through clever advertising) and set prices (by dominating an industry). The rewards to the technocrats who staff these firms are salaries, not profits, and the goals toward which these technocrats move are the assertion and maintenance of their own managerial autonomy. . . .

Professor Galbraith's book appeared at a time (1967) when American businesses were enjoying such unrivaled success that its beautifully crafted sentences seemed to capture some enduring truth. But the passage of time converted many of those eloquent phrases into hollow ones. Within ten years, it had become painfully obvious to General Motors that it could not, in Galbraith's words, "set prices for automobiles . . . secure in the knowledge that no individual buyer, by withdrawing its custom, can force a change."[17] Competition from Toyota, Nissan, and Honda had given the individual buyer great power; coupled with an economic slowdown, that competition led GM, like all auto manufacturers, to start offering cash rebates, cut-rate financing, and price reductions. And still the U.S. firms lost market share despite the "power" of their advertising and saw profits evaporate despite their "dominance" of the industry.

But Galbraith's analysis had more serious flaws than its inability to predict the future; it led many readers to draw the erroneous conclusion that "all bureaucracies are alike" because all bureaucracies employ salaried workers, are enmeshed in red tape, and strive to insure their own autonomy. The large corporation surely is more bureaucratic than the small entrepreneur, but in becoming bureaucratic it has not become a close relative of a government agency. What distinguishes public from private organizations is neither their size nor their desire to "plan" (that is, control) their environments but rather the rules under which they acquire and use capital and labor. General Motors acquires capital by selling shares, issuing bonds, or retaining earnings; the Department of Defense acquires it from an annual appropriation by Congress. GM opens and closes plants, subject to certain government regulations, at its own discretion; DOD opens and closes military bases under the watchful guidance of Congress. GM pays its managers with salaries it sets and bonuses tied to its earnings; DOD pays its managers with salaries set by Congress and bonuses (if any) that have no connection with organizational performance. The number of workers in GM is determined by its level of production; the number in DOD by legislation and civil-service rules.

What all this means can be seen by returning to the Registry of Motor Vehicles and McDonald's. Suppose you were just appointed head of the Watertown office of the Registry and you wanted to improve service there so that it more nearly approximated the service at McDonald's. Better service might well require spending more money (on clerks, equipment, and buildings). Why should your political superiors give you that money? It is a cost to them if it requires either higher taxes or taking funds from another agency; offsetting these real and immediate costs are dubious and postponed benefits. If lines become shorter and clients become happier, no legislator will benefit. There may be fewer complaints, but complaints are episodic and have little effect on the career of any given legislator. By contrast, shorter lines and faster service at McDonald's means more customers can be served per hour and thus more money can be earned per hour. A McDonald's manager can estimate the marginal product of the last dollar he or she spends on improving service; the Registry manager can generate no tangible return on any expenditure he or she makes and thus cannot easily justify the expenditure.

Improving service at the Registry may require replacing slow or surly workers with quick and pleasant ones. But you, the manager, can neither hire nor fire them at will. You look enviously at the McDonald's manager who regularly and with little notice replaces poor workers with better ones. Alternatively, you may wish to mount an extensive training program (perhaps creating a Registration University to match McDonald's Hamburger University) that would imbue a culture of service in your employees. But unless the Registry were so large an agency that the legislature would neither notice nor care about funds spent for this purpose—and it is not that large—you would have a tough time convincing anybody that this was not a wasteful expenditure on a frill project.

If somehow your efforts succeed in making Registry clients happier, you can take vicarious pleasure in it; in the unlikely event a client seeks you out to thank you for those efforts, you can bask in a moment's worth of glory. Your colleague at McDonald's who manages to make customers happier may also derive some vicarious satisfaction from the improvement but in addition he or she will earn more money owing to an increase in sales.

In time it will dawn on you that if you improve service too much, clients will start coming to the Watertown office instead of going to the Boston office. As a result, the lines you succeeded in shortening will become longer again. If you wish to keep complaints down, you will have to spend even more on the Watertown office. But if it was hard to persuade the legislature to do that in the past, it is impossible now. Why should the taxpayer be asked to spend more on Watertown when the Boston office, fully staffed (naturally, no one was laid off when the clients disappeared), has no lines at all? From the legislature's point of view the correct level of expenditure is not that which makes one office better than another but that which produces an equal amount of discontent in all offices.

Finally, you remember that your clients have no choice: The Registry offers a monopoly service. It and only it supplies drivers' licenses. In the long run all that matters is that there are not "too many" complaints to the legislature about service. Unlike McDonald's, the Registry need not fear that its clients will take their business to Burger King or to Wendy's. Perhaps you should just relax. . . .

Notes

1. John F. Love, *McDonald's: Behind the Arches* (New York: Bantam Books, 1986), 140ff.
2. James S. Coleman, Thomas Hoffer, and Sally Kilgore, *High School Achievement* (New York: Basic Books, 1982).
3. Steven Kelman, *Procurement and Public Management* [Lanham: American Enterprise Institute, 1990].
4. John T. Tierney, *The U.S. Postal Service* (Dover, Mass.: Auburn House, 1988), 101–2.
5. Tierney, *U.S. Postal Service*, 94–97.
6. John T. Tierney, *Postal Reorganization: Managing the Public's Business* (Boston: Auburn House, 1981), 67.
7. Ibid., 68–73.
8. Ibid., 72.
9. 18 *U.S. Code* 1696.
10. General Accounting Office, *Progress and Challenges at the Defense Logistics Agency.* GAO report NSIAD-86-64, Washington, D.C., 1986, p. 2.
11. Wendy T. Kirby, "Expanding the Use of Commercial Products and 'Commercial-Style' Acquisition Techniques in Defense Procurement: A Proposed Legal Framework," Appendix H in President's Blue Ribbon Commission on Defense Management (the "Packard Commission"), *A Quest for Excellence: Final Report*, June 1986.
12. I discuss these matters in chap. 17.
13. Kirby, "Expanding the Use," 106–7.
14. 41 *U.S. Code* 10(a).
15. Kirby, "Expanding the Use," 82–83, 91.
16. Quoted in Graham T. Allison, Jr., "Public and Private Management: Are They Fundamentally Alike in All Unimportant Respects?" in Frederick S. Lane, ed., *Current Issues in Public Administration*, 2d ed. (New York: St. Martin's Press, 1982), 13–33. The academic literature on public-private differences

is summarized in Hal G. Rainey, Robert W. Backoff, and Charles H. Levine, "Comparing Public and Private Organizations," *Public Administration Review* 36 (1976): 233–44.
17. Galbraith, *New Industrial State*, 46.

Questions for Discussion

1. According to James Q. Wilson, in what ways is managing a private organization different from managing a public one?
2. Wilson suggests that "red tape" is more often the result of democratic politics than the preferences of bureaucrats. What does he mean by this? Would increasing citizen and group participation in politics lead to more or fewer bureaucratic rules and regulations?

 12.3

Finding the Civil Service's Hidden Sex Appeal

Nicholas Thompson

Although the number of federal employees has fallen since the 1980s, government still needs to recruit tens of thousands of people each year to fill vacancies in administrative units that range from the Foreign Service to the Center for Disease Control to the National Oceanic and Atmospheric Administration. Although government salaries have never rivaled those in the private sector, the difference in wages has grown wider in the 1990s. Moreover, the high level of security offered by a government job does not make up for the slow pace of advancement through the bureaucratic ranks.

Nicholas Thompson argues that a crisis is building as growing numbers of aging government workers begin to retire in coming years. Federal agencies must respond by offering younger workers both interesting challenges and the potential for advancement. Thompson offers encouraging evidence that such challenges and career growth do exist, although more effective publicizing is required. In a sense, Thompson is writing to college students, urging them to consider govern-

Nicholas Thompson is an editor at the *Washington Monthly.*

ment service, where they may well find the opportunity to make a difference early in their careers.

The cover of a brochure given out by the federal Office of Personnel Management shows a young man in sunglasses crouching like a surfer and holding a model spaceship labeled "United States." The brochure bellows "Look Ma! I'm a Bureaucrat!" in a funky yellow font and notes that the cover model, Dan Ridge, is the 24-year-old program director of the computer crime division at NASA. He "wears jeans to the office" and "uses supercomputing technology to protect NASA's worldwide computer system." The brochure goes on to profile more hip young people working in the public sector, including the new, fast-paced, reinvented government. The message: If you're young, ambitious, and looking to make a difference helping other people and the country, you too can be like Dan Ridge!

But if you call NASA to ask Ridge about his wonderful government job, you'll have some trouble finding him. Turns out he left town not long after posing for the brochure. Now he develops supercomputing technology called Beowulf clusters for Scyld, a startup company in Maryland. He didn't leave because he wanted more money—he's earning about the same amount now—or because he didn't like his job. He left because there just wasn't anywhere to move up to without sticking around for another 10 years. "My work was fantastic. I loved it. But it was clear that there was no further path for advancement."

Ridge's complaint is all too familiar. Despite the Office of Personnel Management's (OPM's) efforts, time still seems to move more slowly inside the federal government than outside: It takes longer to get hired, it's nearly impossible to get fired, and the promotional fast track moves like molasses compared to the private sector. Although that has been true for at least a century, the problem is getting worse. The private sector has vastly improved at scooping up talented young people, the call to service rings less loudly for young people today, and the civil service seems specifically designed to repel anyone born after about 1970.

The government's recruitment shortcomings threaten to become a national crisis. The flood of people who entered the federal government in the '60s and '70s is getting ready to start collecting social security, and there's a thin bench ready either to replace them or to move up the ranks. Sixty-five percent of the Senior Executive Service, the government's most elite managers, will be eligible to retire by 2004, and only about five percent of the civil service is under 30. That doesn't mean they will all leave, but according to a recent National Academy of Public Administration report, "the flow of high-quality new hires in federal departments and agencies has decreased dramatically while the average age of workers has risen."

It's not time to flee to Canada, but civil-service reform should be an urgent priority for the next administration. The government needs talented new recruits for the sake of people who drink tap water, drive the highways, or buy securities; and the potential consequences of the looming exodus are unnerving. Clinton and Gore should be applauded for making government reinvention a priority, but they didn't shake up the rules in a way that would significantly attract young people. They improved procurement, and they made the government smaller; but they didn't scour the agencies to determine where people are plotting innovative policy solutions, and where they are simply plotting their next conference trips to Maui.

That's a shame because what's going to pull bright young people in won't be a shrunken bureaucracy, or even higher salaries, but a civil service where they can find exciting and useful jobs with real responsibility and high ceilings—just what Dan Ridge wanted.

Kids Today

According to a recent study by Paul Light of the Brookings Institution, the percentage of students from top graduate schools of public policy and management—the folks most likely to be interested in government careers—who go on to work for government has dropped from 76 percent in 1974 to 55 percent in 1988 to 49 percent today, with state, local, and federal government all losing their appeal. The percentage of master's graduates from Syracuse's Maxwell School and Harvard's Kennedy School of Government who actually pursue the careers their schools were designed for has plunged by 50 percent over two decades.

From the inside, the numbers look equally grim. The percentage of Presidential Management Interns who stay in government, the young people on the fastest possible track into the civil service, is stuck at 50 percent; the number of applications to the White House Fellows program has sunk. According to the National Association for Law Placement, the percentage of law school graduates going into the government has declined slowly but steadily for 25 years, from about 20 percent to 13 percent in 1998. If government were a stock, everybody would be selling it short.

These trends in government service partly reflect the generational shift in attitudes toward government itself. They don't much trust it, and they don't vote in high numbers. According to a 30-year study of freshman attitudes by Alexander Astin at UCLA, the percentage of students who say that they "want to keep up to date with political affairs" has skidded from above 50 percent in the late '60s and early '70s to below 30 percent today.

But this withdrawal doesn't come, as many critics of Generation X argue, simply because recent graduates are too busy dreaming about hundred-dollar bills, thousand-dollar suits, and million-dollar homes. In Astin's study, for example, the percentage of students who consider it critical to be "very well off financially" has famously risen from just under 40 percent in 1970 to 74 percent today. But the percentage was even higher in 1986. Plus, there are some trends moving in the direction of civic engagement: The number of young people who perform some sort of volunteer work is at an all-time high and, according to Light's study of graduates from public management schools, only 17 percent said that salary was a very important consideration for their first job. Eighty percent cited the opportunity to do challenging work.

The real reason young people have withdrawn from government is that government has developed a reputation as a place where the wheels spin endlessly and great ideas are filed away into a bottomless heap of paper. According to Greg Wright, a young Stanford honors graduate who wants to work for the government eventually, but went from college to a consulting group and a dot-com instead of joining a dot-gov: "I want to make as big a splash as I can. Government keeps you in the kiddy pool unless you know someone, have a lot of money, or you have been working in the basement for 20 years."

Executive Insufficiency

Wright's attitude shouldn't be surprising considering that the men who have dominated the federal government for the past 25 years have all treated it with something between lukewarm praise and outward hostility. Ronald Reagan set the tone in his inaugural address—"Government is not the solution to our problem. It is the problem!"—and then placed a team of anti-bureaucrats at OPM. Led by Donald Devine, OPM seemed to strangle recruitment efforts, terminating, for example, all promotional material for VISTA, the Great Society program that sent young people into poor areas to teach and work. One OPM official, Terry Cutler, wrote in the *Wall Street Journal* in 1986, "Government's goal should not be employee excellence but employee sufficiency."

Reagan's rhetoric wasn't an anomaly. Every president since Jimmy Carter has come to office by swinging at the bureaucratic bugbear. Clinton's most famous line is "The era of big government is over," and Gore began his report on reinventing government with this zinger: "The federal government is not simply broke; it is broken." Gore's criticism was in the context of useful suggestions for change, but neither that, nor his repeated boasts about how much the government has shrunk in the past eight years, are quite as good an invitation to service as: "Ask not what your country can do for you. Ask what you can do for your country."

The recruitment problems aren't simply a failure of rhetoric from the top; they're also a failure of execution in the middle. When Wright was a college senior, the consulting group he eventually joined socked his campus newspaper full of ads every day, interviewed him twice, and then flew him to L.A. for a dream weekend complete with a Mustang convertible. Government recruitment was nowhere to be seen, and if Greg had called its toll-free job line he would have been met by an awkward robotic voice blurting out an endless stream of nearly incomprehensible job numbers. If he had called the Smithsonian Institution, for example, he would have been encouraged to listen to a tutorial on the endless codes, terms, and processes necessary to apply, including "the definition of important technical terms you will need to understand to become a competitive applicant."

To be sure, Al Gore's reinvented government has begun to clean these problems up, and job postings are now available through an extensive Web site. But even these efforts have fallen short—in no small part because the federal personnel workforce, the people in charge of recruitment, has declined by 20 percent from 1991 to 1998.

The Civil Service

Although you wouldn't know it from the toll-free job-hunt line, government can still be a great place to work. And this is where federal public relations efforts really fall short. Rarely do you hear, for instance, that the percentage of federal employees reporting that they are satisfied with their jobs is higher than the comparable number in the private sector, according to a 1999 Reinventing Government survey. For example, Jason Goldwater, a 30-year-old employee of the Health Care Financing Administration (HCFA), has spent the last two years at the Centers for Disease Control and Prevention (CDC) and HCFA designing a common data set of Medicaid users—data that will vastly improve our ability to track the incidence of health problems like asthma. He loves his job both because it's exciting and because, "when I go home, I want to think about what I've done, not just a paycheck." Martin Yeung, 25, left investment banking to join the Office of Management and Budget (OMB) and now works there as assistant to the deputy director of management. That may sound boring, but Yeung has got a great job and he loves his work. The OMB controls how legislation across the government is implemented—from airline safety regulation to federally financed student loans—and sits consistently in the middle of conflicts between agencies, the White House, and Congress. According to Yeung, "It's as fast as 'The West Wing'; it's bare knuckles; it's Olympic wrestling. The only way to outmaneuver opponents is to be on top of everything."

But there aren't enough great jobs like Yeung's and Goldwater's and, unfortunately, far too many young people get stuck in boring ones and leave before they can find real job satisfaction. Out of college, I entered a fellowship program with about 40 other graduates interested in public service careers. We all got jobs with the federal government and lived together in Washington. None of us stayed more than two years. The only two people continuing the work they started with were the only two who didn't join the civil service but instead went to work for Congress.

Government simply deserves part of its bad reputation. The federal civil service remains locked in a structure built in the early 1880s after a disaffected job seeker assassinated James Garfield because so many jobs had been doled out through the patronage system. The solution then was to essentially put the civil service in a lock box. Federal employees are guaranteed stability and consistent, slow promotions—from GS-13 to GS-14 after two years and so on. They can't get fired except through a tortuous review process.

This means that the main way to open up jobs is to create new ones, instead of clearing out old ones. And, in the anti-bureaucratic fervor of the past 20 years, that has been nearly impossible. According to Fred Smith, a deputy assistant secretary of defense who has spent his whole career working for the country: "It is extremely difficult, if not impossible, to hire anyone from the outside. We've had maybe four young people come in this year, and all were from the Presidential Management Internship program." Smith has only been able to fire one person in 22 years, and what happened then is instructive. "I tried for three years but two weeks before the process worked through, he chose early retirement and took a $25,000 bonus," said Smith.

In addition, the rules of the civil service don't just block job openings; they also create a bureaucratic mentality that encourages survival over innovation. Agency funding gets renewed every year, even if the work has become obsolete, as long as it can stay below Congress' radar. Salary and rank are based on the number of people supervised, not on the amount of work accomplished. Lastly, once you've left government it's very hard to come back in, a policy that prevents conflicts of interest but also blocks out innovative employees who wanted to step out for a few years and learn about another business culture. In the 1999 government survey of federal employees, only 33 percent said that creativity and innovation were rewarded by the government.

This system limits political meddling and provides safe harbor for saintly civil servants who have been quietly serving for years, but it also makes the civil service singularly unappealing to this generation of young people. In part because of the booming economy and the tremendous opportunities for growth in information technology, this has become the "free agent generation." As Aparna Mohan, a Presidential Management Intern working at the Agency for International Development, says, "Our goal is to have the career be the sum of all the jobs we've had—not to just get one job and make it a whole career."

In short, the advantages of government employment—long-term stability and structure—are the last things that young people seem to care about. The average member of the elite Senior Executive Service, for example, has been working in government for 23 years, more than a lifetime for today's graduates; the average 32-year-old has already worked for nine different companies and is looking around to bounce to a few more. Government just doesn't seem to offer the new thing. As Phil Keisling, the former secretary of state of Oregon and now a vice president at PROdx, a Portland internet consulting firm, puts it, "The rate of change curve is just steeper in the private sector relative to government and the gap is widening."

Uncle Sam Needs You

The government's talent shortage should worry us all. Government employees research asthma at the CDC; they keep planes from crashing at the FAA; and they're the one's who decide when it's safe to set off Forest Service-controlled burns near your house.

Moreover, without top young talent, government is no match for the private sector it is supposed to regulate. Corporations that don't want to pay taxes hire lawyers who compete with the IRS. Mining companies that don't want to pay royalties hire smart lawyers who work wonders with federal law. The government is now entering a critical high-stakes battle with the private sector to see who controls the patents to our DNA. Does anyone really want first-rate people on the corporate side and second-rate people on the public's side?

In addition, a great deal of government work is now contracted out—from the administration of welfare programs to the management of private prisons. But contracting work out doesn't preclude the need for smart people in government: You still need smart people to make sure that the public isn't sold a bill of goods. Many of the security problems at the Los Alamos nuclear laboratory in New Mexico, for example, weren't just caused by the Department of Energy, but rather by lax oversight from the University of California at Berkeley, the main contractor running the lab.

This isn't to say that there's something bad about working for corporate America and the private sector. We're lucky that Henry Ford didn't work for the Department of Commerce, just as we're lucky that executives like IBM's Lou Gerstner and private inventors like Linus Torvalds are improving the ways that America runs. The growth of our private businesses is a primary reason for the current economic boom and its bounties.

The problem is one of balance. A society in which every ambitious environmentalist goes to work for the EPA or a nonprofit would fall apart because there would be no one to help develop non-polluting effluent systems or to argue internally for the limitation of greenhouse gas emissions. A society in which every ambitious environmentalist goes to work for [consulting firm] McKinsey and GE would fall apart because there would be no one to write the regulations and to test pollution levels. Unfortunately, we seem to be shifting to the latter.

Give Youth a Chance

The obvious solution to attracting better people to government is to pay them more. Money does help bring people into government, particularly if targeted to those who need it most, like OPM Director Janice Lachance's recent initiative to allow agencies to pay back student loans as part of the government's often-invoked program to provide relocation, retention, and recruitment bonuses. But even that seems unlikely to reverse current trends. Government will never be able to pay as much as the private sector, no matter how much it tinkers on the margins of federal salary structures. To improve recruitment it needs to rely on its prime advantage: the ability to allow young people to serve others with useful work. According to Lily Batchelder, a 28-year-old law school student who has worked both for a consulting group and the Justice Department: "The problems you try to solve working in government are complex and fascinating. Working in a place where you are focused on profit is like going to a good action movie. It can be fun, but it doesn't hit your soul."

Whether you work in the State Department or the Federal Emergency Management Agency, you have the clear chance to make other people's lives better. This is a powerful incentive, and it's the prime reason that government still attracts as much talent as it does. But the potential to do good doesn't mean much if you can't actually do anything. An idealist who joins an organization only to find her work stifled by rules, regulations, and a boss who comes in at noon, won't stay an idealist for long. If Lily Batchelder finds herself in an agency that's spinning its wheels, she won't stay a government employee for long.

What government needs to do is to improve the ratio of useful to useless work that new employees can do. Fortunately, there are examples right in government—like the White House, the one place in Washington where young people always seem to want to work. In fact, the draw is such that more than 10 million people watch the television program "The West Wing" weekly. They don't watch because they can see the Forest Service and the Bureau of Land Management cross wires. They watch because they can see young people who struggle with moral dilemmas, move quickly, and make everything from the Census to potential war, seem interesting.

In the Clinton White House, similarly, no rules lock employees into place or scuttle promotions, and the days move as quickly as in any dot-com. George Stephanopolous, Rahm Emanuel, and Gene Sperling rose to the top of the hierarchy on plain merit, not because they spent 16 years in the basement of the Interior Department. According to 25-year-old-speechwriter Joshua Gottheimer, who joined the White House after college and a brief stint scooping ice cream at Ben and Jerry's: "There's no defined hierarchy based on age. If you are willing to work hard and put in the hours, you can do almost anything."

In part, the advantage the White House has is that the stakes are higher. It's often only when the work becomes less important that strict hierarchies cement themselves into place. The greatest opportunities for young people in the government came during the New Deal and New Frontier, when they were needed to push forward ambitious and innovative new programs. Even during the arms race, young people were frequently promoted into positions of power. According to James Woolsey, who joined the SALT I negotiating team at age 27 and was counsel to the Senate Armed Services Committee before he turned 30: "Any time there is something brand new like arms control, there are opportunities for young people. The bureaucracy isn't entrenched yet."

The Department of Justice has similar success by placing few limits on the kind of work you can do when you come to it. At the U.S. Attorney's office in Washington, D.C., for example, everyone enters a four-year program that throws them into the middle of important and exciting cases. On Capitol Hill the story is the same. Staffers join their representatives knowing that they can't prepare for 30 years in government because their boss might be booted out in two. If a staff becomes stultified, it's likely their boss would soon be looking for new work.

In the rest of the federal government, the story's different. You can't come and go; you can't move around much; and frequently the good works that you planned to do bear no fruit. But there is hope. Even the Minerals Management Service can draw bright people in if reformed the right way. Consider Stephen Warren, the senior budget analyst of the chief financial officer of the District of Columbia, a city job that overlaps with the federal government which has final say over the city's budget. In a sense, Warren's job is just about looking over spreadsheets and developing revenue-collection models. But to Warren, a 28-year-old who worked for Marriott after graduating from Hampton University, it's an opportunity to improve the lives of the people around him. His proudest moment was when a revenue collection model he'd pored over for six months was approved by Congress, sending millions of dollars to the District. "You do a day's work. You can see something happening. You know, it makes you feel good," says Warren.

Warren didn't go into government thinking that he would be locked into a 30-year career with steady promotions and a group of deadwood co-workers. His boss when he started, Tony Williams, now Washington's mayor, "doesn't say that this is the last job you are going to have. He said that he wants this place to be a platform for young people to start their careers and do something good. If you choose to stay, you choose to stay."

Warren has been there for a bit more than four years and he plans to stay a little longer because he's learning, he's using his skills to serve people, and he's doing something important and useful without being stifled by bureaucracy. And, he adds, "when you come right out of school, you're not quite ready to turn your brain off."

Questions for Discussion

1. Have you ever considered working for the government at any level? Do any of Thompson's examples (e.g., lots of authority at an early age as a House staff member) seem attractive?
2. Is there anything that the government could offer that might induce you to seriously consider working for the government?

12.4

The Confirmation Clog

Norman Ornstein and Thomas Donilon

When a candidate wins the presidency, among his spoils is the right to choose 8000 full- and part-time appointees for positions ranging from secretary of state to deputy attorney general to a host of unpaid jobs on presidential commissions. The top 700 to 800 of these positions are extremely important, in that a chief executive needs to have loyal lieutenants who can carry out the administration's policies. Although the salaries of these jobs cannot compete with those in the private sector, the positions have traditionally attracted highly capable individuals who are called to challenging work and the rewards of serving the public. Since the 1970s, however, obstacles to Senate confirmation have grown steadily. Many well-qualified individuals simply refuse to consider public service, even in key positions.

Norman Ornstein and Tom Donilon, longtime observers of appointment politics in Washington, argue that both the president and the Senate must work to streamline the confirmation process, as well as to make it easier on appointees. Not only is a new president hurt by not getting his appointees in place in a timely manner, but the nominees are also left hanging, and prospective nominees are discouraged from serving. Still, with an evenly divided Senate and in the wake of a contentious presidential election, it may be too much to ask to take politics out of the confirmation process in 2001.

Running Through Molasses

On August 1, Peter Burleigh, one of America's most seasoned and effective diplomats, quietly tendered his resignation after 33 years in the U.S. Foreign Service. Burleigh's nomination to be ambassador to the Philippines had been held up for nine months in the Senate. With no prospects for movement through the remainder of the year, Burleigh decided to move on with his life. He had been in limbo not because of questions about his qualifications or actions, but because Senator Charles Grassley (R-Iowa), upset about the State

---

Norman Ornstein is a resident scholar at the American Enterprise Institute and codirector of the Transition to Governing Project. Thomas Donilon is executive vice president for law and policy at Fannie Mae and served as assistant secretary for public affairs and chief of staff at the State Department from 1993 to 1996.

Department's treatment of an American whistle blower at the United Nations, had exercised his senatorial prerogative to hold up Burleigh's nomination and two other ambassadorial appointments indefinitely.

Burleigh was no stranger to delays in appointments. Previously, he had served as the acting U.S. representative to the United Nations for more than a year while the administration's nominee for the post, Richard Holbrooke, was himself the victim of long executive and legislative branch delays. The Burleigh and Holbrooke examples stand out because of the importance and visibility of the positions, but sadly they are not unusual. More and more top executive jobs are sitting unfilled or filled on an acting basis for months or even years. Without significant changes in laws, rules, and norms, the incoming president of the United States faces the prospect of waiting for nearly a year after his inauguration on January 20 for his team to be set in place—not to mention the headaches any subsequent vacancies will cause.

Forty years ago, when John F. Kennedy became president, cabinet and sub-cabinet officers were nominated and confirmed expeditiously. On average, the 196 top-level executive positions requiring Senate confirmation were filled less than two and a half months after the presidential inauguration. Thirty-two years later, when Bill Clinton assumed the presidency, it was a different story. The 786 top-level Clinton nominees requiring Senate confirmation took an average of almost nine months after inauguration to assume their posts—meaning they missed more than a sixth of the presidential term! Thanks to a president who moved slowly to name top officials, a glacial presidential vetting process, slow FBI background checks for nominees, and a balky Senate confirmation process, securing a top appointed position was like running a marathon in molasses. In some respects, those initial nominees were lucky: many who came later were denied the Senate's predisposition to confirm a new president's people. Nearly all nominees after the first wave were left hanging in the Senate for months after their formal nominations. Many went through the further indignity of anonymous holds by senators, leaving them twisting in the wind for additional months or even years. . . .

That the nomination and confirmation process is broken is a truism now widely accepted by both Republicans and Democrats. It is also clear that the problems did not start with Clinton's administration but have been building for at least 30 years. . . . The average time from inauguration to confirmation of initial administration employees has been increasing since J.F.K.'s presidency, jumping particularly during the Bush and the Clinton eras. This trend applies to all executive appointments, not just those made at the beginning of an administration.

The lag in getting people into office seriously impedes good governance. A new president's first year—clearly the most important year for accomplishments and the most vulnerable to mistakes—is now routinely impaired by the lack of supporting staff. For executive agencies, leaderless periods mean decisions not made, initiatives not launched, and accountability not upheld.

Moreover, the problems persist into an administration's second year. The average tenure of top government positions is only about 14 months, mostly because of promotions and reassignments, which open up gaps in leadership. The gaps become even greater when a top position becomes vacant midway through an administration. Many major positions now routinely go unfilled for a year or more, and sometimes—as in the case of the assistant attorney general for civil rights in the Clinton administration—they are blocked by the Senate for the duration of a presidential term.

The damage to governance is matched by the damage to individual nominees. For many selected to serve at the beginning of an administration, a year or more in limbo is typical. This wait leads to widespread frustration and demoralization for individuals who must give notice to their employers, plan moves across the country, coordinate school schedules for their children, and make home sales and purchases. A survey of 435 senior-level appointees from the Reagan, Bush, and Clinton administrations . . . found "a nomination and confirmation process that exacts a heavy toll on nominees, leaving them exhausted, embarrassed, and confused." The frustration, they found, increases at every stage of the process.

Jumping Through Hoops

Time unfortunately, is only one part of a larger problem. Nominees to executive posts must fill out thick stacks of financial disclosure and conflict-of-interest forms to comply with the ethics requirements of both the executive and legislative branches. Simply filling out the forms—which requires one to list every foreign trip ever made and every foreigner met, every speech given over the past several years, and every investment and income item—takes weeks of effort and a considerable amount of money. One cabinet officer estimated it cost about $20,000 in legal and accountants' fees to ensure the forms were complete and accurate. Most of the information on the forms goes into public files for any inquisitive neighbor, opposition researcher, or reporter to peruse and even publish.

All nominees requiring Senate confirmation must go through full FBI background checks—including agent interviews of family members, neighbors, coworkers, friends, and adversaries—designed to compile every bit of negative information, including rumors and unsupported allegations, into raw FBI files that are then frequently shared with Senate committees and occasionally disclosed to the press. A move from one appointed position to another can require another FBI investigation, starting from scratch.

The full FBI field investigations date from a 1953 executive order. Most of the required forms stem from the Ethics Act of 1978 and subsequent revisions, which were usually responses to new scandals or allegations. But together, these rules and requirements have contributed to a political atmosphere that is unremittingly hostile to nominees. If public service was once considered an honorable calling, these days political appointees are, in the words of one participant, considered "guilty until proven innocent." Joycelyn Elders, who served as surgeon general in the Clinton administration, gave her reaction to the process as she left government: "I felt it was more a mechanism to destroy me than anything else. I came to Washington, D.C., like prime steak, and after being here awhile I feel like poor grade hamburger."

The destructive "mechanism" that Elders described included the scrutiny she received from the press and political adversaries once she took office. For many public officials, the smallest misstep or misfortune of being in the wrong meeting at the wrong time can trigger an investigation, leading to bad publicity and ruinous legal fees. A high-ranking White House aide was overheard saying, "How can I work this way? If I simply go to the wrong meeting my kid's college fund could be gone."

Help Wanted

This disheartening political atmosphere creates problems in recruitment. People with direct experience and expertise in a policy area are often considered unfit to manage that area because they cannot be trusted to oversee their previous employers or patrons. The Clinton administration, for example, had great difficulty filling key Energy Department positions overseeing the disposal of nuclear waste because most experts in the field came directly or indirectly from the nuclear industry and were thus rejected for their perceived conflicts of interest.

Finding top-flight people to serve in government for brief periods in their professional lives has always been a challenge. It requires individuals either at the peak of their professions or on their way up to leave midstream, uproot their families, learn new jobs and skills, adjust to a system without the bottom-line standards present in business and many professions, absorb political flak, and usually take sizable pay cuts. But in recent years the challenge has transformed into a nearly insurmountable one, especially for posts below the prestige level of the cabinet. It is one thing to face these challenges once one has assumed a position of responsibility. It is quite another to make the leap of faith and then wait for months or years of uncertainty accompanied by poking and prodding into one's personal life and financial records, to see if one can even be considered for the job.

No systematic, quantitative evidence suggests a drastic drop-off in the recruitment of America's best and brightest to top public policy positions. But every available piece of anecdotal evidence suggests that the recruitment problem has mushroomed into a recruitment crisis. Fewer and fewer prominent people in business, industry, or professions such as law, medicine, architecture, or science will even consider positions in the federal government. Fewer students in public policy programs aspire to jobs in Washington. If the sheer number of resumes submitted to presidential candidates or presidents-elect has not declined, the quality of the applicants, according to those who look at them, has. More and more positions fit the pattern of the deputy secretary of defense during the Bush administration, when more than 20 qualified possibilities were contacted before a willing candidate who lacked insurmountable conflicts of interest emerged.

Blockage Points

This crisis in public service and governance has structural, legal, cultural, and political causes. The following is a partial list:

1. A steady expansion in the number of executive appointees—what Brookings Institution fellow Paul Light calls "the thickening of government"—has clogged the machinery at every stage of the nomination and confirmation process.
2. Incremental changes in the law and executive orders, each a directed response to an actual or alleged scandal, have accumulated into an unworkable morass of rules intended to legislate morality. At the same time, they cumulatively contribute little to real safeguards of ethical standards, instead bordering on harassment and voyeurism for potential and actual nominees.
3. A more individualistic Senate culture has turned the "hold" from an occasional instrument of modest delay into a lethal weapon used regularly to hold nominees hostage to the whims or unrelated demands of individual senators.
4. The general rise in litigation has found its way into politics; lawsuits and the discovery process have become political tools, used increasingly to embarrass or bankrupt political adversaries.
5. The post-Watergate rise of investigative reporting has increased the media focus on scandal over substance and added to a cultural climate in which public figures are deemed guilty until proven innocent.

Clearing the Path

These dangerous trends in the executive appointment process have been widely noted for more than a decade. In 1989, the National Commission on Public Service chaired by former Federal Reserve Chairman Paul Volcker found that, "if these trends continue, America will soon be left with a government of the mediocre." In 1997 G. Calvin Mackenzie, the leading scholar on the subject, declared "the appointment process had its worst year in its history." Mackenzie goes on to conclude, "The process grows thicker and slower. Vacancies grow longer. Talent grows thinner. Governing becomes more difficult." Still, there has been no serious effort to reform or streamline the appointment process.

The problem will not be easy to solve. The most difficult barrier is a cultural one, as cynicism about public figures has replaced the healthy skepticism that was once a hallmark of American democracy. But culture can be changed, beginning with small but significant steps to reform laws, rules, and norms that signal the society's intention to rethink its ethos. Both Republicans and Democrats now agree that the process is broken and that enough blood has been spilt on both sides of the aisle over the last 20 years. With the election of a new president, perhaps both parties can "call it even" and work to construct a more civil and rational system to staff the senior ranks of government.

First, as several panels have recommended, the president-elect should name his chief of staff and key White House staff as early as possible—ideally the week after the election. President Clinton has said that not moving on the White House staff early was his biggest regret about his own transition. Why? Naming early the chief of staff and key White House staff gives the transition ballast and focus, eliminates a great deal of useless jockeying, and allows a president-elect to operate as a fully staffed president two months before the inauguration.

Second, the president-elect and congressional leaders need to expressly recognize the crisis in convincing America's best to take up public service. They should meet immediately after the election and instruct their top aides to report within 45 days on specific steps to rationalize and streamline the appointment process. The goal would be to publish an agreement on the appointment process by January 1, 2001. The agreement could include the following steps:

1. Implement a common electronic nominations form.   Today, a nominee for a Senate-confirmed position at the State Department must complete three separate background forms for the State Department Diplomatic Security Division, the White House Counsel's office, and the Senate Foreign Relations Committee. The candidate must also complete a financial disclosure form for the Office of Government Ethics. This multiplicity of forms is common to all executive departments. Most of the required information is redundant; much of it is irrelevant. . . . The next president should direct all the appropriate agencies and authorities to accept these computer-produced forms and work together to eliminate unnecessary repetition and unnecessarily intrusive questions.

2. Decriminalize the appointment process.   Today, a misstatement on a nominee's financial disclosure form, a violation of a postgovernment employment ban, or any contact with one's prior government agency is subject to criminal investigation and prosecution. This means that even filling out the forms prior to nomination or having dinner with a former colleague after leaving one's agency for private-sector employment are quite literally dangerous activities. . . .

Such criminalization is unnecessary and gravely damaging to recruitment efforts. Two steps make sense: first, decriminalize the appointment process by having the Office of Government Ethics enforce the disclosure and postemployment statutes as civil or regulatory matters. Second, repeal by executive order the additional postemployment bans put in place by President Clinton in 1993. These largely unenforceable restrictions go beyond the statutes and provide additional opportunities for mistakes with little gain in ethics.

3. Streamline the FBI background check. Beginning with the Eisenhower administration, most executive appointees have been subject to the FBI's "full field investigation." For national-security.posts and other sensitive positions, the investigation makes sense. For most executive positions, it is a Cold War relic and a waste of the FBI's good resources. Surely Washington can move to graduated levels of investigation: full field investigations for national security and other sensitive posts, abbreviated background checks for most appointees, and simple identification checks for part-time and other minor positions. The savings in time and resources would be immense. . . .

4. Protect FBI files. The FBI usually does not edit or judge the information it gathers in its full field investigations. As a result, FBI files contain both accurate and inaccurate information, both legitimate, well-sourced facts and rank hearsay. . . . Given the damage FBI files can do to a nominee, access should be limited to the chair and the ranking minority member of the relevant committees.

5. Change the "hold" custom in the Senate. A "hold" occurs when any single senator asks that a piece of legislation or a nomination not be brought to the floor of the Senate for an unspecified period of time, even though it has passed out of committee. It is an informal practice, has no time limit. and until recently could be totally secret. This past winter—after a good deal of admirable effort—Senators Grassley and Ron Wyden (D-Ore.) persuaded the Senate leadership to agree that a senator who places a hold must tell not only the leadership but also the sponsor of the legislation and the chair of the relevant committee. This was heralded as the end to secret holds.

Not so. When [Richard] Holbrooke's nomination [for U.N. Ambassador] passed out of the Senate Foreign Relations Committee, chaired by Jesse Helms (R-N.C.), it took another two months to get a Senate vote. It turns out that four senators had put holds—three of them secret—on Holbrooke for reasons unrelated to his qualifications for the position. . . .

Holds, mentioned nowhere in Senate rules, are antidemocratic and probably unconstitutional (although not likely subject to judicial review since the courts tend to be deferential to political questions). The Constitution, by requiring a two-thirds Senate vote on executive appointments, reflects the idea that a simple majority is an inadequate check on the executive's power to appoint. Yet the hold subjects nominations to a single senator's veto. The Grassley-Wyden reform should be revisited with an eye toward limiting a hold's duration (to, say, a week, long enough for the legitimate purpose of meeting with or getting additional information on a nominee) or eliminating holds altogether in the case of nominations. At a minimum, the reform should be strengthened to ensure that secret holds are truly not permitted.

6. *Enact other Senate procedural reforms.* The Constitution's provision for senatorial approval of nominees suggests that a president should be permitted to choose his team, that the team should be subject to the political process, and that the president should be held ultimately accountable to the nation for the team's performance. Three Senate procedural reforms . . . could reaffirm these principles and aid in recruitment. First, an executive nomination should be scheduled for a floor vote within 20 legislative days after the nomination has been voted out of committee. If a senator has problems with a nomination, he or she can vote against the nomination—or even filibuster—and let the Senate as a whole make its judgment. Second, committees should use their authority to waive hearings on lower-level positions. . . . Third, the Senate should take former President Bush's 1991 suggestion that the Senate meet in executive session to review a candidate's personal or other sensitive matters. This allows the Senate to do its job while respecting the privacy of nominees.

7. *Start with national security.* Following tradition, the foreign relations, armed services, and intelligence committees should hold pre-Inauguration Day hearings on the nominees for the secretaries of state and defense; on Inauguration Day they should vote on them. . . .

8. *Reduce the number of political appointees.* Currently the executive branch appoints more than 3,000 political positions, roughly a third of which require Senate confirmation. Senators John McCain (R-Ariz.) and Russell Feingold (D-Wisc.) have sponsored a bill to reduce that number to 2,000, as recommended by the Volcker Commission. Most scholars of public administration believe that this streamlining would actually promote more accountable management by political appointees. It would also make the remaining political appointments more prestigious and desirable and would unclog the nomination and confirmation process for them.

9. *Stop the legal assault on the executive branch.* The executive branch is constantly under legal assault—a major deterrent to public service. Very few of Clinton's aides have avoided retaining a lawyer and appearing before a grand jury or other legal processes. Congress made a step in the right direction last year when it let the independent counsel law expire; that law should be buried for good. Other steps should also be taken. First among them, Congress should repeal *Clinton v. Jones,* in which the Supreme Court held that Paula Jones could bring her civil action for sexual harassment against the president while he was in office. The opinion would be rather quaint, with its citations of ancient presidential memoirs, if not for the carnage it has caused over the last few years and the carnage it promises for future presidents. . . .

But the Court [did] at least . . . ask . . . Congress to review its decision. Congress should accept the Court's invitation—and soon—because civil litigation against the president will surely be used again as a political tactic.

These steps will not solve everything. The media's skepticism about government and its obsession with scandal will persist no matter what changes are made in ethics laws or otherwise. A top federal manager's salary is now barely more than half that of a first-year associate at a major law firm. This "wage gap" is likely to widen before it narrows, and candidates for public service simply have to resign themselves to serious financial sacrifice.

But Washington can convert cynicism back to skepticism and remove some of the unnecessary obstacles, annoyances, and harassments from the executive appointment process. These changes should be embraced before the 2000 election and enacted as soon as possible after the election. Governing in the twenty-first century will be difficult enough without the handicap the American political system has placed on its public managers.

Questions for Discussion

1. Why are well-qualified private citizens eager to serve in political jobs, even when the confirmation process is so exasperating?
2. Consider the "reforms" noted here. Which ones seem the most likely to be adopted? Least likely? Are members of the Senate likely to give up many of their prerogatives? Why or why not?

 Chapter 13

THE SUPREME COURT

Barely outlined in the Constitution, the Supreme Court and the American judiciary have been forced, almost from the beginning of the republic, to define their own roles within the political system. Historically, this has meant that the Court has engaged in a long-term balancing act, adhering to the rule of law while remaining conscious of the political environment of the times. At the heart of the American court system is a central irony: We rely on a profoundly undemocratic institution to safeguard our democratic state as well as to check the likely excesses of popular rule.

The Court's major tool in its work has been the power of judicial review: The Court determines whether federal laws and regulations and state statutes are in accord with the Constitution and constitutional principles. Although the principle of judicial review was incorporated into American law with Chief Justice John Marshall's 1803 decision in *Marbury* v. *Madison* (see selection 13.2), the Court has not, over the course of two centuries, invalidated many federal laws. Indeed, there was a fifty-four-year gap between *Marbury* and the next such ruling, the 1857 Dred Scott decision, which struck down the Missouri Compromise. Since the New Deal, however, the Court has been somewhat more willing to overturn federal laws, especially when individual rights are at stake (see Chapter 3). State laws have received even more attention; almost a thousand such statutes have been declared unconstitutional. In a federal system, the power to strike down state legislation is essential, whereas the capacity to overrule national laws is less so.

It is surely conceivable that Congress or the executive branch could interpret the Constitution as well as the Court does. Still, the Supreme Court's role provides for a rough balance of power among the three branches. Lacking the authority to enforce its decisions, the Court can scarcely act in an arbitrary or capricious fashion. That does not mean, however, that it cannot have an impact, as indicated by its decisions on subjects such as school desegregation, the rights of the accused, access to executive branch material (the Nixon tapes case), and the separation of powers (the *Chada* case, which invalidated legislative veto sections of approximately two hundred laws). In these and a host of other decisions, the Court clearly has acted in a policymaking role.

Despite the continuing controversy over whether the Supreme Court should make policy or merely interpret the Constitution in light of the framers' intent, the fact remains that it has consistently rendered policy decisions from its earliest days. It can hardly work in any other way. For example, in *Boyle* v. *United Technologies* (1988), conservative justice Antonin Scalia, writing for a five-to-four majority, argued that members of the military service could not sue the manufacturers of possibly defective military equipment (such as a helicopter that crashed). Scalia reasoned that allowing suits would ultimately increase the cost of defense materiel to the federal government and the American taxpayer. But as dissenting justice William Brennan observed, "the Court lacks both authority and expertise to fashion [a rule that exempts military contractors from civil suits], whether to protect the Treasury of the United States or the coffers of industry. . . . I would leave that exercise of power to Congress, where our Constitution places it." Justice Brennan, however, had previously written a broadly worded ruling that rendered the states almost superfluous in the face of federal power (*Garcia* v. *San Antonio Metropolitan Transit Authority*). In the end, both the conservative Scalia and the liberal Brennan have interpreted the Constitution broadly when doing so has suited their policy preferences. For further discussion of the question of intent and interpretation, see Richard Posner's article (selection 13.3) on the problematic notions of original intent and strict construction.

Mechanically, the Court sets its policy agenda by accepting a relatively small number of cases on which to rule. Although Congress and the president seem to have greater flexibility in setting their agendas, the Court can choose from among some 6,000 to 8,000 submitted cases in selecting the 100 or so that it will hear in its annual October-through-June session. In fact, its docket often includes controversies from which Congress and the president traditionally have shied away. The most notable example is school desegregation, which the Court addressed in 1954, a full decade before Congress passed a major civil rights bill.

Reprinted in this chapter, Alexander Hamilton's *The Federalist,* No. 78, and John Marshall's opinion in *Marbury* v. *Madison* provide the foundations for the Supreme Court's constitutional role. Hamilton articulates the classic formulation of the judiciary as "the least dangerous branch" because it "has no influence over either the sword [the executive] or the purse [the legislature]. . . . It may truly be said to have neither Force nor Will, but merely judgment; and must ultimately depend upon the aid of the executive arm even for the efficacy of its judgments." Marshall demonstrates the accuracy of Hamilton's observations in the *Marbury* decision, which involved a relatively trivial appointment but permitted Marshall to establish the principle of the judicial review of legislation.

In the last two articles, legal journalist Stuart Taylor Jr. and Federal Appeals Court Judge Richard Posner, who also writes on an array of legal issues, address the ever-relevant issue of judicial activism from a contemporary point of view. Although Posner is sometimes labeled a conservative, his intellect and range make him difficult to classify. But Posner does not sit as a judge merely to apply the Constitution in some rote manner or to determine what the framers' "original intent" might have been. Taylor provides a fair-minded assessment of the debate over judicial activism as it has evolved in the 2000–2001 Supreme Court. In particular, Taylor places in context the differing charges of judicial activism thrown at the Court's moderate faction and the more conservative faction, led by the pugnacious Associate Justice Antonin Scalia. Although we often focus on the relations between the federal government and the states and how the Court shapes the federal balance of power (see Chapter 3), the most important contemporary struggle may play out between the Court and Congress. Scalia and his faction of justices see Congress as out of control in extending the reach of federal intervention—even in an era when Republicans have control of Congress.

Taylor wrote before the Supreme Court's momentous decision in *Bush* v. *Gore,* but most legal scholars were amazed (and many appalled) at the activism exhibited by the Supreme Court when it essentially determined the result of the 2000 presidential election. Long considered the most legitimate branch of government, the Court risked its reputation by entering the political thicket.

13.1

The Federalist, No. 78

Alexander Hamilton

Of the three branches of government, the judiciary is the least fully outlined in the Constitution. To an extent this vagueness reflects the framers' greater concerns with the legislature and the executive, but it also indicates their perception that the judiciary simply did not pose the dangers the other branches did. For Alexander Hamilton, the key problem was to ensure that the judiciary remained independent of the legislature and the executive. One way to provide for this separation was to make court appointments lifetime positions, with removal impossible as long as the incumbents maintained "good behaviour"—a purposefully vague term.

Hamilton also laid out the case for judicial review of legislation. He observed that "no legislative act . . . contrary to the Constitution can be valid." And it is the Supreme Court that makes the final judgment on constitutionality. This seemingly great grant of authority is tempered, however, by the Court's inability to enforce its decisions without cooperation from the executive.

T*o the People of the State of New York:* We proceed now to an examination of the judiciary department of the proposed government.

In unfolding the defects of the existing confederation, the utility and necessity of a federal judicature have been clearly pointed out. It is the less necessary to recapitulate the considerations there urged; as the propriety of the institution in the abstract is not disputed: The only questions which have been raised being relative to the manner of constituting it, and to its extent. To these points therefore our observations shall be confined.

The manner of constituting it seems to embrace these several objects—1st. The mode of appointing the judges. 2d. The tenure by which they are to hold their places. 3d. The partition of the judiciary authority between different courts, and their relations to each other.

First. As to the mode of appointing the judges: This is the same with that of appointing the officers of the union in general, and has been so fully discussed in

Alexander Hamilton was the first secretary of the treasury and a consistent supporter of strong central government.

the two last numbers, that nothing can be said here which would not be useless repetition.

Second. As to the tenure by which the judges are to hold their places: This chiefly concerns their duration in office; the provisions for their support; and the precautions for their responsibility.

According to the plan of the convention, all the judges who may be appointed by the United States are to hold their offices *during good behaviour,* which is conformable to the most approved of the state constitutions; and among the rest, to that of this state. Its propriety having been drawn into question by the adversaries of that plan, is no light symptom of the rage for objection which disorders their imaginations and judgments. The standard of good behaviour for the continuance in office of the judicial magistracy is certainly one of the most valuable of the modern improvements in the practice of government. In a monarchy it is an excellent barrier to the despotism of the prince: In a republic it is a no less excellent barrier to the encroachments and oppressions of the representative body. And it is the best expedient which can be devised in any government, to secure a steady, upright and impartial administration of the laws.

Whoever attentively considers the different departments of power must perceive, that in a government in which they are separated from each other, the judiciary, from the nature of its functions, will always be the least dangerous to the political rights of the constitution; because it will be least in a capacity to annoy or injure them. The executive not only dispenses the honors, but holds the sword of the community. The legislature not only commands the purse, but prescribes the rules by which the duties and rights of every citizen are to be regulated. The judiciary on the contrary has no influence over either the sword or the purse, no direction either of the strength or of the wealth of the society, and can take no active resolution whatever. It may truly be said to have neither Force nor Will, but merely judgment; and must ultimately depend upon the aid of the executive arm even for the efficacy of its judgments.

This simple view of the matter suggests several important consequences. It proves incontestibly that the judiciary is beyond comparison the weakest of the three departments of power; that it can never attack with success either of the other two; and that all possible care is requisite to enable it to defend itself against their attacks. It equally proves, that though individual oppression may now and then proceed from the courts of justice, the general liberty of the people can never be endangered from that quarter: I mean, so long as the judiciary remains truly distinct from both the legislative and executive. For I agree that "there is no liberty, if the power of judging be not separated from the legislative and executive powers." And it proves, in the last place, that as liberty can have nothing to fear from the judiciary alone, but would have every thing to fear from its union with either of the other departments; that as all the effects of such an union must ensue from a dependence of the former on the latter, notwithstanding a nominal and apparent separation; that as from the natural feebleness of the judiciary, it is in continual jeopardy of being overpowered, awed or influenced by its coordinate

branches; and that as nothing can contribute so much to its firmness and independence, as permanency in office, this quality may therefore be justly regarded as an indispensable ingredient in its constitution; and in a great measure
as the citadel of the public justice and the public security.

The complete independence of the courts of justice is peculiarly essential in a
limited constitution. By a limited constitution I understand one which contains
certain specified exceptions to the legislative authority; such for instance as that
it shall pass no bills of attainder, no *ex post facto* laws, and the like.* Limitations
of this kind can be preserved in practice no other way than through the medium
of the courts of justice; whose duty it must be to declare all acts contrary to the
manifest tenor of the constitution void. Without this, all the reservations of
particular rights or privileges would amount to nothing.

Some perplexity respecting the right of the courts to pronounce legislative acts
void, because contrary to the constitution, has arisen from an imagination that
the doctrine would imply a superiority of the judiciary to the legislative power.
It is urged that the authority which can declare the acts of another void, must
necessarily be superior to the one whose acts may be declared void. As this doctrine is of great importance in all the American constitutions, a brief discussion
of the grounds on which it rests cannot be unacceptable.

There is no position which depends on clearer principles, than that every act
of a delegated authority, contrary to the tenor of the commission under which it
is exercised, is void. No legislative act therefore contrary to the constitution can
be valid. To deny this would be to affirm that the deputy is greater than his
principal; that the servant is above his master; that the representatives of the
people are superior to the people themselves; that men acting by virtue of powers
may do not only what their powers do not authorise, but what they forbid.

If it be said that the legislative body are themselves the constitutional judges
of their own powers, and that the construction they put upon them is conclusive
upon the other departments, it may be answered, that this cannot be the natural
presumption, where it is not to be collected from any particular provisions in the
constitution. It is not otherwise to be supposed that the constitution could intend
to enable the representatives of the people to substitute their *will* to that of their
constituents. It is far more rational to suppose that the courts were designed to be
an intermediate body between the people and the legislature, in order, among
other things, to keep the latter within the limits assigned to their authority. The
interpretation of the laws is the proper and peculiar province of the courts. A
constitution is in fact, and must be, regarded by the judges as a fundamental law.
It therefore belongs to them to ascertain its meaning as well as the meaning of
any particular act proceeding from the legislative body. If there should happen to

---

* A bill of attainder is a legislative act that inflicts punishment without a judicial trial. Crimes are
thus defined by statutes that are general in nature, and the courts interpret those statutes. An *ex
post facto* law either makes an act illegal after the fact or removes the legal protection from
behavior after that behavior has been performed.

be an irreconcileable variance between the two, that which has the superior obligation and validity ought of course to be preferred; or in other words, the constitution ought to be preferred to the statute, the intention of the people to the intention of their agents.

Nor does this conclusion by any means suppose a superiority of the judicial to the legislative power. It only supposes that the power of the people is superior to both; and that where the will of the legislature declared in its statutes, stands in opposition to that of the people declared in the constitution, the judges ought to be governed by the latter, rather than the former. They ought to regulate their decisions by the fundamental laws, rather than by those which are not fundamental.

This exercise of judicial discretion in determining between two contradictory laws, is exemplified in a familiar instance. It not uncommonly happens, that there are two statutes existing at one time, clashing in whole or in part with each other, and neither of them containing any repealing clause or expression. In such a case, it is the province of the courts to liquidate and fix their meaning and operation: So far as they can by any fair construction be reconciled to each other; reason and law conspire to dictate that this should be done. Where this is impracticable, it becomes a matter of necessity to give effect to one, in exclusion of the other. The rule which has obtained in the courts for determining their relative validity is that the last in order of time shall be preferred to the first. But this is mere rule of construction, not derived from any positive law, but from the nature and reason of the thing. It is a rule not enjoined upon the courts by legislative provision, but adopted by themselves, as consonant to truth and propriety, for the direction of their conduct as interpreters of the law. They thought it reasonable, that between the interfering acts of an *equal* authority, that which was the last indication of its will, should have the preference.

But in regard to the interfering acts of a superior and subordinate authority, of an original and derivative power, the nature and reason of the thing indicate the converse of that rule as proper to be followed. They teach us that the prior act of a superior ought to be preferred to the subsequent act of an inferior and subordinate authority; and that, accordingly, whenever a particular statute contravenes the constitution, it will be the duty of the judicial tribunals to adhere to the latter, and disregard the former.

It can be of no weight to say, that the courts on the pretence of a repugnancy, may substitute their own pleasure to the constitutional intentions of the legislature. This might as well happen in the case of two contradictory statutes; or it might as well happen in every adjudication upon any single statute. The courts must declare the sense of the law; and if they should be disposed to exercise WILL instead of JUDGMENT, the consequence would equally be the substitution of their pleasure to that of the legislative body. The observation, if it proved any thing, would prove that there ought to be no judges distinct from that body.

If then the courts of justice are to be considered as the bulwarks of a limited constitution against legislative encroachments, this consideration will afford a strong argument for the permanent tenure of judicial offices, since nothing will contribute so much as this to that independent spirit in the judges, which must be essential to the faithful performance of so arduous a duty. . . .

That inflexible and uniform adherence to the rights of the constitution and of individuals, which we perceive to be indispensable in the courts of justice, can certainly not be expected from judges who hold their offices by a temporary commission. Periodical appointments, however regulated, or by whomsoever made, would in some way or other be fatal to their necessary independence. If the power of making them was committed either to the executive or legislature, there would be danger of an improper complaisance to the branch which possessed it; if to both, there would be an unwillingness to hazard the displeasure of either; if to the people, or to persons chosen by them for the special purpose, there would be too great a disposition to consult popularity, to justify a reliance that nothing would be consulted but the constitution and the laws.

There is yet a further and a weighty reason for the permanency of the judicial offices; which is deducible from the nature of the qualifications they require. It has been frequently remarked with great propriety, that a voluminous code of laws is one of the inconveniences necessarily connected with the advantages of a free government. To avoid an arbitrary discretion in the courts, it is indispensable that they should be bound down by strict rules and precedents, which serve to define and point out their duty in every particular case that comes before them; and it will readily be conceived from the variety of controversies which grow out of the folly and wickedness of mankind, that the records of those precedents must unavoidably swell to a very considerable bulk, and must demand long and laborious study to acquire a competent knowledge of them. Hence it is that there can be but few men in the society, who will have sufficient skill in the laws to qualify them for the stations of judges. And making the proper deductions for the ordinary depravity of human nature, the number must be still smaller of those who unite the requisite integrity with the requisite knowledge. These considerations apprise us, that the government can have no great option between fit characters; and that a temporary duration in office, which would naturally discourage such characters from quitting a lucrative line of practice to accept a seat on the bench, would have a tendency to throw the administration of justice into hands less able, and less well qualified to conduct it with utility and dignity. In the present circumstances of this country, and in those in which it is likely to be for a long time to come, the disadvantages on this score would be greater than they may at first sight appear; but it must be confessed that they are far inferior to those which present themselves under the other aspects of the subject.

Upon the whole there can be no room to doubt that the convention acted wisely in copying from the models of those constitutions which have established *good behaviour* as the tenure of their judicial offices in point of duration; and that so far from being blameable on this account, their plan would have been inexcuseably defective if it had wanted this important feature of good government.

The experience of Great Britain affords an illustrious comment on the excellence of the institution.

Questions for Discussion

1. Why might a lifetime term for judges and justices be considered a good policy? Why did the framers make officeholding contingent on continued "good behaviour" rather than on some more specific criterion?
2. Why did the framers consider the Supreme Court the weakest of the three branches? How can this be so if the Court has the final say over what the Constitution means?

 13.2

Marbury v. Madison (1803)

In March 1801, during the waning hours of his administration, President John Adams appointed William Marbury to be a justice of the peace in Washington, D.C. James Madison, the secretary of state under incoming President Thomas Jefferson, refused to deliver Marbury's commission, following Jefferson's instructions. Marbury subsequently applied to the Supreme Court to obtain the position.

This minor controversy offered a great opportunity to John Marshall, whom Adams had appointed chief justice in the last months of his tenure. Marshall, no friend of Jefferson's, found in this case a way to establish the Court's power to declare a federal law unconstitutional. Although Hamilton argued strenuously in favor of the judicial review of legislation in *The Federalist,* No. 78 (selection 13.1), the Constitution did not speak definitively on the topic. In this case Marshall ruled specifically that Marbury was entitled to his commission but the Court had no legitimate authority to order Madison to deliver it to him because the federal statute providing the Court with the power to provide the appropriate remedy was unconstitutional. In short, this decision answered the open question posed by the Constitution: Who has the authority to declare a statute unconstitutional? In *Marbury* v. *Madison,* Marshall won that power for the Supreme Court.

M r. Chief Justice Marshall delivered the opinion of the Court.
At the last term on the affidavits then read and filed with the clerk, a rule was granted in this case, requiring the secretary of state to show cause why a *mandamus** should not issue, directing him to deliver to William Marbury his commission as a justice of the peace for the county of Washington, in the district of Columbia. . . .

In the order in which the court has viewed this subject, the following questions have been considered and decided.

1st. Has the applicant a right to the commission he demands?

2dly. If he has a right, and that right has been violated, do the laws of his country afford him a remedy?

3dly. If they do afford him a remedy, is it a *mandamus* issuing from this court? . . .

This . . . is a plain case for a *mandamus*, either to deliver the commission, or a copy of it from the record; and it only remains to be inquired,

Whether it can issue from this court.

The act to establish the judicial courts of the United States authorizes the supreme court "to issue writs of *mandamus*, in cases warranted by the principles and usages of law, to any courts appointed, or persons holding office, under the authority of the United States."

The secretary of state, being a person holding an office under the authority of the United States, is precisely within the letter of the description; and if this court is not authorized to issue a writ of *mandamus* to such an officer, it must be because the law is unconstitutional, and therefore absolutely incapable of conferring the authority, and assigning the duties which its words purport to confer and assign.

The constitution vests the whole judicial power of the United States in one supreme court, and such inferior courts as congress shall, from time to time, ordain and establish. This power is expressly extended to all cases arising under the laws of the United States; and, consequently, in some form, may be exercised over the present case; because the right claimed is given by a law of the United States.

In the distribution of this power it is declared that "the supreme court shall have original jurisdiction in all cases affecting ambassadors, other public ministers and consuls, and those in which a state shall be a party. In all other cases, the supreme court shall have appellate jurisdiction."

It has been insisted, at the bar, that as the original grant of jurisdiction, to the supreme and inferior courts, is general, and the clause, assigning original jurisdiction to the supreme court, contains no negative or restrictive words, the power remains to the legislature, to assign original jurisdiction to that court in other cases than those specified in the article which has been recited; provided those cases belong to the judicial power of the United States.

---

* A writ of *mandamus* is a binding directive, issued to individuals within the executive branch, that requires some action.

If it had been intended to leave it in the discretion of the legislature to apportion the judicial power between the supreme and inferior courts according to the will of that body, it would certainly have been useless to have proceeded further than to have defined the judicial power, and the tribunals in which it should be vested. The subsequent part of the section is mere surplusage, is entirely without meaning, if such is to be the construction. If congress remains at liberty to give this court appellate jurisdiction, where the constitution has declared their jurisdiction shall be original; and original jurisdiction where the constitution has declared it shall be appellate; the distribution of jurisdiction, made in the constitution, is form without substance.

Affirmative words are often, in their operations, negative of other objects than those affirmed; and in this case, a negative or exclusive sense must be given to them, or they have no operation at all.

It cannot be presumed that any clause in the constitution is intended to be without effect; and, therefore, such a construction is inadmissible, unless the words require it.

If the solicitude of the convention, respecting our peace with foreign powers, induced a provision that the supreme court should take original jurisdiction in cases which might be supposed to affect them; yet the clause would have proceeded no further than to provide for such cases, if no further restriction on the powers of congress had been intended. That they should have appellate jurisdiction in all other cases, with such exceptions as congress might make, is no restriction; unless the words be deemed exclusive of original jurisdiction. . . .

To enable this Court, then, to issue a *mandamus*, it must be shown to be an exercise of appellate jurisdiction, or to be necessary to enable them to exercise appellate jurisdiction. . . .

It is the essential criterion of appellate jurisdiction, that it revises and corrects the proceedings in a cause already instituted, and does not create that cause. Although, therefore, a *mandamus* may be directed to courts, yet to issue such a writ to an officer for the delivery of a paper, is in effect the same as to sustain an original action for that paper, and, therefore, seems not to belong to appellate, but to original jurisdiction. Neither is it necessary in such a case as this, to enable the court to exercise its appellate jurisdiction.

The authority, therefore, given to the supreme court, by the act establishing the judicial courts of the United States, to issue writs of *mandamus* to public officers, appears not to be warranted by the constitution; and it becomes necessary to inquire whether a jurisdiction so conferred can be exercised.

The question, whether an act, repugnant to the constitution, can become the law of the land, is a question deeply interesting to the United States; but, happily, not of an intricacy proportioned to its interest. It seems only necessary to recognise certain principles, supposed to have been long and well established, to decide it.

That the people have an original right to establish, for their future government, such principles as, in their opinion, shall most conduce to their own happiness is the basis on which the whole American fabric has been erected. The exercise of this original right is a very great exertion; nor can it, nor ought it, to be frequently repeated. The principles, therefore, so established, are deemed fundamental. And as the authority from which they proceed is supreme, and can seldom act, they are designed to be permanent.

This original and supreme will organizes the government, and assigns to different departments their respective powers. It may either stop here, or establish certain limits not to be transcended by those departments.

The government of the United States is of the latter description. The powers of the legislature are defined and limited; and that those limits may not be mistaken, or forgotten, the constitution is written. To what purpose are powers limited, and to what purpose is that limitation committed to writing, if these limits may, at any time, be passed by those intended to be restrained? The distinction between a government with limited and unlimited powers is abolished, if those limits do not confine the persons on whom they are imposed, and if acts prohibited and acts allowed, are of equal obligation. It is a proposition too plain to be contested, that the constitution controls any legislative act repugnant to it; or, that the legislature may alter the constitution by an ordinary act.

Between these alternatives there is no middle ground. The constitution is either a superior paramount law, unchangeable by ordinary means, or it is on a level with ordinary legislative acts, and, like other acts, is alterable when the legislature shall please to alter it.

If the former part of the alternative be true, then a legislative act contrary to the constitution is not law: if the latter part be true, then written constitutions are absurd attempts, on the part of the people, to limit a power in its own nature illimitable.

Certainly all those who have framed written constitutions contemplate them as forming the fundamental and paramount law of the nation, and, consequently, the theory of every such government must be, that an act of the legislature, repugnant to the constitution, is void.

This theory is essentially attached to a written constitution, and, is consequently, to be considered, by this court, as one of the fundamental principles of our society. It is not therefore to be lost sight of in the further consideration of this subject.

If an act of the legislature, repugnant to the constitution, is void, does it, notwithstanding its invalidity, bind the courts, and oblige them to give it effect? Or, in other words, though it be not law, does it constitute a rule as operative as if it was a law? This would be to overthrow in fact what was established in theory; and would seem, at first view, an absurdity too gross to be insisted on. It shall, however, receive a more attentive consideration.

It is emphatically the province and duty of the judicial department to say what the law is. Those who apply the rule to particular cases, must of necessity expound and interpret that rule. If two laws conflict with each other, the courts must decide on the operation of each.

So if a law be in opposition to the constitution; if both the law and the constitution apply to a particular case, so that the court must either decide that case conformably to the law, disregarding the constitution; or conformably to the constitution, disregarding the law; the court must determine which of these conflicting rules governs the case. This is of the very essence of judicial duty.

If, then, the courts are to regard the constitution, and the constitution is superior to any ordinary act of the legislature, the constitution, and not such ordinary act, must govern the case to which they both apply.

Those, then, who controvert the principle that the constitution is to be considered, in court, as a paramount law, are reduced to the necessity of maintaining that courts must close their eyes on the constitution, and see only the law.

This doctrine would subvert the very foundation of all written constitutions. It would declare that an act which, according to the principles and theory of our government, is entirely void, is yet, in practice, completely obligatory. It would declare that if the legislature shall do what is expressly forbidden, such act, notwithstanding the express prohibition, is in reality effectual. It would be giving to the legislature a practical and real omnipotence, with the same breath which professes to restrict their powers within narrow limits. It is prescribing limits, and declaring that those limits may be passed at pleasure.

That it thus reduces to nothing what we have deemed the greatest improvement on political institutions, a written constitution, would of itself be sufficient, in America, where written constitutions have been viewed with so much reverence, for rejecting the construction. But the peculiar expressions of the constitution of the United States furnish additional arguments in favour of its rejection.

The judicial power of the United States is extended to all cases arising under the constitution.

Could it be the intention of those who gave this power, to say that in using it the constitution should not be looked into? That a case arising under the constitution should be decided without examining the instrument under which it arises?

This is too extravagant to be maintained.

In some cases, then, the constitution must be looked into by the judges. And if they can open it at all, what part of it are they forbidden to read or to obey?

There are many other parts of the constitution which serve to illustrate this subject.

It is declared that "no tax or duty shall be laid on articles exported from any state." Suppose a duty on the export of cotton, of tobacco, or of flour; and a suit instituted to recover it. Ought judgment to be rendered in such a case? ought the judges to close their eyes on the constitution, and only see the law?

The constitution declares "that no bill of attainder or *ex post facto* law shall be passed."

If, however, such a bill should be passed, and a person should be prosecuted under it; must the court condemn to death those victims whom the constitution endeavours to preserve?

"No person," says the constitution, "shall be convicted of treason unless on the testimony of two witnesses to the same overt act, or on confession in open court."

Here the language of the constitution is addressed especially to the courts. It prescribes, directly for them, a rule of evidence not to be departed from. If the legislature should change that rule, and declare *one* witness, or a confession *out* of court, sufficient for conviction, must the constitutional principle yield to the legislative act?

From these, and many other selections which might be made, it is apparent, that the framers of the constitution contemplated that instrument as a rule for the government of *courts*, as well as of the legislature. . . .

It is also not entirely unworthy of observation, that in declaring what shall be the *supreme* law of the land, the *constitution* itself is first mentioned; and not the laws of the United States generally, but those only which shall be made in *pursuance* of the constitution have that rank.

Thus, the particular phraseology of the constitution of the United States confirms and strengthens the principle, supposed to be essential to all written constitutions, that a law repugnant to the constitution is void; and that *courts*, as well as other departments, are bound by that instrument.

Questions for Discussion

1. What was the precise legal issue at the core of *Marbury v. Madison*? Why is this case so important to the ultimate workings of the separation of powers?
2. Is it absolutely imperative that the Constitution be interpreted as the supreme law of the land? Why shouldn't the legislature's interpretation of what is constitutional be weighed equally?

13.3

What Am I? A Potted Plant?

Richard A. Posner

Since the 1960s, there has been a continuing political debate over the appropriate amount of discretion that appeals court judges and Supreme Court justices should exercise in interpreting the Constitution. Liberals have generally argued for substantial leeway, noting that the framers could not have anticipated many key contemporary policy debates, such as those about abortion or the regulation of nuclear plants. By and large, conservatives have made a case for less discretion and a more literal interpretation of the Constitution. Nevertheless, some liberals, such as the late Supreme Court justice Hugo Black, have adopted a literalist position, while some conservatives, such as Court of Appeals judge Richard Posner, have taken a more discretionary approach.

Here, Posner reacts to the strict constructionist or "legal formalist" view, labeling it virtually impossible to carry out. "Judges," he notes, "have been entrusted with making policy from the start." Posner endorses this notion in large part because of his tendency to approach legal reasoning from an economic perspective—one that has little, if any, grounding in the Constitution or the ideas of the framers. What is clear from his point of view is that all judges make policy and that both liberals and conservatives can benefit from expanded judicial discretion.

Many people, not all of conservative bent, believe that modern American courts are too aggressive, too "activist," too prone to substitute their own policy preferences for those of the elected branches of government. This may well be true. But some who complain of judicial activism espouse a view of law that is too narrow. And a good cause will not hallow a bad argument.

This point of view often is called "strict constructionism." A more precise term would be "legal formalism." A forceful polemic by Walter Berns in the June 1987 issue of *Commentary*—"Government by Lawyers and Judges"—summarizes the formalist view well. Issues of the "public good" can "be decided legitimately only with the consent of the governed." Judges have no legitimate say about these issues. Their business is to address issues of private rights, that is, "to decide

Richard A. Posner is a judge on the U.S. Court of Appeals for the Seventh Circuit and a senior lecturer at the University of Chicago Law School. He served as a mediator in an unsuccessful attempt to resolve the Justice Department's antitrust lawsuit against Microsoft.

whether the right exists—in the Constitution or in a statute—and, if so, what it is; but at that point inquiry ceases." The judge may not use "discretion and the weighing of consequences" to arrive at his decisions and he may not create new rights. The Constitution is a source of rights, but only to the extent that it embodies "fundamental and clearly articulated principles of government." There must be no judicial creativity or "policy-making."

In short, there is a political sphere, where the people rule, and there is a domain of fixed rights, administered but not created or altered by judges. The first is the sphere of discretion, the second of application. Legislators make the law; judges find and apply it.

There has never been a time when the courts of the United States, state or federal, behaved consistently in accordance with this idea. Nor could they, for reasons rooted in the nature of law and legal institutions, in the limitations of human knowledge, and in the character of a political system.

"Questions about the public good" and "questions about private rights" are inseparable. The private right is conferred in order to promote the public good. So in deciding how broadly the right shall be interpreted, the court must consider the implications of its interpretation for the public good. For example, should an heir who murders his benefactor have a right to inherit from his victim? The answer depends, in part anyway, on the public good that results from discouraging murders. Almost the whole of so-called private law, such as property, contract, and tort law, is instrumental to the public end of obtaining the social advantages of free markets. Furthermore, most private law is common law—that is, law made by judges rather than by legislators or by constitution-framers. Judges have been entrusted with making policy from the start.

Often when deciding difficult questions of private rights courts have to weigh policy considerations. If a locomotive spews sparks that set a farmer's crops afire, has the railroad invaded the farmer's property right or does the railroad's ownership of its right of way implicitly include the right to emit sparks? If the railroad has such a right, shall it be conditioned on the railroad's taking reasonable precautions to minimize the danger of fire? If, instead, the farmer has the right, shall it be conditioned on his taking reasonable precautions? Such questions cannot be answered sensibly without considering the social consequences of alternative answers.

A second problem is that when a constitutional convention, a legislature, or a court promulgates a rule of law, it necessarily does so without full knowledge of the circumstances in which the rule might be invoked in the future. When the unforeseen circumstance arises—it might be the advent of the motor vehicle or of electronic surveillance, or a change in attitudes toward religion, race, and sexual propriety—a court asked to apply the rule must decide, in light of information not available to the promulgators of the rule, what the rule should mean in its new setting. That is a creative decision, involving discretion, the weighing of consequences, and, in short, a kind of legislative judgment—though, properly, one more confined than if the decision were being made by a real legislature. A court that decides, say, that copyright protection extends to the coloring of old black-and-white movies is making a creative decision, because the copyright laws do not mention colorization. It is not being lawless or usurpative merely because it is weighing consequences and exercising discretion.

Or if a court decides (as the Supreme Court has done in one of its less controversial modern rulings) that the Fourth Amendment's prohibition against unreasonable searches and seizures shall apply to wiretapping, even though no trespass is committed by wiretapping and hence no property right is invaded, the court is creating a new right and making policy. But in a situation not foreseen and expressly provided for by the Framers of the Constitution, a simple reading out of a policy judgment made by the Framers is impossible.

Even the most carefully drafted legislation has gaps. The Constitution, for example, does not say that the federal government has sovereign immunity—the right, traditionally enjoyed by all sovereign governments, not to be sued without its consent. Nevertheless the Supreme Court held that the federal government has sovereign immunity. Is this interpolation usurpative? The Federal Tort Claims Act, a law waiving sovereign immunity so citizens can sue the government, makes no exception for suits by members of the armed services who are injured through the negligence of their superiors. Nevertheless the Supreme Court has held that the act was not intended to provide soldiers with a remedy. The decision may be right or wrong, but it is not wrong just because it is creative. The 11th Amendment to the Constitution forbids a citizen of one state to sue "another" state in federal court without the consent of the defendant state. Does this mean that you can sue your own state in federal court without the state's consent? That's what the words seem to imply, but the Supreme Court has held that the 11th Amendment was intended to preserve the sovereign immunity of the states more broadly. The Court thought this was implied by the federalist system that the Constitution created. Again the Court may have been right or wrong, but it was not wrong just because it was creative.

Opposite the unrealistic picture of judges who apply law but never make it, Walter Berns hangs an unrealistic picture of a populist legislature that acts only "with the consent of the governed." Speaking for myself, I find that many of the political candidates whom I have voted for have failed to be elected and that those who have been elected have then proceeded to enact much legislation that did not have my consent. Given the effectiveness of interest groups in the political process, much of this legislation probably didn't have the consent of a majority of citizens. Politically, I feel more governed than self-governing. In considering whether to reduce constitutional safeguards to slight dimensions, we should be sure to have a realistic, not an idealized, picture of the legislative and executive branches of government, which would thereby be made more powerful than they are today.

To banish all discretion from the judicial process would indeed reduce the scope of constitutional rights. The framers of a constitution who want to make it a charter of liberties and not just a set of constitutive rules face a difficult choice.

They can write specific provisions, and thereby doom their work to rapid obsolescence or irrelevance; or they can write general provisions, thereby delegating substantial discretion to the authoritative interpreters, who in our system are the judges. The U.S. Constitution is a mixture of specific and general provisions. Many of the specific provisions have stood the test of time amazingly well or have been amended without any great fuss. This is especially true of the rules establishing the structure and procedures of Congress. Most of the specific provisions creating rights, however, have fared poorly. Some have proved irksomely anachronistic—for example, the right to a jury trial in federal court in all cases at law if the stakes exceed $20. Others have become dangerously anachronistic, such as the right to bear arms. Some have even turned topsy-turvy, such as the provision for indictment by grand jury. The grand jury has become an instrument of prosecutorial investigation rather than a protection for the criminal suspect. If the Bill of Rights had consisted entirely of specific provisions, it would have aged very rapidly and would no longer be a significant constraint on the behavior of government officials.

Many provisions of the Constitution, however, are drafted in general terms. This creates flexibility in the face of unforeseen changes, but it also creates the possibility of multiple interpretations, and this possibility is an embarrassment for a theory of judicial legitimacy that denies that judges have any right to exercise discretion. A choice among semantically plausible interpretations of a text, in circumstances remote from those contemplated by its drafters, requires the exercise of discretion and the weighing of consequences. Reading is not a form of deduction; understanding requires a consideration of consequences. If I say, "I'll eat my hat," one reason that my listeners will "decode" this in non-literal fashion is that I couldn't eat a hat if I tried. The broader principle, which applies to the Constitution as much as to a spoken utterance, is that if one possible interpretation of an ambiguous statement would entail absurd or terrible results, that is a good reason to adopt an alternative interpretation.

Even the decision to read the Constitution narrowly, and thereby "restrain" judicial interpretation, is not a decision that can be read directly from the text. The Constitution does not say, "Read me broadly," or, "Read me narrowly." That decision must be made as a matter of political theory, and will depend on such things as one's view of the springs of judicial legitimacy and of the relative competence of courts and legislatures in dealing with particular types of issues.

Consider the provision in the Sixth Amendment that "in all criminal prosecutions, the accused shall enjoy the right . . . to have the Assistance of Counsel for his defense." Read narrowly, this just means that the defendant can't be forbidden to retain counsel; if he can't afford counsel, or competent counsel, he is out of luck. Read broadly, it guarantees even the indigent the effective assistance of counsel; it becomes not just a negative right to be allowed to hire a lawyer but a positive right to demand the help of the government in financing one's defense. Either reading is compatible with the semantics of the provision, but the first better captures the specific intent of the Framers. At the time the Sixth Amendment was written, English law forbade a criminal defendant to have the assistance of counsel unless abstruse questions of law arose in his case. The Framers wanted to do away with this prohibition. But, more broadly, they wanted to give criminal defendants protection against being railroaded. When they wrote, government could not afford, or at least did not think it could afford, to hire lawyers for indigent criminal defendants. Moreover, criminal trials were short and simple, so it was not ridiculous to expect a person to defend himself without a lawyer if he couldn't afford to hire one. Today the situation is different. Not only can the society easily afford to supply lawyers to poor people charged with crimes, but modern criminal law and procedure are so complicated that an unrepresented defendant will usually be at a great disadvantage.

I do not know whether Professor Berns thinks the Supreme Court was usurping legislative power when it held in the *Gideon* case [selection 3.5] that a poor person has a right to the assistance of counsel at the state's expense. But his article does make clear his view that the Supreme Court should not have invalidated racial segregation in public schools. Reading the words of the 14th Amendment in the narrowest possible manner in order to minimize judicial discretion, and noting the absence of evidence that the Framers wanted to eliminate segregation, Berns argues that "equal protection of the laws" just means non-discriminatory enforcement of whatever laws are enacted, even if the laws themselves are discriminatory. He calls the plausible empirical proposition that "separate educational facilities are inherently unequal" "a logical absurdity."

On Berns's reading, the promulgation of the equal protection clause was a trivial gesture at giving the recently freed slaves (and other blacks, whose status at the time was little better than that of serfs) political equality with whites, since the clause in his view forbids the denial of that equality only by executive officers. The state may not withdraw police protection from blacks (unless by legislation?) but it may forbid them to sit next to whites on buses. This is a possible reading of the 14th Amendment but not an inevitable one, unless judges must always interpret the Constitution as denying them the power to exercise judgment.

No one really believes this. Everyone professionally connected with law knows that, in Oliver Wendell Holmes's famous expression, judges legislate "interstitially," which is to say they make law, only more cautiously, more slowly, and in more principled, less partisan, fashion than legislators.* The attempt to deny this truism entangles "strict constructionists" in contradictions. Berns says both that judges can enforce only "clearly articulated principles" and that they may invalidate unconstitutional laws. But the power to do this is not "articulated" in the Constitution; it is merely implicit in it. He believes that the courts have been wrong to interpret the First Amendment as protecting the publication of foul

---

* Oliver Wendell Holmes (1841–1935) served first on the Massachusetts Supreme Court and then on the U.S. Supreme Court between 1882 and 1932. He was labeled "the Great Dissenter," and many of Holmes's minority opinions became the fodder for subsequent Court majority reasoning.

language in school newspapers, yet the words "freedom of speech, or of the press" do not appear to exclude foul language in school newspapers. Berns says he deduces his conclusion from the principle that expression, to be within the scope of the First Amendment, must be related to representative government. Where did he get that principle from? He didn't read it in the Constitution.

The First Amendment also forbids Congress to make laws "respecting an establishment of religion." Berns says this doesn't mean that Congress "must be neutral between religion and irreligion." But the words will bear that meaning, so how does he decide they should be given a different meaning? By appealing to Tocqueville's opinion of the importance of religion in a democratic society. In short, the correct basis for decision is the consequence of the decision for democracy. Yet consequences are not—in the strict constructionist view—a fit thing for courts to consider. Berns even expresses regret that the modern Supreme Court is oblivious to Tocqueville's opinion "of the importance of the woman . . . whose chastity as a young girl is protected not only by religion but by an education that limits her 'imagination.' " A court that took such opinions into account would be engaged in aggressively consequentialist thinking rather than in strict construction.

The liberal judicial activists may be imprudent and misguided in their efforts to enact the liberal political agenda into constitutional law, but it is no use pretending that what they are doing is not interpretation but "deconstruction," not law but politics, because it involves the exercise of discretion and a concern with consequences and because it reaches results not foreseen 200 years ago. It may be bad law because it lacks firm moorings in constitutional text, or structure, or history, or consensus, or other legitimate sources of constitutional law, or because it is reckless of consequences, or because it oversimplifies difficult moral and political questions. But it is not bad law, or no law, just because it violates the tenets of strict construction.

Questions for Discussion

1. Can the notion of "original intent" be defended as a serious legal doctrine according to Posner? Why not?
2. Do all judges make policy at least part of the time?
3. Posner has frequently been mentioned as a prospective Supreme Court nominee. Do you think the sentiments articulated in this article make his nomination and confirmation more or less likely? Why?

13.4

The Tipping Point

Stuart Taylor Jr.

The Supreme Court is many things: a set of nine justices who have their individual quirks; groupings of ideological blocs with shifting memberships; a lynchpin of democracy with life-tenured members; a powerful institution that has no independent authority with which to enforce its rulings. Over its history, many times the Court has been balanced closely, with a single vote making all the difference in a 5–4 ruling. In the wake of the 2000 election, Al Gore certainly understands the significance of such a vote. Of particular importance in the current Court is the larger-than-life presence of Associate Justice Antonin Scalia, who is simultaneously charming, acerbic, brilliant, and arrogant. Scalia has clear views about the so-called conservative direction in which he would like to lead the Court: The Constitution would be read more literally, and Congress would delegate fewer powers through vague, ill-defined laws.

In this article, Stuart Taylor Jr. presents a contemporary (June 2000) overview of a Court that leans, but barely, in Scalia's direction. In particular, Taylor addresses the Court's recent antagonism toward Congress; he quotes Scalia, who justifies the Court's willingness to declare laws unconstitutional with the observation, "Congress is increasingly abdicating its independent responsibility to be sure it is being faithful to the Constitution." Ever pugnacious and self-righteous, Scalia is eager to take on Congress. But confrontations between institutions have costs in a separation-of-powers system, and—on the heels of its December 2000 foray into presidential politics—the Court may well risk its legitimacy by picking too many fights with the legislative branch that sits 200 yards away on Capitol Hill.

Justice Antonin Scalia's demeanor was charming, his delivery witty. But his message was serious, and some of his words were blunt. Scalia's subject at a . . . [2000] symposium hosted by Michigan State University in a Washington hotel was "judicial activism." The 64-year-old Reagan appointee's main targets were "the liberal [Supreme] Court of the '60s and '70s"—which he said sometimes used "phony and disreputable" reasoning to distort the meaning of laws—and the U.S. Congress of more recent years, which he accused of "legisla-

Stuart Taylor Jr. is an opinion columnist at *National Journal*.

tive activism." And his conclusions went to the fundament of our constitutional system.

Countering academic critics who have turned the old imprecation of activism against Scalia and his conservative colleagues, Scalia said that "the current Court is considerably less activist . . . than the Court of a few decades ago." He acknowledged that "conservatives are just as willing to play this game as liberals are now," and that "we are striking down as many federal statutes from year to year as the Warren Court at its peak." But he noted that the Court has been voiding fewer state and local statutes than it did in previous decades. And he stressed that most federal and state laws that have fallen lately have "involved attempts by a legislature to do something quite novel and often even downright bizarre." He lingered on "bizarre."

As one example Scalia (a devout Catholic) cited Congress's Religious Freedom Restoration Act of 1993, which sought to force the Court to require governments to provide more accommodations to religion than the Justices (in a 1990 opinion by Scalia) had found required by the First Amendment's guarantee of freedom of religion. This act was, Scalia said, the only statute he had ever seen in which Congress had "purported to direct the Supreme Court to interpret the Constitution in a certain way." The Court struck that law down in 1997 in a 6–3 vote. Scalia blasted another law as a "congressional search for some patsy to pay the welfare benefits that it was unwilling to appropriate out of public funds." That one, which the Court struck down 5–4 in 1998, was a 1992 statute retroactively assessing companies that had left the coal business as long ago as 1965 for the cost of health benefits for miners, their widows, and children. And he assailed a provision of the Communications Decency Act that had effectively barred Internet transmission of sexually explicit materials protected by the First Amendment. The Court voided that law unanimously in 1997. Laws such as these are so clearly unconstitutional, Scalia suggested, that judicial decisions striking them down are "more an indication of legislative activism than of judicial activism."

"Congress is increasingly abdicating its independent responsibility to be sure that it is being faithful to the Constitution," Scalia asserted. "My Court is fond of saying that acts of Congress come to the Court with the presumption of constitutionality. . . . *But if Congress is going to take the attitude that it will do anything it can get away with and let the Supreme Court worry about the Constitution . . . then perhaps that presumption is unwarranted.*" [emphasis added]

In the works at the time, as Scalia knew, was a 5–4 decision in which he and his fellow conservatives had voted to strike down part of the Violence Against Women Act of 1994, which had swept through Congress by wide bipartisan majorities, as an invasion of the traditional domain of the states. When that decision (*U.S. vs. Morrison*) came down on May 15, Chief Justice William H. Rehnquist's majority opinion gave lip service to the familiar "presumption of constitutionality." But the Court's bold action—lopping off a provision that had authorized victims of rape, domestic violence, and other "crimes of violence motivated by gender" to file federal civil rights lawsuits against their suspected assailants—spoke louder than Rehnquist's typically bland words.

It was only the second decision since 1935 holding that some crimes and other matters are so clearly noncommercial and so clearly within the domain of the states that Congress lacks the power to punish them by invoking its power to protect interstate commerce. It was also the 22nd congressional enactment that the Rehnquist Court has struck down in the past five years—a near-record pace. The 23rd came a week later, when a 5–4 majority invoked the First Amendment to void a law that had effectively required many cable television systems to limit sexually explicit programming to late-night hours. . . .

Justice David Souter warned in his opinion for the dissenters in *Morrison* that by intruding into Congress's domain, the majority had taken what "can only be seen as a step toward recapturing the prior mistakes" that had "in large measure provoked the judicial crisis of 1937." The Bush-appointed Souter, who has proved to be fairly liberal, was alluding to the long-discredited line of Supreme Court decisions striking down a succession of federal regulatory laws passed before and during the New Deal. These decisions inspired President Franklin D. Roosevelt's court-packing plan of 1937, which in turn helped prompt the Court to back down. For the next 55 years, it virtually abandoned any pretense of curbing the reach of congressional power, while gradually expanding its protection of civil liberties, especially in cases pitting individuals against states. Joseph R. Biden Jr., D-Del., the main Senate sponsor of the Violence Against Women Act, was more blunt than Souter in his criticism of *Morrison* in an interview with *The Los Angeles Times:* "These folks are judicial activists."

Perhaps so. But the same can be (and has been) said of the Court's four liberals, who see the Constitution as a tool to push for social reform. The activist label is apt for all nine justices to the extent that judicial activism includes invoking novel or debatable interpretations of the Constitution to strike down democratically adopted state or federal laws and practices that offend one's moral or political beliefs, while showing relatively little deference to the other branches of government and the voters. Among the cases in which the Court's liberals (joined by one or both of the centrist conservatives, Sandra Day O'Connor and Anthony M. Kennedy) have done this are a 1999 decision striking down state and federal laws limiting new residents of California to the welfare benefits they would have received in their home states; another voiding a Chicago ordinance that gave police broad powers of arrest to sweep suspected gang members and those who associate with them from neighborhood streets; two 1996 decisions expanding gay rights and casting a shadow of doubt over the constitutionality of all single-sex education; a 1995 decision sweeping away all laws limiting the terms of members of Congress; and a 1992 decision barring public schools from sponsoring prayers (even nonsectarian, nondenominational ones) at public school graduations.

One paradox behind all the finger-pointing about judicial activism is that the Supreme Court—nine unelected, life-tenured, black-robed lawyers who keep striking down popular laws adopted by the people's elected representatives—has always fared far better than Congress and substantially better than the executive branch in polls measuring public confidence in the three branches ever since such polls began in 1966. And the gap has been widening in recent years.*

The recent go-rounds in the Justices' battle over the direction of American law came during the run-up to a presidential election that may well—should one or more Justices retire—have a dramatic impact on the Court's ideological balance, perhaps for decades to come. Even a single strategic appointment (a liberal replacing a conservative or vice versa) could tip the Court decisively to the liberal or conservative side on issues such as affirmative action, racial gerrymandering, public aid (including vouchers) for religious schools and their students, and the battle over federalism-based curbs on congressional power that has produced identical 5–4 splits in *Morrison* and nine other decisions since 1992. . . .

Already this year O'Connor and Kennedy have teamed with the Court's three most conservative members—Rehnquist, Scalia, and Clarence Thomas—in 5–4 decisions barring Congress from subjecting state governments to the federal law that bars discrimination against older employees; voiding the Clinton administration's efforts to regulate tobacco; making it harder for the Justice Department to require that election districts be redrawn to help elect black and Hispanic candidates; making it easier for police to stop and frisk people who flee when approached; and voiding the Violence Against Women Act. Liberal-leaning John Paul Stevens, Souter, Ruth Bader Ginsburg, and Stephen G. Breyer (the latter two are Clinton appointees) have dissented from all these decisions. The same was true of, for example, the Court's 1997 decisions striking down a portion of the Brady gun control act and overruling a 1985 precedent that had barred public school teachers from teaching federally financed remedial classes at religious schools, and its 1995 decision curbing federal affirmative action preferences.

Two June 5 [2000] decisions, on the other hand, illustrate how simplistic it is to see the Justices solely as two undifferentiated ideological blocs. In the first case, an eclectic majority—O'Connor, Rehnquist, Ginsburg, Breyer, Souter, and Thomas—held that a Washington state law took too little account of the constitutional rights of parents in permitting a judge to order visiting rights for grandparents over a mother's objection, while splintering as to the constitutional rationale; Stevens, Scalia, and Kennedy dissented for very diverse reasons. In the second case, an 8–1 majority (with only Rehnquist dissenting) ruled that Kenneth W. Starr, then the Whitewater independent counsel, had violated a plea agreement with Webster L. Hubbell by indicting him for tax evasion on the basis of thousands of pages of personal financial records Hubbell had produced under a grant of immunity.

For its next term, which begins in October [2000], the Court has already scheduled a major test of the sweeping, open-ended powers that Congress has for

---

* This may have changed in the wake of the Courts' intervention in resolving the 2000 election.

decades delegated to agencies such as the Environmental Protection Agency under various regulatory laws. One issue in that case (*American Trucking Associations* vs. *Browner*) is whether to reinterpret the Clean Air Act to require the government to weigh the economic costs against the public health benefits of proposed regulations mandating reductions in air pollution. In another case (*University of Alabama* vs. *Garrett*), the Court will consider whether states are constitutionally immune from suit under the Americans With Disabilities Act. In a third (*Solid Waste Agency* vs. *U.S. Army Corps of Engineers*), the issue is whether to curb federal power over matters such as a local government's plan to fill (for use as a waste-disposal site) an isolated intrastate wetland that could provide habitat for migratory birds.* These are big, important issues.

And in the next few years, the Court is likely to decide the fate of the thousands of federal, state, and local race and gender preferences and racial gerrymanders of election districts. Despite a succession of 5–4 decisions curbing (but not flatly barring) use of such racial classifications, many such programs have survived the cautiously worded majority opinions and concurrences of the often-ambivalent O'Connor. Also in the pipeline are cases in which the Justices will be asked to rule on tuition vouchers for religious schools, various campaign finance restrictions, gay rights issues, the parameters of "right to die," privacy, crime, freedom of speech, property rights, and more—and on now-unforeseen issues that will become important as technology races ahead.

What the Election Could Do

The outcomes of many such future cases will probably depend on who appoints the Court's next one, two, or three members. Any or all of the three oldest justices—Stevens (80), Rehnquist (75), and O'Connor (70)—might well retire in the next four to eight years. It's also possible that others will step down. . . .

[A] conservative Bush Justice replacing a liberal—or O'Connor—could wipe out most or all preference programs maintained by federal, state, and local governments; loosen restrictions on church-state links, including aid to religious schools; and move the Court further down the states' rights road. A one-vote swing to the conservative side might also lead to approval of incremental restrictions on abortion procedures. But President Clinton overstated the Bush threat to abortion rights when he said at a Democratic fund-raiser in January: "There is absolutely no question in my mind that whether *Roe* vs. *Wade* is preserved or scrapped depends on what happens in the presidential vote." In fact, the basic right to have an abortion seems a strong bet to survive a one-term Bush presidency and a reasonably good bet to survive two terms. That's because six of the current Justices—O'Connor, Kennedy, and the four liberals—support *Roe* vs.

---

* The Court decided that state and local authorities had the responsibility, in a January 2001 ruling.

Wade. It would fall only if two of these six were to retire, if Bush were to nominate replacements bent on overruling *Roe*, and if both were to survive what would most likely be Senate confirmation battles of unparalleled ferocity.

A conservative nominee seen as a likely balance-tipping vote to junk *Roe* would face an assault by Democrats at least as intense as the one that ended in the 58–42 Senate vote rejecting Bork in 1987. And although the Senate has since moved from Democratic to Republican control, it voted 51–47 in October to endorse *Roe* as "an important constitutional right" that should not be overturned. Would Bush invite two successive Bork-like brawls? Or might he turn instead to someone whose views are less hard-edged or unknown?* That's what Reagan did in appointing the more moderate Kennedy after Bork went down, and what President Bush did in choosing Souter, the so-called stealth nominee, in 1990; his votes and opinions have appalled conservatives and delighted liberals ever since. In all, two of the three justices added by Reagan (Kennedy and O'Connor) and one of the two added by Bush (Souter) voted in 1992 to uphold *Roe* vs. *Wade*. . . .

Nine Judicial Activists

The justices' eagerness to remain above (or at least outside) the world of politics was one reason for their nine empty front-row seats at President Clinton's final State of the Union address on Jan. 27. Some had medical excuses or pressing family business, and others have skipped such speeches for years. But this was the first time in memory that not one had showed up, excepting 1986, when the speech was postponed because of the disastrous explosion of the space shuttle *Challenger*. This year's absences were not a gesture of disrespect for President Clinton, one justice explained privately. Rather, some of the Court's members have for years felt uncomfortable sitting silent and immobile in their black robes at what has increasingly become a made-for-television political show, with Democrats applauding one line and Republicans the next as the President makes a speech exuding thinly veiled partisanship.

But it's difficult to decide so many politically charged cases and to strike down so many democratically adopted laws without being accused of politically moti-vated judicial activism by someone. All nine members of the current Court have been so labeled—sometimes by one another, as in Stevens' dissent from the age discrimination ruling handed down on Jan. 11. Stevens accused the five conser-vatives of engaging in "judicial activism" by substituting their will for that of Congress.

"Judicial activism" has long served as a campaign slogan for Republicans railing against the Warren Court, the 1973 ruling in *Roe* vs. *Wade*—which was seen at

---

* This question remains open, in the wake of a 50–50 Senate division, and Bush's appointment of hard-line conservative John Ashcroft to serve as Attorney General.

the time as a usurpation of legislative power even by many liberal scholars—and many other decisions during the years after Warren E. Burger succeeded Earl Warren as Chief Justice in 1969. Many of these critics were more unhappy with the political results of the Court's decisions than with its aggressive use of judicial power per se, and thus have welcomed the conservative judicial activism of more recent years.

Activism is contagious. It would take more self-restraint than most judges have to watch their ideological adversaries pursue politically tinged agendas without responding in kind. So it has become fashionable for liberals in Congress (such as Biden), the media, and academia—many of whom find judicial activism congenial when it produces results they like—to join Stevens in turning the old charge of activism against the conservatives themselves. Such charges have become a staple of liberal professors and publications such as *The New York Times*, which blasted the Court the day after *Morrison* for "weakening civil rights" in an editorial headlined "Violence Against the Constitution." Some moderates also assail *Morrison* as "an unwarranted interference by the Court with ordinary democratic politics," as professor Larry Kramer of New York University puts it. "The kind of role the Court is creating for itself is one in which it sets itself up as the final arbiter of how necessary or expedient federal legislation is, a kind of judgment they have no business making for the rest of us," Kramer adds.

While avoiding overt criticisms, Clinton-appointed Solicitor General Seth P. Waxman stressed in a May 1 speech that "the extraordinary act of one branch of government declaring that the other two branches have violated the Constitution has become almost a commonplace." Recalling "the New Deal's head-on collision with the Supreme Court in the tumultuous '30s," Waxman noted that in the succeeding decades the Court had "reiterated time and again that 'the judicial power to hold an act unconstitutional is an awesome responsibility calling for the utmost circumspection in its exercise.' " The Justices struck down only 128 federal laws during the Court's first two centuries, he observed; the current Court has struck down 21 in the past five years. (Two more have fallen since his speech.)

Some critics fault the Court's liberals and conservatives alike for overextending their powers. One such critic is Jeffrey Rosen, a law professor at George Washington University who also writes for *The New Republic* and other magazines. Last June, he criticized as "judicial legislation of the most sweeping kind" a 5–4 decision in which the liberals (plus O'Connor) opened the way for students of all ages to bring federal lawsuits against their schools for possible sexual harassment by other students. In January, Rosen asserted that "the five conservative justices have . . . turned themselves into the mirror image of the judicial activists whom they have spent their careers attacking" in their push to revive federalism-based limitations on congressional power. "This Court is activist in all areas, across the board," adds Kramer.

But judicial activism "means many things to many people," as Scalia noted in his April 18 speech. The phrase has become so protean in its connotations as to be an all-purpose label for decisions one does not like. Thus, some critics call it activism to depart from precedents, while others call it activism to adhere to precedents that are clearly inconsistent with the text or original meaning of the Constitution. In abortion-rights cases, therefore, the charge is hurled both at the justices who would overrule *Roe* vs. *Wade* and at those who seek to preserve it.

Definitions of unwarranted judicial activism tend to fit the patterns of results that are politically congenial to the person doing the defining. Scalia, for example, defines judicial activism as including "decisions that hold unconstitutional practices that were not only approved at the framing but that were continuously viewed as constitutional by at least a substantial portion of the American people," down to the present day. Scalia is honest enough to denounce some decisions even when the results are politically congenial. His dissent in the parents' rights case, for example, stressed that although he agreed that the visitation statute was a bad law, nothing in the Constitution empowered the Court to strike it down. But on most issues, Scalia's judicial philosophy appears to align with his conservative political and moral beliefs: He has evinced deep moral disapproval of abortion and affirmative action preferences; he is skeptical of the need for more federal regulation; he approves of the death penalty and other tough-on-crime measures; he is a practicing Catholic who disapproves of homosexual conduct and supports federal aid to religious and other private schools; and he has assailed as unwarranted judicial activism a variety of decisions that happen to be offensive to those who hold such beliefs.

Almost all liberal justices since the 1960s, on the other hand, have argued that the Court should construe and update the Constitution to serve (their own) evolving notions of human decency, and to give federal civil rights laws and regulatory statutes favored by liberals a sweeping interpretation to serve their "remedial purposes."

Perhaps the most ideologically neutral, and least pejorative, definition is the rather elastic one suggested above: Judicial activism involves invoking novel or debatable interpretations of the Constitution to strike down democratically adopted state or federal laws and practices that offend one's moral or political beliefs, while showing relatively little deference to the other branches of government and the voters. By that standard, all nine Justices are indeed activists at least some of the time. Former Acting Solicitor General Walter Dellinger, who teaches at Duke University Law School and practices law in Washington, puts it this way: "This is a very confident Court." Confident that it knows best. Confident that its rulings will be enforced, not defied. Confident enough to sweep away laws so popular that hardly anybody in Congress would dare vote against them.

Not So Conservative

[I]f measured against poll data indicating the views of the broad American public on the big issues, the current Court is about as centrist as it could be. The Court's balance of power is held not by its three solid conservatives (Scalia, Thomas, and Rehnquist), but by O'Connor and Kennedy. On ideologically polarizing cases, the three conservatives need both of their votes to win. And those votes often come with a hedge, because if O'Connor or Kennedy doesn't want to go as far as the three, then the reach of the decision can be limited. Here's how it has worked out on some of the most controversial issues:

Abortion. The Court's jurisprudence seems very much in sync with public opinion, perhaps a bit to the left of center. There is clear majority support for the basic right of an adult woman to have an abortion. But the public doesn't want to go so far as to use tax dollars for Medicaid abortions, to allow abortion on demand for minors, or to say that anything goes as far as late-term abortion procedures are concerned. That's about where the Justices have come down—although they have probably made minors' access to abortion easier than most voters would like—with O'Connor and Kennedy joining the four liberals in protecting the basic abortion right and parting company with them on how broad that right should be.

Affirmative action preferences. Polls show that solid majorities like "affirmative action" and dislike race and gender "preferences." This reflects both the broader, vaguer, and more inclusive connotation of "affirmative action" and a considerable degree of public ambivalence. This ambivalence is mirrored on the Court. The three conservatives and perhaps Kennedy would apparently like to abolish racial preferences, or come close to doing so. The four liberals would open the door wide to such preferences. O'Connor, who holds the balance of power, is keeping her options open, which helps explain why the Court has not taken up a major affirmative action case since 1995. And although the 1995 decision and resulting media coverage gave "the surface impression of an attack on race-based classifications even for affirmative action purposes," says Harvard Law professor Laurence Tribe, such a view "seems misleading" because O'Connor's mushy, deliberately ambiguous majority opinion left officials and lower courts considerable latitude to keep preference programs.

Religion in schools. On issues such as school prayer, the Court seems to be to the left of public opinion, which has long supported the kinds of organized school prayer that the Justices have barred. The public also wants the Ten Commandments posted on classroom walls, which the Court has also barred. As for tuition vouchers for religious schools, which the Court's conservatives seem likely to approve and the liberals seem likely to find unconstitutional, they are not unambiguously conservative: Black and Hispanic people seem to lopsidedly support them while teachers' unions fervently oppose them. And what was so "conservative" about the 5–4 decision in 1997 to reinstate a federal program designed to help disadvantaged children by sending public school teachers into religious schools to provide remedial services?

Federalism. Even on this front, where the five more-conservative Justices vote as a cohesive bloc, the Court seems to be moving in the same general direction as public opinion. Friedman stresses that the Republican sweep in the 1994 elections, and the accompanying enthusiasm for devolution of power to the states, indicated that the voters were becoming more skeptical of big government in Washington. So did the laws limiting the terms of members of Congress— which the Court struck down, putting itself to the left of public opinion on that issue.

So we really have a centrist, activist Court—one that is too liberal for most Republicans, too conservative for most Democrats, and too eclectic to outrage most of the people much of the time. The next President might (or might not) have an opportunity to change this balance in a big way, as Franklin Roosevelt did by appointing eight of his supporters between 1937 and 1943. Or he might go the way of Harry S. Truman, who named four Justices between 1945 and 1949, only to end up complaining: "Packing the Supreme Court simply can't be done. . . . I've tried it and it won't work. . . . Whenever you put a man on the Supreme Court, he ceases to be your friend."

Questions for Discussion

1. Should members of the unelected Supreme Court have as much power as they do? How are the Justices limited in the scope of their decisions? Are the Scalia conservatives really conservative? Or are they as activist as their more liberal counterparts?
2. Do you think that the Court decision in *Bush* v. *Gore* should alter any of Taylor's conclusions about the nature of the Court? Does the decision affect your view of the Court? Why?

Chapter 14

POLICYMAKING

The policymaking process brings together almost all of the elements in the structure of American politics. We can think of the Constitution as providing a framework within which policies are made—a framework that does not guarantee speedy action or governmental responsiveness to the wishes of the citizens. In addition, public opinion, as expressed through elections or interpreted in the media, is a basic element in policy formulation, yet it is often subject to change and adaptation. After all, presidents and legislators work diligently to generate public support for their own proposals.

The constitutional relationships outlined by the separation of powers and federalism impose serious limitations on policymakers. For example, education has traditionally been a state and local function in the United States; among national institutions, the Supreme Court, with its desegregation rulings, has affected local school districts more than the Congress or the president has.

Beyond these basic rules of the game, contemporary policymaking takes place within the context of a large and growing governmental establishment. Given an annual budget of roughly $1.95 trillion (an almost unimaginable sum), the permanent government of the federal bureaucracy is difficult for elected officials to control. In addition, the government extends its reach by providing guarantees in potentially risky undertakings (the banking industry, student loans, crop damage). The growth of government has produced two other hallmarks of contemporary policymaking: (1) the extensive use of regulation, which has generated substantial debate, and (2) the influence of annual budgetary actions on almost all domestic policy decisions.

Traditionally, students of public policy have focused much of their attention on the legislature and its decisions. But as the reach of government has grown and problems such as environmental pollution have become increasingly complex, Congress has delegated more and more policymaking authority to the bureaucracy and to independent agencies such as the Food and Drug Administration. In terms of the gross number of policies, regulations far outstrip legislation. Both Congress and the president have sought to control this proliferation. Congress has enacted large numbers of legislative veto provisions, which gave it the opportunity to review various regulations, but in 1983 the Supreme Court declared these vetoes an unconstitutional violation of the executive's authority under the separation of powers. The president has had greater success in monitoring regulation. Through the Office of Management and Budget, the executive reviews regulations to determine their consistency with existing policies.

Since the late 1970s, movements toward less new regulation and substantial deregulation have gained ground. Although the Reagan administration generally reduced the number of new regulations, the first moves toward deregulation came in the Carter administration, when economist Alfred Kahn, then chairman of the Civil Aeronautics Board (CAB), began action to curtail regulations within the airline industry. In the end, Kahn succeeded in eliminating the CAB. Increased fare competition among airlines was one short-term result of deregulation, although in the 1990s airline consolidation and higher fares seemed the order of the day. Still, as Pietro Nivola argues (in selection 14.3), despite high-profile deregulation, the overall impact of regulation for the society at large has steadily increased, much to the benefit of attorneys and targeted interests.

Although deregulation proved a mixed bag in the 1990s, a pair of major governmental initiatives—eliminating budget deficits and reducing overall federal debt—was more successful. Building on an important 1990 budget deal, President Clinton adopted the elimination of budget deficits as a centerpiece of his economic planning. A second budget deal in 1993 and a strong economy allowed the budget deficit to decrease from $290 billion in 1992 to $200 billion-plus in 2001. Budget scholar Allen Schick (14.4) argues that our surpluses can keep rising (and our debt shrinking) if we can hold down discretionary spending—no mean feat when times are good. Likewise, tax cuts can put the surplus at risk. Schick notes that we may have divided government, even gridlock, to thank for the surpluses, seeing as "neither party can achieve its budgetary vision" of spending (for Democrats) or large tax cuts (for Republicans).

No set of readings can adequately capture the diversity of domestic policymaking. In selection 14.1, Christopher Georges discusses the general problems of implementing policies. Georges argues that means for effective implementation need to be built into new initiatives, especially when local officials will ultimately be responsible for carrying out the legislative mandates. In an excerpt from her book *Policy Paradox,* Deborah Stone describes how narratives—essentially stories—can define policy problems and possible solutions (selection 14.2). In a policymaking environment that is very complex and is filled to the brim with information from various sources, decision makers need stories to understand, and to help the public understand, how policies operate. Ironically, as we are faced with more and more information, the more valuable we will find narratives in allowing us to appear to understand complicated policies that respond to difficult problems like telecommunications reform or the impact of environmental regulations.

Sign It, Then Mind It

Christopher Georges

The stepchild of American politics and American political science is policy implementation—what happens *after* Congress has acted and the president has signed the legislation. However noble, the intentions of policymakers often, perhaps inevitably, become twisted in the process of implementing laws. With a $1.95-trillion annual budget and literally thousands of separate governmental regulations, it is no wonder that policies regularly change as they are implemented.

Christopher Georges argues here that policy engineers must give more thought to effective implementation when they are designing new legislation. Drawing on past programs beset with implementation problems (1970s crime legislation and 1988 welfare reform), Georges calls for careful construction and sensitive administration of policies put forward by the Clinton administration. Still, when reading this, we might wonder if implementation will ever be high on the list of those who write legislation. Can the government learn from its mistakes? That is a question worth pondering.

Ross Perot recently asked me for $15. Against my better judgment, I'm sending him a check. I did not vote for Perot. I hope he never becomes president. Even so, he earned my contribution based on a single remark midway through the second presidential debate. "Please understand," he said, "there are great plans lying all over Washington that nobody ever properly executes."

If the Clinton administration takes one lesson from Ross Perot, that should be it. It's no secret that the new president has more programs than Microsoft. Many are smart. Some are desperately needed. But most will surely follow the same failed path as the ones they are intended to replace—unless the Clinton administration pays heed to more than just turning good ideas into laws. Just as important is focusing equal attention on the nuts and bolts of how to *make the plans work* on the ground level.

The late Christopher Georges was an extremely talented young journalist who reported and wrote on politics and policymaking.

Let's face it, policy implementation is boring. It's complex, and it makes terrible TV. But it's also the missing gene of American politics. Few people focus on it; even fewer care. But getting it right is especially relevant now as Washington gears up to push Clinton's brash new agenda. "All the pious announcements, all the laws that are passed will mean nothing," explains Richard Nathan, director of the Rockefeller Institute of Government at the State University of New York at Albany, "unless there is a commitment to carrying them out. Our failure to do this has been *the* endemic problem of American government."

And what exactly does that mean? It's no secret that countless plans, whether under Johnson or Reagan, in areas from crime to welfare, have failed to live up to their promise. Little matter that the best policy minds designed them, that ambitious new laws were passed, that billions were funneled to federal agencies and the states. Inevitably, it seems, our social ills have become worse. And when that happens, it's back to the drawing board to try a newer, better plan.

The assumption here is that the solutions—the laws themselves—are flawed. And in some cases that surely is part of the problem. But lawmakers and policy designers rarely stop to consider whether, for example, police officials charged with implementing the latest federal plan for community policing know how to train officers for the task, or whether welfare caseworkers actually sanction welfare recipients who fail to take job training classes, as the latest welfare law requires. In short, when the laws are written, is there enough thought given to how to implement the new policies?

In a word, no. Why not? Presidents and congressmen earn their stripes by passing legislation, not by making sure it works. To the constituents back home, a new law sends a signal that their man in Washington is on the ball, doing something—anything—to solve a problem. To the media, slavishly covering the signing of a new bill—as they did in broadcasting images of President Reagan's White House signing of the 1982 Garn-St. Germain Act, which helped cause the savings and loan disaster—is easy. Schlepping out to the hustings, on the other hand, to decipher the impact of the law on the banking industry, wasn't. About the only ones who seem to pay any attention at all to the implementation gap are professor-filled, blue-ribbon panels. (Foremost among them in recent years have been the 1990 Volcker Commission on Public Service,* the 1992 National Commission on State and Local Public Service, and a Brookings Institution team.) . . . Many have gone to great pains to illustrate that even the best laws will fail when implementation is ignored. Such warnings, however, seem to fall on deaf ears.

Of course, all politicians want their laws to succeed, but there is little incentive while designing new legislation to worry about the fine points of how it will be carried out. Unfortunately, it may take the failure of Clinton's vaunted agenda to prove the point. That's a particularly unsavory notion these days, as policy flops

---

* Former Federal Reserve Board chairman Paul Volcker headed the commission.

in the nineties will be more costly than those of the past. Considering the need to slash the deficit, we simply can no longer afford to play loosy-goosy with social programs; every penny spent must be producing tangible results. Just as important, further failures will push public confidence to the brink: How many times can Washington spend billions on reforms and then have nothing to show for them before taxpayers abandon faith in government solutions altogether?

There is, however, an easier way than waiting for the bright new agenda to become a wasted one: looking back to the causes of failed laws. Two areas, crime and welfare—where fully-debated, smartly-designed policy ideas in recent years failed—make the case.

Disorganized Crime

No issue was hotter in the 1968 election than crime. In the three years leading up to the election, the nation had been bled by riots in more than 100 cities. A 1968 Gallup poll revealed that most Americans believed lawlessness was America's number one domestic problem. After months of debate and with the input of special task forces comprised of the brightest stars in the field, Congress and the Johnson administration unveiled the 1968 Safe Streets Act. The cure to the crime problem would start with the creation of the Law Enforcement Assistance Administration (LEAA), through which $300 million in grants would be doled out to police departments across the nation. In order to win the grants, however, localities had to promise to use the money to fund crime prevention programs that the think-tank task forces had endorsed, namely plans like community-based policing, drug treatment on demand, hiring more police officers, and school-based drug education. Sound familiar? If you've followed Clinton's $3 billion crime program, it should. Of course, Clinton's plan is not identical (he's also pushing tougher ideas like boot camps for juvenile offenders), but the overlap is significant.

The bad news for Clinton is that the Safe Streets Act and the LEAA were dismal failures. (The LEAA, after a controversial, sorry existence, was abolished in 1982.) The good news, however, is that the failure had almost nothing to do with the quality of the policies proposed. In fact, libraries full of studies since 1982 have concluded that such reforms can, and have, worked—which helps explain why they're back on the agenda.

Instead, the failure was largely a product of how the act was carried out. Under Safe Streets, local police departments would submit funding proposals to "state planning boards," which would modify them as they saw fit and pass them along to the Washington-based LEAA for approval. If the plans contained the types of programs Congress and the administration had endorsed, the money would be released to the state boards, which would then dole it out to the local police units.

Of course, fighting crime, as the Safe Streets Act properly recognized, should intimately involve—and ultimately be controlled by—local governments, and not micromanaged from Washington. But Safe Streets' LEAA made a crucial blunder. It essentially threw the money at the states and the state planning boards. It cared only about who got what amount of money. When it came to considering whether the money was being used properly, and more importantly, what results the funding was producing, it was essentially hands off.

And how did that play out in towns and cities across America (where few Washington bureaucrats care to look)? For one, the state planning boards—made up for the most part of academics who were sold on the reforms—invariably locked horns with local police officials, blue-collar types who were often set in their ways. To the local officials, many of whom were quite comfortable running their local fiefdoms, the pointy-headed planners were perceived as a threat to their autonomy. Massachusetts's state planning board, made up mostly of liberal Harvard types, not surprisingly found itself slugging it out with the street-wise Boston police. "Morale here is zero," one Massachusetts state planner told the press in the early seventies. "We have no friends, no political base, no power." One southern state planner at the time said, "The police chiefs in this state come out of the Salem witch hunt. If a police chief doesn't want a training program, you can't do anything about it."

It wasn't long before the agenda began to unravel. While some local departments never applied for funds, others did and then used the money as they saw fit. In 1970, 37 percent of the LEAA funds had been used to pay for programs completely unrelated to crime. (The governor of Indiana, for example, dipped into the LEAA trough to buy himself an airplane.) And in 1971, it was later discovered that more than a dozen states had used LEAA funds for illegal purposes. "What had appeared to be a law officer's dream for badly needed help," stated a congressional report examining the LEAA in the mid-seventies, "was becoming merely a politician's dream for the biggest pork barrel of them all."

Even when the money did filter down to the local level, the new-fangled ideas were often resisted by local police officials wedded to their ways. Consider the Georgia sheriffs who, after a plan had been approved, refused to allow their local jails to be replaced by a multi-county prison slated as a model in providing the latest in rehabilitative programs. Why the stubbornness? To the sheriffs, local jails offered status, provided free labor when needed, and in many cases allowed them to put their wives on the county payrolls to cook meals for the inmates.

In the end, the local police simply beat the planners to a pulp. They were better organized and more politically connected. Linked by vocal, visible, and well-funded groups such as the International Association of Chiefs of Police and the American Correctional Association, they rolled over the friendless and politically unsophisticated planning agencies.

And what was Washington doing during the meltdown? "Their biggest concern was to get the money out in the field," explained one state planning official to the authors of *U.S. v. Crime in the Streets*, a late seventies study of the failure of the Safe Streets Act. "It's as if the people there held an amoral attitude about program standards—they just wanted to get the money out into the hands of the police." Federal myopia meant chaos ruled. Nevada's crime program, for example, failed to include an organized crime component. New York's had just one page detailing how it would deal with the state's drug problem (whereas Vermont's included 320 pages on the same problem). None of this seemed to matter to the LEAA, which approved the plans all the same.

Equally damaging was the fact that evaluation from the LEAA was virtually nonexistent. By the mid-seventies, the Office of Management and Budget (OMB), the General Accounting Office, and the White House had all concluded independently that the LEAA was in a fog. One 1976 OMB report criticized the LEAA for paying for millions of dollars worth of "interesting but unnecessary equipment." In fact, it wasn't until four years after the LEAA was created that Congress made the embarrassing discovery that the agency had not a single employee charged with collecting information on the success of programs.

Given the sloppy implementation of this act, it's little wonder that by the early eighties Washington was no longer enamored of the new crime-fighting ideas. But a decade later, we've come full circle. There is no question that localities must be tightly involved in implementing a federally initiated crime agenda, but unless the Clinton team is aware of why the grand ideas flopped the last time around, history is destined to repeat itself.

Class Act

Of course, the bungling of crime reform may well be the exception. Safe Streets' grand ideas, after all, were being *imposed* on local governments from faraway Washington—a situation sure to inspire distrust no matter how well the regulations were implemented. Perhaps the bulk of the blame in this case really lies with local governments, which were reluctant to accept the fashionable new programs in the first place.

The best way to test that objection is to examine a failed federal reform that was not handed down but was instead inspired by the states themselves—welfare reform.

Clinton's tough campaign rhetoric in this area, such as his promise to "scrap the current welfare system," played no small part in putting him in the White House. While he embraced the foundation of current federal law—forcing welfare recipients to enroll in job training programs—he went a step further, offering a plan that essentially would cancel benefits for those who fail to find a job after two years on assistance. That's no minor suggestion, and one that would require a reprogramming of Aid to Families with Dependent Children (AFDC).

Clinton's no-nonsense talk is justified. Public polls show that Americans are not happy with the welfare system, and plenty of policy experts agree. Nearly 5 million families receive AFDC benefits and the average aid recipient is on the rolls for more than six years. The most recent reform, the 1988 Family Support Act, sought to fix that. The sweeping measure, which came after nearly a decade of debate, turned the philosophy behind welfare inside out. Instead of simply providing recipients with money, the law demanded that those receiving aid must in return prepare themselves for a job through training courses, enrolling in college, or the like.

To make the new idea work, the 1988 law, in creating a program known as JOBS, turned much of the implementation responsibility over to the states. The federal government agreed to release more than $3.3 billion over five years in matching funds to state welfare agencies, which would be charged with creating specific programs to provide job counseling and training. The beauty of the 1988 act was that, unlike Safe Streets, many states, such as Arkansas and Massachusetts, had already experimented with so-called "welfare-to-work programs," giving Congress the confidence that it wouldn't be throwing money at a completely untested idea which the states didn't want.

The first round of evaluations of the act are just now filtering in, and while they don't point to a disaster on the scale of Safe Streets, about the brightest face that can be put on it is "mildly successful." In California, for example, welfare recipients who went through a job training program now earn an average of $1,900 a year. Those who did not, now earn an average of $1,600. Nationwide, the number of people on welfare in the past four years has gone sharply up—not down. "The hope that states would use JOBS to signal a change in the mission of the welfare system has not been realized," was the conclusion of the largest, and thus far only, in-depth study of the act, *Implementing JOBS*, a review of the welfare-to-work programs in 10 states by Jan Hagan and Irene Lurie of the Rockefeller Institute of Government in Albany, N.Y. The pace of progress has in part prompted Clinton and others to push the more radical reform agenda.

But before we leap into the next welfare overhaul, what exactly has gone wrong with the last one? While some critics of the act argue that the law itself is not tough enough (job training requirements, for example, can be fulfilled through taking self-esteem classes), the larger problem is that the act is "underrated and under-implemented," explains Richard Nathan, author of a review of welfare implementation over the past three decades, *Turning Promise into Performance. . . .*

And what does that mean on the front lines? For one, there hasn't been enough money to make it work—partly because the federal government's $3 billion outlay isn't adequate, but also because the states simply have been slow to collect it. (Remember, the federal seed money is not a direct giveaway. In order for each state to receive its share, it must put up matching funds.) Of the $1 billion available to the states in 1991, only $600 million was actually claimed. Of the 10 states studied by Hagan and Lurie, only one, Oregon, even came close to pulling down all the funds to which it was entitled. And often the poorest states, which need the money the most, put up the least—and thus pull down the least. Mississippi, for example, drew less than 15 percent of the federal funds to which it was entitled.

In some cases, states facing serious fiscal problems simply haven't been able to make the investment. But in others, it's also a matter of leadership—or lack of it. In fact, in none of the 10 states studied by Hagan and Lurie did welfare agencies make any "organizational changes" in the administration of their programs to incorporate the new federal mandates. Caseworkers, for example, were rarely trained for the dramatic shift from distributors of checks to counselors. Instead, in places like Tennessee, county welfare directors were taught how to market the JOBS program, but caseworkers were never trained for the tougher job of educating welfare recipients about where to get the actual job training and education.

In some cases, the failure of leadership is apparent not so much in what state officials do but in what they neglect. Some governors, such as Maryland's William Donald Schaefer and Massachusetts's Mike Dukakis in the eighties, sparked their welfare-to-work programs by holding press conferences to emphasize positive results, pushing for ad campaigns and the like. Others, such as Texas's Bill Clements in the late eighties, sat on their hands. While part of the resistance to push JOBS programs in some states may have been due to a lack of funds, some of it was more intentional. "Don't underestimate the politics of it all," said one Texas welfare official, referring to the Clements administration. "They knew they could win political capital by keeping a safe distance from any program that smacked of welfare."

But as with Safe Streets, the implementation vacuum starts in Washington and filters down to the local level. National leadership has made little effort to inspire local welfare agencies to make the new plans work, allowing them to fall back on old ways. In Michigan, says Nathan, "Social workers simply did not believe in the idea of the program. That's what implementation is about, changing the mindset of the people, not just at the top but at the local level." Consider the attitude of welfare bureaucracy in New Jersey. Crucial to the success of the 1988 act, policy planners say, is sanctioning welfare recipients who refuse to take job training courses by withholding part of their welfare checks. But, explains Allan Zalkind, a top welfare administrator in Newark, which has one of the largest welfare populations in the nation, "We oppose the mandatory aspect of the act. We don't like to sanction anyone unless we feel it is absolutely necessary. Our job is not to hold the gun to someone's head."

One fallout from the lack of wallet and will has been that JOBS programs in most every state have been limited to helping only those who volunteer to get job training—in other words, those recipients who actively want to get off welfare. (In some states, like Minnesota, it is official policy to serve only those who voluntarily ask for job training.) That's fine for the volunteers, but it doesn't help much in ultimately lowering the number of people receiving benefits. Those who volunteer for assistance in finding a job are often the most ambitious who, with or without JOBS, would have left the dole after a relatively short period. It's the hard-core cases who are at the heart of America's welfare problem, and JOBS has offered little help in moving them off welfare. "Serving mostly volunteers means we are not reaching into the caseload," explains Judith Geuran, president of Manpower Development Research Corporation, a not-for-profit group that specializes in welfare reform. "The law has potential, but we are a long way from making it work."

The Promise Land

Making the Family Assistance Act or any law work should be just as high a priority as passing it—for Congress, the White House, and especially the federal agencies. Fortunately, there are road maps for this kind of success, especially on the state level. One is Massachusetts's Employment and Training welfare-to-work program. Here Chet Atkins, who headed the state's welfare agency in the eighties, not only played a hands-on role in creating the policy, but once it was designed, took his show out to the field, working with welfare workers across the state to ensure that the plan was accepted and understood. Atkins realized that before he could change the behavior of those receiving aid, he had to change the attitude of those handing it out.

Recognizing the significance of this missing link in American policy may well be the toughest step. Longtime friend of Bill and Hillary, Marion Wright Edelman, sure to be on the "A list" of White House guests, would do well on one of her visits to leave a copy of a speech she gave six years ago at the Kennedy School of Government's commencement ceremonies. There she spoke of the need for change—but not the kind of policy change most closely associated with Clinton's campaign. "Pay attention," she urged the new graduates, "to the nitty gritty steps of implementation. Passing a law or drafting a regulation is the easiest part of the change process. Making it work, informing the public . . . and getting and training sensitive and skilled personnel to administer it is just as crucial."

Questions for Discussion

1. Are the goals of legislators and bureaucrats different when it comes to implementing policies? How so, and with what implications?
2. Georges distinguishes between top-down policymaking (Safe Streets) and bottom-up efforts (JOBS), yet both run into great difficulties. Can top-down legislation ever succeed? Why didn't the bottom-up policy produce better results?

14.2

Stories

Deborah Stone

The context of policymaking in American politics has become increasingly complex over the past forty years. The government and its often overlapping policies have grown steadily; regulations have increased; new rights have been created (by, for example, the Americans with Disabilities Act). And the number of interest groups has kept pace (see Chapter 9). Moreover, legislators, executives, and administrators are deluged with information—from the press, from organized interests, from think tanks, and increasingly from citizens using the Internet. In this "data smog" both decision makers and citizens must try to make sense of an almost incomprehensible world.

Although economists and some political scientists would willingly see the world in simplified, economic terms, such simplification does not direct much policymaking (or explanations of policy decisions). Rather, as Deborah Stone points out, we often rely on stories to help us understand broad issues. In this selection, Stone briefly notes two common story lines that are used to justify decisions first to consider a certain problem and then to act on it. These "stories of decline" and "stories of control" are narratives used over and over in the discussion of why a certain issue needs to be addressed by government action. Data and information are included in these stories, but their power comes not from the information but from the construction of the stories themselves. And we may often enact policies in response that make little economic sense or do not improve the quality of societal life (see selection 14.4). Nevertheless, the narratives create their own realities that virtually demand some governmental response.

Definitions of policy problems usually have narrative structure; that is, they are stories with a beginning, a middle, and an end, involving some change or transformation. They have heroes and villains and innocent victims, and they pit the forces of evil against the forces of good. The story line in policy writing is often hidden, but one should not be thwarted by the surface details from

---

Deborah Stone is the David R. Pokross Professor of Law and Social Policy at Brandeis University.

searching for the underlying story. Often what appears as conflict over details is really disagreement about the fundamental story.

Two broad story lines are particularly prevalent in policy politics. One is a *story of decline*, not unlike the biblical story of the expulsion from paradise. It runs like this: "In the beginning, things were pretty good. But they got worse. In fact, right now, they are nearly intolerable. Something must be done." This story usually ends with a prediction of crisis—there will be some kind of breakdown, collapse, or doom—and a proposal for some steps to avoid the crisis. The proposal might even take the form of a warning: Unless such-and-such is done, disaster will follow.

The story of decline almost always begins with a recitation of facts or figures purporting to show that things have gotten worse. Poverty rates are rising, crime rates are higher, import penetration in U.S. markets is greater, environmental quality is worse—you have heard these all before. What gives this story dramatic tension is the assumption, sometimes stated and sometimes implicit, that things were once better than they are now, and that the change for the worse causes or will soon cause suffering. . . .

The story of decline has several variations. The *stymied progress story* runs like this: "In the beginning things were terrible. Then things got better, thanks to a certain someone. But now somebody or something is interfering with our hero, so things are going to get terrible again." This is the story told by every group that wants to resist regulation. In the 1970s and 1980s, the American Medical Association, fighting government cost-containment efforts, reminded us about the days of plagues, tuberculosis, and high infant mortality, and warned that government restrictions on the profession would undo all the progress doctors had brought us. Biotechnology firms, through their trade association known as "BIO," told a very similar story to fight President Clinton's medical cost-containment plans in the 1990s: biotechnology had brought us miracle medicine, but Clinton's planned regulation and price controls threatened the very survival of the nascent industry.[1] Manufacturing concerns, such as automakers, steel companies, and textile firms, tell a story of how minimum wage legislation, mandatory health benefits, and occupational safety regulations threaten to destroy America's once-preeminent position in the world economy. The CIA tells us that restrictions on its operating methods prevent it from maintaining the security it once could provide, and the Pentagon tells how budget constraints have undermined our once-dominant military position.

Another variant of the decline story is the *change-is-only-an-illusion* story. It runs like this: "You always thought things were getting worse (or better). But you were wrong. Let me show you some evidence that things are in fact going in the opposite direction. Decline (or improvement) was an illusion." Examples of the revisionist story are everywhere. Medical researchers tell us that the improved survival rates for cancer patients are really an artifact of measurement; it is only because we can now diagnose cancer at earlier stages that patients appear to live longer.[2] Child abuse (or rape or wife-battering) is not really on the rise; it only appears to have increased because we have more public awareness, more legislation, and more reporting.

The other broad type of narrative in policy analysis is the *story of helplessness and control*. It usually runs like this: "The situation is bad. We have always believed that the situation was out of our control, something we had to accept but could not influence. Now, however, let me show you that in fact we can control things." Stories about control are always gripping because they speak to the fundamental problem of liberty—to what extent do we control our own life conditions and destinies? Stories that purport to tell us of less control are always threatening, and ones that promise more are always heartening.

Much of the analysis in the areas of social policy, health and safety, and environment is a story of control. What had formerly appeared to be "accidental," "random," "a twist of fate," or "natural" is now alleged to be amenable to change through human agency. For example, much modern economic policy—the use of government fiscal and monetary tools to stabilize fluctuations in the economy—is based on a grand story of control. In the 1930s, when national economies had lurched into rampant inflation and disastrous depressions, they seemed to behave more like the weather than like social institutions. Lord Keynes* wrote a highly influential treatise whose central premise was that seemingly random fluctuations in economies are really manageable through government manipulation of spending and money supply.[3] The story of control governs in a vastly different policy area—public health—as well. Cancer, previously thought to strike victims unpredictably, now turns out to be related to diet, smoking, and chemicals—all things humans can control. Increasingly, cancer is linked to mutant genes, and though we cannot control our genes, the knowledge of genetic contributions to cancer can help us target screening and prevention programs, and may eventually help design genetically based therapies. Stories that move us from the realm of fate to the realm of control are always hopeful, and through their hope they invoke our support.

A common twist on the control story is the *conspiracy*. Its plot moves us from the realm of fate to the realm of control, but it claims to show that all along control has been in the hands of a few who have used it to their benefit and concealed it from the rest of us. Ralph Nader's famous crusade against automobile manufacturers was a story that converted car accidents into events controllable through the design of cars, and even willingly accepted by automakers. Advocates of industrial policy tell a story in which unemployment, thought to be intractable, is actually caused by "capital strike" (businessmen refuse to invest in new plants and ventures) and "capital flight" (businesses invest their capital in other

---

* John Maynard Keynes's theories of state intervention in the economy dominated governmental policies and economic theories from the Great Depression until the Reagan-Thatcher era of the 1980s.

regions or other countries). Conspiracy stories always reveal that harm has been deliberately caused or knowingly tolerated, and so evoke horror and moral condemnation. Their ending always takes the form of a call to wrest control from the few who benefit at the expense of the many.

Another variant of the control story is the *blame-the-victim* story.[4] It, too, moves us from the realm of fate to the realm of control, but locates control in the very people who suffer the problem. In one recent analysis of homelessness, "it was the fact that unskilled women not only married less but continued to have children that pushed more of them into the streets."[5] Homelessness, in this view, is the result of women's knowing choice between two alternatives:

> Few unskilled women can earn enough to support a family on their own. For many, therefore, the choices were stark. They could work, refrain from having children and barely avoid poverty, or they could not work, have children, collect welfare and live in extreme poverty. Many became mothers even though this meant extreme poverty.[6]

There are many versions of the blame-the-victim story. The poor are poor because they seek instant pleasures instead of investing in their own futures, or because they choose to live off the dole rather than work. Third World countries are poor because they borrow too eagerly and allow their citizens to live too extravagantly. The sick are sick because they overeat, consume unhealthy foods, smoke, and don't exercise. Women are raped because they "ask for it." Workers succumb to occupational diseases and injuries because they refuse to wear protective gear or to act with caution. Just as the conspiracy story always ends with a call to the many to rise up against the few, the blame-the-victim story always ends with an exhortation to the few (the victims) to reform their own behavior in order to avoid the problem.

What all these stories of control have in common is their assertion that there is choice. The choice may belong to society as a whole, to certain elites, or to victims, but the drama in the story is always achieved by the conversion of a fact of nature into a deliberate human decision. Stories of control offer hope, just as stories of decline foster anxiety and despair. The two stories are often woven together, with the story of decline serving as the stage setting and the impetus for the story of control. The story of decline is meant to warn us of suffering and motivate us to seize control.

Notes

1. "BIO" stands for Biotechnology Industry Organization. See Peter H. Stone, "Lost Cause," *National Journal* Sept. 17, 1994, p. 2133.
2. Alvan R. Feinstein et al., "The Will Rogers Phenomenon: Stage Migration and New Diagnostic Techniques as a Source of Misleading Statistics for Survival in Cancer," *New England Journal of Medicine* 312, no. 25 (June 20, 1985): 1604–8.
3. John Maynard Keynes, *The General Theory of Employment, Interest and Money* (New York: Harcourt & Brace, 1936).

4. The phrase became a byword in social science after William Ryan's *Blaming the Victim* (New York: Random House, 1971).

5. Christopher Jencks, *The Homeless* (Cambridge, Mass.: Harvard University Press, 1994), p. 58.

6. Christopher Jencks, "The Homeless," *New York Review of Books*, April 21, 1994, p. 25.

Questions for Discussion

1. Relate Deborah Stone's discussion of "stories" to the other selections in this chapter. Why does the use of stories to think through complex issues seem so attractive?
2. Who gets to tell the stories that Stone alludes to: the public, the president, members of Congress, lobbyists, the media? How is the politics of getting our attention different from the politics of affecting decisions?

 14.3

Regulation: The New Pork Barrel

Pietro S. Nivola

Since the deregulation of air travel set off a spate of similar actions in banking, telecommunications, and other fields, the conventional wisdom has been that the United States has become a less highly regulated society. At the same time, although "pork" continues to be distributed in the legislative process, the conventional wisdom holds that there is less governmental "pork" than in years gone by. Regulations, however, continue to be written, as legislators and administrators attack social ills ranging from toxic waste to deaths in automobile accidents. What has gone largely unnoticed, at least by the general public, is that many regulations confer benefits on particular groups (and costs on many others). In other words, "pork" lurking under the cover of "good policy" decisions may lessen the cost-effectiveness of policies.

In this selection, Brookings Institution scholar Pietro Nivola argues that many regulatory policies cost the government little or nothing but cost society at large a

Pietro S. Nivola is a senior fellow in the Brookings Governmental Studies program.

great deal, and he points out that these dispersed costs often funnel specific benefits to particular interests within society. The Superfund law, for example, has generated huge costs and substantial profits without doing much for the environment. Nivola recommends following the money to see who wins and who loses when the government decides to regulate an activity or require that certain standards be met. Not always, but often, the costs to society are substantial, and particular groups benefit from the regulatory requirements. The source of this type of "pork" may not be the old pork barrel from which legislators distributed benefits to their friends and supporters, but it does reflect a kind of politics that benefits organized interests (such as the waste disposal community) but does little for society at large (such as to improve environmental quality).

As the federal government's discretionary spending in the 1990s has become less lavish, so has the supply of old-fashioned lard in the U.S. budget. But if you think this means the era of big government is over, think again. Another pork barrel is burgeoning. Along with preferential micromanagement of the tax code, the bacon these days takes the form of unfunded mandates and regulatory programs and of public facilitation of private lawsuits.

Figure 14.1 tells most of the story. Led by robust military budgets during the late 1970s and the 1980s, discretionary spending increased. Until 1988 the estimated costs associated with federal regulatory activities declined in constant dollars as the economy realized tens of billions in savings from deregulation of the transportation and energy industries and from the Reagan administration's concerted efforts to curb costly new regulations. Afterward, however, regulatory costs turned up sharply and have been on the rise ever since. A profusion of new rules and legal liabilities increasingly bore down on business decisions about products, payrolls, and personnel practices. By the mid-1990s these costs were approaching $700 billion annually—a sum greater than the entire national output of Canada.

Explanations

Whatever else explains this trend, surely it demonstrates that fiscal constraints have not limited the ingenuity of politicians and their clients. Policies that are barely visible on the budget books can still intervene massively on behalf of special interests—and can do so, conveniently, without worsening the deficit or imposing transparent tax increases.

For instance, rules that have encouraged the use of ethanol (a fuel made from corn) are a kind of pork for corn farmers, only less obvious than, say, appropriating millions for irrigation projects in Corn Belt states. Often costing billions of dollars per cancer prevented, the Superfund law to remove carcinogenic toxins

Figure 14.1
Comparison of Federal Regulatory Costs and Discretionary Budget Outlays, 1977–1996

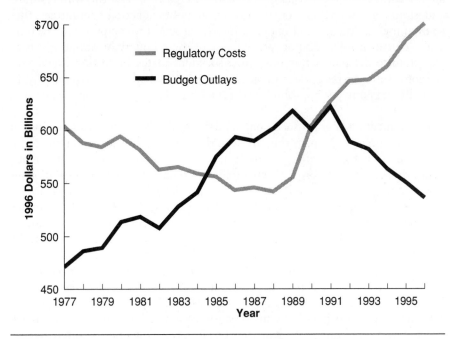

from waste dumps is charging society a small fortune. But Superfund's congressional appropriation is suitably modest, and the program is a gravy train for particular groups, like the thousands of lawyers engaged in cleanup litigation. Similarly, antidumping provisions in the trade laws, devised to regulate "unfair" foreign price competition, require small budgetary outlays to administer. At times, however, these regulations force consumers to pay markedly higher prices to protect a handful of domestic companies. The practice of crafting protections and preferences for selected groups in the name of civil rights is a relatively low-budget operation too. But this regulatory regime nonetheless reaches deep into the private sector, dispensing rewards to the regime's extensive vested interests. There is no shortage of examples of Washington's off-budget spoils system.

Though the regulatory pork barrel frequently serves well-organized constituencies, its scope tends to be broader than the traditional treats (a new post office here, a new road or sewer there) that members of Congress offered to their districts. In contemporary American politics, this difference is an added advantage for members of Congress who need increasingly to curry favor with *national* lobbies and pressure groups that provide valuable political backing. The pattern of influence and obligations is reflected in congressional campaign finance. Whereas candidates in House elections, for example, used to rely for support almost entirely on local constituents and state parties, now the winners draw almost 40 percent of their contributions from political action committees, that is, from the funding arms of national interest groups. Prosaic projects, reaching only hometown folks, do not satisfy many of these hungry organizations; they expect, instead, a diet rich in ubiquitous social mandates: more safety devices in *all* motor vehicles, pure water in *any* river, equality of athletic programs within virtually *every* university, prohibition of smoking from sea to shining sea, and so on.

The number and cost of such commandments also keep mounting because of the extraordinary legitimacy they are accorded. In part, this situation reflects the skill of their advocates and patrons at marshaling notions of fairness or rights. Thus, the trump card played by champions of rigid antipollution regulations is that all citizens have "an inherent right" to a pristine environment. The mandating of benefits for each new class of disadvantaged people reflexively summons the Fourteenth Amendment, rather than a plainspoken demand for government funding. The clinching argument in many product injury verdicts seems to be that buyers should bear no responsibility for the risks they run since consumers are entitled to be absolutely safe. The time-honored defense of antidumping regulations is that they uphold the economic rights of firms and workers victimized by foreign predators who employ "pauper labor."

Because regulatory pork barreling is presented not as a system of special favors, but as a means of honoring solemn legal claims, the claimants are often given a direct hand in enforcement. Many regulatory activities, in other words, gain momentum because they deputize vigilantes. Most environmental statutes and consumer protection laws invite citizen suits to ensure compliance. Of late, the employment laws have induced a surge of job-bias class actions. Various interests are parties to these lawsuits or become beneficiaries of them. Besides awarding significant sums to nonprofit advocacy groups, settlements have ordered a bevy of purchasing contracts and franchises to designated for-profit organizations and produced a billable hours bonanza for the contingency lawyers and for a cottage industry of diversity management consultants.

Concerns

Does all this pose a problem? A prosperous, civilized country should be expected to regulate harmful types of economic fraud and abuse, to reduce socially corrosive inequities, to bar morally repugnant forms of discrimination, and to protect the health and safety of its citizens. Despite the soaring costs of the policies produced by these exertions, their net worth is sometimes impossible to measure. Even though many of them advantage certain groups while disadvantaging others, society may have decided that such uneven outcomes are virtuous and just. And the fact that politicians pull in campaign funds and votes with the decisions does not, in itself, invalidate them. Pork, courtesy of other people's tax payments or of regulatory exactions, is a staple of politics. Without it, democratic government would lose some muscle as well as flab.

What is unsettling, however, is the seeming ease or insouciance with which current political arrangements seem to crank out expensive directives that invoke high principle to conduct . . . "public affairs for private advantage." The old pork barrel, stuffed as it was with federal bricks, mortar, and macadam, at least had to be paid for with tax dollars or with deficit spending. The favoritism was explicit, concrete (often literally), and visibly priced. Even the subtler fiscal delicacy, targeted tax relief, has had reasonably obvious budgetary implications, which sooner or later would alarm deficit hawks. Wasteful as these expenditures and tax measures frequently are, at least they have borne clearly the signatures of elected officials, who occasionally might be asked to answer for the consequences of their actions.

The new system is murkier. Its contents extend far beyond earmarked appropriations or tax breaks to a stack of selective legal strictures that appear budget-neutral and "tax free," and that are partly in the custody, so to speak, of unaccountable private attorneys general. In contrast to honest spending and tax bills, no consistent effort is made to score the economic impacts of the voluminous mandates, especially those that emanate from the executive branch. Hence, as [economists] Robert Hahn and Robert Litan recently reported, approximately half the federal government's social regulations issued between 1982 and mid-1996 generated costs plainly in excess of social benefits, yet remained unchallenged.

The rise of legal and regulatory burdens may seem of trivial consequence to America's formidable economy, but in fact the productivity and incomes of Americans would have grown more rapidly if the nation's cost-oblivious penchant for regulatory sanctions and suits had been brought under better control. As a conservative estimate, just ridding the *Federal Register* of the manifold rules since 1982 that flagrantly flunked an elementary cost-benefit test would have increased the size of the economic pie by almost $300 billion. Fixing countless other programs whose net benefits are not being maximized would "grow the economy" further. The penalty for not seizing these opportunities now while the going is good is likely to worsen substantially in the years ahead. In the next millennium, the competitive heat of the global marketplace will intensify and so will the incentives for firms to outsource across borders. Especially if encumbered by too many injudicious laws and lawsuits, more U.S. businesses will simply off-load more of their operations. In the course of this industrial upheaval, millions of American workers are likely to be sacked or, at a minimum, to see their wages stagnate.

Prudent Corrections

Not unaware of this prospect, the [1995–1996] 104th Congress made some tentative progress toward redressing abuses of the regulatory state. Legislation was passed requiring federal agencies to weigh the costs and benefits of major new mandates and to submit their studies to Congress for review. Narrower statutes were enacted eliminating zero-tolerance standards for health risks in some consumer goods (processed foods, for example) or at least requiring regulators to publish cost justifications for safety standards (as for drinking water). In an attempt to curb the excesses of what might be called privatized social regulation—in particular, the rampant civil litigation that purports to protect consumers—Congress succeeded in setting minimal limits on the rewards to shareholders and plaintiffs' attorneys for suing companies frivolously.

To call such steps anything but a bare beginning, however, would be a delusion. The shareholder "strike" suits bill should have, but didn't, clear the way for a broader legal reform proposal that would have restricted punitive damages in product liability cases generally. (President Clinton vetoed both bills, but only one of his vetoes was overridden.) So far, the new procedural requirements for the formulation of executive rules, in turn, have proved mostly exhortatory. In only one case, the Pipeline Safety and Partnership Act of 1995, is an executive bureau expressly enjoined from promulgating standards whose costs are unjustified by benefits. In the rest, administrators are only asked to consider and report their cost-benefit assessments and to explain any rule-making that discards them. The provisions for congressional oversight of proposed rules are constrained by tight statutory time-frames, presidential veto power over resolutions of disapproval, and too limited a role for the legislative branch's top economic analysts. (The 1995 Unfunded Mandates Reform Act authorizes the Congressional Budget Office to "score" regulatory acts of Congress, but not those of the executive. The latter's rules, according to the Small Business Regulatory Enforcement Fairness Act of 1996, are to be examined by the General Accounting Office, arguably under unrealistic deadlines.) Perhaps least satisfactory is the grandfathering* of existing laws and rulings. With a few notable exceptions—such as the Delaney clause, which barred any level of risk in food additives—old regulations, no matter how questionable, remain on the books.

Some of these deficiencies might be partially remedied by more fine-tuning. A pending bill, the so-called Regulatory Improvement Act authored by Senators Fred Thompson (R-TN) and Carl Levin (D-MI), would try to ensure, for instance, that agencies take seriously their evaluations and risk assessments of new rules by introducing a process of independent peer review. The bill would also extend methodically a similar review process to extant regulations.

---

* To "grandfather" a policy into law means that a current policy will be exempted from the impact of a newly enacted statute.

Even these corrections, however, will not suffice to sharpen the lines of political accountability for regulatory pork. A proliferation of agency analyses, peer committees, and reporting requirements is no substitute for democratic *choice*. Ultimately, the buck ought to stop with Congress itself, where members should have to cast transparent up or down votes on all the government's off-budget activism, just as votes are recorded on other important taxes and expenditures. But unless these decisions are well-informed, legislators will render them meaningless, if they render them at all. One way to minimize evasion might be to expand the capacity of the Congressional Budget Office to delineate for the legislature society's gains and losses from every major regulatory initiative, much as CBO performs this annual service with every big budgetary item. A joint report by the American Enterprise Institute and the Brookings Institution published last July suggested experimenting along these lines.

Beyond these institutional adjustments lie larger priorities. Sooner or later, policymakers in the United States will have to face the fact that inordinate legal contestation pervades the way this society seeks to regulate itself. Much of this punitive "adversarial legalism" . . . lines the pockets of lawyers and professional litigants while accomplishing little else. The resulting drag on American economic performance, though little noticed at the moment, may become considerably less affordable in time. Part and parcel of serious regulatory reform, therefore, has to be a reasonable contraction of federal enactments that stimulate, indeed sometimes sponsor, our seemingly insatiable appetite for litigation. This won't be easy, for it will mean rolling back an oversupply of suits everywhere, from the workplace to the doctor's office, as well as entertaining fewer complaints about sagging stock quotations, risky products, and many of life's hazards, misfortunes, and disappointments.

Questions for Discussion

1. The essence of traditional pork barrel politics has been the distribution of favors for political support (including, but not limited to, campaign contributions). What is the difference between what Nivola terms "regulatory pork" and traditional spending on roads, military spending, or public works projects?
2. As Georges notes in selection 14.1, implementing policy is a difficult and frequently unrewarding task. Does the new pork barrel regulation suffer from an absence of attention to how policies are implemented? How could oversight of such policies be improved?

14.4

A Surplus, If We Can Keep It

Allen Schick

Without question, the most profound development in the context of American politics during the 1990s came in the drop from huge budget deficits to sizeable and growing surpluses. No one predicted such a reversal, and the rising surpluses, projected to total more than $4 trillion by 2010, have allowed politicians to consider large tax cuts and major spending initiatives, as well as to encourage paying down the national debt. The decline in the deficit resulted from some important bargains between Congress and the president in 1990 and 1993, along with a booming economy that increased governmental revenues. A large deficit constrained legislators' plans for spending or cutting taxes; surpluses offer the possibility of setting lawmakers free from such limitations.

In 1787 Benjamin Franklin was asked what kind of government the framers had constructed. He replied, "A Republic, if you can keep it." Budget scholar Allen Schick knowingly paraphrases Franklin in the title of this piece, as he conveys the difficulty officeholders may have in keeping their hands off the growing surpluses. Although we traditionally decry divided government, Schick argues that a bit of gridlock may be a good thing because it prevents the forging of consistent majorities that might reduce the surpluses, which have been central in holding down interest rates and maintaining a strong economy.

"It's the economy, stupid." The battle cry of Bill Clinton's 1992 presidential campaign as been recycled to explain how a $290 billion budget deficit has been transformed into a $100 billion surplus that is expected to quadruple in the decade ahead. I would argue, however, that the hand of Washington has had as much to do with liquidating the deficit as the economy's invisible hand. Policies matter. Wrong decisions in the 1980s condemned the nation to a decade of high deficits; right ones in the 1990s have liberated it from past budgetary misdeeds.

Liquidating the deficit ranks as one of the supreme budgetary accomplishments in American history. In 1993, the Office of Management and Budget projected that the fiscal 1998 deficit would be $339 billion; the Congressional Budget

---

Allen Schick is a visiting fellow in the Brookings Governmental Studies program. He is the author of *The Federal Budget: Politics, Policy, Process* (Brookings, 1995; revised edition forthcoming).

Office projected $357 billion. That was not the only year for which budget experts were wide of the mark. In both their five-year projections and their annual budget estimates, OMB and CBO persistently overestimated the deficit. In 1993, CBO projected that policies then in place would yield cumulative deficits of $1.5 trillion over the next five years. Actual deficits totaled less than a third that.

An analysis of economic performance, spending policies, and revenue trends during the 1980s and 1990s makes clear how the federal budget was balanced. Whether it will still be balanced a decade from now when the first wave of baby boomers reaches retirement is much less certain.

The Economic Boom

Every budget is hostage to the economy. Congress and the president cannot balance the budget when national output is declining and unemployment is soaring. Budget receipts are highly sensitive to changes in economic conditions, spending less so, but even a small shortfall in economic performance can affect the budget in a big way. CBO has estimated that if the annual real growth rate over the next decade were just 0.1 of a percentage point less than it has assumed, the fiscal 2010 budget surplus would be $40 billion below current projections.

When the deficit peaked in 1992, the United States was emerging from a brief recession. When the budget was balanced in 1998, the economy was completing the seventh consecutive year of growth, during which 13 million jobs were added and inflation averaged less than 3 percent. The budget was the beneficiary of economic success. Revenues escalated as corporate profits and personal incomes rose; spending dropped as welfare rolls declined, the crisis in the banking sector was resolved, and inflation in the health care sector moderated.

But economic good times alone do not account for the budget's unexpected turnaround. Measured in terms of growth rates, the eight consecutive years of expansion during the 1980s (from the end of the Reagan-era recession in 1982 to the onset of the Bush-era recession in 1990) outperformed the boom of the 1990s (see table 1). The two expansions were structured differently, which may partly explain their different revenue impacts. During the 1980s expansion, which followed a decade of "stagflation," growth began at a high rate and tapered off. The 1990s expansion, which followed a long period of growth that was briefly interrupted by the 1990–91 recession, began with low growth that accelerated as the expansion continued.

Spending Policies

Although a cooperative economy made the budget surplus possible, the surplus would not have materialized if budget policy in the 1990s had repeated the

Table 1

Economic Performance, 1983–90 and 1992–99

Economic Indicator	1983–90	1992–99
Average real GDP growth rate[a]	4.0	3.5
Average annual civilian unemployment rate[b]	6.7	5.7
Total civilian jobs added (millions)[c]	18.0	15.1
Cumulative increase in real per capita disposable income[a]	20.5	14.1
Average annual change in consumer price index[b,c]	3.9	2.6
Average ten-year Treasury note rate[b]	9.5	6.2
Cumulative increase in productivity[d]	12.5	13.3

Sources: *Economic Report of the President,* January 1999; Bureau of Economic Analysis (November 1999); Bureau of Labor Statistics (November 1999); and Treasury Department (September 1999). Data are through preliminary September 1999, except for average ten-year Treasury note rate, which is through June 1999.

[a]Based on chained 1996 dollars.

[b]Calendar year average.

[c]For all urban consumers.

[d]Output per hour of all persons in business sector.

mistakes of the 1980s. Differences between the revenue and spending paths taken during the two decades led to quite different budgetary outcomes.

On the spending side of the ledger, the key differences were in budget enforcement rules, defense spending, discretionary appropriations, and entitlements.

During the 1980s, Washington postured against deficits with futile gestures that reflected the inability of a Republican president and Democratic Congress to agree on tough budget measures. The 1985 Gramm-Rudman-Hollings (GRH) law promised annual cuts in the deficit and a balanced budget within six years. Although the law threatened the automatic cancellation of budget resources if the projected deficit exceeded the target, the actual deficit was above the statutory limit every year. With clumsy and unworkable sequestration procedures, GRH induced Congress and the president to lie about the deficit by substituting illusory cuts for real ones and by pretending that the budget picture was better than it actually was.

In 1990, with the projected deficit spiraling out of control, the warring branches replaced GRH with the Budget Enforcement Act (BEA), a law that focuses on revenue and spending rather than the size of the deficit. Almost a decade later, BEA remains in effect, and although it has not always been strictly enforced, it has helped improve the budget condition. It has two principal rules—a limit on annual appropriations and a requirement that any revenue or spending legislation that would increase the deficit (or decrease the surplus) must be offset. In sharp contrast to GRH, it does not regulate changes in the budget caused by fluctuations in economic conditions or in the cost of existing entitlement programs. It controls only the parts of the budget that the president and Congress directly influence—and thus holds politicians accountable only for the things they control.

Congress and the president have had a complicated budgetary relationship under BEA. At times, one branch has deterred the other from violating the rules; at other times, both have conspired to evade the rules by designating routine expenditures as emergencies, manipulating the effective dates of tax legislation to hide the full budgetary impact, and using a bewildering variety of bookkeeping tricks. BEA has elevated "scoring" (measuring the budgetary impact of legislation) to a valued political art, but it also has dampened the ability of vote-seeking politicians to cut taxes or boost spending. As with other budget rules, its effectiveness has weakened over time as claimants for federal money have devised means to outwit the process or disable its controls. Hefty surpluses have also weakened BEA. Budget controllers cannot enforce the rules with the same zeal when money is abundant as they can when resources are tight.

Discretionary Spending

It is difficult to separate the impact of BEA from the conditions under which it has operated. Had there been no discretionary caps, defense spending still would have been held down by changes in world affairs, domestic spending pressures, and oversize deficits.

The 1980s began with a steep boost in defense spending; the 1990s, with the collapse of the Soviet empire and the end of the Cold War. Defense spending, which began to level off during the second half of the 1980s, continued to fall through most of the 1990s. Adjusted for inflation, defense outlays were almost $100 billion less in 1998 than they had been a decade earlier. If the Cold War were still raging, there probably would be no surplus.

As after past wars, some defense savings were reallocated to domestic programs. Because the budget enforcement rules built a "firewall" between discretionary appropriations and direct spending, domestic appropriations reaped most of the savings. These programs, which fell more than 15 percent during the 1980s, grew more than 25 percent during the next decade. In fact, real discretionary domestic spending is much higher today than it was when Ronald Reagan launched his campaign to roll back social programs. As a share of gross domestic product, however, discretionary domestic spending has fallen—from 4.5 percent in 1981 to 3.2 percent in 1999.

During the 1990s, the president and Congress exploited BEA spending caps to demonstrate their commitment to control the budget and to reduce the size of the government while spending somewhat more than the BEA rules intended. Led by Clinton, the Democrats came out ahead in this contest; they got credit for fiscal prudence while securing more money for popular programs. Outmaneuvered, congressional Republicans reluctantly approved the increases, sometimes after getting billions more for defense. But the marginal growth in discretionary appropriations was too small to derail the march to a balanced budget.

Direct Spending

Spending growth in entitlements was held down during the 1990s by the BEA pay-as-you-go rule requiring legislated increases in these programs to be offset by cuts in other direct spending or by revenue increases. But even in the absence of PAYGO, big deficits would probably have inhibited the president and Congress from establishing new entitlements and impelled them to seek savings in old ones. After all, few initiatives made it through Congress during the pre-BEA 1980s. And despite PAYGO, Clinton won some new entitlements, such as the children's health insurance program enacted late in the 1990s.

The PAYGO decade did see some publicized cutbacks, though their net effect on federal spending has probably been small. Medicare was nicked repeatedly, with some of the claimed savings used to offset the cost of benefit enhancements. At the century's end, Clinton transformed the Medicare debate from worrying about the coming retirement boom to adding prescription drugs to the list of eligible benefits. Welfare was converted from an open-ended entitlement to a fixed block grant to states, and changes were made in eligibility rules and program benefits to move recipients from welfare to work. When the reforms were enacted in 1996, a six-year savings of $54 billion was projected. Steep, largely unexpected declines in welfare rolls—6.5 million fewer recipients in 1998 than 1993— boosted short-term federal spending above what it might have been had the old AFDC program continued. Nevertheless, over the longer term, welfare spending will decline if the reforms endure. Congress also overhauled farm price supports in 1996, but the projected savings will probably not materialize. Whenever farmers run into trouble, politicians pour in billions of dollars of emergency money.

All told, the 1990s were a fiscally static period in entitlement policy.* Leaving aside deposit insurance, mandatory spending was a higher share of GDP in 1999 than in 1990. Means-tested entitlements grew the most, both because of new legislation (such as increases in the earned income tax credit) and because of built-in growth in old programs.

Tax Policy

If the economy and spending changes do not adequately account for the surplus, the only other place to look is on the revenue side of the budget. During the 1990s, tax policy largely reversed actions of the previous decade. During the

---

* Fiscal policy is essentially overall spending policy and its effects on the economy.

1980s, the highest marginal tax rate (50 percent on earned income and 70 percent on unearned income—interest and dividends) was reduced to 28 percent (or 31 percent if a "bubble" in the rates is included). But in the 1990s, the rate was boosted to 39.6 percent, and with various phase-outs of exemptions and deductions included, the effective rate is now above 40 percent. The first tax increase was enacted in 1990 when George Bush was president; the second in 1993 when Bill Clinton was in the White House. The first deprived Bush of reelection; the second helped the Republicans take over Congress in 1994 but ultimately aided Clinton's reelection. While politically risky, the tax increases pumped up federal revenues. Federal receipts rose from 18.2 percent of GDP in 1990 to 20.5 percent in 1998, adding $190 billion in revenue. If the 1989 tax structure were still in place, there would be no surplus to discuss.

The targets of the 1990 and 1993 rate hikes were upper-income taxpayers. By contrast, during the 1990s the income tax burden on low-income Americans was greatly eased. Because of the widened income gap between low and high earners, the government took in much more revenue than it would have if the tax increases had been spread evenly across income brackets. *The government taxed the winners during the 1990s, redistributing income while boosting its revenues. By design or accident, sound social policy coincided with responsible budget policy.* [emphasis added]

Will the Surplus Persist?

Anyone who has made or used budget projections during the 1990s should be exceedingly guarded in forecasting the budget future. Although the medium-term (five to ten years) outlook is cloudy, the longer-term forecast is clear. Under current policy, the budget will incur large and growing deficits when the surge in the over-65 population forces the Social Security fund to draw down the trillions of dollars of accumulated surpluses.

The sure prospect of resurgent deficits makes it urgent that policy mistakes not imperil the surpluses projected for the first decade of the new millennium. Last July CBO estimated that annual budget surpluses would rise from $161 billion in 2000 to $413 billion in 2009. If the forecasts are right, Washington would accumulate almost $3 trillion in surpluses during the next decade—two-thirds in Social Security funds, the rest in the general fund.* Although the projected surpluses are enormous, the economic and revenue assumptions on which they are based are modest. The CBO does not build a recession into its forecast, but it assumes that the economy will grow only 2.4 percent a year over the next decade—much more slowly than it has in the recent past. It also expects federal

---

* In January 2001, the estimates for surpluses rose to $5.6 trillion by 2010.

revenues to rise only $75 billion a year during the next five years, as opposed to the almost $115 billion averaged during 1993–98.

The weakest part of the CBO projection is the assumption that discretionary spending (capped through fiscal 2002) will remain tightly in check. The recent actions of Congress in evading the caps for fiscal 2000 appropriations make it highly unlikely that this part of the budget scenario will play out according to the CBO script. Responding to real and imagined emergencies, boosting defense spending (something Democrats and Republicans alike support, though they differ as to how much), raising discretionary domestic appropriations in line with price increases, and adding billions here and there for national priorities such as education would consume almost three-quarters of the projected non-Social Security surpluses. If, as is likely, taxes are also cut, the remainder of the surplus would be at risk.

These possibilities counsel two prudent steps on the part of Washington politicians: do not spend the surplus before it is earned and do not repeat the policy mistakes of the early 1980s. Prudence in fiscal management cannot ensure that surpluses will persist, but it can guard against a return of runaway deficits.

The 2000 election may have much to say about the future budget health of the nation. Divided government has blocked Republican ambitions for large tax cuts and deterred Democrats from big increases in social spending. If either party were to win all the national political sweepstakes in 2000, it would have a clear field to pursue its pent-up budgetary agenda. Perhaps the surprising lesson of the conversion of deficits into surpluses is that fiscal prudence can reign when neither party can achieve its budgetary vision.

Questions for Discussion

1. Why would it be useful for the federal government to maintain revenue surpluses over the 2000–2010 period?
2. Why were we able to produce surpluses in the last years of the 1990s? What threats to maintaining surpluses does Schick see as the most important?

CREDITS

Beard, Charles A. Reprinted with permission of Scribner, a Division of Simon & Schuster, Inc., from *An Economic Interpretation of the Constitution of the United States* by Charles Beard. Copyright © 1935 by Macmillan Publishing Company, copyright renewed 1963 by William Beard and Miriam Beard Vagts.

Binder, Sarah A. From *Brookings Review*, Winter 2000, pp. 16–19. Reprinted by permission from The Brookings Review.

Birnbaum, Jeffrey H. Reprinted from *The American Enterprise*, a Washington-based magazine of politics, business, and culture.

Broder, David S., and Richard Morin. © 1999, The Washington Post. Reprinted with permission.

Cannon, Carl M. Copyright 2001 by National Journal Group Inc. All rights reserved. Reprinted by permission.

Cigler, Allan J., and Burdett A. Loomis. From *Interest Group Politics*, Fifth Edition, by Allan J. Cigler and Burdett A. Loomis. Copyright © 1998 Congressional Quarterly Inc.

Cohen, Richard E. Copyright 1999 by National Journal Group Inc. All rights reserved. Reprinted by permission.

Dahl, Robert A. Reprinted by permission of *Political Science Quarterly*, 105 (1990): 355–372.

Derthick, Martha. From *Brookings Review*, Winter 2000, pp. 24–27. Reprinted by permission from The Brookings Institute.

Donahue, John D. From the *Disunited States* by John D. Donahue. Copyright © 1997 by John D. Donahue. Reprinted by permission of BasicBooks, a subsidiary of Perseus Books Group, LLC.

Dreyfass, Robert. Reprinted with permission from *The American Prospect*, Volume 11, Number 23: November 6, 2000. The American Prospect, 5 Broad Street, Boston, MA 02109. All rights reserved.

Ehrenhalt, Alan. Reprinted with permission, Congressional Quarterly, Inc. Copyright 2000.

Ehrenhalt, Alan. Copyright 2000 by National Journal Group Inc. All rights reserved. Reprinted by permission.

Friendly, Fred. From *Minnesota Rag* by Fred W. Friendly, copyright © 1981 by Fred W. Friendly. Used by permission of Random House, Inc.

Georges, Christopher. Reprinted with permission from *The Washington Monthly*. Copyright by The Washington Monthly Company, 1611 Connecticut Avenue, NW, Washington D.C. 20009. (202) 462-0128.

Ginsberg, Benjamin. From *The Captive Public: How Mass Opinion Promotes State Power* by Benjamin Ginsberg. Copyright © 1986 by Basic Books, Inc. Reprinted by permission of BasieBooks, a subsidiary of Perseus Books Group, LLC.

Hamilton, Lee H. Reprinted with permission. Copyright © 2000 by Lee H. Hamilton. All Rights Reserved.

Ladd, Everett Carll. Reprinted from *The American Enterprise*, a Washington-based magazine of politics, business, and culture.

Lawson, Kay. From "Why We Still Need Real Political Parties" by Kay Lawson, from *The Democrats Must Lead* by James MacGregor Burns et al, pp. 13–24. Copyright © 1993 by Westview Press. Reprinted by permission from Kay Lawson.

Meyrowitz, Joshua. From *No Sense of Place* by Joshua Meyrowitz, copyright © 1985 by Joshua Meyrowitz. Used by permission of Oxford University Press, Inc.

Milbank, Dana. © 2000, The Washington Post. Reprinted with permission.